Jacob K. Olupona, volume editor, is Professor of African American and African Studies at the University of California at Davis. He is the author of *African Traditional Religions in Contemporary Society.*

AFRICAN SPIRITUALITY
Forms, Meanings, and Expressions

World Spirituality

An Encyclopedic History of the Religious Quest

1. Asian Archaic Spirituality
2. European Archaic Spirituality
3. African Spirituality
4. South and Meso-American Spirituality
5. North American Indian Spirituality
6. Hindu Spirituality: Vedas through Vedanta
7. Hindu Spirituality: Postclassical and Modern
8. Buddhist Spirituality: Indian, Sri Lankan, Southeast Asian
9. Buddhist Spirituality: Chinese, Tibetan, Japanese, Korean
10. Taoist Spirituality
11. Confucian Spirituality
12. Ancient Near Eastern Spirituality: Zoroastrian, Sumerian, Assyro-Babylonian, Hittite
13. Jewish Spirituality: From the Bible to the Middle Ages
14. Jewish Spirituality: From the Sixteenth-Century Revival to the Present
15. Classical Mediterranean Spirituality: Egyptian, Greek, Roman
16. Christian Spirituality: Origins to the Twelfth Century
17. Christian Spirituality: High Middle Ages and Reformation
18. Christian Spirituality: Post-Reformation and Modern
19. Islamic Spirituality: Foundations
20. Islamic Spirituality: Manifestations
21. Modern Esoteric Movements
22. Spirituality and the Secular Quest
23. Encounter of Spiritualities: Past to Present
24. Encounter of Spiritualities: Present to Future
25. Dictionary of World Spirituality

Volume 3 of
World Spirituality:
An Encyclopedic History
of the Religious Quest

AFRICAN SPIRITUALITY

FORMS, MEANINGS, AND EXPRESSIONS

Edited by
Jacob K. Olupona

A Herder and Herder Book
The Crossroad Publishing Company
New York

*This book is dedicated with gratitude
to the faculty, students, and staff of
The University of Edinburgh, Scotland,
and especially to the Faculty of Divinity
for conferring on me
the Honorary Degree of Doctor
of their University
on July 21, 2000.*

The Crossroad Publishing Company
481 Eighth Avenue, Suite 1550, New York, NY 10001

Copyright © 2000 by The Crossroad Publishing Company

Printed in the United States of America

Library of Congress Cataloging-in-Publication Data

African spirituality : forms, meanings, and expressions / edited by
  Jacob K. Olupona.
      p. cm.
   "A Herder and Herder book."
   Includes bibliographical references and indexes.
   ISBN 0-8245-0794-0 — ISBN 0-8245-0780-0 (pbk.)
   1. Spirituality—Africa. 2. Africa—Religious life and customs. I.
Olupona, Jacob Obafemi Kehinde.
BL2462.5 .A375 2000
200'.89'96—dc21

                                              00-010546

1 2 3 4 5 6 7 8 9 10   05 04 03 02 01 00

Contents

PREFACE TO THE SERIES   xi

FOREWORD, *by Charles Long*   xiii

INTRODUCTION   xv

Part One:
Cosmologies and Sacred Knowledge

1   Some Reflections on African Spirituality
Dominique Zahan   3

2   African Shrines as Channels of Communication
Benjamin Ray   26

3   The Lake Goddess Uhammiri/Ogbuide: The Female
Side of the Universe in Igbo Cosmology
Sabine Jell-Bahlsen   38

4   Ancestral Spirituality and Society in Africa
Ogbu U. Kalu   54

Part Two:
Authority, Agencies, and Performance

5   *Pa* Divination: Ritual Performance and Symbolism
among the Ngas, Mupun, and Mwaghavul
of the Jos Plateau, Nigeria
Umar Habila Dadem Danfulani   87

6   Some Thoughts on Ideology, Beliefs, and
     Sacred Kingship among the Edo (Benin)
     People of Nigeria
          Flora Edouwaye S. Kaplan   114

7   Spiritual Beings as Agents of Illness
          David Westerlund   152

8   Witchcraft and Society
          M. F. C. Bourdillon   176

9   Mami Water in African Religion
     and Spirituality
          Kathleen O'Brien Wicker   198

10   Art and Spirituality
          Wyatt MacGaffey   223

11   Spiritual Foundations of Dagbamba
     Religion and Culture
          John M. Chernoff   257

Part Three:
Africans' Encounter with Other Religions

12   The Task of African Traditional Religion
     in the Church's Dilemma in South Africa
          G. C. Oosthuizen   277

13   African Muslim Spirituality: The Symbiotic
     Tradition in West Africa
          Patrick J. Ryan, S.J.   284

14   Patterns of Islam among Youth in South Africa
          Abdulkader I. Tayob   305

15   Sufism in Africa
          Louis Brenner   324

16   Roman North African Christian Spiritualities
     Margaret R. Miles   350

17   Asante Catholicism: An African Appropriation
     of the Roman Catholic Religion
     Pashington Obeng   372

Part Four:
African Spirituality in the Americas

18   Forms of African Spirituality in Trinidad and Tobago
     Rudolph Eastman and Maureen Warner-Lewis   403

19   The Music of Haitian Vodun
     Gerdès Fleurant   416

20   African-derived Religion in the African-American
     Community in the United States
     Mary Cuthrell-Curry   450

CONTRIBUTORS   467

PHOTOGRAPHIC CREDITS   469

INDEX   470

Preface to the Series

THE PRESENT VOLUME is part of a series entitled World Spirituality: An Encyclopedic History of the Religious Quest, which seeks to present the spiritual wisdom of the human race in its historical unfolding. Although each of the volumes can be read on its own terms, taken together they provide a comprehensive picture of the spiritual strivings of the human community as a whole—from prehistoric times, through the great religions, to the meeting of traditions at the present.

Drawing upon the highest level of scholarship around the world, the series gathers together and presents in a single collection the richness of the spiritual heritage of the human race. It is designed to reflect the autonomy of each tradition in its historical development, but at the same time to present the entire story of the human spiritual quest. The first five volumes deal with the spiritualities of archaic peoples in Asia, Europe, Africa, Oceania, and North and South America. Most of these have ceased to exist as living traditions, although some perdure among tribal peoples throughout the world. However, the archaic level of spirituality survives within the later traditions as a foundational stratum, preserved in ritual and myth. Individual volumes or combinations of volumes are devoted to the major traditions: Hindu, Buddhist, Taoist, Confucian, Jewish, Christian, and Islamic. Included within the series are the Jain, Sikh, and Zoroastrian traditions in order to complete the story, the series includes traditions that have not survived but have exercised important influence on living traditions—such as Egyptian, Sumerian, classical Greek and Roman. A volume is devoted to modern esoteric movements and another to modern secular movements.

Having presented the history of the various traditions, the series devotes two volumes to the meeting of spiritualities. The first surveys the meeting of spiritualities from the past to the present, exploring common themes

A longer version of this preface may be found in Christian Spirituality: Origins to the Twelfth Century, *the first published volume in the series.*

that can provide the basis for a positive encounter, for example, symbols, rituals, techniques. The second deals with the meeting of spiritualities in the present and future. Finally, the series closes with a dictionary of world spirituality.

Each volume is edited by a specialist or a team of specialists who have gathered a number of contributors to write articles in their fields of specialization. As in this volume, the articles are not brief entries but substantial studies of an area of spirituality within a given tradition. An effort has been made to choose editors and contributors who have a cultural and religious grounding within the tradition studied and at the same time possess the scholarly objectivity to present the material to a larger forum of readers. For several years some five hundred scholars around the world have been working on the project.

In the planning of the project, no attempt was made to arrive at a common definition of spirituality that would be accepted by all in precisely the same way. The term "spirituality," or an equivalent, is not found in a number of the traditions. Yet from the outset, there was a consensus among the editors about what was in general intended by the term. It was left to each tradition to clarify its own understanding of this meaning and to the editors to express this in the introduction to their volumes. As a working hypothesis, the following description was used to launch the project:

> The series focuses on that inner dimension of the person called by certain traditions "the spirit." This spiritual core is the deepest center of the person. It is here that the person is open to the transcendent dimension; it is here that the person experiences ultimate reality. The series explores the discovery of this core, the dynamics of its development, and its journey to the ultimate goal. It deals with prayer, spiritual direction, the various maps of the spiritual journey, and the methods of advancement in the spiritual ascent.

By presenting the ancient spiritual wisdom in an academic perspective, the series can fulfill a number of needs. It can provide readers with a spiritual inventory of the richness of their own traditions, informing them at the same time of the richness of other traditions. It can give structure and order, meaning and direction to the vast amount of information with which we are often overwhelmed in the computer age. By drawing the material into the focus of world spirituality, it can provide a perspective for understanding one's place in the larger process. For it may well be that the meeting of spiritual paths—the assimilation not only of one's own spiritual heritage but of that of the human community as a whole—is the distinctive spiritual journey of our time.

EWERT COUSINS

Foreword

OUR DISCOURSES ABOUT Africa in the modern period have centered around two major meanings of the modern world, the African slave trade and the intellectual movement referred to as the Western Enlightenment. From the former we are able to understand how African peoples have been dispersed throughout the world, especially within the worlds of the Americas. The Enlightenment as an intellectual movement debased the meaning of African cultures and placed their meanings under the scrutiny of abstract analytical categories as fodder for the deferral of the fraternal and egalitarian ideals of its vision. So neither on the empirical historical nor on the intellectual levels have Africans been introduced into the world of modernity as human beings who were involved in the many ordinary and extraordinary acts of work, thought, and imagination that all human cultures undertake to cope with the several issues of human existence.

Because of this limiting perspective on the reality of the peoples and cultures of Africa in the present, the understanding of the continent and its people in the past is seldom noted. The continent was formative, and continues to be a sustaining meaning in the constitution of the Mediterranean, Atlantic, and Indian Ocean worlds. Africa also looms large in any serious consideration of the originative structures of the worlds of the Ancient Romans, the Western Semitic traditions, Christianity, and Islam.

Africa as a geography and container of several cultures has thus been at the crossroads of all but one of the major cultural contacts that created world cultural systems. The majority of the essays in this volume treat modern and contemporary issues of African peoples and cultures. They attest to the fact that African peoples continue to express an essential element in the formation and sustenance of modern cultures in various parts of the globe and how the African meaning is still alive in the orientations of the modern and post-colonial worlds.

While each essay is devoted to a precise and concrete form of African spirituality, all of them depict a distinctive mode of an African understanding and orientation in the several worlds in which they find themselves. They show how Africans in diaspora and at home, in contact and in exchange with other cultures, have kept alive the possibilities for the perception of another world and the imaginative endeavors involved in the "making of worlds" of human meaning.

CHARLES LONG

Introduction

JACOB K. OLUPONA

IN SPITE OF Western assumptions of absence of spirituality, this volume on African spirituality is the product of collaborative efforts from a diverse number of scholars—Africans and non-Africans who have been working on various aspects of African religions and culture for many years. The current focus on many elements of Africans' spiritual and cultural heritage, which often puzzles foreigners and the global community, should continue to receive serious scholarly attention as the world moves into the next century. African peoples today, especially the elders, look at their classical religious heritage with a nostalgia for a paradise lost. In the beginning, they often argue, was a deep religious and spiritual heritage vouchsafed in myths, rituals, and symbols. But as a result of Africa's contact with the outside world, especially under very ignominious circumstances—exploration, slave trade, and colonialism—significant aspects of these traditions were lost or modified to conform to the taste of the conquerors and the new rulers. A central event in the African's encounter with colonialism was the former's conversion to Islam and Christianity and their imbibing of new religious traditions from the Middle East and Europe. Africans responded to this encounter with resistance and fierceness and in most cases adopted the new spirituality by domesticating the new traditions and making them truly African. It is very difficult to continue to call Islam and Christianity in Africa foreign religions because they have been thoroughly changed and adapted to African taste and sensibility. A similar domesticating process affected African religions that were transported to the New World mainly by Africans who left against their will as slaves to labor on the plantations in the Caribbean, as well as those of North and South America. There, in their new environment, the slaves adapted their masters' religion but still kept on praying to their African deities and dancing to their music in the new land. From this encounter a new "syncretistic" faith has emerged more African than European in structure, style, and content.

A major question is how to characterize African indigenous spiritual traditions, which are diverse and complex but yet enduring? One approach to understanding is to enumerate their essential features without debating whether or not these traditions fit into the pattern of religion already mapped out by theologians, historians, and religions that use Western religious traditions as standards for constructing what religion should look like in other parts of the world. First, one can say that in the African spiritual worldview, myths about the origin of the world, of death, of various institutions are thought to be the key to understanding traditional life. From these myths information is derived about the nature, characteristics, and function of the deities. These myths, which differ from one ethnic group to another, yield images of the different supernatural entities. The first, of course, is the Supreme Being, who remains supreme but like Juno or Jupiter is not beyond being influenced.

Second, I argue significantly that the relationship between the human being and divine being is expressed and achieved in ritual. Ritual is often thought to be the acting out of myth. It is only recently that scholars have given ritual a significant place as a tool for explaining religion in its own right. Third are the human agencies, religious functionaries, and those who have undergone apprenticeship in ritual technique such as priests attached to specific shrines, diviners, and more informally herbalists. This category of religious functionaries includes sacred kings and chiefs, whose participation is crucial in most rituals. Although not exclusively religious functionaries, kings and chiefs as key political, social, and economic leaders play a major role in the religious sphere that legitimizes those positions of leadership, which in turn legitimize religion. Along with practitioners of African medicine, kings and chiefs are regarded as sacred and as intermediaries between their clients and the divinities. Less conspicuously, artists play important roles since they provide the plastic and performance media that express the meaning, the essence, of belief systems.

Perhaps no feature is more revealing of the traditional religious systems than the method of divination that each religious tradition employs. Among the Yoruba, for example, *Ifa,* like other divination processes, has a very complex process of "explanation, prediction and control of space-time events." Ifa is a major religious legacy that Yoruba traditional religion bequeathed to the Americas through the African Diaspora. The divination system employs a set of poetic verses which the diviner recites in the process of consultation.

In our contemporary world, as African traditional religion faces modernity, a significant aspect of the modernization process is the change in traditional beliefs, ideology, and practices. As I observed above, sacred kingship and chieftainship form a critical part of the belief system and social structure in traditional society. The kingship ideology and rituals complement the role of traditional festivals in the personal and social formation of community. The rituals of kingship are concerned with the renewal of the community as much as of the cosmos. In recent times, kingship ideology and rituals have increasingly assumed the function of public or civil religion. Conversion to Islam and to Christianity created a climate of religious plurality. In most traditional societies, kingship ideology and rituals naturally responded to these changes by providing an overarching sense of protection for the community and society, a sacred canopy under which indigenous religion, Islam, and Christianity can coexist in an atmosphere of tolerance and mutual trust. Contrary to this ideal situation that existed in several communities, today new forms of Islamic and Christian traditions are becoming highly intolerant of each other and are creating a new crisis as they attack this last bastion of peaceful coexistence in communities.

These common elements in African religious experience—ancestorhood, multiplicity of gods, medicine, divination, sacred kingship, rituals, and festivals—pose great challenges to contemporary African societies. Unlike previous accounts of these traditions that tend to denigrate them and plead for their destruction, recent scholarship focusing more on the content, structures, and meaning of the traditions has pointed to the vitality of the myths, rituals, festivals, and values, and the ethical principles they espouse. African religions continue to be a source of social stability and cohesion in African communities, especially in the midst of rapid socioeconomic change. They also form the sources for African traditional religious ethics and values, which Africans will continue to cherish and preserve for posterity.

The Divine and the Sacred

African spiritual experience is one in which the "divine" or the "sacred" realm interpenetrates into the daily experience of the human person so much that religion, culture, and society are imperatively interrelated. The significance of this interaction is that there is no clear-cut distinction between religious and secular spheres or perspective of the ordinary life experience.

The African concept of time is as important as a holistic approach to life. I am not talking here about the debate about whether time is cyclical or linear; to the African mind, time is an event and not something that is pursued like setting a time for a board meeting, where every member is guarded by the company laws. Africans have refused to rush to the future! They allow it to come to them and it is then utilized. Their belief that no condition is permanent allows them to face life with patience, endurance, and perseverance.

Another feature of African religious experience supports and encourages pluralism. While religions exist as a potential cleavage within societies of multifaiths and multicultures, the unifying elements for monotheistic religions have either been a theistic concept of God or the sacred kingship and chieftain ideology. In African religious heritage, there is an emphasis on pluralism and, inevitably, tolerance toward other religious and cultural traditions. Clearly, many traditions are eclectic; they accept differences in religious experiences of adherents. Such eclectism produces an attitude of tolerance and peaceful cohabitation toward other traditions and culture. In several countries in Africa, the contemporary religious exclusivism and intolerance characteristic of Christian and Islamic fundamental revivalism have led to serious crises among adherents of these two religions and to violence and suspicion in society.

Women have a significant place in African religious heritage. Indeed, the complementarity of male and female principles and values, as argued in several essays in this volume, is portrayed as essential for the survival of any African community. It is partly the recovery of this ancient heritage in their theology, rituals, and beliefs, that contributed to the progress of African established churches, in which women play leadership roles as founders, priests, and prophets.

More than anything else, Africa's religious heritage bestows upon its people a worldview and a value system; it bestows a personal and social orientation to life. As Africa enters the twenty-first century, it faces new spiritual, social, and economic challenges, which it must surmount with resources from its own religious and cultural heritage. Africa has much to offer society by the way it utilizes these resources. Africa's sense of the family, holistic approach to life, her dancing, singing, expressing herself freely in an uninhibited manner and her patience are great assets to the global community. Further, Africa's indigenous healing process and her sense of community are values which if properly channeled would lead to the transformation and renewal of life.

The essays in this volume do not constitute all the features in the African spiritual universe. Nevertheless, they provide adequate examples of the core spiritual values and the complexity of the religious situation in the continent, which I hope future studies will tackle with equal candor and depth. The essays examine various aspects of African spirituality, drawing specific examples from the area of the continent best known to the authors:

North, West, East, Central and Southern Africa. Recent studies show that these traditions represent a strong continuity with Africa's past. Further, the African Diaspora is included, because it shows the religious heritage that the continent bequeathed to the Americas and to Europe.

Cosmology, God, and Ancestral Spirit

In the first chapter, Dominique Zahan provides the general characteristics of African spirituality. He begins with very forceful philosophical statements that African traditional religion lacks the notion of original sin and redemption. This distinguishes it from Christian religion, to which it is often compared. Unlike Western Christianity, which has a linear conception of time, African traditions are cyclical, repetitive, and lack the notion of eternity—what Mircea Eliade has often referred to as "the myth of eternal return." In theological terms, however, African religion is not completely devoid of the notion of redemption and salvation. Rather, African religion presents a proximate form that places the responsibility of salvation primarily in the hands of individuals and not a transcendent being, as it is in other world religions. In addition, African tradition maintains a familiarity with the Supreme Being, and practitioners are of the view that they "share the same advantages and disadvantages, the same rights and the same duties," whereas Christian tradition purports an unequal relationship between God and the human beings. By conceiving of a Supreme Being as a leader in a hierarchy of beings of which one is also a part, humans see God as only a more perfect being than an order that separates the divine from the human. This attitude, Zahan argues, enables humans to maintain the feeling of respect, fear, adulation, and even pity toward God. Zahan also examines very briefly African mystical tradition, a theme rarely touched on by scholars of African religion. He is of the view that "African mysticism brings to the surface the way in which God's possession of the believer is realized" (p. 4).

Three aspects of African spirituality are further discussed in detail: (1) creator and creation; (2) spirituality and the cult of ancestors; and (3) shrines, priests, and prayer. The Supreme Being is central to the African religious universe, and the ideas about the Supreme Being are conveyed by religious specialists to initiates during ceremonies. With idioms, metaphor, metonymy, and symbols, elders and priests relay various images of God to those undergoing initiations into the secret knowledge of their groups. Further, Africans utilize their material cultural and environmental objects to convey the secrets and wisdom of the Supreme God. Zahan provides plausible explanations to the most difficult issues in the understanding of

African cosmology. One is the notion that God is remote and distant from
the world of the living. Various myths suggest that at the beginning time,
heaven, and earth were formed together; they were severed only as a result
of human offense against God. In this context, Zahan notes: "The distancing of God creates a religious need within the human being; absence engen
ders the search for what is absent—a search that is finally accomplished by
less noble but perhaps more efficient intermediaries" (p. 6). Next to the
Supreme God are spiritual agencies, often regarded as intermediaries.
According to Zahan, they are "directors of major events" occurring in the
life of their communities. A significant number are connected with natural
phenomena such as rain, thunder, and lightning. While the primary function of God is to create the universe, the "secondary" divinities are in
charge of the day-to-day life of the community. Outlining the ideas and
beliefs surrounding ancestor veneration and providing the qualification for
ancestorhood in African communes, Zahan underscores the importance of
ancestral traditions in African spirituality. The rituals of propitiation to
ancestors are also examined, as are the role they played in the lives of their
communites. One central belief relating to ancestorhood is the relationship
of ancestors to the living. The ties between the two are represented in symbolic and artistic forms in various West African traditions. Finally, Zahan
provides a description of shrines, priests, and prayer—major aspects of
African religions.

In "African Shrines as Channels of Communication," Benjamin Ray
examines the forms of shrines in African indigenous religions and the role
shrines play as the medium for facilitating communication between gods
and humans. Shrines primarily act as "symbolic crossroads between two
worlds and instruments of social unification" (p. 26). In African religious
practice, a reciprocal relationship is maintained between, on the one hand,
the gods and ancestors and, on the other hand, humans. The spiritual
beings are placated, fed and honored by humans, and in response the gods
and ancestors bestow blessings upon humans and rejuvenate the cosmos for
the benefits of society. Through the agency of priests and devotees of the
deities, the gods show up on occasions of ritual activities. Dance and trance
provide paths by which the gods visibly manifest themselves to humans.

Based on his field research among the Ganda of Uganda, Ray provides a
phenomenological description of the royal shrines of the Ganda of Central
Uganda and the ceremonies accomplishing Maya mythic and historical
events in the life of the Ganda people. Ganda royal shrines serve as an
important entry point not only to the ideology and rituals of kingship but
also to the cosmology and social life of the Ganda people. Royal shrines are
the storehouse of the royal power, which the king accesses for the mainte-

nance of his kingdom. The royal shrines are maintained by the mediums of the royal ancestors who live around the shrine. The mediums convey messages from the ancestors and the gods to the king, who resides in the capital city, the political center of the kingdom. Ray further examines forms and functions of shrines among various African communities, especially the Kung San of Botswana and Namibia, the Igbo and Yoruba of Nigeria, the Dinka and Nuer of southern Sudan, and the Ashanti of Ghana and the Fang of Gabon. In all these cases, Ray argues that shrines provide the most vital communication within the sacred reality, though this is accomplished by various channels. What has been the impact of Islam and Christianity on African shrines? How has conversion of Africans to the two world religions affected the status of shrines in African society? With conversion to Christianity, there is no longer emphasis placed on a sense of fixed location and shrine, though one may also argue that sacred presence set apart by members of indigenous Christianity functionally play the role of shrines in African Independent Churches. One often hears of "holy land," holy place, as places of power and emphasis, where communication is maintained between the humans and the spiritual realm.

Sabine Jell-Bahlsen's essay, "The Lake Goddess, Uhammiri/Ogbuide: The Female Side of the Universe in Igbo Cosmology," is based on beliefs and ritual practices of the water goddess Nne Mmiri of the Igbo people of Nigeria. This deity is in charge of the crossroads of life, death, and rebirth. She controls procreation and continuity of the process of life. Jell-Bahlsen resuscitates a core traditional Igbo spirituality, namely, the abundance of female divinities apparently suppressed during the colonial periods. This is also shown in her treatment of the water goddess among the rural Oru Igbo people, where the goddess is locally know as Uhammiri/Ogbuide, the spirit woman of Ugwuta Lake. With her husband the river god Urashi, Uhammiri is often represented as part of a divine pair. Jell-Bahlsen argues that Uhammiri is a quintessential deity; she responds to various aspects of life problems of her peoples, as well as the quest for wealth, children, and long life. She is related to healing and medicine; her cult is visited by people with mental illness and gynecological problems. Within this structure, Jell-Bahlsen outlines Igbo religious cosmology and locates the place and role of Ogbuide/Uhammiri within this structure. In the complex Igbo religious universe, the Supreme God, Chi-Ukwu, occupies a central place and presides over an assemblage of male and female deities, spirits, and human agencies. The whole structure is embedded in the Igbos' social matrix. Ogbuide/Uhammiri appears in this complex cosmology as an important nature deity symbolized in water.

Jell-Bahlsen identifies two central principles guiding the Igbo universe:

(1) "the significance of balance and the need to reconcile antagonistic forces," and (2) "the notion of circular time and of the life force/soul/*chi* traveling eternally within the cycle of life and death" (p. 41). She examines the significance and aesthetics of balance through references to evidences in Igbo arts (sculpture and painting), social norms and cultural idioms and the struggle to preserve balance and harmony in nature and society. Coupled with the idea of balance is the notion of the immortality of the soul, the belief that one's life force or *chi* undergoes a cycle of life, death, and rebirth in an eternal cycle of time. The latter is played out in the rites of passage humans undergo in their lifetime. In her case study conducted in the town of Ugwuta, Jell-Bahlsen shows the importance of two female deities in Igbo religion and society: Uhammiri/Ogbuide (the water goddess), discussed above, and Ani/Ala (the earth goddess). In coming to earth (birth), the individual encounters one of these two goddesses, at which time the person is given the choice to retain the original destiny bestowed by the Supreme God or to change to another dictated by either of these two deities. The goddess ultimately forms a part of the drama of human existence and sojourns in this world. Jell-Bahlsen examines the ecological and economic significance of Ogbuide's belief and practices, the relationship between the environment and religious ideology, and gender relations in the cultic and ritual deity. The author concludes by underscoring the importance of the female elements of Igbo cosmology and the significant contribution of women to African spirituality and, by extension, to personal, economic, and social well-being. She observes that the female side of the universe is not only complementary to the male but also pivotal to man for his procreation, reincarnation, and continued existence within the circular flow of time.

In his essay "Ancestral Spirituality and Society in Africa," Ogbu Kalu cites a quotation from Birango Diop, "Those who are dead are never gone: the dead are not dead," to encapsulate the essence of African spirituality and the consequent perception of the cosmos. For the Igbo people of Nigeria, life is a cycle that moves from birth to death and, passing through the spirit/ancestral world, comes back to reincarnating birth—a worldview that culminates in the ancestral belief that death is only a transition from the human plane to the spirit/ancestral world.

As a case study, Kalu adopts the culture-area approach with Odo ancestral cult among the Igbo of Southern Nigeria. While the people believe in the Supreme Being, they look up to the ancestors for life's practical needs. Every child is initiated into a soul covenant relationship with the ancestral world. The advent of a gospel shared the New Testament worldview and a new covenant with Jesus Christ that threatened the old covenant. Hence the interplay, the contact and clash of the traditional and Christian covenants caused major social unrest and revealed that the existence of the gospel among the people has been a strained and compromised one. Thus, the questions arise, How long and how well can this old wineskin hold the new wine, and what implications will it have on the African society? Kalu calls this "bundles of dilemma" that defy a visible viable solution.

Spiritual and Human Agencies

Part 2 concerns the spiritual and human agencies, beliefs, and performative traditions, especially arts and music in African religions. Danfulani's essay, "*Pa* Divination: Ritual Performance and Symbolism among the Ngas, Mupun, and Mwaghavul of the Jos Plateau, Nigeria," focuses on *Pa* divination practice among a group of people in the middle-belt zone of Nigeria. *Pa* divination, which is similar to some other African divination systems, involves the use and casting of pebbles to uncover hidden secrets and truths. It is used as a mechanism through which a reconciliation of the human and spiritual beings is achieved. The author identifies some important dimensions of this aspect of religiosity, including ritual and symbolism as they affect both individuals and the community. As a heuristic device, *Pa* divination is a medium through which explanations of the causes of afflictions, conflicts, and crises are made and solutions proffered. Danfulani discovers that *Pa* divination is a strong indicator of ritual time for most social and religious practices among the people. While calendrical rituals of passages of life follow the twelve lunar months, *Pa* diviners, through their divination practice, set particular dates considered to be the most auspicious days for various festivals. The "auspiciousness" of the days is understood in terms of social balance, peace, and ritual cleanness of the land, which is believed to be in control of spiritual forces. Hence the need for ritual ceremony and redress. *Pa* divination, with its attendant rites, like most African systems of divination, plays significant roles not only in an individual's total life but also in resolving national calamities. National calamities, the author notes, would include contagious diseases and natural disasters such as famine and drought. *Pa* divination rituals, in both the symbolic and the structural mode, reinforce the transitional stages within an individual's life cycle and unite the individuals with spiritual forces in order to cushion, absorb, and pacify the pains of passages through life, time, and space. Danfulani further notes that symbolism is a strong feature of *Pa* divination practice which is visible in ritual arrangement, gestures, words, color, and objects that are used during the process of divination and ritual prescription. The significance of Danfulani's essay is that it contributes to our knowledge of a seemingly obscure religious life of a people whose indigenous religiosity has not been given significant academic treatment.

"Some Thoughts on Ideology, Beliefs, and Sacred Kingship among the Edo (Benin) People of Nigeria," by Flora Edouwaye S. Kaplan, focuses on the significance of sacred kingship in a West African kingdom. Among the Edo (Benin) people of Nigeria, an aura of sacredness surrounds the institution of obaship (kingship). According to Flora Kaplan, the *Oba* is believed to be a living deity in this world, the intermediary and earthly counterpart of other deities and divine forces. This aura of sacredness is protected and maintained through various yearly rituals during which the Oba is worshiped. Because the Oba embodies the soul of the state, his state of mind determines the well-being of the state as a whole. According to Kaplan's field research, the Oba negotiates between the visible human world and the invisible world of deities and spirits, *agbon* and *erinmwi*. The unbroken link between them—all in this one enity, he is both the "living past" and the "living present."

In "Spiritual Beings as Agents of Illness," David Westerlund focuses on the relationship between religion and medicine. Africans have various explanations for the cause of illness in their midst. Some diseases are ascribed to biological factors, others to social problems, and yet others to the interference of the supernatural in human affairs. Westerlund examines three African cultures to account for the belief in the supernatural as agents of illness: the hunter-gathering San of Southern Africa, the pastoral Maasai, and the agricultural Sukuma of East Africa. Westerlund asserts that although there are points of difference in the three cultural perceptions of the nature of the Supreme Being and other spiritual beings and in the manifestation and observance of their religious obligations, these perceptions converge in the notion that there is a supernatural and spiritual dimension to the cause of illness and healing. However, the degree of involvement of spiritual beings varies. For instance, the San believe that virtually all these beings are involved, although a greater emphasis is placed on the lesser deity and the spirits of the dead. Among the Maasai, the major agent of disease and health is God. In the religion of the Sukuma, ancestral spirits are often involved in the cause of illness as a means of ensuring strict moral order among living relatives. On the whole, Westerlund concludes, all three cultures agree in varying degrees that omnipotent God is the "ultimate cause of disease and death," for no other agents can succeed without his sovereign approval.

In "Witchcraft and Society," M. F. C. Bourdillon treats the pervasiveness of the belief in witchcraft in the whole of Africa as he draws examples from many African societies to show the multifarious interpretations attached to this belief system. Although African societies view and interpret witchcraft differently, it is closely associated with "moral outrage" and "with misfortune, death, immorality, the night and darkness, certain dangerous animals, secrecy, power, spirits, caprice, and other sources that threaten good social order." How much of the belief in witchcraft is founded on empirical evidence? How justifiable are interpretations of, and reactions to, accusations of witchcraft? Bourdillon submits that witchcraft is often a social and material problem, and that individual's and society's tensions and inexplicable misfortunes deepen the reality of witchcraft in people's minds. The term "witchcraft" is very problematic. While some support their opinions on the impression that witches make confessions, not even confessions can be a sufficient proof because they may be made out of social frustration or psychological problems. Therefore confessions, if and when they are made, hold insufficient evidence in themselves, though scrutiny of the situation surrounding the confessions and "corroborative evidence" may provide a substantial—but yet unempirical—proof. Even when there is empirical evidence for witchcraft practices with bizarre manifestations, such evidence cannot logically account for bad treatment meted out to witchcraft suspects.

Kathleen O'Brien Wicker's essay, "Mami Water in African Religion and Spirituality," focuses on extensive field research in Ghana carried out with Asare Opoku of the University of Legon, Ghana. In the last few decades, the phenomenon of Mami Water, "a class of female and water divinities and Spirits" has been gaining currency in West African and New World studies. This essay examines the importance of Mami Water in Africa and in non-Africans' devotional lives; the possible origins and growth of the phenomenon; and the ideological constituents and ritual practices related to Mami Water spirituality. Wicker observes that its appeal among Africans may be due to its unique ability to connect with both "the empirical and meta-empirical worlds." She begins with the recognition that Mami Water arose from an amalgam of various religious and cultural traditions from West Africa and beyond. It is a highly "syncretistic" tradition that developed in Africa and the Black Atlantic world. Theoretically, she situates her interpretative framework of the Mami Water phenomenon with Paul Gilroy's analysis of "Black Atlantic" cultural productions. In New World black culture, Mami Water functions "both transformatively and subversively."

As a background, Wicker provides an overview of the place of African water deities within African religious and sociocultural universe. Water deities are characterized by "fluidity of disposition, race, and representation" that endear them to larger and diverse groups of devotees. Like the water they symbolize, these deities represent both beneficence and capriciousness; they sustain and destroy; they heal and make sick; though they are often represented as female-gendered deities, they have both male and female aspects. Wicker also examines the influence of European strands on the Mami Water tradition represented in the mermaid/merman and the snake-handling women.

While we may not be able to ascertain the precise nature or time of the European tradition that influenced West African Mami Water, the "foreign" influence is undoubtedly very visible and quite compelling. The author also examines the interaction of the Africa tradition on the New World Mami Water tradition represented in the local religious traditions. Again one sees a syncretistic tradition incorporating both elements of the two traditions. Another important influence one notices is the Indian strand in the Mami Water tradition. Wicker suggests that the encounter of Africans with the Gujurat merchant of the Asian Indians along the West African coast may have contributed to this influence. Concluding with a descriptive interpretation of a Mami Water shrine at Adome in the eastern region of Ghana, Wicker examines various representations and functions of Mami water in indigenous, Christian, and Islamic contexts. From extensive interviews conducted with Adewuso Dofe, who bears the title "Abidjan Mami water," Wicker interprets the syncretistic nature of this local tradition, which borrows from indigenous, Islamic, Christian, New World, and Indian elements.

Wyatt MacGaffey, in "Art and Spirituality," examines the relationship between art and religion. He begins by raising deep conceptual and theoretical issues, especially as to whether what Western scholars call art and spirituality really exists. MacGaffey provides a brief review of the development of African arts as a field of study and concludes that it did not gain respectability until the 1960s, when most African states obtained independence. The nineteenth-century evolutionary thinking in Europe colored Western construction of African arts and scholarship. Africa did not succeed in wresting itself out of this European mind-set until the 1960s, when after independence African arts began to gain worldwide respectability.

A useful departing point for MacGaffey is to show how the origin and meaning of "arts" and "spirituality" in Western discourse differ from the African meanings and contexts. The vastness of the African continent makes it literally impossible to speak of a unilateral notion of arts in the continent, and equally complex is the relationship between arts and religion. MacGaffey observes, following the works of Henry Drewal that most African art with religious functions can be found in the middle of the

African continent, in an area characterized by a heavy forest whose inhabitants belong to the great Niger-Congo linguistic family.

The Yoruba masquerades and Yoruba masking tradition in Southwestern Nigeria examined in Drewal (1988) and Drewal and Drewal (1991) provide a good entry point for MacGaffey's interpretation of this phenomenon. A human person is (like) a mask and possesses a masklike dimension of the visible exterior that conceals an interior soul or spirit that constitutes the being and essence of that person. The Yoruba metaphor of the inner spirit head (*ori inu*) and the outside physical head (*ori ode*) represents two interconnected realms in the human person. MacGaffey rightly observes that the central feature of the African mask is that it is "an outside covering for (an inner) vital spirit." With this key observation, MacGaffey provides us with a detailed illustration of how this is manifested in a variety of art forms associated with the sacred kingship, medicine, cosmology, and social relations and rituals. In all these instances, the role of women and the feminine essence runs through the various illustrations provided by the author. This is a major contribution to gender discourse in African arts. From all indication, the feminine is normally portrayed as more powerful than the masculine, as the mask for the Nowo water spirit clearly shows. Here, the east/upward direction is associated with the feminine and is regarded as the source of life. The west/downward side is masculine and is associated with the sunset and death.

John M. Chernoff is an ethnomusicologist who focuses on "Spiritual Foundations of Dagbamba Religion and Culture" and examines the role and significance of two African traditions—Islam and indigenous religion in the social and cultural life of the Dagbamba people of northern Ghana. He looks at the historical, geographical, and cultural contexts in which the Dagbamba exist in this part of Ghana. Islam, he observes, was introduced to the aboriginal inhabitants about three to four hundred years ago. Chernoff presents the structure of Dagbamba indigenous religions from the prism of a lineage-based guild of drummers who are considered the traditional historians of the area. The knowledge of ancient history is secretive and is only revealed under strict religious guidance. The Dagbamba rulers were warrior immigrants who, under their leader, came and conquered the aboriginal group. Through wars of conquests they conquered towns and villages and placed Dagbamba chiefs over them. However, the places were also under the rulership of local priests, whose very title (*tindana*) signifies the autochthonous symbolism of their spiritual roles. Each was regarded as the "owner of the land" and was in charge of town shrines and gods (*bu a*). Although "stranger" chiefs usurped the political authority of places, the important spiritual role of sacrificing to local deities remained squarely in the hands of the *tindanas*. This arrangement seems to be a common pattern of West African society.

There are numerous pantheons of deities in Dagbamba society and culture. They are distributed throughout the villages and towns and even beyond the borders of their territory. One significant characteristic of these shrines is that participation is irrespective of ethnic origins. Islam was officially introduced into the region at the beginning of the eighteenth century, almost two centuries after the formation of the Dagbamba state. Although traces of Islam could be found in the region before the eighteenth century, this date marks the beginning of institutionalized Islam, after which Islam gained major control over the ritual and social lives of the people. Conversion to Islam has been inconsistent. The Dagbamba often identify three types of Muslims: first are those who read the *Qurʾan*, such as the clerics; second are those who cannot read but are nevertheless very devout; and third are those who mix Islam with indigenous religious practices. In general, Islam among the Dagbamba is nonmilitant. Chernoff also claims that "the overall impression is one of a society in which the practice of Islam was tempered by a number of other cultural factors" (p. 269). Dagbamba Muslim festivals represent a continuity and discontinuity with their past, a mixture of "pure" Islamic rituals and indigenous belief, practices, and chiefly traditions. Islamic and Christian encounters with indigenous African religions produced significant results—African Islam and African Christianity with their unique tone and identity.

African Traditional Religions' Encounters with Islam and Christianity

Part 3 of this volume looks at the impact of the two global religions on African indigenous traditions. Gerardius Oosthuizen's essay, "The Task of African Traditional Religion in the Church's Dilemma in South Africa," examines the relationship between African indigenous religions and the African derived churches. Oosthuizen begins with the premise that the strength of a religion lies in the meaning and significance of its central practices. In African traditional religion the lack of recognition of those who practice these traditions by scholars has meant a total misunderstanding of the traditions. Echoing Jacob Olupona's statement, the author suggests that African traditional religion should be regarded as a world religion on a par with other religious traditions around the globe. For African people, religion constitutes an integral part of life. It is intrinsic to their daily life. Oosthuizen also examines the role of African independent churches in preserving aspects of indigenous religions that mainline churches would have long ago destroyed. Unlike mainline churches that measure success in terms of conversion figures, African traditional religion measures success by its meaning and significance to its practitioners. Finally, Oosthuizen looks at personhood in the African spiritual universe and observes that in the African thought system, the person is very much linked with the community and the extended family. The author concludes by outlining the future role of African independent churches in preserving African indigenous spirituality and African humanity, noting that the church in South Africa faces two choices: either tread the path of indifference to Africa's orientation and aspiration or respect and identify with the African's spiritual reality. The church's dilemma in Africa generally, and particularly in South Africa, arose out of a dual obligation: the responsibility of adhering to the idealistic ecclesiastical structure wherein the African cultural and religious worldview stands the risk of perpetual stigmatization, and a desire to influence the people. The "mainline" (mission) churches that hold tenaciously to Western orientation and interpretation would rather uphold theology for its own sake, and so they are fated to be on the margin of the religious life of South Africa. However, the African indigenous churches (AICs), like the new South Africa, have been emerging out of mental and spiritual decolonization. They wield a great deal of influence on the populace. The AICs can see in the African traditional religions certain elements of "true" African spirituality that are indispensable to the spread of Christianity in Africa.

Patrick Ryan's essay, "African Muslim Spirituality: The Symbiotic Tradition in West Africa," focuses on the encounter between Islam and indigenous African tradition, as well as on the role of the religious synthesis that emerged out of this encounter in the daily lives of Muslims. Ryan observes that although reform-minded Muslims in Africa often claim that the "mixing variety of Islam" is fast disappearing, in reality this is not so, and that indeed, even the reform-minded Muslims often take part in African indigenous traditions. He shows how this popular tradition reveals "a spirituality of people who live on religious frontiers." The first encounter of Sub-Saharan Africans with Islam was through their encounter with North African Berbers. Through commercial contacts with the Western Sudanese empire, especially Mali, the Sudanese gradually developed great admiration for Muslim trading partners and their religious beliefs. These peaceful encounters became the basis for gradual Islamization of ancient West African states. Several Berber holy men and scholars often called *Ibadis* traveled and lived in the Sudanese kingdoms as "strangers" in foreign lands where there they prospered and established religious posts patronized by the indigenes. The Islamic encounter with the ancient kingdom of Ghana presents an interesting case study here. At first, the small Muslim community lived in a quarantine, separate from the central city populated by the local indigenous non-Muslim community. However, the Muslim leaders served as advisers to the king and were accorded a highly privileged status and great respect by the citizens. Ryan underscores the enduring importance of this first African encounter with a moderate form of Islam tolerant of African ritual practices and traditions. This tolerance prevailed before the more militant eleventh-century reform movement of the West in Sudan that sowed the seeds of Islamic militancy in the region.

Ryan further illustrates the history of the symbiotic Muslim spirituality in West Africa by examining events in the medieval Mali empire of the eleventh century. Here the ruler of the kingdom employed the spiritual power of the Muslim stranger-guests to assist in periods of crisis. Illustrated in Ali-Bakri's writings, the ruler of Mali sought the help of his Muslim guest to solve the problem of a great drought in his town. This case points to the continued importance of the Muslim clerics in the West African region during this period. Such dramatic events led to the conversion of the people of the kingdom, and Islam was adopted as the official state religion. The importance of the conversion to Islam, which occurred only after the cleric, through his fervent prayer, delivered the king and his subjects from a great drought illustrates, as Ryan has said, that the "spirituality of symbiotic West African Islam takes an instrumental attitude to prayer" (p. 290). When the empire of Mali collapsed at the end of the fourteenth century, Mali traders called Dyula and Wangara migrated to other parts of the region planting the seeds of Islam in their newly found homes in Sierra Leone, the Ivory Coast, and Nigeria, intermingling with local inhabitants, but remaining tolerant of indigenous practices. Ryan also examines the impact of North African Muslim immigrants and the Malain Diaspora on the forest region of West Africa. Among the Yoruba a large number of people converted to Islam. Indigenous religion and Islam interacted peacefully, but at times conflicted. The Yoruba situation differs from the Akan people of Ghana in which the matrilineal kinship system and disdain for circumcision make them less likely to convert to Islam. Yet Akan rulers did not hesitate to harness the esoteric knowledge of Islam to their advantage. On the whole, Islam bequeathed to West Africa the literate culture it espouses. Muslim knowledge of Arabic script and Qurʾanic scripture fascinated a largely illiterate population, so much so that in the governance of their territories, rulers sought the friendship of the Muslim clerics.

Tayob Abdulkader's essay, "Patterns of Islam among Youth in South Africa," examines Islamic spirituality among the Muslim youth. Abdulkader begins with the premise that religious practices are heavily influenced by cultural, social, and political values, and that those practices and values dovetail. The paper identifies the core values of the Muslim Youth Organization in the second half of the twentieth century. He outlines a brief historical trajectory of Muslims in South Africa who constitute only about 10 percent of the total population of South Africa even though Islam has been present in the Cape region since 1658. According to the author, Islam was established from two main sources: (1) a first wave of Muslim immigrants from the Mali Archipelago and around the Bay of Bengal, and (2) a second wave of immigrants, indentured Indians who came to work in the sugar cane plantations of Natal province. It was after the Second World War that Muslim youths, the descendants of these two immigrant groups, began to assert themselves as a response to institutionalized apartheid. Providing a historical outline of the emergence of dominant youth organizations, the author observes that the death of the famous youth leader Imam Abdullah Haran in 1969 at the hands of the state constituted the watershed for the more visible social and political role that Muslim youth organizations were to play in South Africa. From 1969, the youth movements became national as opposed to their regional postures prior to this date. One significant change in the new identity they then assumed is the strong interest they took in the application of Qurʾanic principles and values, especially concerning such issues as women and workers' rights. Tayob examines the contribution of Islam to the development of Muslim youth, especially in a highly racial society. The author observes that Islam alleviated the crisis that apartheid caused. Today there is still much division among Muslim youth, especially between those who favor a traditional role and hence are opposed to political involvement and those who clamor for modernization and are engaged in political struggles and human rights activities. It will be interesting to watch the role of the Muslim youth in the post-apartheid era, especially in the Cape Coast region, where Muslims organized to fight the evil of drug addiction and armed robbery in their communities.

Louis Brenner's "Sufism in Africa" begins with a theological and linguistic explanation of the origin and meaning of Sufism (*tasawwuf*). Sufism, he argues, is a "spiritual discipline" that aims at liberating "the human spirit from its corporeal shell so that it can move closer to God." There are two major approaches to the study of Sufism—the outsider's intellectual pursuit and the insider's "revelatory" approach, an approach described by Ibn Khaldun as "Supernatural perception." These two qualitatively different methods have caused major dissension between Sufis themselves and their "intellectually oriented" adversaries. Sub-Saharan African Sufi tradition and practice were spared such conflicts because, until recently, practice and intellectual pursuit were combined by Sufi adherents. Brenner examines the theology of leading African Sufi exponents, especially Ahmad Ibn Idri, who focused on three central concerns: (1) the epistemological context in which Sufi ideas are formulated, (2) the ritual practices in which Sufi ideas are carried out, and (3) the relationship of Sufism to social environments.

Sufism shares with non-Muslims in Africa a common epistemology in which supernatural occurrences and activities are regarded as real. Unlike Brenner's term "rationalistic paradigm of thought" characteristic of Western epistemology, the Sufis' "esoteric paradigm" appears to be quite crucial to the religious cultural milieu in which Sufis operate. A central idea in Sufi epistemology is that reality has two aspects, the manifest (*zahir*) and the hidden (*batin*), "external" and "internal." These two forms of knowledge are not accessible to all Muslims. While the "external" is for the general Muslim and can be obtained through obedience to the *sharia* (divine law), the "internal" is deeper and more restricted and is meant only for those who undergo the "spiritual discipline of the *tariqa*." For centuries, such "hierarchical conceptualization of knowledge" has been a major aspect of Africa's Islamic thought. Brenner provides a detailed outline of Islamic teaching in Africa showing how Sufism and Sufi ideas are privileged in religious knowledge. The practical dimension of Sufi ideas is equally espoused. He calls "applied Muslim religious science" the practice of tapping the "esoteric power" of the *Qur'an* for the good of society. The esoteric knowledge of the *Qur'an* became the basis of popular Islam, especially in healing and medicine. Healing is a central component of African life and society to which Islam has made major contributions. Muslims and non-Muslims alike tapped into these popular practices in spite of the condemnation of the Ulama that the practices constitute mere superstition. The author also observed that "because healing by its very nature is a pragmatic process, Muslim and non-Muslim religious experts have tended to interact rather freely in their roles as healers" (p. 337).

Lastly, the paper examines the devotional practices of the Sufi order (*tariqa*). Through the *tariqa* Muslim Sufi are able to go through prescribed spiritual training and to submit to the rigorous disciplinary rules necessary for their spiritual development. Through the help of a guide or spiritual leader, the path to perfection is accomplished by a Sufi initiate. The role and the significance of the two largest Sufi orders in West Africa, the *Quadriyya* and the *Tijaniyya* brotherhoods are discussed by the author.

Margaret Miles's paper, "Roman North African Christian Spiritualities," provides ample information about a region of the world that is often neglected in the treatment of African Christianity. From an "ecumenical and comparative perspective," she presents an overview of the intellectual and ethical contributions of North African Christianity to the growth of early Christianity, a neglected aspect of church history. Even though some of the dominant interpretations of Christian beliefs and practices take place in this part of the world, these interpretations later became branded as heretical and schismatic from the orthodox viewpoint. At the time these ideas and viewpoints were in currency, they were viewed not as heretical but as alternative interpretations of Christian belief and values that were attractive and appealing to certain people. The author further examines the important contributions of North African church fathers such as Tertullian, Cyprian, and Augustine in the development of religious life of Africans in the region.

This trio played major roles in the issues of church discipline, the establishment of an authoritative church hierarchy, and the crafting of a viable relationship between church and state. Miles acknowledges that the church fathers' interpretations of Christian values, lifestyles, and institutions became the standard for North African Christianity, but also influenced greatly the development of the Catholic Church across the Roman empire. Miles further examines the African Christian preoccupation with martyrdom and the emphasis placed on "the working of the spirit." From archaeological and literary evidence, she provides a descriptive interpretation of Roman African "pagan" religion. The focus was on the Saturn cult, a public religion adopted by the Berbers, especially the lower classes in Roman North Africa, in which child sacrifice was a central part. Only in the second century, she observes, when the cult of Saturn was romanized was there a substitute of animal for human sacrifices. Miles places the practice of violence against children within the context of a culture of violence that prevailed in the region. She raises the possibility of continuity between the human sacrifices and the Christian martyrdom referred to earlier on. In the last section, Miles analyzes the characteristics of various Christian groups, organizations, ritual practices, and worldviews in Africa during this period such as the Manichaeans, the Donatists, and the Montanists. Her treatment of these groups illustrates the divergence of North African Christianity in this period. Finally, she examines the nature of North African Catholics, looking at them through the prism of the venerable and prolific bishop Augustine of Hippo. She observes that Augustine was singularly responsible for transforming Roman-African Christianity into a much broader outlook in consonance with the universal Catholic Church and a global Christianity. One lasting legacy of Augustine, portrayed in his great works Confessions and the City of God was his views on the place of the body in Christian faith and practice.

"Asante Catholicism: An African Appropriation of the Roman Catholic

Religion," by Pashington Obeng, examines aspects of Africa's response to the Roman Catholic religion. Obeng's thesis is that as two cultures with divergent worldviews and values come into contact, the result is often conflict, but if there are parallels between their belief systems and practice, a sort of reciprocal influence emerges. Obeng surveys the specific situation of an indigenous African religious experience, the Asante tradition, in contact, in clash, and in continuity with the Roman Catholic faith. The product of this phenomenon he terms "Asante Catholicism." Obeng explores three main areas in highlighting the "cultural permutation" between Asante cultural values and Catholic belief. These three areas are (1) the Asante Catholic mass, (2) healing practices, and (3) the celebration of Corpus Christi. Mass is said in Asante Twi; there is singing and dancing, and the Catholic Church uses medals, vestments, and holy water. It believes in guardian angels and prayers for the dead, all symbolic for the Asante indigenous religious experience, providing convergence between the Roman and Asante cultures. The Catholic sacrament of anointing of the sick for healing fuses easily into the Asante belief that there is a spiritual dimension to ailments and that spiritual cures should be sought. Overall, the Asante try to maintain a canonical link with the Roman Catholic faith as well as to appropriate the new faith for their old indigenous religious experience. A complex and multifaceted spirituality is born—Asante Catholicism.

African Spirituality in the New World

African religion has been termed a global tradition in the sense that it has become an important tradition in the Caribbean and the Americas. The last part, therefore, examines some aspects of this tradition. In "Forms of African Spirituality in Trinidad and Tobago," Rudolf Eastman and Maureen Warner-Lewis document some retentions in African Diaspora, particularly in the Caribbean islands of Trinidad and Tobago. The authors examine the three formal African-derived religious organizations: Orisha, Vodun, and the Spiritual Baptist faith. There are differences in the mode of worship and in religious observances, but African ritual, like trance-possession, initiation, noncentralized shrines, and priesthood processes, cut across the three religious congregations. The fourth religious expression with considerable African retention and spirituality is referred to as "Obeah," signifying manipulating spiritual forces for good or evil through magical, herbal, and spiritual knowledge. A symbiotic relationship exists between these African religions just as their memberships also overlap with memberships of other religions in that cultural milieu.

Gerdès Fleurant's essay, "The Music of Haitian Vodun," explains the prejudices against Vodun, one of the most maligned African-derived religions in the Western Hemisphere. Vodun differs from and is similar to Western monotheistic traditions at the same time. For example, the theistic concept *Iwa*, which is often translated as "god," normally refers to spiritual entities. Fleurant provides an ethnographic history of Haiti as a background to a descriptive interpretation of Vodun. Before Africans were brought from the continent in 1502, aboriginal groups of Native American (Indian) tribes lived in the Americas. African slaves came from different parts of the continent but predominantly from West Africa, with diverse and rich cultural traditions. On their arrival Vodun tradition emerged as a synthesis of these diverse indigenous African religions and provided "the cement that bonds together all of these people." Following the slave revolt and war of liberation (1791–1803), Haiti became an independent state. Vodun belief and practices are generally classified into two broad though exclusive ritual or worship patterns, *Rada* and *Kongo/Petro* rites.

The Rada represents those whose music and structure came from Fon/Ewe and Yoruba of Dahomey (Benin) in West Africa and the Kongo represent those that began from the period of slavery in Haiti. Like the African religions from which it came, Vodun is family-based and displays structures similar to African traditions. Belief in a Supreme Being and several spiritual entities often coexists with belief in Catholic saints. The spiritual forces are *Legba*, the spirit of the gate keeper; *Ezuli*, the spirit of love; and *Ogooun,* the spirit of defense and war. Vodun is a highly pragmatic and practical religion. Its devotees propitiate their deities in exchange for favors and interventions in periods of crisis. Fleurant underscores the important role of music in Vodun spirituality. According to him "dancing, drumming, and singing are the main components of the music of Vodun." Vodun connects very much with African music, and a knowledge of the structure and workings of the music is essential to Vodun religion. However, Vodun music is complex and varies. Fleurant uses samples of music for major Rada and Kongo/Petro Iwa in Bopo and other towns in Haiti to illustrate that music provides very deep meaning. This music relates to the social, historical, religious, and communal ideas and feelings of the people. The author observes that some rhythms and dances of Vodun music are symbolic of specific "action, either impending or in progress." Moreover, the music is inclusive, allowing for the active participation of everyone present.

In "African-derived Religion in the African-American Community in the United States," Mary Cuthrell-Curry traces the history and growth of African-derived religion in the United States. Beyond African-inspired religions, a term she defines as religion as practiced today by "native born African-Americans" in the United States but which had its origin in Africa, Cuthrell-Curry claims that the Yoruba-derived religions in the United States were first introduced to America through the slave-trade link. The Yoruba religion (called *Santería*, *Ocha*, or simply the Religion) operates on a system of beliefs and practices that include notions of destiny and reincarnation; perception of a universe where humanity stands in between various forces; and complex ritual ceremonial systems. The author then examines the ritual practices of Yoruba religion, arguing that they constitute the core of the tradition. Unlike in Santería, Afro-Cuban religion, practitioners of Yoruba religion in the United States are gradually purging the tradition of its Catholic elements.

Acknowledgments

The African volume in the World Spirituality series was coordinated in its earlier stage by Charles Long, who passed it on to me to develop and complete. I am deeply grateful to him for the scholarly insights and personal support he gave me throughout the different stages of this work. I also wish to express my sincere thanks to all the authors for their contributions and for their patience over many years.

I owe special thanks to Connie Zeiller and Aklil Bekele for secretarial support. Connie worked under enormous pressures of time during the last phase of the work. For their assistance in bringing the project to a successful conclusion, I owe a debt of gratitude to Mark Davis, my research assistant; David Ogungbile, my former student in Nigeria and now a graduate student at Harvard Divinity School; and Debbie Klein, a postdoctoral research scholar currently working with me. Finally, I am grateful to the editorial staff of The Crossroad Publishing Company and to Maurya Horgan and Paul Kobelski of The HK Scriptorium, Inc., for their diligence in producing this book.

Part One

COSMOLOGIES AND SACRED KNOWLEDGE

Some Reflections on African Spirituality

DOMINIQUE ZAHAN

FROM THE MANY STUDIES and research projects undertaken in recent decades on the subject of African religion, one fact consistently arises: the traditional spirituality of the peoples of the so-called Dark Continent includes distinctive characteristics compared with those generally ascribed to the spirituality of so-called revealed religions.

The latter religions are above all else based on relationships with the Invisible and are the products of a code of love. The religious experience in this case results from the love of God for his creatures and the love of these creatures for their Creator. The spirituality of *l'Homme Noir,* on the other hand, does not appear to confine itself to such a conceptual construction. Traditional African religion is devoid of the notion of original sin. The African lives in a state of *anamartesis,* which cannot be fully appreciated by revealed religions. The destiny of the African is linked neither to the original drama in which the primordial ancestor played the leading role nor to the tragedy of redemption in which the essential role is played by God himself. The absence of original sin and of redemption necessarily implies the absence of final judgment.

The two kinds of spirituality that have just been identified do in fact place human destiny in two different durations. The religious experience of upholders of revealed religions has a linear time scale; humanity, in this case, is on a path that has neither a beginning nor an end. The experience of the followers of traditional religions, however, is the product of a cyclical, repetitive time that lacks the mark of eternity. But this does not mean that the latter religion is totally devoid of the notion of salvation. In cyclical time salvation itself becomes a repetitive undertaking of which the protagonist is the individual. The preoccupation of the "believers" consists here not in the handing over of their redemption to a transcendent being but in their taking upon themselves their own redemption by appropriate spiritual techniques. In traditional religions salvation is conceived of as the supposedly indeterminate return of the human being to this world.

From all this we can easily note the great difference that exists between the spiritual portrait of the African person and that of a person of non-African cultures. The latter is steeped in justice, reverence, love, and fear with anguish and anxiety coloring the notions of life and death which underlie one's destiny. The former, on the other hand, maintains a kind of equality between the human and God. In traditional religions the believers and the Supreme Being in whom they believe share the same advantages and disadvantages, the same rights and the same duties. From this ensues the familiarity and simplicity which characterize the religious procedures of Africans in their spiritual quest. These attitudes do, however, also contain prototypical elements. The Invisible toward which believers strive becomes for them a model which, in the hierarchy of beings, is like the leader above the believers who possesses the same qualities as believers but tends toward perfection. This explains the feelings of respect and fear, and indeed of pity and adulation, that can be found in African spirituality.

There is, however, a culminating point which resides in the mystical emotion that the religious experience provides for believers being carried along the dark path of their relationships with divinity. Until now this aspect of African religion has been little studied. It does, however, reveal the time dimensions of the religious beliefs of the African people. African mysticism brings to the surface the way in which God's possession of the believer is realized. It also shows the demands made by God on the believer as well as the feelings of the latter toward the invisible possessor.

Creator and Creation

As strange as it may seem, the Supreme Divinity is not generally the pole toward which the innumerable threads of African spirituality converge. It does, however, constitute the ultimate stage of recuperating the vital human elements released at the moment of death. Altars are sometimes dedicated to him and offerings are made; but sometimes his name, if not his very existence, is unknown. As for mystic phenomena, especially those concerning possession, there is rarely any connection with the Supreme Divinity. More often than not it is the secondary divinities who have the monopoly on the piety and fervor of the believers. Such is the case, for example, among the Songhai people, the Nagos-Yoruba, the Fon, the Hausa, and the Ewe, to name but the best-known populations in West Africa alone.

Ideas concerning the Supreme Being are not recorded in any corpus, nor do they constitute a form of teaching that is reserved for specialists who could possibly be considered in the same light as our own theologians. The initiates come to understand the nature of God with the help of icons, metaphors, metonymies, and symbols that are presented to them in various forms during initiation meetings. God the "reaper" of human lives thus appears in the image of the hunter (a widespread theme in West Africa). His immensity is often skillfully depicted as the elephant and the hippopotamus (Bambara, Bozo, and generally among forest dwellers and those living beside the stretches of water where this latter mammal can be found). His majesty and justice are often conveyed through the metaphor of the lion. Finally, what may seem to Westerners to be "obscene" rites can symbolize a man's joy at being beside his God (Bambara).

Africans may use all the materials that their environment puts at their disposal in order to express their ideas about God. For them everything that surrounds them exhibits a sort of transparency that allows them to communicate directly with heaven. Things and beings are not obstacles to the knowledge of God; rather they constitute signifiers and indices which reveal the divine being (Zahan 1979, 15).

In order to have a better understanding of Africans' knowledge of the Supreme Being, the tendency in recent years has been to study theophoric names of individuals at the time they are given or at the time of their integration into initiatory societies. Researches carried out on this subject in West Africa (Mossi and Bissa in Upper Volta, Kabyadina and Moba in Northern Togo, and Sara in Chad) are not convincing. Theophoric names tend rather to be "stylistic devices," usually hypallages, behind which is concealed a very anthropomorphic notion of the Supreme Being.

Among the significant elements of the knowledge of the nature of God, the distancing of him is undoubtedly the most widespread and the most firmly rooted in the beliefs of Africa. Humans, earth dwellers par excellence, see the Divine Being, both in space and in emotional perception, as an entity so distant that it is sometimes impossible to name it and especially to address invocations or to devote cults to it. Among the Dangaleat people of Chad, God is neither named nor invoked. The Bura of Mali name him but have no cult surrounding him. But this distancing has not always been this way; it represents the last stage of the mythical drama telling of the relationships between humans and God. In the past, according to the tales of many African peoples (Bwa, Dogon, Lobi, Mossi, Ewe, and others) heaven was close to earth, if not in fact joined to it. As for God, he lived among humans, who, not knowing about food products acquired through work, would feed themselves by taking slices from the nearby firmament.

Divinities as Intermediaries

Most myths emphasize certain structural motifs in the present universe. Heaven and the divinity moved away once and for all and adopted the position they currently occupy, abandoning human beings to their tasks and obliging them above all to invent for themselves intermediaries in order to reestablish a link with the Invisible. The strategy of mythical thought is clear here. The distancing of God creates a religious need within the human being; absence engenders the search for what is absent—a search that is finally accomplished by less noble but perhaps more efficient intermediaries.

In "primal" theology these intermediaries constitute punctilious divinities, economic gods, such as the Orishas of the Nagos-Yoruba or the Voduns of the Fon. They are the directors of major events such as war and hunting. They are assimilated to atmospheric phenomena such as wind and rain, thunder and lightning, or rainbows; or even elements on which human life depends such as the earth, rivers, the sea, the sun, and so on. Among these divinities the "master" of smallpox enjoys special consideration in the form of Sakpata for the Fon and the Ewe, and Ojuku for the Ibo. The importance attached to this illness is not, as we might think, due to its highly contagious and epidemic nature, nor to its exceptional gravity. To understand it we have to know that the cultures of West Africa where smallpox is venerated affirm a correlation that they believe exists between this illness and the Lord. The royal nature of the illness has already been pointed out by G. Parrinder (1950), but he took it no further. Now, according to agricultural and royal traditions recorded by me among the Kourouba people in the northern regions of Upper Volta, the first Lord of this people descended from heaven, his body riddled with smallpox. He was cured by his subjects, the farmers, who had issued from the depths of the earth. The pimply eruptions that characterize smallpox make of it a heavenly illness because the skin of those affected by it resembles the celestial dome littered with stars. Descended from heaven, with which he identifies himself in a way, the first Lord was a smallpox victim, his skin showing the signs of the starry firmament. This allows a further understanding not only of the way in which certain gods are "born" into African religion but also of their nature and perhaps of the rites that emerge from their cults. Thinking of this in another way allows us to understand the ideas of

Africans concerning the origin of certain illnesses as well as their treatment.

Smallpox, supposedly an illness from heaven, owes its cure to those who, in mythical times, rose from the bowels of the earth. It is also, therefore, connected with the chthonian world, while the divinity by which it is represented is at the same time God of heaven and of earth. Through an inability to understand these correlations, researchers have often been bothered by the cult devoted to this divinity, whose followers were once, as Parrinder points out, "more numerous than those of all other gods."

Attempts have sometimes been made to draw up exhaustive lists of the divinities who constitute the "pantheon" of certain peoples, especially in the area around the Gulf of Benin. Some researchers have come up with three hundred and even as many as five or six hundred of them among the Ewe. These figures are interesting in that they show the extent to which everyday reality is considered sacred. It is as if human beings were trying to attain everything beyond their immediate powers not by means of "lay" technology but rather through religious know-how. Apart from this practical aspect, however, the inventories in question do not seem to offer much of scientific interest for the understanding of the religion of the various peoples.

Unlike the roles played by the "secondary" divinities, the function of the Supreme God is essentially that of Creator. This is his prerogative and his alone, even though he may not play a part in every aspect of creation. For example, the task of creation may be assigned by the Creator himself to an Assistant, who thus becomes the principal mediator between the divinity and humans. This can be seen with the Bambara (Faro being the Assistant of Bemba), the Dogon (Nommo is the Assistant of Amma), and the Bwa (Do is the Assistant of Debwenu). Although this idea of an "Assistant" (*Moniteur*) has not yet attracted the interest of West African ethnic groups apart from those mentioned above, it is a reasonable assumption that the idea of providing the Creator with an efficient helper fits into the mainstream of traditional African thought concerning power. Power has always been conceived of by Africans in the least despotic light possible. The more important it is, the more reason to share it in order to avoid the individualization that could generate social abuses and disturbances. This, I think, helps us to understand the existence of divine couples: among the Fon of Dahomey we find Lisa and his female partner Mawu; Obatala (male) and Odudua (female) are the "partners" of Olorun according to the Yoruba people. There is much variety in the accounts of African origin concerning the act of creation. Once again it can be said that no methodical study has been made concerning this aspect of African culture. (Syntheses, especially, are greatly lacking in this area.)

The Supreme Being and Chains of Creation

Accounts of creation seem to put forward four modes of accomplishment: (1) the exteriorization of signs and thoughts actually conceived within the divinity (Dogon, Bambara); (2) the "thingification" of the Word of God (Dogon, Bambara); (3) the manual act (most African cultures); (4) creation, through vomiting, by the Supreme Divinity. We will not linger on the first three modes, though they are worthy of interest. They are well known to experts and even to the informed public. Our attention will focus on the fourth mode because of its rarity on the African continent, which is partly why researchers know so little about it. Until now we have encountered it only among the Bakuba people of Zaire, for whom the story of their origins is closely linked to, and is on a parallel with, the performance of initiation rites.

These people tell of how, one day, the god Mboom (Mbuma) suffered from painful cramps. He proceeded to spew forth the sun, the moon, and the stars, which brightened up the water-covered and darkened earth, over which he had always reigned. The heat from the sun evaporated the primordial waters. Mboom began to vomit again, bringing up from his stomach nine animals and many human beings. Among the nine animals was lightning in the form of a black quadruped resembling a leopard. These animals were the forerunners of their species; each one began to vomit and brought up his species; the universe was formed in a succession of vomiting spells which separated one species from another.

At a given moment a certain Woot appeared in the human species, a cultural hero and founder of the Kuba dynasty. He is on earth what God is in the grand scheme of things. Woot is the symmetrical equivalent of Mboom, and he gives life to nine children, corresponding to the nine primordial animals of the creation. They are not, however, born through vomiting but by what could be called natural means. A woman, in this case the sister of Woot, gives birth to them after an incestuous union between herself and her brother.

The sons of Woot provide the basis of the Kuba initiation system. In order to punish them for a breach against him, Woot makes them undergo tests that would become the present initiation rites. The first ordeal consists in making the novices cross a ditch that lies to the west of the village, and which is supposedly the inhabitants' defecating area; in actual fact it is not. After passing through this area the novices run to cleanse themselves of their symbolic filth, and then undergo further daily ordeals that are intentionally omitted from this study.

What we are concerned with here is the structural scheme according to which Kuba cosmogony and initiation are bound together on the basis of ascent and descent. One fact concerning this springs immediately to mind. The god Mboom and the cultural hero Woot are beings who, in one way or another, reject what has been introduced into their bodies, rejection being the result of ingestion. However, from a functional point of view there is a great difference between God and humans (in this case Woot). The first is a being with one essential orifice: the mouth. The second has openings at both of the body's extremities. We can therefore assume that what is ingested by God does not pass through his body but enters and leaves through the same opening in a movement of descent and ascent, whereas that which is ingested by a human passes through his body in a downward movement. The state of the evacuated substances is therefore different in both cases. In vomit the ingested substances are not completely transformed. Fecal matter, on the other hand, no longer has anything in common with what was ingested. In traditional cultures excrement represents not only a total transformation of ingested matter but also the most adequate example to symbolize the human being at the beginning of initiatory life, at the moment when he begins the attempt to surpass himself. In one African culture that is geographically distanced from the Bakuba (the Bambara in the Republic of Mali), where similar ideas concerning excretion can be found, it is said: "Man issues from the mouth of God, the sage issues from the buttocks of man." Who is the Kuba who would refuse to accept such a statement?

We now have a better understanding of the initiation system that involves the defecation ditch toward which the Bakuba neophytes are driven. The initiation is a complex operation, but it stems from a seemingly simple principle which, in African thought, can be summed up as follows: to be initiated is to surpass oneself, but in order to achieve this one has to compare oneself to human excrement.

The second affirmation that can be made concerning the example around which Kuba cosmogony and initiation are structured involves the relationship, in the eyes of the Kuba, between the mouth of God and the sexual organs of a woman. What is born from the mouth of God is the equivalent of that which is born from the sex of a woman, with the following difference: God gives birth to beings of cosmic dimensions whereas a woman gives birth to beings who must conquer their cosmicality through initiation rites. In the Kuba myth concerning the origins of the world, it is said that Mboom also gives birth, through vomiting, to three sons. They are not, however, evoked in any self-surpassing process. On the contrary, they behave like their creator: The first vomits white ants; the second, a plant from which originates all vegetation. The third is the kite, a unique bird that was vomited by the egret (one of the nine primordial animals). The conquest of cosmicity by the children of woman proceeds with a descending-ascending movement and is thus inversely symmetrical to that of the beings who come from God. This first descent of a human from the mother's uterus to the outside world should be insisted upon here. The Bakuba, like most human cultures, hold with the descent of the child head first because it corresponds to entry into this world and is synonymous with life. The inversely symmetrical descent (feet first) is considered a bad omen; it corresponds to the exit from the world—in other words, death. This is why dead bodies are always carried feet first to their place of burial. The upward movement of the human being begins with his obtaining knowledge through initiation.

The ascending-descending movement in which is inscribed the cosmogonic myth of creation, and the ascending-descending movement that characterizes human destiny, go hand in hand with the diurnal and the nocturnal regime of the sun. Our world is one of darkness that can be thwarted and dissipated only by initiatory knowledge. This explains the parallelism between the Mboom and the Woot cycles. The latter is in fact continually striving toward the former. Humans can surpass themselves only by putting themselves on equal footing, so to speak, with God, which is a common mystical attitude among African cultures.

Spirituality and the Cult of Ancestors

The question of the ancestor cult is crucial to African spirituality. The veneration of the respected dead constitutes one of the commonest features of African liturgies, but it bears only a slight resemblance to our "cult of the dead." Ancestor worship in Africa has some specific features that it is important to point out.

Generally speaking, the death of the individual is the necessary condition for becoming an ancestor throughout Black Africa. This is because death does not represent the end of human existence, but rather a change in its status. This demand is not absolutely necessary because of another aspect of the notion of death. This creates a solution of continuity between the living and the dead, a solution marked by the differential distance on the scale between these "creditors" (the dead) and these debtors (their "heirs"). Because this distancing begins even before the last breath of the elderly has been breathed, in certain societies they become ancestors during their own lifetime. Therefore a great-grandfather belonging to the Mossi people in the Republic of Upper Volta, for example, may be considered an ancestor long before his death. This example is by no means an exception: It has already been noted among the Bantu people in southeastern Africa among others. We should point out, however, that it is neither a question of true ancestor worship, nor is it metaphorical. The great-grandfather in question is an ancestor because he represents for his descendants the image of the archetypal model whose outlines have been traced and defined by the society into which they have both become integrated. As an ancestor, he may, should the case arise, return in one of his heirs, but may receive cult status from them only after his death and especially after the differential distancing which becomes apparent only during the second funeral ceremony, or when modifications are made to his tomb.

It is important also to note that not all dead people automatically attain the status of ancestor and that death is not always a requirement for it. The notion of ancestor implies the idea of selection. It is necessary that it correspond, before any other consideration, to a social model based on the idea of exemplification, in the strictest sense of the word. Thus, the ancestor is someone who has reached a great age and who, during his lifetime, has acquired a vast experience of life, human beings, and things. He is also someone who dies in a way that conforms to the rules of society to which he belongs: death by "ill reputed" disease (such as leprosy) or by accident (especially if provoked by lightning) means exclusion from the society of the ancestors. The same goes for all those who do not enjoy their physical, psychic, and moral integrity. The latter stems, above all, from the mastering of the self and of one's word. Finally, only he who is an organic member of the family, of the lineage, or of the tribe to which he belongs can be an ancestor. Slaves and outsiders, even if integrated into a social unit, can never attain the status of ancestor.

Another specific feature of ancestor worship lies in the position occupied by the ancestors on the scale of values. The society of these glorious dead represents a perfect community. Unlike the society of the living, where we find "good" people and "bad" people, "pure" people and "impure" people, "handsome" people and "ugly" people, that of the dead is exempt from contradictions, tensions, and oppositions. The world of the ancestors is one that is free of antitheses and violence because it resides in a slow time. Ancestors can, of course, become incensed and they are even susceptible to suffering. It is, however, always the living who bring about these mood changes and these feelings in them.

Even though the life of the ancestors is characterized by slow time, this does not imply that their society is inert, like still water. The contrary is the case. The ancestral community is in a constant state of renewal which is affected in two ways. First, the "newly dead" invariably keep the earthward side of their universe updated and on its feet. Second, there is the continual disappearance of a part of them, the heavenly side, which has become useless because of the weaknesses in the collective memory of those in this world. So for each African community the useful part of the world of the ancestors (for the living) is reduced to a meager slice (sometimes just a few generations) which is, however, constantly being renewed. Parallel to this dynamic of the world of the ancestors, under the signs of "Entrance and Exits," we find another that could be called the "exit into touch" of the ancestors.

In most African societies, it is thought that the newborn of both sexes, while being the result of fertilization of woman by man, carry within them (in forms defined by each individual society) an ancestor. This is likened to a soccer ball or a rugby ball "thrown in" from the imaginary sideline which is the demise or distancing brought about by age. The back-and-forth movement of the ancestors constitutes, in itself, a certain dynamism; it is clothed with another, more subtle this time, which consists in the acquisition, by those who go back to this world, of cultural enrichment achieved by the welcoming committee since their departure from this world. We can thus talk of a parallel "cultural enrichment" of the world of the living and of the world of the ancestors. This means that the tradition and the social and religious behavior of the living invoked by the upholders of a common culture are not fixed realities. They are, of course, the result of experiences lived by the living, the sum of the wisdom of a society at a given moment in its existence and gradually stored up in "the Beyond" by its most eminent dead. They are at the same time results that change imperceptibly, like branches whose buds swell continually.

The second point, opposing the opinion of those who would like to see in the world of the ancestors a fixed world, is related to the trade between the living and the ancestors by way of libations and sacrifices. Though this aspect of ancestor worship is usually invoked by researchers because it is most apparent, still the tendency has been to concentrate only on certain elements found within it. Succinctly, there is a certain structural logic in the system of giving offerings to the ancestors. Generally speaking, libations precede the bloody sacrifice, which always involves victims that are white in color. For an African with a sense of traditional values, the reasons behind this are clear. Libations constitute the "introduction" to trade with the ancestors, and the sacrifice its high point, engaging the living, in a radical fashion, in their quest and their wait, and the dead in their obligation to reply favorably.

Libations provide a means of exploring "Heaven"; through them it is hoped to discover the ancestors' dispositions and to provoke their reactions with regard to one undertaking or another, for which their intervention is sought. They are usually constituted of three media: fresh water, millet flour mixed with water, and millet beer (or palm wine). Each of these three "materials" possesses a particular virtue. Fresh water is an emollient; it attracts the attention of the person to whom it is offered, because it is a tender and affectionate touch on the part of the one who pours it onto the ancestral altar. If it were not for the sensual connotations, we could say that fresh water is like a caress. Water mixed with millet flour is more than just a sacred "touch." It awakens. It causes swallowing and its immediate and involuntary reaction is digestion. It drives the ancestor to act, to carry out the sure, fair gesture whose consequences, expected by its seeker, will escape, so to speak, even from his own control. Millet beer and palm wine are stimulants. As an offering, the beer stimulates and exalts the ancestors. It causes them, as it were, to lose control of themselves and react just as the living would like. In the order of libations, fresh water precedes and sometimes introduces the other two. Fermented beer follows the other two. It is the last recourse of human beings to the will of the ancestors before the most noble gift offered to them through bloody sacrifice. This represents the most important invention by religious humanity concerning its communication with the Invisible. This kind of offering is equivalent to millet flour mixed with water. Both are vital substances. Blood, however, goes further in that it calls to mind the durable action that resembles the life of the animal. All major moments of the ancestral cult end with bloody sacrifices, the victims of which are usually white chickens (male or female), or goats. Sometimes if the royal house is involved, horses and even human beings, as was the case in Mossi country (Upper Volta), in Dahomey, among the Malinke, and elsewhere.

Ancestral altars do vary. It would, however, be possible to establish a typology without linking each type to specific societies. They usually consist of one or several stones placed on the ground. Sometimes they take the form of seats (as in Asanti, Ewe, Attie), pottery, clay cones, or simply the uprights from each side of the entry of the dwelling place. The officiating priests of the cult of ancestors offer less variety. Such a priest is either the oldest member of the lineage or tribe, or he is someone specially chosen by his group. There are also cases, for example, among the Dogon people, where this role is partially filled by someone chosen by the ancestor himself.

In appearance, the cult of ancestors seems very simplistic, whereas in reality it is as complex as the public cult of Christian churches. One of the commonest elements of the cult is the use of small wooden objects of varying lengths, cut into a Y shape, with notches in the shape of steps all along one side. They look like ladders, well known throughout West Africa, especially where the dwellings have terraced roofs, to which the ladder often provides access. The Dogon do in fact call them "ladders" (*bilu*). They are found from one end of West Africa to the other. These objects are usually placed near the ancestral altar, along with other ritual objects (pottery, acorn cups, small statues, etc.). They can also be found on the tombs of the deceased, as is the case in Guinea. These miniature ladders, as liturgical objects, are intended to master and harmonize trade with the souls of the dead. They permit the souls to rise to heaven sometime after the death of the person, and then to come back and consume the food that is offered to them. Finally, it allows them to be reincarnated in the bodies of their descendants. By extrapolating the meaning of those objects from what we know of the Dogon, it can be said that these ladders cement the link between the living and the dead in three main ways:

1. By causing the intervention of the feet and the legs, the ladder authenticates communication between the visible and invisible worlds; as something essentially human among the living, it is the leg which assures communication in space.

2. By causing the intervention of the organs, the ladder facilitates the climb and avoids the fall; it integrates the communication in a moderate rhythm which suits the slow time in which the lives of those departed flow by.

3. By its Y shape, the ladder brings to mind the pubis and the sexual organs of both man and woman; it is a sign of both masculinity and femininity, and places the communication into the symbolic realm of fertility. All trade between the two worlds which departs from this framework can only inspire mistrust and fear among the living.

The cult of ancestors constitutes a humanized liturgy. Although women have as many rights to ancestor worship as men, in matrilineal societies female ancestor worship takes precedence over male ancestor worship, whereas in patrilineal societies the opposite is the case. It seems, however, that in all cases the woman is the soul of the cult and the man its obligatory agent. Without woman and the role she plays in the society of the living, the cult of ancestors would probably have no reason for existence.

The Shrines

What was always surprising to the Western person traveling in Africa was the absence of great shrines dedicated to the public cult and, on the other hand, the presence of innumerable places of prayer that are sometimes marked simply by a tree, a copse, a stone, a water hole, a lake, a river, or even the sea or mountains. Generally speaking, we can say that the African has accorded more attention to the "source" of the cult, to the altar, than to the shrine intended to shelter it. There are exceptions to this general remark. In Nigeria, Dahomey, Ghana, and Mali, there are still real religious edifices of which a part is allocated to the public and the rest to the protection of the liturgical material. "Public" is not to be taken in the same social sense as we understand it. It masks the ideas of initiation. Generally, the only people admitted to the common part of the shrines are the followers who have been introduced to the understanding of the "mystery" evoked by the place of the cult, while the "reserved" section is accessible only to the high dignitaries belonging to the cult in question. What is more, the members of this community may not penetrate into a shrine erected to another mystery if they are not initiates of that one too. In practice this means that religion poses not only problems of faith and affective adhesion to a system of beliefs but also, and above all, problems of understanding. The religion is divided up, so to speak, into as many sectors, whether they be exclusive or complementary to each other, as there are different realms of understanding. Only the follower initiated into all of these can enter all of the particular shrines. It should be added that because a shrine belongs to a particular group it does not necessarily follow that other groups with the same cultural background have access to it. Thus, even if we can talk about "one" African religion as a "system of beliefs" resting on the same principles, it can be divided into as many different "departments" as there are cults and men who practice it.

The dividing up of religion, suggested here by the multiplicity of shrines, can be compared to the dividing up of land into many properties, each with its own "shrine heraldry." The great number of these cult places should not, however, discourage us from trying to establish a systematic classification as original as it is close to African thought. The four "basic" elements: air, earth, fire, and water provide an evocative outline of this viewpoint.

In many parts of West Africa, water, as a natural element, is a factor that inspires at the same time feelings of uncertainty, fear, assurance, and security. Seen essentially as a source of life, it is closely linked to human existence. Shrines are erected in any place where water is found or where it may be found. Rivers and lakes contain, in the image of the water that they carry along or enclose, deeply religious representations. Each one has its genie, if it is not, metonymically speaking, both a kind of "water god" to which riverside dwellers devote a cult, or a "water temple" into which the believers enter respectfully carrying their offerings. Not much is known about sacred representations in connection with water, because of their great valorization. In West Africa only the Niger River, and to a lesser extent the smaller river in Nigeria, have been explored in this light, along with the Bosomtiwi, Debo, and Faguibine Lakes. The part of the Niger that crosses Bambara country is purported to be the body of Faro (the water genie) with whom are associated fertility, multiplication, and the proliferation of all living things. Among the Yoruba people of Nigeria, it is believed that Yemoja (the daughter of Obatala and Odudua) gave birth to all waters in the country, but she is above all "in charge" of the Ogun River, her favorite shrine. We are reminded by G. Parrinder that the temples erected in her honor shelter vases that contain holy water from the river. For the Bini, in the same country, all the waters in the region belong to Oba. In Ghana and the Ivory Coast rivers and still waters are the property of Tano and Bia, two renowned divinities. Before a major fishing trip Lake Debo receives (from the Bojo people) a goat whose throat has been cut, as well as fresh water and certain kinds of cereals and plants. Springs, permanent swamps, and temporary water holes, so numerous that they cannot possibly be listed here, are also "water temples" connected with female fertility and the psychoreligious evolution of the individual. How many deep and indiscernible autochthonous considerations we can discover by delving deep into the thought of humble villages lying by a stretch or a body of still water that the rains replenish each year!

Fresh water is, by its nature, favorable to life; it is human water. Sea water is inhuman and wild; as the Africans see it, special means are required in order that this water be tamed. Moreover, if there are sacrificial grounds or places of prayer which face the sea, these marine temples do not, it seems, enjoy the renown of inland temples. However, the Ashanti, the Fante, and the Ga of Ghana, the Yoruba and the Bini of Nigeria, as well almost all the peoples occupying the lagoons, coastal regions, and islands in the ocean, such as Bidjoko, for example, are naturally carried toward a sea religion.

Shrines that have connections with the earth have as many variations as, if not more than, those mentioned earlier. We must keep in mind that at least 75 percent of Africans are settled farmers, that the earth is for them the true source of life, just as the woman is the vital receptacle for lineage and class. From this comes the symbolic assimilation of the two realities, which is often found in Africa. Also stemming from this is the mythical theme, mentioned earlier, concerning the emergence of the first farmers from the bowels of the earth. This idea is so widespread among African peasants and so well known by Western researchers that it is unnecessary to go into detail here. It would be better to concentrate on the shrines dedicated to the soil.

The shrines dedicated to the soil have specific characteristics wherever they are found on the African continent: they are not temples properly speaking; the earth has no edifice; it is a religious and sacred monument in itself. This is why it would be inappropriate to want to limit it or to claim to imprison it within walls. Earth shrines can be found wherever human beings make the gesture of deference to the ground that feeds them. Mountains, caves, rocks, and stones that awaken the religious imagination, holes and crevices that open out into the unknown and the mysterious lend themselves admirably to the metamorphosis of such features into cult places. With no prior preparation they become altars, churches, temples. Cultivated fields are especially suited to being regarded as sacred. Before working a field, the farmer (whether he be Asanti, Mossi, Bambara, or other) pours in the four corners of the field a little millet flour and water, as well as the blood of a white chicken sacrificed by himself. This is his offering. It increases the feeling of veneration for the soil and the food given to the ancestors. Through these actions the field becomes a cult place, or even a shrine.

In much of West Africa, and especially between the Niger and Cavaly Rivers, to the east and west respectively, a whole section of the population belonged to the category known as earth chiefs. It is among these that the agents of earth cults are recruited, who are also in charge of various rituals concerning agriculture and the establishing of political leaders. These latter are, despite their power, tributaries of the first—who naturally assure them their sustenance.

The temples in harmony with the air are the most numerous and the closest to the disposition of the believers. These temples, however, consist of sacred trees and groves. These vegetal species, and the limited groupings that they constitute without human intervention, are thought of as aerial because they are linked to concrete time, marked by atmospheric changes and the seasons. Trees (and all vegetal matter) follow the "movement of the air": they "are" of an aerial nature.

There is not a single African community that does not show great consideration toward this type of vegetation. The fact that the traditional pharmacopoeia is largely dependent on it certainly helps explain this infatuation, but it does not explain everything. The real reason seems to stem from the fact that the tree seems to act as an intermediary between human beings and spiritual powers.

This mediation is often so strong that humanity is considered to emanate from vegetal matter. The Bambara believe in a kind of metempsychosis in which one of the milestones is in fact the tree. This belief ties in somewhat with those found among the Fon of Dahomey: certain of their myths tell of how men and women descended *in illo tempore* from the branches of an iroko tree. It is also apparent in the widespread African practice in which women hoping to become pregnant ask a tree to help the child come; such trees include iroko, kapokier, acacia, acajou, baobab, palms, and so on.

The mediatory power of the tree comes from its nature too. The tree lives after the fashion of the human being. It even serves as an example for a human being, offering itself to him or her as a model. It has a soul and it lives in the true sense of the term; it dies without the destruction of its body and is then reborn to continue its existence.

There is, therefore, a deep-rooted and unsuspected link between humanity and the tree. A tree is not felled without having first been given offerings to subsidize the needs of its soul. There is no confusion between the vegetable matter and the objects that human beings can get from it. But a lack of respect for the harmony between the two realities causes the object to no longer be able to fulfill its mission. Rites involving drums, as well holy seats among the Akan people, are incomprehensible without this information. The tree takes on an even more intense religious value when it is integrated into the copses used by people for religious assemblies and initiation rites. These sacred copses can be found everywhere in Africa. They are naturally offered up by the ecological milieu; one can sometimes rearrange their central part in order to make a clearing. These are in fact air temples, and access to them is made difficult by the very nature of the vegetation, which usually consists of sharp prickly thornbushes, as well as by pathways that are hidden.

From what we already know about the symbolism of the sacred copse among peoples of the Mossi, the Bambara, and the Senufo, it can be said that this kind of shrine is loaded, in the minds of its users, with representations concerning knowledge, mystery, and secrets. Further, the inner clearing represents the end of the path of knowledge—the sky and holy space. Nowhere else do African liturgies contain more meaning than in these aerial sanctuaries.

The most humble African temples are those concerned with fire. They are also the closest to daily life and the most widespread. First, there is the hearth where the African woman prepares the food for her household. It is not the heat that gives the hearth its reverential character but the fire that transforms it and accords its users both light and heat, and which is the mediatory element between the living and the dead. We cannot grasp the full importance of the hearth in religious terms without considering this triple dimension. By taking it into consideration, we can explain not only the ritual offering of food cooked on the hearth, which is as common as fire rituals, but also the significance of ashes in fire ceremonies. This residue from the most intimate part of the house can in fact replace any sacrificial victim which the believers do not possess due to lack of resources. Both the past and the future of the inhabitants of the house reside in the ashes. The hearth which gives light makes their substance as rich and as full of life as the fire that creates them.

The notion of the forge accompanies the ever-present "fire temple" in most West African agglomerations, although the blacksmith's profession is not always considered to be reserved for a "caste." The forge is not simply a workshop but also a cult place. The ground it stands on is sacred; shoes are not worn there, since footwear could contaminate the place. The forge is also a haven of peace; no argument is tolerated there. It is also a place of refuge, where human justice gives way to the leniency of the sky. But the most typical characteristic of the forge lies in the fact that it is a place of creation, comparable to the place where the Creator himself began the creation of the world. This explains why it is a shrine in which the "prayer" of the sterile womb hoping for fertility will, according to the believers, be answered. The work of maternity, the blacksmith's trade, and God's creative enterprise are, in this temple, all caught up in the same mainstream of liturgical logic.

The most impressive fire temples for human beings are the natural phenomena which the human being considers to be sacred. This occurs in the case of the active volcanoes situated along the great fault line of East Africa. In Rwanda, the Ryaangoomba cult centers around the Muhabura volcano, on the summit of which this mythical hero made his home and where, they say, he still grows tobacco, sorghum, and banana trees. Certain women of the Nyanga people become the wives of the volcano and are in charge of a permanent cult based upon these fire shrines emanating from the bowels of the earth.

Priesthood and Prayers

Generally speaking, African religion is usually a male affair. Women, however, especially after menopause, often become the true agents of a cult whose spiritual power is parallel, complementary, and sometimes superior to that of males, and yet independent of them. We should remind ourselves here of the Guere, the Oubi and the Wobe peoples of the Ivory Coast, the Dogon of Mali, the Mende of Sierra Leone, and especially the Yoruba and the Ibo peoples of Nigeria. The fact remains, however, that the true master in this field is the man, because of a prerogative attached to his masculinity which gives him the power to put to death, therefore to sacrifice, which does not suit femininity, which is in charge of the giving of life.

The religious attributes of the agent of a cult are handed down in order of priority to the oldest member of a group, who is, because of his age, at the limit of this world and of the world of the dead. He is considered, therefore, to be in a good position to assure relations with the invisible. But, generally speaking, it is not customary in African religion to concentrate spiritual powers in the hands of an individual. Prayers and offerings are often the concern of a patriarch, whereas the carrying out of sacrifices is the responsibility of an official sacrificer. It could almost be claimed that African religion tends toward the multiplication of agents and of functions concerning the spiritual life of human beings.

These functions are often many and varied, and they all contain an oral liturgical element which is of primordial importance. Researchers have called this element "prayer." But this term is not altogether suited to the reality it claims to cover in Africa; in this case prayer is not indifferent to its verbal expression. The oral formation of the imprecation, of the request, or of the wish, plays an essential part in its efficacy; it gives it life since the word that is invested with characteristics of both water and heat, is supposedly their fertilizing power. Prayer becomes in our eyes an incantatory formula, whereas for the African it is the soul of the act that it accompanies. One cannot claim to know all the liturgical prayers that are employed even in one culture alone because they are not all worded in a set way. From what we already know in this field, we can easily grasp the eminent value accorded by the African to the efficacy of his word accompanied by gestures directed toward the Invisible.

"Revelations" and Mystical Life

African mysticism should not be understood in the sense of our mental perception in which the shadow of the Christian mysticism of our own societies rides high. Nor should it be understood in the sense attributed to it by Lucien Lévy-Bruhl. It does, of course, concern an experience of the invisible world, which is distinct from that which concerns the visible world, although the one is not more "cognitive" or "emotional" than the other. It can even be said that the mystical life of an African is based on a more cognitive experience than that which underlies the ordinary and practical life. One is not born a "mystic" in Africa; one becomes it. This is where recourse to initiatory methods comes into play. One sees the human body as the starting point of religious and mystical feeling. This is taken so far that the body becomes, in a way, the authentic symbol of the elevation of the human being to the heights of spirituality. That is to say that the mystical in African religion does not remove the human being from the earth; on the contrary, it allows him to live there again and again on an indefinite basis.

These two religious phenomena come into contact on various levels in numerous countries in Africa whether they be pastoral or agricultural. It would seem that in the latter rites are practiced that show the deep tendencies of their spiritual life. These are oriented toward the transformation of the human being symbolized in the image of the seed which, buried in the earth, "dies" in order to be reborn in an infinite variety of forms. The theme that emphasizes the symbolism of the human being to the seed is found in various forms among many sedentary African tribes of which the Venda, Dogon, and Bambara are perhaps the best known. Elsewhere the theme is expressed in a more precise way. Among the Abidji people (northwest Abidjan, Ivory Coast), cultivated plants are "born" from the body of a dismembered human being and buried in the earth. The permutation of human flesh and the seed (or the cultivated plant) forms, so to speak, the most accomplished example of initiation during which the neophyte, by his symbolic death, reaches the same position as the seed.

It is not possible in a study of this scale to take into account all the initiatory rites practiced in Africa. A limited number of rites can be used for illustrations, since the structure and the aim of these "introductions to knowledge" are basically similar.

A closely conducted study reveals that these rites are destined to assure participation for those who assume them in a life other than daily life, which ensues from adherence to the world which we neither see when born nor feel when growing up, but which is there and is more real than the concrete world of everyday life. It is this feeling which defines the deep spirituality and the mystical life of the African. The acquisition of this "interior disposition" stems from what may be called "spiritual technology," the application of which is different for each society.

Two fundamental aspects of this technology are put forward by initiatory societies: one concerns the education and the mastering of the body; the other the acquisition of the feeling of the abolition of finitude. The "spiritual person" here is the one who has controlled one's body to the point of perfect mastery and who has also acquired the certainty of having conquered death. Asceticism and immortality are the principal ideas of the African mystic. It should, however, be added that the periods allowed for initiatory rites represent only the "strong" moments of spiritual "discoveries"—because the initiation does not end in fact until the moment when one breathes one's last breath.

Although there is still a great deal to be learned about African initiatory rites, it would seem that these latter examples fit into a double "typology." Over a vast geographical area that includes Nigeria, Benin, Dahomey, and Ghana (for example, among the Yoruba, Ewe, Fon, and Asanti peoples), initiation is of a type that could be called epispanic. From the Greek *epispaō* ("to attract"), the initiates are a group of people who attract divinity to themselves, and the impact between the two beings reveals itself in the form of the possession or the trance of the neophyte. When such people are noticed, their introduction to spiritual life and their preparation for it are realized either by individual training, with the follower choosing an experienced teacher who will supervise his education for about two to three years (as is the case with the Asanti and the western Yoruba peoples) or by collective training in "monasteries" (as is the case among the Ewe and the Fon, the eastern Yoruba and the Tsha peoples). This model of initiation is open to both men and women. There is, however, a difference between the two. The pious women, or Woyo, undergo an apprenticeship that lasts only a week; they enter a state of trance only about once a year, whereas the instruction of the men lasts two or three years and they enter a state of trance whenever clients go to them for individual consultations.

The physical tests imposed on the neophytes during their training have a specific aim, although this may not be revealed by their teachers. It is not simply a question of subjecting the body to the "sights" of the mind, as it would seem if looked at from a "Manichaean" perspective, but rather of a spiritualism of the functioning of the human "machine" and especially of the organs of sight, hearing, and taste. The eyes, ears, and palate of the novices undergo treatments that underline the concern of the master initiators to raise these organs above the conceptions that ordinary mortals (the uninitiated) have of them. The eye should learn to see what an "ordinary" person cannot; ear should hear what others do not hear; the tongue should be able to appreciate what others find tasteless (such as meals served intentionally without salt) or simply disgusting (as is the case with coprophagy). All these means of transcendence, as well as the materials they employ, are little known by specialists in African studies.

As well as this kind of *epispanic* initiation, there can be found, from Ghana to Guinea, to the north and to the south of the equator, another kind of initiation, which we can call *allotactic* initiation. Here the neophytes go in search of the "Other," that is to say, God. It should be added here that these two initiatory systems are not, geographically speaking, mutually exclusive. The proposed distinction is rather a statistical one. Allotactic initiation appears to be more intellectual than epispanic initiation. In other words, it is more concerned with "inventing" all manner of means and techniques with a strong symbolic value, in order to reach its proposed goal. Whether it be a question of the Thonga initiation in Transvaal, the Kuba initiation in Zaire, or the Bambara and Senufo initiations in Mali, the investment by society in terms of initiatory materials and techniques is of a wealth and ingenuity that surpass all expectations. The expenditure of energy and the physical and mental effort of the novice are also considerable. It is a question of true asceticism, which here touches on heroism with its contempt for the body. This aspect of the initiatory code can also be found in epispanic initiation, but to a considerably lesser degree, making the neophyte seem passive in comparison with the expenditure of energy required of the allotactic initiate.

On the knowledge to which the neophyte should aspire, the two types of initiation are equally instructive. In epispanic initiation the novice is "chosen" by the divinity, who "mounts" him with no prior preparation by any human enterprise; he then learns how to be a "mount" worthy of his divine rider. In allotactic initiation the important aspect is the acquisition of a transforming knowledge which will bring the initiate closer to God and allow the initiate to be something like God. This striving toward immortality is the only means of assuring the human being of a chance to return to this world through reincarnation. This return corresponds to the idea of salvation, which is more in evidence here than in epispanic initiation. Rather than a "universalist" concept of salvation, this is limited to the individual.

This transforming knowledge cannot be acquired in a few weeks or even in a few months. In the past, several years were necessary for the initiate to achieve it. Among the Senufo people of Mali and the northern regions of the Ivory Coast, the initiation into the society of the Poro lasted more than twenty years. Among the Bidjogo people of Guinea in West Africa the duration has no limit. Several years of isolation in the forest, followed by a "black period" (so called because of the hard tasks that the initiates had to accomplish and the ill treatment they were forced to endure during this time), lasting from eight to ten years and spent outside of the village, were necessary for their preparation.

There is an important feature of allotactic initiation which concerns the sharing of knowledge by men and women. Usually women are excluded from masculine initiation and vice versa. It is also assumed that the woman is automatically exempted from having to acquire a transforming knowledge. Sometimes, however, female initiation includes a very interesting feature. It is destined in a way, to subsidize the fault of masculine initiation by outlining the "potentiality of salvation" which the woman carries within herself. Among the Bidjogo, mentioned earlier, the Defuntos comprise a female initiatory society with a priestess, former initiates, and novices. The latter represent boys who died before being able to complete their own initiation and who have thus sustained a serious loss. The young virgins replace the deceased (hence the name Defuntos) and undergo initiation in their place, but without male intervention. As soon as the girl receives the soul of one of the dead, she "becomes" that person and his mother even considers her as her own son (Gallois-Duquette 1983).

This initiatory system reveals the leitmotif of African spirituality, present in allotactic initiation, which consists in human beings' struggle to protect themselves against the total erosion of their existence. It also shows the economy of the initiatory process based on a framework with social characteristics. Not only do those involved in the training of neophytes fall into a structured, hierarchical group (supreme leader, instructors, sacrificers, etc.), but also the neophytes themselves are categorized and classed according to their level of instruction. All of them, both masters and novices, form an *initiatory brotherhood.*

Transforming knowledge often falls within the competence of a single initiatory brotherhood. But it is sometimes the province of several groups which combine to form a vast initiatory group with the last, in chronological order, being the most sacred and destined to allow the follower to haul himself up to the summit of spirituality. Such is the case among the Bambara of Mali, for whom the Kore constitutes the summit of the religion to which every "noble" person should aspire (lower-class people and slaves are excluded from it).

Finally, it is important to note, when speaking of African spirituality and mysticism, that the nature of the relationship between the believer and the Invisible when they finally meet is seemingly very different for each of the two initiatory processes. The supreme God does not gain "possessions" by means of ecstatic trance. His "possession" consists rather in the believer's awareness of a complete surpassing, which is for him the Being he wishes to join and toward whom he is invited to go, by aspiring to be something like that Being and yet without losing his own identity. "Secondary gods," on the other hand, take possession by means of ecstatic trance during which the believer becomes the "other" (the god who "mounts" him) with a momentary loss of his own identity.

It appears as if the religious capacities of the human being throughout Black Africa were of a univocal nature. But the "spiritual load" he assumes is of an equivocal one, so strong and even "explosive" where the spirituality

based on allotactic initiation is concerned; moderate and easier to bear
(even though the spectacle of ecstatic possessions may at first sight seem terrifying) than in the case of spirituality based on epispanic initiation. The
first of these initiatory systems could be said to denote heroism and conquest and to conceal a promethean significance. The second deals with the
acceptance and the upkeep of values granted by the Invisible. Here the
believer is the object of spiritual mutations, whereas in the former the
believer is their subject.

References

Gallois-Duquette, D.
>   1983   *Dynamique de l'art bidjogo (Guinee-Bissau).* Lisbon: Instituto de
>   Investigacao Cientifica Tropical.

Lafargue, F.
>   1972   *La religion traditionnelle des Abidji.* Thèse de Doctorat de 3e
>   Cycle, Université Rene Descartes, Paris.

Parrinder, G.
>   1950   *La religion de l'Afrique occidentale.* Paris: Payot.

Thomas, L.-V., and R. Luneau
>   1975   *La terre africaine et ses religions.* Paris: Larousse.

Zahan, D.
>   1979   *The Religion, Spirituality, and Thought of Traditional Africa.*
>   Chicago: University of Chicago Press. Translation of *Religion,*
>   *spiritualité et pensée africaines* (Paris: Payot, 1970).

2

African Shrines as Channels of Communication

BENJAMIN RAY

A FRICAN SHRINES ARE CHANNELS of communication between the human and the spiritual worlds. In Africa shrines may be purely natural in form, such as forest groves, large rocks, and trees where gods and spirits dwell. Almost every African landscape has sacred places of this kind which are the focus of ritual activity. Human-made shrines vary in form, from large buildings to simple tree branches stuck into the ground. Whatever its form, the shape and design of the shrine indicate its function as a symbolic crossroads between two worlds and instruments of social unification. The ritual and social focal point of the shrine is often an altar where offerings are placed. Families, lineage groups, village members, and townspeople join together at shrines in order to provide sustenance for the gods and ancestors so that they, in turn, will renew the moral and spiritual life of the people. Every shrine is therefore a bridge between divinity and humanity whose convergence at the shrine brings moral and spiritual benefit to the human community. Priests and lay people may also go into trance states at shrines in order to bring down spiritual beings "onto their heads." In this way people may identify closely with their gods, and professional mediums may also communicate the words of the gods directly to the people.

Each of these characteristics is well illustrated by the royal shrines of the Ganda of central Uganda. The Ganda shrines are large, conical-shaped buildings, approximately eighty feet in diameter and two stories high. They are identical to the palace of the living king, for they are the "houses" of the spirits of the royal ancestors. Although the kingship of Uganda was abolished in 1967, twenty-three royal shrines still exist, approximately one for each royal ancestor.

The interior of the shrine is divided into two sections by a bark-cloth curtain. The front section is where the people sit; the rear section, which no one enters, is the inner sanctum, called the "forest." This is where the spirit of the deceased king dwells. In the past when the king died, his jaw-bone was removed and placed in the darkened "forest." It was put on top of a tall frame and wrapped in layers of bark cloth in the form of an effigy of the dead king. According to Ganda mythology, Kintu, the founder of the kingdom, did not die but "disappeared" into a forest next to his palace. The symbolism of this mythic event was incorporated into the shrines of Kintu's successors, each shrine having its own "forest" sanctuary for the effigy and spirit of the dead king. Like Kintu, the kings of Buganda were not said to have died but to have "disappeared" or to have "gone away."

Later, their spirits took up residence in the "forests" of their shrines. In front of the curtain is a raised platform fenced off by spears. This is the empty throne of the king. It connects the spirit world behind the curtain with the front part of the shrine where the people sit. When the cere-monies begin, the curtains partly open so that the royal spirit may come out of the "forest." The medium of the king's spirit sits on the throne and becomes mildly entranced by the spirit which is said to mount the medium "on the head." The medium dances before the people, and they greet it with royal greetings and sing songs in honor of the royal "twin." The king's twin symbol, a large-handled vase, which contains the royal umbili-cal cord, stands on the throne platform facing the people. Pots and baskets holding offerings of beer and coins also sit in front of the throne. In the past ceremonies were held once a month at the time of the appearance of the new moon. The shrines were, and still are, places of pilgrimage for members of the royal family and for descendants of palace officials.

The shrines are located in the ancient heart of the kingdom. A main road connects the shrine of the king's predecessor to the royal capital. Messen-gers from the mediums of the royal ancestors traveled along this road to advise the king. He, in turn, sent offerings to his ancestors at their shrines. The kingship of Buganda thus consisted of two parts: the spiritual realm of the royal ancestors who dwelt in their shrines and the political realm of the reigning king centered at the royal capital. The shrines were the foundation of the sacred dimension of the kingship. They acted as a sacred pivot of the kingdom, uniting its mythic and historical foundations together with the living members and departed spirits of the royal class of Buganda.

The essential feature of an African shrine is that it creates a sacred space which joins together human and sacred realities. This function may be pres-ent even in the absence of permanent architectural form, as among hunting and gathering peoples such as the Kung San and Mbuti.

For the Kung San of Botswana and Namibia, communication with sacred reality occurs during the "dance of power," called *n/um tchai.* Until recently, this dance was the main religious ceremony of the Kung, which they performed about once a week. The men dance all night around a fire in the midst of the huts while the women sing and clap. The fire, the songs, and the dance contain the sacred force of *n/um*. The dancing and singing activate *n/um* in the men, who go into trance states which the Kung call "half death." In this condition, between life and death, the men are able to "see" what is troubling the people. They bend over the women and children and flutter their arms about them to draw out illnesses and the causes of misfortune. Some of the men run through the fire and rub coals on their heads to help increase the power of *n/um* . Fortified in this way, men run from the sacred dance circle into the bush and chase away the malevolent spirits of the dead which hover around the margins of the encampment and send sickness to the people. The ceremony reaches its climax at dawn, when the sun, which is also a source of *n/um* , appears on the horizon. For the Kung the dance of *n/um* is thus a channel between themselves and sacred power. Hence it serves the basic function of shrine, transmitting sacred life-giving power to the people.

Like the Kung, the Mbuti pygmy hunters of eastern Zaire also lack permanent buildings. But they too have created a shrinelike channel to the sacred. It is a long hollow tube, called the *molimo* trumpet, through which the Mbuti sing their songs of the forest. The Mbuti live part of the time in the Bantu villages near the great Itrui forest and part of the time in the forest itself. The Mbuti call themselves the "children of the forest," and the forest is their true home. It provides them with food, shelter, and a peaceful life; it is also their God. Periodically, the Mbuti leave the forest to live in the Bantu villages, where they trade the products of their hunting and gathering in return for garden foods and an opportunity to earn money. But, when things begin to go bad for them in the villages, for example, too many sicknesses, an unfortunate death, or bad hunting, the Mbuti leave the villages and return to the forest to put things right. In the forest they perform the *molimo* ceremonies, whose purpose is to "awaken" the spirit of the forest. The Mbuti say that things go wrong when the forest falls asleep and fails to look after them. Thus they sing their joyous *molimo* songs in order to awaken the forest so that everything will go well again. Everyone contributes food and firewood for the all-night ceremonies. The women and children remain indoors, while the men sing the *molimo* songs around the burning *molimo* fire. Some of the young men sing the songs through the *molimo* trumpet, which amplifies them and carries the sound further into the forest. During the daytime the trumpet is hidden deep in the forest. It is brought out only at night and during the early predawn hours. As the young men sing through the trumpet, they conceal it by holding it in their midst. The words of the *molimo* songs are simple and repetitious, saying mainly, "the forest is good." It is not the words but the sound of the songs that are joyous and powerful in waking up the forest. The trumpet is cooled by being placed in a stream to "drink" water, which is said to improve its "voice." The trumpet is also passed through the flames and coals of the *molimo* fire, and hot ashes are rubbed on it to increase its effectiveness. Between songs the trumpet emits the sounds of animals—leopard, buffalo, and elephant—and women and children are told that the trumpet is a fearsome forest animal. The trumpet is both of the forest and of the people, sending the people's enlivening songs deep into the forest and bringing something of the mystical reality of the forest among the people. As the only sacred object the Mbuti possess, the *molimo* trumpet is their means of communication with ultimate reality.

More settled peoples require more permanent architectural forms, even though they may be quite simple in nature. The most common shrine among the Nuer and Dinka cattle herders of the southern Sudan is a forked tree branch stuck into the ground. People make this type of shrine (called *rick* or *yik*) when they wish to offer sacrifice to a spiritual power which is troubling them. Once the spirit is identified, a man cuts a large forked branch from a tree known to be preferred by the spirit. The branch is stuck into the ground so that its limbs point upwards. The purpose of the shrine is to establish permanent contact with the afflicting spirit. If the spirit is a human ghost, the shrine is called a "ghost house." Bracelets are hung on the shrine as gifts for the spirit, together with the tokens of sacrifice, animal ears and horns, and maize from the gardens. Animal skulls are set at the base. The Dinka leave the ground around the base of the shrine in its natural grassy state in contrast to the cleared ground of the village courtyard. Such a place is not of human beings but of spiritual power; it is both the dwelling place of a spirit and the means of access to it.

The treelike form of the shrine is also significant. Nuer and Dinka myths tell about the creation of the first human beings by the supreme God at the foot of a tamarind tree. Nuer say that the Tree of Creation still stands in their land, and they regularly place offerings at its base. Like the original tree, each forked-branch shrine stands as an *axis mundi*, linking the sky realm of the gods and spirits to the earthly realm of humanity. Thus the shrine joins together the spiritual and the human in the midst of the village courtyard.

Throughout Bantu-speaking central Africa, there are a number of healing cults, called cults of affliction, which people join in order to be cured and protected from a variety of misfortunes and illnesses. Each cult association has its own shrines. For the Ndembu of northwest Zambia, initiation into the Chihamba cult involves the making of a personal shrine, called *kantong'a*, near the hut of the initiate. The shrine is made of several items: a bundle of medicinal twigs set into the ground; a clay pot containing tree bark and medicinal leaves, water, and beer; and a large section of cassava root, which is half dried near the pot. Seeds of beans and maize are planted in a circle around this assemblage.

The main element of the shrine is the cassava root. It represents the body of Chihamba, the ancestress of the cult, whose spirit resides in the shrine until the conclusion of the initiation rites. The root also stands for the male ancestor spirit, Kavula, who is sacrificed in effigy during the rites, prior to the symbolic killing and rebirth of the initiates themselves. The shrine is consecrated by the sacrifice of a chicken whose head and blood are for Chihamba. The initiates wash twice daily in the medicines contained in the pot of the shrine in order to cure their afflictions. The pot and the bundle of twigs contain samples of every kind of medicine used by the Ndembu, and thus the bundle represents the total system of curative rituals. The washing is both a cure of the initiate's immediate problems and a prophylactic against all future ones. The washing ceases when the bean and maize seeds begin to sprout and grow up around the shrine. At the conclusion of the initiation rites the spirit of Chihamba leaves the shrine. Henceforth, the shrine stands as a memorial to Chihamba and to Kavula, and as a reminder of the initiation process itself. It reminds the initiate that he or she has been reborn into a new community of cult members who are protected from the evils of this world, a purified society which is good, healthy, and fertile.

A similar intention underlies the building of the large, houselike *mbari* shrines of the Igbo of eastern Nigeria. In the past the Igbo moved their villages to nearby sites every thirty or fifty years, following a catastrophe, such as an unusually high number of infant deaths or a severe drought. Later, certain misfortunes would prompt the people to consult a diviner. His verdict would reveal that the senior god or goddess of the village needed a new *mbari* shrine as a testament to the people's faith and pride in their deity; then all would go well in the village. A few years later, sufficient funds would be collected and laborers organized for the work. In addition to the master builder and his apprentices, workers are recruited from each of the lineages of the village to build the shrine. Refusal would mean risk of death at the hands of the deity, while compliance would mean health and prosperity for the worker and for his lineage. Construction would take about two years and would be conducted in ritual seclusion behind a high fence.

The *mbari* shrine house consists of an enclosed central room surrounded on all four sides by a wide, roofed porch. The porch area is filled with dozens of nearly life-size, painted clay sculptures. The sculptures depict men, women, deities, and animals of all types. Some are fearful, some are good and beautiful, some are forbidden, and some are humorous. All are "children of the god" and make the shrine beautiful. Artistically, the purpose of the shrine is to depict the world both as it is and as the villagers hope it to be, prosperous, healthy, and productive. When the shrine is completed, the soul substance of the deity is placed in a bowl inside the central room. The deity's statue, the largest sculpture and focal point of the shrine, sits in front of the closed doorway to the inner room. Although numerous ceremonies have gone into the building of the shrine, no further ceremonies are held after the shrine is opened to the public view. The shrine stands as a "thing of pride" both for the town and for the deity. As the result of years of planning, work, and considerable monetary expense, the shrine is the villagers' offering to the god in the hope that the deity will respond by sending down blessings upon them.

The shrine is thus a visible reminder of the covenant between the villagers and their god. Indeed, the building of the shrine repeats the original creation of the world. In the beginning, the Supreme God Chineke built a house representing the world and placed all things, man, woman, gods, animals, trees, and food in its four rooms. The *mbari* shrine and its four porches represent the original house of God's creation. It is built to honor the village deity so that he or she will help to maintain the world in its original prosperity. Because the shrine may not be repaired, it eventually deteriorates and collapses after forty or fifty years. But, in the cyclical nature of things, a generation or more later, the village will build a new shrine. Thus a new representation of the world expressing a revitalized faith will again take shape for the prosperity of all things.

The Ashanti of Ghana also build large shrine houses. These contain the ceremonial stools of deceased kings, queens, and clan chiefs. The wooden stools, which are shaped like small benches, serve both as shrines for ancestor spirits and as altars upon which vegetable and meat offerings are placed. Inside the stool house the blackened blood-encrusted stools sit on a raised platform. In front of them lie the swords, weapons, and musical instruments associated with the ancestors together with bowls and cups used in feeding the spirits and offerings made by private individuals seeking help.

The stool ceremonies are performed on Sundays and Wednesdays in a forty-two-day cycle. The king and his officials enter the shrine wearing old clothes to show their inferiority to the ancestors. They pour out water on the floor so that the spirits may wash their hands before eating. Spoonfuls of mashed plantain are placed on each stool, and the spirits are requested to eat and to bring prosperity to the town. A sheep is taken into the shrine and the ancestors are again asked for prosperity. The officials smear blood from the sheep's throat upon the stools. Later, they place skewers of roasted meat on the stools and wrap intestinal fat around the center columns of the stools.

When a ceremonial stool is made for a person in authority, it is constructed by a ritual process. For the stool is regarded as the repository of the owner's soul. The soul is said to be fastened by miniature fetters "to chain it down" to the central column supporting the seat and the base. At death, the stool is blackened by smoke or by being coated with soot mixed with egg yoke. The blackened stool continues to be the residence of the soul which has now become an ancestor spirit. Henceforth, the stool is kept in the stool house and becomes both an altar and a shrine for the ancestor spirit.

The gods of the Ashanti must also have containers in which to dwell. These are brass pans which, when consecrated, become the repository of the spirit of a deity. Because the Ashanti gods are universal, they may be present in many shrines at the same time. A god may take possession of someone, whereupon he or she may appear to have gone mad. A priest will be consulted, and he may discover that a deity has come upon the person. A brass shrine must be made so that the god can be transferred from the person to the shrine. This will enable the afflicted person to communicate regularly with the deity and to become its servant, thus normalizing the relationship. When all preparations have been made, the possessed person will dance, accompanied by drumming and singing, sometimes for as long as two days. At some point in the ceremonies, the dancer will leap into the air and catch something by hand or plunge into a nearby river and emerge holding something in the hands. Water will be sprinkled on it to cool it, and it will be thrust into a brass pan and covered up. The priest will then gather some clay from a sacred river, medicinal plants, tree roots, leaves, and a gold nugget. These he pounds together and puts into the pan. Then he tells the god why he is being enshrined, and he prays for the prosperity of the village. Sacrifices are made and blood is allowed to fall upon the contents of the brass pan. Henceforth, the pan will stay in the dark interior of its house, seated on its stool, and the newly made priest will place offerings before it.

People may come to the shrine to receive advice from the god about their sufferings and ailments. The priest stands in front of or behind the curtain covering the doorway of the shrine and becomes possessed by the god. The priest's spokesman interprets his words and tells the supplicant how to solve his or her problem. During the New Year's (Apo) ceremony, the shrines of all the gods are taken out of their houses and carried on the priests' heads down to the sacred rivers of Ashantiland to be purified by water. Afterwards, they are returned to their houses for the next year.

One of the most widely venerated gods among the Yoruba of southern Nigeria is Ogun, the god of iron, war, and hunting. His shrines are usually simple altars located outdoors in the open air at the foot of a sacred tree, by the side of a wall, or in a smithy's workshop. Iron is the essential element in Ogun's shrine. The shrine can be as simple as two pieces of iron put together and stuck into the ground. The shrine is consecrated and "becomes Ogun" when palm oil is poured over the iron.

Generally, an Ogun shrine is made up of a living tree, sacred to Ogun, whose branches are trimmed to about four feet. This provides a platform for the sacrifices. A skirtlike woven garment, called "the dress of Ogun," is tied around the tree. At the foot, iron rods and staffs may be driven into the ground. Iron bells and machete which are used during the ceremonies may also be seen nearby on the ground. Ogun's personality has both destructive and creative aspects, and the symbolism associated with the shrine expresses these different aspects. The color red, sacrificial blood, and the foods of Ogun represent the destructive (cruel, violent) principle; the color white, fluids from snails, the woven skirt, and the drinks of Ogun represent the creative (pure, calm) principle. During the course of the ceremonies, each of these symbolic elements is placed upon the shrine. The intention of the rituals is to pacify and control the destructive side of the deity. In this way, people hope for protection against accidents involving iron, such as machetes, industrial machinery, automobiles, and accidents from weapons, such as knives and guns. By sacrificing Ogun's animals (snails, tortoises, and dogs) and by offering Ogun's foods and drink (yams and palm wine) at this shrine, people hope to avoid the violent and destructive misfortunes of everyday life.

The meeting house of the Bwiti cult among the Fang of Gabon is a different type of shrine. Here the purpose of the shrine is not merely to communicate with sacred reality but also to create within the shrine itself an entire sacred world. Through song and dance and the use of a hallucinogenic drug (*eboha*) the members of the Christian-influenced Bwiti experience rebirth during the transition from life to death, from this world to the world of the ancestors, and back again. In the course of this all-night ceremony lies the promise of their own ultimate salvation in the world of the saved ancestors. This experience is made possible by the symbolic architecture of the Bwiti chapel.

The plan of the chapel is based upon the idea that life proceeds along a path, a red path of birth and death, which all people follow. If people follow this path well, they will arrive at the land of the dead; if not, their souls at death will be left to wander aimlessly in the dark forest. Bwiti ritual keeps people's souls on the right path by periodically reorienting them toward the land of the dead through the visionary experiences induced by the drug *eboha*.

The philosophy of Bwiti is symbolically expressed in the carved, central pillar of the chapel, the *axis mundi* of Bwiti. The pillar is divided into three sections, separated by two holes, one above the other. The top section of the pillar represents the land of the gods and spirits; the middle section represents the land of the living; and the bottom section represents the earth and graves of the dead. At death, the souls of the dead ascend to the sky through the upper "death hole." At birth, the souls descend to the land of the living through the "birth hole." Thus there is a circulation of spirits on this axis of the world. During the ceremonies, people touch the pole to help free their spirits from their bodies so that later at death they may pass more easily through the "death hole" to the spiritual realm.

The Bwiti ceremonies begin when the members enter the chapel through the right-hand doorway, the red, female path of birth. They proceed along the right side of the chapel into the front section, which is associated with human life. Several hours later, after many songs have been sung, they go past the central fireplace, called the "fire of the life of the chapel," to the rear section, which is associated with death. At the extreme rear of the chapel behind the altar is a space called the "sea." It is the abode of many spirits. Beyond the "sea" lies the realm of the sun (male) and moon (female), where God and his Sister dwell together with the saved ancestors. The altar is the place where the people communicate with this realm of the dead. Hanging from the roof above the altar is an open circle made of raffia, called a "circle of grace" or "death circle," where the spirits of the living pass over into the land of the dead. A similar circle hangs over the fire. It is where the spirits of the dead pass their blessing down to the living. At the end of the ceremonies, the people leave the chapel by the door on the left side, which represents the white, male path of death. Thus, one "dies" out of Bwiti back into this world. The chapel of Bwiti is therefore both the link to the sacred world and the very image of that world in symbolic form.

African shrines often contain carved images of gods, spirits, and ancestors; indeed, such images may serve as shrines themselves. Carved figures may function as altars for communication with spiritual beings or as physical embodiments of spiritual powers.

Among the Yoruba, when a twin child dies, a wooden statuette, known as *ere ibeji*, is made as a substitute. The Yoruba regard twins as sharing the same soul between them. If one twin should die, an *ibeji* statuette is made to house its half soul. Otherwise the other half in the surviving twin might want to "leave" and join its partner. Because of the presence of the half soul in the statuette, it is treated like a living child; it is symbolically fed and bathed at the same time as the surviving twin. Both wear identical clothes. If both twins should die, which is a common occurrence, two statuettes are made, and they are treated as living children in the hope that they will soon be born again, either singly or together, to the same mother. If this does not happen, the twin statuettes serve as household shrines, embodying the souls of the twins. The mother ritually washes, dresses, feeds, and puts them to bed at night to gain protection and wealth for herself and for her other children.

The Yoruba ancestor mask, called *egungun*, is also a vehicle for the soul of the dead. The mask, which is worn by a dancer, is to honor a family ancestor and to enable his soul to visit his people. Although everyone knows that a human being is under the mask, they believe that the rituals which the masquerader must undergo before putting on the mask have made him a true medium for the soul of the ancestor. The masquerader and his mask thus become a temporary shrine, making possible communication between the living and the dead.

Similarly, the Dan-speaking peoples of Liberia and the Ivory Coast carve wooden masks to embody spirits of the forest so that they may appear before the people. Unlike human beings, the forest spirits have no physical bodies, hence they require masks and human masqueraders in order to manifest themselves. In this way they entertain the people of the villages and perform certain moral and legal roles.

As mentioned at the beginning, a shrine may also be a feature of nature. Among the Yoruba, for example, rivers, lagoons, trees, rocks, and mountains are regarded as dwelling places of divinities. Their significance is usually explained in myths which tell how such natural phenomena became important in human experience. Shrines are set up to establish communication with the gods and ancestors associated with these sacred places. The Nigerian city of Ibadan, which is the largest black African city south of the Sahara, is said to have been founded by an outlaw chieftain named Lagelu. After consulting a diviner, Lagelu founded Ibadan on a hill called Okebadan, which overlooks the present city. Lagelu lived there with his followers, naked and in a state of social licentiousness. A goddess named Atage Olomu Oru also lived on the hill. She became the fertility goddess of the people of Ibadan, and one of Lagelu's descendants became the chief priest of the shrines on the hill. Every year, usually in March, the priest of Okebadan determines the date of the festival in honor of the founder of the city. It is a raucous, carnival-like affair. At night the priest stays in the shrine on the hill, naked like his ancestor, with the goddess of the hill. Children born on this day are dedicated to the goddess.

The coming of Christianity and of Islam to Sub-Saharan Africa has resulted in large numbers of converts to these religions. In the case of Christianity, Africans have created indigenized churches alongside those of European origins. The independent churches are adaptations of Christianity to the African religious context. Like the traditional religions, the independent churches emphasize treatment of illnesses and social problems. But this is not accomplished through the use of shrines. It is done through the power of the Holy Spirit, transmitted through the founders and leaders of the church. Because the Holy Spirit is universal and available to everyone, it does not dwell in a local shrine. It dwells within the community, especially its prophetic founder and leaders. No shrine in the physical sense is therefore needed. There are over six thousand such groups in tropical Africa, and many have no church buildings and hence worship outdoors. This is entirely appropriate because the Holy Spirit is both "no place" and everywhere. Like the Kung and the Mbuti, the independent Christians have discovered a sacred reality whose presence can be evoked without recourse to a fixed sacred place. It can be evoked within the midst of the community itself. Through prayer and moral and physical purity, each member of the church has direct access to the healing powers of the Holy Spirit in the context of the community's worship. The human community is thus the channel for the sacred. Wherever the community is, the Holy Spirit will come.

One of the basic principles of African thought is the unity between matter and spirit, between body and soul. The African shrine, whether a building, an object, a feature of nature, or the ritual community itself, is the necessary material foundation for the communication with spiritual reality.

References

Awolalu, J. Omosade
   1979   *Yoruba Beliefs and Sacrificial Rites*. London: Longman Group Ltd.
Barnes, Sandra T.
   1980   *Ogun: An Old God for a New Age*. Occasional Paper, No. 3. Philadelphia: Institute for the Study of Human Issues.
Cole, Herbert M.
   1982   *Mbari: Art and Life Among the Owerri Igbo*. Bloomington: Indiana University Press.

Evans-Pritchard, E. E.
1956   *Nuer Religion*. Oxford: Clarendon Press.
Fernandez, James W.
1982   *Bwiti: An Ethnography of the Religious Imagination in Africa*. Princeton: Princeton University Press.
Lawal, Babatunde
1977   "The Living Dead: Art and Immortality among the Yoruba of Nigeria." *Africa* 47, no. 1.
Lienhardt, Godfrey
1961   *Divinity and Experience*. Oxford: Clarendon Press.
Marshall, Lorna, and Megan Biesele
1974   *N/um Tchai: The Ceremonial Dance of the Kung Bushmen, A Study Guide*. Somerville: Documentary Educational Resources.
Rattray, R. S.
1923   *Ashanti*. Oxford: Clarendon Press.
1927   *Religion and Art in Ashanti*. London: Oxford University Press.
Ray, Benjamin C.
1976   *African Religions*. Englewood Cliffs, N.J.: Prentice-Hall.
1977   "Sacred Space and Royal Shrines in Buganda." *History of Religions* 16, no. 4.
Turnbull, Colin
1962   *The Forest People*. New York: Doubleday.
Turner, Victor
1975   *Revelation and Divination in Ndembu Ritual*. Ithaca, N.Y.: Cornell University Press.

3

The Lake Goddess, Uhammiri/Ogbuide: The Female Side of the Universe in Igbo Cosmology

SABINE JELL-BAHLSEN

Nne Mmiri is a female deity with variants of local names, e.g., *Idemmili*. She is the mother of a group of water spirit beings who journey to and from the land of the living and the dead. Her abode and empire is the water. Her life begins and ends there. . . . With the arrival of Europeans to this part of the world, *Nne Mmiri* became known as "Mami Wota"—a translation which enabled the local inhabitants to communicate the existence and exploits of this female deity to foreigners. (Achebe 1986, 15)

FEMALE DIVINITIES and their social manifestations were ignored and suppressed during colonial times.[1] In the aftermath, pre-Christian female deities in particular were attacked by religious fanatics from various churches.[2] Colonial administrators and their successors were inspired by European male-biased beliefs and power structures and, in addition, were driven by their desire to control the land and its people. Consequently, researches on its political and administrative implementations[3] have focused on the male divinities including those of ancestor worship and other divinities, and on the conservative male aspects of custom, *omenala*, at the expense of the dynamic, innovative, and creative female side of custom (Jell-Bahlsen 1998a; Obiora).

My case study takes a close-up look at female spirituality manifested in the water goddess and her worship in the lives of the rural Oru Igbo.[4] There, the goddess is known locally as Uhammiri/Ogbuide, the spirit woman of Ugwuta/Oguta Lake.[5] Uhammiri's husband is the river god Urashi. The divine pair harbors cosmic balance, creation, and procreation.

Uhammiri, the goddess of Ugwuta Lake, occupies an important space and (with other female divinities) and represents the female side of the universe in Igbo cosmology. She presides over the crossroads of life, death, and rebirth. One of her local names is Idemmili, "pillar of water," a force that cannot be pinned down, while supporting and renewing local custom. Obiadinbugha, the hereditary male priest of the goddess in Orsu-Obodo, while addressing Uhammiri at her shrine would say:

> This is what I have to tell you, Uhammiri, and your husband, Urashi. What we ask is what you should manifest to us: we ask for children, wealth, and life.[6] Uhammiri Ogbu-ama, the sparkling one, here is kolanut! . . . I am asking you to protect and guide his life, . . . Let him have good things. Good thing is having wealth. Good thing is having offspring. Good things is life.[7]

The goddess Uhammiri also compensates for losses and disappointment. Her priests and priestesses often are renowned healers of various illnesses, treating particularly gynecological and mental problems. The water goddess protects, encourages, and empowers those who cannot or would not live up to society's norms, ancestral custom, and the laws of the land, *omenala*, and of *ani/ala*, the earth goddess. Although the water has its own set of rules that govern much of Ugwuta's daily life, the element of the flexibility, mystery, and unpredictability of the liquid balances the static, earth-bound side of the universe. The fluid, female side of Igbo cosmology harbors creative energies that are both challenging and innovative. The Oru people in general, and women in particular, still derive much spiritual strength, psychological and economic empowerment from the lake goddess and other water deities, despite and against the encroachments of Christianity, Islam, and foreign power structures.

Chi-Ukwu, Ogbuide/Uhammiri, and the Igbo Pantheon of Deities

The Igbo universe has a complex cosmology with Chi-Ukwu presiding over a pantheon of lesser nature spirits, deities, ancestors, and humans within their social and natural environment, and the flora and fauna around them. Chi-Ukwu is beyond shape and gender. This force is too abstract to be depicted in human images and too large to be contained in temples. Only missionary-trained local and foreign-influenced scholars or artists would attach gender to the Supreme God and narrow his image down to a European male with long hair and a long beard, an idea alien to the African context.

Chi-Ukwu is the creator who bestows life force, death, and rebirth. This force can manifest itself through the royal python, *eke*.[8] The meaning and symbolism of the snake are quite distinct from Judeo-Christian beliefs.[9] Prominent in classic African art, the snake, particularly the python, and her consorts symbolize creation, procreation, and death.[10] Below Chi-Ukwu there is a pantheon of highly localized female and male deities, nature spirits, and ancestors. Although an individual may pray directly to Chi-Ukwu in private, the Supreme God is publicly more appropriately addressed through messengers at the shrines and temples of these nature deities and ancestors.

It is almost impossible to describe the Igbo belief system in Western terms,[11] because the people conceive of their cosmology differently. Their deities and divine forces of nature are evasive, flexible, and multidimensional. For the purpose of communicating to the reader the notion of the water goddess within the pantheon of Igbo deities the major elements of this cosmogram could be illustrated thus:

Chi-Ukwu
(The Supreme God of creation and destiny, gender neutral)

Pantheon of Deities and Spirits

Nne Mmiri	**Ala/Ani**[12]
The water goddess (fem.)	The earth goddess (fem.)
Arishi (nature deities and spirits)	**Nde Mmuo** (ancestors)

female and male
white and red
cool and hot

These forces are associated with:
transitions, flexibility vs. unwritten laws, fixed norms,
innovation/*widernis* vs. custom/*omenala*
creative/challenging forces vs. conservative forces
unusual/unpredictable vs. normal/predictable

change vs. continuity

Messengers and Mediators

(pythons, diviners, priest/esses, male and female elders)

Humans

Figure 1. Oru-Igbo Cosmogram

Chi-Ukwu creates and presides over the universe. Below Chi-Ukwu there is an entire pantheon of gods and goddesses. Among them are the nature spirits as well as the ancestors. These forces are associated with different qualities and intents. Some are more conservative and static, others are more volatile and innovative; they sponsor challenges of custom. According to local myths, the ancestors established the people in their present location; they invented the way people have until recently made their living off the land, and they laid down custom, *omenala*, the laws of the land/the earth goddess, Ani/Ala. Custom was invented by those who died for the continued well-being of the people, for those who are living and for those yet to be born.

Among those living, the elders are closest to the ancestors and in charge of transmitting their traditions to future generations in order to preserve and perpetuate the heritage and ideas conceived by the ancestors. There are also spiritual, social, and natural forces challenging this order. Custom ascribes certain types of behavior to human culture and other forms of behavior to the domain of nature, for example, twin births are regarded as normal for certain animals, but multiple births were customarily shunned in humans (Uchendu 1966). But nature may play tricks on people and challenge their traditions, for example, when a woman bears twins, or when an individual cannot or will not live up to society's norms and expectations. In Ugwuta, these nonconformist individuals could find refuge, consolation, and even empowerment through dedicating themselves to the lake goddess, Uhammiri/Ogbuide. As a result, there is a perceived antagonism between different cosmological forces: on the one hand, there are those forces, divinities, and people, perceived as static and conservative, and, on the other hand, there are also unpredictable, challenging, mysterious, and dynamic forces of nature, particularly of the water.[13] There are those who easily live up to society's expectations, who conform to and abide by the norms, but also others who, for one reason or another, cannot or will not fulfill these norms, and as a result are perceived as nonconformist, unusual, creative, or innovative, yet they are often highly successful individuals. In Ugwuta, these extraordinary individuals are frequently women who travel and trade, who want more from life than "the joys of motherhood,"[14] or who cannot fulfill society's expectations of raising many children of their own.[15]

Two major underlying principles emerge from the Igbo universe: (1) the significance of balance and the need to reconcile antagonistic forces, and (2) the notion of circular time and of the life force/soul/*chi* traveling eternally within the cycle of life and death.

Chaos, Balance, and Cosmic Harmony

The universe is made up of different components and forces that may be antagonistic. Balance emerges as an all-important value opposed to potential chaos; balance is necessary to maintain continuity of life, health, and prosperity of the people. If one side of the universe, of people, society, or life takes control over the other, there is imbalance. Innovation and change are important to secure progress. This is always an intrinsic part of Igbo custom.[16] On the other hand, too much innovation may distort people's ethics and ultimately harbor crime and impoverishment, as evidenced in contemporary societies. While one group amasses much wealth and power, others are ruthlessly exploited and driven to the brink of extinction.

By contrast, pre-Christian Igbo cosmology, ethics, and aesthetics strove for balance against social, economic, political, psychological, and mental imbalance. Balancing the antagonistic forces of the universe in life and society is a major task, as local people struggle to meet various norms, standards, and requirements of society, of the ancestors, of contemporary life, and the challenges of nature, personal interest, and aspirations. The notion of cosmological balance is expressed in social norms and aesthetic ideas, as evidenced in the arts of space, for example, classic sculpture and painting, featuring balanced composition, symmetry, and harmony of contrasting colors. The ideal of balance is also evidenced in personal appearance—grooming and posture, hair styling, and dress codes. Dreadlocks, uncut hair, untidy clothes, or jerky dance movements are normally rejected, but could be integrated when associated with particular spirits, for example, water spirit calling, spirit possession, prophecy, but also temporary mental derangement. In the arts of time including music, lyrics, oral literature, choreography, ritual performance, masquerade and dance, balance is constantly emphasized. But at the same time, possession by a water spirit may induce a socially accepted form of dancing out of control.

Humans' Life Cycle of Time and Eternity

Besides the importance of balance, the notion of the indestructible soul/life force, *chi*, and its continuous journey through life, death, and rebirth within the eternal cycle of time is equally basic to Igbo cosmology. The individual's eternal cycle of life, death, and rebirth is illustrated in figure 2.

In this view, the soul/life force, *chi*, travels in an eternal cycle of time, corresponding to different stages of human life and death. This is marked by several transitions. First is the transition into life: birth/rebirth; second is the transition that involves naming and entry into society and childhood;

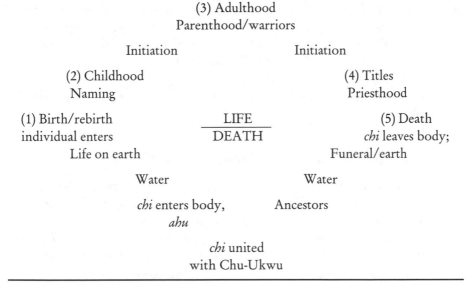

Figure 2. The Individual's Journey and Transitions in the Cycle of Time

the third transition is the period of puberty, adolescence, and initiation into adulthood, marriage, parenthood, and being a warrior; the fourth transition is old age and initiation into titles and priesthood; the fifth transition includes death and funeral. At death, one half of the cycle is complete, and the soul/life force, *chi*, leaves the body, traveling on to join the ancestors, and ultimately to be one with the Supreme God, the great *Chi*, Chi-Ukwu. When the *chi* departs from Chi-Ukwu again, to enter a new body, the life cycle begins anew, and a new person is reborn in another body.

Each of the major phases of life is marked by a point of transition, ritually signaling initiation into a new stage of the life cycle. At that point, the individual is given a new name and identity, while his/her old name/identity is left behind. The old individual dies metaphorically or literally, and a new one is born. All of these transitions are marked by special rituals and color symbolism.

The color white is used in the form of white limestone, called chalk, *nzu*, in all rituals marking critical transitions from one stage of the life cycle to the next, for example, in birth, naming, initiation, and funerary rites. White chalk is also used in all ritual activities to signal esoteric involvement with the spirit world and communication with divine forces. The color white is the symbolic color of the water goddess, Uhammiri/Ogbuide, the goddess of the crossroads and mythical guardian over the transition into and from life and death. Within the ritual context associated with the water goddess Uhammiri/Ogbuide, the color white is displayed. It symbolizes femininity. This color is an important component of rituals honoring the goddess Ogbuide/Uhammiri, exhibited in the costumes worn by her priests and priestesses and worshipers, and paraphernalia used in the healing rites performed to enlist the goddess's help to preserve an individual's life, health, and sanity.

The Mother Water Goddess of the Crossroads

Among the many deities of the Igbo pantheon of gods and goddesses, the supreme mother water goddess known as Uhammiri/Ogbuide in Ugwuta, and the mother earth goddess Ani/Ala are the most prominent, ever-present spirits in Ugwuta and its environs. Chinwe Achebe elucidates the significance of this female force in Igbo cosmology (Achebe 1986). According to Ms Achebe, V. Uchendu, and others, the Igbo Supreme God, Chi-Ukwu, is also known as the god of destiny (Achebe 1986; Uchendu 1966). When the yet-to-be-born individual receives his/her life and personal chi[17] from God, the person makes a commitment about his destiny and course of life on earth, witnessed by Chi-Ukwu. Yet, before entering into and exiting from this world, the individual must cross a river. Because the concept of time is circular, one must cross a river twice—not only once, as in the crossing of the river Styx at death in ancient Greek mythology. When crossing the river to enter life on earth, the individual is challenged, either by the supreme water goddess Nne Mmiri/Uhammiri or by the earth goddess of the wild bush, Onabuluwa. At this point, the individual's destiny, his/her sacred pact with the Supreme God, is at stake. The person may accept and defend his or her destiny, or may change its course by forming a pact with the mother water goddess. This not only alters the individual's life and destiny; it also dedicates the person to the goddess as her devotee.

If the individual later tries to evade both his/her destiny and the goddess's claim by refusing to conform to either his/her original destiny or the goddess's demands to fulfill her requirements, then this may cause illness, mental derangement, continued loss of children, spouses, and eventually premature death. At death, a person's chi returns to the sky god, Chi-Ukwu. The individual is eventually reborn, although not with the same chi. Before reincarnating, the new person must again confront the goddess to sort out his/her destiny. After birth, it must be determined who reincarnated in the new being.[18] This task is taken very seriously by local people, for failure to determine correctly "who reincarnated the newborn child" could have fatal results later in life.

As divine mother, the water goddess is imperial in challenging or confirming one's destiny. She is not only present but also pivotal for one's entry into and exit from this world. The divine woman is believed to be an eternal, intrinsic, and dominant force of our very nature, our existence, our life course and destiny, *akarakara* (Achebe 1986, 20–25).

Divination

The complexity of Igbo cosmology is evident here. It is not everybody who lives in this world who is aware of all the details of his or her existence. In analogy to the complicated power play of the forces of the universe, there are daily problems confronting individuals. To avoid mistakes in naming a child, to determine the causes of sudden illness, to improve one's lot, to overcome barrenness or other medical, social, and psychological problems, one consults a diviner, *dibia*, who sorts out, explains, and advises on dealing with this complex social and cosmological web of forces. Correct behavior is difficult, yet essential. It must be learned and constantly maintained. Mistakes could upset the cosmic balance and cause illness and misfortune. Conversely, regaining balance can reestablish health. This is achieved by appeasing the offended forces through ritual offering and performances including music and dancing. In Ugwuta, many prominent diviners, though not all, are also priests and priestesses of the goddess of Ugwuta Lake, Uhammiri/Ogbuide.

The Goddess in the Daily Life of the People

The crucial position of the water goddess echoes the economic importance in Oru life of the waters of Ogbuide Lake and her tributaries.

The precolonial economy of the Oru people was based on farming, fishing, and trading. During colonial times, oil palm was promoted in this area as a major cash crop by the John Holt Company. Today there are many other professions and trades, and mineral oil is pumped nearby. Yam and cassava are the most prominent staples, supplemented by plantains, rice, and a variety of beans, vegetables, palm oil, fish, small game, goats, sheep, poultry, and an occasional cow. Before the advent of roads, the rivers and lakes provided the most important means of transportation for people, materials, produce, and goods for trade. The waterways provided a major source of communication and an important resource in the trading networks controlled by women.

Ogbuide Lake, the river Niger, and its tributaries form an interrelated network of waters, of vital natural resources, upon which the Oru towns' very existence and continued well-being depend. The annual flood impacts the water levels of the farmland and thereby determines the beginning of the planting seasons, in coordination with the ritual calendar of the towns.[19] However, while determining the cycle of life, subsistence, and cultural activities, the water levels are not always predictable, and the flood cannot be easily controlled. Moreover, the rivers have provided access to foreign intruders.

The supreme economic importance and threat posed by these waters are echoed in the importance and awe attached to the goddess of the lake, Ogbuide, as well as to the deities of the adjoining rivers and creeks. They are the most important yet most unpredictable forces, potentially benevolent but also harmful to the adjacent villages.[20] The nourishment and kindness of the mysterious, awesome, and divine waters are perceived as essential to human life and existence. To ensure continued favors from this volatile force, people maintain good relations through paying homage and offering sacrifice, in properly timed and performed rituals, supervised by priests and priestesses who maintain and serve the water deities' shrines. To this end, proper timing is important in ritual performance, as it is in farming and other economic activities.

The Igbo market week has four weekdays: *Nkwo, Eke, Orie,* and *Afor.* Two four-day market weeks make up an eight-day rhythm, and seven four-day market weeks make up one month of twenty-eight days in the lunar calendar. This calendar underpins all major rituals and town festivals in Ogwuta. Each of the Igbo market weekdays is associated with a particular market. For example, Ugwuta holds its market on *Nkwo;* Orsu-Obodo holds its market on *Eke;* Izombe holds its market on *Afor,* and so on. In addition, each day is associated with a particular deity worshiped on this day, just as Christians attend church on Sundays. In Ugwuta, *Orie* day is sacred to the goddess of the lake, Uhammiri/Ogbuide. The rituals performed in honor of the goddess and her husband, the river god Urashi, normally take place on *Orie* day. Alternative days are *Afor,* and also *Eke* night, going into *Orie.* This is also the time when devotees must also abstain from sexual activities and fully dedicate themselves to the goddess. On *Orie* day, the goddess's worshipers meet to perform rites in honor of the goddess at her shrines, either in a priest's or priestess's house or traveling to the water deities' sacred groves on the lake and riverbanks away from town.

The goddess's priests and priestesses are chosen on several levels, operating within the carefully balanced different ritual domains of men and women. Oru society revolves around patrilineal village kindreds. As a result, there are hereditary male priesthood titles associated with the shrines of the most important local deities, including the goddess of the lake, Ogbuide/Uhammiri, and her husband, Urashi. In addition, any person can take up serving the shrines of the all-important water deities through possession or spirit calling and initiation. The latter avenue of priesthood is chosen especially by women who become devotees and/or full-time priestesses of the divine pair of water deities (Jell-Bahlsen 1998a). This type of priesthood is often associated with the art of divination and/ or healing, with spiritual powers held in awe and highly recognized. An individual may at first resist this spirit calling and devotion. But the refusal to serve a shrine invariably causes tremendous social and psychological pressures. The resulting personal problems often involve illness, locally interpreted as related to personal destiny and a breech of the prenatal vow to serve the water goddess.[21] A man or woman may join a group of water worshipers and gain access to esoteric knowledge and ultimately ritual leadership, because of his/her own personal problems, or desires, or on behalf of his/her child.[22]

The priests and priestesses of Ogbuide/Uhammiri respond to the needs of any villager or stranger who may call on them for help in mediation with the spirit world. Major priests and priestesses of Uhammiri/Ogbuide treat cases involving fertility, gynecological problems, repeated deaths of children, questions regarding reincarnation and naming, mental illness, and a host of other problems.[23] On one level, all physical and mental disorders are regarded as social disorders, caused by individual spirits or an imbalance in the essential unity of the personal, social, spiritual, and natural domains of being (Jackson 1983). There is no rigid dividing line between the illness of body and mind, physical and mental, or spiritual well-being; healers are at the same time priestesses, attending to both their clients' spiritual and physical needs.

When the personal balance is disturbed, a man/woman may suffer a physical or mental breakdown, or break with social norms, such as marriage arrangements. This antisocial and often destructive behavior is locally interpreted as a form of mental disorder requiring healing by an herbalist commonly called a "native doctor," who is, above all, a priest or priestess of Uhammiri/Ogbuide. This healer-priest reconciles the individual with his/her personal *chi*, with his/her destiny, and with local custom. The healer-priest channels spirit possessions and thereby heals the individual by restoring his/her personal balance. In some cases, the healer-priest may turn a former patient into an initiate and apprentice of religious worship and a trainee in the art of healing. During the course of healing and initiation, the patient regains his/her psychic, social, and cosmic balance and may ultimately obtain ritual leadership status.

Conclusion

Female elements, like water spirits, have a very special place in Igbo cosmology, with regard to the circular flow of time, reincarnation, challenge, and innovation. The contributions of women (and water) are known to be complementary and decisive in procreation, and for ensuring the continuation of life—of people's very existence, health, personal and economic growth—in real life as in cosmology.

The water goddess embodies female control over the crossroads between the ordinary and the extraordinary, between spirits and humans, between life and death. This perception of gender contradicts patrilineal ideology, power, and inheritance patterns reinforced in colonial times. Like divine pairs, men and women are different yet equally important economically. In Ugwuta women are also equally powerful ritual leaders. Both male and female are important components of the delicate balancing of cosmic powers. Igbo cosmology endows womanhood with extraordinary status and powers, ascribing to women not only complementary importance expressed in the beauty of a mature woman, but also awe-inspiring qualities, embodied in a maiden's premarital beauty.

The female side of the universe is not only complementary to the male but also pivotal to man, for his procreation, reincarnation, and continued existence within the circular flow of time. This is expressed in ritual and in the water goddess's power to challenge man's destiny. By balancing patrilineal kinship structures, women's ritual leadership reiterates the concept of complementarity between static and dynamic elements, conservative and creative forces, continuity and change, ancestors and water spirits, men and women. The water goddess, Ogbuide, through her priesthood emphasizes and reinforces several major aspects of womanhood in Igbo cosmology: a nourishing mother, a destructive, wild beauty beyond reach, and a force mediating one's destiny. The goddess Ogbuide compensates both men and women for deprivations, losses, and misfortunes. In addition, the goddess is a source of healing for her devotees and a source of empowerment for women, who personify the female side of the universe.

Notes

1. Igbo women actively resisted these encroachments in the Igbo women's war of the 1920s. See Jell-Bahlsen 1998a; VanAllen; and Rogers.

2. Evidenced, for example, in the beheading of the shrine sculptures for the river goddess, Ava, near Nsukka. See Jell-Bahlsen, *Ava* (a video), 1994. See also the rhetoric of certain Christian videos distributed in Nigeria, as described by Oha.

3. For a critical evaluation of the colonial literature against contemporary work especially by Igbo scholars, see, e.g., Grau, *Die Igbo*.

4. The Oru Igbo are a subgroup of the Igbo peoples of southeastern Nigeria. The Oru are a subgroup of the riverine Igbo, a group made up of several towns along the river Niger, including Ugwuta/Oguta and Onitsha. The oldest, ancestral town of the Oru is Orsu-Obodo, while Oguta is their most prominent and wealthy city, and their administrative center today. The major strand of the Oru/Oguta population has migrated to its present location east of the Niger from the Benin kingdom west of the Niger River, some ten generations ago, according to local oral historians. The Oru display certain cultural peculiarities and speak their own dialect of Igbo, differentiating themselves from other Igbo groups. At the same time, Oru and Igbo share major aspects of Igbo language and culture.

5. The Igbo town Ugwuta was given the English name Oguta during British colonial occupation. This name is still used in Nigeria today for administrative purposes and on road maps and street signs. The town of Ugwuta is located on a lake associated with a spirit being, the lake goddess Uhammiri. This goddess is also known as Ogbuide, a name probably derived from Benin, as a large strand of Ugwuta's population migrated into their present location from the kingdom of Benin west of the river Niger, some ten generations ago.

6. Obiadinbugha, the chief male hereditary priest of the goddess Uhammiri/ Ogbuide of Umudei village in Orsu-Obodo, Oguta II, addressing the goddess when performing a sacrifice of a white ram to her at her shrine in Orsu-Oboro, on behalf of Chief Francis Ebiri, April 1979. This event was documented on film by Sabine Jell-Bahlsen and Georg Jell and can be seen in the film/video *Divine Earth-Divine Water, Part I: Offering to Uhammiri*, Ogbuide Films, New York, 1982.

7. Obiadinbugha: "Uhammiri Ogbu-ama ki Orji!" Group: "Ise." O. : "Asim gi zo ya ndu, si gi zo siya ike." Group: "Ise." O.: "Ifeoma biani ya ife oma bu ego, ife oma bu nwa, ife oma bu ndu." Oiadinbugha, the hereditary male chief priest of Uhammiri performing a sacrifice at the goddess's shrine on Dec. 14, 1978.

8. The python symbolized both the life-giving force of procreation and the eternal cycle of life and death. The creature may appear whenever an abomination is committed against the water goddess, for example, in local Oru myth and in the chapter on "Idemmili" in Chinua Achebe's novel *Anthills of the Savannah*. In Ugwuta, as in many parts of Igbo land, the python is sacred and must not be killed, or if accidentally killed it must be buried like a human. See also Williamson 1972, 108; and Parrinder 1967.

9. Parrinder 1967. See also Jell-Bahlsen 1997.

10. See also Robert Farris Thompson's description of the Yoruba notion of *Ashe* and its manifestation in the snake (Parrinder 1967; Jell-Bahlsen 1997). The idea of the python symbolizing death, eternity, and continued life was clearly expressed by Palmer in an interview. The Owu Mmiri, priest of the water deities of Egbema in a chalk drawing can be seen in the documentary film by Jell-Bahlsen, *Mammy Water: In Search of the Water Spirits in Nigeria*, University of California Extension Center, Berkeley, 1991.

11. Chinua Achebe, private converstation, December 10, 1995.

12. There are several different aspects associated with the earth goddess Ani/Ala. There is the supreme mother earth goddess of the town who presides over the adherence to custom, *omenala*. Then there are the earth goddesses of individual compounds, of individual farmlands, and of the wild bush, *onabuluwa*. According to Chinwe (Ms) Achebe, *Onabuluwa* challenges human destiny like the water goddess (*World of the Ogbanje*).

13. A similar distinction is described by R. Horton on Kalabari water spirits.

14. To paraphrase the title of a novel by Buchi Emechata. See in particular the novels by Flora Nwapa and also the interview.

15. Examples are the heroines of Flora Nwapa's novels *Efuru* and *Idu*, both set in Ugwuta.

16. Leslye A. Obiora has convincingly argued for the flexible nature of African customary law, custom that does allow for change and includes innovation in contrast to foreign interpretations that have attempted to freeze customary law into a static entity serving colonial and neocolonial purposes. See Obiora 1993.

17. *Chi* could be roughly translated as "life force," or soul.

18. See, e.g., Jell-Bahlsen 1989, Celia's account of the circumstances surrounding her child's illness, in the ethnographic documentary by Jell-Bahlsen, *Mammy Water: In Search of the Water Spirits in Nigeria*, 1991. See also Jell-Bahlsen 1998a.

19. Proper timing of planting in accordance with the water levels appropriate for the germination of the crops and coordination with the ritual calendar are important. Each new planting season is initiated by the *Agugu* festival honoring Owu, a mysterious gift from the water, recalling the Owu myths, and displaying the Owu masquerade. This festival is documented in S. Jell-Bahlsen, *Owu: Chidi Joins the Oloroshi Secret Society* (video), Columbus, Ohio, National Black Programming Consortium, 1994.

20. The ambivalence and awe are reflected in possible translations of the name Ogbuide: (a) she who floods or gives excessively, or (b) she who kills with flood. See the letter by Victor quoted in Jell-Bahlsen 1998c.

21. As evidenced in the story of the priestess Eze Mmiri in the ethnographic documentary by Jell-Bahlsen, *Mammy Water: In Search of the Water Spirits in Nigeria*, University of California Extension Center for Media, Berkeley, California, 1991, and in the story of Eze Nwata, narrated in the ethnographic documentary by Jell-Bahlsen and George Jell, *Eze Nwata: The Small King*, Ogbuide Films, New York, 1983.

22. As evidenced in story of baby boy Urashi narrated on camera by his mother in the documentary film by Jell-Bahlsen, *Mammy Water: In Search of the water Spirits in Nigeria*.

23. Jell-Bahlsen 1995b; 1998a. See also Nwapa 1966; 1970; and her unpublished manuscript *The Lake Goddess*.

References

Achebe, Chinua
1959   *Things Fall Apart.* London: Heinemann.
1972   *Girls at War.* London: Heinemann.
1987   *Anthills of the Savannah.* New York: Anchor Books.
Achebe, Chinwe (Ms)
1986   *The World of the Ogbanje.* Enugu: Fourth Dimension Press.
Acholonu, Catherine O.
n.d.   *Trial of the Beautiful Ones.* Owerri: Totan Publishers.
Akpan, E., and V. Ekpo
1988   *The Women's War of 1929.* Calabar: Government Printer.
Amadi, Elechi
1966   The *Concubine.* London: Heinemann.
Amadiume, Ifi
1987   *Male Daughters, Female Husbands.* London: Zed Books.
Aniakor, C., and H. Cole
1984   *Igbo Arts: Community and Cosmos.* Los Angeles: UCLA Press.
Boone, Sylvia A.
1986   *Radiance from the Waters: Ideals of Female Beauty in Mende Art.*
            New Haven: Yale University Press.
Grau, Ingeborg Maria
1998   *Die Igbo sprechenden Völker Sudost Nigerias: Fragmentation and*
            fundamentale Einheit in ihrer Geschichte. Ph.D. diss., Univ. of
            Vienna, 1998. Reviewed by Jell-Bahlsen in *International Journal*
            of African Studies 30, no. 1A (1996): 13–14.
Horton, Robin
1967   "African Traditional Thought and Western Science." *Africa*
            37:150–81.
Jackson, Michael
1983   "Thinking through Body." *Social Analysis* 14:127–49.
Jell-Bahlsen, Sabine
1989   "Names and Naming: Instances from the Oru-Igbo." *Dialectical*
            Anthropology 13:199–207.
1994   "This Native Something: Understanding and Teaching the
            African Experience." *Dialectical Anthropology* 19:373–86.
1995a   "The Concept of Mammy Water in Flora Nwapa's Novels."
            Research in African Literatures 26, no.2:30–41.
1995b   "Mammy Water: Weltbild Ritual and Heilung: Beobachtungen
            bei den Oru-Igbo in Sudost Nigeria 1978-1992" [Mammy Water:
            Cosmology, Ritual and Healing: A case study of the Oru Igbo in
            Southestern Nigeria]. In *Jahrbuch für transkulturelle Medizin und*
            psychotherapie 1993, ed. Walter Andritzky. Berlin: Armand
            Aglaster Verlag.

1997   "Ezi Mmiri di Egwu: The Water Monarch is Awesome: Re-Considering the Mammy Water Myths." In *Queens, Queen Mothers, Priestesses and Power: Case Studies in African Gender,* ed. Flora Edouwaye S. Kaplan, vol. 810, 103–34. New York: New York Academy of Sciences.

1998a   "Female Power: Water Priestesses of the Oru-Igbo." In *Sisterhood, Feminisms, and Power: From Africa to the Diaspora,* ed. Obioma Nnaemeka, 101–31. Trenton, N.J.: Africa World Press.

1998b   "Flora Nwapa and Uhammiri/Oguide, The Lake Goddess: An Evolving Relationship." In *Emerging Perspectives on Flora Nwapa,* ed. Marie Umeh, 77–110. Trenton, N.J.: Africa World Press.

1998c   "Interview with Flora Nwapa." In *Emerging Perspectives on Flora Nwapa,* ed. Marie Umeh, 633–60. Trenton, N.J.: Africa World Press.

Kaplan, Flora Edouwaye S., ed.
1997   *Queens, Queen Mothers, Priestesses and Power: Case Studies in African Gender.* New York: New York Academy of Sciences. Vol. 810.

Kasfir, Sidney
1994   "Review of 'Mammy Water' . . ." *African Arts* 27:80–82, 96.

Mundibe, V. Y.
1988   *The Invention of Africa: Gnosis, Philosophy and the Order of Knowledge.* Bloomington: Indiana University Press.

Nnaemeka, Obioma
forthcoming   "Bringing African Women Into the Classroom? Rethinking Pedagogy and Epistemology." In *Borderwork: Feminist Critiques of Comparative Literature,* ed. M. Hignonet. Ithaca, N.Y.: Cornell University Press.

Nnaemeka, Obioma, ed.
1998   *Sisterhood, Feminisms, and Power: From Africa to the Diaspora.* Trenton, N.J.: Africa World Press.

Nwapa, Flora
1966   *Efuru.* London: Heinemann.
1970   *Idu.* London: Heinemann.
1979   *Mammywater.* Enugu: Tana Press.
1992   *Never Again.* Enugu: Tana Press.
1998   "Interview w. S. Jell-Bahlsen and Francis Ebiri." In *Emerging Perspectives on Flora Nwapa,* ed. Marie Umeh. Trenton, N.J.: Africa World Press.
forthcoming   [posthumously] *The Lake Goddess.* Unpublished manuscript.

Obiora, Leslye A.
1993   "Re-Considering Customary Law." *Legal Studies Forum* 17, no. 3:217–51.

Oha, Obodimma
    1997   "The Rhetoric of Nigerian Christian Videos: The War Paradigm of *The Great Mistake.*" In *Nigerian Video Films,* ed. Jonathan Haynes, 93–98. Jos: Nigerian Film Corporation.

Parrinder, G.
    1967   *African Mythology.* London: Paul Hamlin.

Rogers, Susan
    1980   "Anti-Colonial Protest in Africa: A Female Strategy Reconsidered." *Heresis* 3, no. 1, issue 9:22–25.

Thompson, Robert Farris
    1984   *Flash of the Spirit.* New York: Vintage Books.

Uchendu, V.
    1966   *The Igbo of Southeast Nigeria.* New York: Holt Rinehart & Winston.

Umeh, Marie, ed.
    1998   *Emerging Perspectives on Flora Nwapa.* Trenton, N.J.: Africa World Press.

VanAllen, Judith
    1972   "Sitting on a Man: Colonialism and the Lost Political Institutions of Igbo Women." *Canadian Journal of African Studies* 6 no. 2:165–81.

    1976   "'Aba Riots' or 'Igbo Women's War'? Ideology, Stratification and the Invisibility of Women." In *Women in Africa: Studies in Social and Economic Change,* ed. Nancy Hafkin and Edna G. Bay. Stanford: Stanford University Press.

Williamson, Kay
    1972   *Igbo English Dictionary.* Benin City: Ethiope Publishing Co.

Ethnographic Documentary Films Cited

Jell-Bahlsen, Sabine. *Ava: A Water Goddess Near Nsukka, Nigeria 1978–1992.* New York: Ogbuide Films, 1993.

——. *Mammy Water: In Search of the Water Spirits in Nigeria.* Berkeley: University of California Extension Center for Media and Independent Learning, 1991.

——. *Owu: Chidi Joins the Okoroshi Secret Society.* Columbus, Ohio: National Black Programming Consortium, 1994.

Jell-Bahlsen, Sabine, and Georg Jell. *Divine Earth—Divine Water: Part I: Sacrifice to the Goddess of the Lake, Uhammiri.* New York: Ogbuide Films, 1982.

——. *Eze Nwata: The Small King.* New York: Ogbuide Films, 1983.

4

Ancestral Spirituality and Society in Africa

OGBU U. KALU

The Problem

THE INFLUENCE OF ANCESTRAL SPIRITS in Africa is very pervasive, and devotional concerns over them loom so large in the primal religious structures that emergent religious forms must perforce reflect the encounter with ancestral covenants. Years ago the Senegalese poet Birago Diop observed that in Africa,

> Those who are dead are never gone:
> > they are there in the thickening shadow.
> The dead are not under the earth:
> > they are in the tree that rustles,
> > they are in the wood that groans;
> Those who are dead are never gone:
> > they are in the breast of the woman,
> > they are in the child who is wailing
> > and in the firebrand that flames.
> The dead are not under the earth:
> > they are in the forest,
> > they are in the house.
> *The dead are not dead.* (Jahn 1961, 108)

Death is a mere passage from the human world to the spirit world. The passage enhances the spiritual powers so that one could now operate in the human environment and especially in the human family as a guardian, protective spirit/power/influence. The structure of this belief about dead people requires much explanation. But the reality of the dead-among-the-living attracts so much religious devotion that in many African societies the ancestors occupy more devotional attention than God/Supreme Being. In

54

some communities, no cultic attention is paid to the divinities; in others the divinities are scions of the ancestral spirits for prediction and control of space-time events.

Two scholarly predilections betray this fact in *God: Ancestor or Creator?* (1970), in which the Sierra-Leonian scholar Harry Sawyerr outlined a path of development for African contribution to Christian theology that would explain the reality of God through the pervasive African understanding of the ancestor. A brand of social anthropology argues that, indeed, Africans conceive of a High God but, in daily cultic ritual, this God is remote or hidden. The ancestor deputizes. Some anthropologists, such as Cyril Nwa-nunobi, argue that Africans transposed their social transaction model to their relationship with God. The ancestors are intermediaries. The doyen ethnologist J. B. Danquah says of the Akan ancestors: "They act as friends at court to intervene between man and the Supreme Being and to get prayers and petitions answered more quickly and effectively" (Opoku 1978, 37).

Other ancillary matters, such as whether the ancestor is *worshiped* or *venerated*, are of little consequence here. In *Gods as Guests*, Robin Horton showed that masquerades, dances, and festivals constitute means by which the gods return as guests to the human world. Thus, while their influence operates at the spiritual level, sometimes they physically reenter the human world. The belief in reincarnation further confirms that ancestors do return through children. The sincere desire of each person in primal society was this: "May my name never be lost." The Igbo of southern Nigeria call it *ahamefula*. It is believed that the dead pass through the spiritual world and return for yet another pilgrimage.

Ancestral beliefs, in summary, underscore certain social ideals: the vibrant reality of the spiritual world or "an alive universe," the continuity of life and human relationship beyond death, the unbroken bond of obligations and the seamless web of community. The sense of *communitas* stands above the individual even in death. Kofi Opoku adds a cogent element:

> ancestral beliefs act as a form of social control by which the conduct of individuals is regulated. The constant reminder of the good deeds of the ancestors act as a spur to good conduct on the part of the living; and the belief that the dead can punish those who violate traditionally sanctioned mores acts as a deterrent. Ancestral beliefs, therefore, represent a powerful source of moral sanction for they affirm the values upon which society is based. (Opoku 1978, 39)

A certain worldview sustains the rationality of this central belief. As figure 1 shows, the African perception of time is cyclical: life moves from

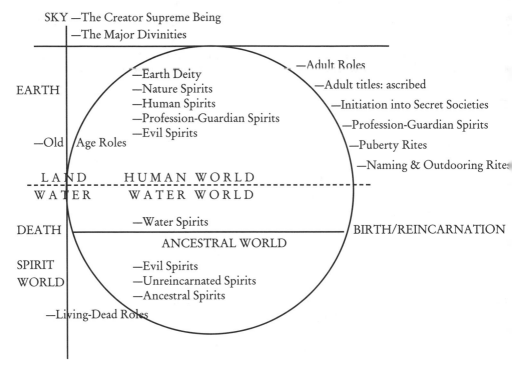

SKY —The Creator Supreme Being
—The Major Divinities

EARTH
—Earth Deity
—Nature Spirits
—Human Spirits
—Profession-Guardian Spirits
—Evil Spirits

—Adult Roles
—Adult titles: ascribed
—Initiation into Secret Societies
—Profession-Guardian Spirits
—Puberty Rites
—Naming & Outdooring Rites

—Old Age Roles

LAND   HUMAN WORLD
WATER   WATER WORLD

DEATH
—Water Spirits
ANCESTRAL WORLD
BIRTH/REINCARNATION

SPIRIT
WORLD
—Evil Spirits
—Unreincarnated Spirits
—Ancestral Spirits

—Living-Dead Roles

Figure 1. African Worldview[1]

birth to death, through the ancestral world to reincarnating birth. The ancestral world is a mirror of the human world. Thus, an achieved, titled person in the human world sojourns as an achieved chief in the hereafter.

This explains the burial of the ancestor's servants along with him. He would, presumably, continue to need the services of these valets.

To put matters in their proper context: Africans operate with a three-dimensional perception of space: the sky, the earth (land and water), and the ancestral or spirit world, which is located under the earth. This can be deduced from funerary rites and the pouring of libations on the ground. Each space dimension is imbued with divinities (principalities), territorial spirits (powers), and a host of minor spirits (localized to specific professions, places, and objects—for instance, a river, a hill, a stone, and so on). Evil spirits pervade. On the whole, the human world is inhabited precariously by spirits for good or evil while human beings maneuver to tap the resources of the benevolent spirits to ward off the machinations of the devouring spirits. To achieve this vicarious goal, human beings weave enduring covenants with these spirits. Cultic practices are devoted to initiations into the covenants, nurturing of the covenants, and renewal of the covenants at major festival points in time. The kernel of spirituality lies in these covenants.

It is argued here the covenants with ancestral spirits loom very large because these spirits not only dominate the spirit world but operate pervasively in the human world to the extent that, in some communities, they monopolize cultic devotion.

But who are ancestors? Some of the literature leaves the impression that only old men become ancestors. There are reasons for this deduction: an ancestor must have lived a morally worthy life and must have died a good death. This means that the person was not killed by lightning or a falling tree, did not drown (betraying the sanction of the gods) or commit suicide, and was not killed by a strange disease such as smallpox or leprosy. There is no gender differentiation; both males and females could be ancestors. An ancestor must have received a second or third burial to smooth the sojourn through the spirit world to reincarnation. Obviously, those who died bad deaths or did not get fitting burials do not reincarnate and, indeed, turn

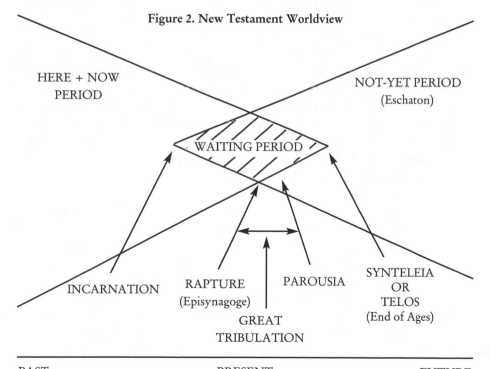

Figure 2. New Testament Worldview

HERE + NOW
PERIOD

NOT-YET PERIOD
(Eschaton)

WAITING PERIOD

INCARNATION   RAPTURE   PAROUSIA   SYNTELEIA
                (Episynagoge)   OR
                                          TELOS
                    GREAT   (End of Ages)
                  TRIBULATION

PAST   PRESENT   FUTURE

into malevolent spirits which hound their progeny for failing to bury them properly.

There are communities where the schematization is not clear and all the dead who did not die bad deaths become ancestors. The masquerades, therefore, represent various genders, characters, and age groups.

Figure 2 shows that the New Testament perception of time, which dominates Western imagination and yields a rationalistic worldview, differs from the African perception. Thus, the incursion of the Christian gospel into Africa involved at the same time challenges of worldviews and covenants. The covenant with Jesus was not proffered in conflict with the covenant with the spirits in the sky, land, water, and ancestral world. A new spirituality emerges in the contemporary period as people adjust to the new in the midst of the old.

Method

This reflection explores the dilemma in the process of adjustment. The dilemma is excruciating because of the tensile strength of the enduring covenants and the persuasiveness of ancestral spirituality. There is awareness that the size of Africa and her multifarious cultures lead to a unified hypothesis model in the analysis of her spirituality. Thus, the worldview articulated contains some common features, but the richness of Africa's culture and the complexity of the problem could best be understood by focusing on a community here and an ethnic group there.

This reflection will use a case study from the Igbo of southern Nigeria. A survey was conducted in 1990–91 on the deities of Igbo land. A sample of 615 deities was analyzed, as shown in table 1. If the data on ancestral spirits were combined with those on guardian patron spirits (since both categories perform within the same religious band), the conclusion would be that over 31 percent of the deities which occupy religious devotion are ancestral. This constitutes the largest category and, therefore, the predominant form of spirituality.

Utilizing the culture-area approach, it becomes obvious that the semi-savanna, northern Igbo devote the highest attention to ancestral spirits. Understandably, marine (water) spirits dominate cultic attention in culture areas located along waterways. The task, then, is to examine how communities of northern Igbo land, whose social harmony has been built around ancestral cults, responded to the embattlement launched by the Christian covenant and the pattern of spirituality that has emerged. This has wider significance for the travails of African theology, especially the ruminations on inculturation theology.

Table 1
Covenanting Deities: Distribution of Igbo Gods

Culture Area Distribution	Nature of Deity						
	Earth	Nature	Water	Guardian Patron	Oracular	Spirit Force	Ancestral
Percent	9.59	9.91	21.18	12.35	2.76	24.45	18.86
North	3	14	5	9	2	14	21
Northeast	3	9	12	5	2	18	8
Northwest	1	11	16	6	-	26	5
West	1	1	8	3	-	6	4
Central I	16	2	19	6	2	5	15
Central II	13	4	34	18	1	21	25
Central III	7	6	25	12	4	3	14
South	12	9	10	8	3	20	14
Southwest	1	2	7	2	-	4	1
East	2	4	7	7	3	32	9
TOTAL	59	61	134	76	17	151	116

Explanations:
1. Central I: Owerri, Mbaitoli
2. Central II: Orlu, Isu Nkwerre, Ideato
3. Central III: Mbaise, Etiti, Mbano, Isuikwuato
4. Nature deities include sky gods such as Lightning, Sun, etc.
5. Depth of sampling in the southwest and west—slighter than in the rest.

A Bundle of Dilemmas

The Roman Catholic Holy Ghost Fathers evangelized the semi-savanna northern Igbo land in the 1900s. Within the first three decades, they staked out bounds, and the process of consolidation followed thereafter. Rapid vertical expansion in the first phase raised much Christian hope riddled with illusions. Thus, when the second wave of christianization sought to domesticate Christian values, it touched off a violent reaction from primal religionists, as the novelty wore off. The heart of the conflict was a cultural

peculiarity of the subculture of Igbo land, namely, the centrality of an ancestral cult called Odo. These are ancestral spirits who periodically visit and
dwell among humans for long periods ranging from six to nine months.
Even when they return to the ancestral spirit world, their influence on
human communities persists. The cycle of return, departure, waiting
period, and return controls the spiritual life of their human progeny. They
thus create a covenant tradition that is enduring and powerful.

When Christianity comes into such a culture theater, a dilemma is created: a new covenant and spirituality are proffered which reject the viability of the traditional covenant at the core level, especially as the Christian
messengers are challenged to build a new fellowship which is integrated
into the old life and culture of the people. The challenges are (a) to express
the Christian message in the people's idiom; (b) to weave a new bond of
loyalty which confronts the old through Christian nurture and proclamation. In recent times, the receptor communities have become concerned
that, after many years of Christian contact, the church has existed as a
stranger. The clarion call has gone out that the message should be adapted,
indigenized, contextualized, incarnated, and inculturated (Ukpong 1984).
There is the feeling that the message has not developed enduring roots and
that the new covenant has not overthrown the old and that Christian spirituality has not supplanted the primal. The resilience, persistence, or
endurance of the traditional covenants is palpable. Christians call for a new
strategy to tackle the apparent failure because the mission has neither been
accomplished nor the challenge duly met. A bundle of dilemmas weighs
heavily on the Christian agents.

As a caveat, a sage quipped that, given the number of centuries within
which the traditional deities held sway, it would be too much to expect
Christianity to wipe out the old covenants in less than two centuries.
Therefore, the effort should rather focus on extolling the gains made and
revamping the tools for the assault on new grounds. This is an optimistic
exit which begs the question about viable tools for a new assault and does
not resolve the bundle of dilemmas.

Beyond the problem of posing the question, scholars have had problems
with the answers articulated. Some argue that the essential message of the
gospel could be proclaimed, even from the rooftop, in any native idiom;
that the universality of the gospel does not wear contextual garb. One
wonders whether the core issue is theologizing in an African idiom. The
innate quality of translatability of the Christian gospel, which Lamin
Sanneh has ably argued, should have sufficed. Perhaps it is not a mere matter of communication (Sanneh 1989). As walls have ears, so do cultural
forms have nuances. Old social anthropology such as Ruth Benedict's pat-

terns of culture, argued that each ingredient of a culture only makes meaning within the total culture. When it is borrowed for a different cultural setting, problems arise.

Others have argued that the index of indigenization is through dialogue and integration. Amidst the competing solutions there is the final dilemma that such theological solution lacks practicability in the midst of a real-life conflict. The gap between theological reflection and grassroots reality is the point of departure for this article. What does the church do when a cultural form is central to the life of a community and when the church perceives that cultural form to be inimical to the affirmation of the gospel and the ecclesiastical tradition? How do "dialogue and integration" operate in the heat of conflict? Experience has shown that rejection and affirmation of the unique claims of the gospel merely exacerbate matters.

The dilemma of grassroots inculturation of the gospel could be illustrated with the conflict between the Aku community (northern Igbo land) and the Roman Catholic Church over the celebration of the Odo ancestral cult. Such conflicts burst as from dark clouds occasionally in other communities within the culture theater, but this particular case is well documented. By 1983 the dark clouds started gathering and broke in mid-1989. The shattered unity of the community and the strained relations with the church hierarchy occupied the rest of the year.

The Gathering Clouds:
The Structure of the Odo Cultus

In Igbo language, "Odo" represents the yellow color, and this is the traditional color of the Odo ancestral cult. But the meaning of the term is different. Local informants surmise that "Odo" is an elliptical version of Odomagala, meaning "setting things right," and suggesting that these ancestral spirits return into the human world to set right human affairs that might, by disorder, incur the wrath of the gods. Odomagala, therefore, emphasizes the function of the cult and contains or encapsulates a wealth of Igbo philosophy of life (Kalu 1985).

In northern Igbo land, a sample study of sixty-eight deities (tables 2 and 3) shows that the dominant concerns of the primal religion are nature deities, ancestral deities, and spirit force—that is, spirits which enhance, preserve, or destroy life and fortunes. They are linked: land is sacred because the ancestors are esconced in her womb and the ancestors imbue spirits which assist their progeny to live and enjoy the good things of life to a venerable old age. These deities provide protection from the envy and competition of others. Spirit forces could be tapped for both salient and

Table 2

Distribution of Deitites in Northern Igbo Land

Nature of Deity	Number	
Earth	3	
Nature	14	
Water	5	
Guardian/Patron	9 }	
Ancestral	21 }	30
Oracular	2	
Spirit Force	14	
Total Sample	68	

destructive purposes. Thus, the core element of the primal religiosity in this culture theater is the cult of ancestors.

The Odo ancestral cult looms so large in the religious consciousness of this region that people name their children after the cult—Odo, Odoaja, Nwodo, Odeke, and so on. It must be added that the semi-savanna Igbo land could be divided into two subculture zones identifiable by the prevalent ancestral cult. In the Nsukka area, the Omabe is predominant. Its structural features are similar to Odo. The provenance of Odo is in three subsectors known generally as Igbo-Odo (the part of Igbo land controlled by Odo ancestral spirit). These consist of (i) northeast of Old Nsukka Division: Ikem, Neke, and Eha-Amufu; (ii) southeast of Old Nsukka Division: Ukehe, Aku, Akpugo, Udueme, Ohebe-Dim, Umunko, Umuna, Onyehe, Ochima, Ikolo, Idoha, and Diogbe; (iii) north Udi District: Umuoka, Umulumgbe, Affa, Nze, Ukana, Akpakwume, Egede, Ebe, Awhum, Okpatu, Abo, Nsude, and Ngwo.

It is believed among these communities that a certain spiritual linkage binds them to the ancestral world, in spite of the intervening distances in the human world and that the Odo ancestors start their journeys from Eha-iheyi in the Eha-Amufu area and weave their ways into all the eighteen communities.

Thus, from the age of twelve, every male child must be linked to his ancestors through an initiation ritual. Even when Christianity came and the school calendar became disruptive, uncles and fathers would act as surrogates to weave the covenant of identity and belonging. As soon as the

Table 3

Sample of Ancestral Deities of Northern Igboland*

Name		Location	Function**	Sacrificial Animal***
1. Okwesili Nwodo		Ukehe	Protection; Moral Control	cock, goat
2. Ngwu Nwa Omeje		Owerre Ani	"	goat, cock
3. Ohabuenyi Ugwuebonyi		Opi	"	"
4. Attama Nwa Mba		Eha-Alumona	"	"
5. Ezomo Nwa Atta		Nguru	"	"
6. Ezcokpaka		Item	"	"
7. Ugwueke Oloto		Ibegwa	"	"
8. Nnumokwome	F.	Obukpa	Military Prowess	
9. Adoro	F.	Alor, Ero Uno	Military Prowess; Adjudication	cow, sheep
10. Nkwu	F.	Nsukkn Asndu	Fertility, Health	black dog, cow
11. Eshuru Nkwa		"	Assistant and Husband to Nkwo Deity	"
12. Idenyi Nkwo	F.	"	Assistant and daughter to Nkwo Deity	"
13. Odo		Widespread		cock, cow, goat
14. Omabe		Widespread		pig, cow, goat
15. Ojiyi		Aku	Uniting force	cock, goat
16. Abere		Imilike	Adjudication	dog, cock
17. Ezogwuda		Leke	Adjudication	dog, cock
18. Ekpala	F.	Eha-Alumona	Moral Control	fowl, goat
19. Ugwuekpe Adoro		Alor/Ero Uni	Assists Wife	"
20. Ngwu Adoro	(Son)	"	Fertility	"
21. Nwada Adoro	F.	"	Assists Mother	"

*Derived from my "Gods of the Fathers: A Taxonomy of Deities in Igboland" (Research Project).

**The range of functions emphasizes the concern of ancestors to protect their offspring, ensure moral probity, adjudicate controversies, and uphold unity and social harmony.

***The quality of sacrifices indicates the degree of importance in the communal consciousness.

grand ancestral spirit called Odo Ububa would enter the human world, new entrants would inquire from the controlling priest about the initiation requirements and date. It must be on an Nkwo market day. Initiation was obligatory for these youths and, as an informant insisted, it could serve as a form of census of births. It was presumed that from such an age, a child could learn to keep the cult secret and other confidential things from women and uninitiates. Thus, it would be quite impossible to be a native of these communities without being covenanted to the ancestral spirits.

From a sample of the liturgy in the celebration of the cult, the dwellers in this culture zone believe that these spirits are their protectors and guardians and that they constitute their life support. Prosperity and health come from the ancestral spirits. For instance, at Ukehe, when the Odo-Ububa masquerade dances in the village square, the priest would call out: "Odo-Ububa Ubeke, were oji" (Odo-Ububa Ubeke, here is kola). This is repeated five times, substituting the varied manifestations of the ancestors—for instance, Ajima Nwazenyi, Elumule Umuacha, Efoke Onyi, and Etoke Okupe. Then the priest would move into the petitions:

1. *Please, we solicit for your protection.*
   As you have returned, our lives are in your custody.
   Never you accept any evil to befall us.
   You are the great kings of a great town.
   You are aware of all that happened in the past, in the
   present and the ones that will happen in future.

After extolling the omniscience of the ancestral spirits, he would catalogue the specific requests:

2. *Odo, you are welcome;*
   Protect us;
   Give us good life;
   Give us long life;
   Give us prosperity. (Nwokwor 1990)

These ancestral spirits are assigned most of the attributes of God and are expected to perform all the duties of a Creator. They are worshiped. The sacrificial materials include tender palm fronds, eagle feathers, kola nuts, palm wine, richly cooked food, goats, cocks, rams, cows, and articles of clothing (in rich colors). It is believed that lavish gifts and food offered to the Odo spirits will ensure bountiful rewards in one's business and life endeavors.

A critical informant made three observations: (1) Most men spend a lot of money and time that could have been used reasonably for other things through the long period of six to nine months when Odo spirits are in residence. (2) Much food is wasted because more food is carried to Odo shrines than could be consumed and women are not allowed to eat the leftover food when it is taken home. (3) A lot of money that could have been used in the education of children and other productive ventures is squandered during the Odo festival period. The bias betrays an educated indigene, but the point is that people spend much in the hope that the spirits will reward their generosity in equal measure.

The origin of the cult is somewhat uncertain. A sixty-four-year-old priest from Uwelle Amokufia, a village in the Ukehe group, said in 1990:

> The story of Odo cult originated from a particular woman fetching firewood, who saw the first Odo in the bush. The strange sight terrified her; she ran home and reported to the husband who hurried to the spot with the wife. When the man saw the strange figure, he exclaimed, "Ele O!" The strange figure responded, "Ele nwa m." From that time, "Ele" became a password for Odo masquerade.

It became also the pseudonym for the secret cult. Variations of the myth of origin abound.

Another vision claims that the woman was returning from market where she went to purchase kola nut.

> Even in fright, she offered the strange figure some kola nut; when the kola nut was broken by the strange figure, it yielded three lobes. The Odo appreciated this offer and established a relationship with the woman. He accompanied her home, protecting her against invaders. But when they reached the outskirts of the village, the Odo took refuge in the bush. The woman reported to the village folk. On inspection, they saw and exclaimed, "Ele O!" The strange figure responded, "Ele, umu m" (Ele, my children). A diviner betrayed the fact that the strange figure was their ancestor who came from the land of the dead, wanting to commune with them.

They offered sacrifices and solidified the cultic relationship. The details that (1) the figures were more than one and (2) each carried a machete, come from a third myth of origin. These are aetiological myths precisely because current practices combine all the layers of the various traditions. E. Eze (1980) emphasized further aspects, namely, the elaborate ritual of propitiation with cows and the like as well as the protective covenant woven with the ancestral spirit. He added that when Cross River Igbo people (Abiriba, Ohafia, and Abam) raided northern Igbo communities, they failed in the areas where the Odo cult predominated because the protective ancestors routed the invaders and created a secure cordon over their progeny.

Beyond these aetiological and a historical myths of origin, some efforts have sought more historical origins. A. J. Shelton's study of Igbo-Igala Borderland (1971) traces the origin of Odo and Omabe to Igala land. Local sources vehemently dispute this as baseless in spite of obvious links between the Igala and Nsukka Igbo. In the Aku community, there is still another tradition linking Odo with one of the bastions of Igbo historiography.

Some Aku elders trace their origin to Nri and aver that Odo, therefore, came from Nri, and that this explains the dirge on the day before Odo departs to the Spirit World:

> **Igbo:**   Nshi Namoke Nwa Okporo odudu, Ezitere Odo na onoghalu n'igbo.
>
> **English:**   Nri Namoke, son of Okporo Odudu, has sent a message that Odo has overstayed outside.[2]

Before Odo departs, each leading Odo in Aku would give out three lamenting wails (iwa-oka):

> **Igbo:**   Shim Oka!
>
> **English:**   I am from Awka (in the Nri hegemony)! (Ezike 1983)

This would inform all the shrines of the imminent departure. However, this linkage offers little help because the whole of northern Igbo land labors under two claims of origin—Igala and Nri. These were dominant military and ritual centers. It was as fashionable to weave such a linkage as for many western and northwestern Igbo to look to Benin, another military center. The Nri-Awka origin contradicts another version which says that the full name of Odo is Ugwuoke Elechi while Omabe is Ugwuoke Aleke and that both cults represent a great ancestor, Ugwuoke (Male Hill). The ascent of Odo hill must be in his honor!

The Odo represents not an ancestor but many ancestors—male adults, women, youth—and betrays the character traits of many individuals—the jovial, wise, wild, and decorous. Each Odo type is represented by a masquerade. Thus, each ancestral spirit emanates in the form of a specific masquerade spirit. Broadly, the Odo ancestral spirits are grouped into five, each broad type containing many characters, as illustrated in table 4. Each community has its own names but the types are the same.

Category 1 masquerades are owned by a clan. Within the clan or group of villages, each village owns categories 2–5 masquerades. Each masquerade

Table 4
Typology of Odo Masquerades

	Function	Main Type	Subtypes
1.	Soul of the Community (village group)	Odo Eworozara Odo Mbiaraka	
2.	Soul of the Village	Odo Agu	Odo Nkpukpe Odo Agu Odo Onuagu Odo Onugwu
3.	Great Grand Ancestors	Mnema or Ewuru	Odo Ububa Elumule Umacha Efoke-Onyi Etoke-Okpue Ugwu-Uti Ajima Nwazenyi Odo Amadim Ofiagu-Ogule Olenyi-Omaga Ogbu-Ogele
4.	Spirits of the Departed Youths (strength, power for war and business)	Obadike	Odo Uroko Omego Odo Ubuchiruvo Uroko Ibule
		Ogadike	Odo Ugba Odo Achara
5.	The Great Spirit	Odo Ukwu	(controller of morals)

or subtype has a priest chosen from specified families, based on tradition. Some ancestral spirits have groves or shrines, while others are housed in the homes of the oldest person, Onyishi, who also serves as the priest. Before the return of the ancestral spirits from the netherworld, such shrines and homes are cleaned and fenced to guard against the prying eyes of women or uninitiates. As one of the Odo songs teases:

> Omalu Igorigo Ezehe?
> Omalu Igorigo, omalu, omalu
> Omalu igotegh zau?
> Omalu ime agaa?

Free Translation:
> Gaping woman
> What will you do?
> If you know, even if you know,
> Won't you buy fish for Odo?
> If you know, what will you do? (Nwokwor 1990)

To repeat a caution: in each community, different names may be given to the Odo types and subtypes, but the functions and generic functions remain the same. There are three important sequences in the nine-month return of the gods as guests: (1) the return or entry into the community, (2) the ascent of the hill, and (3) the departure.

Ceremonies attend the whole nine-month period, but some communities put a premium on the entry period while others turn the departure event into a climactic community affair. It must be emphasized that all three stages are important. The specific case study, Odo Aku, lays much emphasis on the departure event called Ula Odo Aku (The Departure of the Odo in Aku Community). In some communities this stage is rather low-keyed and sad. Some men cry that the ancestors are leaving. A cynic calls it "Monday Blues" after a long festival of ease. A second point of emphasis is that the calendar of return, ascent, and departure is fixed by divination and cannot be amended. Thus, if the departure day falls on a Sunday (in the Christian calendar), it cannot be shifted. For instance, in those christianized parts of Igbo land, if the village's market day fell on Sunday, usually the market would not be held. But within Igbo-Odo (those parts of Igbo land where Odo cult exists), no such amendment is allowed in the Odo calendar.

There is a dramatic quality to the Odo cult. Scholars dub it "magic theater." As is typical of any festival, the drama starts with the preparation period, through the beginning of the returns (Mgbafu Odo), followed by the return of the rest of the ancestors (Nluamlua). The middle section of the drama consists of a grand outing of all the masquerades celebrated with festivities. The ascent of the Odo hill heralds the beginning of the departure (Ula Odo) in the ninth month.

The first category of ancestors to return are the Odo Eworozaka. Many others return in the Nluamlua period. Then the date for the great-grand ancestors—Nnema and Ewuru Odo—comes. This heralds the period when new initiates can be covenanted (Ofufu Ama). The wild Obadike and Ogadike spirits, then, emerge from the spirit world. Odo Ukwu, the Great One, will also visit. He will eat sumptuously and humorously castigate wrongdoers and depart on the same day. Various ritual celebrations, at the clan, village, and family levels, will occupy the months. Gifts are exchanged and the roots of the people are secularized and solidified.

The most colorful point is just before the ascent of the Odo hill, when all the masquerades invade the market square. Women are allowed to dance to the melodious music supplied by "spirits" from enclosures. The entire community surges out in their finery. It is revelry galore. Some of the Odo masquerades have to be rescued from female consorts to embark on the arduous ascent at dusk. The village square becomes deserted as people anxiously wait to hear whether the ancestors made it safely to the hills. Once in a while, a loud shrill of "wahoho!" rends the night air, announcing a successful ascent of yet another ancestor.

This event signals that the final departure is near. Preparations begin. Sacrifices, petitions, and vows are made. Those who will escort the spirits are chosen and begin to arm themselves with empowering charms. Such journeys are hazardous, as ritual taboos gird the movements. For instance, an incautious escort who moves in front of an ancestral spirit is killed.

In some communities, such as Aku, a mass return of sons and daughters is prescribed before Ula Odo. Meetings are held to sort out the affairs of the community amidst the rituals of Odo. Thus, the whole community is recovenanted to the ancestral spirits. In some communities, the paraphernalia of the Odo spirits are taken around the villages to pay final homage to every family and reassure them of ancestral protection during the two-year absence. The day of departure is a dangerous period: women, uninitiates, and strangers in the community, including government workers, teachers, and boarders in secondary schools, are not allowed outdoors. The secrets of the cult as well as the gory rituals are shrouded from certain sectors of the populace. The ancestors finally leave the human world.

Critics point to the wild activities of the youthful and exuberant Ogbadike group of Odo masquerades and to the restrictions put on women. This should not suggest that women do not play any roles in Odo cult. In Aku, women feature in the following ceremonies shown in table 5.

However, only males undertake certain aspects, such as Egorigo, Ntibe Uhamu, Ofufu Ama (initiation), Ogbugba Uham, Otutu Odo (hailing Odo), Osuso Odo (running around with the masquerade), looking after it, singing his song, making the shrine or homestead, clearing his route, preparing the animal sacrifice, and so on. Women do all the cooking; they receive and give gifts and enjoy the festivity—colors, music, clothes, and revelry. In Aku, for instance, the Odo-Ayi or Gberere is nicknamed Oyi-Umaunwanyi (women's friendly Odo). He does not molest them, as do the

Table 5
Female Roles in Odo Cult: The Aku Example

Ceremony	Required Items
1. OBU-EGBA-ODO (fixing the Calendar of Odo: women join in celebrating the announcement	black beans, rice, fish, palm wine, tobacco
2. MPIGIRI (celebrating the return of Odo)	kola, maize, beans, money
3. IPAFU NRI ODO (providing food when Odo music is played)	food with meat, fish, wine
4. OGUGO ODO (worship)	yams, money, fowl
5. OBUBO ODO (cleaning the shrine)	money, fowl
6. OHUHE ODO (sighting Odo and dancing Odo dance)	money, lambs, fowl
7. OKWUKWE NA OHUHA OBURU (making vows and fulfillment of vows to Odo)	as per vows
8. ODO IJE BE ADA (Odo visits first daughters)	gifts
9. ODO IJE BE NNE OR NWUNYE (Odo visits mothers, wives)	gifts
10. Provision of accoutrements	obejiri (knife), ute (mat), odo (yellow chalk), otanjele cloth (woven by women)

boisterous Ogada and Ugwu-Ugwoke (Ogadike subtypes). Rather, Ayi demonstrates dance styles and gives men and women kola nut from his pocket in anticipation of monetary returns. But Odo season is a tense period for women because of costs, extra work, taboos, and restrictions. The molestation of females is rampant during the Odo season.[3]

In Aku, the ancestral spirits visit for six months. They must depart on an Nkwo market day. On that day, no woman or uninitiate goes out from morning till night. On the previous day, Afor market day, people slaughter goats, pigs, cows, sheep, and fowl to celebrate the end of the season. The departure is conducted in utmost secrecy on a long defined route.

The Rains: The Conflict of 1983

As mentioned earlier, the process of chrisitanization within "the part of Igbo land in which Odo is celebrated," Igbo-Odo, started in the second decade of the 1900s. The discovery of bitumen coal in the Udi hills in 1909 turned the attention of the colonial government to this area. An evacuation railroad, running from Enugu to Port Harcourt (on the Atlantic sea front) was completed between 1913 and 1916. Meanwhile, the aftermath of the Aro expedition opened the Igbo hinterland and attracted the missionary bodies from the coastal areas into the hinterland in the wake of "pacification." A competition for spheres of influence ensued (Kalu 1992a).

Another determining factor was the career of a local chieftain, Chief Onyeama of Eke. His community bordered on the coal deposit and his foresight and friendly disposition toward the new colonial agents were important. He organized the supply of labor for government projects. Chief Onyeama was an enlightened despot who sought to lift his people up (Onyeama 1982). A colonial officer described the Igbaja-Udi group of villages as being extremely fractious. They gloried in intercommunal warfare, but once a year they would lay down arms and celebrate at an ancestral shrine located at Nsude. Chief Onyeama was a man of his people. He typified them in his aggressive obstinacy and by force of character became a ruler and a cohesive force. He traveled around settling disputes. This man, about whom numerous anecdotes of violence abound, became the chairman of a native court. His ambition was to raise a number of educated indigenes who could deal with the colonialists. He, therefore, approached the Anglicans in nearby Awaka. They sent a black priest, Isaac Ejindyu, to evangelize Onyeama's suzerainty. But the Anglicans' policy was to teach the junior classes in the vernacular. The import of this for the communication of the gospel and development of the Igbo language was immense but unappreciated. The chief was astounded and argued that his people already knew enough Igbo language and wanted English for political survival. He threw out poor Isaac and molested Anglicans all over Igbaja-Udi. He then sent to Igbariam, near Onitsha, for the Roman Catholics. They made an initial contact but lacked the personnel for consistent evangelization. The outbreak of the First World War put severe strains on personnel, and the Alsatian priests were withdrawn from a British territory for security reasons.

Roman Catholic missionaries took up the challenge seriously in the inter-war years. From the Oji River to Nsukka and throughout the Igbo-Odo culture theater, Chief Onyeama eased the paths of the Roman

Catholics and blocked the chances for the Anglicans. Between 1918 and 1938, most of the communities in northern Igbo land witnessed Roman Catholic influence. As the fame of Onyeama spread, friendly contacts widened. Many admired him. Some, such as Chief Attama Nwa Mba of Eha-Amufu, imitated him to become a bastion of colonial support. Others were cowed down while the school strategy as well as the personality of the white missionaries ensured initial success. For instance, in Aku, Chief Ugwu Manu, an admirer of Chief Onyeama, invited the Roman Catholics to visit from Aguleri in 1922. Local sources recall Fathers Murray and Grandin as the early evangelizers. A school started and, by 1952, Aku became a parish with over a dozen outstations. It grew so much that in 1977, Ukehe Parish was carved out of Aku Parish (Eneasato et al. 1985).

A key characteristic of Christian presence in northern Igbo land was the measure of Roman Catholic success: Anglican rivalry was strong in Igbaja-Udi, at the one end, and Nsukka, at the other end, leaving the intervening area, which constitutes the heart of Igbo-Odo, solidly Roman Catholic. This explains why the controversy was against the latter.

Chief Onyeama died in 1933 at the time when the process of consolidation of Christianity was starting. The domestication of Christian values coincided with the economic crunch of the depression, and local resistance arose. The Aba Women's Riot occurred in 1929–1930, but before then, the Nwaobiala Dance by women in 1927 was a harbinger of protest. The reaction to the colonial revolution was discussed in religious terms: the ancestral gods were angry at the attack on traditional mores. The worldview was predicated on a religious moral order. Admittedly, the colonial government possessed neither enough ethnographic data to understand the problem nor enough workers for the task of governance. The Warrant Chief system collapsed while intelligence reports were used to dig into the debris (Afigbo 1966).

The strategy of the missionaries also created a superficial existence. Court alliance often deterred aggressive evangelism. A shortage of personnel in the face of rapid expansion weakened the depth of the process, and neither the colonial government nor the missions had developed a viable culture policy. The Roman Catholics actually took a liberal stance, namely, to ignore the "pagan" cultures and baptize as many as possible into the fold, in the hope that they would become true believers later. The hope remained unfulfilled as primalists struck back on behalf of the embattled gods. A liberal culture policy bred a compromise stance in the early period which made it difficult for the church to reassert a Christocentric social ethics later. This explains why a commentator observed that, when Bishop

Eneja was the first parish priest in Aku in 1952, he did not dare oppose Odo cult as his agents would in 1989. As the ruler of the community informed the parish priest on June 26, 1989, "I am bringing to your notice that almost all your so-called Christians are Odo worshipers."

We argued earlier that the centrality of Odo ancestral cult in this subculture zone is important for understanding the nature of Christian presence. In the early period, rivalry among mission bodies and the desire to stake large claims weakened the ability to root the gospel. Thus, certain areas of controversy simmered over a long period of time. Some have argued that the *école-église* method ate up so much time in education that proclamation and pastoral care suffered. Bishop Shanahan saw matters differently: school was in the service of evangelization, and the capture of the minds of the young was seen as a more virulent attack on the mores of the people than a confrontation could achieve. This still has much merit both in logic and empirical results. But, initially, accommodation was not an official policy. Indeed, the official policy was *extra ecclesiam, nulla salus est* (no salvation outside the church). The liberating air of Vatican II worked closely with the large-scale development of indigenous clergy and political independence to create a new atmosphere in the period 1970–1990. Dialogue, attached to Vatican apron strings, became the new official attitude toward non-Christian religions (Kalu 1978).

In Igbo land, this period was characterized by new forces which changed the pattern of Roman Catholic evangelical strategy. First, before the civil war (1967–1970), the Aladura, or Independent churches, grew wings in Igbo land. For years they proliferated in Yoruba land, as John Peel (1968) has shown, while the Igbo people took the mission churches to be "the real thing." R. C. Mitchell's study has confirmed this. Even the neighboring Ibibio were more enthusiastic toward religious independence. Igbo adventurism preferred nationalist African churches, but the real concern was to pioneer secondary schools in the 1940s. By 1961, communal and privately owned secondary schools were more in number than mission and government secondary institutions. During the civil war period (1967–1970), ordered mission activities were disrupted. Relief services kept the priests busy and relevant, but the Aladura grew. The return to traditional culture, the prevalence of magic, medicine, and easy solutions served as religious balm to war-torn communities.

Something else happened: secular ideology mushroomed during the desperate part of the war, 1969–1970. The Ahiara Declaration blared an anti-Christian, Marxist ideology running as a deep undercurrent. Finally, the immediate postwar period witnessed the inexplicable Pentecostal wind.

Charismatic movements grew within the mission churches and outside. By 1977, the Festival of African Culture was elaborately celebrated in Nigeria, giving African cultural renaissance a new fillip. It overflowed into the theological scene as advocacy intensified for indigenization, moratorium, and African theology. African theology either talked of power and social ethics or tackled inculturation (Kalu 1992b).

The attack by the Aladura religious movements became acute with the growth of messianic groups and the nativistic types. The disruption caused by the civil war was traumatic, and miracles and wonders magnetized many. The cultural nationalists created a pervasive system which intertwined with the hubris fueled by oil money. The lure to conform to such world systems put much pressure on the church. This explains the debates on whether Christians should be barred from taking the *Ozo* title. This debate tore the peace of the church apart. The charismatic movement constituted a serious challenge because of a scriptural base. On the sideline was the new and open garb of respectability accorded to theosophic societies such as the Rosicrucian Order, Freemasonry, the Grail Message, Eckankar, the Aetherius Society and the like. An embattled church fought back to redefine its doctrinal stance.

In 1983, the raindrops increased. The Ula Odo Aku fell on Sunday, August 21. The last time this had occurred was on July 16, 1967, and no protests came from the church as the bugles of the civil war sounded in the background. But by 1983, the forces that we described earlier had forced the church to become more defensive and alert.

A prominent Catholic layman, Emmanuel Idike, gathered a cross-section of the Aku community to discuss the new awareness of the Christians toward the oppression of primal religionists. As he argued:

> Since the inception of Christianity in Aku, there have been continuous misunderstanding and bitter controversy between the Christians and traditional worshippers in the town. The traditional worshippers want to impose their ways of worship upon Christians in order to preserve and perpetuate the traditional system of worship of our forefathers. Most of these practices are simply seen as Omenala (customs) opposed to Christian faith and Christian ways of life.

He catalogued the models of victimization of Christians:

1. Excommunication of Christians in the community
2. Imposition of heavy fines on the Christians
3. Denial of rightful shares
4. Exploitation of Christian women
5. Demolition of the victim's house and the destruction of household property.[4]

Idike traced the areas of conflict through the rites of passage to Odo ancestral cults and pleaded for harmonious coexistence. He drew attention to the embarrassment caused to government officers, teachers, and secondary school boarders who are not indigenous. The interesting aspect is that Emmanuel Idike later became the chairman of the Aku General Assembly (AGA), whose motto could be liberally translated to mean "We thrive through our Ancestors." He became central in the thunderstorm of 1989.

In 1983, the appeal for peaceful coexistence did not deter the Odo cultists. They drew up guidelines to restrain the flagrant harassment of female school boarders and in 1987 made a deliberate effort, under the leadership of Idike, to discipline some masquerades from Umuori and Amogwu villages who molested some girls.[5] These were forced to pay compensations for the scarves seized from the girls. However, the position of the Aku General Assembly was that such discipline could only be carried out by the ruler of the community, Igwe O. C. Manu III.

The Thunderstorm: The Crisis of 1989

By Easter 1989, it had become apparent that the Odo season was near and that the calendar indicated that the Ula Odo Aku, the departure of Aku ancestors, would fall on a Sunday, with immense potentials for conflict. The Roman Catholic parish priest Rev. Fr. J. A. W. E. Nnadozie agonized over the matter. It could be surmised that change in ministerial formation among the Catholics had yielded a band of younger clerics who were articulate, conscientious, and deeply concerned with the problem of inculturating the gospel. At both the pastoral and theological levels, Archbishop/Cardinal Francis Arinze had paid much attention to this problem before moving to Rome, where he heads the unit on dialogue with non-Christian faiths.

On May 20, 1980, Fr. Nnadozie organized a seminar on inculturation as a preparation to the "faithful." It was centered on four questions:

1. How far do the values obtained in the Igbo cultural major feasts and traditional rites resemble, differ, supplement, contrast, contest, complement the Christian values?
2. Do you think that the Church is a tenant in Africa looking at the good news of Jesus Christ the Son of the Living God, the Lord of the Universe?
3. How in your opinion can the obstacles on the way to Inculturation in Aku Parish be best solved? Suggest some ways of removing the obstacles.
4. What claims has Christianity to universal validity?[6]

This seminar was crucial in defining the ideology for battle. It sought to

evaluate traditional culture in the light of Christian norms, especially the
Odo and Omabe. The conferees affirmed the beauty of Odo music and the
joys of reunion but condemned the pagan sacrifices, brutality, and waste of
resources. They roundly condemned the curfews on women and the uninitiated, the orgies, and the charms. The seminar reaffirmed the existence of
Christianity on African soil. It could not be a stranger because God created
the whole universe. The Igbo acknowledged God as supreme before missionaries came, and, therefore, worshiping nature deities was wrong,
pagan, and based on ignorance. Based on Christ's attitude to Jewish culture, the grass-roots Christians in Igbo land had the task of "amending the
culture that involves the worshiping of false gods." Christ is the "father of
all cultures." They then zeroed in on defining the path of interaction and
dialogue—also from a Christian perspective. They took specific examples
of core cultural forms such as the New Yam festival, Onyisi office, and
Ozo title. They concluded that sacrifices in the New Yam festival should
be removed, turning it into a merry-making festival. The Onyisi (eldest
man) in a kinship group deserves honor and gifts, but the libations are
counter to Christianity. Many of the rituals in the Ozo title-taking process
were condemned as un-Christian. From here, it was a short step to the
apology for the Christian cause extolling the universality of Christianity
and its socio-moral contributions to uplifting of Igbo people. In spite of the
merit–demerit approach, the focus was normative ethics based on Christian values.

The parish council, then, wrote the traditional ruler of the community
and the Aku General Assembly alerting them to the approaching thunderstorm. The council informed the police on June 14, 1989, that the activities
of Odo on a Sunday would likely cause a breach of peace in Aku.

The traditional ruler quickly countered the church and intervened with
the police arguing: (a) The activity slated for July 16, 1989, was a custom
from immemorial time, and there are Dikwus (cult leaders) from sixty-five
wards to ensure proper conduct. (b) The Aku General Assembly has
devised an exit: church services should be held from 6 to 9 A.M. The ritual
curfew would follow thereafter. He affirmed that "this happened in 1983
on Sunday, August 31, Nkwo, and there was no hitch." The onus was on
Christians to maintain the compromise. (c) The prospect of trouble was
through the invidious activities of the parish priest, who used his sermon
on June 11, 1989, to reveal Odo secrets. According to informants, "there
was great hissing and walk-out by Christians, both male and female from
the church." (d) The government's cultural revival, Manwu festival (festival
of masquerades), is an encouragement. (e) Efforts have been made to visit
secondary schools and to admonish everyone to be decorous.[7] These facts

stood out: the church's discussion of the matter from the pulpit and the easy resort to the police infuriated both the traditional ruler and the Aku General Assembly and made the position of Emmanuel Idike, the president of AGA and a patron of the church, very difficult. The protagonists insisted that Aku Christians were in favor of Odo and that women were not protesting.

On June 29, the St. James Catholic Parish Council lodged an official complaint to the chairman of the local government authority Igbo-Etiti rejecting the compromise on the time of the service based on the specious legality that (a) "universally Sunday is the Day of the Lord, Dominica Die"; and (b) observances are obligatory and last through the whole day. They rejected the curfew and the decretal form of the order from the Aku General Assembly. They concluded that:

> For justice, peace, law and order, secret cult people could be made to keep to Odo shrines and path ways. For all Christians be they active or lukewarm cannot accept this trafficking in lawlessness by Odo fans, operating under the guise of tradition and culture.

On July 3, the parish priest alerted the police commissioner, Anambra State Command, Enugu, echoing the same points. This aggravated the crisis potential. The matter had gone beyond the local government to the state government level. The Aku General Assembly held an emergency meeting on July 6 to issue a nine-point peace formula. They couched the language carefully—for example, both Sunday services and Ula-Odo should be held on the basis of "live and let live." Yet this reaffirmed the time limit without mentioning so. The impression was left that everyone was free to move about. Yet they did not remove the curfew. They admonished Odo celebrants to use the traditional routes while the main roads should remain free. But the town had spread into the "traditional routes" and the "main roads" were not the points of contention precisely because the Odo people could not enforce any obstruction there.

On July 11, the state governor's office intervened, possibly at the prompting of the bishop of Enugu. The traditional ruler read the ominous reminder by the commissioner: "I am to warn that you will be personally held responsible for any breakdown of law and order that may arise from the attempt of the Aku General Assembly to tamper with the religious program of any Christian church in Aku."[8]

The day of reckoning came. The bishop of Enugu came to St. James Church, Aku, in person. Busloads of "faithful" arrived from all over the parish, and the mass lasted the entire day. Twenty-four priests ministered as the church refused to allow the Odo cultists to determine when they could worship. Culture and the gospel clashed in spite of sixty-seven years of compromise. As the parish priest told the police, "Odo fans continued to chant and parade and operate around the church precincts to distract a large crowd of the congregation," brandishing sharp machetes.[9] The police intervened. The worshipers stayed in the church till dusk. Many were beaten and attacked with machetes on their way home. But the chief claims that he visited all wards to ensure that there was calm. On August 17, 1989, he decided to reply to the government's letter.

The combative tone was an aspect of the aftermath—the trickles after the heavy downpour. It was also reported that a systematic vengeance was meted out to offending Christians; for instance, here a landlord would order the tenant to quit, there a father would refuse to pay the school fees of a "religious" daughter.[10] The Aku Road Transport Union decided that Catholics should not ride commercial vehicles to farms and markets. Attacks on Christians at funerals increased. Many more subtle forms of punishment continued as the chorus mounted that the parish priest should be removed. A reinvigorated consciousness to protect traditional culture suffused the community.

A certain staunch, educated Catholic, U. P. Udenigwe, wrote the bishop in obvious dismay over the conflict. He contended that the unsavory aspects of Odo had been removed; it was not merely a cultural event. The battle of evangelization could not be won by confrontation, and Aku people neither wanted a non-indigene priest to fight their battle nor did the women seek liberation. The battle was perceived as a reverend father's personal war of vengeance.

Analysis

The clash betrays how Christianity has been received in Igbo-Odo. In 1985, as part of the centenary celebration of the Roman Catholic missionary enterprise in Igbo land, a book was produced entitled *The Advent and Growth of the Catholic Church in the Enugu Diocese*. It documents forty-seven parish and monastic activities of the church with much satisfaction and emphasis on growth. Little attention is paid to areas of conflict. Yet these conflicts betray the nature of the expansion. This can be represented by the diagram on the following page.

The two concentric squares indicate that the community preserved the core covenants with the ancestors as the sustenance of the community. The need to cope with the colonial fact created a field of interaction where the encounter with the Christian change-agent occurred. In that threshold, ecological or socioeconomic and political factors determined the pattern of

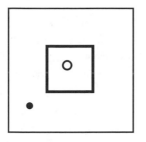

O epicenter (core covenant)

● epicycle (field of interaction)

horizontal growth. Patronage of Christianity served as an instrument to achieve a host of needs: education, wealth, status, individual and communal rivalries. In the process of encounter, the communities moved from a patronage period, when they invited missionaries, through a persecution period, when primalists reacted violently to the process of domesticating new Christian values, to a compromise period, when the new change-agent was routinized. A *modus vivendi* was created so that both the church and the shrines were there as aspects of the community. Conflict arose only when one party asserted itself over the other. In this Aku conflict, the weak Anglican Church kept to the previous compromise. The chief congratulated them. That compromise ensured that the church and the gospel did not attack the spirits which governed the land. The covenant with the gods of the fathers was still the dominant force in Igbo-Odo. The seminar exposed the breadth of the failure of the church.

The eclectic approach of the adaptation strategy was exposed by the 1983 solution. It assumed that certain aspects of the culture could be picked out for negotiation with the villagers. The demand to "amend" these betrayed ignorance about the nature of spiritual warfare. It drew attention to the lack of depth in biblical moorings of some scholarly theologizing on indigenization. Many African scholars ignore the reality of principalites, powers, rulers of darkness, wicked spirits in high places, and demons. A vestige of missionary ethics ignores the "alive universe," which is the context of evangelical battle. Some have missionized in ignorance of the clash of worldviews to the detriment of the gospel.

The seminar betrayed the gap between scholarly theologizing in the African church and the spiritual reality at the grass roots. None of the answers proffered by inculturation theologians could be applied. Those who thought that the ancestors could be *communio sanctorum* found that Paul never said in 1 Corinthians 15 that unbelievers resurrect. Besides, they could not perceive Odo as communion of saints. The participants virtually abandoned the gymnastics of liberal theologians on the culture–gospel interface and reaffirmed the old religion. The wonder is why they did. Commentators fell upon the personality of the parish priest. Was he motivated by the new wind of renewal blowing through the church? Two other aspects stand out: the seminar in theory perceived culture as "God-given" but in practice confronted it as "satanic." This is an unresolved dilemma in modern African spirituality and theology. Second, and arising from the above, is the doffing of the hat to the "continuities" between African and Christian spirituality in theory while emphasizing the "discontinuities" in practice.

Of much interest is that both parties indulged in a war of subterfuges. It was obvious that the clash was between a new covenant proffered by Jesus and the old covenant with the gods of the fathers. Yet Udenigwe claimed that the spiritual elements in Odo had been removed, including the charms. This is untrue. The chief claimed to be protecting culture. This ignored the spirits at work within cultural forms. These forms are not aesthetic, dramatic forms but rituals in which powerful spirits are at work. Western rationalist tradition may demur, but the reality persists.

The Christians took a legal high road—protection of women and freedom of worship. These ignored the core of the matter because of a desire to attract the lightning rod of the secular government of the heads of the Odo people. Nigeria is a secular state, so the level of the government's intervention remains limited. Quite often, political considerations determine the reaction to each situation. But the law enforcement agents are so corrupt that their presence taints. Many believe that law officers were paid to protect the churchgoers. Others presumed that the bishop used his personal relationship with some government officials. The impression was strong that the reverend fathers fought the Aku people for reasons beyond the theological; after all, the compromise between Christians and Odo lasted for a long period. Besides, the silence of Anglicans was noteworthy. Police presence diminished the image of the church and did not constitute a viable solution.

The mop-up activity of the Odo people indicated strongly that, at the grass-roots level, neither the question of inculturation theology nor any viable answers (that would enable theology to assist Christian living) had emerged. Thus, when the reverend father exposed the secrets of Odo cults in his sermons, the congregation hissed in disapproval. Some walked out. The challenge to African theologians remained because cultural theology is fraught with problems. An example is Fr. J. P. C. Nzomiwu's article in *Africana Marbugensia* in the year of the crisis, 1989. He stated: "The inculturation or indigenization of Christianity in Igbo culture would, therefore, mean no opposition between Christian values and the good values of the

Igboman, such that the Igbo is truly and fully an Igboman and a Christian at the same time, not either/or" (Nzomiwu 1989, 17).

In the Aku grass-roots context, how does this aid the people to experience the presence of the kingdom and yet celebrate Ula Odo Aku? If they eliminated the sacrifices and covenant renewals, would Odo be the same? Will the people accept such amendments? Thus, the dilemmas heap up without a viable solution. When pneumatic theology supersedes cultural theology, an exit will emerge. A spiritual problem requires a spiritual approach. Scholarly reflections dependent on Western traditions continue to be out of depth and contact with African spirituality in the modern period.

Notes

1. Adapted from Kalu 1978.

2. Interview with Okafor, August 19, 1983.

3. E. Idike, "Suggestions on how to improve the relationship between Christians and Traditional Worshippers in Aku and Ensure Peaceful and Harmonious Co-existence in the Society," January 16, 1983.

4. Ibid.

5. C. U. Okechukwu, "Ula Odo Aku on 16 July 1989: Maintenance of Peace," June 26, 1989.

6. Patrick Ochiam, "A Communique Issued by St. James Parish, Aku, at the end of a Seminar on Inculturation held at St. Michael's Catholic Church, Ikolo, on 29 May 1989," July 10, 1989.

7. Igse O. C. Manu III, "Conduct likely to cause a breach of peace in Aku," June 26, 1989.

8. J. C. Udeaguala, "Maintenance of Justice, Peace, Law and Order in Aku, Igbo-Etiti LGA," July 11, 1989.

9. A. J. W. E. Nnadozie, "Reports on Sunday Services held in Aku on 16/7/89 being Nkwo Ula Odo Aku Day," July 18, 1989.

10. Akubue S. Obetta, "Activities likely to bring about War in the Town," August 25, 1989.

References

Published Materials

Afigbo, A. E.

    1966   "Revolution and Reaction in Eastern Nigeria: 1900–1929." *Journal of the Historical Society of Nigeria* 3, no. 3:539–51.

    1972   *The Warrant Chief.* London: Longmans, 1972.

Eneasato, M. O., et al., eds.

    1985   *The Advent and Growth of the Catholic Church in the Enugu Diocese.* Onitsha: JET Publications.

Eze, E.
    1980   "Ekewo in Ukehe Contemporary Society." *IVOM* 1.
Ezike, J. N.
    1983   "Aspects of the Pre-Colonial History of Aku." B.A. thesis, History, University of Nigeria, Nsukka.
Horton, R.
    1961   "Gods as Guest." *Nigerian Magazine,* special edition. Federal Ministry of Information, Lagos.
Imo/Anambra River Basin Authority Reports
    1985   O. U. Kalu, "Socio-Economic Profile, Amadium-Olo Project"; "Socio-Economic Profile, Agba Umana Project."
Jahn, J.
    1961   *Muntu: An Outline of Neo-African Culture.* London: Faber & Faber.
Kalu, O. U.
    1978   *African Cultural Development.* Enugu, Nigeria: Fourth Dimension
    1985   "Socio-Economic Profile, Amadium-Olo Project"; "Socio-Economic Profile, Agba Umana Project." Imo/Anambra River Basis Authority Reports.
    1992a   "The Christianization of Igboland 1857–1967." In *Ground of Igbo History,* ed. A. E. Afigbo, 488–521. Lagos: Vista Books.
    1992b   "Unconquered Spiritual Gates: Inculturation Theology in Africa Revisited." *Journal of Inculturation Theology* [Catholic Inst. for W/Africa] 1, no. 1.
Kalu, O. U., with R. O. Onunwa and D. Inyama
    1989   "Gods of Our Fathers: A Taxonomy of Igbo Deities." Research Project. A report on this was presented to the Seminar on Igbo World View, Institute of African Studies, University of Nigeria, Nsukka.
Mitchell, R. C.
    1970   "Religious Change and Modernization: The Aladura Churches among the Yoruba of Southwestern Nigeria." Ph.D. diss., Northwestern University.
Nwanunobi, C.
    1984   "The Deus Otiosus Concept: An Examination through Transactional Analysis." *Anthropos* 79:145–54.
Nwokwor, C. O.
    1990   "The Resilience of African Traditional Religion: A Case Study of Ukeje." B.A. Thesis, Religion, University of Nigeria, Nsukka.
Nzomiwu, J. P. C.
    1989   "Inculturation: Its Meaning and Implication for the Nigerian Church." *Africana Marbugensia* 13:11–23.

Onwuejeogwu, M. A.
1981   *An Igbo Civilization: Nri Kingdom and Hegemony.* Benin: Ethiope Publishing Company.
Onyeama, D.
1982   *Chief Onyeama: The Story of an African God.* Enugu: Delta Publications.
Opoku, K. A.
1978   *West African Religion.* Singapore.
Peel, J. D. Y.
1968   *Aladura.* London: Oxford University Press.
Sanneh, Lamin
1989   *Translating the Message: The Missionary Impact on Culture.* Maryknoll, N.Y.: Orbis Books.
Sawyerr, H.
1970   *God: Ancestor or Creator?* London: Longmans.
Shelton, A. J.
1971   *Igbo-Igala Borderland.* Albany: State University of New York Press.
Ukpong, J.
1984   *African Theologies Now: A Profile,* Spearhead 80. Eldoret: Gaba Publications.

Unpublished Documents

Aku General Assembly. Circular from the Secretary, AGA Executive Meeting. Agendum: To discuss the strained relationship between Christians and non-Christians which is greatly affecting the peace, unity, social life and development in the town. August 22, 1989.

Akubue, Sebastian O. (Sec. Parish Council). "Maintenance of Justice, Peace, Law and Order in Aku." To the Chairman, Igbo-Etiti Local Government Authority, June 29, 1989.

Idike, E. "Suggestions on how to improve the relationship between Christians and Traditional Worshippers in Aku and Ensure Peaceful and Harmonious Coexistence in the Society." January 16, 1983.

Manu, Igwe O. C. III (Traditional Ruler). "Conduct likely to cause a breach of peace in Aku." To parish priest, St. James, Aku, June 26, 1989.

——. "Maintenance of Justic, Peace, Law and Order in Aku during Ula Odo Aku Festival on Sunday 16th July 1989." To Commissioner for Special Duties, Military Governor's Office, Enugu, August 17, 1989.

Nnadozie, Rev. Fr. J. W. E. Awazie (Parish Priest, St. James Aku). "Maintenance of Justice, Peace, Law and Order in Aku, 3/7/89." To the Commissioner, Anambra State Command, Police HQ, Enugu, July 3, 1989.

——. "Reports on Sunday Services held in Aku on 16/7/89 being Nkwo Ula Odo Aku Day." To Commissioner of Special Duties, Enugu, July 18, 1989.

Obetta, Akubue S. (Teacher, Boys Secondary School, Aku). "Activities likely to bring about War in the Town." General Distribution. August 25, 1989.

Ochiam, Patrick (Sec. St. James Parish, Aku). "A Communique Issued by St. James Parish Aku at the end of a Seminar on Inculturation held at St. Michael's Catholic Church, Ikolo, on 20 May 1989." July 10, 1989.

Okachi, Ezike (Onyishi Aku). "Resolutions by Aku Community on Maintenance of Peace, Law, and Order during Ula-Odo Aku on Sunday, Nkwo, 16th July, 1989." July 7, 1989.

Okechukwu, C. U. (Sec. Aku General Assembly). "Ula Odo Aku on 16 July 1989: Maintenance of Peace." To parish priest, St. James, Aku, June 26, 1989.

——. "Maintenance of Peace, Law and Order—Ula Odo Aku on 16/7/89." To the Sec., Catholic Church Council, Aku, June 26, 1989.

Udeaguala, J. C. (Director-General, Office of the Military Governor, Anambra State, Enugu). "Maintenance of Justice, Peace, Law and Order in Aku, Igbo-Etiti LGA." To HRH Igwe O. C. Manu, III, July 1, 1989.

Udenigwe, O. P. "Ula Odo Aku." To Rt. Rev. Dr. M. U. Eneja, Bishop of Enugu, July 30, 1989.

Part Two

AUTHORITY, AGENCIES, AND PERFORMANCE

Pa Divination: Ritual Performance and Symbolism among the Ngas, Mupun, and Mwaghavul of the Jos Plateau, Nigeria

UMAR HABILA DADEM DANFULANI

IVINATION AS A UNIVERSAL phenomenon and a standardized process of deriving hidden or secret knowledge from a learned cultural tradition based on an extensive body of knowledge (Peek 1982, 1) is of different types in African societies. It ranges from simple beliefs about and the interpretation of omens, dreams, and the flipping of a coin, to complicated methods such as graphology, gambling, horoscopes, tarot cards, *I Ching*, and a game of cards. In its simplest dimension, divination has to do with options and choices within a range of probabilities. It appears to be one of the strongest viable systems in African thought patterns that penetrates the spiritual realm and serves as a vehicle for reconciling the human and spiritual worlds. It is through such systems that human beings communicate with spiritual agents and vice versa.

The diviner[1] thus stands at the crossroads between the spiritual and human worlds. S/he is the intercessor, mediator, and bridge of communication between the two worlds. As an agent between the human and spiritual worlds, s/he explores and exploits the mystical world to normalize, ameliorate, restore, and reconcile estranged relationships for a harmonious and habitable universe. S/he uses a specialized body of knowledge in manipulating and controlling the spirit world for the benefit of the human and spiritual communities.

This chapter examines the ritual symbolism and performance of divination among the Chadic-speaking groups of the eastern and southeastern Jos Plateau (in Nigeria), focusing on the Ngas, Mupun, and Mwaghavul.[2] *Pa* divination—lithomancy—is the major form and most reliable system of divination practiced among the people. The paper discusses the ritual framework of *Pa* divination as an indicator of ritual time and places it within the scope of communal and individual affliction, conflict, and crises caused by both spiritual and human agents. It analyzes the ritual process of this system of divination. Ritual symbolism, purification of *Pa* divination pebbles and other paraphernalia for divination, and the processes of divination are described and interpreted. In all these rituals, *Pa* divination is noted to have constituted part of *tok kum*, communication with the deities through redressive rites.

The Etymology of the Term *Pa*

Pa is a term that denotes finding out the spiritual forces that underpin the causes of illness. In a technical sense, *Pa* refers only to lithomancy, that is, divination with pebbles. Etymologically, *Pa* means "to cover something." It has to do with something that is secret and hidden. However, the ritual performance and act of divination are known as *kos Pa* in Mupun and Mwaghavul, and *kis Peh* in Ngas.[3] *Kos Pa* means "to cast" or simply "casting," denoting "to uncover hidden secret" or "to uncover truth" in its most minute details. *Pa* ideally provides a solution to every human problem. *Pa* divination is the system of revealing all secrets and hidden knowledge, whether human, mystical, or spiritual. Furthermore, *kos/kyes Pa* means "to cast" or "grind" the divination pebbles and by so doing to discover/read the divine wishes of the spirit realm and solve human problems. Thus, the diviner is called *ngu-kos-Pa* (or *ngo-kis-Peh*), the shuffler and caster of pebbles. It goes beyond this to denote one who diminishes or eliminates human problems. *Pa* is associated with every agent capable of causing fortune or misfortune, health and ill-health, restoring normalcy or rendering havoc in both human and spirit worlds.

The Ritual Framework of *Kos Pa*

Among Chadic speakers the process of *kos Pa* is located around their concept of disease—the causal agent(s) of affliction and the redressive rites needed to avert, remedy, and exorcise affliction. In most parts of Africa, the spiritual world is reflected in the human world and vice versa. For instance, disease is not regarded merely as ill health, nor is health simply viewed as the absence of disease. The concept of health and ill health transcends the *terra firma* into the spiritual realm. Though its consequences are seen and felt in the human world, ill health, and indeed any anomaly in the human world, mirrors occurrences in both the world of human beings and that of spirits. Affliction, whether personal or communal, symbolizes a negation of natural and spiritual principles. It symbolizes a breakdown, an interruption, or a termination of the normal relationship and patterns of interaction that should exist between human and spirit beings. Since affliction, crisis, and conflict represent ill health, they must be eliminated at all costs from human society.

Pa divination is a mechanism through which social conflicts are excluded and resolved. Rituals are introduced as a device to look beneath the surface of social regularities into the hidden contradictions and eruptions of conflict in society. *Pa* rituals are employed in case of crisis and a breach of regular norms governing social relationships in human society. Thus, individuals and communities are integrated through rituals.

Pa Divination and Ritual Time

Central to understanding the ritual process and divination among these people is the concept of time. Ritual time in the practice of divination and sacrifices is related to the agents that cause affliction, conflict, crisis, and misfortune. Chadic speakers view the world, life, time, and space in terms of a fluid cyclical process. The past is capable of being repeatedly reenacted in the present and future. For instance, Chadic speakers observe changes in the seasons, the marked differences between day and night and between the here and now, this place (the human world) and the hereafter, that place (the spiritual world). Time is not determined by a series of successive moments, but it is related to observable natural phenomena that determine and express objective time. The principal markers of this cyclical worldview and history are the sun, the moon, and the stars, climatic and seasonal changes, animal and human conditions, and plants. These become reference points because of their rhythmic, repetitive, and cyclical patterns. Time is located within experience, that is, in historical events.

Time in its two-dimensional nature is conceived in terms of binary opposition modes, such as day and night, morning (east) and evening (west). These binary opposition modes are reflected in the ritual time of *Pa* divination. In the underground world of the ancestors, time is reversed, in that the sun rises for them in the west and sets in the east, reemerging in the world of humans in its cyclic journey around celestial space. These two time frames and realms are the inverse of each other and are represented in terms of opposition—spirit/human, sacred/profane, and there/here, mortality/immortality. These two opposing features of time are harmonized and reconciled only in ritual, most especially in *Pa* divination and post-divination rites. Ritual time is cyclical; it is an interruption of ordinary linear time, when human beings reestablish contact with the creative events of the cosmogonic period. In ritual, the mythical past is thus constantly recoverable. It is not an irretrievable "grave yard of time" but a constant source of ontological renewal. Ritual time thus harmonizes and reconciles two worlds, because, while it is conducted in the human world, it penetrates the spirit world.

Tok Kum in Calendrical Rituals of Passages

The passage of the years and seasons and the events conducted within them are ritually important for Chadic speakers. To keep a strict record of rites within the passing years, the high priest uses a calendar consisting of twelve lunar months. Knowing that after three years he would have fallen behind the civil calendar by one lunar month, he alters the calendar by a month within that period. Chadic speakers, like other Jos Plateau peoples, thus operate a twelve-month lunar year, with each month counted as "one moon," roughly corresponding to the lunation of the moon. Seasons of particular festivals are also referred to in terms of moons, for example, the moon for sowing, the moon for cultivation, and the moon for harvesting. Time is thus reckoned according to the phases of the moon and the seasons.

Among the Ngas, Mupun, and Mwaghavul, *Pa* divination plays an important role in setting the dates for various festivals which are mutually determined by chief priests and high priests, all of them operators of *Pa* divination. *Pa* divination is conducted to ascertain the most auspicious days for the various festivals that celebrate the passage of the seasons, such as the Ngas beer festivals of the shooting of the moon (*mostar*), fifteen ancestral and nine hunting festivals of the Mwaghavul, and the Mupun festival of the dead (*bwenene*).

In divination for hunting, the diviner may start by chanting the praise names of famous ancestor-hunters and warriors who were known to have killed large animals, followed by names of animals revealed through *Pa* divination to be killed at the hunt. He does not mention the names of dangerous animals such as leopards, lest the youths become frightened.

All these ceremonies call for careful and expert choice of auspicious days according to their seasons. The diviner ascertains the peacefulness and ritual cleanness of the land before any festivals, to ensure that the earth is not "sick" or "hurt" due to the spillage of human blood, otherwise things may go wrong in human society. *Pa* rites are therefore conducted before rites of passage to purify and reconcile "mother earth" to human beings and to herself. Redressive rites are performed where the land has been defiled and polluted to avert national affliction and calamity that may follow in the near future. *Pa* also avails a high priest the opportunity to see what the future holds, whether "the land is cool," "quiet," and peaceful and, if not, to warn the elders "to put things right" by performing the necessary redressive rituals. Such rituals are usually performed discreetly so that witches and sorcerers do not disrupt the various rites and render them useless.

Tok Kum for National Calamities

The rituals conducted for national disasters are similar to those for the calendrical rituals of passage, the difference being that the role of the diviner is here reversed. Calendrical rituals of passage are the opposite of national disasters. In the former, the diviner tries to avert such disasters through peaceful and nonredressive rites, whereas in the latter, affliction has already occurred and redressive rites are conducted to remove the calamity, purify the land, and guard against future occurrences. As a rule, *Pa* rites are much shorter in the former than in the latter, which may take days, even weeks, to complete. National calamities include famine, "when the earth turns white," drought, "scorching heat," and locusts, pests, caterpillars, blight, and mildew, which destroy crops. All these may usher in a year of hunger. Other national calamities include smallpox and other epidemics that may affect both human beings and livestock. In times of such national catastrophes, *tok kum* rituals take the form of *Pa* divination, conducted on the basis of the extended family, the clan, and the village to reveal the causal agent(s) of affliction. Redressive rites then follow, ending with an invitation to the ancestors, who emerge from the underground in the form of different masquerades charged with the responsibilities of taking away such afflictions and calamities.

Pa divination rites are also important in rainmaking. Rituals of rainmaking are not annual events, but are resorted to only in time of drought. Rainmaking is a communal affair among Chadic speakers. The rites are the closest rituals to instituting a direct worship of *Naan* (God). It is the only ritual where *Naan* (God) is directly called upon to act in mercy and save the people from total annihilation. Some extended families among Chadic speakers possess the secret medicines for making rain. The rainmaker is a diviner, a medicine man who possesses intuitive powers. The rite of rainmaking is a post-divinatory one. Priests purify the land through redressive rites (*tok kum*) before calling upon the rainmaker to make or "catch rain" through certain mystical influences and arts.

The neglect of deities and ancestors, wickedness engendered by witchcraft, sorcery, and unjust wars (for instance when one people declares war on another in a year of peace), could among others be the causes of drought. *Pa* divination attributes guilt to a whole village population, then to particular clans and then to extended families, who are then indicted. Individual culprits may be detected within the extended family, but they are never publicly exposed. Later, the family can settle those affairs at home, since "dirty linen is not washed in public." Clan and extended family heads are fined in the form of goats, millet, and *fonio* flour for the performance of redressive rites (*tok kum*). As the representatives of the ancestors, heads of clans contribute goats, millet, and *fonio* flour. Goats received as fines for the breach of moral law, especially adultery, may be used for such occasions. The heads of the affected clans and extended families publicly confess the shortcomings of their members and beg *Naan* (God), the deities, and the ancestors for mercy. The tokens of libation, sacrificial blood, meat, and meal are then offered to spiritual beings, by the high priest, who asks *Naan* (God), the deities, and the ancestors to accept them and bless the people with rain. It is after these redressive rites that the rainmaker secretly sets aside a day as revealed through *Pa* divination for rituals of rainmaking.

Tok Kum in Life Crisis Rituals

During life crisis rituals, divination rites play the role of cushioning, absorbing, and pacifying the pains of passages through life, time, and space. Chadic speakers perform *Pa* rites at every major stage of the life of the individual, from pregnancy and birth to death and rebirth. Life crisis stages include puberty, marriage, installation, and burial rites.

In Mupun and Mwaghavul lands, a diviner may recommend, as part of pregnancy rites, the veneration of a particular deity for the protection of an unborn child. For example, during first pregnancies, the Mwaghavul of Mangun placate a type of household deity, while others may rely on the compound deity (*Kumbong*). *Pa* divination may also be conducted together with pregnancy and birth rites. This is known as "divination for a baby." The ritual of nailing calabash pieces above the door of the expectant mother's room may be performed by a diviner to safeguard against threatened miscarriage. The diviner, moreover, sets the time for other prenatal rituals such as the "washing off dirt" performed for the pregnant bride within the second trimester. This signifies the washing away of any guilt committed before marriage. It is believed that without this ritual, the bride may experience a difficult labor. A ritual for sacred places is performed to protect the young mother from affliction in case she violates certain taboos or desecrates sacred places in her pregnant condition. The ritual of "inquiring from the pregnancy" (the fetus) is performed when a woman experiences frequent miscarriages. This is a divinatory rite in which a diviner asks a pregnant woman to sit down on a ritually treated calabash, which is turned upside down on the ground. The diviner holds some ritual leaves in his hands and inquires from the fetus the causes of previous miscarriages, while he shakes the leaves. The breaking of the calabash in the process of inquiry signifies that the woman is responsible for her past miscarriages. Herbal medicines are administered after such redressive rites. *Pa* divination is performed to discover the cause if the calabash does not break. *Pa* divination becomes necessary if an expectant mother becomes ill or experiences difficult labor. In the case of the latter, a local midwife may ask the woman to confess hidden wrongdoings while *Pa* divination is in progress.

After the birth of a child, some societies consult the *Pa* diviner to know which ancestor has visited them, but this is seldom the case. The more common practice is to wait and see whether the child will become emotionally attached to a particular life already lived by a deceased person. For instance, there have been a few cases of children who, right from early ages, begin to talk about the previous experiences of their former lives. The *Pa* diviner is called in here to confirm the identity of the ancestor. Thereafter, rites of veneration are carried out and further rites are performed to make the child forget its former life. This is to enable the child to begin a new and normal life.

Puberty rites for boys start with *Pa* divination to determine the date and predict events surrounding the period. The elders who usually conduct the exercise are renowned *Pa* diviners and men with intuitive powers, the "powers of second sight." As the neophytes stay in the shrine, they are taught, among other things, the art of *Pa* divination in a formal school environment. *Kos Pa* is similarly required to select the most auspicious day for the initiation rites of priests of divinities, as well as that of chief priests, high priest, diviners, medicine persons, rainmakers and other religious functionaries.

Pa is also conducted at all levels of marriage negotiations to ensure that the match is suitable, that all parties involved accept each other, and that both families are free from witchcraft, sorcery, terrible diseases, and scandals that may affect marriage. Furthermore, divination ensures that a suitable middleman is chosen. This is because such a man is crucial in the case of "wife stealing." The middleman announces in a "wailing" or "mourning" manner the theft of a wife to the bride's parents and makes sure that the bride-wealth is redeemed.

Tok Kum for Individual Afflictions
Caused by Spiritual Agents

In both calendrical and national rites, it is noted that the target of *tok kum* is the group or community. In ill health, however, the focus is the afflicted individual. The most common and recurrent forms and reasons for *kos Pa* among Chadic speakers are personal conflicts and afflictions. Causal factors for personal affliction include, among others, God, the free spirits, the deities, ancestors, and living human agents. Afflictions caused by spiritual agents are usually meant for benevolent reasons, except those from some free spirits that are malevolent.

An affliction is attributed to "the hands of God" *(sar nNaan)* only when no other agent is found to be responsible. In such a case, the diviner informs the relations of the patient that *Naan* (God) is involved and he does not know why. They will leave and then perform redressive sacrifices to the ancestors and deities, pleading with them to implore *Naan* (God) to "release" the patient. When the free spirits are blamed as the cause of an affliction relating to personal illness, *tok kum* takes the form of rites of exorcism and appeasement, because free spirits are considered most dangerous to human beings. After these rites, the patient will continue with medication to ensure a cure for his/her affliction.

The most common sources of affliction by spirit forces are believed to be the deities and ancestors. For instance, *Tau,* a deity *(Kum)* that ensures the welfare and protection of the whole of Ngasland, may cause the land to become "sick" and polluted when he is neglected. *Tenpe* afflicts through a poor harvest, and blesses by bestowing the people with a bumper harvest. *Kumyer* is symbolized by a bunch of grasses tied to a twig and planted on a farm or hanged from a tree crop, to guard and protect property from trespassers and thieves. When a taboo is violated, the deity "catches" culprits by afflicting them with edema. *Kampaal,* like *Nyer,* checks theft too, but more importantly, adultery and immorality. It afflicts culprits with paralysis, stomachaches, impotence in men, and barrenness (matter of the dry tree) in women. *Kumbong* is a deity symbolized by a long sacred stick planted at the gate of the compound or opposite it, to ward off witches, keep peace in the compound and "catch" an adulteress by causing her to stumble at the compound gate.

Tok Kum for Individual Afflictions
Caused by Human Agents

The most common sources of affliction emanating from human agents given by *Pa* diviners are anger *(dor),* witchcraft, sorcery, and the evil eye.

During ordinary divination sessions, most afflictions from human sources are blamed on anger or witchcraft. Sorcery manifests itself in the form of leprosy. However, an attack through the evil eye is rare. Anger in whatever form (whether from the ancestors, kinsmen, neighbors, or parents) is considered dangerous; thus children are implored not to make their parents and relatives angry. It is believed that fostering anger in the heart renders a ritual ineffective and can kill another person. Intense or unconfessed anger is sometimes equated with witchcraft. Chadic speakers, however, distinguish between ordinary anger (*túp*),[4] and intense anger (*dor*). The second type could be forgiven only through ritual intervention. However, *dor* is considered dangerous when a parent is enraged by his/her child but not the other way round. When there is no reconciliation, the child may suffer as a result because *dor* may turn into a curse placed on the child's head. It manifests itself in the form of loss of blessing, and the victim may become insane, impotent/barren or materially poor, demonstrating that s/he is still searching for that lost blessing. The patient may not know about it until s/he visits a diviner. In this way rituals make explicit and conscious those powerful and dangerous thoughts that are liable to become repressed (cf. Turner 1969, 23). Chadic speakers find the importance of confessing anger by "speaking out," admitting it, seeking for reconciliation and expressing goodwill, in *tok kum* rituals.

Rites of reconciliation between children who suffer from loss of blessing and their parents may be prescribed by a *Pa* diviner, whereby they are requested to make peace. In such rites, there is confession of anger, of quarrels, and of rejection of anger, repeatedly expressed in the rituals, symbolized by the sharing of communal meals between the warring parties, family members, and their ancestors. Reconciled parties share the same meal and drink beer in pairs or threes, simultaneously from the same calabash. They place their mouths side by side, with one touching the other along one edge of the calabash. The confession of guilt and of *dor* here becomes the essence of *tok kum*. The pacified parent(s) "spit out the spittle of blessing" on the ground to cancel the anger (*dor*) they have been nursing. The ancestors who are said to be living in the ground are invited by this act, the chanting of prayers and their names to come and witness the rites. The Mupun thus express parental blessing, which is absolutely vital for personal well-being, in the act of "spitting on the child," or "anointing the child with spittle."

Rites for Invoking a Deity to Avenge Injustice

How is the diviner involved in the divinity's "catching" of the culprit who violates his or her law? Chadic speakers believe that sometimes the culprit automatically incurs the wrath of the deity immediately when s/he violates its taboos and is thereby afflicted with one of the diseases associated with that deity. At other times, the victim of a violation or injustice may have to report his/her case formally to a particular deity in a simple invocation rite, urging the deity to come to his/her aid and to render justice by exposing the culprit or wrongdoer. This rite is known as *pak kum*, suppressing spirituality by laying a complaint before a divinity and invoking the divinity to punish and expose an offender. The deity is invoked by the presentation of *fonio* flour (thereby lodging a complaint before it), through its high priest. The *fonio* is presented in the form of a flour mix to the deity in the presence of witnesses who also partake of the sacred drink as witnesses. After this brief rite, usually conducted in the grove, the priest and elders present disperse. In most cases, *pak kum* manifests its symptoms in a culprit after some days, weeks, or months through the swelling of the stomach or acute stomachache.

Fonio flour is a sacred whitish substance that symbolizes holiness, purity, and innocence. By drinking the ritual flour mix, the elders are not only professing their innocence, but they thereby identify themselves with both the victim of injustice and the deity, as witnesses to the sacred contract entered with the divinity. The victim of theft must also partake of the drink as a witness to himself. This demonstrates the genuineness of his case and his frustration, for if he is telling lies, the affliction will turn on him.

When affliction sets in, it is important that the *Pa* diviner do his job without telling the culprit the cause(s) of affliction, even though he must tell the kin of the afflicted who consult on behalf of the patient. Though a sick person has the right to be present during a divination session, s/he must leave before the final verdict is made by the diviner. Instead, "somebody who could talk to him/her," for example, a close kin, friend, wife, or any person with whom the patient intimately shares his/her secrets, goes and gently leads him/her to confess wrongdoing, guilt committed, or prohibitions violated. Such a person must be asked to carefully question him/her in such a manner that s/he freely confesses his/her guilt and becomes well again, without conveying to him/her the verdict of the diviner. In this way a diviner may unveil many wrongdoings, conscious and unconscious, committed by the culprit during the process of confession, since the causes of ill health may be several. A diviner should always be careful in pursuing all the angles concerned with a case, so that affliction is dealt with once and for all. A patient may, therefore, not need several journeys to the diviner or contemplate visiting different diviners.

As demonstrated above, the efficacy of the rites of *tok kum* in this case lies in the power of the confession of guilt and reconciliation. The redressive rites may be properly carried out and the diviner reliable and truthful; however, if the patient does not confess all "with one mind," the affliction will persist. It is for this reason that the diviner first finds out the type of affliction/disease and its medicinal remedies, followed by the (spiritual and human) causal agents of affliction or illness, before performing the redressive rites required. An animal victim may be slaughtered in the place of a condemned culprit or offender. The animal victim becomes the mediating symbol in such a transaction, because it partakes as a witness in the events of both human and spiritual worlds. It lives in the human world, but its life belongs to the spiritual. It symbolically links the human world with the divine, and it makes the divine accessible and subject to human control. The sharing of the victim in a sacrificial-communion feast, in both its flesh and blood, confirms the spiritual bond which exists between human beings and the deities and ancestors, to whom the life (blood) and portions of the flesh are given. The spiritual and the human realms who are the victims of injustice and the culprit/offender are thereby appeased. Hence, a restoration of the proper mode of interaction and channel of communication between the vertical and horizontal planes (that is, between the human and the supernatural realms and between one human being and fellow human beings) is guaranteed. *Pa* divination seeks for the causal agent(s) of affliction, abating these by appeasing the divinity and releasing the culprit through redressive rites. It reconciles the culprit with, and rehabilitates and reintegrates him/her into society, satisfying the victim of injustice, who goes home gratified.

From the above, it is clear that *Pa* divination deals with human problems, ranging from personal to more communal issues. Affliction on the community or an individual could be benevolently caused by Naan (God), the deities, or ancestors, or malevolently by the free spirits or human beings. However, some human beings may unwittingly cause affliction to manifest itself in others, as is the case with anger (*dor*). In most cases, affliction is removed and health and well-being restored through redressive sacrificial rituals of reconciliation. The *Pa* diviner acts as the mediator between the victim of affliction and the afflicting spirit being. He intercedes between the victim and the afflicting agent by penetrating into the spirit realm and returning with an intelligible etiology of the ill health. The *Pa* diviner recommends what should be done to restore health and well-being. From the ritual process of *Pa* divination, therefore, a normal pattern of interaction is resumed between the individual and the spirit realm, and with fellow human beings.

The Ritual Process of *Pa* Divination:
Ritual Symbolism

Ritual is a prescribed formal behavior, a sequential stereotype of activity involving symbolic gestures, words, and objects performed in sequestered places and designed to influence supernatural entities or forces on behalf of the actors' goals and interests (Turner 1977, 183). It is all forms of mechanical human behavior ranging from the simple custom of hand shaking and the daily etiquette of greeting, to such complex and solemn acts of ritual as sacrifices (Leach 1982, 523). Rituals are repeatable over a period of time in human and cosmic life. *Pa* divination rituals involve the shuffling and casting of divination pebbles, the writing of symbols, and their interpretation. They are conscious and voluntary, repetitious and stylized symbolic bodily actions, centered on cosmic structures and/or sacred presence (Zuesse 1987, 405). *Pa* divination rituals are repetitive symbolic behavior expressed during the times of crisis, misfortune, conflict, and affliction. They communicate in a stylized overt form the values and concerns of a particular group or individual (Honko 1979, 373).

Pa divination rituals are intrinsically inseparable from the different symbols that give them meaning. *Pa* divination symbols, which are usually marked out on the divination board, represent their mode of writing. It uses a language entirely different from that of everyday speech. This oracular speech is cryptic and full of symbols. *Pa* divination symbols denote the paraphernalia, acts, relationships, and linguistic formations used in *Pa* rites. Its ritual symbols are therefore used in the divination process, beginning with finding out the causes of conflict, affliction, and misfortune. The reason is that rituals are generally associated with notions that their performance in some mysterious way by a process of sensory control affects the well-being of the participants and their land, by protecting and aiding them in other ways to achieve their well-being.

Pa divination symbols are pregnant with meaning discernible by persons versed in both the people's language and oracular speech. The verses, narratives, and stories, when decoded, reveal hidden meanings. The rituals of *Pa* divination are expressive actions of human behavior; in other words, "ritual is communication." It has a sender (the client/patient), a receiver (the spirit world), and a reply and receptor (oracular messages decoded by the diviner). It is a traditional, prescribed way of communication between human beings and the sacred. Not only do *Pa* rituals link Chadic speakers with the supernatural; they also serve as a reservoir of knowledge about history, ecology, philosophy, theology, psychology, sociology, anthropology, biology, medicine, and many other experiences of life.

The key to understanding *Pa* divination lies in learning its ritual process and, more importantly, the various meanings of the ritual symbols embedded in *Pa* oracular speech, acts, and paraphernalia. The statements of the diviner are considered efficacious through the meaning they convey. Meaning is to rituals very much what sound is to language (Sörensen 1993, 23). It is the emphasis placed on the search for meaning in rituals, especially in *Pa* rituals, that makes them mechanisms for reducing, excluding, or resolving social conflicts in society. They serve as storage bags filled with information. *Pa* rituals have therefore consequently preserved a part of the rich cultural heritage of the Chadic speakers.

The Ritual Significance of Pebbles

The paraphernalia of *Pa* divination are similar to, even though they differ in many respects from those of *Fa*, *Ifá*, and *Afa* divination systems of the Fon of Benin, Yoruba, and Igbo of Nigeria, respectively. Chadic speakers use the following instruments in *Pa* divination: divination pebbles (*hik Pa*), a cow or bull's horn, a tortoise shell, a divination board or the bare ground, *Pa* divination powder or wood ash, and, finally, the diviner's hands and fingers. The diviner also has special regalia for divination. The divination pebbles (*hik Pa*) are, however, the most important items among all these.

A diviner requires thirty (or twenty) plus one or two pebbles for performing *Pa* divination rituals. Each pebble is roughly half an inch in diameter. The pebbles replace the sixteen sacred palm nuts, other nuts, seeds, and pods used in divination with sixteen basic figures by ethnic groups of central and southern Nigeria, particularly in Yoruba *Ifá*, Igbo *Afa*, and Fon *Fa* divination systems. As in the Yoruba myth of origin of divination system, the sixteen sacred palm nuts (*ikin*) were believed to have been brought down to earth by Orunmila, the Yoruba deity of divination. Chadic speakers believe that the divining pebbles, were brought from heaven by *dakur* the tortoise in his shell. Pebbles are kept inside the tortoise shell during divination ritual performances.

Pa diviners seek for divination pebbles in several sources. The first source, considered the most important, is caverns found in lakes or ponds along streams and rivers. The diviner who goes to collect the pebbles from the river sharpens his powers of second sight by remaining ritually clean. He should be brave, healthy, and strong, since while on such an errand, he is said to be traveling to the land of the spirits. He starts out without disclosing his mission to anybody and does not rest along the way, but goes directly to the lake or pond along the river. He makes only brief replies to salutations, and if people inquire about his destination, he tells them indirectly that he is on a clandestine mission. As a good swimmer, he dives swiftly into the lake and fetches the divining pebbles in great haste. He gets out of the water and goes home immediately without looking back.

The pebbles belong to the river, which is their home. The spirits that possess them are "the river beings" (river spirits). For this reason, every morning after sunrise and in the afternoon after the sun has tilted toward the west, the spirits are thought to come from the river to witness divination sessions and guide the pebbles to tell the truth. The divination pebbles can also be picked up when a lake or pond dries up. Divination pebbles are also found in crocodile stomachs. A soft-wooded but gummy plant is thrown into a lake and the crocodile sinks its sharp teeth into it. It is then dragged out of the water and slaughtered. Divination pebbles are sometimes found in the process of tin mining, and others are said to be waste products of vultures that is, "spirits." Another form may be obtained from a plant in the forest. It is, however, necessary for divination pebbles to be multicolored, consisting of creamy white, dark, light brown, and light blue types, which *Pa* diviners refer to in dual (black/white or dark/light) color terms, representing human skin complexions.

The diviner uses a bull's horn (acquired from a dwarf or long-horned cow) for storing divination pebbles. Where the horn is not available, a gourd in the shape of a horn is used. The pebbles are loosely wrapped in a strip of cloth and carefully stuffed into the horn. While Yoruba *Ifá* diviners keep the sixteen sacred divination palm nuts (*ikin*) in beautifully decorated wooden bowls, *Pa* diviners store *Pa* pebbles in the hollow part of a stone, carefully chipped and shaped for that purpose. Water is poured into the hole daily to reenact the natural condition the pebbles had enjoyed in the pool or lake. In such a favorable environment the pebbles are claimed to be recharged with mystical energy. When they are kept in the cow's horn, water is sprinkled over them to make them feel comfortable. Fine ritual dust is spread over them to enable them to maintain their smoothness.

A tortoise shell, a small calabash, or a wooden receptacle curved in the form of a tortoise shell constitutes the divination bowl. These items are used as a symbol for the shell of the tortoise where he had hidden the pebbles while coming from heaven. This treatment enables the pebbles to "hear," "see," and "speak the truth." The efficacy of the divination process is ensured only if the diviner scoops the pebbles in his hands, casts them, and replaces them sequentially into the tortoise shell. Chadic speakers use a divination board or tray measuring about three by two feet, curved from soft wood, most commonly from the black palm. These are also known among *Ifá* and *Afa* diviners, whose divination trays are more elegant than those of Chadic speakers. The board is mostly used by *Pa* diviners in the wet season, when the ground is damp and wet. It is rarely used during the dry season when the bare ground becomes more convenient. The *Pa* symbols are written on the divining board or on the bare ground.

To facilitate the writing of *Pa* symbols, fine brown dust, ground from light brown clay, is spread on the divination board. The refined divining ritual powder, like those of Igbo and Yoruba diviners, possesses medicinal qualities. Chadic speakers use refined clay from special locations that is not used for pottery by women. In the absence of the powder, wood ash is used. *Pa* symbols are inscribed in this powder. Chadic speakers use the term "inserting" or "imprinting" the *Pa* symbols, rather than "writing." This is because the imprints of *Pa* symbols are engraved with human fingers in the divining powder. The *Pa* diviner also uses his hands to take the divination items out of his divination bag, to empty the divining pebbles from the bull's horn into the divining bowl (the tortoise shell), and to scoop them up for counting and cross-checking. He uses his hands also for shaking the pebbles properly (so that they can judge well and render the correct verdict), for casting the pebbles, and for recording the results on the divining board.

Pa diviners use special regalia whenever they sit down to perform divination rituals. These include a triangular loincloth/pant and an animal skin. The diviner wears a triangular loincloth/pant, made from pure white cotton, woven by the hand-loom. This is a normal cloth for men, and therefore not uniquely associated with divination. Some diviners' triangular pants are made from leather, especially from the hide of a goat or of a wild animal. The *Pa* diviner wears a long animal skin over his triangular loincloth/pant, the latter being tied around the waist, joined by two angles, with the third angle passed over the genitals, through the groove of the buttocks and neatly knotted behind. The broader part of the pant covers the pubic area and genitals, but not the buttocks. The animal skin is tied in the reverse direction over the pant, so that it covers the bare buttocks and it is knotted below the stomach (just above the pubic area). The longer part of the skin, which contains the tail, dangles toward the ground. When it is very long, it may sweep the ground as the diviner walks. It is customarily drawn forward, through the legs, over the pubic area, and hooked over the knot made earlier by the skin of the forelimb in front.

It is mandatory for the diviner to wear his animal skin during divination sessions. It forms part of his seat. Instead of sweeping it backwards, he sweeps it forward and sits down on part of it. The significance of the animal's skin is the animal's intuitive power of second sight. Moreover, an animal is the sacrificial victim that mediates between the human and the spiritual worlds. Its blood expiates the guilt of humans because it partakes in both the spiritual and the human world. The *Pa* diviner assumes the role of mediator as he sits on the animal's skin. The animal skin aids the diviner in penetrating the spirit world to bring back secret knowledge in the form of solutions to problems of his clients.

Other items of the diviner's regalia that portray his status and power are a royal roll of cloth, a divining bag, a hat, a walking stick, and a long tobacco pipe. The royal roll of cloth—that is, a piece of thick cloth woven from dyed or undyed cotton threads made by the hand-loom—is of higher quality than the triangular pant. It is worn crosswise over the bare shoulders and drawn down to the waist, where it is either hooked by the animal's skin or is allowed to dangle over it. The roll of ritual cloth signifies status, authority, high birth, and death (being in addition a burial shroud). This is in contrast to *Ifá* priests, who wear light blue flowing gowns, adorning themselves profusely with beads, which they tie to the wrist and neck (Abimbola 1976, 13). Some *Pa* diviners, however, tie strips of wild animal skins around their wrists.

If the diviner is a royal prince, priest chief, or high priest, he wears the following in addition: a crimson red hat, the symbol of his office, worn only by traditionally consecrated chiefs of the royal family; an apron, which he wears in place of modern trousers, symbolic of his high status in society (used instead of the usual triangular loincloth worn by sundry males); a long pipe which symbolizes a high status in society; and a special wooden stick with three iron rings around it, similar to the ornamental *Ifá* staff, curved and decorated from wood, wrought iron, or ivory. This last item is both a symbol of his legitimacy and the staff of authority of his office. Other diviners with lesser sociopolitical powers wear hats with other colors besides red, symbolic of their lower social rank and political status. The roll of cloth and the red hat symbolize title, political power, and authority.

The *Pa* diviner's bag is locally woven from jute or sisal fibre. Another type is of leather, procured from the careful removal of an animal's skin in such a manner that it comes out whole without being cut up. The skin is removed carefully from the cut neck down to the tail, by gentle probing and pulling, after air has been blown into the space between the skin and the flesh through tiny holes made on the edges of the hind and fore limbs. The diviner then dries the skin in the sun, oils it daily, and massages it into fine leather. The diviner hangs the divination bag over his shoulder. No diviner goes out without his divination bag, which is big enough to contain his apparatus and concoctions of herbs if he is also a medicine man. Personal items and token gifts, such as tobacco, *fonio*, the two pieces of iron for making fire by friction, tobacco pipe, some money, sacrificial meat, and other personal effects are also kept in the bag. Some *Pa* divination bags are decorated with cowries; *Ifá* and *Afa* priests use this type of bag in addition to a different type made from cloth.

A diviner carries his bag because, like the Western family physician, his duties involve itinerancy, thus "carrying" his profession with him wherever he goes, because that is his station in life. He cannot refuse a client by lamely giving the excuse that he forgot to carry his divination bag. Moreover, a crucial decision needing his attention may arise at any time, since affliction "does not knock on the door before coming." The paraphernalia for *Pa* divination are always kept ready in the bag so that the diviner can perform divination for anybody, anywhere during the day. Medicine persons and other people, male and female, carry bags. These, therefore, are by no means particular to the diviner, but those carried by women differ from those carried by men of title and rank and religious functionaries, such as diviners.

The Ritual Purification of Divination Pebbles

To keep *Pa* divination instruments in perfect condition, ritual cleanness of the diviner and his instruments, especially the divination pebbles, is necessary. "Ritual cleanness" here includes moral uprightness, absence from anger and ill feeling toward others, as well as abstinence from sexual contact before the diviner goes in search of divination pebbles and medicines for the ritual purification of the divining pebbles and for his patients if he is also a medicine man. The diviner observes certain moral taboos particular to his office, such as eating food and drinking beer moderately, to enable concentration on the ritual process (since Chadic speakers associate gluttony with witchcraft), and not eating food or drinking beer or gruel prepared by a menstruating woman or a nursing mother. Moral misconduct, such as theft, incest, and adultery, immediately discredits him as diviner.

The diviner prepares the instruments for use in his office with utmost care and ritual attention. The most important of all these is the ritual purification of the divination pebbles. Freshly acquired pebbles, for instance, are said to be "blind, deaf, and dumb" and cannot therefore be used for divination unless they are purified. *Pa* divination pebbles may also lose their power to communicate with the spiritual world if they are not purified from time to time. The purification rite is described as "washing the divining pebbles" or "washing divination." When neglected, the pebbles lose their ability "to see, hear, speak and know things" and events, becoming "mute, dumb, blind and ignorant." Yet they cannot become completely useless, except when they are burnt in fire. The ritual "washing of *Pa*" makes them alert and effective, by recharging their energy, sensitivity, and perception.

Pa diviners use the following ingredients for making the medicinal concoctions for washing the pebbles: (1) a species of water lily that floats on top of water; (2) a parasitic plant that grows on the white cactus; (3) sand from a river bed; (4) a small plant that grows close to the ground; (5) a spongy, sharp-edged itchy species of weeds that grows in river valleys; (6) ritual red ochre; and (7) two species of some wild leaves. All these items are blended together into "medicine for washing the divination pebbles" or "medicine for purifying divination" with a few drops of beer and/or gruel made from *fonio* flour, added to the concoction, as libations. *Pa* diviners insist that other medicines, which cannot be disclosed to the public, are also added. Most of these items, however, come either directly from or are associated with the river (valley), the vicinity from which most divination pebbles are collected.

It is mandatory for the diviner to ritually vivify the divining powers of the pebbles under one of the following conditions: first, newly acquired divination pebbles such as those to be used in the initiation ceremony of a novice; second, after the pebbles have just passed a verdict of death on a patient; third, depending entirely on the judgment of the diviner himself, since the pebbles are supposed to be purified after a length of time.

Invocation Rites in *Pa* Divination

Among Yoruba and Igbo, some diviners use wooden, ivory, and/or metal rattles, jingles, and drums for invoking the deity of divination. *Pa* diviners believe that river spirits are always present during divination sessions to guide the divination stones, if favorable conditions are created. Thus, no serious invocation is needed, as in *Ifa* or *Fa* divination practices. River spirits are children of God who aid *Pa* divination as long as ritual cleanness of the ritual apparatus and the diviner is maintained. The *Pa* diviner is careful not to work before sunrise, at noon, and after sunset, when the spirits are believed to go back to the river to bathe, take a nap, and rest. *Pa* diviners, thus, work only during daylight hours. A diviner may, however, ask a desperate client who wakes him up early in the morning to go out and see whether the sun is out yet. Ngas, Mupun, and Mwaghavul diviners believe that a diviner who operates his apparatus at noon, before sunrise, and/or after sunset does so in vain. He will not arrive at the right solutions to his clients' problems. During these periods the owners of *Pa* divination, that is, the river spirits, are not present to witness and guide the pebbles to take the right decisions.

The diviner, therefore, faces the sun always during shuffling and casting of the pebbles in divination sessions. The caster of the pebbles faces the east (sunrise) before midday, and, after a compulsory break at noon, when the sun tilts toward the west, he faces the west (sunset), suggesting a phallic symbolism, which in a nonerotic sense preserves the vitality of the divination instrument. The interpreter of divination symbols does just the opposite, facing the sunset before noon and the sunrise after the noon break.

The moment he begins to take out his divination apparatus from his divining bag, the *Pa* diviner starts to utter inaudible incantations and prayers to *Naan* (God), the deities, and ancestors. From a seated position on a stone, a low stool, or the bare ground, he takes the pebbles out of the horn from his bag, unwraps them from the piece of cloth and pours them into the tortoise shell already placed in front of him. Bending forward, he selects the mother of the pebbles (usually the smallest in size, along with the father of the pebbles, if he has it), and places it into a tortoise shell (which is not being used). The whole process of *kos Pa* is based on binary opposition modes, represented by mother/father, female/male, dark/light, and so on. He bends forward again and places his left hand by the narrow end of the shell. Using his right hand, he scoops all the pebbles into the left, covering them with the right and holding them up. Rapidly, he begins to count them in pairs, dropping them back into the tortoise shell. As he does so, he begins to chant some phrases, indicating that the journey of divination has begun.[5] This initial ritual is a head count of the pebbles to make sure they add up to thirty. The *Pa* diviner then scoops them up again from the tortoise shell, with one hand sweeping them into the other. He holds them up in both hands and shakes them noisily to enable them "to speak well." The counting and shaking of the pebbles constitute invocatory rituals in *Pa* divination. These are conducted throughout the process of divination. Thus the repeated process of scooping, shuffling, shaking and casting, replacing and scooping again forms the invocatory process of *Pa* rituals. The noise of the pebbles may take the place of rattles that are used in other systems of divination, and, as a result of these processes, *Pa* divination is indeed a very noisy rite.

The Process and Structure of *Pa* Divination

The efficacy of the divination process is ensured if the diviner scoops the divination pebbles in his hands, casts them in pairs, and replaces them sequentially into the tortoise shell without dropping any one of them. To do otherwise is to declare a particular round of casting null and void, forcing the diviner to repeat the whole procedure.

The general ritual process of *Pa* divination consists of three standard stages:

1. The first is referred to as *le sar/sar ngu-kos-Pa*—"placing the diviner's hand" (which may be regarded as his signature). This consists of the first row of symbols obtained from the first casting of the day. They refer to the diviner and reveal to him whether his "hands are clean," that is, if he is ritually favored by the spirit world to consult on that day or not. If this preliminary casting is not favorable, the diviner directs his clients to another diviner, while he consults a diviner within the kin group to know why he is ritually unclean.

2. The second stage is *tal Pa/kos Pa muut*—"inquiring from *Pa* divination the cause(s) of the problem/illness." As soon as the diviner is certified to consult for the day, he begins fresh rows of castings below his "hand" (signature), in search for the problems of his client. If it is personal, he asks for the name of the patient, not the client, because very often the patient is represented by a client. He calls out the name of the patient as he casts the pebbles, urging them to reveal what has gone wrong. If it is for a national calamity or for a communal activity, such as drought or hunting, he mentions the problem by name throughout, asking the pebbles to tell him what they see. Observations at *Pa* diviners' sessions show very clearly how diviners rhetorically ask the pebble to reveal all that they see about the causal factors of the problem under consideration. *Tal Pa/kos Pa muut* is inquiring after the cause(s) of misfortune, conflict, and affliction.

The diviner does not work alone. *Kos Pa* divination is a public affair which is conducted by more than one person. The caster of the pebbles needs two other diviners, one to write and another to interpret what he is casting. In more ordinary cases, however, he is assisted only by the interpreter, who sits opposite him. In such a case, he will both cast and write out the symbols himself. In national crisis rituals, however, as many as twenty to thirty diviners, casting, writing, and interpreting simultaneously may be needed for each village.

3. The third stage is *tok kum* rituals in which the diviner provides human, spiritual, medicinal, and ritualistic remedies to the problems of his clients. Once the cause(s) of the problem(s) has been located through the casting sessions, medicinal and redressive rituals such as sacrifices are carried out. The second structural framework of *Pa* divination, that is, inquiring for the cause(s) of problem/illness is examined in detail, because it is this session that involves actual *kos Pa*, that is, the casting of the pebbles. This ritual process of *Pa* divination is simply called *kos Pa*, "casting the divination pebbles." It constitutes three stages and distinct activities: (a) the

shuffling and casting process, (b) the inscribing (writing) process, and (c) the process of decoding the messages from the inscribed symbols in the divining powder.

Shuffling and Casting *Pa* Divination Stones/Pebbles

The first stage of *kos Pa*, the shuffling and casting of divination pebbles, is done through a number of steps.

Step 1   The diviner scoops the divining pebbles (twenty or thirty of them) from the tortoise shell, with the right hand into the left hand (some diviners reverse the hands). He lifts up all of them in both hands (closed together) and shakes them so that they will "speak well," "tell the truth," and "decide among themselves" which pebbles should be used for that round of casting.

Step 2   The diviner separates his hands, which divides the pebbles into two groups. He returns the pebbles in his right hand to the tortoise shell and uses the ones in his left hand to begin the casting session. No conscious effort is made on the part of the caster to divide the pebbles equally or unequally between the left and right hands.

Step 3   The caster counts the pebbles rapidly in pairs into the free hand, replacing them continuously into the tortoise shell, until only one or two pebbles remain in his hand.

Step 4   Starting from the top right-hand corner of the divining board, he records his findings in the powder, already spread out on the divination board.

Step 5   The caster repeats the same procedure for each round of casting, until he has the desired numbers of *Pa* symbols and rows on the divining board.

Inscribing *Pa* Divination Symbols

Jwal Pa/Ran Pa, the second stage in the process of *Pa* divination, is the marking of *Pa* impressions (symbols/letters) in the powder spread out on the divination board. This is *jwal Pa*, "inserting" or "imprinting" *Pa* symbols. The *ngu-kos-Pa* diviner starts the writing of *Pa* symbols according to the results of his castings, from the top right-hand corner of the board toward the left. As already indicated, a second diviner (apart from the caster) may assume this role in serious problems such as homicide, manslaughter, national calamity, swollen stomach, or a difficult illness (that is, where the patient is likely to die). He is called *ngu-jwal-Pa,* the scribe or inscriber of *Pa* impressions. This specialist inserts the *Pa* symbols in the powder spread out on the divination board. However, with more ordinary problems such as headache, inquiring about the outcome of a journey, and less risky problems, the same diviner simultaneously performs both roles. The steps in writing out the *Pa* symbols thus follow from those of the casting described above:

Step 6   The diviner marks one stroke on the divining board when only one pebble remains in his hand and two strokes when two pebbles remain in his hand at the end of the first round of casting.

Step 7   In the second round of casting, the diviner starts a second vertical row (instead of continuing with the first) to the immediate left of the stroke(s) of the first round, marking single or double strokes, depending on the number of pebbles that remain in his hands. This is the second round of casting.

Step 8   The diviner then returns to the first vertical stroke(s) and records the result of the third round of casting beneath it.

Step 9   He continues this process, alternating his results between the pair of vertical rows, recording the results immediately under previous strokes until a complete (four) round(s) of castings per vertical row or set of strokes is obtained. Since the diviner must consecutively shuttle between two vertical rows, a complete round with full strokes goes over eight rounds (2 x 4 = 8), thereby giving us two *Pa* symbols after every round. This round forms a complete "head of divination," and is counted as the "first head of divination." Each head produces a total of no fewer than eight strokes (if both rows are made of single strokes, 8 x 1 = 8), and no more than sixteen strokes (if both rows scored double strokes each, 8 x 2 = 16).[6]

Step 10   The diviner continues to cast the pebbles, recording his findings from the right-hand side to the left-hand side of the board. The third and fourth rows are taken together, and they form the "second head of divination." The third and fourth, fifth and sixth, seventh and eighth heads of divination, are obtained through the same procedures. This completes the first row of *Pa* divination. At the end of a row, the diviner must have made no fewer than thirty-two single strokes (if he records single strokes throughout the eight vertical rows or four heads, 8 x 4 = 32), and no more than sixty-four strokes (if he records double strokes throughout the first row, 8 x 8 = 64). *Le sar/sar ngu-kos-*

Pa, "the diviner's hand" (signature), must go over the first row of casting. Recordings of subsequent castings begin on a new row below the first, again from right to left, after a line has been drawn across the board, just below the first row. He wipes out the long "tails" of the symbols written above, leaving behind just dots in the divination powder to represent them. The diviner levels the powder below the rows from time to time. By the end of four vertical rows, which is considered enough for an ordinary problem,[7] the diviner must have written not fewer than 128 strokes (4 x 32) and no more than 256 strokes (4 x 64). Sometimes, however, a third or even a fourth row may not be necessary since, when the causes and symptoms of affliction are clear, the medicines and sacrifices may not be farfetched. At other times, more than four rows are needed, and divination sessions may last for days, even weeks, particularly in cases of national calamities, when many rows by many diviners will be needed to produce desired results.

Interpreting *Pa* Divination Symbols

Chan Pa, the third and last stage of *Pa* divination, means "cutting," "passing," or "handing down the verdict." The *ngu-chan-Pa,* interpreter of *Pa* divination, must be different from the caster of pebbles and writer of the *Pa* symbols. When the *ngu-kos-Pa* is shuffling and casting the pebbles, the writer (if he is another person) must observe and record the results. The two, caster and scribe, therefore work together (most often the same man does both tasks). However, the *ngu-chan-Pa* interpreter need not directly observe the casting and writing procedure, nor the caster/writer the interpretation, as long as they are within hearing distance of each other. One party may be a short distance away; it is still legal if they can hear each other. The caster, writer, and interpreter very often interchange their roles, but only in different divination sessions. Thus there are no special categories of casters, writers, and interpreters in *Pa* divination. Every *Pa* diviner knows the three activities very well.

Notes

1. The diviner is often also a medicine person and/or a priest.
2. These ethnic groups speak Chadic, a subfamily of the Afroasiatic or Hamitoasiatic language group spoken on the Jos Plateau. Some languages spoken by some of these groups are mutually intelligible (or mere dialects), for example, the rela-

tionship between Mupun and Mwaghavul. In this chapter I refer to these three ethnic groups collectivly as Chadic speakers.

3. The Mupun also refer to it as *kyes Pa* ("to cast" or "to finish something").

4. *Túp* (ordinary anger) stands for the human heart, while *dor* denotes burning anger similar to the sting of a scorpion. Thus the term also means scorpion in both Mupun and Mwaghavul.

5. This opening phrase is very common among Mwaghavul diviners. Other diviners use other opening remarks, even the praise names of grandparents and maternal uncles who taught them how to divine, including their own personal praise names. A *Pa* divination session is regarded as a journey. The *Pa* symbols travel one to the other through the pebbles, leaving behind different symbols and interpretations.

6. It is unlikely, however, for the *ngu kos Pa* to come up very often with either of these results in the probability arithmetic involved in *Pa* divination.

7. The first row being *le sar,* "the diviner's hand," the second to determine the cause of illness, the third to prescribe the medicinal remedy, and the fourth for *tok kum,* that is, to prescribe redressive sacrifices that are needed.

References

Abimbola, Wande
    1976   *Ifa: An Exposition of Ifa Literary Corpus.* Ibadan: Oxford University Press.
Bascom, William R.
    1969   *Ifa Divination: Communication Between Gods and Men in West Africa.* Bloomington and London: Indiana University Press.
Bell, Catherine
    1992   *Ritual Theory, Ritual Practice.* New York and Oxford: Oxford University Press.
Danfulani, Umar H. D.
    1995   *Pebbles and Deities: Pa Divination among the Ngas, Mupun and Mwaghavul in Nigeria.* Ph.D. diss., Uppsala, 1994. Frankfurt: Peter Lang.
Honko, Lauri
    1979   "Theories Concerning the Ritual Process: An Orientation." In *Science of Religion: Studies in Methodology,* ed. L. Honko. The Hague: Mouton.
Leach, Edmund
    1982   *Social Anthropology.* London: Fontana.
Mendonsa, Eugene
    1982   *The Politics of Divination: A Processual View of Reactions Illness and Deviance Among Sisala of Northern Ghana.* Berkeley/Los Angeles/London: University of California Press.

Peek, Philip M., ed.

1982   *African Divination Systems: Ways of Knowing.* Bloomington and Indianapolis: Indiana University Press.

Sörensen, J. P.

1993   "Ritualistics: A New Discipline in History of Religions." In *The Problem of Ritual,* ed. Tore Ahlbäck. Åbo: The Donner Institute for Research in Religious and Cultural History.

Turner, Victor

1969   *The Ritual Process: Structure and Anti-structure in African Rituals.* Chicago: Aldine.

1977   "Symbols in African Rituals." In *Symbolic Anthropology: A Reader,* ed. J. L. Polgin, D. S. Kemnitzer, and D. M. Schneider. New York: Columbia University Press.

Zuesse, Evan M.

1987   "Divination." In *The Encyclopedia of Religion,* ed. Mircea Eliade. New York: Macmillan.

Figure 1. *Pa* divination pebbles in tortoise shells and an empty gourd. The river pebbles are of slightly varying colors. Photographed by the author in 1993 at Larpya Village, Jing, in Mupun land.

Figure 2. Two *Pa* diviners simultaneously divining, with one diviner facing the sun and the other with his back to it (in the absence of a board, the bare ground is used). Photographed by the author in 1993 in Larpya Village, Jing, in Mupun land.

Figure 3. Casting divination pebbles in pairs. Photographed by the author in 1993 in Larpya Village, Jing, in Mupun land.

Figure 4. A divining board (notice the inscriptions in the divining powder across the upper part of the board). Photographed by the author in 1993 at Abwor-Dyis Village of Mupun land.

6

Some Thoughts on Ideology, Beliefs, and Sacred Kingship among the Edo (Benin) People of Nigeria

FLORA *EDOUWAYE* S. KAPLAN

ENIN HISTORY IS KNOWN from its early foreign contacts with Western expansion in the last quarter of the fifteenth century, later occasional reports of European travelers and traders, and from indigenous oral tradition and court art. Twentieth-century ethnography that records the ideas and beliefs of living and contemporary people supplements these and other historical sources. They all affirm a long tradition of Edo ideology and beliefs that persists in the context of ongoing and sometimes wrenching change. The combined study of religious beliefs, history, ethnohistory, archaeology, and ethnography, thus, calls attention to the power of culture, as evidenced in people's words, actions, motivated by the ideas and values they hold in their minds in a changing world. These shape people's choices and modify behavior as they are passed on from generation to generation.[1]

Living remembrances about Benin kings and customs were first collected from very old people in the late 1920s and 1930s in Benin by Chief Jacob U. Egharevba, an untrained local historian, who published a series of pamphlets locally (1933–1976) (see Usuanlele and Falola 1994; and Eisenhofer 1995). His best-known work, *A Short History of Benin*, became a minor classic and went through a number of editions, with revisions along the way (1936, 1953, 1960, 1966, and 1968). The University of Ibadan Press published several editions in the 1960s. Egharevba's pioneering efforts produced a chronology of kings and set down a body of oral tradition that, despite its problems, have informed the work and speculations of virtually all scholars who followed. A historiography of his work is long overdue that would draw on new archival data, extensive archaeology, and systematic comparison with other groups in the region.[2] More than forty years ago the University of Ibadan history project had as one of its goals an integrated picture of Benin culture and colonial history. It involved British and Nigerian scholars, some of whom mined available archival, historical, and colonial records (Ryder 1969) and others who did ethnographic fieldwork (Bradbury 1957; 1959; 1961; 1964; 1970).[3] Robert Bradbury's field notes and publications have been touchstones for most researchers who have worked in Benin from the late 1950s and 1960s to the present.[4] More recently, researchers in Nigeria have focused on political issues, women's reproduction, and problems of economic development. Others in the late 1980s and 1990s started down the several "roads" leading to Benin. The present study draws on extended fieldwork in Benin and looks at those aspects of Benin ideology and beliefs that underlie and illuminate the institution of sacred kingship and its persistence into modernity.

Colonialism and Sacred Kingship

British colonial ambitions clashed openly with sacred kingship toward the end of the nineteenth century, when the destruction of the Benin kingdom and the Oba's independent rule was being orchestrated in England. Diplomatic and commercial interests in London, Liverpool, and Glasgow set a collision course with the Oba (Home 1982), in whom religious and secular powers were conjoined. Some ethnic groups subject to Benin wished to collaborate with the British and free themselves of Benin control, but had been kept in check by the threat of the Edos' potent military force, and fear of human sacrifice used to sustain the Oba and his supernatural powers. "The juju and fetish rule of the king of Benin," as the British termed it, enabled him to periodically bring to a halt all trading on the rivers and creeks in the region. The Oba's political and economic might stiffened British resolve to end his rule.

The excuse they needed came in 1897. A party of British officials, diplomats, and others, led by Acting Consul General Captain James R. Phillips, was ambushed and slain in what was called the "Benin Massacre." Only two members of the party escaped death. The uninvited visitors had provoked the Benin chiefs by their deliberate disregard of annual religious observances and Benin sovereignty (Home 1982) (fig. 1). The British quickly seized this opportunity to retaliate and launched a major military offensive against the Benin kingdom. Their superior weaponry and firepower prevailed. After a mock trial was held in Benin by the victors, several chiefs were executed for their role in the ambush, and the Oba was exiled to Old Calabar in eastern Nigeria. The royal palace was looted of some two thousand works of art that had been stored there over the centuries. They were shipped to England to pay the expenses of what has been called in history books the "Punitive Expedition." The art constituted the historic records of the eight-hundred-year-old dynasty. Thus, the visual collective memory was diminished, as were the kingdom's treasury and the Benin repertoire of material culture (Kaplan 1991).

Sacred kingship, so deliberately and ruthlessly brought down in 1897, was reinstalled by the British after Oba Ovonramwen passed away at Old Calabar. His son was crowned Oba Eweka II in 1914. Thereafter, Benin kingship survived nearly a half-century of colonial rule in a rapidly changing and increasingly pluralistic society. It has remained firmly in place through alternating periods of military and civilian rule after Nigerian independence in 1960. Insight into the resilience of the institution of sacred kingship may be gained by examining Benin ideology and belief embedded in its religious system.

Ideology, Ritual, and Sacred Kingship

A now ubiquitous seventeenth-century engraving published by Olfert Dapper in Amsterdam (1668; 1686) shows the Oba of Benin surrounded by chiefs, nobles, and retainers in a procession outside his walled city palace, where his people could see him. The Oba reportedly did this only once or twice a year, which state of affairs obtained up to the time of Oba Ovonramwen and the British military assault at the end of the nineteenth century (Kaplan 1981, 78; pl. 9) (fig. 2). Inside his palace the Oba performed secret religious rites throughout the year to ensure the well-being of his people and the continuity of the state. He literally stood (and still stands) for the Benin polity and for the spiritual and physical health of his people. Religious and political power are joined in his person. Court art and especially the famed cast bronze plaques, heads, and sculptures mark important events in each Oba's reign and serve as historical documents (Kaplan 1991) (fig. 3). The art works show him as both a warrior and a sacred ruler. Other works represent important personalities and events to be remembered: conquests, foreign contacts and visitors, victories, rare found objects; and a succession of Obas, Iyobas (queen mothers), court attendants, local rulers, warriors, town chiefs, and palace chiefs accompanied by their attendants (Kaplan 1990; 1993b).

As a sacred king and living deity, the Oba is believed to be the intermediary and earthly counterpart of other deities and divine forces. For example, he is the "Lord of the Dry Land," the counterpart of the deity Olokun "Lord of the Waters," the giver of wealth and children. Men and women alike often have personal shrines to Olokun in their homes. Those wealthy enough have life-sized figures of Olokun sculpted in mud for their shrines. Successful Olokun priests and priestesses also keep elaborate shrines. These shrines replicate a royal court sculpted in clay, complete with a kingly central figure of Olokun, surrounded by his wives and children and many offerings. White, the color associated with the god Olokun and worn by his followers, symbolizes prosperity, peace, and purity.

The Oba mediates between the two worlds envisioned by the Benin and communicates with both the visible world of human beings, *agbon*, and the invisible world of deities and spirits, *erinmwi*. Both the visible and the invisible worlds are ruled by a high god, Osanobua, the Supreme Deity and god of creation. However, he is too remote and powerful for direct human approach and is never represented in human form. He is reached only through lesser deities, priests, and the Oba.

The Oba personifies the living realities of spiritual beings and deities and is worshiped at yearly rituals tied to the agricultural cycle, which are still performed today. *Ugie Erha Oba* honors the Oba's deceased forebears and *Igue* strengthens his personal powers. Two sacrifices are offered to appease the spirits at *Ugie Erha Oba*: one is for the restless and insignificant spirits who are thought to be hanging about on these occasions to steal a share of the sacrifices, and the second sacrifice is for witches and those spirits who would otherwise cause trouble. Both sacrifices are intended to make the world safe for another year.

The *Eghute* is a ritual performed to protect the fertility of women, and the festival *Isiokuo* honors Ogun, the god of iron and of war. Like Ogun, the Oba is feared because he has the potential for destruction as well as creation. He, like Ogun, is associated with the color red, which is believed to combat evil. In Benin, bronze (leaded brass) is described as red and is reserved for royal usage. Its sheen and durability are also symbolic of the enduring nature of divine kingship. Coral beads are red. The color red is powerful, and the Oba wears red clothing on certain occasions. The sacred coral beads are renewed each year with blood sacrifice in a special festival that venerates the ancestors. The chiefs must also bring their coral beads to the palace for this festival. They wear only a white thread around their necks during the period of these observances. In the past, human blood was used to renew the beads; now a cow or goat is sacrificed.

Seated on his throne, the Oba of Benin is awe-inspiring. He alone possesses the royal coral-bead regalia—the crown, the staff, and the royal coral-bead shirt and wrapper (fig. 4). He is living proof of the cogency of sacred kingship and his ability to control the beneficent and destructive forces of the earth. In the past, he had the power over life and death. This power is still attributed to him through his pronouncements, which, it is believed, will come to pass.

The color red is also associated with Osun, the god of medicine and herbs. Osun specialists are skilled native doctors and diviners whose knowledge of the medical arts is highly developed in Benin (fig. 5). On occasion they carry special iron staffs to guard and protect the Oba. These staffs are wrought in complex and variable arrangements of flames, birds, chameleons, and snakes—symbols mustered to battle witches and evil forces. Because the Oba is the embodiment of the Benin people, his health must be carefully safeguarded. His health is a literal reflection of the state and of its temporal and spiritual affairs.

In addition to the state rituals mentioned here, there are other personal rituals. The Oba honors his head and his hand. And so do the Iyoba, the queen mother, the chiefs, and those Benin who are worshipers of indigenous gods (the latter are called "animists" in Nigeria today) (fig. 6). Royal altars-of-the-hand, *ikegobo*, were cast in bronze (leaded brass) and symbolized the personal achievements of the kings and queen mothers, princes, and chiefs. Chiefs' altars are carved in wood. The animals used for sacrifice are represented on altars-of-the-hand and alternate with tools of various crafts, trades, subsistence, and warfare on the flange of its base. They signify the different ways in which the celebrants achieved success and wealth in this life. Among these offerings the crocodile is the most highly valued sacrifice to an altar-of-the-hand, according to Bradbury. It remains an important sacrifice for curing and other magical purposes. Today, instead of human beings, cows and rams are offered as sacrifices to one's head and hand.

The head and the hand are central symbols in Benin art and culture. They express the ethos of the people—their individualism, exuberance, and competitive spirit. These qualities are expressed in daily life as well as in in rituals. The Benin think that the good things of life are to be enjoyed without guilt or shame, and they take open pleasure in being fortunate. So, an exchange of greetings between members of a chiefly family might begin: "Good morning, God of Iron." To which an answer might be: "Thank god, what wealth has done for me. I am glad to be in comfort." Celebrating one's hand and head expresses prevailing ideas about a person's pre-destiny and a future open to individual personal achievement. The head is the locus of reason in Benin and enables a person to realize his or her destiny and potential in this life. The hand is the means of winning wealth and prestige through one's own efforts and skills. Both the hand and the head are cult objects, although the hand was more widely worshiped in the past than it is

today. The worship of the Oba's hand is private, whereas the ritual veneration of his fathers, represented by the royal heads on the ancestral palace
altars constitutes a central public ritual of sacred kingship.

Pre-destiny, like personal achievement, is a key concept in Benin. It
implies that a person does not have total control over events. Each person
is said to have a chosen destiny upon leaving the spirit world for this one.
The *Ehi*, each person's spirit counterpart, is thought to be located at the
nape of the neck and therefore is never seen. It assists one in realizing one's
chosen path of worldly destiny. Related to these ideas is a widely held
Benin belief in reincarnation. The newborn infant is critically studied by
parents and other relatives to ascertain his or her resemblance to a deceased
relative, who is then said to have "come back" in this or that child. Their
judgment finds expression in the naming ceremony for a child, which customarily takes place seven days after it is born, and fourteen days after
birth if it is a child of the royal family. Everyone is believed to come back
(to be reincarnated in another person) fourteen times. Every Benin person
can tell you who he or she is supposed to be. Of course, no one is sure
which of the fourteen times is represented by any one reincarnation.

The belief in reincarnation based on shared characteristics with a
deceased relative serves to create strong ties with the ancestors and the
familial past in each generation. The ideas of individual uniqueness and of
continuity with the past are expressed also in the naming ceremonies of
Obas prior to being crowned. For example, after the 1897 British military
assault and the "interregnum" in Benin City that lasted until 1914, the heir
to Benin's throne took the name "Eweka II" in a traditional ceremony that
involved divination. In so doing, Oba Eweka II called attention to the
antiquity of kingship in Benin and the continuity of the eight-hundred-
year-old dynasty founded by Oba "Eweka I."

These notions of rebirth and continuity, of pre-destiny coupled with reason (head) and individual effort (hand) are recurrent themes in many oral
traditions about the great kings throughout Benin history. They explicate
what is asserted here—that the struggles and actions of early "warrior
kings" are not so different from those most scholars contrast them with—
the later "sacred kings" living mostly in seclusion. Indeed, oral tradition
and written history make it clear that the vicissitudes and challenges to
"sacred kings" from the seventeenth century to the nineteenth were no less
than those of "warrior kings." The personal triumphs of all kings were necessary demonstrations of their essential divine right to rule.

Divinity and pre-destiny are conjoined in the person of the Oba in
Benin. Pre-destiny should be seen as integral to Benin belief in individual
action and personal responsibility. Both are needed by kings as well as ordi-

nary people in order to achieve their destiny (Kaplan n.d.; 1993b; 1991). Benin's kings are "sacred" by virtue of their centrality to life and the continuity of the spiritual and worldly agricultural domains. In this, they resemble other divine kings formerly widespread elsewhere in the world (Hocart 1927; 1936).

The dichotomy that has been posited in the literature of Benin between secular and sacred kings is more compatible with Western thinking than indigenous ideas (Kaplan n.d.; 1993a; 1990). Rather, we should think in terms of a continuum and the whole. The pressing need for kings who fought wars of defense and conquest early in Benin history lessened over time, especially as the kingdom expanded and was secured with the assistance of guns and Portuguese mercenaries in the sixteenth century. The Obas' greater seclusion in the seventeenth and eighteenth centuries and the reports of him as a sacred king did not do away with conflicts over the succession or with challenges to the Oba by his chiefs. Such conflicts continued from the fifteenth through the nineteenth century, up to the 1897, when the British conquest and colonialism ended the Oba's autonomy. Sixteenth- and seventeenth-century bronze (leaded brass) plaques represent the king as a victorious warrior. The Oba is usually shown accompanied by two or more supporters, attendants, and servants carrying weapons and musical instruments, and holding offerings of incense, boxes for kola nuts, and other gifts customarily presented to the gods.

Early Obas took vigorous practical steps in the early period to solidify their earthly power. Oba Ewedo (ca. 1255–1280 C.E.) moved the palace to its present site in the center of Benin City. Ewedo diminished the authority of the noble council, the *Uzama*, and arrogated to himself sole power to award titles, creating many new ones. Oba Ewedo is said to have established the *eghaevbo n'ore*, town chiefs, "with the lead title that came to be *Iyase*" (Oba Erediauwa, personal communication, July 3, 1995). Oba Ewedo also invented the prison and made a number of laws (Egharevba 1960, 9–10). Oba Oguola (ca. 1280–1295 C.E.) is reputed to have begun the earthworks in and around Benin City to create defense system between himself and his greatest threat, the Akpanigiakon of Udo, to the west of Benin, across the Ovia River (Egharevba 1960, 11). Sometime later in the fifteenth century, Oba Ewuare (1440–1473 C.E.), who had suffered greatly at the hands of the nobles and palace chiefs, enlarged the new order of town chiefs and made other changes that redefined their relationship with the palace chiefs—shifting the balance of power between them. Oba Ewuare was the first Oba to have contact with the Portuguese in the last quarter of the fifteenth century (Egharevba 1960, 13–14). He extended the city walls, attesting to his successful expansion and to the increasing conflicts between Benin and other ethnic groups (ibid.).

Even Oba Ewuare "The Great" at first had to hide from his enemies, the chiefs, before taking the throne. He was aided by two of society's most unfortunate creatures the slave Edo and a childless market woman, Emotan. Ewuare is later said to have immortalized the slave, adopting his name for all free Benin people, who still refer to themselves as "servants of the Oba," meaning that they owe the king unquestioning dedication and loyalty. The childless Emotan, with no one to remember her, the condition considered the most pitiable of all in Benin, is still remembered to this day in all chieftaincy rounds and burial rites in Benin for her service and faithfulness to Oba Ewuare. "Emotan was always faithful to the Oba," is both a saying and proscription among the Benin people (Chief A. S. Guobadia, personal communication, July 29, 1995).

The tribulations, defeats, and problems encountered by the early and later Obas should not be seen as inconsistent with the concept of sacred kingship as most scholars now believe. Rather, the seclusion of later Obas and elaboration of ritual should be seen as results of the more settled conditions and increased leisure that followed Benin military suzerainty across southern Nigeria in the sixteenth and early seventeenth centuries.

Twentieth-century archaeological surveys reveal many miles of extensive outlying earthworks around Benin City (Connah 1975, 102, 101–6, 275). The walls and ditches, and the dates associated with them, are consistent with events recorded by Egharevba associated with the named Benin kings (1956; 1960). These monumental earthworks and recorded oral tradition attest to the early Obas as warrior kings. However, they do not refute that they were also sacred kings. There has been acceptance by most Benin scholars (but questioned here) of the proposition that the early warrior kings of Benin were eventually transformed into sacred kings who retreated into the palace and were secluded and increasingly surrounded by rituals and taboos. This change is thought to have occurred sometime in the seventeenth century, the period shown in Dapper's engraving (Kaplan 1981).

The Obas and the Ancestors

Bradbury (1973) observed that, for the Benin, many religious activities centered on the dead. These include the unincorporated dead who had been neglected by the living and who had to be appeased; and the incorporated dead, the ancestors, and the elders who resided in the land of the dead and who had to be commemorated, propitiated with offerings, and satisfied to protect and respond to the requests of the living.

Ancestor worship is central to Benin religion, and each male head of extended family is charged with the responsibility of maintaining and making appropriate offerings at the shrine in the family house. Such shrines are maintained today even in family houses where most members have converted to denominations of Christianity. The Oba, like his subjects, serves his ancestors who came before him. He honors them before a series of royal circular, polished mud altars in the house of the fathers, Ugie Erhioba, at the palace. The display of bronze heads of past kings, ivory tusks, and other ritual furnishing and decoration on the ancestral altars are seen during public rituals. They are visible evidence of the longevity of Benin kingship and the divine right to rule (fig. 7). The cast bronzes include, besides ancestral heads, bronze bells for invocations, sculptures, figures, and carved ivory tusks, altarpieces that commemorate historic events. There are carved wood rattle staffs to "call" the ancestors and mark their passing, and large polished stones, ancient celts that the Benin call "thunderstones" (fig. 8). The Obas' shrines are propitiated both for his family and for all Edo-speaking peoples.

The Oba's most important duty, like all firstborn children, is to "plant" or bury his father. In performing the rituals necessary to mark his father's "death-journey," the firstborn son marks his own journey toward full adult status and the right to assume his father's vacated roles. When the cycle is complete, the Oba has a head of his father cast in bronze and placed on an ancestral altar in a palace compound. It is this compound, with its display of heads and other sculptures on ancestral altars that is opened for the most important annual ceremonies. It is where the Oba is seated during the ceremonies, and where the chiefs come before him to pay homage.

The royal furnishings for these ancestral altars and the regalia worn and used by the Oba, his family, and members of the court were produced by guilds of palace artisans. The very materials used in this highly ranked society reflect an individual's status. Ivory is reserved for the Oba's personal use; and to a lesser extent, sculptures, ornaments, and tusks were also carved for the Oba's mother, the Iyoba. She had altars to her predecessors and the gods at her palace at Uselu, on the outskirts of Benin City. In the past one tusk of every elephant killed had to be given to him before the hunter could trade the other or be rewarded for his skill. Bronze too was reserved for palace use, especially the ancestral heads and sculptures of kings and other things (fig. 10). Coral beads are the most important item of Benin court dress, and each chief, on taking his title, receives some beads from the Oba, to which he adds his own to the extent his wealth allows. When the chief dies, the beads are returned to the palace by his family, before they are given the white cloth for his burial.

Special artisans make the tools and objects needed by members of guilds, initiates, followers, and village elders. They make the different things used by priests, priestesses, diviners, native doctors, farmers, hunters, and traders: staffs, ornaments, hoes and adzes, weapons, and musical instruments; leather fans and containers; carved wood boxes, staffs, heads, and stools; clay pots, cloth; beaded jewelry, bangles and other ornaments. Oba Eweka II restored the royal guilds in the 1920s after the palace was rebuilt. (He himself is reported to have been quite a good carver.) These newly trained craftsmen at the palace also began to work for the tourist and commercial markets in the twentieth century, some creating new traditions in ebony and metal, as well as recreating the old ones. Their traditional repertoire was much reduced by the 1897 looting of the palace. It was stimulated in the early 1980s by illustrated catalogues of foreign exhibitions of Benin art and other books with examples of early castings (Kaplan 1991).

The year-long cycle of funeral ceremonies for an Oba who has passed is both like and unlike those of ordinary men. The eldest son performs the funeral rituals on behalf of all one's children, but in the crown prince's case his father's "children" are all the Edo-speaking peoples, not just the extended family of an individual. The royal funeral ceremonies are political as well as religious: they recapitulate the history of the Benin kingdom and legitimate the Oba-to-be as rightful ruler. An ordinary man's eldest son earns the right to assume all his father's roles as head of family in simple rituals that vary in scale of celebration depending on the available resources. The crown prince journeys from child to youth to novice to prince to maturity as king: all the stages of a lifetime are compressed and reenacted in the context of a single year. The scale is national, and the ceremonies also mark the crown prince's, the *Edaiken*'s, transformation from human to sacred and divine earthly ruler as the Oba of Benin.

His unique status is reflected in other practices associated with the Oba. It is believed that he does not eat or drink as ordinary mortals do, and that the Oba does not die, nor is he allowed to be sick. On being present at an important meeting in the early 1980s between (then) military governor Useni, at the Oba's palace, I witnessed what happened when the Oba happened to cough. Almost immediately, three hundred chiefs seated in the courtyard for this meeting coughed as one! When I inquired of a chief near me, he replied, "They are taking the cough from him!" An important visitor to the palace might be told, "The leopard is resting," meaning the Oba is sleeping or otherwise unavailable. All references to him are indirect, and he is protected from any knowledge of sickness, illness, and death while living, since his state of mind is the state of the state.

The passing of Oba Akenzua II in 1978 was publicly announced by the Esogban of Benin, Chief Ize-Iyamu, acting for the Iyase, who cried out "The White Chalk is broken," and cast it on the ground. The white chalk lay scattered before the clay statue of Ozolua, at Ughe Ozolua in the main palace compound (Kaplan 1981). As Oba Akenzua II had performed the royal funeral cycle in 1933 for Oba Eweka II, Oba Erediauwa performed the ceremonies for Oba Akenzua II in 1978, prior to being crowned. The year-long cycle of royal mourning began as they all do, with the announcement that the "White Chalk" was broken. White chalk, symbolizing purity and peace, stands for the Oba himself. In assuring his father's safe passage to the next world into the land of the dead, the Oba makes many offerings (in the past these included human beings, many of them said to be condemned prisoners). Today, cows and rams are sacrificed before the royal altars. The cycle of ceremonies reenacts dynastic history, affirms the continuity of the Edo people, purifies the land, and strengthens the Oba's powers and the allegiance of the chiefs to him (Nevadomsky and Inneh 1983; Nevadomsky 1984a; 1984b).

The Oba's Court

In each generation Benin history and culture were writ large in court art, and rewritten by chiefly service, royal marriages, and ritual reenactments at court and in Edo villages and towns that pay homage to the Oba of Benin. The palace occupies a site that dates to the thirteenth century, and possibly to the eleventh or earlier. The fire of 1897 razed most of the original structure, which was rebuilt by Oba Eweka II after 1914. Although smaller than the original palace, it occupies the equivalent of several large city blocks and is surrounded by a series of now deteriorating earthworks, roads, and wards in which live chiefly families, guilds, retainers, and servants. The palace precincts may be entered only by those initiated into the various palace groups, and members of the royal family may visit the living quarters of their "home." Within the vast palace are numerous rooms, compounds, and courtyards, each belonging to a different group, whose members have sworn oaths of secrecy and fealty to the Oba. Members of each group may enter and use only the section of the palace assigned to that group; members of the royal family may not enter any of these. Only the Oba, as chief priest, moves freely among all sections of the palace.

The Oba is served by three groups of chiefs: the *Eghaevbo n'ogbe*, the palace chiefs; the *Eghaevbo n'ore,* the town chiefs; and the *Uzaman'ihiron,* seven hereditary nobles who rank next to the Oba: Oliha, Edohen, Ezomo, Ero, Eholonire, Oloton, and the Edaiken, the latter the heir apparent to the Benin throne (fig. 10). The palace chiefs, the *Eghaevbo n'ogbe,* dominate the activities of the royal court, which is comprised of three male associations: the *Iwebo,* the oldest of the three, whose members are charged with crafting and caring for the Oba's wardrobe, regalia, and treasury; the *Iweguae,* who attend to his person and household; and the *Ibiwe,* responsible for the royal harem and the Oba's children. All Benin chiefs are sworn to keep the secrets of their orders upon pain of death, and to dedicate themselves to the service of the Oba. These ideas of secrecy and service underlie social, political, and religious life in Benin.

Of the palace associations, the *Eghaevbo n'ogbe* have the largest membership, the most wide-ranging duties, and the greatest impact on society. Rank within all the associations is achieved, and members are advanced or not by the Oba from one level to the next according to their character and demonstrated abilities. Other special male associations who serve the palace include the slaughterers of sacrificial animals; the various singers and musicians; the Oba's doctors and ritual specialists, the *Ewaise;* the palace warriors, *Asiemwero;* and others identified with the crown prince, the *Efiento;* and the various royal guilds including artisans. The *Eghaevbo n'ogbe,* together with the seven hereditary nobles, the *Uzama n'ihiron,* and the association of town chiefs, the *Eghaevbo n'ore,* constitute the Oba's main ministers. The Oba confers chiefly titles at his discretion and creates new ones.

When given a title a chief celebrates first by coming to the palace with his followers to thank the Oba publicly. He then visits a prescribed route of special shrines, "dancing" around the city with his followers to express his great joy at this happy event. There is feasting and modest offerings are made to other chiefs. Homage is paid to the ancestors. Kola nuts are ubiquitous at these and virtually all other ritual events because, it is said in Benin, "He who brings kola nuts, brings life." The *eben,* a ceremonial sword made of iron, the handle sometimes embellished with bone or ivory, is a symbol of office granted each chiefly title-holder. The *ada,* a special sword, is rarely given. Chiefs thereafter salute the Oba by "playing" the large *eben* before him, twirling and tossing it in the air and catching it with one hand, in a display of strength, personal skill, and as a gesture of respect and fealty. It is said, "The respect that an *ada* and *eben* give to the king is what you give to me."

Chiefly titles reflect belief in the Oba's extraordinary qualities and powers so central to Benin worldview. For example, the *Aisagbonrioba,* a senior

Iweguae palace chief's title, may be translated, "The Oba is not made on earth" (meaning he is predestined to rule). Bradbury's informants described the Oba in such terms as the following: "the child of the first light of the day that has no end" (meaning limitless wealth); "the child of one who looks at someone and does not blink his eyes"; "the child of the sole of the foot that does not make the earth jealous"; "the child of the earth that one begs not to sink" (i.e., kill one); "the child of the sky that one begs not to fall (and) cover one" (i.e., kill); and "the child of the king for whom silence is made" (i.e., no one should talk when Oba is talking).

Most titles are conferred for the lifetime of the holders, except for a few hereditary titles, and they cannot be taken away. However, the Oba can banish a chief from court if he is very displeased with him. In rare cases, he can cast the offender outside Benin society altogether, by naming him an "enemy of the Oba." This was tantamount to a death sentence in the past. Such a chief and his family would be totally ostracized by the community, making it impossible for them to survive. No one would serve them, trade with them, talk, visit, or otherwise engage with them. The guilty chief would likely either kill himself or, in some instances, be killed by members of his family to lift the ban. As recently as 1990, in a rare modern occurrence, three chiefs were named Oba's "enemies." Intensive negotiations followed, initiated by their supporters, to allow them to beg forgiveness and be received at the palace again (eventually, the Oba agreed). The populace was angered by the offenses, and the three chiefs suffered great discomfort and public embarrassment. Such is the respect the Oba engenders and enjoys as the key, living symbol of Benin identity, pride, and polity.

Supremacy is central to the institution of sacred kingship, but Obas are vulnerable as well. This vulnerability is protected in traditional accounts of actual events. Oba Ehengbuda (ca. 1578–1608) is reputed to have been a great native "doctor" and a magician who lived a very long time. His life is counted as follows: two hundred years as *Okoro* (a prince), two hundred years as the *Edaiken* (the crown prince), and two hundred years as Oba (the king). Two hundred in Benin means "many" or "too numerous to be counted," and in this case, it clearly means Ehengbuda lived a very, very long time. According to one account, Ehengbuda had grown tired of living, but showed no signs of dying in the normal way; so he decided to go voluntarily and visit the spirit world, *erinmwi*—that is, die. But when he arrived in *erinmwi*, he was told that he could stay only if he first went home and came back in the usual way. So he returned home.

Bradbury suggested that this story was invented to hide a real disaster that is thought to have befallen Ehengbuda on a visit to the territory that his father, Oba Orhogbua, acquired in Lagos. It is said that a terrible storm blew on the creek, on the Oba's way to Lagos, and some of his followers were drowned. The Oba's body was recovered and brought back to Benin—an incident, Bradbury believed, that would not have been told to the common people. Ehengbuda's visit to the spirit world, *erinmwi*, could also have been invented to hide a disaster that befell him. At the same time, the widespread belief in the supernatural powers of Ehengbuda makes the story credible in Benin. The most widely accepted account is that he went to heaven through the sea (Oba Erediauwa, personal communication, July 3, 1995).

Ehengbuda, as a great magician, was not to be born in the natural way, but is said to have emerged from his mother's thigh. He is considered a great Oba, second only to Ewuare (ca. 1440–1473 C.E.). He is said to have traveled a great deal, particularly in western Ibo country, where he is still worshiped in many places. If Bradbury is correct (the widely held beliefs about Oba Ehengbuda all have reference to his being a powerful magician and "traveling" a lot—which has several meanings, among them many "conquests"), these stories illustrate the Benin penchant for cloaking meaning. They suggest that an ideology of sacred kingship was in place in the late sixteenth century (and/or was possibly recast at a later date).

While succession in Benin is based on primogeniture, competition between brothers born of different mothers in the Oba's polygynous household continued up to the late nineteenth century. Because queens always gave birth outside the palace (in the homes of chiefs), there were many possibilities for mischief. The queen, *oioi*, who gives birth to the firstborn son acknowledged by the Oba, will eventually become the *Iyoba*, the queen mother (named three years after her son ascends the throne)—as she was predestined to do. The prince predestined to rule as the Oba also had to prove himself fit by his deeds (Kaplan 1993b).

A good example of the intertwining of beliefs in predestiny and in a good "head" and "hand," as applied to "sacred kingship," is found in the many stories of rivalry between Oba Esigie (ca. 1504–1550 C.E.) and his brother, Prince Ahrauran, a giant warrior. Ahrauran was born in the morning but did not cry right away (consequently, his birth was not announced to the Oba); Esigie was born of a different mother that afternoon and cried lustily. The late-fifteenth- to early-sixteenth-century triumphs of Esigie over the giant Ahrauran from childhood on are well known in modern Benin. In each story Esigie demonstrates the cleverness and even trickery essential for kingship and success and that brains rather than brawn are to be admired—and are needed to rule (Kaplan 1993b). Not incidentally, the strained relationships and rivalries among wives and siblings in traditional polygynous Benin households echo through the centuries of oral tradition.

So too oral tradition about palace societies who follow the king illustrates enduring cultural values that give rise to behavior in Benin. Members of the *Ibiwe society* who first followed Oba Ozolua (ca. 1481–1504 C.E.) are called "the left hand of the leopard," because of their faithfulness to him. Is is said that Oba Ehengbuda asked the *Iwebo* to accompany him to the sea, but they refused saying they needed to look after his valuable regalia; and *Ibiwe* also declined to accompany Ehengbuda because they needed to look after the Oba's wives. "It was only the *Iweguae* who volunteered to accompany Oba Ehengbuda to the sea," an event that is still reenacted today in a special Iweguae dance (that never comes out)" (Oba Erediauwa, personal communication, July 3, 1995). In another version it is only the *Ibiwe* who were willing to follow him. Seeing that they were trustworthy, Oba Ehengbuda decided to leave them behind to look after his wives and children (which they do to this day). Oral tradition shows the king's good judgment, an important leadership quality; and the different versions show why one or another of these societies may be trusted and are close to the king. These and other stories extol the still-held and deeply rooted values of service, secrecy, and loyalty.

The Sacred King and His Wives

The Oba's person is so sacred and suffused with taboos that he is dangerous to others. He cannot be touched by ordinary people or by women other than his wives and daughters. Any woman he touches becomes his wife. The Oba's wives, the *iloi*, his queens, are themselves taboo and live in seclusion because of their direct contact with him. They avoid contact with men, by accident or otherwise. Their families and kin come to see them at the palace for much the same reasons that other Benin do—to petition for things and assistance and, through them, to seek the Oba's help.

The queens' quarters, the harem, *erie*, is on the left side of the palace. There petitioners and visitors gather in the outer courtyard waiting for the queens to "come out." They include people who are related to a queen or know a relative, a friend, or a chief. Among these people are men who may be allowed to speak to one of the royal wives from a distance in the courtyard. Chiefs, male relatives, and petitioners, even a queen's own father or brother cannot come closer. Female relatives may be privileged to speak with a queen in one of the inner reception rooms, but they cannot enter the harem: only those who are her servants may do so. The wives and daughters of chiefs have their own palace associations and come to the women's quarters at the palace to sing and play their gourd rattles, to dance and to make the queens happy. These women have their own roles to play in town as mothers, cultivators, traders, and so on. They act as the eyes and ears of the queens, keeping them informed of public sentiment, problems, events, social and economic opportunities (Kaplan 1993a).

The Oba's wives, the *iloi*, serve him by giving him children, by offering prayers and songs on his behalf, and by secretly performing prescribed rituals. The queens are, in turn, served by the young women "betrothed" to the Oba, whom they are obliged to instruct in court etiquette. The queens are also served by attendants, relations, and by other women of the harem. Like all Benin women, they serve their husbands and take care of their children. Queens, princes, and princesses kneel to the Oba; chiefs and commoners kneel to princes and dukes as well as to the Oba; and among themselves, chiefs kneel to those of higher rank. The wives, children, and junior relatives of a man, however humble his position, kneel to greet him, and they too serve him.

The Oba, like his subjects, reveres his mother. He honors her and raises her to the status of queen mother, the *Iyoba*, three years after his own coronation. He builds a palace for her at Uselu, where she is attended by servants and by her own chiefs. In the past the Oba provided lands and villages for her support. The Oba grants his birth mother various insignia of high rank, denoting her new gender status, equivalent to a male chief (Kaplan 1991). He may grant her the privilege of using both ceremonial swords, like himself—the *ada* as well as the *eben*—as did Oba Erediauwa in 1981 (fig. 6). When she dies, the Oba has a shrine built for her at Uselu and decorates the altar in the palace where the *Iyobas* are venerated.

Thus, the Oba presents a role model to be emulated by other Benin sons (and daughters), who must give respect to the women who bore them. Benin men often set up an altar to their mothers in their houses, apart from the shrine in the family house that honors the patrilineal ancestors. A son nowadays will decorate her tomb and, if wealthy enough, commission a life-size or larger statue of his mother that is installed on the grounds of his own compound or in a house built by his mother.

Service, Secrecy, and Society

Individuals fulfill their destiny through their own efforts by using their heads and their hands. One important way of doing so is by serving those who rank above you in age and position. Such service is expected to bring rewards in material benefits; service leads to recognition and advancement, which are marked by increased access to information and knowledge. Knowledge is power in Benin, and its flow is consciously controlled from one individual and group to another; the transfer takes place within the male palace associations—and, more informally, among the town chiefs, who are not charged with the personal care of the Oba, his family, and regalia.

Secrecy, then, is crucial to power over others. It suffuses the rituals and charms that defend against enemies, both seen and unseen. By regulating power and advancement in society, secrecy effects political cohesion as well as conflict. The Oba holds the reins of knowledge and power. He is surrounded by and adorned with secret charms to safeguard his person and the polity he embodies. He is the ultimate source and the goal of all activities that emanate from the inner depths of the male palace associations. He dispenses the rewards, which in the past were measured in lands and wives, both sources of the wealth and children so eagerly and traditionally sought by Benin males.

Membership in the main associations of palace and town chiefs is open to all males. Chieftaincy titles, once awarded, are kept for the lifetime of the recipient and, with a few exceptions, are not hereditary. This allows both for stability and for social mobility based on achievement, and makes for flexible and dynamic political relationships within the city, and between the center and the periphery, the palace and the villages and towns. Fathers, who are often chiefs themselves, may bring a young son to the palace to serve the Oba. Children may be promised at birth in gratitude for a favor granted, or to win the Oba's good graces. A child is the greatest gift a parent can offer the Oba. It also gives the father the possibility of access to the palace, and the child the opportunity of rewards for service. A boy as young as seven may be given, and he becomes an *Omuada*, or *Ibieguae*. For the first seven days of training and initiation, the boys are also introduced to the palace language. At the end of this period, the senior chief of the Iweguae, the *Isere*, announces which of the palace associations will claim the initiates; and he places the distinctive brass anklets on the *Emuada*, palace pages, which they wear until they reach puberty (or later), and are released from service. Their heads are shaved except for a small circle of hair, *ovie osusu*, after which there are ceremonial acceptances.

Their duties include carrying messages for the Oba, and to and from the harem. From among the most senior pages a few boys are chosen to carry the Oba's symbolic swords of state, the *ada* and *eben*, at public and ritual functions. The Emuada are celibate and cannot touch or be touched by a female until they are discharged from palace service. Formerly, the Oba would reward good service with land and a wife from among the young girls given to the Oba but not taken by him as brides. The Ibierua were similarly rewarded, but they could remain in palace service after marriage and could live in their own home outside the palace. Unlike the Emuada, who in pre- and early colonial times went naked until they left service, the Ibierua wore a cloth wrapper (later, in the 1920s, some type of covering was adopted for the pages and young girls).

Emuada are found only in the Iweguae society, but Ibierua are found in the other two associations, the Iwebo and the Ibiwe. Between the entry and highest levels there are as many as five levels of membership. Some individuals remain where they enter for life, whereas others steadily climb, and some pass over intermediate levels, directly to titled positions. On entering the palace, all initiates are called by the same name as a bride, *oha*. They enter in a pure state, which must be maintained until they reach manhood and are dismissed at the discretion of the Oba.

The palace associations contrast with the loyal opposition, the association of town chiefs, the *Eghaevbo n'ore*. Town chiefs attain their positions through success in life and earn respect through their achievements and contributions to Benin society (fig. 11). They come to the palace on ritual occasions, at Igue, the main series of annual observances. They demonstrate their loyalty to the Oba by playing their ceremonial sword, the *eben*, saluting the Oba with the time-honored gesture. Each town chief is accompanied by a crowd of his followers, relatives, and supporters, men and women who will dance and sing and join him in swearing fealty to His Highness. The size and composition of the group that "follows" a chief are indicators of his importance and popularity in the town and rest on his deeds. Thus, in demonstrating their allegiance to the Oba, one by one, the senior chiefs act both to validate both their own status in society and to affirm the continuity of their associations. Unless called upon by the Oba to perform specific tasks, the town chiefs pursue their own affairs and attend to their followers, would-be followers, and kin. Such tasks include arbitrating disputes between parties, ascertaining the facts in cases brought before the Oba for settlement, rendering advice on civil and secular matters, and attending ceremonies.

The palace chiefs, the *Eghaevbo n'ogbe*, however, have regular duties to perform each day in the special sections of the palace assigned to them. The members of one association are forbidden to enter the sections of the others within the Oba's vast palace. Prior to the British conquest in 1897 and the fire that razed much of the old palace at that time, it was an even greater complex of buildings and courtyards. The Oba alone may enter all the Palace rooms, a physical affirmation of his centrality to the whole enterprise. The rituals of each palace association are secret and known by members, according to their rank in the association. It is only the Oba who, as sacred king, has knowledge of all the rituals; he is a living divinity, a ruler, and a high priest. Priests in Benin may be either males or females, but are not otherwise ranked, except by popular reputation and renown for their personal powers and demonstrated efficacy (figs. 12, 13). The Oba's powers are his by virtue of birth and ritual transformation.

In the performance of his duties the Oba has the opportunity, as does everyone else, to gain individual recognition through the innovations he devises in his reign and the quality of his service. As members rise in the internal hierarchy of Iwebo, Iweguae, or Ibiwe, greater knowledge and secrets are passed down as needed, a little at a time, from those at the next highest level. However, these are given only as needed, bit by bit, a little at a time. Confidences, like all else in Benin society, are hard-earned. Palace chiefs, like town chiefs, devote most of their time to their own affairs, especially if they have growing families and are still active in their businesses, professions, jobs, and farms. Others who are either retired or younger devote themselves mainly to the daily welfare of the Oba and his family. This is a heavy burden, since the Oba, as a living god and a sacred king, must be venerated, perpetuated, and obeyed without question. Before the British, the Oba had the power of life and death over his subjects; he was both feared and adored.

This combination of affection, fear, and awe marks the Oba's present aura as well. His health and happiness are still considered to be a literal representation of the state of the state's conditions and fortunes. Today the Oba lives in semi-seclusion, but moves about the city and country with his chiefs and entourage more frequently than in the immediate colonial and precolonial past. He visits disaster sites and dedicates and opens schools, colleges, and other institutions; he meets with Nigerian Heads of state, military and civilian presidents at their invitation, either at his palace or in Abuja, the country's capital; and he may, on occasion, preside at important public functions in Benin, Lagos, and in other parts of Nigeria. Because his person is taboo, his movements must be carefully planned when he travels. The present Oba Erediauwa has served as Pro-Chancellor of the University of Ibadan, and he has been head of the state's Council of Traditional Rulers.

Contemporary Ideas and Beliefs

Benin, men and women alike, will speak and refer to themselves still, as they did up to the end of the nineteenth century, as "the Oba's servants." This may seem a contradiction among a people who for centuries were and are served themselves by others: household servants, young children and men and women given to them to train or educate according to their ability and service, as well as by slaves captured in wars and raids up to the late nineteenth century. But the idea of service is at the heart of ideology and beliefs governing relationships in Benin. Therefore, the self-referencing oneself as a servant of the Oba calls attention dramatically to the devotion of the Edo-speaking peoples to the Oba and his welfare, and subtly through the contrast between their free state and highly valued individualism and the voluntary nature of their subordination.

Indeed, historically the most powerful political check on an Oba who abuses his power is desertion by his people. If made truly unhappy, his chiefs will stop coming to the palace; and the villagers, townspeople, and others will cease bringing foodstuffs, livestock, and gifts for the Oba's use and redistribution (Kaplan 1990). For example, Oba Ohen in the mid-fourteenth century suffered this fate (Egharevba 1960). Conversely, among the Oba's most powerful weapons were banishment from the court; declaring a person "the Oba's enemy," putting him or her beyond the pale of society; and the Oba's injunction to commit suicide, "Go and take your feet off the ground." Offenses against the king were punished severely, because they threatened to disrupt the delicate balance of power in society. Such sanctions, however, were applied sparingly and rarely invoked.

The chiefs, whether palace or town leaders, serve the Oba and their own ancestors in their family houses. Each adult Benin male, titled and untitled, serves his own forefathers with offerings, prayers, and sacrifices at the family shrines, according to his seniority, status, and wealth. Young men serve older men, and children serve their parents, elders, and others as they pass through the age grades from youths, to marriageable adults, to mature men, and elders. So too, Benin women serve their parents, husbands, and others of rank and deserving of respect. The lessons of service are embedded in the often-told stories and myths of Benin.[5]

Oral tradition makes it clear that no one, not even the Oba, is above serving in order to merit assistance and to be served himself. For example, according to oral tradition, the father of idia, Esigie's mother, was the Ohen Ovia at Udo Unuame. He was an old man and Idia was his only daughter. When she grew up, Oba Ozolua married her. She bore him a son who later became Oba Esigie. When Esigie was still young, his body became red (i.e., he had leprosy). They said only his grandfather, the Odionwere at Unuame, could cure him. So the old man was sent for and cured him. Again, Esigie caught leprosy and was cured. After he became Oba he had leprosy a third time, but when the Odionwere was sent for, he refused, saying that after he had cured him last time, the Oba had forgotten him.

He was an old man with only one daughter, and when he died there would be no one to serve Ovia for him. Esigie then went to Unuame and served Ovia with him. They swore juju together that every Oba would go there to serve Ovia. Having served, Esigie was cured.

This oral tradition carries a lesson that endures beyond the agricultural world of the sixteenth century. It was living history for the Benin, who continued to worship Ovia in villages in the largely rural society that obtained through the 1960s. And it has meaning in present-day relations between family members, in-laws, and between age and youth.[6] Beyond the 1960s and even now, many Edo speakers are still living in villages of four hundred to five hundred people, while others live in large towns of more than one thousand. The villages and towns and Benin City itself were divided into wards with one or more patrilineal extended family and relatives. Today Benin City, like other cities in Nigeria, has grown dramatically in size and diversity since the 1950 census, when some 50,000 mostly Edo-speaking people were counted. By the 1990 census, some 250,000 people of different ethnic and religious affiliations lived in the capital city. Nonetheless, most people still identify with their age mates, now often their schoolmates as well—even after they move to large towns and cities in other parts of the country and abroad. It is not unusual to hear people talk of so-and-so who was his or her "schoolmate" or is my "age mate" (often used as equivalents); and this connection is used as a basis for greater confidence and trust in contemporary business and social relations.

In the villages and towns away from the Oba's palace and the city, the eldest male in a patrilineage commands the most respect among the others in a locale; and he, like the senior person in other male ranked hierarchies, is called the *Odionwere*. For example, the most senior of the Oba's many *emuada* is a young man, but he is also called "Odionwere" as the most senior person in that group. Society is ordered in a three-tier age-grade association in Benin, much as Bradbury described it nearly a half-century ago: the elders, *edion*, comprised of males above forty or fifty years of age; adult males, *eghele*, from twenty-five to thirty years; and youths, *iroghae*, from about sixteen years of age. The age grades prove useful today in different ways and underlie city life as a basis of male (and female) bonding not only within lineages, but in many different kinds of associations, including church groups, business, social, and professional associations which cut across kin lines. The age grades, palace and town associations, guilds, and other groups in the past had long served the Oba well, indissolubly linking the palace and the hinterland over the centuries.

The Odionwere sometimes shared authority with a chief or a duke, *enogie*, assigned to the village. The *enogie* is the eldest son in a local ruling royal patriline. In the past, the dukes, *enigie*, who are junior brothers of the Oba, and their descendants, served by collecting and transmitting tribute from one or more villages, by supplying labor and military recruits, by keeping the peace, and otherwise administering an area. Some appointees were from among the palace and town chiefs, the *Uzama* nobles. The Oba's mother, the *Edaiken*, and even some of the Oba's wives used to be absentee administrators of village tribute units, whereas today, in some cases, they act as advisees and may receive gifts. In 1988, Oba Erediauwa named ten of his brothers *enigie* of villages in various parts of Edo State (fig. 14).

Conclusions

Benin, a forest kingdom that predated fifteenth-century European contacts, offers a documented, ongoing, if imperfectly known, case study of indigenous African sacred kingship. The present dynasty has lasted some eight hundred years into the twenty-first century—through violent conquest and a period of more than sixty years of colonial rule in the twentieth century. It produced the largest extant body of cast bronzes in Africa over five centuries—works that constitute the kingdom's historic records. It also produced one of Africa's most valued and humanistic art traditions, much admired around the world. In addition to the tangible remains of Benin history in art and material culture, there is a rich oral tradition that is now partly recorded and still very much alive. These offer insights into the durability of the institution of sacred kingship in Benin, when analyzed in the context of the living culture and relevant information. While arguments will undoubtedly increase over the succession of kingship, chronology, and contacts—both greater clarity and complexity will ultimately emerge from more extensive and systematic archaeology in the region, historiography, and other research—and will prevail beyond reigning opinion.

The attempt here was to recover more than possible "historical facts" of oral tradition, art, religion, and ethnohistorical writings. The effort was to find the "cultural verities" contained in the ideology, behavior, ethos, values, and worldview of the Benin. These verities lie at the core of continuities in Benin daily and religious life; and being held in the mind, they are found beneath the surface of events, symbols, myths, and stories. They illuminate patterns of thinking and beliefs about the way the world is ordered and how the Benin should behave in it. Such underlying verities manifest themselves in myriad ways in speech and observable actions, in everyday life, in work and play, in worship and rituals. Such truths are expressed symbolically, without words, in art and material culture. They may also be cloaked in words and wrapped in the colorful imagery of narratives, myth, and story. Cultural verities may be discernible and visible for brief moments in the ephemeral performances of religious and other events. They are obtained in ethnographic fieldwork and from ethnohistoric documents; they are discovered in oral tradition, art objects, and artifacts; and they are uncovered in archaeology (Kaplan 1990; 1991).

Today in modern Nigeria, Oba Erediauwa, the great-grandson of Oba Ovonramwen reigns as the thirty-eighth Oba in an unbroken line of succession by primogeniture and patrilineal descent, and conventionally, if not verifiably, dated to the twelfth century. Crowned king on March 23, 1979, Oba Erediauwa praised the vision of his father, Oba Akenzua II. And he declared in his speech, "Our custom and tradition shall form the bedrock on which this era will be built." He represents the living past of more than eight hundred years of Benin political and spiritual continuity.

Oba Erediauwa is also a symbol of the living present: a sacred king who is also the product of a Western secular education. He is a graduate of Kings College, Cambridge, England, where he read law. As crown prince, he was district officer in Ahoada, working also in Enugu in the old Eastern Region of Nigeria. After the civil war he served in the Ministry of Mines and Power, actively participating in the reorganization of Nigeria's oil relations with OPEC. In Bendel State he became commissioner of finance, until he resigned to assume his traditional role as Oba of Benin. It is significant that no breath of scandal is attached to any of the posts he held before his coronation as Oba. His experience and moral and ethical behavior are acknowledged by virtually all ethnic groups in Nigeria, according him widespread respect in his role as a traditional ruler.

This blend of old and new, of tradition and modernity in the person of Oba Erediauwa, attests to the durability of the Benin belief system and the capacity of its key symbols to acquire new meanings and to fill different public roles. The present Oba is one such symbol in the modern secular nation-state of the Federal Republic of Nigeria. No longer an autonomous head of state, he continues to wield influence as a traditional ruler, spiritual leader, and adjudicator, especially in land and inheritance disputes. As a visual manifestation of cultural continuity and spiritual power, central to the worldview of the Edo-speaking peoples, the Oba continues to create the very power he embodies through the emanation of multiple meanings attached to him as a sacred king and to his office, which bears the weight of history (fig. 15).

Notes

1. The ideology and beliefs surrounding sacred kingship in Benin were derived from ongoing ethnographic fieldwork, readings, and collections. This includes the art and material culture, Western historical records, and ethnographic sources. I remain deeply grateful to His Royal Highness *Omo N'Oba N'Edo Uku Akpolokpolo Erediauwa*, the Oba of Benin, for his kind permission to conduct this research and for his critical reading, valuable comments, and discussions of earlier drafts of this and other articles. I began ethnographic fieldwork in Benin in 1982 and continued in 1983–1985 as a Fulbright Associate Professor, Department of Sociology and Anthropology, University of Benin, and at CenSCER (Centre for Social, Cultural and Environmental Research). Additional periods of research in Benin followed yearly, from 1986 to 1995.

2. Sometime in the 1920s and 1930s information was gathered from elderly persons, chiefs, and other informants who were alive at the time of the 1897 British military assault against Benin. From 1933 on these stories and accounts were published privately and locally mostly by Chief Jacob U. Egharevba, an untrained historian, who had collected them. His work provides a written record (necessarily fragmentary) of events, places, and people, made within memory of the British conquest. His now disputed chronology of Benin kingship and other oral tradition nevertheless (despite anticipated modifications), "will always remain a valuable, indeed an indispensable, pioneering work," Bradbury wrote in his "Foreword to Third Edition," of Egharevba's now classic *A Short History of Benin* (1960; 1968, ix). (See Eisenhofer 1995; and Usuanlele and Falola 1994, for bibliography and current commentary.)

3. Many important publications resulted from the University of Ibadan history project and were published in the Ibadan History Series (K. O. Dike, general editor, and later, J. F. A. Ajayi). These publications show that profound administrative and judicial changes took place in traditional areas of Nigeria as a consequence of punitive raids, new legal institutions, and colonial policies. The British manipulated traditional leadership in the north to create what they termed "indirect rule." They found it more expedient, in Benin, to reinstall the rightful heir to the throne as Oba, in 1914. In the mid-1950s a group of British and Nigerian multidisciplinary scholars (anthropologists, historians, and archaeologists) produced an invaluable body of publications at the University of Ibadan on Benin history and culture. The Ibadan scholars drew heavily on known European documentary sources and oral history; and some archaeological surveys and test site excavations were carried out. The challenge was to fit the various pieces of information "together into an integrated picture of the past" (Ryder 1969, ix).

Bradbury's pioneering ethnographic fieldwork in Benin was ended with his untimely death at age forty-nine in 1970. His meticulous research and copious field notes, including some photographs, archived at the University of Birmingham, England, were among materials copied and collected in the early 1980s and brought back to Benin City at the behest of the Benin Traditional Council and the

University of Benin (CenScer), by Joseph Nevadomsky and Daniel Inneh, a historian and the Oba's private secretary (1983, 87). Bradbury's notes have provided valuable data for many later well-known Benin researchers, among them Paula Girshick Ben-Amos, Barbara Blackmun, and others. The Benin linguist Rebecca Agheyisi-Nevadomsky has been a more recent source of information and translation for some scholars.

4. "Benin" refers both to the culture and the people themselves. Benin City is the present capital of Edo State, Federal Republic of Nigeria, and was the ancient center of the kingdom of Benin and the seat of the Oba. The Benin kingdom was an empire from medieval times that extracted tribute from subject peoples and controlled much of what is southern Nigeria at different times over the centuries. The first Portuguese contact was in 1472. The Edos include the Benins proper, centered in and around Benin City, the Ishan, and the Northern Edo, among whom are the Ivbiosakon, Etasako, Northwest Edo, and the Ineme. The Urhobo and Isoko of the Niger Delta (with small pockets extending as far as Rivers State), speak markedly different dialects (Bradbury 1957, 13, 61, 63–64, 85, 100–101, 112, 123–24, 129–30, 174, 177–80). Edo-speaking peoples are linked by their origins to Benin court history, by shared traditional religious beliefs, and by rituals, values, and ideas about the way the world is and how people are supposed to behave in it.

5. Oba Erediauwa expanded on this in his letter to me of July 3, 1995, saying that he has often tried (in private conversation) to correct the English translation of "Ovien Oba," usually given as "slave of the Oba." He goes on to say that there are three groups who serve: "The correct equivalent of the English 'slave' in Benin is 'Oghunmwun,' and all Benin people are not 'Oghunmwun' to their Oba. 'Ovien Oba' is simply 'servant of the Oba' and all Benin people (who are not 'Oghunmwun') are truly 'servants of the Oba' . . . for distinction, 'Ovien' is subservient while 'Oghunmwun' is servile. The third group in this 'Master-Servant' relationship is 'Oguomwandia' which may be translated 'househelp.'"

6. Olokun, god of the sea, children, and wealth, one of the four sons of the high god, Osanobua, had his faults, according to oral tradition. Olokun was guilty of boastfulness, proclaiming himself greater than his father. Osanobua answered that he was still his father, but agreed to meet him at Uzamokon. Olokun dressed himself in his finest clothes, and he sent word he had arrived. Osanobua said that he would send him his messenger because he was having his bath. Osanobua said that if Olokun was better dressed than his servant, then he would come to meet him. If the servant was better dressed, then Olokun should go home and put on better clothes. Osanobua sent the chameleon who said, "Your father greets you. If you are better dressed than I, you are to wait here. If I am better dressed, you are to go home and dress again." The chameleon held up the mirror that Osa had given him, and Olokun saw a reflection of himself. Four times the chameleon came, and four times Olokun saw him dressed like himself. Olokun then gave up and sent to tell his father, Osanobua, that his servant had as much as Olokun himself.

These events in the invisible spirit world, told and retold in Benin, the world of human beings, convey important ideas about how to comport oneself properly, no matter how great you are. The story shows the foolishness of excessive vanity and boasting, the need to understand your place, and the respect due to your elders. In turn, the elders show patience, and their greater wisdom and wit in dealing with the excesses of youth. These are important lessons, because Olokun is the most widely worshiped god in Benin.

References

Bradbury, R. E.

1957 *The Benin Kingdom and the Edo-Speaking Peoples of South Western Nigeria.* Ethnographic Survey of Africa, Western Africa, Part XIII. London: International African Institute, Oxford University Press.

1959 "Chronological Problems in the Study of Benin History." *Journal of the Historical Society of Nigeria* 1, no. 4:263–87.

1961 "Ezomo's Ikegobo and the Benin Cult of the Hand." *Man* 61, 165:129–38.

1964 "The historical uses of comparative ethnography with special reference to Benin and the Yoruba." In *The Historian in Tropical Africa*, ed. J. Vansina, R. Mauny, and L. Thomas. London: Oxford University Press.

1973 *Benin Studies.* London: International African Institute, Oxford University Press.

Connah, Graham

1975 *The Archaeology of Benin.* Oxford: Clarendon Press.

Dapper, O.

1668 *Nauwkeurige Beschrijvinge der Afrikaansche Gewesten.* 2nd ed. Amsterdam.

1686 *Description de l'Afrique.* Amsterdam.

Egharevba, Jacob U.

1947 *Concise Lives of the Famous Iyases of Benin.* Lagos: Temi-Asunwon Press.

1956 *Bini Titles.* Benin City.

1960 *A Short History of Benin.* 3rd ed. Ibadan: Ibadan University Press.

1969 *Some Prominent Bini People.* Benin City: Ribway Printers.

Eisenhofer, Stefan

1995 "The origins of the Benin kingship in the works of Jacob Egharevba." *History in Africa: A Journal of Method* 22:131–63.

Hocart, A. M.

1927 *Kingship.* London: Humphrey Milford, Oxford University Press.

1936 *Kings and Councilors.* Cairo: Printing Office Paul Barbey.

Home, Robert

1982 *City of Blood Revisited: A New Look at the Benin Expedition of 1897.* London: Rex Collings.

Kaplan, Flora *Edouwaye* S.

1990 "Männerdienst und Geheimnis am Königshof von Benin." In *Männer Bände, Männer Bunde,* ed. Gisela Volger and Karin von Welck, 1:289–94, plates XVIII, XIX. Cologne: Rautenstrauch-Joest Museum für Völkerkunde.

1991 "Benin Art Revisited: Photographs and the Documentation of Museum Collections." *Visual Anthropology* 4, no. 2:117–45.

1993a "Images of the Queen Mother in Benin Court Art." *African Arts* 26, no. 3:55–63, 86–88.

1993b *"Iyoba,* The Queen Mother of Benin: Images and Ambiguity in Gender and Sex Roles in Court Art." In *Representations and the Politics of Difference,* Special Issue, *Art History* 16, no. 3:386–407. London and Cambridge, Mass.

n.d. *In Splendor and Seclusion: Art and Women at the Royal Court of Benin, Nigeria.* London: Thames & Hudson. Forthcoming.

Kaplan, Flora S. ed.

1981 *Images of Power: Art of the Royal Court of Benin.* New York: New York University.

Nevadomsky, Joseph

1984a "Kingship Succession Rituals in Benin, Part 2: The Big Things." *African Arts* 17, no. 2:43–47, 90–91.

1984b "Kingship Succession Rituals in Benin, Part 3: The Coronation of the Oba." *African Arts* 17, no. 3:48–57, 91–92

Nevadomsky, Joseph, and Daniel E. Inneh

1983 "Kingship Succession Rituals in Benin, Part 1: Becoming a Crown Prince." *African Arts* 17, no.1: 47–54, 87.

Ryder, A. F. C.

1969a "A Reconsideration of the Ife-Benin Relationship." *Journal of African History* 6, no. 1.

1969b *Benin and the Europeans 1485–1897.* Ibadan History Series, O. Dike, general editor. London and Harlow: Longmans, Green.

Talbot, P. Amaury

1926 *The Peoples of Southern Nigeria.* 4 vols. London.

Usuanlele, U., and Toyin Falola

1994 "The Scholarship of Jacob Egharevba of Benin." *History in Africa: A Journal of Method* 21:301–18.

Figure 1. Memorial cross erected to mark the place where British officers with Acting Consul General James R. Phillips and others were killed, January 4, 1897, Ekehuan Road, Benin City. Collection of Flora E. S. Kaplan. Photograph by S. O. Alonge, 1938.

Figure 2. Oba Ovonramwen under arrest aboard the British Protectorate yacht *Ivy*. Photograph by J. A. Green, 1897. Manchester Museum, University of Manchester.

Figure 3. Plaque, European soldier who served as a mercenary, the Royal Court of Benin, Nigeria. Bronze, sixteenth century. Private Collection.

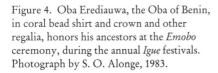

Figure 4. Oba Erediauwa, the Oba of Benin, in coral bead shirt and crown and other regalia, honors his ancestors at the *Emobo* ceremony, during the annual *Igue* festivals. Photograph by S. O. Alonge, 1983.

Figure 5. Staff of Osun, god of medicine and herbs, nineteenth century. Collection of the Brooklyn Museum. Photograph courtesy of the Brooklyn Museum.

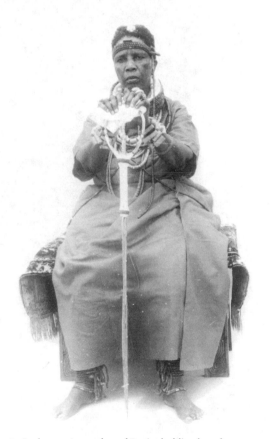

Figure 6. Iyoba, queen mother of Benin, holding her *eben*, a sword symbolic of her male chiefly status. This is one of several formal portraits taken during her title-taking ceremonies. Collection of Flora E. S. Kaplan. Photograph by S. O. Alonge, 1981.

Figure 7. Ancestral head of Oba, Royal Court of Benin, Nigeria. Bronze, late eighteenth–early nineteenth century. Courtesy of the Glasgow Museums and Art Galleries, Scotland.

Figure 8. The Queen Mother's rectangular polished clay altar to the god of the sea, Olokun, bringer of wealth and children. Benin City, Edo State, Nigeria. Photograph by Flora E. S. Kaplan.

Figure 9. One of the three main ancestral shrines in the Oba's palace, the center of Benin religious and political life. This type of circular, polished clay altar can be used only for the Obas. During the annual ceremonies at Igue, the Oba is seated in front of these shrines and calls upon his ancestors to assure the well-being and prosperity of all Edo-speaking peoples in the coming year. These altars were and still are elaborately decorated with fine castings of leaded brass ancestral heads, sculptures, bells, carved ivory tusks, and polished stone celts, the Benins call "thunderstones." Each of the wooden ancestral rattle-staffs stands for a departed ancestor and is struck on the ground and shaken to communicate with the ancestor. The rattle-staffs, *ukhure,* bear unique royal designs. The shrines are located at Ughie-erha Oba, the Oba's fathers' chamber, in a separate compound on the palace grounds. Benin City, Edo State, Nigeria. Photograph by Flora E. S. Kaplan, April 1989.

Figure 10. A group of chiefs line up in the center of the compound of the Oba's fathers' chamber, Ughie-erha Oba, at the palace. Kneeling in the center, his arms supported by members of the Iwebo palace society, a chief has come to make obeisance to the Oba in thanks for the title he has been given. In a series of ritual gestures the chief will press his hands on the sacred ground, and first touch his right hand to his left shoulder, then his left hand to his right shoulder, press the ground, then touch his forehead, rise and salute the Oba, walk forward, then kneel again. He repeats the series of gestures until he reaches the Oba's throne and is acknowledged. The joy on the faces of the chiefs accompanying him in this solemn ritual demonstration of gratitude and loyalty to the sacred king expresses the male solidarity and mutual support they give to each other and to the king. This takes place in the Oba's palace compound where annual sacrifices are offered to the ancestors on behalf of the Edo-speaking peoples. Photograph by Flora E. S. Kaplan, December 1986.

Figure 11. The *Esama* of Benin, Chief G. O. Igbinedion, holding his sword of office, the *eben*, and wearing full ritual regalia during Igue festival. His red cloth regalia is cut out in a pattern to resemble the pangolin's skin. Senior chiefs wear this cloth to symbolize the pangolin, an animal that "respects itself." The *Esama* ranks fifth among the town chiefs, the *eghaevbo n'ore*. He is accompanied by his followers during the ceremonies at the palace; he "plays" the *eben*, twirling and tossing the sword high into the air with one hand, to demonstrate his skill, as well as his loyalty and respect for the Oba. The Oba's palace, Benin City. Photograph by Flora E. S. Kaplan, December 1984.

Figure 12. Olokun priest, native doctor Osemwegie Ebohon, in his ritual dress of white cloth, with shirt thickly covered with cowrie shells; his wrapper has coral beads, shells, and brass charms attached, as well as other substances. A red cap is tied around his chin, and he carries a side-blown carved ivory horn, sounded during the dancing that accompanies worship at his center. While all priests, male and female, wear similar garb, the richness of beads, cowries, charms and other items of wealth reflect the success of the practitioner. Ebohon Cultural and Religious Centre, Benin City, Edo State. Photograph courtesy of Priest O. Ebohon, 1988.

Figure 13. Olokun priestess dancing, holding a fan that "cools" her, as she whirls to receive the spirit that will possess her. Benin City, Edo State. Photograph by Flora E. S. Kaplan, 1988.

Figure 14. Prince Edun Akenzua, Enogie of Obazuwa-Iko, in his coral beads and headband, *udahae*. A white feather will show that he is one who leads the way. Photograph taken when he was named a "duke" by his brother, Oba Erediauwa, Oba of Benin, in 1988, and given a district to administer. Photograph courtesy of the Enogie of Obazuwa-Iko.

Figure 15. His Royal Highness, Omo N'Oba N'Edo Uku Akpolokpolo Erediauwa, the Oba of Benin, on his throne, with royal *eben* held by attendant to his right; his wives and children are seated to the left of his throne. He holds the "leaves of happiness," that mark the end of the annual Igue ceremonies, attended by chiefs, state and federal government officials, civic leaders, visitors, and the populace. Photograph by Flora E. S. Kaplan, December 1992.

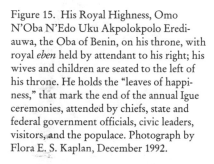

Figure 16. Chief's altar-of-the-hand, Benin, Nigeria. Wood, twentieth century. Collection of Morton Lipkin.

Figure 17. Ancestral head placed on altar of a chief's family house, Benin, Nigeria. Wood, late nineteenth century. Collection of Morton Lipkin.

Figure 18. Ancestral head placed on altar in the family house of a member of the guild of royal bronze casters. Clay, nineteenth century, Benin, Nigeria. Collection of Morton Lipkin.

Figure 19. Juju house in the back of the queen's compound. Benin, Nigeria, 1897. Collection of the National Museums and Galleries on Merseyside, Liverpool. Photograph courtesy of the National Museums and Galleries on Merseyside, Liverpool, England.

7

Spiritual Beings
as Agents of Illness

DAVID WESTERLUND

IN AFRICAN CULTURES, spiritual beings may be seen as important causes of illness, although it should be emphasized at the outset that, in many cases, nonreligious etiologies of disease may be as significant as, or even more significant than, the religious ones. As Steven Feierman remarked, "popular African medicine has strong pragmatic elements and gives weight to natural explanation" (1985, 107). Human agents of disease, such as "sorcerers" or "witches," are well known in many parts of Africa. It should be emphasized also that there is often an overlap between spiritual or religious causes and those that are natural or biological and human or social. This essay, however, will mainly provide examples of the spiritual aspects of the causation of illness.[1] Thus, the focus will be on the interrelationship between spiritual beings and disease, and there will only be some final notes on natural and social illness causation. Instead of giving a broad phenomenological overview, the examples will refer to three specific peoples and cultures: the hunting-gathering San of southern Africa, the pastoral Maasai, and the agriculturalist Sukuma, both of East Africa. In his classical work on Nuer religion, British anthropologist E. E. Evans-Pritchard remarked that, besides being of interest per se, a study of those factors to which people attribute illness, as well as other misfortunes, may reveal the predominant motif in a certain religion (1956, 315). This is clearly the case with the three examples of the San, Maasai, and Sukuma that will be presented here.

The cultures chosen as examples are basically different in religious as well as in economic, social, and political respects. Today around fifty thousand people may have a San (Bushman) identity, and a minority of them still live as hunters and gatherers. The San live in separate groups, often called "tribes" in the ethnographic literature, which are linguistic and cultural entities. The most well known tribe is the Kung of Namibia and Botswana, and the following presentation of San spirituality and illness causation will focus on that group.[2] The term *Maasai* refers to some Nilotic and mainly pastoralist "tribes" or sections (*iloshon*) in southern Kenya and northern Tanzania, who today may number about four hundred thousand. The dominant section in the northern part of the territory inhabited by the Maasai is the Purko, and in the south it is Kisonko.

For the pastoral Maasai, cattle play a central role not only economically but also culturally and religiously. For example, while sheep and goats are often slaughtered for food, cattle are reserved for rituals and ceremonial feasts. The Bantu-speaking Sukuma live south of the Maasai, in central Tanzania, and number around three million. Sukuma may be seen as a generic name for people with different origins, and it is important to keep the provisional nature and contextual relativity of such an ethnic label in mind. They are closely related to the neighboring Nyamwezi to the south, and it was not until the colonial period that these peoples became established and were perceived of as two distinct and separate groups.[3] The Sukuma economy is based primarily on agriculture, although the economic and social significance of animal husbandry has increased considerably. Like San and Maasai, the Sukuma have a tradition of living dispersed in small settlements.

These three groups of people also share a reputation for being "conservative," and neither Christian nor Muslim missionary attempts have been very successful in areas where they live. The Maasai, in particular, have been very resistant to conversion, and the great majority of them still adhere to their indigenous religion. Needless to say, this does not mean that important religious and other changes have not taken place among the San, the Maasai, and the Sukuma. This essay, however, will not focus on aspects and possible causes of change. By and large, rather, the "ethnographic present" will be used.

Heavenly Beings and Illness Causation among the San

The sky is the dwelling place of all the divine beings and spirits in !Kung belief. (Marshall 1986, 171)

Severe internal pain and sickness which make one feel genuinely ill all over . . . are called "sickness of the sky." (Marshall 1969, 370–71)

The religion of the Kung, as well as other San groups, differs from most other indigenous African religions in that, as a rule, it does not include any spirits of nature. Thus, spirits or divinities are not associated with trees, hills, rivers, or other parts of the earth. The abode of spiritual beings is above the sky, which holds the sun, moon, and stars. When referring to this abode, I will here use the term "heaven." Among the Kung the category of illnesses that are caused by heavenly beings may be designated "sickness of the sky" (*kwi naa*). Such heavenly diseases can manifest themselves in grave internal ailments of which people are aware, but they can also exist in a person without that person knowing it. This spiritual category of illness is distinguished from another category which includes mild, localized ailments visible on the surface of the body, common aches, and minor injuries.

Another general characteristic of San spirituality is that it has little bearing upon economic and social life. Moreover, several scholars have stressed the extraordinary dearth of communal rituals, which contrasts sharply with many overgeneralized presentations of African religions as being particularly rich in terms of such rituals. Mathias G. Guenther even holds that paucity of ritual is "*the* remarkable feature about traditional Bushman religion" (1979, 111; emphasis added).

As a rule, initiation rituals and trance dances are the only elaborate communal rituals. Since the spiritual agents of disease figure very prominently in the trance dance, this type of ritual will be studied in some detail here. Before that, however, the heavenly beings—the Supreme Being or God, a lesser deity, and the spirits of dead human beings—should be presented briefly.

God the creator is the highest being.[4] The nature of the Supreme Being is somewhat ambivalent, although the good and helpful qualities are stressed. For instance, based on the analyses of her impressive amount of material from various periods of time, Ingrid Thurner draws the conclusion that the creative and beneficial rather than the destructive aspects predominate (1983, 391). The lesser deity, who among Kung and other San groups may be called Gauwa—a term that may also be used for designating the evil aspect of the Supreme Being—is ambivalent too, but in this case the evil or destructive aspects are the most characteristic traits. It is possible that at one time there was a single being.

Nowadays, however, most San seem to conceive of God and the lesser deity as two distinct beings, if closely associated with each other. Whereas there are many examples of prayers to the former, there are very few examples of prayers to the latter. Both the name and certain attributes appear to suggest that the lesser divinity is closely allied to the spirits of the dead, who may be called *gauwasi*.[5] Like the deities, they are ambivalent spiritual beings associated with the heavenly realm, where they live eternally. Being spirits, they are usually invisible but may occasionally be seen, particularly by healers in a state of trance. As in the case of the lesser deity, the negative or evil traits seem to be the predominant ones. Although they may act independently, they appear more often to be regarded as servants of the Supreme Being and the lesser deity; and there is usually no organized cult or veneration of the deceased. In a classical book from 1930, for instance, Isaac Schapera concluded that the San did not have any organized "family or tribal ancestor worship" or any form of religious practice in which the spirits of the dead were regularly invoked or propitiated (1965, 171, 395).

The heavenly beings presented above figure prominently in the important trance dance, which has been described and discussed in many different sources from various periods of time. Even rock paintings indicate that this dance, which has also been labeled, for example, "medicine dance" or "therapeutic dance," was a most essential element in San religion many thousand years ago (see further Lewis-Williams 1981). There are certain differences between various groups of San in terms of performance and contents of the trance dance. Yet the similarities are more conspicuous, and there seem to have been few changes in time. There is even a marked similarity between southern San dances, evidenced in rock paintings, and current dances performed by Kung and other San groups. As a background to the presentation of the heavenly beings as agents of disease, I will sum up briefly, and with special reference to Kung, the major features of the trance dance (see also Marshall 1969; Lee 1979, 103–18; Katz 1982).

A trance dance usually starts at dusk and frequently goes on until dawn the following day. The central purposes are prevention and healing of serious affliction, but there may be important elements of recreation and entertainment also. Moreover, such a dance is an event when healers gather and transmit to other participants important information about how things are in the spiritual world, and how people in this world would do best to relate to them. Dances are not necessarily restricted to members of one particular band, nor is participation based on kinship ties. The number of participants and spectators, sometimes including Bantu people or other "outsiders," may range from a few dozen, or even less, to a few hundred. The trance dance takes place around a fire, either inside or outside an encampment. It can be planned but may also begin spontaneously, usually by women who start singing and clapping. Most women and girls sit at the fire, very close together, while the men who join in, and occasionally a few women, dance in either direction around them After some time of intensified dancing the trance comes to some of the dancers, and then they start treating the other participants.

A key idea in connection with the trance dance is the concept of *num*.[6]

This has been described as a "spiritual energy" (Katz 1982, 34), which normally resides in the stomach. Kung hold that it was created by God, who gave it his own power. He does not wield it or command its every working, but he can stop it from working any time he wishes.

Not only human beings have *num;* it exists in many other things too. *Num* is always strong, and sometimes so strong that it is dangerous. If ordinary mortals come too close to God, for instance, God's *num* would automatically kill them. "It seemed to me that num had several attributes similar to those of electricity. Like electricity, num is powerful and invisible, capable of beneficent effects, but highly dangerous if too strong" (Katz 1982, 41). In the trance dance, *num* is activated, and when it is "boiling," it rises up the spine to the head. This "boiling energy" (*kia*), to use the title of the book by Richard Katz, is a strong healing power, which exudes from the body in the form of sweat.

The state of trance is induced by the repetitive dancing, the singing, and the fire.[7] Hence, *num* resides not only in the dancers or healers but also in the songs and in the dance fire. The songs, which are named after "strong" things such as certain animals, usually have sounds rather than ordinary words and complex melodies. Kung, among others, believe that *num* songs are created by God and revealed in dreams and visions. Like the songs, the dance fire augments the concentration of *num* at a trance dance, Unlike many shamans in South America, for instance, Kung and other San healers usually do not make use of intoxicants. Likewise, there are few, if any special paraphernalia, although the use of rattles, wound around the legs of the dancers, and sticks has been reported.

In the state of trance, healers may perform feats such as touching the fire, eating burning coals, seeing at a great distance, and obtaining special information. They claim that if their own *num* is hot enough, they will not be burnt by the fire. At least in the past, some powerful healers were believed to be able to transform themselves into animals such as lions. When healers are in deep trance, a comatose or sometimes unconscious state, when they are said to be half dead or dead, their souls are believed to leave their bodies to travel to the world of spiritual beings. This shamanistic feature of out-of-body travel is an important element in San religion. One important reason for a healer's travel in extracorporeal form is the diagnosis of "soul loss," which is another striking similarity between San religion and religions among hunting-gathering peoples in America and elsewhere. Taking the souls or spirits of living humans away is one of the various means used by the spiritual beings to bring diseases and other types of misfortune; and the trance dance is the occasion when they are most likely to bring afflictions. Since it occurs normally at night, when the spiritual beings are very alert, they are attracted by the event.

In order to grasp the idea of soul loss, an examination of San conceptions of soul or spirit is needed. Both of these terms have been used in the literature on San to designate the part of human beings that is normally considered to be invisible and immortal. Here the ideas of the Kung will be presented.

When a Kung person dies, spirits of the dead come to take that person's spirit[8] by pulling it through the head of the corpse. Likewise, it is through their heads that the spirits of the healers in trance leave their bodies temporarily to encounter the spiritual being, who lurks in the shadows around the dance fire, and it is through the heads that the spirits return. The spirit that is taken from the corpse when a person dies is distinct from "life,"[9] which is put inside the body of a person or animal and held there by God. It exists in the vital organs of the body, including the head, but not in the arms and legs. Whereas wounds in the former parts can be lethal, somebody may even lose a limb and survive all the same. Eventually "life" dies in the body and stays there, but the spirit does not die.

When the healers encounter the spiritual beings in the trance dance, they often lack the respectful attitudes they normally have. Kung, among others, do not argue with God and the lesser deity in daily life and may fear to utter their ordinary names, using expressions such as "the one in the east" or "the one in the west" instead. The attitudes observed in trance dances can be more open and straightforward. Although more cautious means such as cajoling or pleading with the spiritual beings occur in trance dances as well, the healers often become aggressive and swear at them.

Sometimes burning sticks are hurled at them and indecent invectives are used. When a healer's soul leaves his body to try to rescue the lost soul of a seriously sick person, he enters into very close contact with the spiritual world, and the struggle becomes intense.[10] According to Katz, "this struggle is at the heart of the healer's art and power" (1982, 43).

Besides soul loss, another major reason for serious illnesses is intrusion. In that case some object, originating from a spiritual being, is believed to have entered the body of a person. Apparently, the intruding object is most often thought of as a miniature arrow. From the Kung area, for instance, there are reports about invisible arrows shot by the spirits of the dead. Whether invisible or not, such arrows or other things that have made people seriously ill must be removed by the healers by, for instance, sucking or drawing them out. Important as these methods may be, maladies and deaths caused by spiritual beings can be brought about in other ways too. Among Kung, for example, they can influence wild animals to attack people, and they can be the cause of a person's falling from a tree.

Lightning can be used by the spirits of the dead to kill people when God and the lesser deity so command. Like lightning, a whirlwind is a "death thing" in Kung belief. A whirlwind is called *gauwa a,* which means "*gauwa* smell." The spirits of the dead come in whirlwinds too, but neither they nor the lesser deity can be seen or heard in these winds. People who encounter such winds must try to get away, lest they become sick or die.

Sometimes sickness seems to be a very abstract notion. A person may or may not be aware of having sickness. Yet even those who are unaware of being ill are treated by the healers in the trance dance. A healer in trance may "absorb" a person's affliction into his or her own body and let it run its full course there. Although this can be painful for the healer, his/her "hot" state of trance makes it possible for him/her to endure and survive. With regard to Kung, Katz has drawn the following conclusion:

> Sickness is more an existential condition or level of being than a particular illness or symptom. Everybody has some sickness, and so everybody who is at a dance is given healing. In most persons, this sickness remains incipient, neither serious nor manifested in symptoms. In some persons, the sickness is actualized into what westerners would call an illness. . . . Persons who are ill get especially intensive and extensive healing. Num is for prevention as well as treatment. (1982, 102)

There are not different words to distinguish potential illness from illness that is specific or manifested in symptoms. In both cases the term *xai* is used. Hence, the distinctions are created by the context of usage.

As a rule, it does not seem possible to differentiate clearly between the spiritual beings as agents of disease and death, although some general tendencies may be discerned. Among Kung, it seems that the spirits of the dead are the primary direct causes of serious afflictions. Yet it must be remembered that they are often commanded by the more powerful beings. God is seldom a direct cause of illness, but he may send diseases and death through the lesser deity and the spirits. Being all-powerful, he is ultimately responsible for death. According to Marshall, the lesser deity was previously, when the idea of God's omnipower was less significant, thought of as the death-giver (1969, 234). He is now conceived of more as messenger, although, like the spirits of the dead, he can act independently as well. If they are in a benevolent mood, they may be placated by the healers in the trance dance. That is unusual, however, and the healers must then try to drive them away instead. Sometimes they succeed in doing so, but at other times they lose the battles with these spiritual beings. God is confronted by the most powerful healers only, whose souls travel to his home, at the greatest risk to their very lives.

Why, then, do the heavenly beings cause maladies and deaths? The basic San answer to this question appears to be some reference to their ambivalent and unpredictable nature. In works by scholars of the Catholic-inspired Vienna school, founded by Fr. Wilhelm Schmidt, the moral aspect of San thoughts about the reasons for diseases and deaths has clearly been exaggerated (see, e.g., Gusinde 1963–64; 1964–65, 38). The idea of afflictions as punishment for misbehavior was not prominent among those Kung studied by Richard Lee, and Lorna Marshall concludes that the concept of sin as an offense against spiritual beings is vague. One person's wrongdoing against another is corrected or avenged within their social context and not by God, who punishes people for his own reasons, which can be quite obscure. The somewhat unpredictable nature of God is exemplified by the story about the hunter who died after eating the meat of a gemsbok he had killed, because God had changed himself into that particular gemsbok. The informant who told Marshall this story said that God might regret having done such a thing—killing a man who was just hunting to feed his children—and to make amends he might particularly favor that man's son (Marshall 1962, 245).

Marjorie Shostak provides a Kung example of how the spirits of the dead, as it were, may punish the punished. A spirit can exercise his or her power against the living if, for example, a certain woman is not being treated well by her husband and other people. In such a case the spirit may conclude that no one cares whether or not she remains alive and, for that reason, "take her to the sky" (Shostak 1981, 291). Moreover, the spirits of the dead may bring sickness simply because they are longing for the living. The process of a person's death can thus be seen as a struggle between two loving sets of relatives, one living and the other dead, each wanting the individual for themselves. Even though a variety of San explanations to the problem of why the heavenly beings cause diseases and deaths have been rendered in the sources, there is clearly no systematic or coherent theological answer to that question. Like other issues of San religion, this is characterized by flexibility and fluidity. Besides, Lee's conclusion that the Kung do not spend much time in pondering over religious or philosophical problems such as this (1979, 109) seems to be applicable to other San groups as well.

The Role of God as an Agent of Illness among the Maasai

God, who created the world and human beings, who gives and maintains life, is also the ultimate cause of disease and death. (Arhem 1989, 80)

Many of the scholars who have studied the Maasai religion have emphasized its uniqueness in the African context. The most striking feature is its monotheistic character, but the lack of such things as sacred buildings, religious images, priesthood, spirits of ancestors, and, as a rule, even of belief in an afterlife has been seen as evidence of the unique character of this religion. Certainly it seems that some of these characteristics are particularly pronounced among the Maasai. By and large, however, their religion is similar to the type of religion that is found among other pastoral peoples in Africa. Maasai religion differs from San religion in that, among other things, it is richer in terms of ceremonies and rituals. Above all, there are elaborate ceremonies connected with initiations at certain ages, for example, the circumcision ceremony. The major age-group ceremonies and rituals involve features such as ritual head shaving, continual blessings, slaughter of animals, paintings of the body, singing, dancing, and feasting. Another difference between Maasai and San religion is that in the former leadership functions are more strongly dominated by men. Maasai elders are the most prominent authorities in both religious and secular affairs.

The most important name, or the proper name of the Supreme Being or God among the Maasai is *enkAi*. The word *enkai* can be translated "heaven," or "sky," and "rain" too. As suggested by the name, God is associated particularly with the heavenly realm, although he is said to be omnipresent. God is the creator and giver of everything, the master of life and death. He is the sustainer of the world as of all living things. Because the Supreme Being is actively involved in daily life, prayers and sacrifices to him are common. What human beings need, enkAi provides, and the Maasai are, above all, provided with cattle. Through the gift of cattle, God has established a special relationship between himself and the "people of cattle," although enkAi is God of all peoples. Morally, he is described as good and merciful. God is like a father and mother of all creatures, and he "appears to have many of the highly respected attributes associated with extreme age, only more so" (Spencer 1988, 49).[11]

According to the quotation at the beginning of this section, God is the ultimate cause of illness and death. This has been stated also in a number of other sources. For instance, J. G. Galaty concludes that "God himself is thought to operate at levels of ultimate principles behind all fundamental processes in life," even though "[t]his monad of fundamentality does not adequately explain the particularities of individual life events" (1977, 320). In particular, it seems that serious diseases that may lead to death and death itself are frequently believed to be occasioned by God. A disease or death immediately caused by God is referred to by the term *enkea*. Such a disease or death is distinguished from illnesses and deaths ultimately caused by God but mediated by healers (*iloibonok*), who themselves derive their powers from God. Thus, *enkea* represents the unmediated and destructive intervention in the lives of living humans. This may be compared, for instance, to the view of birth as a result of the creative intervention by God. As implied in the concept of *enkea*, disease is conceived of as a kind of death. An *enkea* is a serious affliction which, in a sense, is a forestate of death. Mild ailments such as headache or stomachache, which are not serious or mortal, may generally be referred to by the term *emoyan*. If a person is weaker than what is considered normal and this weakness is believed to be due to blood loss, it is regarded as something distinct from disease proper. Such weakness is cured not by medicine but by the consumption of large amounts of blood and fat. Notions of strength and weakness are usually described in the idiom of blood. Hence, a strong person is full of blood, whereas a weak person is said to lack blood (Arhem 1989, 80–81, 84).

In his classic study from 1904, M. Merker seems to indicate an element of predestination when he says that a human being dies when the life span of that person, which has been "predetermined" by God, has come to an end (1904, 196). To the best of my knowledge, however, this statement has not been confirmed in other sources. It may be compared, for example, to H. Fokken's conclusion that a human being does not die until God ends the course of life of that individual (1914, 32). Merker himself says that, in the hope of recovery, a dying person may sacrifice a bull to God (1904, 192).

In a sense, however, death and disease are beyond human comprehension, since nobody can predict the actions of God. When causing afflictions and death, God may use natural elements such as lightning and strong winds. If somebody is hit by lightning, people may say that the "red God" has hit that person.[12] As is the case with San, among whom destruction caused by whirlwinds is associated with the lesser deity Gauwa, the "red" aspect of enkAi appears in destructive winds. Earthquakes and the eruption of volcanoes are other means by which God may make his presence known in a destructive way.

Tord Olsson concludes that it is in certain types of discourse, such as myth and liturgy, that God is seen as the ultimate cause of events in cosmos, nature, society, and history. On such levels of discourse, or in such speech situations, observable facts such as lightning and volcanoes are thought of as being employed by God as "instruments" or "methods" (*impukonot;* singular, *empukonoto*). In other words, particular events or states, like ailments, can be discussed at different levels of discourse involving an empirically observable cause or an unobservable and intentional dimension.

When Maasai discuss origins of diseases, they are, thus, often heard to apply arguments according to the following lines of thought. First they try to find out what may be the empirically observable cause, and if it is considered a sufficient cause they try to find some remedy. Although the established cause may also be regarded as necessary, it may be that in some ensuing speech situations it is no longer regarded as sufficient. The empirically observed cause is then regarded as guided by some unobservable entity, or, more precisely, guided through a nonempirical or nonconcrete dimension of it. The "cause" is employed as an instrument by some "guiding cause" (Olsson 1989, 236).

It is emphasized by Olsson that empirical and nonempirical causes should not be seen as alternatives. As appears from the quotation above, nonempirical causes are rather thought of as being complementary to empirical ones. This is in accordance with the situation among other peoples. Hence, it should be stressed that the employment of terms such as "spiritual" and "natural" causes does not necessarily imply that these are alternatives. Jan Voshaar holds that all objects that are used in daily life have a meaning and efficaciousness beyond their immediate purpose. Thus, "a club is not just a club" (1979, 199).

Things like milk, grass, and fire are symbolically meaningful and efficacious of themselves and are used in various rituals. Other things, such as tobacco containers and walking sticks, are imparted with an extra meaning and power through blessing and consecration by elders. For instance, after the birth of a baby, objects for personal or family use are blessed by the spittle of elders. In part, this is done in order to protect the mother and the child from sickness and death (Voshaar 1979, 199–201).

Mythical Maasai versions of the origin of illness and death tell that the first beings had to suffer these evils because they had disobeyed God by eating the fruit of a certain tree. Disease and death are henceforth implicit in the human condition. However, they may also be interpreted as God's punishment for the transgressions of human beings here and now. According to Merker, elephantiasis is caused by incest, and malformed or stillborn babies are also the result of "sins" punished by God (1904, 51, 175).

Much more recently, Paul Spencer has demonstrated that any deformity of a baby may be regarded as an indication of "some past sin dogging either parent" (1988, 42).[13] There is in all matters concerning birth and infancy, not only among human beings but among all living things, an element of providence expressed as the prerogative of God. To take any life in embryonic form or at young age is regarded as a sin, *engoki*. Misfortune will surely follow the killing of such lives. For instance, persistent misfortune of some elders may occur because they have killed women as warriors, not knowing that the women were pregnant. There is a notion that an infant is a fetus (*olkibiroto*) as long as it is fed wholly on the mother's milk. It is not until milk from the herd is introduced into its diet that the fetus becomes a person (*oltungani*). During the very first period of life, when the child is particularly weak, dependent, and vulnerable, it is thought of as being especially close to God. There are other occasions, also, when the concept of *engoki,* or sin, is applicable. On the whole, evil done when life is weakest is *engoki.* For example, elders and people in situations of rites of passage, that is, when a former state of life is left and a new state has not yet been entered, are vulnerable; and evil done to such categories of people may result in the immediate sickness or death of the perpetrator. The punishment may even affect such an evildoer's family and animals.[14]

Some authors have stressed the connection between "sins" and illnesses as divine punishments.[15] However, a wider comparion of sources indicates that such punishments are not generally believed to be common. It appears that, as a rule, wrongdoers are dealt with by elders rather than by God himself. For example, Kaj Arhem states that he has not heard of maladies that have been attributed directly to moral misconduct or transgression of normative rules (1989, 84). Although the good and creative aspects of God are stressed by Maasai, he is an ambivalent being. Hence, he is considered to embody the dual qualities of good and evil, creation and destruction, within himself.

In his study of the Matapato Maasai, Paul Spencer speaks about "a dualistic perception of God, protective on the one hand and castigating on the other" (1988, 48). Clearly, the sources are somewhat conflicting and do not render any precise conclusions about the issue of illnesses and death as divine punishments. On this question, as well as in other cases, the significance of variations between various Maasai groups and individuals must also be kept in mind. These considerations notwithstanding, it appears that, in most cases, God is not thought of as a moral guardian who metes out punishments in the form of diseases, deaths, and other forms of misfortune. He does not often seem to be involved directly as a cause of illness and death, except in the case of serious afflictions and when people harm certain living things, such as infants and trees, that stand in a particularly close relationship to him. Nevertheless, his role stands out as very important in that he is also indirectly involved in the actions of elders and healers, who wield the power of cursing, which is an important cause of illness. Elders and healers stand in a special relationship to God and use their supranormal power in conjunction with him.

Prayers and sacrifices to God often exist in connection with cases of disease; and it seems that they may be directed to him even when he is not thought of as the direct or immediate cause of the disease in question. In cases when God is believed to be the direct cause of an illness, he is called upon in a special manner to bring redress.[16] When people are wasted by serious illnesses such as epidemics, large numbers of worshipers may be involved and several animals may be slaughtered near mountains or oreteti trees,[17] which are seen as one of the most powerful manifestations of God.[18]

Spirits of Ancestors as Agents of Illness
among the Sukuma

The religion of the Sukuma, in its practical aspects, is composed almost entirely of a direct ritual relationship with the spirits of the ancestors (Tanner 1967, 5). In many overgeneralized, comparative accounts of indigenous African religions, ancestor worship has been depicted virtually as *the* religion of Africa. However, there are many African peoples, such as the pastoral Maasai, who pay little or no attention to spirits of ancestors. It is mainly in agriculturalist cultures without centralized sociopolitical systems that ancestors have a central role in the religion. The Sukuma culture is an example of that type of society in which the "cult" or "veneration" of the ancestors is, or at least has been, a most prominent feature.[19]

Belief in God and spirits of nature is, certainly, a part of Sukuma religion; but "what constitutes the very forces of ritual life" among the Sukuma, Nyamwezi, and other peoples with a similar culture is the relationship between the living and the dead (Brandstrom 1990, ch. 6, p. 10; see also Abrahams 1967, 77; and Hatfield 1968, 16).

Moyo is a Sukuma word that has frequently been translated "soul." It is associated with the heart, the breath, and the shadow of a human being. It is the principle or spirit of life, which is centered in the heart and maintained or manifested by the breath. In a sense, the shadow is a sign that a person is living, and dead people or corpses are said to lack shadows. When a human being dies, *moyo* ceases to exist. Within a human being, however, there is also a spiritual entity, *isamva* (plural, *masamva*),[20] associated with the blood, which survives death. Thus, unlike animals, humans continue existing after death. In the Sukuma afterlife there is no "heaven" or "hell." Hence, "good" and "bad" people do not exist in different abodes after life. As in other religions, Sukuma conceptions of the afterlife tend to be vague and conflicting. In some respects the life of ancestors is similar to the life of living humans. For instance, the social position is not changed in the land of the spirits, and ancestors are offered food products which they enjoyed in life. Spirits of ancestors may be associated with the earth and the graves as well as with the air above.[21]

People do not necessarily have to honor the *masamva* at fixed places, even though rituals or ceremonies are frequently performed at graves. Cult activity may also be localized at small spirit houses built in honor of the ancestors and constructed from specific trees with symbolic meanings. Moreover, animals such as cows, goats, and sheep are kept in remembrance of *masamva*. Such a dedicated animal may not be slaughtered and is kept until it dies. In addition to animals, virtually all kinds of inanimate objects may be consecrated. Some of these ritual paraphernalia are articles which ancestors possessed in their lifetimes, but other objects such as weapons, sticks, skins of animals, necklaces, pearls, and many other things can be dedicated too. In time of illness, for instance, people may bear their venerated objects.

An ancestor or *isamva* is an immaterial or incorporeal but individual or personal power of great importance, and living humans relate closely to their own deceased agnatic as well as cognatic relatives. Since ancestors for their "survival" depend on children and grandchildren, although deceased children and adults without offspring may be included in general terms when *masamva* are invoked, descendants are of vital importance. Normally, ancestors of three or four generations can be remembered and honored by descendants. The cult or veneration of ancestors is manifested in a rich variety of sacrifices, invocations, and dances. There are simple libations of milk and beer as well as more complex rituals with sacrifices of fine and healthy goats, sheep, and cattle in large feasts. When people invoke ancestors, they often invoke the Supreme Being as well. Ultimately, God is the master of life and death, the manifestation of power in its totality. However, his transcendence and noninvolvement in human affairs are pronounced features of Sukuma religion, and there is little or no direct cult of him.[22]

Sickness now seems to be the most important reason for ceremonies of ancestor propitiation. Thus, it is largely in the context of health problems that the construction of spirit houses, the consecration of various objects, sacrifices, initiation of various individuals into secret societies, and similar actions must be seen.[23] Through the various means of propitiation, health can be regained. It seems that ancestors may be thought of as agents of all kinds of illnesses as well as of infertility and other kinds of misfortune, possibly with the exception of death.[24]

Even though there has been a decline in terms of beliefs and practices relating to ancestors, there are still many Sukuma who conceive of these spirits as important agents of sickness. To be "seized" by an *isamva* is to them an undesirable experience associated with some misfortune such as physical or mental affliction. It appears that in general there are no specific diseases that are associated with the actions of ancestors. As a rule, thus, the symptoms of a certain affliction do not indicate if it is an ancestor at work. However, "social" symptoms such as lack of respect for daily life may do so. Moreover, if a child is doing poorly during the days immediately after its birth, that would easily be taken as a sign of ancestor action. In most cases, however, divination is needed in order to find out not only which ancestor is at work but also, in the first place, if it is an ancestor at all. On the other hand, there are some diseases that may not be occasioned by ordinary ancestors. In particular, epidemic illnesses are found in this category. The *masamva* cause afflictions of their own descendants but not of people who are not members of their own families.[25]

Diseases caused by human agents—"witches" and "sorcerers"— can have somewhat more specific symptoms. Hence, it may be possible to conclude from certain symptoms if the disease is not the result of the intervention of an ancestor.

There are many reasons why spirits of ancestors may cause diseases and other types of misfortune. According to Ralph E. S. Tanner, "Sukuma believe that misfortune in all its forms is the result of sin which turns back on its perpetrator and spreads through his family" (1958, 225). In another work Tanner elucidates his use of the term "sin" and argues that Sukuma morals are qualified by relationship, locality, and the circumstances surrounding an incident. A person's primary ties are to his or her family and tend to diminish with increasing kinship distance. "The average Sukuma would seem to grade his ideas of right and wrong according to the degree of relationship he has to the person in the context" (Tanner 1967, 22). This feature is certainly not peculiar to Sukuma, but it tends to be less pronounced in cultures where kinship ties are not quite as important as they are among the Sukuma. Several scholars emphasize the great importance which Sukuma attach to correct behavior within the community of living and dead family members. Lineage rules must be observed and ancestors must be honored, lest illnesses or other problems follow. If grave faults, such as incest, are committed, disaster may threaten not only human fertility but even the fertility of the land. Seeing that they influence their own descendants only, ancestors cannot be depicted as upholders of Sukuma customs and morals in general.

Another way of angering ancestors which may result in illnesses is the failure to name children after them. An ancestor can demand more than one child to be named after him or her. Name-giving is usually done soon after birth, but names may be changed later in life because of illness which has been attributed by divination to a dereliction of filial duty. The head of the lineage will invoke the ancestors and asperse the afflicted person at a formal ceremony. After this ceremony, however, there is no need for him or her to use the new name in everyday life, as the formal ceremony and the mention of the name therein are sufficient to alleviate the troubles. If ancestors are not properly remembered in the prayers and offerings of their descendants, the spirit will occasionally cause misfortune until such remembrance is made. *Masamva* may also affect living relatives in order to air past grievances and to demand satisfaction. Such grudges can be based on past events which may be unknown to or forgotten by the living. A particularly unpredictable and dangerous group of ancestors are those who died in unusual circumstances and whose corpses were mishandled or lost. The absence of a corpse is a breach of lineage unity, which makes the lineage members more exposed to illness. A large proportion of all ceremonies carried out to reduce diseases are directed to the unpredictable "wandering spirits."

A certain amount of unpredictability is a characteristic of all ancestors. Like living humans, spirits of ancestors are not good *or* bad but good *and* bad. As ambivalent beings, they may be contented agents of blessings as well as discontented agents of misfortune. Thus, the surviving relatives ask their *masamva* to assist in providing good harvests, many children, good health, and other good things in life. Since the actions of ancestors are more powerful than the actions of their descendants, the spiritual assistance is important in order to obtain a good life on earth. Ultimately, however, the *masamva* are dependent on God, even though prayers and offerings are addressed directly to the former and indirectly only to the latter.

Since ancestors are able to harm their descendants, there is some amount of awe of them; and, as indicated above, it seems that at least in recent decades, *masamva* have generally been asked to abstain from evil rather than to bring about good. Yet the amount of fear should not be exaggerated. The feelings of living humans toward their ancestors are a complex mixture of affection and awe. In a sense, they are still one with the living members of their families rather than dominating outsiders who aggressively control their descendants. When communicating with their living relatives, ancestors can appear in dreams and possess people. Possession, particularly of women, seems to be a common phenomenon among the Sukuma. A possessed person or "medium" acts as a mouthpiece of the possessing spirit. People who become possessed are both ordinary persons and healers, *bafumu* (singular, *nfumu*). Moreover, an ancestor can reveal himself or herself in the form of an animal, usually a snake, which must be well treated. In divination, it is the living who actively seek to find out which ancestor is the cause of a particular affliction and what complaints or wishes that spirit may have. Simple and common forms of divination are known to ordinary people, while more advanced cases are referred to the *bafumu*, who are highly specialized in various forms of divination and healing. Although there are some *bafumu* who work with medicines or instruments and do not rely on spiritual support, most of them are dependent on the assistance and power of *masamva*. Much of their energy is devoted to the task of maintaining or reestablishing harmony between living humans and ancestors.

Ancestor veneration helps to keep families together. It is closely associated with the Sukuma social system and serves as a kind of social cement. Ancestors are interested in the successful continuation of their lineages, and their presence sanctions the moral behavior of individuals within specific families. The concept of *mhola*, which may be translated "health," refers to the desirable state of life in a most comprehensive sense. Thus, not only health—in a limited sense—but also prosperity, peace, and all the good things in life belong to the realm of *mhola*. It is the "cool" state of peace and good relations between the living as well as between the living and the dead. The state of *mhola* must be attained, maintained, and, time after time, retained. *Busatu*, "illness," is a less comprehensive term than *mhola*. There is no inclusive expression for the state of "non-*mhola*." However, illness and natural calamities like drought and subsequent famine, for example, are spoken of in terms of "not being" or "lacking" *mhola* (see further Brandstrom 1990).

Notes on Natural and Social Causation of Illnesses

Even though this essay has focused on the roles of spiritual beings as agents of disease, it should be stressed that in the illness etiologies of all the three peoples studied here, natural or biological aspects are of great importance. The issue of natural or physical causation is of paramount significance particularly for the Maasai. As early as 1904, for example, Merker reported that in most cases the Maasai thought that illnesses had natural causes (1904, 174); and in his much more recent study Olsson says that "pastoral Maasai prefer to regard disease as physical influence upon, or organic perturbation in the bodies of men and animals" (1989, 235). *Ilabaak* form a Maasai category of medical practitioners who may be referred to as curers, or (secular) doctors, and who must not be confused with the healers (*iloibinok*), whose art of healing has a spiritual dimension. In the medicines used by the *ilabaak*, as well as by ordinary Maasai, it is the physical properties that count but, unlike those of the *iloibonok*, not any spiritual or supernormal qualities.

Like the Maasai, ordinary San and Sukuma have extensive knowledge of household remedies.

The idea of human or social causation of afflictions is not a very prominent feature among the hunting-gathering San and pastoralist Maasai. Concerning the Kung San, Marshall concludes that they do not have "sorcerers" or "witches" (Marshall 1962, 249; Katz 1982, 55, 103), and regarding the Maasai, Dirk Berg-Schlosser says that there is "a general lack of belief in witchcraft" (1984, 170). Because of influence from non-San peoples, there are now a few San examples of "social illnesses" caused by "witchery" (witchcraft and sorcery).[26] Among pastoralist Maasai, human agents of diseases are, and have been, somewhat more important than among hunting-gathering San (see, e.g., Fratkin 1991, 318–33). However, these agents are primarily, or almost exclusively, healers and elders who may use their special power to inflict harm on other people.[27] For this purpose they use the method of cursing or certain witchery practices. The belief in the power of cursing, or blessing, is associated with legitimate authority, which underpins the social order. In particular, curses of elders are considered effective on account of the right order of things and are used or threatened to be used for the benefit of the community or a family. Yet elders seem to show great restraint before they resort to the pronouncement of curses. The ultimate agent of the curse is God himself, and appeals are made to him to punish an alleged offender, which God is expected to do if that person is indeed an offender.

The power of cursing can be misused, and especially healers (*iloibonok*) are believed to use their power occasionally for their own private benefit.[28] In comparison to the illness etiologies of the San and the Maasai, the Sukuma etiology of disease clearly gives more weight to human agents. *Mhola*, the desirable state of everything, is threatened by the activities of *balogi* (sorcerers or witches). Symbolically, witchery (*bulogi*) is associated with the color black; and while the blackness of life-giving clouds of rain and fertility is good, the blackness of witchery is evil. The *balogi* may or may not use special "medicines." *Bugota* (or *buganga*) is a Sukuma concept which has often been translated "medicine." It represents an impersonal power within human reach and can be manipulated by human beings. The term is comprehensive and refers, for instance, to headache powders and injections for bilharzia as well as to protection against evildoers and medicines for revenge. In *bulogi*, the power of *bugota* is utilized aggressively in order to harm people. *Balogi* can instigate all kinds of evil, and illnesses as well as deaths are frequently caused by them.

For instance, incurable diseases are often seen as a result of their evil machinations. If a person whose affliction has been believed to be occasioned by ancestors, God, or natural causes does not get relief, the problem of witchery may be considered. *Balogi* are seen as social and moral deviants with harmful powers rather than as physically or mentally abnormal people.[29]

Concluding Remarks

In all African cultures there is, apparently, a spiritual dimension of illness causation as well as of healing. Frequently, the spiritual agents who cause, or contribute to causing, an illness are also those agents to whom people turn for healing.

The examples provided in this essay show that there may be important differences as well as similarities in terms of spiritual involvement. Among the San, all the spiritual beings, but particularly the lesser deity and the spirits of the dead, play substantial roles as agents of serious afflictions. In the monotheistic religion of the pastoral Maasai, God is an important cause of disease as well as of health, whereas in the Sukuma religion, the spirits of ancestors play a much more significant role as direct agents of ill-health.

Among the San, the moral aspect of disease causation is not very pronounced. Here, rather, the ambivalent character of spiritual beings appears to be the main answer to the question why these beings sometimes occasion maladies. Likewise, among the Maasai, afflictions are not primarily conceived of as a divine punishment for "sins." Indirectly, however, he is involved in the actions of healers and elders, who have a special power of cursing and blessing, which are important causes of illness and health, respectively, because they use this power in conjunction with God in order to defend the moral norms of Maasai society. Sukuma spirits of ancestors are upholders of the morals of their living relatives, and illnesses are one way of punishing the latter for breaking these morals. However, even in this case there is a certain amount of unpredictability.

While focusing on the role of spiritual beings as agents of illness, it has been stressed that natural or physical causes are also a highly significant part of the disease etiologies of the three peoples presented here. Human agents of affliction, such as "witches" or "sorcerers," are of little significance among hunting-gathering San and pastoral Maasai, but clearly more important among the Sukuma. A discussion of this difference and its possible causes would be a challenging theme for another essay!

Notes

1. In a recent article, Robert W. Wyllie uses the term "spiritualistic etiologies" (1994).

2. There is a substantial body of scholarly literature on the Kung. Some works of particular interest are Marshall 1969; Lee 1968; and Katz 1982. In addition to published literature, the unpublished diaries of M. Gusinde, which are found in the Anthropos Institute in St. Augustin, Germany, have been used to a limited extent here. For an interesting article on Khoisan religions in general, see Barnard 1988.

3. The bulk of the archival material used here is from the archive of the White Fathers in Rome and refers primarily to the northern part of Sukumaland, near

Lake Victoria. Among significant published works on the Sukuma and Nyam-wezi, the following may be mentioned: Tanner 1959; Tcherkezoff 1985; and Brandstrom 1990. For more detailed references to works on the San, Maasai, and Sukuma, see Westerlund 1989.

4. There are several names of God, some of which are associated with heaven and greatness.

5. This is a plural form of *gauwa*, which can be translated "spirit."

6. *Num* is a Kung term, but there are equivalent concepts in the languages of other San groups, such as *tsso* among the Nharo of western Botswana.

7. Psychologically, physical exertion and food deprivation may be important factors for understanding the inducement of trance.

8. *Gauwa* is the term used by, among others, Marshall.

9. *Toa* is the Kung concept for "life."

10. On their return from out-of-body travels, the healers may describe the heavenly realm, sometimes in great detail, and recount their fight for the sick one's soul.

11. EnkAi is a feminine form, and it is not uncontroversial to refer to God as "he." Yet the Maasai themselves speak of God as "he," and divine attributes such as greatness and power are associated with men rather than with women. See further, e.g., Hauge 1979, 17.

12. The expression "the red god" (*enkai nanyokie*) is associated with the red color of the sky at sunrise and sunset during the dry season. Whereas "the black god" (*enkai narok*), associated with the dark clouds, brings rain and, consequently, grass to cattle and prosperity to people, "the red god" may bring famine and death.

13. Spencer says that Matapato Maasai are reluctant to discuss family tragedies and that they dispose of dead children unobtrusively. The general absence of con-genital disabilities, he argues, "inevitably raises questions regarding the fate of defective babies" (1988, 42).

14. See further Mol 1978, 70; Voshaar 1979, 190–92; and Spencer 1988, 39, 41.

15. This emphasis is common, for instance, in the Christian-influenced unpub-lished theses found in the archive of the Makumira Lutheran Seminary near Arusha in Tanzania.

16. Jan Voshaar holds that the sacrifices are reminders of life rather than gifts or substitutions for life (1979, 37). God himself is confronted with the facts of life: "See what life is, do this to us no more."

17. Like mountains, the tall oreteti trees (fig trees) rise up toward heaven and are thus, in a sense, close to God. Mountains and trees function as a kind of medium by which prayers and offerings reach him. God, as it were, hears prayers through such entities, as he hears through heavenly bodies.

18. Because of the monotheistic and theocentric character of Maasai religion, there is little or no room for spiritual beings other than God. In recent decades some cases of possession, involving spirits from other peoples, have been reported from some Maasai areas in Tanzania. However, this new phenomenon, which does not seem to exist among Maasai in Kenya, will not be described here. For a study of this phenomenon, see Hurskainen 1989, 139–50. It should be mentioned also

that among agriculturalist Maasai, such as the Arusha in Tanzania, spirits of ancestors may be seen as important agents of illness.

19. Here, as in many other cases, their significance has decreased considerably in recent times. For a discussion of such changes and their possible reasons, see Westerlund 1989, 189, 200–206.

20. The term *isamva* seems to refer to the active power of the ancestors.

21. Since, with the exception of dominant chiefly lineages, Sukuma lineages have not been and are not localized, the land is not considered to belong to the ancestors.

22. The earlier-mentioned spirits of nature have a very marginal position in the Sukuma religion.

23. In 1967, Tanner concluded that "now both the educated and uneducated persons neglect their ancestors for years and consider propitiating them only when they are in trouble, so that the cult of the ancestors has changed from maintaining their goodwill by regular rites as was done in the past to the present intermittent recognition of their powers to harm and the ceremonies, individual rather than collective, necessary to recover their goodwill. It is their interference rather than their benevolence that occasions the ritual" (1967, 24).

24. Power over life and death is the prerogative of God rather than of the ancestors.

25. Previously, chiefs attempted to control, by ritual means, deadly diseases such as smallpox, plague, measles, cholera, and rinderpest. Epidemics sent by chiefly ancestors, as well as their withholding of rains, were lethal threats to large groups of people.

26. For a recent discussion of the general lack of witchery among hunting-gathering San, see Guenther 1992, 83–107.

27. A belief in people with "evil eyes" who can cause illnesses is found also among Maasai. See, e.g., Hauge 1979, 58; Voshaar 1979, 195–96; and Spencer 1988, 43–44.

28. The idea of "sorcerer" or "witch" (*olasakutoni*) who harms people simply out of evil motives or for profit does exist, but it appears to be quite insignificant. See further, e.g., Galaty 1977, 306; cf. Mol 1978, 172.

29. For a study of witchery problems among the Sukuma, see Tanner 1970; see also, e.g., Steves 1990.

References

Abrahams, R. G.
     1967   *The Peoples of Greater Unyamwezi (Nyamwezi, Sukuma, Sumbwa, Kimbu, Konongo)*. Ethnographic Survey of Africa, East Central Africa, 17. London: International African Institute.
Arhem, Kaj
     1989   "Why Trees Are Medicine." In *Culture, Experience and Pluralism: Essays on African Ideas of Illness and Healing,* ed. Anita Jacobson-Widding and David Westerlund, 75–84. Uppsala Studies in Cul-

tural Anthropooogy 13. Stockholm: Almqvist & Wiksell International.

Barnard, Alan
1988   "Structure and Fluidity in Khoisan Religious Ideas." *Journal of Religion in Africa* 18:216–36.

Berg-Schlosser, Dirk
1984   *Tradition and Change in Kenya: A Comparative Analysis of Seven Major Ethnic Groups.* Internationale Gegenwart 3. Paderborn/Munich: Ferdinand Schöningh.

Brandstrom, Per
1990   *Boundless Universe: The Culture of Expansion among the Sukuma-Nyamwezi of Tanzania.* Uppsala: Department of Cultural Anthropology.

Evans-Pritchard, E. E.
1956   *Nuer Religion.* New York: Oxford University Press.

Feierman, Steven
1985   "Struggles for Control: The Social Roots of Health and Healing in Modern Africa." *African Studies Review* 28:73–147.

Fokken, H.
1914   *Spruchweisheit der Masai.* Leipzig: Verlag der Evang.-Luth. Mission.

Fratkin, Elliott
1991   "The loibon as Sorcerer: A Samburu loibon among the Ariaal Rendille." *Africa* 61:318–33.

Galaty, J. G., and D. L. Johnson, eds.
1977   *The World of Pastoralism: Herding Systems in Comparative Perspective.* New York: Guilford Press.

Guenther, Mathias G.
1979   "Bushman Religion and the (Non)sense of Anthropological Theory of Religion." *Sociologus* 29:102–32.
1992   "'Not a Bushman Thing': Witchcraft among the Bushmen and Hunter-Gatherers." *Anthropos* 87:83–107.

Gusinde, Martin
1963/64;   "Aus dem Geistesleben der Hukwe beim Caprivizipfel." *Journal*
1964/65   *S. W. A. Wissenschaftliche Gesellschaft* 18–19:35–42.

Hatfield, C. R., Jr.
1968   "The Nfumu in Tradition and Change: A Study of the Position of Religious Practitioners among the Sukuma of Tanzania, E.A." Ph.D. diss., The Catholic University of America, Anthropology Studies 12, Washington, D.C.

Hauge, Hans-Egil
1979   *Maasai Religion and Folklore.* Nairobi: City Printing Works.

Hurskainen, Arvi
1989   "The Epidemiological Aspect of Spirit Possession among the

Maasai of Tanzania." In *Culture, Experience and Pluralism: Essays on African Ideas of Illness and Healing,* ed. Anita Jacobson-Widding and David Westerlund, 139–50. Uppsala Studies in Cultural Anthropology 13. Stockholm: Almqvist & Wiksell International.

Katz, Richard
    1982   *Boiling Energy: Community and Healing among the Kalahari Kung.* Cambridge, Mass., and London: Harvard University Press.

Lee, Richard B.
    1968   "The Sociology of !Kung Bushman Trance Performances." In *Trance and Possession States,* ed. R. Prince, 35–54. Montreal: Bucke Memorial Society.
    1979   *The Dobe !Kung.* New York: Holt, Rinehard & Winston.

Lewis-Williams, J. David
    1981   *Believing and Seeing: Symbolic Meanings in Southern San Rock Paintings.* London: Academic Press.

Marshall, Lorna
    1962   "!Kung Bushman Religious Beliefs." *Africa* 32:221–52.
    1969   "The Medicine Dance of the !Kung Bushmen." *Africa* 39:347–81.
    1986   "Some Bushman Star Lore." In *Contemporary Studies on Khoisan: In Honour of Oswin Kohler on the Occasion of his 75th Birthday,* ed. R. Vossen and K. Keuthman, 169–204. Quellen Zur Khoisan-Forschung 5/2. Hamburg: Helmut Buske.

Merker, M.
    1904   *Die Masai: Ethnografische Monographie eines ostafrikanischen Semitenvolkes.* Berlin: Dietrich Reimer.

Mol, Frans
    1978   *Maa: A Dictionary of the Maasai Language and Folklore.* Nairobi: Marketing & Publishing Ltd.

Olsson, Tord
    1989   "Philosophy of Medicine." In *Culture, Experience and Pluralism: Essays on African Ideas of Illness and Healing,* ed. Anita Jacobson-Widding and David Westerlund, 235–46. Uppsala Studies in Cultural Anthropology 13. Stockholm: Alqvist & Wiksell International.

Schapera, Isaac
    1965   *The Khoisan Peoples of South Africa: Bushmen and Hottentots.* 1930. Reprint, London: Routledge & Kegan Paul.

Shostak, Marjorie
    1981   *Nisa: The Life and Words of a !Kung Woman.* Cambridge, Mass.: Harvard University Press.

Spencer, Paul
    1988   *The Maasai of Matapato: A Study of Rituals of Rebellion.* Blooming-

ton and Indianapolis: Indiana University Press in association with the International African Institute.

Steves, Guy W.
1990   "Contextualizing the Atonement for the Sukuma Tribe of Tanzania." M.A. thesis, Abilene Christian University, Abilene, Texas.

Tanner, Ralph E. S.
1958   "Ancestor Propitiation Ceremonies in Sukumaland, Tanganyika." *Africa* 28:225–31.
1959   "The Spirits of the Dead: An Introduction to the Ancestor Worship of the Sukuma of Tanganyika." *Anthropological Quarterly* 32:108–24.
1967   *Transition in African Beliefs: Traditional Religion and Christian Change: A Study in Sukumaland, Tanzania, East Africa.* Maryknoll, N.Y.: Orbis Books.
1970   *The Witch Murders in Sukumaland: A Sociological Commentary.* Crime in East Africa 4. Uppsala: Scandinavian Institute of African Studies.

Tcherkezoff, S.
1985   "The Expulsion of Illness and the Domestication of the Dead: A Case Study of the Nyamwezi of Tanzania." *History and Anthropology* 2:59–92.

Thurner, Ingrid
1983   *Die transzendenten und mystischen Wesen der San (Buschmänner): Eine religionsethnologische Analyse historischer Quellen,* Acta Ethnologica et Linguistica 56. Vienna: Fohrenau.

Voshaar, Jan
1979   "Tracing God's Walking Stick in Maa." Ph.D. thesis, Katholieke Universiteit, Nijmegen.

Westerlund, David
1989   "Pluralism and Change: A Comparative and Historical Approach to African Disease Etiologies." In *Culture, Experience and Pluralism: Essays on African Ideas of Illness and Healing,* ed. A. Jacobson-Widding and David Westerlund, 177–218, Uppsala Studies in Cultural Anthropology 13. Stockholm: Almqvist & Wiksell International.

Wyllie, Robert W.
1994   "Do the Effetu Really Believe that the Spirits Cause Illness? A Ghanaian Case Study." *Journal of Religion in Africa* 24:228–40.

8

Witchcraft and Society

M. F. C. BOURDILLON

Belief in Witchcraft

BELIEF IN WITCHCRAFT is widespread in Africa, as in many societies throughout the world. The basic belief is that certain people have special, unnatural powers to harm others, and that they use these powers in perverted ways that contradict the values or norms of society. Witchcraft by definition is thoroughly evil, and a witch is a person who practices witchcraft.

Different societies vary in the details of beliefs about what witches typically do, as they vary in their language about witchcraft. Most African languages have words that can appropriately be translated as "witch" and "witchcraft." And there are some general characteristics of witches and witchcraft that are widely cited in different societies.

Generally, witchcraft involves the reverse of normal values and behavior. Witches are typically believed to act secretly at night, instead of openly by day as honest people do, and to operate with the help of familiar animals of the night, such as hyenas and owls. The special powers of witches are often assumed to come from evil spirits that encourage the witches in their evil practices. Witches are typically associated with death and are often presumed to desecrate graves, to eat human flesh, and to kill people either for fun or to further their own powers. Witches reject kinship loyalties: people say that witches eat even their own kin, and the kin of witches are believed to be in as much danger as anyone. Often witches are believed to be sexually deviant: incest is commonly associated with witchcraft, and in some societies people assume that witches have some kind of sexual relationship with their spirits or animal familiars. Witches are often believed to work in groups or covens, which meet at night to conspire in their wicked plans, and to carry out their strange rituals. These rituals are assumed to include dancing naked, disturbing graves, eating human flesh, and other

176

activities that flout the values of society. Witches are believed to delight in evil for its own sake.

Witches do what others are afraid to do. Witches work in the dark, normally a time of danger. Witches kill and are assumed to be able to protect themselves from revenge. Witches commit incest and break other fundamental taboos that protect the coherence of society. Others are afraid to do such deeds for fear of supernatural punishment: witches are assumed to have special powers even with respect to the world of the ancestors. Witches break the rules of society with impunity and are assumed equally to break the rules of nature.

Witches are powerful and are able to keep their activities secret from outsiders. The more powerful and wicked the witch, the less likely it is that ordinary people will find empirical evidence of his or her activities. The only way to confirm that a person is a witch is through the oracles of someone who has access to even more powerful spirits or even more powerful magic. Because of its secret and antisocial nature, researchers generally cannot observe what witches do or learn from them their point of view.[1] Indeed, many researchers regard witchcraft as a figment of the imagination. Accounts of witchcraft come from popular stereotypes, which are in the public domain.

When a diviner confirms that someone is a witch, that person can do little to avoid the consequences. To deny the allegation would confirm that the witch is stubbornly bent on practicing evil. To concede to the allegation equally convicts a person. In many societies, people say that witches were always killed in the past, before colonial powers stopped the killing of witches, and even now, a convicted witch may be lynched or driven out of the community. It is not uncommon for a person convicted by an oracle of being a witch to commit suicide rather than face society with this characterization. But if a convicted witch is contrite and shows a desire to mend his or her ways, he or she may be ritually cleansed and accepted back into the community over time.

Among the Zande of the southern Sudan, the oracles concerning witchcraft were not made public (Evans-Pritchard 1937, 26–29). When someone dies and suspicions of witchcraft are confirmed by an oracle, the senior relative of the deceased would try to avenge the death through witchcraft by using vengeance magic against the witch. Sooner or later, some misfortune befalls the witch or his family, and the matter is assumed to be resolved.

Many colonial governments responded to the harm done to persons accused of witchcraft by banning both witchcraft and accusations of it. In practice, such legislation was normally used only to convict accusers and diviners, and in the eyes of many people simply served to defend witches against exposure and punishment. Many believed that witchcraft spread without restraint under such colonial protection. The problem remains of controlling the consequences of accusations without the scrutiny of empirical evidence, and many modern governments have maintained the relevant legislation, even if they use it with less rigidity.

Perhaps the problem is not fundamentally different from other forms of deviant behavior that disrupt social interaction. Suzette Heald (1986) compares suspicions of witchcraft among the Gisu of Kenya with suspicions of theft. Elderly impoverished men are often assumed to be witches. Similarly young men, who, against societal norms, delay getting married, are often suspected of being thieves and may occasionally be punished by being beaten to death. This is particularly the case if they are without adequate economic evidence, and because it lies outside the cognitive realm of imported legal systems.

Although the paradigm of witchcraft is evil, the term can be used without all the connotations we have just described. A person may use the term "witch" to connote a real witch who conforms to the paradigm I have just outlined. But the term may depict someone who only occasionally uses harmful magic for a particular reason (a sorcerer in classical anthropological terminology); this category is considered less capricious, less bent on evil, and is less feared than real witches. A sorcerer may act only on provocation, or perhaps the person is designated a witch because he or she simply tends to act secretly.[2] People can apply these different connotations to the term "witch" loosely and differently in different situations. So to call someone a witch is not a descriptive statement; rather, such a statement conveys loosely the negative and suspicious attitude of the speaker toward the person concerned. The term is vague and connotes simply general disapproval.

The term "witchcraft" can be applied even to actions that are not unambiguously wrong. A man might use medicines to protect his property from theft, in accordance with common practice in society. Another who believes he is suffering from such medicines may regard them as witchcraft, acts performed in secret to harm his ancestral spirits to punish rebellious young men who are threatening the coherence of the lineage. When a young man believes he is suffering as a consequence of such an invocation, he may regard this as witchcraft, and when such invocations by an elder become too frequent he may be regarded as a witch (see Middleton 1961, 226–28).

In some societies, traditional healers, who are experts in medicines and who often have the support of spiritual powers, are treated with a mixture of respect and fear. Those who have special powers to do good can use the same powers to harm people. I have heard the view expressed in Shona society in Zimbabwe that all traditional healers are potential witches—which is not to say that they all go dancing naked at night. Indeed, the person who holds such a position is likely to consult a traditional healer in time of need; but he will be sure to pay his fees promptly.

Traditional rulers are often associated with mystical power, including power to kill their enemies and to protect themselves. Some Korekore peoples in the northeast of Zimbabwe assume that members of the chiefly families use witchcraft against each other, and such activity is acceptable as long as the chief is able to rule effectively and for the good of the people. Similarly among the Mijikenda of Kenya, an exclusive secret society of elders commands fear and exercises power to harm or even to kill. This is considered to be a necessary part of maintaining order in society (Parkin 1985). Actions in one context might be judged to be thoroughly evil with all the connotations of witchcraft, and in another context would be viewed as necessary for society.

In all these cases, we find that the concept of witchcraft occurs in a context in which supernatural powers are believed to control society. The distinction between witchcraft and the work of the ancestors is not always clear. The basis of moral judgments that condemn particular actions as "witchcraft" is not always well defined. We return to the idea that the terms "witch" and "witchcraft" express an attitude of the speaker rather than describe a person or an action.

Although witchcraft is closely associated with moral outrage, it cannot simply be equated with moral wrong. Indeed, in some societies, it is said that a person can be a witch without knowing it. As we shall see when we discuss confessions, conscientious persons can fear that they have become witches when things go wrong. In these cases, witchcraft does not involve the moral responsibility of the witch.

Witchcraft is associated with misfortune, death, immorality, the night and darkness, certain dangerous animals, secrecy, power, spirits, caprice, and other things that threaten good social order. The term is neither exact nor analytic, and it does not distinguish between these very undesirable material disasters, and equally undesirable moral depravity. Like many powerful social symbols, its power rests not in any exact meaning but in the range of the connotations it evokes, any or all of which can be called into play on any particular occasion (see Sperber 1975, esp. 137).

Symbolic connotations are also at play in what witches are believed to be today. They desecrate graves, they consume human flesh, they are naked at night, they use symbols of their victims such as images or things that have once been in close contact with them. If we understand magic as action that uses symbols in an attempt to manipulate material events, witches use magic.

The Explanatory Power of Witchcraft

Some people ask why others believe in witchcraft. Those who live in societies where this belief is taken for granted wonder how anyone can deny the existence of witches and witchcraft. To them the evidence is clear. Certain people have been known to confess to witchcraft, and no one could confess to anything so terrible if they were not guilty. This point will be dealt with later. There are overbearing and arrogant people in society, whose confidence must be based on special powers. But most of all, misfortunes befall people for no apparent reason. Such inexplicable misfortunes seem to confirm the reality of witchcraft, especially if there are people around known to be hostile to the unfortunate persons.

In a society built around close personal relations, events are often understood in personal terms (see Horton 1982, 237). The understanding of disease and misfortune often relates closely to the social categories of the society concerned (see Harwood 1970). In such a society, it is not always easy to draw a clear distinction between material misfortunes and the moral blemishes of people.

Sometimes it is easy enough to understand why things go wrong. A lazy person gets poor crops because he has not done sufficient work in preparing the soil and weeding. People get venereal diseases through breaking sexual taboos. Sometimes it is clear why spirits might be displeased and bring sickness and other troubles to the people they should normally care for. But sometimes things go wrong when everyone has done their best, and this is a puzzle. If an explanation is to be found, it must be outside the realm of moral norms.

Witchcraft beliefs are in accordance with the experience of people who hold them, and they comprise rational explanations of empirical events. E. E. Evans-Pritchard, in his discussion of witchcraft beliefs among the Zande (1937, 65–69), gives the example of a granary being eaten by white ants, and collapsing while people were sitting under its shade. Everyone knows that it collapsed because it was weakened by termites. But why did it collapse just when those people were sitting under it?

A skilled wood carver chooses a hard piece of wood and carves it with care. In spite of his knowledge and his care, occasionally the wood splits. He has no explanation other than witchcraft. People brought up in a different way of thinking may talk about chance or the will of God: for people brought up to think in terms of witches, the question of why is answered in terms of witchcraft.

Death in particular is explained in terms of witchcraft in many societies. Sometimes people accept that an old person can die naturally, but the death of a young person disrupts the social relations of the family and their immediate social group. An explanation may be demanded to help people to come to terms with the tragedy. Where there has been open or suppressed conflict in the community, the malice of someone who simply delights in malice is an alternative explanation.

Members of a kinship group are united by ties that cannot easily be broken, and this demands various kinds of social cooperation. Similarly, a small village of small-scale farmers tied together by the land is expected to maintain good social relations with each other. When certain people are unpleasant through being overbearing or boastful, or perhaps particularly successful, others may not normally show hostility toward them. If, however, unpleasant persons have put themselves outside the moral realm by practicing witchcraft, the normal social rules do not apply, and any such person can even be driven out of the community or even killed. Belief in witchcraft provides an explanation for the behavior of such persons and justification for taking action against them.

Witchcraft explains social as well as material problems. I have already pointed out that incest is sometimes associated with witchcraft. Witches have no respect for human life. Witches have no respect for sacred things relating to the ancestors or the spirit guardians of the people. Witchcraft in its extreme form threatens the very basis of social existence.

Belief in witchcraft provides a way of thinking about things, a way of ordering and understanding things that come into the experience of believers. Like any other belief system, witchcraft cannot easily be proved or disproved by empirical evidence. Evans-Pritchard (1937, 63–83) points out that the Zande were able to reason excellently within the system, even at times empirically testing particular oracles; but he argued that they could not reason outside the system since they had no other conceptual framework in which to think (see also Gluckman 1960, 81–108). It is very difficult, and very rare, for individuals to challenge the whole system that provides their framework for understanding the world. More frequently they simply modify the system slightly to cope with particular experiences.

Whatever outsiders may think of the reality of a witch's powers, in the perspective of insiders, witchcraft is a social reality that cannot easily be laid aside. Since the explanatory function of the belief complements, rather than contradicts, the material explanations of empiricism and science, belief in witchcraft does not necessarily fall away with education. Such beliefs are embedded in societies and cultures.

When Christian missionaries and colonial governments tried to suppress accusations of witchcraft, many people believed that they were protecting evil witches. Belief in witchcraft affects, both for good and for bad, the ways in which people understand the world and the ways in which they relate to each other. Witchcraft is a key issue in the spirituality of many Africans. The curing of witches and the eradication of witchcraft are also key issues in many independent Christian churches in Africa. Even the older established churches take seriously the issue of witchcraft (see Lagerwerf 1987, 14–36).

Witchcraft and Social Tension

Some attention will be paid to a number of sociological issues relating to beliefs about witchcraft. My purpose is not to dismiss the beliefs as simply social epiphenomena, but to understand how they relate to particular and different social contexts.

Witchcraft beliefs and accusations invariably reflect areas of particular tension in society. This is not surprising when we remember that the dominant theme in beliefs about witches is that they harm other people. Generally, people do not suspect others of using witchcraft unless there is tension.

Concern about witches and witchcraft is particularly common among groups of people who are forced to live together and to cooperate, and who have no alternative ways of dealing with conflicts that arise. Throughout the world, witchcraft appears in small-scale agricultural societies, in which people are bound together by their ties to the land. Often they are in competition for the land that binds them together. In such societies, mounting tensions between individual members of groups cannot easily be resolved by keeping apart. This is particularly the case among groups of kin who are not supposed to bring their conflicts openly to a public court (people know that witches kill even their own kin). In contemporary African societies, we often find suspicions of witchcraft between co-workers, who are forced together by their need for employment and who compete for favors and promotion from their employers.

On the other hand, concern about witchcraft is rare, if it exists at all, among people who are highly mobile. People who survive on hunting or on pastoralism may believe in witchcraft, but specific accusations of witchcraft are rare. When misfortune occurs in such societies, people may attribute it to some spiritual power, perhaps resulting from the victim's moral faults or conflict with elders; but it is rare to find an explicit accusation of witchcraft. When tensions occur in a social group of this kind, it is easy for the people concerned to part company long before either party puts the other beyond the realm of human morality (see Baxter 1972).

In large cities, people necessarily live close together, but they do not have to maintain close ties with those who live physically close to them (see Marwick 1970). In a rural village, you are expected to be on good terms with everyone: the whole community meets and exchanges pleasantries at social gatherings. In a large city, there are too many people for anyone to maintain friendly relations with everyone, and you can choose those with whom you wish to socialize. When tensions arise between two people, it is usually possible for them to avoid each other. Moreover, many relationships are simple and relate to a specific function: in a city you do not have to socialize with the people from whom you buy your food as you do in a rural village. We still find suspicions of witchcraft among urban co-workers, but we expect witchcraft accusations to become less frequent in the cities.

We still find suspicions of witchcraft in groups of kin and in-laws who may be forced to live together in the absence of alternative accommodation.[3] We still find people thinking in terms of witchcraft if they have grown up in a society in which witchcraft is a dominant theme. But suspicions are often vague and generalized: people fear that there are witches around without making specific accusations (see Mitchell 1965). Even when suspicions are specific and divination is sought, this is not likely to result in a public accusation. Generally, we expect the absence of specific accusations in urban areas to result in witchcraft beliefs becoming slowly less dominant in the cities.

One study, which compared rural and urban Xhosa in South Africa, confirmed this trend (Hammond-Tooke 1970). Urban and rural Xhosa showed little difference in attributing certain misfortunes to ancestors, reflecting the fact that the kinship groups controlled by the ancestors remained important in the city. But city Xhosa were less likely to attribute their misfortunes to witchcraft than were their rural counterparts. When the ancestors were not involved, city people were prepared sometimes to say that misfortune resulted simply from chance or bad luck, whereas rural folk invariably suspected witchcraft.

This change may be partly explained in terms of the contact of urban people, through education and through other forms of communication, with a wider world and a wider range of explanatory systems. Through such contact, urban people have a range of explanatory frameworks to choose from. But even educated people in small agricultural communities often refer to witchcraft in some form.[4] Social changes seem more significant than education in changing people's beliefs.

In societies where witchcraft beliefs are dominant, we find variations that reflect particular areas of tension or concern in each society. The Nyakyusa of southern Tanzania, for example, traditionally believed that witches were people who lusted after meat and milk (see Wilson 1951). They said that witches gnaw at the insides of people thus causing their death, and at the udders of cows causing them to dry up. The main evidence for attacks by witches came from dreams, or from waking up at night in a cold sweat. When people suspected witchcraft, it was always someone in the village community who was suspected and accused, often unrelated neighbors and only very rarely kin. Nyakyusa on the whole lived in villages of age-mates, away from their kin. Wealth, and cattle in particular, was owned by lineage groups. There were conflicting ideals of conserving wealth for the lineage and dispensing liberal hospitality to one's neighbors. The belief in witchcraft reflected a fear of hungry and envious neighbors conspiring to dissipate the family wealth.

The Pondo of South Africa, on the other hand, believed that a witch always works with a familiar—a fabulous hairy being with exaggerated sexual characteristics, and always of the sex opposite to that of the witch (see Wilson 1951). Envy aroused by conspicuous success was said to be the cause of attacks among the Pondo, just as it was among the Nyakyusa. Among the Pondo, the basis of beliefs about attacks of witchcraft was dress, sexual dreams being particularly likely to be interpreted in this way. Unlike Nyakyusa society, witchcraft accusations among the Pondo most frequently occurred between mother and daughter-in-law, sometimes between fellow-workers, and only very occasionally between unrelated neighbors. Monica Wilson makes a number of suggestions about why the Pondo beliefs about witchcraft focus on sexual deviance. One of them refers to problems facing young wives who move into an extended family and compete with their mothers-in law for the husband's resources. A mother, on finding that her newly married son no longer has as much time as before to cut firewood for her, may blame the inconvenience to herself on a daughter-in-law who is suspected of illicitly using up her son's energies.

A study of the Nupe of northern Nigeria in the 1940s showed that, in this society, witches were virtually always assumed to be women, unlike among neighboring peoples, where men or women could equally be suspected of witchcraft (Nadel 1952, 18–22). Among the Nupe, witches were believed to work in organized groups, similar to the groups of Nupe women traders. This belief reflected an antagonism between the sexes in Nupe society, arising from the men's perception that women were neglecting their traditional subservient role in the family and home in order to participate in successful itinerant trading.

In societies where divorce is easy and marital relations are unstable, such as the matrilineal Cewa of Zambia, accusations of witchcraft between husband and wife are rare: if tension arises, the spouses simply separate (Marwick 1965, 146–67). There are more cases of persons accusing their kin of bewitching their spouses. If the husband and wife get on well together, tensions readily arise between the close kin of the wife and the close kin of the husband over how much attention he gives to each group. These people are unable to break up the marriage so easily, and suspicions of witchcraft may arise. In societies in which marriages are bound together by large and complex bride-price payments, divorce is not so simple, and husbands may more readily accuse their wives of witchcraft.

About half the accusations of witchcraft among the Cewa occurred within the matrilineal group, and most of these between members of different segments. On the one hand, there was the Cewa ideal of keeping a large family harmoniously together. On the other hand, when the founder who holds the family together dies, junior segments may balk at remaining under the authority of the head of the senior branch of the family. Unity is no longer easily maintained when the family becomes unmanageably large. If they accuse the new family head of bewitching his predecessor in order to inherit his position, they have a reason for hiving off and maintaining their autonomy. For the Cewa, witchcraft explains why the ideal of large extended families does not work in practice.

In many contemporary African societies, stories circulate about witchcraft involving businessmen trying to make more money through magic, particularly magic involving the murder of innocent victims to provide parts for their potions. Such stories are occasionally supported by empirical evidence brought before a court of justice, and they reflect the ruthlessness of economic competition in an urban environment. People also fear witchcraft in their places of work, where rivals for promotion are assumed to be unscrupulous about who practices witchcraft, and how they do it.

Beliefs about witches may also reflect conflicts of values or expectations. I mentioned the problems of young wives among the Pondo. In many matrilineal societies, young wives are under suspicion when they first move into the extended families of their husbands. This is especially the case when no children appear, or when children are aborted or die in the womb or shortly after birth. When the husband's family has handed over considerable wealth in order to have a wife who can bear children for the lineage, failure to produce healthy children suggests that their resources have been wasted. Although she is not meeting the expectations of her in-laws, the young woman may have a pleasant personality, making it difficult to send her away in anger. If, however, it can be assumed that secretly she is a witch who eats her own children, this is good reason to break up the marriage.

In a witch-cleansing movement among the Ibibio of Nigeria in the late

1970s, one class of people likely to be identified as witches comprised the very wealthy and successful people in a time of economic hardship and decline. Others, and particularly their rivals, assumed that they achieved their success through witchcraft. Another group of people who were identified as witches were very poor old men: these were people who traditionally should be respected on account of their age, but who commanded little respect in a materialistic society on the grounds of their poverty. This conflict between age and poverty was resolved by those people who claimed that such old men must have spent their wealth acquiring witchcraft. On the basis of such an assumption, the elderly poor could be rejected and despised.[5] Similarly, among the Gisu of Kenya, impoverished old men are often accused of witchcraft (just as poor young men are often accused of theft and may be brutally punished for it; see Heald 1986).

An obsession with witchcraft can reflect very generalized tensions in a society. Meyer Fortes (1987, 212–15) attributed the readiness to think in terms of witchcraft among the Ashanti of Ghana to the conflicting patterns of authority and care in which children grow up. Ashanti children have divided loyalties between their father's lineage on one side and their mother's lineage on the other, resulting in an insecure sense of identity. Witchcraft operates like a self-destructive power within the close matrilineal kinship ties of the Ashanti. Fortes contrasts this with the much more stable family structure of the neighboring matrilineal Tallensi, who do not frequently refer to witchcraft and who push witchcraft to the periphery in their understanding of events in their lives.

Men and Women

The example of the Nupe raises the question of gender and witchcraft. Among the Nupe, only women become witches. Men provide guardians against witches. Successful female traders become wealthier than their farming husbands and take over some of the economic responsibilities traditionally attributed to men in this male-dominated society. Moreover, trading women rebel against their traditional role of staying at home and bearing children for their husbands' lineages. Accusations of witchcraft and rituals to remove witchcraft are controlled by men and serve to assert the traditional values of male authority.

Gender is not always so dominant a theme in witchcraft beliefs. Indeed, S. F. Nadel contrasts the Nupe with the neighboring Gwari, among whom men and women could equally be suspected of witchcraft, and among whom trading by women was less well developed. Nevertheless, in many societies dominated by men, women are more frequently suspected of witchcraft than men (see Bourdillon 1991, 200). We have already pointed out how in some societies, a young wife coming into an extended family is likely to fall under suspicion.

Among the Cewa, men are accused of witchcraft more often than women. The Cewa use a single word for the two categories. But they distinguish between real witches, in whom the power and the practices are innate, habitual, and capricious (acting even without any prior quarrel with the victim), and sorcerers, who practice their art and kill only in situations of conflict and for a particular purpose. We find that men form a large majority of people accused of sorcery; those accused of real and capricious witchcraft, however, are mostly women (Marwick 1965, 102).

In traditions about the founding of some chiefly dynasties among the Shona, men were the leaders in war and politics, but the men often depended on their womenfolk, particularly their sisters, for mystical "medicines" with which to destroy their opponents. These legends reflect the more subtle influence exercised by women when formal authority is in the hands of men (see Bourdillon 1987, 53f.). A similar argument could be made concerning the association of women with witchcraft.

The Social Effects of Beliefs in Witchcraft

One obvious social function of belief in witchcraft is social control and the preservation of order. At the simplest level, as part of the process of socialization, adults tell children not to behave in certain ways for fear of being attacked by a witch, or for fear of appearing to be a witch. Belief in witchcraft can also support certain types of authority in society.

I mentioned that among the Nupe, men are assigned the role of defending people against witchcraft. They are supposed to do this through the powers of their secret society. Anyone who rebels against the authority of senior men might find the protection of such men withdrawn and so become vulnerable to the whims of any witch.

Among the Nyakyusa, a witch is believed to operate through having a python in his or her belly. Village headmen also have pythons in their bellies, but these are to protect those under their care from attacks of witchcraft. I have mentioned chiefs among the Shona and elders among the Mijikenda who use powers akin to witchcraft to maintain their positions and their authority.

Among the Zande, the king controls the ultimate oracle that reveals who is and who is not a witch. Zande people assert that the king's oracle cannot make a mistake, and it never accuses a member of the royal lineage of witchcraft.

The use of accusations of witchcraft to justify the splitting of unmanageably large groups can also be considered to facilitate social order. Such accusations enable people to overcome the conflict between the ideological ideal of staying together as the population grows and the practical desirability of keeping populations scattered in farming communities. Alternatively, we could argue that beliefs in witchcraft have prevented people from seeing the practical impediments to their ideals of ever-increasing lineage or village populations. In their view, the ideal does not work because some people are wicked.

Similarly, accusations of witchcraft justify people in breaking off social relations that have become intolerably strained. Equally, such accusations can increase the social tensions that have arisen in a community and make them intolerable. While suspicions and accusations of witchcraft usually reflect areas of social tension, it is also possible that suspicions of witchcraft create tension when things go wrong and exacerbate tensions that already exist. In any case, an accusation of witchcraft changes the nature of a conflict. An accusation of witchcraft makes a moral statement about the world, and about the rights of individuals to have a place within the moral universe.

A young man from a rural family had excelled above his brothers and sisters. He had done very well at school and had gone on to university. He was the family's pride and hope for the future. In the course of his studies he developed an infection. He reacted badly to the antibiotics that were administered, and he died quickly. Tragedy had already hit the family. Now the family delayed the burial while they tried to find out who was the guilty witch responsible for the death. The young man's mother was divined to be the witch and was sent out of the family.

I do not know what family tensions may have lain behind this divination, but it seems likely that the suspicions were created by the sudden death of the young man. The belief in witchcraft diverted attention that might have been more fruitfully paid to the treatment the young man received from medical personnel, and instead created a further split in the bereaved family.

Eradication of Witchcraft

Since death and misfortune in so many societies are attributed to witchcraft, it is not surprising that from time to time such societies try to eliminate all witches and witchcraft. Apart from sporadic accusations of witchcraft, often in response to particular misfortunes, occasionally a community may become so obsessed with witchcraft that they try to discover and eliminate all witchcraft in the community. In such a witch-hunt, previously unsuspected people may be accused of witchcraft.

Witchcraft eradication movements have been a regular feature of many African societies. A series of witch-cleansing movements spreading over eastern and southern Africa were recorded during colonial times (see Richards 1935; Marwick 1950; Willis 1968). They continue in various forms in modern Africa: in one such movement in the Cross River State of Nigeria in the late 1970s, several persons were killed or driven to suicide (Offiong 1991). Usually such hunts occur in times of trouble of some kind, such as economic recession, when people begin to think that the sources of their troubles are malicious persons in their communities. The hunts are consequently popular movements, in which people hope to rid themselves of the sources of their troubles. But they often involve violence to the suspected witches.

A relatively benign form of witchcraft eradication is a common theme in many independent churches, in which accused witches may be treated sympathetically as unfortunate persons possessed by evil spirits and therefore not responsible for their actions. Prophets claim to see witches, and then to exorcise the evil spirits from them, providing the kind of therapy frequently associated with possession trances.

There are several general characteristics of witch-hunts. First, they respond to the fears and troubles of the time. The early movements in eastern and southern Africa corresponded to economic crises and crises caused by rapid social change. The movement in the Cross River State of Nigeria occurred when the oil boom was slowing down and the flow of money into society was rapidly drying up. People's expectations of rapidly increasing wealth were being frustrated. In Zimbabwe, such hunts occurred immediately after independence, when people found that they were not being given all the good things they had been promised while fighting the war. Witch-hunts occurred again when three years of drought added to the country's financial problems, which included rapid inflation and no parallel increases in available income. In a society where events are largely understood in personal terms, people are ready to suspect personal malice as the cause of their frustrations. The social environment is ripe for a witch-hunt to gather momentum.

Second, a leader is required and believed to have special powers to reveal witches through divination and to overpower the witches. Usually these leaders charge considerable fees for their services to communities. Their supposed supernatural powers make them practically immune from rebuttal by the people who are accused.

Third, witch-hunts are to some extent self-validating: accused witches are believed to be thoroughly evil, to conduct all their witchcraft in secret, and to have special powers to conceal their activities from investigation. The refusal to confess by some witches is taken as a sign of their malice and their determination not to reveal the secrets of their cults. If a person revealed and accused by a witch-finder refuses to confess, this is taken as a sign not of innocence but of obstinacy, and such a person is liable to be beaten or even killed. Naturally, under such pressure, some people do confess in order to escape the severest punishment, and this is cited as further evidence of the justness of the hunt.

Those who are accused are usually people who are for some reason disliked by the community as a whole. In the Cross River State, we have noticed that wealthy people and the elderly poor were particularly vulnerable. One movement among the Fipa of Tanzania occurred when there was considerable opposition between those who wanted to conserve traditional values and the younger group who were adopting new political and religious ideas and new ways of life, and also when there was a shortage of accessible land for young men: old people were suspected of bewitching the frustrated youth of village communities (Willis 1968).

There are other means of validating accusations. The witch-finder may go into the homes of accused witches and produce charms and medicines that are supposed to have been used for witchcraft. No amount of denial by the accused person can convince others that these were only for healing or protective purposes, even though most of the population may in fact use protective charms and certain traditional medicines.

Although any society may contain individuals who readily break its most fundamental norms, in a witch-hunt innocent people may suffer and have their lives ruined in the mass hysteria of a community that believes it has found a means of ridding itself of all its fundamental tensions and frustrations. Immediately after a witch-finding exercise, there might be for a time a state of euphoria as people expect an end to their problems, a euphoria that is short-lived as problems continue to emerge. There are parallels between witch-hunts and millenarian movements, which promise the coming of a new order in which there will be no wrong. Indeed, certain witchcraft eradication movements emphasize moral revival and might be classified as religious movements (see, e.g., Marwick 1950).

People believe in witchcraft because things happen that they can explain in no other way: within their view of the world, the evidence points to witchcraft taking place. The symbols of witchcraft provide an explanatory framework within which people intellectually cope with the frustrations that puzzle them. Witchcraft seems to explain the problems, and a witch-hunt seems to provide a solution to them. But beliefs in witchcraft are not precise, and the vagueness of the beliefs often results in a failure to look for the material causes of the problems facing the community.

Confessions and Evidence

One form of evidence supporting beliefs in witchcraft is the fact that occasionally people confess to practicing witchcraft. People argue that no one could confess lightly or falsely to something so evil. Occasionally empirical evidence is brought to support the confession. In Zimbabwe since independence, there have been several cases of persons who could show physical evidence of the rites they had performed with others in a witchcraft cult.[6] A typical pattern is that a person gets drawn into a cult, possibly with the motive of getting medicines for personal or protective use. They are sworn to secrecy and are slowly drawn into more and more compromising practices. Eventually they are asked to kill a relative through witchcraft for one of the cult rites, and find it very difficult to extricate themselves. In such circumstances a person might confess to a powerful traditional healer or a witch-finder in the area, hoping for protection from others of the coven. But confessions of this nature are rare, in comparison with those in which no concrete evidence of witchcraft can be produced.

Deviance of this nature is not fundamentally different from other forms of deviance found in many modern cities, in which people are drawn into drugs, for example, and through addiction into crime in fringe groups. The cultural idiom of witchcraft and the rewards it promises are different; but in each case we can understand how some people may be drawn into practices that run against the norms of society.

The point about confession of such deviant behavior is that the deviant admits he or she has done wrong and so reaffirms the societal values that they have transgressed. The classic illustration of this principle is the religious practice of confession, in which individuals confess their faults with the intention of correcting them: even if the faults occur again, at least the ideal of correcting them is maintained. So societies prefer criminals to confess to their crimes and express regret. We have learned, however, that a confession made under duress cannot be conclusive evidence of a crime without further corroborating proof. Even without apparent duress, people with psychological disorders have been known to confess to crimes they never committed. If a witch confesses and repents, the accusers and the punishment appear justified. To this end, they may demand a confession, but such confessions, especially when made under duress, need not be evidence that the witchcraft has in fact been practiced.

At a different level, certain people accept the implications of witchcraft in order to gain power in a community. Such a person might use threatening language and might avoid making any denial of witchcraft, in order to inspire fear. The motivation for such an attitude is obvious, and people rightly condemn it but the attitude is not evidence that the person in fact practices witchcraft. Similarly, a person may threaten physical violence to get his way without in fact ever being violent.

Some confessions are based on the belief that a person can be a witch without knowing it. A person who is unsure of himself but believes in the system of divination may be surprised to find himself pointed out as a witch. Nevertheless he may accept the divination and confess as the first step in the process of being cured and returning to a normal place in society.

Such a confession may be spontaneous. This is illustrated by the case of a young woman in Nigeria whose first child had died young and whose second child was mysteriously becoming ill. The mother was extremely worried and began to fear that she herself was in some way to blame. This was a time when witch-finders were identifying many witches in neighboring villages, and she eventually decided that she must be a witch. She approached a witch-finder of her own accord in order to confess and seek a cure. The local people took this as further evidence that there were all sorts of unlikely people practicing witchcraft in their communities; but the mother was concerned about the life and health of a child, and this contradicts the typical idea of a witch. It seems more useful to explain the woman's behavior in terms of anxiety and a guilt complex expressed in the idiom of witchcraft. Even in such a spontaneous case, we cannot accept confession as conclusive evidence of crime.

M. J. Field (1960, 149–200) presents a number of cases from among the Ashanti of Ghana of women seeking healing either because they believe they have become witches against their will, or because they are afraid of becoming witches. Field links these cases to patterns of clinical depression sometimes related to personality traits and sometimes to external pressures. A normally conscientious woman finds she can no longer work; she cannot sleep and cannot sit still; her mind becomes restless. Then she knows, or fears, that she has become no good and must be a witch, deserving to be killed. For the woman, the evidence of witchcraft is there; for an outsider, the evidence can be interpreted according to another paradigm.

In some West African societies, such as the Banyang of Cameroon, people do not normally accuse each other of witchcraft (Ruel 1970; see also Wyllie 1973, among the Effutu of Ghana). When misfortune occurs, and particularly serious illness that threatens life, the stricken person is pressured to look for the cause in their own actions, particularly the use of animal familiars to harm others. Malcolm Ruel cites cases in which persons confessed to such activities shortly before dying, in the hope that confession might relieve the sickness. Alternatively, when a diviner cites a familiar animal as a cause for misfortune, the person concerned may refrain from denying knowledge of the animal. Such a denial would not in any case receive credence against the diviner's word. In such cases, again we see confessions arising from social pressure.

Finally, there are very rare instances of confessions by individuals or groups of the bizarre rites associated with witchcraft. In one case, rites included dancing naked at night and playing football with the heads of sleeping persons. The head would be returned to the person before he or she awoke and the victim would know nothing about the sport (see, e.g., Crawford 1967, 44–59). There is no evident motive either for such rites or for their confessions, and psychosis is as likely an explanation of the confessions as anything else.

The point is that confession may be an indication of witchcraft practices, but it is not in itself proof. One has to look very carefully at the circumstances of the confession and at corroborating evidence.

Conclusion

Although we may be skeptical about the evidence of confessions, witchcraft remains a reality for many African peoples. The denial of the beliefs by governments and religious people does not eliminate them. It would be useful to summarize the social realities behind the beliefs.

In most societies, there are a few thoroughly antisocial individuals who reject the norms of the society in which they live, even to the extent of sadistically delighting in harming others. But such persons are rare, and normally we need psychology or psychiatry to understand such people. If in any situation there is evidence that such deviant people are common, then we need to examine what is wrong with society as a whole rather than simply condemn the individuals.

These extremely antisocial people may try to further their aims through the occult powers of witchcraft. These practices are naturally regarded as criminal, and it seems reasonable to treat such practices, when they come to light, as criminal in modern courts. Occasionally, evidence has come to light showing that such sorcery has included murder and the use of parts of the human body. This kind of evidence is, however, very rare and cannot adequately explain accusations of witchcraft.

Occasional empirical evidence has come to light of individuals or groups taking part in bizarre rites in the practice of witchcraft, including the desecration of graves, the murder of children and even cannibalism. Again, such evidence is rare and cannot explain common suspicions of witchcraft.

People can die from witchcraft. Even some Western doctors, who are increasingly seeing the importance of a person's mental state to bodily health, have admitted that a person who believes he is bewitched may give up hope and die, with no observable physical cause of death. Whether or not the powers of a witch can harm someone other than through fear remains a matter of belief.

Especially in situations of social tension, accusations of witchcraft may become common and witchcraft beliefs may become prominent in people's minds. Such accusations are the result of increasing frustration, misfortune, and suspicion.

Finally, we cannot deny disease, death, and other misfortunes that people interpret as resulting from witchcraft. The events that people interpret in terms of witchcraft are real, as is the experience of people accustomed to such interpretations.

I have argued that witchcraft accusations result largely from social conflict when people are forced to live together, particularly conflicts arising from contradictions between ideals and reality. This is not to deny that in such situations people may more readily attempt to practice witchcraft. But, as we saw at the beginning of this chapter, witchcraft is a vague and loose term, defying exact definition and defying empirical proof. Too often an accusation of witchcraft prevents the participants from facing up to the true and material nature of the social problems that confront them. Suspicions of witchcraft may enable people to cope with tense relations, but it does this only by severing them through special separation or social avoidance. Such suspicions never heal damaged relations: they remove the damage only by destroying the relations.

Notes

1. A partial exception is Paul Stoller, whose apprenticeship into traditional magic among the Songhay of Niger brought him into contact with harmful magic (sorcery rather than witchcraft). See Stoller and Oakes 1987.

2. G. L. Chavunduka lists a variety of uses of the term "witch" in Zimbabwe (1980, 132–34).

3. The research of Mary Hull, not yet published, reveals cases of such suspicion among urban residents in Zimbabwe.

4. See, e.g., Favret-Saada 1978, on a small farming community in France.

5. This movement is described in Offiong 1991. The point about poor old men

being accused, however, comes from oral information I received at the time from students living in affected areas.

6. This information comes from as yet unpublished research by G. L. Chavunduka. Such witches hoped for protection and support from the Zimbabwe Traditional Healers' Association, which had government support, and of which Professor Chavunduka was president.

References

Baxter, P. T. W.
  1972   "Absence makes the heart grow fonder: Some suggestions why witchcraft accusations are rare among East African Pastoralists." In *The Allocation of Responsibility,* ed. M. Gluckman. Manchester: Manchester University Press.
Bourdillon, M. F. C.
  1987   *The Shona Peoples: An Ethnography of the Contemporary Shona with Special Reference to Their Religion.* 3rd ed. Gweru: Mambo Press.
  1991   *Religion and Society: A Text for Africa.* Gweru: Mambo Press.
Chavunduka, G. L.
  1980   "Witchcraft and the Law in Zimbabwe." *Zambezia* 8, no. 2:129–47.
Crawford, J. R.
  1967   *Witchcraft and Sorcery in Rhodesia.* London: Oxford University Press for the International African Institute.
Evans-Pritchard, E. E.
  1937   *Witchcraft, Oracles and Magic amongst the Azande.* Oxford: Clarendon Press.
Favret-Saada, J.
  1978   *Deadly Words: Witchcraft in the Bocage.* Cambridge: Cambridge University Press.
Field, M. J.
  1960   *Search for Security: An Ethno-psychiatric Study of Rural Ghana.* London: Faber & Faber.
Fortes, M.
  1987   *Religion, Morality and the Person: Essays on Tallensi Religion.* Cambridge: Cambridge University Press.
Gluckman, M.
  1960   *Custom and Conflict in Africa.* Oxford: Blackwell.
Hammond-Tooke, D.
  1970   "Urbanization and the Interpretation of Misfortune." *Africa* 40, no. 1:25–38.

Harwood, A.
   1970   *Witchcraft, Sorcery, and Social Categories among the Safwa.* London: Oxford University Press for the International African Institute.Heald, S.
   1986   "Witches and Thieves: Deviant Motivations in Gisu Society." *Man* 21, no. 1:65–78.

Horton, R.
   1982   "Tradition and Modernity Revisited." In *Rationality and Relativism,* ed. M. Hollis and S. Lukes. Oxford: Blackwell.

Lagerwerf, L.
   1987   *Witchcraft, Sorcery and Spirit Possession: Pastoral Responses in Africa.* Gweru: Mambo Press.

Marwick, M. G.
   1950   "The Bwanali-Mpulumutsi Anti-witchcraft Movement." *Africa* 20:100–112.
   1965   *Sorcery in its Social Setting: A Study of the Northern Rhodesian Cewa.* Manchester: Manchester University Press.
   1970   "The Decline of Witch-beliefs in Differentiated Societies." In *Witchcraft and Sorcery,* ed. M. Marwick. Harmondsworth: Penguin.

Middleton, J.
   1961   *Lugbara Religion.* London: Oxford University Press.

Mitchell, J. C.
   1965   "The Meaning in Misfortune for Urban Africans." In *African Systems of Thought,* ed. M. Fortes and G. Dieterlen. London: Oxford University Press for the International African Institute.

Nadel, S. F.
   1952   "Witchcraft in Four African Societies." *American Anthropologist* 54:18–29.

Offiong, D. A.
   1991   *Witchcraft, Sorcery, Magic and Social Order among the Ibibio of Nigeria.* Enugu: Fourth Dimension Publishing Co.

Parkin, D.
   1985   "Entitling Evil: Muslims and Non-Muslims in Coastal Kenya." In *The Anthropology of Evil,* ed. D. Parkin. Oxford: Blackwell.

Richards, A. I.
   1935   "A Modern Movement of Witchfinders." *Africa* 8, no. 4:448–61.

Ruel, M.
   1970   "Were-Animals and the Introverted Witch." In *Witchcraft Confessions and Accusations,* ed. M. Douglas. London: Tavistock.

Sperber, D.
   1975   *Rethinking Symbolism.* Translated by A. L. Morton. Cambridge: Cambridge University Press.

Stoller, P., and C. Oakes
1987   *In Sorcery's Shadow: A Mmoir of Apprenticeship among the Songhay of Niger.* Chicago/London: University of Chicago Press.

Willis, R. G.
1968   "The Kamcape Movement." *Africa* 38, no. 1:1–25.

Wilson, M.
1951   "Witch-beliefs and Social Structure." *American Journal of Sociology* 56:307–13.

Wyllie, R. W.
1973   "Introspective Witchcraft among the Effutu of Southern Ghana." *Man* 8:74–79.

Mami Water in African Religion and Spirituality

KATHLEEN O'BRIEN WICKER

ADAPTABILITY, FLEXIBILITY, TOLERANCE, and openness are distinguishing characteristics of African cultures and their religions and spiritualities.[1] These characteristics differentiate African spiritual traditions from Western religions, where faith usually involves acceptance of an articulated set of beliefs posited as absolute truths. Within African religions, however, religion and life are co-extensive. "Fixity of identity is only sought in situations of instability and disruption, of conflict and change" (Young 1995, 4).

Water divinities and spirits are arguably the most adaptable, flexible, and innovative of all African divinities, since fluidity is of the essence of their being (Opoku 1978, 60–65; Horton 1993, 217–19). They are characterized by shifting dispositions, genders, and representations. This dispositional fluidity is probably why many Africans have an ambivalent attitude toward these divinities and spirits. They are, on the one hand, considered beneficent providers of the bounty associated with water, especially fish, but more generally with riches of all kinds: knowledge of healing herbs, spiritual wisdom, creative inspiration, children, beauty in women, gold and gems, success in business. Conversely, they are also capricious spirits who, if offended, could cause disasters by drowning people who are attracted to water, capsizing their boats, rendering them childless, or driving them mad.

The ambiguous nature of water divinities is reflected also in their gender identities and representations. Originally hermaphroditic, they are now more commonly portrayed as male–female pairs. They attract devotees of the same or of the opposite sex. They also assume a number of different nonhuman forms, including the rainbow, python, crocodiles, snakes, and fish. The major symbolic value of water divinities and their representations in African cultures is to express the possibility of bridging worlds. Water divinities demonstrate by their very nature the intimate connection between the divine, the human, and the natural worlds. They express the continuity of life among those not yet born, the living, and the living-

198

timeless. They symbolize the discourse between "the empirical and the meta-empirical worlds" (Akyeampong and Obeng 1996), which is the essence of African spirituality.

African cultures are open and tolerant. They frequently assimilate new traditions into their spiritual strand social systems. They also valorize and reaffirm their traditions through a process called assemblage, in which they accrete new elements from nontraditional sources, often through war and marriage (Blier 1995a, 23–54; 1995b, 75–79). While assimilation may occur simply as the result of exposure to new traditions, intentional religious assimilation and accretion are strategies for obtaining or negotiating power in the spiritual and material worlds. The strategic functions which the process serves may be as fundamental as securing basic survival needs or as pervasive as coping with the realities of modernism produced by colonialism and postcolonialism.

The assimilated or accreted traditions may come from other African communities or from foreign traditions which reach Africa. The old Dahomey state was well known for the practice of enriching its own culture in both ways. More recently, Paul Gilroy (1993, 1–40) has described the process of mutual interaction between Africa and the African Diaspora, which results in syncretistic cultural expressions he calls "Black Atlantic" productions. Colonizing cultures have also afforded Africans the material from which they create a *métissage*, a "braiding" together of diverse elements, or produce what have been called hybridized or creolized cultures (Lionnet 1989, 1–29; Young 1995, 1–28). Such cultural productions function both transformatively and subversively in relation to the traditions which constitute them (Gilroy 1993).

One result of the creolization of African water divinities can be seen in the production of Mami Water. Mami Water is the name applied by Africans to a class of female and male water divinities or spirits that have accreted elements from several European, New World, and Indian cultural traditions. The *métissage* constructed by combining these cultural elements with the traditional African water divinities began as early as the fifteenth century. It defined itself specifically as Mami Water, probably by the end of the nineteenth century. But the process did not end then. Mami Water is an evolving cultural production which continues to be enriched by new elements.

Cultural Strands in Mami Water

The cultural exchanges and accretions that produced Mami Water occurred in a variety of times and places and had the complex cumulative effect of creating a distinctive new tradition. The process of teasing apart its various cultural strands, which will be attempted here, is an effort to reveal the cultural complexity of the Mami Water tradition and the process that produced it. This effort may give the unfortunate impression that a linear process was at work in the construction of Mami Water, with one tradition at a time being accreted to the traditional water divinities until at last the phenomenon called Mami Water was constructed. I do not wish to suggest that this is the case. However, such an exercise can be useful as a means of enabling us to understand and appreciate the complex phenomenon of Mami Water.

The European Strand in the Mami Water Tradition

Africans recognized a similarity between their water spirits and divinities and the mermaids and mermen of the Western tradition, to which they were introduced by merchants and explorers arriving in Africa as early as the fifteenth century (Drewal 1988a, 103–4, 110–24). This tradition became one strand that Africans accreted to their water divinities and spirits. When Europeans arrived in Africa, they arguably had mermaids carved on the prows of their boats and mermaid talismans in their pockets.[2] The Christian faith, which came to the African continent with the traders, colonizers, and missionaries, further familiarized Africans with mermaids and mermen. These half-human, half-fish creatures were included in European bestiaries and in ecclesiastical art to teach moral lessons to the faithful about the spiritual threats posed by sexual seduction and the desire for material wealth (Benwell and Waugh 1961, 51–85).

An ivory salt cellar known to have been produced by the Sherbro of Sierra Leone as a trade item was in Denmark by 1743. It is the earliest extant evidence for the mermaid in African art. This object, which has carved upon it a mermaid, a cross, two human figures and two aquatic creatures, probably crocodiles, might be used to argue for the indigenous character of mermaid/man iconography in Africa. But, because it was a trade item, the salt cellar more probably reflects early European influence in Africa. It also shows that the process of integrating African water divinities, represented by the crocodiles, with European mermaids/men and Christian traditions, had occurred at least as early as the mid-eighteenth century (Fraser 1972, 276–77; Paxson 1980, 30–33).

Two distinct patterns in European mermaid/man mythology probably aided in their syncretistic identification with African water divinities.[3] One pattern focuses on the spiritual dimension of these beings who transcend the limitations of the human sphere and yet are able to interact with it. In this tradition, mermaids/men give humans the gifts of wisdom, prophetic powers, and the healing arts. These are characteristic features of African water divinities as well. The second tradition in its positive aspect emphasizes the ability of mermaids/men to provide favored humans with tangible gifts of gold, jewels, and progeny. Negatively, mermaids/men are also embodiments of sexual and material seduction. Africans also associate these characteristics with the traditional water divinities.

When the African water divinities became hybridized with European mermaids/men in Mami Water, they took on the mermaid form and adopted the typical mermaid features and accoutrements. Mermaids were often depicted in European art and literature as attractive young women with fish tails, having long hair connoting sexual entanglement; a comb, symbolic of the female pudenda and unrestrained sexuality; a mirror, associating them with the moon and Venus; a magical belt or cap talisman, allowing the possessor to negotiate between worlds; pearls, jewels, and other riches, signifying material wealth; musical instruments, expressing the mermaid's ability to lure humans to another realm or to seduce them physically or spiritually (Benwell and Waugh 1961; Griffith 1986; Phillpotts 1980). These symbols have also been incorporated into Mami Water rituals and representations.

The snake-handling woman, popularized by a nineteenth-century German chromolith, was another European cultural element that Africans accreted to their water divinities. This chromolith, showing a woman with long flowing hair, dark complexion, and non-African features, probably depicted the Samoan wife of a German side-show operator who commissioned the chromolith. It has been the inspiration for a variety of iconographic representations of Mami Water in Africa. However, Africans have often interpreted the snake-handler as an Indian divinity, since many of these chromoliths were printed in India and because the woman looked neither African nor European (Drewal 1988c, 169–70).

New World Strand in the Mami Water Tradition

Another major strand in the cultural production of Mami Water was associated with the New World and slavery. Several significant pieces of evidence from Surinam support this assertion (Paxson 1980, 47–54; 1983, 418–19). One is an eighteenth-century traveler's account which mentions a secret dance in honor of *Watra Mamma*, which African slaves performed in Surinam and other colonies in 1750. A second bit of evidence is a 1796 journal entry that refers to a spirit called *Watra Mamma*, which made its home in the river Surinam. A third item is a calabash dated 1831, which features three incised mermaids holding a comb, a baldachin, a leafy twig, and a club (Paxson 1980, 50–54). It is possible that these mermaids are representations of *Watra Mamma*. Other representations on this calabash include snakes and a Christian monstrance for displaying the consecrated host.

This combination of decorative elements clearly suggests that the process of syncretization among traditional African water divinities, the mermaid tradition, and Christianity, similar to that evident in the Sherbro salt cellar, had already begun by the early nineteenth century in the New World. The calabash is reported to have been made by slaves as a gift for a Christian missionary from Germany (Paxson 1980, 54).

A later legend from Surinam tells of the Great Mother of the Inland Waters who delivered Africans from slavery as they made their way up the Mamadam River in two boats with six paddlers each. One interpretation of this legend suggests that its original inspiration was in stories about a woman who aided African slaves in escaping from bondage (Paxson 1980, 54–80). Small boats with six paddlers are found in a number of African Mami Water shrines, perhaps recalling these traditions (Drewal 1988b, 41).

Africans in the New World appear to have preserved their old traditions about water divinities or spirits, hybridized them with local water divinities, and invoked them against the power of their slave masters. The slaves probably found local support for their resistance either in shrines to water divinities of the area or through the assistance of the local people. Alternatively, they may have been able to gain freedom via local waterways. Africans' resistance to slavery was strengthened through this process of assimilation. The veneration of such creolized divinities constituted "transformative practices . . . which, when performed properly by humans, mobilized 'supernatural' forces in order to affect human life" (Blier 1995b, 75). The colonial authorities also recognized these transformative practices as politically subversive acts which they attempted, ineffectually, to suppress.

The Indian Strand in the Mami Water Tradition

Although Africans had encountered Indians on the African continent prior to the twentieth century and perhaps also in the New World, the Indian strand in the Mami Water *métissage* probably derived from contacts with Gujurati merchants along the west coast of Africa around the period of the First World War. Indians set up successful commercial enterprises which brought them to the notice of Africans, who studied their traditions and ritual behaviors. Africans then appropriated elements of Hindu praxis into their rituals in honor of Mami Water (Drewal 1988c, 170–76).

Chromoliths of Indian divinities are part of many Mami Water altars, as are representations of Indian divinities in sculptures and wall paintings. The three-headed male divinity, Bhairava, an incarnation of Shiva, holding a trident and flanked by a bull and three dogs, has been interpreted as a male Mami Water called Densu. The Indian goddess of wealth, Lakshmi, is another divinity popular in Mami Water shrines and rituals, where she is invoked as Mami Titi.

Indian styles of dress such as the sari and the turban have also been adopted by Mami Water priests and priestesses as ritual attire and for official portraits. The lotus position for prayer, the *mudra*, a Hindu ritual gesture, the chanting of mantras and the use of the *bindi*, a forehead mark, are other evidences of Hindu influences in Mami Water ritual, praxis, and representation. Mami Water devotees have also incorporated flowers, blue candles, incense, and perfume, items commonly found on Hindu household altars, in setting up Mami Water shrines.

Construction and Strategic Functions of Mami Water

Diverse constructions of Mami Water within traditional, Christian, and Islamic communities illustrate the creative reinterpretations of these cultural strands in the process of assimilation or assemblage. Based on the strategic function each community uses Mami Water to achieve, they may privilege its African-centered, foreign, or hybridized character. The following examples illustrate the construction of Mami Water in several different traditional, Christian, and Islamic African communities and Mami Water's strategic functions in each context.

Traditional Religions

Mami Water as African-Centered

Mami Water is interpreted in many communities as an African-centered manifestation of traditional water deities despite her apparently foreign iconographic characteristics. Sabine Jell-Bahlsen asserts that iconographic features associated with Mami Water are explained in African terms in a number of Nigerian communities. So, for example, Mami Water's luxurious long hair is *dada-rasta* hair and represents unrestrained fertility, creativity, and spirituality. The white complexion and facial features in Mami Water representations are regarded not as markers of ethnicity but rather as symbolic of the sacred (Jell-Bahlsen 1995a; 1995c).

The use of the names of traditional water spirits, and only secondarily the creolized name Mami Water, and the preservation of traditional rituals to these divinities also emphasize the African-centered nature of Mami Water devotional service. Jell-Bahlsen has documented rituals at an Igbo shrine in Orsu-Obodo, Nigeria, where the spirit of the lake, Uhammiri or Ogbuide, is identified as Mami Water and has as her consort the traditional river god Urashi. At a shrine presided over by the priestess Eze Mmiri, Queen of the Water, devotees meet every fourth day to make offerings and dance in honor of these divinities (Jell-Bahlsen 1989).

Mami Water, identified as the local divinity, functions strategically to alter traditional cultural expectations. Jell-Bahlsen has observed that Mami Water devotional service attracts people, especially women, who are

> extraordinary and creative. They do not easily conform to established norms and they are often marginal, yet highly recognized, in their own communities. Many Mammy Water worshipers are prophets, or mediums of the water spirits. As performing artists they express new ideas and forms. Their native doctors are frequently women who possess extra-ordinary powers. (1995a, 30)

Wealthy trader women often become devotees of Mami Water as well, reinforcing the connection between Mami Water and material wealth.

Mami Water thus validates non-normative cultural and behavioral patterns, while leaving these norms intact for the majority of the community. African communities recognize that initiates into Mami Water have obligations imposed on them which are not part of normal social behavior. After their initiation, devotees set up altars to Mami Water in their bedrooms, where they carry out weekly ritual observances in private. They are also expected to observe one or two days a week of sexual abstinence. Mami Water may also demand additional dietary restrictions and initiation into the service of other divinities with which s/he is associated.

Africans also realize that Mami Water can have a negative impact on their lives. Della Jenkins observes that

> s/he is thought to be responsible for inflicting laziness, madness, infertility, and sickness. . . . A lovely woman of the evening may turn out to be Mammy Wata in bed, bringing gonorrhea a few days later. . . . She wreaks havoc in markets. She talks to and steals children playing near rivers, . . . and as a python, swallows goats and ruins houses. (Jenkins 1984, 75)

Devotees attempt to divert these potentially negative effects of Mami Water by appropriate observances.

Mami Water as Foreign

Observations at traditional Mami Water shrines and analyses of Mami Water rituals and praxis reveal that foreign elements are conspicuous in Mami Water devotional service: non-African iconographic representations of Mami Water; ritual meals in which Western foods are eaten; ritual tables that resemble Hindu and Christian household altars with candles, bells, and incense; and European dressing tables with powder and perfume; ritual behaviors including European dances, books, and Western objects such as sunglasses; and direct claims made by shrine personnel about the foreignness of Mami Water.

Henry Drewal has drawn from this evidence the conclusion that Mami Water's foreignness is essential to her nature and that, in fact, s/he is either an African representation of foreigners or of "an exotic European water spirit." He suggests that because Europeans and Indians came to Africa in ships laden with goods, Africans thought these foreigners belonged intrinsically to the realm of the water spirits and their riches (Drewal 1988a, 101–39; Kasfir 1994, 80).

The construction of Mami Water as a foreign divinity associated with wealth is related to one of the strategic functions that Mami Water has for Africans. S/he is perceived as a potential source for the alleviation of economic hardship. In addition, "[a]s a modern deity, she deals especially with modern problems: gaining entrance to a school or university, passing exams, getting a lucrative 'post,' purchasing a new automobile" (Jenkins 1984, 75).

The emphasis on foreigners, divine or human, in Mami Water ritual and praxis is evidence for Africans' creative appropriation of "the other," in this case Europeans and Indians. Claiming "the other" for themselves allows Africans to gain access to the wealth Europeans and Indians possess, by invoking either the foreigners themselves, personified as Mami Water, or their divinities. Devotees' identification with Mami Water in possession experiences and in ritual and praxis also appear to function as a means for Africans to transform themselves into foreigners, and foreigners into Africans. In so doing, Africans resist their own transcription by foreigners as "the other," and at the same time they negate the efforts of foreigners to resist assimilation into African cultures by claiming them as African.

Mami Water as Hybrid

The hybridity of Mami Water is yet another construction found in traditional communities. This construction privileges neither Mami Water's foreign aspects nor its African-centered character but utilizes both elements strategically (Wendl 1991, 9–37).

One example of the hybridized construction of Mami Water comes from the Lagoon region of Ivory Coast. The traditional water divinities, who were the guardians of fertility, were thought to have become ineffective against the power of witchcraft to cause sterility. Sterility was regarded as a significant problem in the community because it effectively reduced the power of families to produce heirs to inherit family property. "But," says Emmanuel Akyeampong, "it went beyond that. Witchcraft reduced the viability of communities to reproduce themselves socially and biologically. It dented the fabric of communities, not just individual families."[4]

As a result, at the end of the nineteenth century the foreign Mami Water was integrated with traditional water divinities, and they were then collectively given the name Mami Water. Mami was considered the consort of the earth god, Beugre. Together they were responsible for fertility and the prosperity of the community. The strategic functions of this alliance were the revitalization of traditional divinities and protection against witchcraft (Augé 1969, 185, 194–97).

When even this solution did not prove effective, the community turned in the mid-twentieth century to a more inclusive strategy suggested by a religious leader named Papa Nouveau (Dagri Njava) (Walker 1979, 40–41). He was inspired by the syncretistic Mami, whose "spouse" he was, to extend hospitality to the Christian God and to found a church. The result was that Mami Water became a consort of the Christian God in this religious movement. This action was, effectively, a repudiation of the local creator god who, according to tradition, had removed itself from the world after creation, thus empowering malevolent spirits which attempted to prevent procreation. By contrast, the Christian God, who continued to be actively involved in the universe, was considered a more potent force in the subversion of witchcraft, but only in combination with Mami Water.

Witchcraft also manifests itself in forms other than sterility. Physical and mental disorders, business problems, thefts, alienation of affection, family quarrels, accidents and deaths are attributed to witchcraft as well (Wendl 1991, 254–307).[5] These and like problems bring people to Mami Water shrines for assistance and protection. When the problems are explained and effectively addressed at the shrines, clients often become Mami Water devotees. A Ghanaian woman reported her experience at one shrine:

> I was ill and was brought here. . . . When we came here Bosomfo Kow Tawiah said that we had to perform a ritual at the beach for Mami Water. During the ritual I was possessed by the spirit and that suggested to me that Papa Kow Tawiah is a very powerful Bosomfo. For this reason I have put myself under his protection morning, noon and night. . . . The illness disappeared in less than a fortnight. . . . I am here because I am safe. (Biney 1994-95)

This function of protection from various forms of witchcraft is similar to the New World role of *Watra Mamma* as a protector and liberator from slavery.

Mami Water in African Christianity

For many African Christians, Mami Water represents the demonic in traditional religions which their faith requires them to denounce and resist.

This response is consistent with a frequently occurring Christian strategy of demonizing spiritual powers other than its own god. Birgit Meyer has suggested that Christian churches in Africa have even fostered continuing belief in spirits and in witchcraft by asserting that spirits who work evil are false gods, rather than by denying their existence (Meyer 1992, 98–132).

Christianity responds to religious or spiritual phenomena which devotees may encounter in the broader culture or even in their own families or Christian communities by locating them in its cosmological structure of angelic and demonic beings. Some sense of the efficacy of the Mami Water tradition is provided by the place of importance Mami Water is given in Christian demonology in these communities. A Ghanaian Christian woman opined that Mami Water was cast out of heaven with Lucifer at the beginning of time. They then took up residence in the sea, from which Mami Water emerges or sends agents to tempt faithful Christians to sins of sexual excess or materialism (Anyimadu 1994). Mami Water is also charged with fostering homosexuality and lesbianism, which are in general not culturally approved practices in Africa (Eto 1989, 17, 25).

The construction of Mami Water as demonic in African Christianity serves several significant strategic functions. It implicates non-Christian Africans in the colonial project by suggesting that Mami Water devotional service fosters materialism and legitimates the practice of non-African sexual mores. The contemporary Zairian Christian artist Cheri Samba provides a Christian critique of Mami Water in many of his paintings by depicting Mami Water as a voluptuous female mermaid accompanied by snakes and adorned with gold and jewels, representing sexual and material seduction. In addition to seductive mermaids and mermen, he often depicts in the same paintings a person reading a biblical quotation such as Luke 6:24: "But woe to you that are rich, for you have received your consolation" (Vogel 1991, 18–20, 123–24, 132–33). This is the artist's reminder to his audience to resist the temptations of Mami Water, however attractive they may appear.

African traditional religion is also subverted by the construction of Mami Water as demonic. Water divinities are often thought in traditional religion to take specially selected people under the sea with them to teach them philosophic wisdom or healing skills or to give them poetic inspiration. Kofi Awoonor attests to the traditional belief that when persons return from their "under the sea" experiences, they are thought to "exist beyond the purely bodily level" (Goldblatt 1972, 44). By portraying these under-the-sea experiences as opportunities for humans to learn how to carry out demonic interventions against believers, Christians problematize a long-held tradition about the nature and activities of water divinities and the persons they call to their service.

A Christian evangelist who claims to have been taken under the sea by Mami Water, "the Queen of the Coast," testified that he observed the methods demons used to make Christians lapse and the punishments meted out to demonic defectors. He himself was required to kill his uncle. After doing so, he met Lucifer, head of the kingdom under the sea, who instructed him to fight "real Christians" and to destroy the church through money, material goods, and women. Ultimately he was converted to Christianity, but not before strenuous efforts were directed against his conversion by the "Queen of the Coast" and her agents (Eni 1987).

Another strategic function of Mami Water as demonic is to provide a threatening example that will persuade believers not to explore the efficacy of new religious or spiritual phenomena which they may encounter but instead to commit themselves to the superior power of Christ. The threat posed by a spirit like Mami Water, who can intervene in their lives and seduce them even against their wills, makes them even more dependent on the power of their own deity and on solidarity with their own religious communities (Meyer 1995, 47–67).

Mami Water in Islam

In Africa, Islam has reduced the status of traditional divinities by advocating belief in Allah as the high god. Islam adapts to traditional religions by including ancestral and other spirits in the category of *jinn,* spirits who are created by Allah to serve him. *Jinn* are regarded as angelic or demonic, depending on their behavior. Traditional communities have often resisted the assimilation of their primary gods into the *jinn,* but have tolerated the incorporation of nature spirits, especially those related to land and water, into this Islamic category (Trimingham 1959, 102–23).

Islam considers Mami Water a traditional water spirit and includes it among the *jinn.* Stories in pre-Islamic Arabic literature of secret marriages between *jinns* and human spouses may have provided the model for devotees being referred to as "spouses" of Mami Water. Mami Water's strategic function in Islam is to empower traditional priests, diviners, and healers to interpret phenomena through the practice of magic or divination and to suggest cures, charms, or amulets to solve or ameliorate clients' problems. This is a function similar to that which Mami Water plays in traditional religions.

A Ghanaian informant reported that a young woman of his acquaintance had been "bothered" by Mami Water, who told the girl she wanted to "marry" her. Mami Water manifested her presence through direct encounters with the girl in trance, the smell of unfamiliar perfume, money vanishing or increasing, and the girl's attraction to water. When she consulted a diviner to have the spirit "sucked" from her, the diviner responded that no fortune-teller can "suck" that spirit. Because Mami Water is the source of many diviners' power, they cannot use their charms against her (Anyi-madu 1994). Mami Water has proved to be a spirit that is not totally con-trolled by Islamic theology or by its clerics, diviners, and healers. She has eluded the control that her subordinate status as a *jinn* was intended to impose on her.

Mami Water Assemblage

Teasing apart the multiple cultural strands in the Mami Water tradition and analyzing the strategic significance of Mami Water has demonstrated the complex process of assemblage, assimilation, and accretion which has produced Mami Water and the creative responses to her in a variety of African communities. But living religious traditions do not understand themselves as "strands," "constructions," or "strategies." Mami Water as a vital African tradition can best be appreciated when it is seen as an integral whole. The spiritual experiences of one Mami Water priest, Togbe Abidjan Mamiwater, and the Mami Water representations and rituals at his shrine in the Eastern Region, Ghana, provide an excellent example of the African practice of assemblage, in which foreign elements are incorporated into an existing tradition in order to enrich but not replace it.

Historical Background

Adawuso Dorfe, an Avenor Ewe living in Ghana, was born probably in the first decade of the twentieth century. He was not called to Mami Water devotional service until his thirties. During his young adulthood, he con-sulted a Muslim diviner for guidance because he was not a successful farmer. Later, after a profitable day at a market, he visited a prostitute but did not succeed with her. Worried about the situation, Dorfe consulted a local diviner who said that Mami Water had been responsible for his suc-cess and that he had offended her by using his gains on a prostitute.

After returning home, Adawuso Dorfe consulted the Muslim diviner he had visited earlier. That man agreed that he had been called by Mami Water and also mentioned a bowl, which his mother "birthed" from her womb before his own birth. The diviner interpreted the bowl as a manifestation of Mami Water and told the future priest that this was the only icon he should revere and that he should use the bowl for divination.

The diviner gave Adawuso Dorfe the name Abidjan Mamiwater, because the spirit that claimed him originated in the river of that name in Ivory

Coast. He also recommended that the priest consult Mama Shika, at that time the only Mami Water priestess in the Ewe area. This event occurred in the mid-1940s. She prayed for him at the beach, confirmed his calling, and advised him to build a shrine for Mami Water in his room. Since 1945, he has practiced as a diviner, healer, and priest of Mami Water. After a dream revelation, he reestablished his original shrine at Adome on the Volta River, where it remains today.

Theology of Abidjan Mamiwater

The priest Abidjan Mamiwater identifies himself as a practitioner of Vodun. Vodun shares with other African traditional religions the belief in a creator god, primordial divinities, and spirits associated with the elements, the ancestors, and other lesser spirits, who act for good or ill. But it has its own distinguishing characteristics as well.

> The essence of *vodun* . . . lies in the need for one to be calm and composed. One must take the time to sit quietly rather than rushing through life . . . *vodun* constitutes a philosophy which places a primacy on patience, calmness, respect, and order both in the context of acquiring life's basic necessities and in the pursuit of those extra benefits which make life at once full and pleasurable. (Blier 1995b, 79–80)

These are Vodun's "cool" qualities. Vodun also has a "hot" aspect, which encourages people to do whatever they can to change negative life situations, especially through seeking protection from spirits that promote positive changes.

In Abidjan Mamiwater's system, Mami Water has become the feminine counterpart of the male water divinity Tokosu. Mami Water, like other primordial divinities, has her appropriate sphere. But the priest also regards all the primordial divinities as a unity. Thus, he says, "Tokosu, Ablo [divinity of agriculture] and Mamiwater are all one and the same thing. If someone has Tokosu, it means that Ablo and Mami Water are also with him." Further evidence for the construction of Mami Water as a traditional divinity is her association with natural phenomena, such as thunder, rain, crocodiles, and the rainbow.

Representations of Mamiwater at the Shrine

A large roadside sign welcomes visitors to Abidjan Mamiwater Village. On the sign the priest is depicted with *dada-rasta* hair crowned with the four red parrot feathers of Xebieso, divinity of the thunderbolt. He is wrapped in a black, red, blue, and white cloth that ends in a fish tail. In one hand he holds a fly whisk and in the other a pistol. He is flanked on one side by the thunder divinity and on the other by Aziza, the dwarfs. Over all is the rainbow python, Dan (figure 1).

The first building in evidence upon entering the village is decorated with large paintings of Xebieso (figure 2). Additional shrines to Xebieso or Tohono and other primordial divinities including Ablo, divinity of earth, and Tokosu, divinity of water, Aziza, and a host of other lesser spirits are also distributed throughout the shrine complex. The rainbow python is frequently depicted in paintings with Mami Water. Crocodiles, fish, and snakes are also prominently featured in wall paintings (figure 3). Most divinities are represented as female–male pairs, reflecting the traditional Vodun view of complementarity in the divinity (figure 4).

Female and male Mami Waters are represented at the shrine, according to Abidjan Mamiwater, simply because his clients expect to see them.

> We draw and paint Mami Water icons on walls, so that even if you are illiterate the picture will tell you that this is a Mami Water shrine . . . when people come they will know that these are the divinities we revere . . . Mami Water had never come out from water and walked with a fish-tail for anyone to see. . . . It is only the picture of painters that we all see. . . . One should tell the truth for the blessing of God. I have never seen Mami Water with a fish-tail.

The influence of Christianity is also observable in the statues and paintings of Jesus, Mary, and the crucifix found in the shrine area (figure 5). Abidjan Mamiwater claims to have little or no contact with Christians. He knows enough about Christian teaching, however, to say that he finds "some sweetness" in it, but because Christians "condemn us, the devotees of Vodun, that makes their words unpleasant to me." The reason the priest has the Christian representations at his shrine is "to tell those who do not know that there is no difference between what he is doing and what the Christians are also doing . . . all the two systems aim at [is] making people do good to one another, without which there will be no happiness in the world."

These Christian representations should not be understood to have the same symbolic significance at the shrine as they do in a Christian context, however. In Africa and in the African Diaspora, Christian figures have long been equated with Vodun divinities, or used as disguises for the Vodun divinities, as part of the process of accretion. The Christian redemptive symbol, the cross, is identified both in Africa and in the Diaspora with the Vodun cosmogram, which expresses the link between the living and the dead (Thompson 1995, 103; 1984, 103–59).

The centrality of traditional religion at the shrine is dramatized by the subordination and minimalization of Christian representations in relation to traditional iconography and images of the mermaid/man. A large painting in the priest's reception area is dominated by a female Mami Water with African features. She is flanked on either side by two men, who are positioned lower than she is in the painting but on the same level with each other. One of them is the priest and the other is a non-African Jesus. The composition as a whole suggests that both the priest and Jesus gain their power from Mami Water and that they are equally her representatives (figure 6). As another example, a six-headed female figure, modeled on a dream revelation given to the priest, dominates the outer court of the shrine proper. The sculpture stands in a pool of water at the base of which is a niche containing a small statue of Jesus as the good shepherd. The relative size and position of the two sculptures leave no doubt as to which is more important (figure 7).

Chromoliths from India as well as statues and paintings influenced by the iconography of Indian divinities are also displayed on the shrine walls. A major painting of the priest garbed in Indian attire attests to the adaptation of this tradition in Mami Water devotional service (figure 8). But Abidjan Mamiwater also says that he is totally unfamiliar with the Hindu religious tradition.

Rituals at the Shrine

As at all shrines in honor of traditional African divinities, a broad variety of human concerns brings clients to consult the priest and the divinities. The priest summarizes their concerns. "Some people come because prosperity eludes them. Some come because they are childless. Others come because they have all sorts of problems, for example lawsuits harassing them. They also come to be initiated." Mediation between worlds and response to human material and spiritual needs are primary functions of the shrine.

A consultation with the priest begins with a divination, so that he can make an assessment of the client's problem. Abidjan Mamiwater's system of divination reflects his belief in the power of traditional spirits. He divines according to the *Afa* system, but he also uses Muslim divination practices. He interprets his ability to divine effectively as a gift from Mami Water.

Once the priest has assessed the client's problems, he may prescribe initiation into Mami Water. This involves the procurement of a collection of items by the initiant to be used in the ritual, and the observance of particular taboos, such as abstinence from sex and certain foods and drinks, prior to the initiation. The priest may also prescribe certain herbs to deal with the physical problems of the client, if these were revealed to him in divination.

During Mami Water rituals and at the annual festival in honor of the divinities at the shrine devotees dance, using Mami Water dance movements, to a Mami Water drum rhythm (Opoku and Wicker 1994, 18–19). The drum rhythm was revealed in a dream to Abidjan Mamiwater. He was on a long journey when he came to a road lined with white men. In the middle of the road was a white ram. One of the white men told him to lift up the ram, but whenever the white man said "*Adcsu/Yesu*," the priest would be thrown to the ground. The white man would similarly be defeated when the priest said the same formula. The contest ensued, but the priest woke before either party was victorious. He remembered the drum rhythm, however, and taught it to his chief drummer. This drum rhythm is now used in Mami Water devotional service at the shrine and is a popular dance rhythm throughout West Africa as well.

Another practice in Mami Water rituals at the shrine is the throwing of money into the Volta River in memory of the priest's grandfather, Seke, a slave trader, who reincarnated in him. Once, when people tried to rob Seke, who was on a boat trip to purchase slaves, he jumped into the river to escape. In order not to drown, Seke divested himself of some coins which he offered to the river. Though the grandfather did not know Mami Water, the priest carries on the practice of throwing money into the river as part of Mami Water rituals. This act is intended to remind people that life is more valuable than wealth and that too much wealth can lead to destruction.

Conclusion

Bruce Lawrence has described spirituality, as distinct from religion and theology, as "a renewable resource with deep currents and countless rivulets (Lawrence 1995, 6). This seems a particularly apt characterization of Mami Water spirituality. The image suggested by "deep currents and countless rivulets" is of rhythmic movement coming from the center of the universe and connecting all the parts—deity, divinities and spirits, ancestors, human beings, animals and plants—in a dynamic unity. Mami Water is an essential part of that rhythmic movement which pervades and creates the universe. She is connected to her consort, Tokosu, and to the community of gods which constitute a communitarian divinity (Ogbonnaya 1994, 13–32). She also manifests in the natural world as water, the substance without which life cannot continue; as a channel to the supernatural (Akyeampong 1996); as fish, food for sustenance; as healing power, restoring broken connections. Her spirit flows through the generations, linking the living-timeless with their children existing in time, and continues into the animals and plants and around and through the rocks as it circles back to the center of the universe.

The "deep currents and countless rivulets" of Mami Water as celebrated at the Abidjan Mamiwater shrine enable humans to achieve the calmness and creative control of their lives, which is the goal of the practice of Vodun. The drum rhythms of Mami Water move her devotees as smoothly and unresistingly as a swimmer carried along by the gentle movement of the current. Respectful rituals recognize Mami Water's power to give abundant gifts, but at the same time require that devotees give gifts to others as well as receive them for themselves. Unity with the divinity, and the blessings which flow from that unity, can be achieved only when the human community is itself united and in harmony with the natural world.

The "deep currents" of Mami Water flow not only in traditional communities, however. The "countless rivulets" of Mami Water extend their tributaries out beyond those communities into Islam and Christianity, though the cartographers of those religions often assign them other names. In Islam, Mami Water's name and power are recognized, even while she is made a *jinn* of Allah or takes the form of al-Buraq, the winged horse with a woman's head (Roberts 1995, 90). In Christianity, even though the name Mami Water has become synonymous with the demonic, the "deep currents and countless rivulets" of water, blood, and other liquids used in ritual symbolize both the purification and the unity of the community (Akyeampong 1996). They are important expressions of the cultural roots of African Christianity (Turner 1979, 225–30; Thomas 1994, 39–56).[6]

Notes

1. See Hackett 1991, 135–48; Idowu 1973, 203–8; Jules-Rosette 1991, 149–65; King 1986, 112; Lawson 1984, 76; Mbiti 1990, 256–71; Parrinder 1969, 235; Platvoet 1993, 29–48; 1996.

2. Barbara K. Paxson reports that models exist of two European ships from the period of exploration and trade, the Dutch East-Indian *De Zeven Provencien,* 1716–1725, and the French frigate ship *Protée,* 1748–1771 (Paxson 1980, 25–27). Both models have mermaid figureheads on their prows. While the itineraries of these vessels are not known, it is a reasonable hypothesis that these or other ships with mermaid prows may have reached Africa during the period of exploration and trade.

3. Mermaids/men are also found in the mythologies of many other cultures as widely and chronologically separate as ancient Babylonia and Greece, pre-Columbian Mexico and modern China. Though Europe cannot be established conclusively as its sole source, European culture, including its Near Eastern and classical roots, is the most likely origin of the mermaid/men representations in Africa.

4. Emmanuel Akyeampong, personal communication, December 4, 1995.

5. Hans-Jürgen Greschat suggests that African independent churches developed because Europeans did not understand the power of witchcraft and the working of the spirit in African communities (Greschat 1993, 197–209).

6. The Mami Water Project, which produced the research reported in this section, is co-sponsored by The Institute of African Studies, University of Ghana,

Legon, and Scripps College, Claremont, California. Professor Kofi Asare Opoku, of the Institute of African Studies and Lafayette College, Easton, Pennsylvania, and Professor Kathleen O'Brien Wicker, of Scripps College, are the co-directors of the project. The research team for the project includes Mr. K. Ampom Darkwa, field coordinator; Mr. K. Asazu, interviewer and Ewe translator at the Abidjan Mamiwater shrine; Mr. C. L. Biney, interviewer and Fante translator at the Bosomfo Kow Tawiah shrine mentioned earlier; Mr. J. Asmah, cinematographer and video editor; Mr. K. Osei Bonsu, secretary; Ms. Pati Ranieri, student research assistant; Nancy S. Burson, secretary. It gives me great pleasure here to thank Togbe Abidjan Mamiwater and the members of his community; Bosomfo Kow Tawiah and the members of his community; Mami Water priestess Aba Yaba; and Professor Kofi Asare Opoku and the research team for their dedication and cooperation in carrying out this research project. Welcome grants from the American Academy of Religion, Scripps College, the Irvine Foundation, the Hewlett Foundation, and the West African Research Association have made this project financially possible.

References

Akyeampong, Emmanuel
   1996   *Drink, Power and Cultural Change: A Social History of Alcohol in Ghana, c. 1800 to Recent Times.* Portsmouth, N.H.: Heinemann.
Akyeampong, Emmanuel, and Pashington Obeng
   1996   "Spirituality, Gender, and Power in Asante History." *International Journal of African Historical Studies* 29, no. 1.
Anyimadu, Amos
   1994   "Interview with Moses Kakraba." Legon, Ghana, January.
Augé, Marc
   1969   *Le Rivage Alladian: Organisation et Évolution des villages Alladian.* Mémoires Orstom 34. Paris: Orstom.
Benwell, Gwen, and Arthur Waugh
   1961   *Sea Enchantress: The Tale of the Mermaid and her Kin.* London: Hutchinson.
Biney, C. L.
   1994–95   "Interviews at Bosomfo Kow Tawiah Shrint." Moree, Ghana.
Blier, Suzanne Preston
   1995a   *African Vodun: Art, Psychology and Power.* Chicago: University of Chicago Press.
   1995b   "Vodun: West African Roots of Vodou." In *Sacred Arts of Haitian Vodou,* ed. Donald J. Cosentino, 61–87. Los Angeles: UCLA Fowler Museum of Cultural History.
Drewal, Henry John
   1988a   "Interpretation, Invention, and Representation in the Worship of Mami Water." *Journal of Folklore Research* 25, nos. 1–2:101–39.
   1988b   "Mermaids, Mirrors, and Snake Charmers: Igbo Mami Wata Shrines." *African Arts* 21, no. 2:38–45, 96.

1988c   "Performing the Other: Mami Wata Worship in West Africa."
             The Drama Review T 118:160–85.

Eni, Emmanuel
1987   *Delivered from the Powers of Darkness.* Ibadan: Scripture Union
             (Nigeria) Press and Books.

Eto, Victoria
1989   *Exposition on Water Spirits.* Warri, Nigeria: Shallom Christian
             Mission.

Fraser, Douglas
1972   "The Fish-Legged Figure in Benin and Yoruba Art." In *African
             Art and Leadership,* ed. D. Fraser and H. M. Cole, 261–94. Madi-
             son: University of Wisconsin Press.

Gilroy, Paul
1993   *The Black Atlantic: Modernity and Double Consciousness.* Cam-
             bridge, Mass.: Harvard University Press.

Goldblatt, John
1972   "Interview with Kofi Awoonor." *Transition* 41:42–44.

Greschat, Hans-Jürgen
1993   "African Independent Churches and Theological Scholarship in
             Germany." In *Religious Plurality in Africa: Essays in Honour of
             John S. Mbiti,* ed. Jacob K. Olupona and Sulayman S. Nyang,
             197–209. New York: de Gruyter.

Griffith, Lee Ellen
1986   *The Tale of the Mermaid.* An Essay on the Folklore and Mythology
             of the Mermaid, accompanied by Illustrations of Objects from the
             Exhibition. Philadelphia: Philadelphia Maritime Museum.

Hackett, Rosalind I. J.
1991   "Revitalization in African Traditional Religion." In *African Tra-
             ditional Religions in Contemporary Society,* ed. Jacob K. Olupona,
             135–48. New York: Paragon House.

Horton, Robin
1993   *Patterns of Thought in Africa and the West: Essay on Magic, Reli-
             gion and Science.* Cambridge: Cambridge University Press.

Idowu, E. Bolaji
1973   *African Traditional Religion: A Definition.* Maryknoll, N.Y.: Orbis.

Jell-Bahlsen, Sabine
1989   *Mammy Water: In Search of the Water Spirits in Nigeria.* VHS video,
             59 min. Berkeley: U. of California Extension Media Center.
1995a   "Dada-Rasta-Hair: The Hidden Messages of Mammy Water in
             Nigeria." Paper presented at the African Studies Association
             Meeting, Orlando, Florida, November.
1995b   "The Concept of Mammywater in Flora Nwapa's Novels."
             Research in African Literatures 26, no. 2:30–41.
1995c   "Eze Mmiri di Egwu—The Water Monarch is Awesome: Recon-
             sidering the Mammy Water Myths." In *Queens, Queen Mothers,
             Priestesses and Power: Case Studies in African Gender,* ed. Flora

Edouwaye S. Kaplan, vol. 810, 103–34. New York: New York Academy of Sciences.

Jenkins, Della
1984   "Mamy Wata." In *Igbo Arts: Community and Cosmos,* ed. Herbert M. Cole and Chike C. Aniakor, 75–77. Los Angeles: UCLA Fowler Museum of Cultural History.

Jules-Rosette, Bennetta W.
1991   "Tradition and Continuity in African Religions: The Case of New Religious Movements." In *African Traditional Religions in Contemporary Society,* ed. Jacob K. Olupona, 149–65. New York: Paragon House.

Kasfir, Sidney
1994   "Review of *Mammy Water: In Search of the Water Spirits in Nigeria,* by S. Jell-Bahlsen, and *Mami Wata: Der Geist der Weissen Frau,* by T. Wendl and D. Weise." *African Arts* 27, no. 1:80–82, 96.

King, Noel Q.
1986   *African Cosmos: An Introduction to Religion in Africa.* Belmont, Calif.: Wadsworth Publishing Co.

Lawrence, Bruce B.
1995   "Toward a History of Global Religion(s) in the Twentieth Century: Parachristian Sightings from and Interdisciplinary Asianist." Sixteenth Annual University Lecture in Religion. Arizona State University, Department of Religious Studies.

Lawson, E. Thomas
1984   *Religions in Africa.* San Francisco: Harper & Row.

Lionnet, Françoise
1989   *Autobiographical Voices: Race, Gender, Self-Portraiture.* Ithaca, N.Y.: Cornell University Press.

Mbiti, John S.
1990   *African Religions and Philosophy.* 2nd ed. Oxford: Heinemann.

Meyer, Birgit
1992   "'If You Are a Devil, You Are a Witch, If You Are a Witch, You Are a Devil': The Integration of 'Pagan' Ideas into the Conceptual Universe of Ewe Christians in Southeastern Ghana." *Journal of Religion in Africa* 22, no. 2:98–132.
1995   "Magic, Mermaids and Modernity: The Attraction of Pentecostalism in Africa." *Etnofoor* 8, no. 2:47–67.

Ogbonnaya, A. Okechukwu
1994   *On Communitarian Divinity: An African Interpretation of the Trinity.* New York: Paragon House.

Opoku, Kofi Asare
1978   *West African Traditional Religion.* Accra: FEP International Private Ltd.

Opoku, Kofi Asare, and Kathleen O'Brien Wicker
1994   "Abidjan Mami Water Festival 1994." *Religious Studies News* (Nov.): 18–19.

Parrinder, Geoffrey
    1969   *Religion in Africa.* New York: Praeger.
Paxson, Barbara K.
    1980   "Mammy Water: Ideas and Images of a New World Transcen-
                dent Being." M.A. thesis, University of Washington, Seattle.
    1983   "Mammy Water: New World Origins?" *Baessler-Archiv* N.F.
                31:418–19.
Phillpotts, Beatrice
    1980   *Mermaids.* New York: Ballentine Books.
Platvoet, Jan
    1993   "African Traditional Religions in the Religious History of
                Humankind." *Journal for the Study of Religion* 6, no. 2:29–48.
    1996   "From Object to Subject: A History of the Study of the Religions
                of Africa." In *The Study of Religions in Africa: Past, Present and
                Prospects,* ed. Jan G. Platvoet and James L. Cox/Jacob Olupona.
                Cambridge: Roots & Branches; Herare: U. of Zimbabwe Press.
Roberts, Allen F.
    1995   *Animals in African Art: From the Familiar to the Marvelous.*
                Munich: Prestel.
Thomas, Linda E.
    1994   "African Indigenous Churches as a Source of Socio-political
                Transformation in South Africa." *Africa Today* 41, no. 1:39–56.
Thompson, Robert Farris
    1995   "From the ISLE BENEATH the SEA: Haiti's Africanizing
                Vodou Art." In *Sacred Arts of Haitian Vodou,* ed. Donald J.
                Cosentino, 91–119. Los Angeles: UCLA Fowler Museum of Cul-
                tural History.
Trimingham, J. Spencer
    1959   *Islam in West Africa.* Oxford: Clarendon Press.
Turner, Harold W.
    1979   "A Theology of Water," in J. Ade Aina's *Present-Day Prophets,* in
                Religious Innovation in Africa, 225–30. Boston: G. K. Hall.
Vogel, Susan
    1991   *Africa Explores: 20th Century African Art.* New York: Center for
                African Art.
Walker, Sheila S.
    1979   "The Message as the Medium: The Harrist Churches of the Ivory
                Coast and Ghana." In *African Christianity: Patterns of Religious
                Continuity,* ed. George Bond, Walton Johnson, and Sheila S.
                Walker. New York: Academic Press.
Wendl, Tobias
    1991   *Mami Wata oder ein Kult zwischen den Kulturen.* Kulturanthro-
                pologische Studien 19. Münster: Lit Verlag.
Young, Robert J. C.
    1995   *Colonial Desire: Hybridity in Theory, Culture, and Race.* London:
                Routledge.

Figure 1. Roadside sign, Abidjan Mamiwater Village, Eastern Region, Ghana. Photo: Patricia Ranieri, 1996.

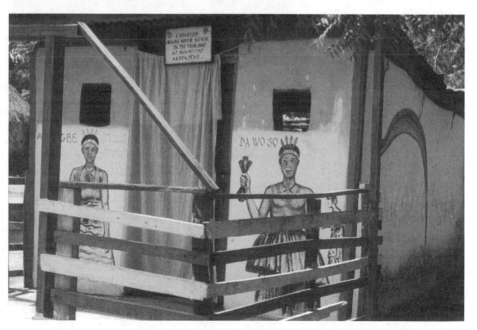

Figure 2. Shrine of the Thunder divinities, Abidjan Mamiwater Village, Eastern Region, Ghana. Photo: Allan W. Wicker, 1994.

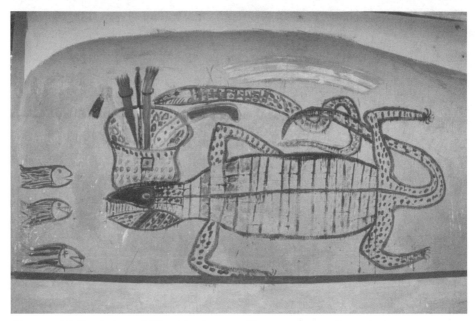

Figure 3. Wall painting, Abidjan Mamiwater Village, Eastern Region, Ghana.
Photo: Allan W. Wicker, 1994.

Figure 4. Mami Water wall painting, Abidjan Mamiwater Village, Eastern Region, Ghana.
Photo: Kathleen O'Brien Wicker, 1993.

Figure 5. Mami Water shrine, Abidjan Mamiwater Village, Eastern Region, Ghana.
Photo: Kathleen O'Brien Wicker, 1993.

Figure 6. Togbe Abidjan Mamiwater in his reception area, Abidjan Mamiwater Village,
Eastern Region, Ghana. Photo: Kathleen O'Brien Wicker, 1993.

Figure 7. Six-headed divinity with statue of Jesus at base, Abidjan Mamiwater Village Shrine, Eastern Region, Ghana. Photo: Kathleen O'Brien Wicker, 1998.

Figure 8. Painting of Togbe Abidjan Mamiwater with Mami Water by A. A. Ofori. Abidjan Mamiwater Shrine, Eastern Region, Ghana. Photo: Kathleen O'Brien Wicker, 1993.

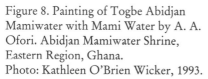

10

Art and Spirituality

WYATT MACGAFFEY

Man's best artifice to snare and hold the grandeur of divinity always crumbles in his hands, and the more ardently he strives the more paltry and incongruous the result. So it were better he did not try at all; far better to ritualize that incongruity and by invoking the mystery of metaphor to hint at the most unattainable glory by its very opposite, the most mundane starkness—a mere stream, a tree, a stone, a mound of earth, a little clay bowl containing fingers of chalk. Thus it came about that the indescribable Pillar of Water fusing earth to heaven at the navel of the black lake became in numberless shrine houses across the country, a dry stick rising erect from the bare, earth floor. (Achebe 1988, 94)

BOTH "ART" AND "SPIRITUALITY" are concepts that should be used with caution in relation to sub-Saharan African cultures. The Ghanaian philosopher Wiredu writes that "belief in countless 'mystical,' 'spiritual,' and 'supernatural' entities has been attributed to the African race. In fact, however, these categories do not exist in Akan thought, for example; they would seem not to exist in the thought of many other African peoples" (1992, 324). Mudimbe questions whether the concept of "art" is applicable to Africa; he quotes the anthropologist Edmund Leach as saying that "the notion of artist is a European one." A Nigerian artist however says that, "It appears that religion has never been able to stand on its own except with the aid of art" (Moyo Okediji, quoted in Harris 1993, 126). The exploration of the tension between these points of view should prove fruitful.[1]

The evolutionary thinking that prevailed in Europe during the nineteenth century and until recently associated art exclusively with what were supposed to be the refined values and sensibilities of "advanced" cultures. At the same time, social scientists could represent Africa as thoroughly spiritual; they asserted that religion pervaded its cultures and mentalities, and they explained social movements in these terms. This evaluation was

223

not entirely a favorable one; according to the concept of social evolution, religion was deemed to precede the more rational thinking supposedly prerequisite to politics, economics, and "advanced" civilization. To be religious was to be pre-political and pre-economic—as well as "pre-artistic." Africanists are still thinking their way out of this paradox, which is enshrined in the term "primitive art."

The reevaluation of African objects as "art" began at the end of the nineteenth century. In a romantic reaction against prevailing tastes, Gauguin drew upon what he supposed were "primitive" themes, although in fact they were mostly projections of European ideas. In the course of his explorations, the first contact between "art" and "Africa" may have taken place in Paris at the Universal Exposition of 1889, where Gauguin seems to have acquired two figurines from Loango, which he subsequently "improved," adding the initials "P. Go." (Dapper 1989, 10). Fifteen years later, Picasso, Modigliani, and a few other bohemians in Paris were influenced by the forms of certain African sculptures, which were beginning to be seen in Europe, fruits of the imperial conquests of the day. Such objects were collected not as art but as souvenirs, trophies, and tokens of barbarism overcome. Serious studies of sculpture, largely restricted to those that seemed to conform to a European aesthetic, were undertaken in the 1950s, but Africa was not generally endowed with art until the 1960s. On the one hand, as the former colonies were admitted to the community of nations they began to be credited with history and art, along with seats in the United Nations. On the other, in Africa itself, nationalist ideologies called for the creation of museums in which indigenous artifacts represented each country's cultural heritage.

In the rest of this chapter, certain themes and topics (for example, gender, or Igbo art) seem to be isolated for comment in the several sections, but in fact the narrative will repeatedly return to each of them.

Art

There are basically two characterizations of art, one that identifies it with experience of the aesthetic, the other defining it by reference to a particular institutional structure and practice. Neither of them is very useful for the task at hand. The first perspective appears to be less restrictive; the concept of the aesthetic (which can be considered universal, even though different peoples may have different ideas about what it means), associates art with the spiritual. J. Maquet links the experience of art to the meditative techniques of Buddhism and continues, "as meditation, aesthetic vision apprehends its object in a contemplative mode of consciousness" (Maquet 1986,

58). But, as Arthur Danto puts it, "anything can become an object of detached aesthetic scrutiny—the teeth of a dead dog, to cite an example of St. Augustine, or the purpled eyelids of his dead wife, as in the case of Claude Monet" (Danto 1988, 20).

In the second, more restrictive perspective, art is the product of persons recognized as "artists," and it is housed where it can be looked at, usually in buildings or other spaces set aside for the purpose. Art of this kind did not emerge in Europe until the seventeenth century; the great age of the museum was the nineteenth. Museums house objects made for display, which Maquet, following A. Malraux, calls "art by destination," but they also show objects originally made for some other purpose, which become "art by metamorphosis" when they are "framed" in the museum environment. The second category can include almost anything made anywhere in the world, and thus all of what is usually called traditional African art.

In practice, the two definitions tend to overlap because the "total disinterested vision" that aesthetic objects stimulate is best achieved when the object is framed in such a way as to set it apart from such distractions as the wealth and social importance of the owner or the owner's family (Maquet 1986, 33). This requirement tends to restrict art to the museum and the experience of it to an artificially narrow, visual mode which many art movements in the twentieth century have challenged.[2]

Until the development of studio arts in Africa, objects were not made there to be "art," although in many areas the skill and creative imagination of experts in many media were (and are) greatly esteemed. Many utilitarian objects (East African headrests, for example, or carved Somali spoons) are made and used with obviously deliberate attention to their aesthetic qualities, that is, the pleasure they give the eye; presumably, this pleasure is experienced during contemplative moments, or perhaps simply in the course of use. Most African objects likely to be metamorphosed into art by collectors and critics do not depend for their visual effect, in their intended environment, on contemplation; on the contrary, they are usually experienced in the midst of noise, dust, darkness, and dancing. Whereas the museum or gallery situation privileges visual experience to the systematic exclusion of all other forms, African art is often deliberately concealed or only partly visible, and the sight of it is accompanied by a variety of other sensual stimuli.

Spirits

"Spirituality," in modern Western usage, can mean anything from theology to alternative medicine, but in Africa, as K. Wiredu indicates, most of what are usually called "spirits" in connection with African religion are not regarded "spiritually." Spirits, trance states, and magical devices do not belong to a supernatural world that follows a logic different from that of everyday life. The activity of spirits and the efficacy of ritual are banalities—facts, not fantasies (Olivier de Sardan 1992, 11)—but although they are mundane, such entities and processes are not normally visible. This fact helps us to limit our topic.

The function of much of what is now called African art is to give a visual impression of the reality of invisible personalities and forces, thereby confirming their truth but at the same time preserving the boundary between the visible and the invisible. Whereas modern art theory assumes that the gallery- or museum-goer can or should be able to see, and so grasp, the work, which is taken to be, as it were, open, the essence of African art may be that in seeing you do not see. Some of the most respected and spirit-related objects are rarely seen by anybody; in the words of A. F. Roberts, "not seeing is believing" (Roberts 1993). In a very broad sense, African art is the art of the mask.[3]

In Africa, knowledge itself is considered to be a kind of spiritual force. It is exclusive, mysterious, and possibly dangerous. Sometimes such knowledge is of the kind that might be called scientific elsewhere, such as the knowledge of working or healing, but Africans did not distinguish this from other kinds of knowledge until the emergence of African philosophy. Knowledge includes not only the experience of spirits and how to deal with them but social and forensic skills based on proverbs, ritual formulae, traditions, and genealogies. Some knowledge consists simply of the privilege of being "in the know," even though the secret is that there is in fact nothing there.

Knowledge and spirits adapt to changes; new cults are imported, old secrets are abandoned. Art objects are traded over distance between different groups, some of whom may specialize in providing their neighbors with masks and the like. Entire masquerades may be copied or purchased. The aesthetic effects of objects, surrounded and augmented by music, rules, dance, and ceremony, may itself facilitate change. The essentially ironic and paradoxical character of masks, in which what is apparent contrasts with intended meaning, what is with what might be, encourages ideological reflection. "[Tabwa cult adepts] are possessed by spirits in a catharsis that brings insight, perception, and solutions to nagging dilemmas, sudden crises, and life-threatening circumstances" (Roberts 1990, 47). The appearance of spirits upsets the normal order and is often an occasion for sexual references and charades that would normally be forbidden (Bravmann 1974, 114). Art causes us to see the world anew.

Inside and Outside

Henry Drewal's description of a Yoruba masquerade (southwestern Nigeria) provides a point of departure (Drewal 1977). Each of the features he mentions is replicated, as we shall see, in many reports from a vast area of Middle Africa, from Sierra Leone to Zambia. The area is generally forested, and the inhabitants all speak languages of the great Niger-Congo family (Greenberg 1966). Most African art with religious functions comes from this area, but the fact is not reducible to the availability of wood or to the nature of language. Certain representatives of the West Atlantic group, the Adamawa group and the eastern Bantu languages (all Niger-Congo), and the unrelated Nilo-Saharan family are associated with arts and cosmologies of quite different character. There are arts, spiritualities, secrets, and religiously sanctioned concentrations of power, but they do not coincide in the same way.

The Yoruba claim that a person has exterior and interior aspects. A person's exterior reveals little or nothing of what sort of person he or she is; it is the inner aspect that controls all thoughts and actions (Drewal 1977, 546). The human being is thus himself (or herself) a mask, an exterior that conceals what we might call a spirit or soul which is the essence of that person. In possession trances, the spirit of a deity takes over control; the individual temporarily becomes someone else. The inner aspect is considered to be more powerful and less easy to discern in women than in men. Because secrecy is thus inherent in femaleness, all Yoruba cults, even those supposedly male and closed to women, have at least one powerful female official (ibid., 547).

The body is a container as well as a mask. Women are more contained, especially older women who no longer menstruate, and therefore have greater inner power than men. These "mothers" are regarded as subordinate only to the supreme deities, Olodumare and Orunmila, and superior to all *orishas;* they are called the white, or cool gods, in opposition to the hot or hard *orishas* (Drewal 1977, 551). Their mystic power can be used destructively if not propitiated. Efe/Gelede masquerades at the start of the agricultural cycle honor the special powers of women, to dissuade them from doing harm. The elders of the cult and the maskers themselves are men, though the costumes are female.

Efe is the night version of the cult; its mask is Iyanla, the great mother, the most sacred mask. "Preliminary masqueraders prepare the entrance of Iyanla, who comes in total darkness. While she is abroad, all lights must be extinguished for no one must gaze on the face of the mother." As she moves in a gentle, slow dance, matching her steps with the drum rhythms, the elders of the cult flock around her to limit the audience's view of the headdress, which is carried in an almost horizontal position and largely obscured by a long white cloth (Drewal 1977, 553). The mask itself is a bold, simple shape, quite unlike the daylight Gelede masks; it consists of a head with a long, flat "beard." When the carver has completed it, using a prescribed type of wood obtained from the forest in a prescribed fashion, the elders apply medicines to empower the mask, which otherwise is just a piece of wood. "The medicines . . . are an essential part of the image and determine, as much as any visible motifs, people's ideas, attitudes, and reactions concerning the form" (ibid., 558). The relatively large size of the mask indicates its importance; the prominence of the forehead suggests that it is swollen with spiritual force; and the long white cloth symbolizes the unity and prosperity of the community. The "beard" is clearly no ordinary beard; it indicates the ambiguous "otherness" of the mother, who possesses two bodies—that is, she embodies both genders, whose relations are at issue—and simultaneously, by analogy, suggests that she mediates between this visible world and the other, more powerful world of spirits.

Because the radiating power of the medicines can cause physical harm to viewers, especially young women, the mask is kept partially or completely concealed in a shrine when it is not in active use. "So while in one sense a performance implies observation by an audience, the audience is purposefully given very limited access to the image and may in fact never see it." Drewal concludes: "What has the greatest impact upon all present is the invisible—the obstructed view and concealed medicine—that gives the mask a special aura of power" (1977, 559).

The Yoruba experience of a mask such as this is radically different from that of the museum-goer who sees it in the antiseptic silence of a museum. The visible form of the wooden object is its least important feature. In contrast, Gelede, the daylight masquerade, is not only more accessible but is composed of "enthralling imagery" (Drewal and Drewal 1983, 152). The costume represents either a male or a female, the latter consisting of an exaggerated structure of breasts and buttocks, decked in an extravagance of brightly colored cloths. The mask proper is the face of a man or of a beautiful woman, surmounted by an elaborately carved superstructure that comments on some aspect of Yoruba life and values, "anchored in certain fundamental beliefs about the spiritual powers of women and the means of channeling them for society's benefit" (ibid., 270). The inventiveness and skill of the sculptors of these masks is endlessly astonishing.

Although the masquerade is serious in its social commentary, it also provides entertainment; the point of the masquerade is to show off the costumes and the skill of the dancers to the whole community, which itself participates in the event. The tension between what is internal, powerful, and secret and that which is external and relatively profane is matched visually in the contrast between the two parts of the cult, nocturnal and diurnal. Such tension is also at the heart of humor everywhere; entertainment and the sacred are intrinsically related.

Persons as Containers, Containers as Persons

The essential idea of a mask, that of an outer covering for a vital spirit at least partly unseen, typifies a continuum of art forms found from Sierra Leone to southern Congo. Variations on the type include masked kings, reliquaries, graves, charms, and the human body itself in modified form.

Kings

Masks are often medicated, although only in a few instances have scholars been able to determine the rationale for the medicines. Yoruba kings (*Oba*) are transformed by the rituals of investiture into exceptional beings. The Oba is masked by his crown, with beads that hang down in front of his face, because no ordinary person may look directly upon him. Most crowns have a generic face on the front, to depersonalize the king and emphasize the perpetual kingship. A crown is medicated so strongly that even the Oba may not look inside it; considered to be itself an *orisha* (spirit), it gives the Oba power over witches and spirits (Pemberton 1989). The crown may be treated with respect, in his absence, as though it were the Oba, but nevertheless the crown needs to be associated with a live king, whose body itself provides continuity with his predecessors; he is one of the essential ingredients of the whole. If an Oba "changes position" he is not said publicly to have died (Lawal 1977, 56). The regalia of the "immortal" Akuapem king (in Ghana) reveal him as the holder of the office: "their outer form is publicly visible but their inner contents remain veiled, just as the sacredness of the kingship is concealed—though visually represented—within the king's person" (Gilbert 1993, 137).

M. D. McLeod makes a useful distinction between "statement art" and "process art." Statement images are those meant to represent that which is formal, fixed, and timeless; they are intended to elevate rulers, whether kings or lineal ancestors, to superhuman status—their function is to deny time, and they communicate that message by their form alone (McLeod 1976). Process images, on the other hand, are deployed to mediate relations between persons in real time. They depend for their message on associated codes such as proverbs or other verbal utterances that adapt their significance to the situation at hand. When the occasion has passed, the images may be abandoned, as is often the case with images used to instruct novices in initiation rites, or masks for annual entertainments. Or it may be that through repeated use their form alters, as they accumulate the residues of sacrifice or other records of processes past, and they become increasingly sacred. But evidently there is a continuum here, not a sharp contrast. The regalia of the sacred king are brought out from time to time as part of the material infrastructure of rituals. The most dangerous masks receive sacrifices even though the human witnesses to the event are few, and the memorial to an ancestor may last no longer than the materials of which it is made. As we will see, the associated codes are many, not only verbal.

Luba Women

The body of the king, itself masked by robes and crown, conceals an extraordinary vitality. The Luba of southeastern Congo, the significance of whose much-admired artworks has recently been investigated in the field by Mary Nooter, entertain strikingly similar beliefs in the powers of women to those of the Yoruba (Nooter 1990). Both the Yoruba and Luba speak languages of the great Niger-Congo language family, but this linguistic relationship is as distant as the geographic one. For the Luba the principal container of spiritual power is the transformed female body. They say, "Men are chiefs in the daytime, but women become chiefs at night," and all Luba emblems of power are based on the female form, expressing the idea that the royal dynasty depends for its reproduction on women. Although the kings were men and this is a patriarchal society organized with matrilineal descent groups, the Luba think of kingship itself as feminine. Womanhood is the source of both art and power; carved female figures on the staffs of chiefs cross their hands over their breasts to show that it is they who keep the secrets of the kingship.

Like the Yoruba, the Luba think that spirits reside in the forest, in the deep of the earth, and in the inner space of the person. The natural bodies of men and women are considered uncivilized; female bodies in particular undergo processes of modification to enhance their sexual attractiveness and thus their fitness to become vessels to contain and transmit political power. The modified body, eroticized by rich scarification, elongated labia and intricate coiffures, is itself a work of art, imitated in sculpture. Probably the best known type of Luba art is the royal stool, its seat supported by the figure of a kneeling woman. Such stools are not to be sat on and are brought out only on rare occasions. A stool represents a spirit capital, the village of a deceased king, where his spirit is embodied in a female spirit-medium. It acquires sacredness not only by its form but also by its use in rituals, where oil and sacrificial blood continue the transformation of the surface.

The female image in sacred sculptures of the Luba, though the feature most obvious to the eye, was not the most significant. Geometric designs on stools and staffs, called "scarification," were essential to their effectiveness as recipients of sacrificial and medicinal substances. The verb "to scarify" also means "to clear the way to the royal capital," and "to embellish" means "to produce order." In the Kongo and Yoruba languages, verbs meaning "to scarify" also mean "to open the way," thus to impose order and civilization.

Kongo Minkisi

The Kongo of western Congo and neighboring territories objectify the body still further (MacGaffey 1993). They think that a soul can be contained in, or transferred into, a human or animal body or an object, and that the container can be animated more or less by powerful spirits. The spirit (or soul) inside an ordinary human being is considered incapable of much; to be able to do remarkable things, its inner resources must be fortified by additional elements. Ritual experts (*nganga*) can only deal with witches by having within them witchcraft substance (*kundu*), itself supposedly derived from the soul of a human victim. The souls of persons killed by sinister means can also be enclosed in, for example, a stoppered bottle, where they are forced to work for their master and generate wealth for him. This is also the generic model of a *nkisi,* whose visual form is intended to suggest the presence of masked forces under control.

The Kongo have had few masks but many *minkisi* ("power objects"; singular *nkisi*) which take the form of an anthropomorphic or zoomorphic figure, an animal horn, a clay pot, a basket, and many others.[4] The container itself is a mere object until it is animated by "medicines," which are of two principal kinds. Chalk, signifying the land of the dead, or earth from a grave brings the power of the dead into the composite. Sinister, violent *minkisi* are thought to contain the souls of victims mysteriously slain for the purpose. The second and more numerous and varied kind of medicines are those that metaphorically or by a kind of pun on their names suggest the purposes to which the power of the dead is to be put. For example, an eagle feather implies that the *nkisi* will strike its victim suddenly and from above, as does a bird of prey; the inclusion of the creeper, *ndandanzila,* "road follower," suggests that the *nkisi* will track down wrongdoers; in these "process images," words are built into what the viewer sees. Some of the animating forces (such as the feather) are visible on the outside of the container; others are contained in tightly wrapped bundles or in resin-sealed packs, often faced by a mirror in which is revealed the direction from which malice approaches. The container of the *nkisi* is part of its metaphorical description of itself. A bag full of white powder, bearing sea or snail shells, announces its relation to the life-giving force of terrestrial waters; a male statue with threatening spear upraised promises violence. Even anthropomorphic figures are never images of the spirit of the *nkisi;* the assemblage summarizes the process of interaction between the spiritual entity and the object of its action.

Properly composed, the *nkisi* takes on the attributes of a person: it can be cajoled, invoked, mobilized, even insulted. Each of the many types of *minkisi*, identified by name and reputation, is associated with the service or group of services it is believed to be able to perform, if its rules and rituals are properly observed. As a Kongo commentator put it, "One would not, for example, take *nkisi* Mwe Nsundi for a headache, or Mbwanga for stomachache." Sacred objects, like persons, display their sacredness in the behavior they impose on people around them, in the form of avoidance, obeisance, food taboos or the nonuse of certain words, for example; such behaviors, though not collectable, may be significant according to the same principles as those that govern the composition of the object, and may thus be part of it.

The two principal classes of *minkisi* are those said to be "of the above," which are thought of as predominantly masculine, red, and violent in the retribution they inflict on malefactors, and those of the below, which are thought of as predominantly feminine, cool white, and productive of fertility and good health. This contrast is broadly similar to that which Yoruba draw between different kinds of *orisha.*

Chiefs were, in precolonial times, a kind of superior *nkisi*, ritually fabricated and then tested for efficacy, like ordinary *minkisi*. In the rite of investiture, continuity with the dead and with past chiefs was provided by the sacred white clay, *mpemba*, a word that is also the name of the land of the dead. Medicines metaphorically spelled out the powers of the ruler, which were maintained only by respecting prohibitions which extended the metaphors in time. The Kongo king was in fact called *nkisi* (in the sixteenth century), just as the Kuba king, in central Congo, was called by a cognate term, *ngesh.*

Occasional Masks

The spirit contained in a body and partly revealed by the body's appearance may be temporarily replaced by another, as in cases of spirit possession. When possession happens, the unusual behaviors of the body, including but not limited to trembling, trance, glossolalia, and the like, signify the inward change. These signs may be supplemented by special masks (Kramer 1993). In elaborate possession traditions, the costumes and behaviors reveal the identity of the particular spirit who is present, as one of a roster of possibilities. Elsewhere, as among the Kongo, the possessing spirit is and apparently always has been nondescript (the multiplicity of figured *minkisi* seems to have made other kinds of masks generally redundant).

Initiation, often represented as a death, a liminal period of change in another world, and a rebirth, usually requires seclusion, so that the novice becomes a "secret," and a mask or costume indicating that he or she is, at this moment, no ordinary being. So the women returning from initiation school have their bodies smeared with white and wear special costumes and nonfigurative face masks, which literally deny them their ordinary identity. A Tabwa diviner in a state of possession is smeared with white, partially masked, and costumed with signs that indicate his mediating role between the seen and the unseen (Nooter 1993, 67, 87). "Artworks" of this kind are not collectable, but are otherwise logically indistinguishable from other masks and sacred vessels.

Cosmology and Social Relations

Although the logic of the spirit world does not sharply contrast with that of the world of the visible and everyday, which it often strongly resembles, recognizing the difference between two worlds presupposes that there is a certain cosmology, which is itself often represented in African art. The invisible world is white, a color that connotes the presence of the dead but also the virtues of inner tranquillity, wisdom, and innocence. Black tends to be associated with the visible world, especially with the obscurity of witchcraft and with the unruly, organic processes of sorcery, procreation, and war. Some masks and other sculptures are halved in black and white, or have Janus heads, indicating that they mediate between worlds. The color red marks states of danger, transition, and liminality. Colors may be combined in significant ways, but meaning is situational and can never be read automatically; one cannot write dictionaries of symbolism in African art.

Apparently decorative geometrical patterns may have a more profound cosmological significance than an anthropomorphic component of the same sculpture. In West Africa, a tight, zig-zag pattern indicates water, celestial or terrestrial, one of the three cosmological domains. In Tabwa art (in southeastern Congo), a simple pattern that appears purely decorative conveys a basic cosmological idea that is also the key to a profound philosophy. Called "the rising of the moon," it consists of a row of isosceles triangles arranged in such a way that their bases form two parallel lines. For the Tabwa, the new moon is a time of renewal; the darkened moon is a time of danger, when witchcraft threatens (Maurer and Roberts 1985, 3).

In Benin (south central Nigeria) a pendant in the form of a cross identifies the agent of the creator god and is itself a sign of the creation, the act of dividing the universe into the two worlds (Ben-Amos 1980, 40). The deity Olokun is identified with the passages of death and birth across the waters between the worlds, which "meet at the riverbank" (Ben-Amos 1972, 30). Whereas the everyday world is beset by dangers, Olokun's kingdom abounds in wealth, peace, and joy. The riverbank is the source of mud, halfway between worlds, between earth and water, from which sculptures are made for the shrines of Olokun, portrayed as the king of the spirit world. He and other spirits of this kind are cool, symbolized by white; they are contrasted with Ogiuwu, bringer of death, symbolized by black, and with the red of Ogun and Osun, associated with violence, fire, and blood (Ben-Amos 1980, 49). P. Ben-Amos shows how Olokun symbolism is generated by an underlying cosmographic image, within which individual artists find their themes.

The similar cosmology of the Yoruba is often visualized as either a spherical gourd, whose upper and lower hemispheres fit tightly together, or as a divination tray, both of which forms become finely carved works of art (Drewal and Pemberton 1989, 14). The tray, upon which the diviner begins by inscribing a cross to mark the four cosmic directions and the intersection of the worlds, has at its head the figure of Eshu, mediator between humans and gods. At the center of a Yoruba town, the crossroads, the spirit Agan, who must not be seen by anyone, is heard opening the festival of Egungun (Drewal and Drewal 1983, 4). A similar cosmology, with a similar though less developed cast of spirits, is found among the Kongo in western Congo and the Americas (Thompson and Cornet 1981).

Temne women (in Sierra Leone) belong to the Bondo association, into which they are initiated as girls in a ritual dominated by a helmet mask called Nowo. This mask, the epitome of female sexual allure, is black (as is the costume) with a strip of white cloth attached to the helmet. All female Temne spirits are black, black being thought of as a positive color, the color of beautiful people and the sign of the physical world in its "civilized" form. White refers to the spiritual, but is regarded by Temne as the predominant color of male spirits; it is possible, however, that the black raffia of the costume represents the spiritual forces of the masculine and death-bringing forest (Lamp 1985, 30, 43).

Nowo is a water spirit. A cult leader narrates his experience with Nowo:

In a dream Nowo appeared to me and told me to go to the river and beat drums. I went into the river and stayed for three days to arrange for the taking of Nowo. But the water that I went under was not the water of this world (that is, it was the water of the way to the other world). I had arranged a group of people on the shore who began to beat drums. They began to play and sing, and I saw Nowo coming, little by little. Then I arose out of the water. I took the head of Nowo—only the head, not the raffia body—and I carried it out with me. Then I prepared a raffia dress for it. (Lamp 1985, 33)

The mask itself shows the elaborate hairdo proper to an elegant woman, suggesting the refinement of civilization. Both it and the girls undergoing initiation are compared to the chrysalis of the butterfly—a metaphor for the transformation of immature and sexless girls into beautiful, powerful women. The neck rings of the mask correspond to the basal rings of a chrysalis, to the ripples of the water as the mask emerges, and to ideals of both male and female beauty.

The form of the mask is also cosmographic. The direction east, which is also upwards, is feminine, the source of life; west, which is also downwards, is masculine, associated with the decline of the sun and with death. Features of the top of the mask refer to the germination of new life, since fertilizing spirits are believed to enter the head from above. In the ideal village, east is the direction of the gardens, west of the untamed Poro bush; the mask's braided hair recalls that, in myth, the cultivated earth is described as the braided hair of a "great person." The cosmos consists of the physical world, "the place of braiding," and the spiritual world, the place of the "penetration" of the invisible. Between them is the river, which the dead cross (Lamp 1985, 40-41). Lamp notes the similarity between the cosmologies implicit in this mask and in Kongo art and thought.

Architecture

Microcosms and macrocosms take a variety of artistic forms. In Central Africa, the house is seen as analogous to the female body and the procreative capacity; its parts may be identified, decorated, and medicated accordingly: the male housepost, the doorway as vagina, and the back door (or a hole in the back wall) as the way of death. In the modern religious movement called Bwiti, in Gabon, the chapel carries complex cosmographic significance, elaborated in three dimensions, as in the Nowo mask. The two sides of the chapel: the left (facing away from the altar, toward the entrance and exit) is associated with birth, women, the moon, and red color; the right, with death, sun, men, and white. Movement within the chapel proceeds counterclockwise from the left-hand doorway, past the pillar of earth and heaven and the life of the visible, into the realm of the unseen and back through the right-hand doorway. The altar, beyond which lies the land of the dead beyond the great water, dominates the zone of the unseen (Fernandez 1982, 280). The carved central pillar represents the vertical dimension of the red road of birth and death; two holes in it represent birth (large and near the ground) and death (small, and as close to "heaven" as possible). The hole in which the pillar stands is medicated, and the pillar itself blessed (ibid., 374, 395).

The traditional homestead of the Dogon of Mali responds to an entirely different cosmology. The plan of the building is said to represent the demiurge Nommo, in the form of a man lying on his side, procreating. The kitchen represents the head, whose eyes are the stones of the hearth; the trunk is symbolized by the central room, the arms by two lines of storerooms, and so forth. "The whole plan is contained in an oval which itself represents the great placenta from which have emerged, in the course of time, all living beings, and everything in the world" (Griaule and Dieterlen 1954, 97–98).

Male and Female

Closely related to cosmology, as we have already seen, are the foundational social relations of gender and generation, whose constitution is sacred in every society. Generation is the social dimension explicit in ancestor cults; it is always built on hierarchy. What matters about gender is not maleness or femaleness as such but the ambivalent interdependence of the two, always at least latently competitive. Among the Wan people of the Ivory Coast, neighbors of the Baule, a group of three masks called Goli, whose particular names can be translated Youth, Man, and Woman, play an important role at the burial of an adult man and later at his funeral (Ravenhill 1988). Each masquerade costume includes a wooden mask that is its "head," a bark fiber cape and skirt, bracelets and anklets, and an animal skin attached to the back. In the costumes we find expressed a set of oppositions, simultaneously cosmological and social. The Youth mask is black; it includes references to solitary animals, and it behaves in an uncouth manner. The Man mask is predominantly red, to suggest violence; he represents the ancestors and thus both death and the continuity of the lineage. Unlike Youth's, his power derives from experience rather than brute force. The Woman mask is a relatively naturalistic representation of the cultural ideal of female beauty: scarification, elegant coiffure, earrings, chipped teeth. Cape and skirt are as clean and white as possible, whiteness being associated with purity, water, well-being, and coolant. White animals are sacrificed to water spirits. In the set of three masks, animal (in the forest) is opposed to human (in the village); they express the fundamental relations of life and death, gender and generation. Individually they are associated, respectively, with the cosmological domains of earth, sky, and water. A similarly constructed triptych, contrasting male and female, elder and youth, is found in the *kifwebe* masquerades of the Songye in eastern Congo, employing a related but considerably more complex grammar of animal, chromatic, and cosmological significance (Hersak 1990).

Among the We of Ivory Coast, most masking is the exclusive business of men and it is considered dangerous to women. But the women have a masquerade of their own in which a respected woman dances in costume, performing functions similar to those of the male maskers but with only this difference. Her performance is not called "a mask" and her face is covered with paint instead of wood (Admas 1986). It would seem that women are regarded as already "masked."

In the sculptured couples of the Senufo (Ivory Coast), the female is usually larger than the male. This makes "a succinct declaration, in plastic terms, of core Senufo social and religious concepts: the procreative, nourishing, sustaining role of both mothers and Deity; the priority of the uterine line in tracing relationships and determining succession rights to title and property; and the special role of women as intermediaries with the supernatural world" (Glaze 1976, 51). Like the Temne, the Senufo stress to an unusual degree, at least in their rituals, the complementarity and interdependence of the sexes. Women are considered more important than men in securing the goodwill of the deity, the ancestors, and bush-spirits. The more secret the activity, the greater the importance of women (ibid., 48). At funerals, senior initiates of the women's Tyekpa society dance over the body, holding the large imposing female sculptures above their heads, threatening death to male viewers. Here, sculpture is animated by dance and music, in a way usually associated with masks, and the intimidating role usually adopted by male associations is taken over by women, who do not need to be masked (ibid., 87). Tyekpa, like Bondo, is the women's version of Poro. "An elder woman discovered the bush spirits drumming and dancing by a stream; she exclaimed at the beauty of the dance and was then told she could take for herself the bush spirits' Tyekpa" (ibid., 85).

In one of the best-known types of Senufo art object, a maiden carved at the top of the "champion cultivator" staff, associated with the men's agricultural competitions, carries on her head a sort of bowl containing secret medicines that strengthen the champion and defend him against hostile magic (Glaze 1976, 34). In Senufo sculpture, red usually implies the danger-ous knowledge possessed by older men, but the bowl on the staff is "a hot red . . . this lion, this juice of red peppers."

All Senufo masquerades are performed by males organized into various kinds and levels of the exclusive Poro association. Besides the village Poro, or "Large Sacred Forest," there are also specialized ones for smaller settle-ments and occupational groups. The true head of Poro, however, is a woman, and the role of the female is intrinsic to the functions of the associ-ation. Helmet masks, showing an open-jawed animal, signify death and masculinity; face-masks signify femininity, fertility, and communal well-being, but even the helmet masks are complemented by staffs carrying female figures (Glaze 1986, 30). The glossy black of face-masks connotes ideally beautiful femininity, but black in the form of old sacrificial encrus-tations on a helmet mask refers to male Poro and the shedding of blood (ibid., 32).

Each village of the Afikpo (southeastern Nigeria) supports a fraternity to which all adult men belong and with which the village masquerades are associated. But whereas Senufo emphasize the special role of women, even in the men's associations, the Afikpo say their association is intended to keep women in their place. Women are afraid of it, and if one should see the activities forbidden to women she would no longer conceive. The soci-ety is directed by a group of senior title-holders and one of ritual specialists (Ottenberg 1975, 9). Putting on a mask "turns a man into a spirit, *mma*" a manifestation of the society's deity (*egbele*), which remains in the sacred bush. No one is supposed to know who the masker is, although many do. *Mma* is also a term for any unknown thing, such as a white man or type-writer. The most popular Afikpo masquerade is *okumpkpa*, a series of satir-ical skits commenting on real people, at which a hundred maskers may be present. In a pattern we have already encountered, the darker and "uglier" Afikpo masks are worn by older men, the more "feminine" by younger men (ibid., 11–13).

Ancestors

The role of "ancestors" in African religion has been greatly exaggerated; not all of those who normally inhabit the land of the dead are ancestors, recognized by groups of descendants (Siroto 1976). Others of the dead include "heroes" (whose historical reality is usually in doubt) and the spir-its of natural forces whose powers serve the interests of local communities rather than descent groups. Among the most striking and distinctive of African sculptures are those that represent Tshibinda Ilunga, the great hunter and civilizer who founded chiefship among the Tshokwe (Cokwe). Sculptors transform his chief's winged headgear into a majestic structure. He carries his gun, knife, charms, and other equipment necessary for hunting; his huge hands and feet signify his skill and endurance (Bastin 1994, 41). Of nature spirits, we have already encountered a number.

The term "ancestor" is used, loosely enough, to refer to spirits of historical, remembered, or purely hypothetical forebears, usually male (even in societies with matrilineal groups). In general, they are severe authority figures and will visit afflictions upon their descendants if they feel neglected in the matter of palm wine, tobacco, or other good things they enjoyed in life. When a man dies, "his strength grows greater and his vision sharper" (De la Burde 1972). The respect due to them is similar in kind, though greater in degree, to that owed to living elders. Not everybody goes on to become an ancestor, only those who were distinguished in their lifetime, or who left many descendants. Often enough, an ancestor is simply a projection of the identity of the group whose unity he represents.

Images of ancestors include masks, fixed shrines, graves, and portable images. Among Edo-speakers in south central Nigeria, a wooden ram's head representing the ancestor is placed on the family shrine, and sacrifices are made to it (De la Burde 1972). Sometimes shrine figures are roughly anthropomorphic; at other times merely a forked stick or a clay mound. Figures placed in shrines are not usually medicated containers, though they may receive a coating of sacrificial materials such as blood and millet beer; they identify the shrine and share sacredness with it.

The Yoruba "have succeeded in neutralizing the power of Death, using art as a weapon." Myth tells how the first Egungun mask was invented to overcome Death, which formerly invaded life's marketplace unopposed. Death, in Yoruba as in Kongo thought, is not the end of life; it is merely a dematerialization of the vital soul. Heroes such as Shango, worshiped by the whole community, are thought of as not having died in the ordinary way but, for example, as having turned directly into stone sculptures; the ordinary human body is regarded, like sculpture, as a mere mask of temporal existence (Lawal 1977, 50–52).

Egungun *paaka* are masks for the lineage ancestors, who have to be kept happy lest they withhold the blessings of children, wealth, and prestige. They take many forms; one of the most powerful has "small gourds filled with powders, packets of herbs. . . . [P]owerful concoctions made of crushed leaves of various plants, feathers, bits of animal flesh and bone hang from the base of the carved portion and are secreted in the folds of the red cloth that is woven among the black cloths beneath the carving that crowns the masquerade. The dancer wears additional pouches of medicine." An ancestor mask, even when it is identified with a named individual, is not made to recall his original, historically contingent appearance; its presence among the living "is swathed and enshrouded in layer upon layer of cloths, bird plumage, bones of animals, the skin of a snake." It is essential that the dancers be not easily seen; "in the ancestral force they represent all traces of individuality and of time fall away" (Pemberton 1978, 41–46). The mask separates the worlds of physical and metaphysical action, thus denying the power of death, which can act only on the physical. People know that the mask hides a dancer, but they believe that the preparatory rituals have depersonalized him; he is "a mask within the mask." The dancer's voice, also, is guttural and otherworldly (Lawal 1977, 54, 59).

The Yoruba use a sculpted likeness of the deceased during the second-burial rites to demonstrate that he has "changed position," and also to impress upon him that "having cast off his earthly mask, he must now proceed to heaven to join the souls of his predecessors and to team up with them to help the living." The destruction of his effigy implies that his former mask can never be reused. The better to make use of the power of the departing soul, his descendants may build a shrine for him, with a stylized, generic effigy into which, his last mask, he moves at the moment of invocation (Lawal 1977).

Farther east, near the confluence of the Niger and Benue Rivers, Eku masks of the Igbirra also represent deceased elders. The great variety in the style of the masks may be explained by the fact that the magical substances attached to it, not the mask itself, are sacred (Unrug 1983). The Bangwa of Cameroon regard ancestor statues as portraits; though they are memorials, not shrines (unlike the ancestral skulls), they are treated as persons and may be handled with ritual precautions.

An *nkisi* in Kongo is a sort of portable shrine to a spirit identified by the service it performs. Although it belongs to the class of "the dead," its powers are invoked only by those who suffer from the problem with which it is identified. An ancestor is one whose descendants are entitled to approach him at his grave, a fixed shrine localizing his spirit. Because art has to be collectable, salable, and therefore portable, graves (like human bodies) do not usually enter into the category, but reliquaries do. The Bembe (northern Kongo) made ancestor figures, either carved figurines or somewhat sticklike, wrapped "dolls" (*muzidi*), which did not usually contain any physical relic of the ancestor but into which his spirit was ritually induced to enter. They were made only for families experiencing misfortune (Kavuna 1995; Søderberg 1975). The Fang, Kota, and neighboring peoples in Gabon made figures in the form of highly abstract, two-dimensional representations of the human head, covered (among Kota) with brass or copper; the figures were placed above bundles containing skulls, which served as the "body" of the figure and endowed it with power. The whole can be regarded as a special development of the mask, with the relics as its medication and as its connection with the sacred past. In Calabar (southeastern Nigeria), family groups who could afford it installed a screen to commemorate a wealthy member. These screens were complex constructions carrying a central figure flanked by others (Oelman 1979). In northwestern Nigeria, the Dakakari decorate the family grave mounds of important and wealthier men with flat stones and grave sculptures in terra-cotta, in a style quite different from those of the south (Bassing 1972). In these examples, and many others, it is difficult (and probably inappropriate) to disentangle the components of ritual and display. Modern funerary monuments in cement are among the few classes of objects that are clearly related to the spiritual and may also be intended, in some sense, to be "contemplated," although the contemplation of a splendid screen or tomb is usually intended to induce respect for the social position of the deceased and his family. Admiration for its appearance may well enhance its significance as a shrine.

The Miji Kenda of northeastern Kenya carve grave posts (*vigango;* singular *kigango*) for deceased, influential elders, erecting a grave post when it is believed that the elder is causing misfortune to the living because he feels neglected. The long, narrow, planklike post is a focus for offerings placed in a bowl at its foot. The ritual that sets it up includes a blood sacrifice, and the hole in which it is set contains medicine. When the family moves, it does not take with it the post, which will eventually rot. Posts show a highly stylized human body marked out with triangles and other flat, abstract forms. The head is often more realistic, but is intended to be not a portrait but a representation of an ideally beautiful face. Apparently a post is not comparable to a container or a mask.

Social Hierarchies

The universal relationship between weighty seniors and the juniors from whose ranks will come their successors is formalized in some societies into a succession of grades. In many African societies, ritual procedures, unsatisfactorily called "initiation," introduce boys or girls to the lowest grade of an exclusive association of men or women. The highest grade is that of the "elders," or perhaps of people who by reason of their knowledge, skill, wealth, family connections, or other abilities have become community leaders. The number of intervening grades varies, as does the degree of exclusiveness, which sometimes properly attracts the label "secret society."

The visual language of initiation rituals becomes increasingly abstract and metaphorical in the advanced grades (Nooter 1993, 25). Together, such grades share responsibility for such functions as the settlement of disputes, the administration of justice, punishment, and communal defense against the attacks of sorcerers and malicious spirits.

Not only the knowledge acquired by the members but also their personal identity may not be publicly known. Particular grades may manifest their exclusiveness and their public responsibilities dramatically in masquerades, impressing others by the character of the masks, the skill of musicians and dancers, and the pervasive sense of mystery. Masks and masquerades are empowered by spirits, but it is not usually useful to think of the spirit as an entity existing apart from the performance; the mask is the spirit, on the occasion of the performance, and the spirit is the mask. Much the same fusion is true, in general, of ancestral figures and shrines. Behind the power attributed to the spirit lies the real force, moral and physical, of the group that reforms it or prays or sacrifices to it. Bangwa Night Society masks are carved to resemble terrifying, powerful men; they are carried, never worn, and would kill anyone who tried to do so.

Among the Igbo there are thousands of masks. The masking organizations vary in their social base—secret fraternity, age-grade, grade, village cult—but are overwhelmingly male and are hierarchically organized (Cole and Aniakor 1984, 111). Their masks are likewise ranked. All masks are considered to be spirits, the returning dead, not ancestors in the lineal sense.

Ideally "beautiful" and feminine masks belong to younger grades; horns, teeth, smelly medicines, and other natural ingredients compose the threatening masks danced by successful, middle-aged men. These "great male spirits," deliberately unpleasant, often carry strong medicines and are so destructive they may have to be restrained by ropes; they must be appeased by sacrifices, and the dancer must be protected and strengthened by medicines (Cole and Aniakor 1984, 114, 131). They are assembled over a long period of time and require a levy on all the men of the village to pay for them; villages compete with one another to have the most powerful masks. These masks represent the collective power of the older men who accompany them. They turn out in terrifying array to convey the soul of a deceased elder to the land of the dead. They also had effective and final governmental powers (ibid., 134). The contrast is evident between masks that are light, beautiful, and predominantly white and those that are heavy, ugly, black, and male, but this oversimplification breaks down amid the multiplicity of Igbo mask representations, which can include "the European," "the Hausa diviner," a mother, a hunter, and many others (ibid., 113).

Where the hierarchy of authority is explicit, as it is by definition in king-doms, the images that express and confirm it tend toward "status art"; though stylized, they are relatively realistic and do not need accompanying explanations. The bronze memorial head on the altar to a deceased Oba of Benin looks like a live Oba in his royal regalia. Ben-Amos tells us that the palace shrines honoring the royal ancestors are the only ones that are national in scope; the art objects found on them reflect the hierarchical structure of the kingdom (Ben-Amos 1980, 60, 64). This hierarchy is not simply secular, however; the Oba is considered to be a force for moral good, and he must also exercise the powers of sorcery. He is the counter-part of Olokun on earth (Ben-Amos 1972, 31). Conspicuous consumption, political emblems, and reference to spirits lie on a continuum.

"Realism" in royal memorials does not amount to portraiture, however; the memorial, though it represents a named individual, shows a generic Oba. The identities of the beautifully carved *ndop* "portrait" statues of Kuba kings (central Congo) are revealed by the emblem each carries, not by facial features. Realism, in this sense, is also characteristic of some very ordinary ancestral figures and many others that are "spirits" lacking social biogra-phies. In any case, what a given sculpture "represents" depends on the degree of knowledge of the person who is looking at it. A relatively recog-nizable Senufo hornbill mask, with its long beak and swelling belly, is a bird but also evokes ideas of procreation, while the leopard carved on the back of it combines the terrestrial with the aerial, and perhaps death with life.

Cool Spirits

However they may be identified, ancestors, who have biographies and descendants, are about the dimension of time in social life, about social reproduction from generation to generation. Local communities, consist-ing of members of more than one descent group, have as their common interests such concerns as the fertility of the soil, the benevolence of the weather, and the incidence of disease. Such interests are represented in cults of "nature" or "bush" spirits, tutelary deities of space, of particular locali-ties; they are often identified with streams, sacred groves, or rocks. Though these spirits are dangerous and can cause harm, they are principally associ-ated, as we have seen, with prosperity, tranquillity, and feminine character-istics.

Minkisi are believed to originate with nature spirits, such as occur gener-ally throughout the forest areas of West and Central Africa. Among the Dan of Liberia, it is thought that when nature spirits, unhappy with their invisible, bodiless nature, want to make themselves useful, they arrange to incorporate themselves in objects. In a typical narrative that could as well be Kongo, it is said that the spirit appears in a dream to a sympathetic person to whom it can give future-telling powers, animal strength, or political influence, among other good things.

> In return, the spirit dictates the manner in which it should be manifested and sustained. Its appearance can be static, in the form of a bundle of fur, antelope horns or a small snail shell filled with various ingredients. . . . At other times a spirit may ask for a mobile, living materialization and urge the chosen person to incarnate him, to perform him, with a mask. (Fischer 1978, 18)

In that case, the masker is the spirit itself, not just an impersonation. "The masks, as spirits, are believed to be alive, and it is said they can be heard gnashing their teeth." Like *orishas* and *minkisi,* the masks and the spirits they embody deal with virtually all human concerns (Fischer 1978, 23).

Water-spirit cults are widespread in Nigeria and Cameroon. Idoma, near the Benue River in southeast Nigeria, believe that *anjenu* spirits inhabiting streams and termite hills must be propitiated at shrines, which contain among other items images of the spirits in the form of seated women (Kasfir 1982). Every village of the Abua in Calabar has a masquerade representing a water spirit, whose myth of origin closely resembles others, but which also makes clear that a mask gives shape to something that otherwise lacks it: "The first spirit was found floating on the river as a shapeless piece of wood . . . eventually a cap mask was carved to represent it" (Eyo 1974, 52). Not far away, the Urhobo celebrate, every decade, the festival of Ohworu, a spirit of the deep waters and deep bush. In this instance, the man who first saw the spirit dancing on the surface of a river was given a complete performance kit; he learned its songs, dances, and music and acquired two face-masks, a slit-drum, and a pot of medicines (Foss 1972).

In the north-central Igbo region, community deities are housed in a common temple, appropriately more ornate than other dwellings, where offerings are placed. The deities are tutelary spirits associated with rivers, the market, and lineage ancestors; their anthropomorphic forms are those of ordinary people (Cole and Aniakor 1984, 89). Around Owerri are found unfired, therefore impermanent, mud houses called Mbari, containing wall paintings and sometimes dozens of figures. In this "Spiritual art gallery" are all kinds of realistic scenes of everyday life, including some representations that would normally be improper (Cole and Aniakor 1984, 195). The entire house is a representation of the community, the gods, and the universe. It renews the world. Mbari are made as sacrificial offerings to the community's tutelary deities in times of trouble, by groups of men and women initiated as "spirits" and secluded to serve the deity by building

Mbari. The preparation has something in common with a masquerade, in that although the public admires the outcome they are not privy to the production process. Diviners direct the rituals, order sacrifices, and supervise the proceedings. The importance of the whole thing is the process of creating it; it is not preserved ever after as a work of art.

Spirits in Many Media: Sculptures in Sound

An African artwork in a museum is only part of the material infrastructure of the performance that once manifested the spirit. The infrastructure itself, including a costume now perhaps missing, various medicines and other attachments, auxiliary masks, musical instruments, special houses and screens, was only one dimension of not only the performance but also the experience. A sacred object realizes its sacredness in the behavior it imposes upon the people around it, whether avoidance, food taboos, prescribed forms of speech or music, or demands for food and drink. Such behaviors are as much part of the total representation as the object itself and are often readable in the same metaphorical terms. A performance requires an audience who respond to the demands of the spirit by being frightened, entertained, or excluded.

Most obviously missing from objects that become art by metamorphosis are the effects of sound and movement. A Guere mask from Ivory Coast wears a whole ruff of metal bells. Dancing a mask can be a considerable athletic feat in the case of heavy masks such as the Senufo hornbill mask or *Ijele,* the largest and most expensive of Igbo masks (southeastern Nigeria). *Ijele* is a vast structure of appliquéd cloths, tassels, mirrors, and human and animal figures on a frame, up to eighteen feet high and eight feet wide. Sacrifices are made to the mask when it is completed or reassembled. In this case, the dancer is known and applauded for his heroic effort (Cole and Aniakor 1984, 140). For other masks the expected style may have to be learned; the dancers who perform best are thought of as contributing to the spiritual effectiveness of the mask.

Masks often speak in a special "spirit voice." In the case of "acoustic masks," which are not unusual, the "mask" consists solely of strange voices heard in the night. The Sapo of southeastern Liberia distinguish between "dressed" and "naked" masks. The dressed, or costumed, daytime masks are controlled by young men, who demonstrate their physical powers by bringing these masks out of the forest to entertain with speeches and songs in strange language that must be translated by a speaker. The naked mask, meaning one in which the performer's face is uncovered, belongs to a restricted association of the leading lineages. It appears at nightfall, just outside a village, in the form of a man wearing amulets and a "wig" reminiscent of British-style judges—this being a judicial mask—whose voice is "masked" by the use of a device containing a membrane (Lifschitz 1988).

The art forms of the Bembe of eastern Congo reflect the heterogeneity of the historical influence upon this people. One of their associations is *elanda*, whose mask may be danced only by the head of the association's local cell. The mask expresses power and prestige but also requires skills, including shivering and trembling dance movements, and a way of speaking in a raucous, ventral voice, which may have taken months to learn in secret (Biebuyck 1972, 19). The mask may not be an ancestor, nor is it a nature spirit. It is an *'ebu'a*, something hidden, unseen, unrecognizable, and indefinable. Outsiders are frightened by it, but it reinforces the collective solidarity of initiates, who engage in various forms of law enforcement.

Musical instruments are commonly thought of as voices of the dead. The activation of Kongo *minkisi* was accompanied by specific instruments (rattles, whistles, bells, wooden gongs) that were often exquisitely carved. So close was the association between musical sounds and the powers of the spirits that instruments were often converted into *minkisi* themselves by the addition of medicines, and the constituents of *minkisi* sometimes included miniature versions of the appropriate instruments. In West Africa, large drums were often works of art. The sacred drums of the Yoruba Ogboni cult were rubbed with blood of sacrifices; only initiated members might see their carved decoration (Ojo 1972).

Other Religions, Other Arts

Art intended to suggest the reality and character of spirits is not universally distributed in sub-Saharan Africa. The speakers of Nilo-Saharan languages, found mostly in the savanna zones north of the equatorial forest, entertain subtle ideas of the spiritual. But these ideas, including the cosmologies presupposed in them, are very different from those we have been considering, and their spirit entities are not generally represented or addressed in sculptural or masquerade form.

Dogon

Although the Bamana and Dogon peoples in the arid environments of Mali speak languages belonging to the Niger-Congo family and have produced some of the best-known types of African art, their art forms and the associated cosmologies are very different from those of the forest. The most familiar case is that of the Dogon, whose remarkable cosmogonic theories were reported by Griaule and his associates, beginning in the 1930s. Whereas the Yoruba cosmology, for example, is cyclical and static, that of the Dogon emphasizes the process of differentiation of an original cosmic "egg." Most of Dogon art was deemed to represent the primordial demiurges, often twins, who appeared in the myths. The three principal types of mask (*kanaga, ammata,* and *sirige*) are supposed to refer to three different cosmogonic stages; other masks represent historical events. According to the Dogon sage Ogotemmeli, "the society of masks is the entire world . . . it dances the system of the world" (Dieterlen 1989). Unfortunately, not much has been reported on the context in which masks are actually used, and recent research has cast doubt on the authenticity of Griaule's understanding of Dogon cosmology; critics are now reluctant to interpret the significance of the art. In modern times, masquerades have become primarily public entertainments, rehearsed as such (Imperato 1971).

There is no doubt that Dogon art is religious in intent, oriented toward a series of spirit entities intermediate between the founder of a lineage up to the "first ancestor," called Lebe, the spirit of the fertile earth (Ezra 1988). All Dogon men belong to the Awa association, which performs at men's first and second funerals, and they also participate in the great *sigi* festival, which occurs every sixty years. *Sigi,* somewhat like Egungun, recreates the "great mask" made to contain the force released by that death. Between Lebe and lineage ancestors come the totemic spirits of the clans, remote ancestors who have returned to earth in the form of animals in order to be helpful.

The Griaule school identified nearly all images as versions of Nommo, which are "sons of God," personifications of elements of the creative process, and prefigurations of man (Griaule and Dieterlen 1954). Human figures, often in pairs and couples, sometimes with both male and female sexual attributes, correspond to the frequent appearance in the creation stories and in ritual of twinlike couples and other expressions of balance, complementarity, and fruitful duality. The figures, often encrusted in sacrificial material, are remarkable for the exaggerated vertical and horizontal forms discovered in the human body, and their striking combination. Research has shown that abstract and realistic forms occur in the same historical periods and may be combined on the same sculpture; it is not known why. Such figures are secluded in shrines; little is known about them, and scholars disagree whether the striking and frequent gesture showing both arms upraised represents the creative activity of Nommo or prayer for rain (Ezra 1988).

Masks, on the other hand, are well documented. Griaule listed more than eighty types, constituting an inventory of everything in the Dogon world—people, animals, and things (Ezra 1988, 22). The great mask is never actually worn; other masks were made to deal with subsequent deaths and the dangerous energy released by them. A mask that is not painted or repainted in brilliant colors is nothing but a piece of wood. None of them, apparently, is otherwise "medicated," nor has the attributes of a "container." Hundreds of maskers may appear at an important funeral. The sculptures are made by blacksmiths whose creative powers give them a special role as mediators between heaven and earth.

Komo

Among the Bamana of Mali we find four principal "power associations," each supposed to enhance the community's well-being while controlling its economic and political functions and providing an arena for deadly competitions between persons of power and persons of knowledge (McNaughton 1979). Any undertaking by an association involves sculptures considered so powerful in themselves that merely seeing one is dangerous for the uninitiated. Sculptures are of three types: *boli,* horns, and masks. Each association usually possesses all three kinds, kept secret from all but initiates. All three are composed of more than one kind of material; the secret techniques for assembling them are believed to generate "massive amounts of useful energy."

Komo is the largest and most complex of the societies; the leader in any local community is also the masker. In the course of the association's weekly dance, "he will don his mask and costume and, in a marvelous orchestration of ritual, theater, music, and mobile sculpture, he will respond to the requests that have accumulated during the week." He speaks or sings through a voice-disguising instrument, his words interpreted by a bard who follows him around. The dance performance itself, lasting all night and demanding great skill and strength, is awesome and intimidating (McNaughton 1979, 17, 39).

Masks enable men to harness useful amounts of the enormous and potentially dangerous forces of the universe. A mask is constructed in the bush over a period of weeks, although the carving itself may only take an afternoon. Masks are made and danced by blacksmiths, who of all occupations need the most cosmic energy. One can be born with large amounts of this energy, but can also acquire it in the form of packets of knowledge, consisting of lists of animal, vegetable, and mineral substances, where to find them, how to combine them properly, and the rituals of their use. Packets of knowledge are bought from those who have them and are known to use them well (McNaughton 1979, 24–28).

Komo association masks are the most complex assemblages of such packets of knowledge. The costume is built on a framework of bamboo, which is covered with amulets. The mask itself, intended to be horrific, is in three parts: horns, mouth, and a dome which supports extensions, front and back. At the back, large antelope forms emerge, signifying the dangerous powers of the bush and the animals there; in front, a long, ominous mouth, well furnished with teeth, depicts overwhelming power capable of eating sorcerers. Vulture feathers, suggesting celestial knowledge and medication, and porcupine quills, implying knowledge of sorcery and poisons, are attached to the top of the mask, with other aggressive things. Most masks are coated, except for the feathers and quills, with sacrificial blood, clay, and medicines attached with resins, as the owning blacksmith receives additional packets of knowledge. "These coatings are a kind of visual record of power harnessed through knowledge." The greatest masks are praised as "wild beasts"; seen in a museum, they can be impressive works of art, but in performance they are terrifying (McNaughton 1979, 35).

An association's horns, generally in groups of three, are considered to be an extension of the *boliw* (singular *boli*) and are stored with them. Horns are thought of as storage places for power; like both *boliw* and masks, they come to be coated with sacrificial materials. *Boliw* are among the most enigmatic of objects; assemblages of bones, vegetable matter, honey, and metal, they vaguely resemble animals, but their accumulated coatings of clay and sacrificial materials are intended to render them inscrutable. Their contents and symbolic rationale are known only to initiates.

Other Spirits, Other Bodies

In eastern and southern Africa many different art forms exist, usually without relation to spirits (Krieger 1990). "Until the present century, the vast majority of East African societies did not require visual representation of ancestral or other spiritual forces to enhance their essential life-cycle rituals" (Hartwig 1978, 62). The speakers of Nilotic languages (Eastern Sudanic) in southern Sudan and northern Uganda believe in spirits so abstract as to be barely personified at all; they do not use plastic forms to reinforce belief or to suggest the presence of the invisible (Buxton 1973; Burton 1981). The celebrated artistic traditions and inventions of the Mangbetu (Central Sudanic) and their neighbors in northeastern Congo, for example, were almost entirely devoted to the personal adornment and conspicuous display associated with the aristocracy of the kingdom (Schildkrout and Keim 1990).[5]

On the other hand, "masking" traditions in the form of possession cults are strong in savanna areas bordering the forest.[6] L. Frobenius was so impressed by the apparently contrasting distributions of possession and sculpted figures that he thought they belonged to entirely different civilizations, but this view has long since been discarded; there is nothing incompatible between "possession" and "masking" in the abstract, but they have different contents in different religious traditions (Kramer 1993, 161).

Artists

The museum-goer's expectation that objects are remarkable primarily for their visual characteristics, which are open to all who have eyes to see, parallels the Western theory that knowledge is a free good to which everyone should have access. According to the African values we have been considering, the opposite is true. Knowledge is dangerous and should not be available to ill-intentioned people. The more powerful the knowledge, the more restricted it should be, and the more dangerous it is not only to outsiders but to those who have acquired it. The necessary boundary between those who know and those who do not is made apparent by devices which conceal in revealing, and which by their strangeness set in opposition to everyday reality a theory of how the world works, an explanation for good and evil, a mechanism for correcting problems, and a demonstration of the structure of reality. Such foundational theories are always sacred.

In general, the "better" an artwork is, the more effective for the control of knowledge—but better may not mean aesthetically pleasing. Art may be deliberately frightful or deliberately amorphous. The artwork, or the object that will metamorphose into art, is not at first a sacred thing or a repository of power. A Dogon mask is just a piece of wood until it is painted, and so is a Kongo *nkisi* until medicines have been added to it, and a Yoruba ancestral figure until sacrifices have been made to it. There may therefore be a division of labor between the sculptor and the ritual expert who ordered the work and deploys it, but equally, as among the Bamana, the creative processes may be combined and carried out by the same individual.

The status of the artist varies greatly in African societies. The Gola artist is considered to be in league with supernatural forces. Fang carvers are people of no importance; the Afikpo carver is silly (D'Azevedo 1973, 283). Among the Bangwa, carving is an honorable occupation that almost all men try. Some carvers are professionals; traditionally they were slaves. Nominally all important Bangwa works were carved by the chief, and all are sold through him. Chiefs are still the principal patrons and brokers of art (legally and illegally) (Brain and Pollock 1972, 39). African sculptors are and have often been sensitive to market demand, producing not only for their own communities but for others; whole masquerades, with songs and medicines, have traveled over long distances. As in the case of the Mangbetu, many of the classical art forms emerged from about 1860 onwards in response to European tastes (Schildkrout and Keim 1990).

Societies that include art galleries and museums, in Europe or Africa, attempt to distinguish "art" from religion, politics, and education, but art nevertheless does perform moral, supervisory, and tutelary functions. Art museums, as repositories of important values, have much in common with temples, so that people make pilgrimages to them, dragging their children along for their good. One reason for recognizing objects as "art" at all is that they are otherworldly, nonfunctional in a materialist sense, and nonrepresentational—a painting, no matter how realistic, is only representational by convention. They are something other than what they seem, and only specially trained custodians and experts fully understand them.

Artists may work by "inspiration," but that is regarded as a force that comes from within rather than from the land of the dead. Museum art is not dangerous to the artist or to those who go to "see" it, but perhaps only because it is exhibited in conditions of reduced sensory experience which neutralize its potential force (Freedberg 1989). In Africa today, some painters, such as Emmanuel Jege, speak of themselves as inspired in the same sense as do the sculptors of masks, but clearly, for the viewer of the work, its impact is reduced as compared with Eyanla or the Komo mask (Derrick 1972). Other artists use traditional religious themes to express Christian values, and some use them simply as cultural icons or as sources of "inspiration," like dreams. A number draw upon them very directly as a means of reflecting upon the African heritage and modern predicaments.

In Ghana, members of a local church, African in leadership though Catholic in inspiration, build sculpture gardens with saints and angels in cement, in which to perform healing rituals and store holy medicine (Breidenbach and Ross 1978). Art and spirituality continue their complex relationship in new forms.

Notes

1. In a study of this kind, unfortunate omissions and unreliable generalizations are inevitable. In their astonishing inventiveness, both spirituality and art in Africa resist summary and paradigm, but in the effort to impose some unity on the argument I believe I have not forced it into an arbitrary framework. Among the obviously neglected topics are those of diffusion and change—hence the uncertain wavering of tenses.

2. Maquet implies some distaste for artworks that lack an aesthetic quality, despite being shown in a museum (1986, 129).

3. The most thoroughgoing exploration of this theme is the book *Secrecy,* associated with the exhibition of the same name at the Museum for African Art, to which the rest of this paper is indebted (Nooter 1993). The references cited in this paper are not intended to be exhaustive; the choice is biased in favor of items that are readily accessible. The best annotated overview of African art is Susan Vogel's *For Spirits and Kings* (1981).

4. Although *minkisi* abound in collections of African art, those made since about 1921 no longer take the spectacular forms of the past.

5. According to Greenberg's classification, the large, independent language family Nilo-Saharan includes Songhai in West Africa, Saharan in the central Sahara, and Chari-Nile, which includes the Eastern Sudanic and Central Sudanic groups (Greenberg 1966).

6. The literature here is enormous; items of interest include Fry 1976; Ngubane 1977; and Boddy 1989.

References

Achebe, Chinua
    1988   *Anthills of the Savannah.* New York: Anchor Press.
Admas, M.
    1986   "Women and Masks among the Western We of Ivory Coast."
                African Arts 19, no. 2:46–55.
Bassing, A.
    1972   "Grave Monuments of the Dakakari." *African Arts* 6, no.
                4:36–39.
Bastin, M.-L.
    1994   *Sculpture Angolaise.* Lisbon: National Ethnographic Musem.
Ben-Amos, P.
    1972   "Symbolism in Olokun Mud Art." *African Arts* 6, no. 4:28–31.
    1980   *The Art of Benin.* London: Thames & Hudson.
Biebuyck, D.
    1972   "Bembe Art." *African Arts* 5, no. 3:12–19, 75–83.
Boddy, J.
    1989   *Wombs and Alien Spirits.* Madison: University of Wisconsim
                Press.
Brain, R., and A. Pollock
    1972   *Bangwa Funerary Sculpture.* Ondon: Duckworth.
Bravmann, R. A.
    1974   *Islam and Tribal Art in West Africa.* London: Cambridge University Press.

Breidenbach, P. S., and D. H. Ross
 1978   "The Holy Place: Twelve Apostles Healing Gardens." *African Arts* 11, no. 4:28–35.
Burton, J. W.
 1981   *God's Ants: A Study of Atuot Religion.* Sankt Augustin: Anthropos Institute.
Buxton, J.
 1973   *Religion and Healing in Mandari.* Oxford: Clarendon Press.
Cole, H. M., and C. C. Aniakor
 1984   *Igbo Arts: Community and Cosmos.* Los Angeles: Museum of Cultural History, University of California.
Danto, A.
 1988   "Artifact and Art." In *ART/artifact,* 19–32. New York: Center for African Art.
Dapper, F.
 1989   *Objets interdits.* Paris: Fondation Dapper.
D'Azevedo, W. L., ed.
 1973   *The Traditional Artist in African Societies.* Bloomington: Indiana University Press.
De la Burde, R.
 1972   "Ancestral Rams' Heads of the Edo-speaking Peoples." *African Arts* 6, no. 1:28–34.
Derrick, J.
 1972   "Artist from Ekiti, Emmanuel Jegede." *African Arts* 6, no. 1:42–43.
Dieterlen, G.
 1989   "Masks and Mythology among the Dogon." *African Arts* 2, no. 3:34–43.
Drewal, H.
 1977   "Art and the Perception of Women in Yoruba Culture." *Cahiers d'etudes africaines* 68, no. xvii-4:545–67.
Drewal, H. J., and M. T. Drewal
 1983   *Gelede: Art and Female Power among the Yoruba.* Bloomington: Indiana University Press.
Drewal, H. J., and J. Pemberton II
 1989   *Yoruba: Nine Centuries of African Art and Thought.* New York: Center for African Art.
Eyo, E.
 1974   "Abua Masquerades." *African Arts* 7, no. 2:52–55.
Ezra, K.
 1988   *Art of the Dogon.* New York: Metropolitan Museum of Art.
Fernandez, J. W.
 1982   *Bwiti: An Ethnography of the Religious Imagination in Africa.* Princeton: Princeton University Press.

Fischer, E.
    1978   "Dan Forest Spirits: Mask in Dan Villages." *African Arts* 11, no. 2:16–23.

Foss, P.
    1972   "Festival of Ohworu at Evwreni." *African Arts* 6, no. 4:20–27.

Freedberg, D.
    1989   *The Power of Images.* Chicago: University of Chicago Press.

Fry, P.
    1976   *Spirits of Protest.* Cambridge: Cambridge University Press.

Gilbert, M.
    1993   "The Leopard Who Sleeps in a Basket: Akuapem Secrecy in Everyday Life and in Royal Metaphor." In *Secrecy: African Art That Conceals and Reveals,* ed. M. H. Nooter. New York: Museum for African Art.

Glaze, A.
    1976   *Art and Death in a Senufo Village.* Bloomington: Indiana University Press.
    1986   "Dialectics of Gender in Senufo Masquerades." *African Arts* 19, no. 3:30–39.

Greenberg, J. H.
    1966   *The Languages of Africa.* Bloomington: Indiana University Press.

Griaule, M., and G. Dieterlen
    1954   "The Dogon." In *African Worlds,* ed. D. Forde, 83–110. London: International African Institute.

Harris, M. D.
    1993   "Resonance, Transformation and Rhyme." In *Astonishment and Power.* National Museum of African Art. Washington, D.C.: Smithsonian Institution Press.

Hartwig, G. W.
    1978   "Sculpture in East Africa." *African Arts* 11, no. 4:62–65.

Hersak, D.
    1990   "Powers and Perceptions of the Bifwebe." *Iowa Studies in African Art* 3:139–54.

Imperato, P. J.
    1971   "Contemporary Adapted Dances of the Dogon." *African Arts* 5, no. 1:28–33, 68–72.

Kasfir, S. L.
    1982   "Anjenu: Sculpture for Idoma Water Spirits." *African Arts* 15, no. 4:47–51.

Kavuna, S.
    1995   "Northern Kongo Ancestor Figures." Trans. and ed. W. MacGaffey. *African Arts* 28, no. 2:48–53.

Kramer, F.
    1993   *The Red Fez.* New York: Verso.

Krieger, K.
1990   *Ostafrikanishce Plastik.* Berlin: Museum für Volkerkunde.
Lamp, F.
1985   "Cosmos, Cosmetics and the Spirit of Bondo." *African Arts* 18,
            no. 3:28–43.
Lawal, Babatunde
1977   "The Living Dead: Art and Immortality among the Yoruba of
            Nigeria." *Africa* 47, no. 1:50–61.
Lifschitz, E.
1988   "Hearing Is Believing: Acoustic Aspects of Masking in Africa." In
            West African Masks and Cultural Systems, ed. S. Kasfir, 221–30.
            Tervuren: Musee Royal de l'Afrique Centrale.
MacGaffey, W.
1993   "The Eyes of Understanding." In *Astonishment and Power.*
            National Museum of African Art. Washington, D.C.: Smith-
            sonian Institution Press.
Maquet, J.
1986   *The Aesthetic Experience: An Anthropologist Looks at the Visual
            Arts.* New Haven: Yale University Press.
Maurer, E. M., and A. F. Roberts
1985   *Tabwa: The Rising of the New Moon.* Ann Arbor: University of
            Michigan Museum of Art.
Mcleod, M. D.
1976   "Verbal Elements in West African Art." *Quaderni Poro*
            1976:85–102.
McNaughton, P. R.
1979   *Secret Sculptures of Komo.* Philadelphia: Institute for the Study of
            Human Issues.
Ngubane, H.
1977   *Body and Mind in Zule Medicine.* New York: Academic Press.
Nooter, M. H.
1990   "Luba Art and State Formation." Thesis, Columbia University.
Nooter, M. H., ed.
1993   *Secrecy: African Art That Conceals and Reveals.* New York:
            Museum for African Art.
Oelman, A. B.
1979   "Nduen Fobra." *African Arts* 12, no. 2:36–43.
Ojo, J. R. O.
1972   "Ogboni Drums." *African Arts* 6, no. 3:50–52.
Olivier de Sardan, J.-P.
1992   "Occultism and the Ethnographic 'I.'" *Critique of Anthropology*
            12, no. 1:5–25.
Ottenberg, S.
1975   *Masked Rituals of Afikpo.* Seattle: University of Washington
            Press.

Pemberton, J.
    1978   "Egungun Masquerades of the Igbomina Yoruba." *African Arts* 9,
                 no. 3:41–47.
    1989   "Dreadful God and the Divine King." In *Africa's Ogun: Old
                 World and New.* Bloomington: Indiana University Press.
Ravenhill, P.
    1988   "An African Triptych." *Art Journal* (summer).
Roberts, A. F.
    1990   "Tabwa Masks: An Old Trick of the Human Race." *African Arts*
                 23, no. 2:36–47.
    1993   "Insight, or Not Seeing Is Believing." In *Secrecy,* ed. M. H.
                 Nooter, 65–79. New York: Museum for African Art.
Schildkrout, E., and C. A. Keim, eds.
    1990   *African Reflections: Art from Northeastern Zaire.* New York:
                 American Museum of Natural History.
Siroto, L.
    1976   "Essay." In *African Spirit Images and Identities.* New York: Pace
                 Primitive and Ancient Art.
Søderberg, B.
    1975   "Les figures d'ancêtres chez les Babembe." *Arts d'Afrique noire*
                 13:21–33.
Thompson, R. F., and J. Cornet
    1981   *The Four Moments of the Sun: Kongo Art in Two Worlds.* Washing-
                 ton, D.C.: National Gallery of Art.
Unrug, K.
    1983   "Eku Masks of the Igbirra." *African Arts* 16, no. 4:54–59.
Vogel, S., ed.
    1981   *For Spirits and Kings: African Art from the Tishman Collection.*
                 New York: Metropolitan Museum of Art.
Wiredu, K.
    1992   "Formulating Modern Thought in African Languages: Some
                 Theoretical Considerations." In *The Surreptitious Speech: Presence
                 Africaine and the Politics of Others, 1947–1987,* ed. V. Y.
                 Mudimbe, 301–32. Chicago: University of Chicago Press.

11

Spiritual Foundations of Dagbamba Religion and Culture

John M. Chernoff

THIS ESSAY DESCRIBES the multifaceted religious environment of the Dagbamba people of northern Ghana.[1] Among the Dagbamba, Islam and indigenous religion are the dominant religious forms. There is, however, an increasing penetration of Christianity, although Catholic presence had taken root for some time. This essay begins by placing the Dagbamba in a regional and multireligious context. It discusses the Dagbamba kinship system as the cultural foundation of religious sentiment. It concludes with a critical examination of the diverse areas of religious manifestations in Dagbamba land.

The Dagbamba People

The ancient state of Dagbon in northern Ghana is home to the Dagbamba people. The boundaries of Dagbon are roughly an oval surrounding two towns that generally appear on global maps, Tamale in the west and Yendi in the east. The boundaries are over a hundred miles east to west and about seventy miles north to south. About 450,000 people currently speak the local language, Dagbani, which belongs to the Oti-Volta group within Central Gur, though the number of Dagbani speakers includes some smaller cultural groups who are shifting from their earlier languages. Dagbani is the most widely spoken indigenous language of the northern and upper regions of Ghana (see Naden 1989).

According to an oral tradition, there were eight chiefs between the one who led the group of warriors to northern Ghana and Naa Gbewaa, Naa Nya si's grandfather. It was during the time of these leaders that many of the customs surrounding the Yaa-Naa's chieftaincy were established. The earliest leaders were not Dagbamba chiefs but *tindanas*, or land-priests.

They had taken over a *tindana*'s chieftaincy and had become a part of the *tindana*'s line, and only later did they extend their rule and establish the chieftaincies of the towns under one family. In that genealogy, it is significant that both the father's side and the mother's side of the chieftaincy line should enter and mingle with *tindanas*. In contrast, it is not unusual for conquering groups or ruling elites to hide their relation to their mother's side, which in time includes the line of the conquered or indigenous people from whom the conquerors took wives and gave birth. The secrecy with which this connection is hidden obviously supports the status quo, the idea that the elite are separated from the commoners, and thus the stratification of the state makes more sense to all concerned. Apart from a few drummers, the subtleties of the assimilation of the chiefs is not something people even think to inquire about. The reason this issue takes on religious significance is that the political system has been a major focus of spiritual intensity. The replacement of *tindanas* with chiefs may have taken only several generations, but the more immense cultural movement occurred gradually: the transition from ancestorism within affiliated or isolated lineages to a system in which a single descent group gave a unified conception of a tribe or people. Along the way, the Dagbamba developed a complex set of institutions surrounding chieftaincy (see Drucker-Brown 1975).

The generally accepted historical account of the region claims that the Dagbamba arrived in the region from the east, probably from a Hausa area during the fifteenth century. They had passed through the Guruma areas of Burkina Faso and occupied various places in northeastern Ghana before arriving at an area about twenty miles north of where Tamale now is. With horses and spears in their military technology, they conquered the indigenous inhabitants and imposed their chieftaincy over the area that became Dagbon, a politically elaborate centralized state that has existed for centuries under a single dynasty. The modern chiefs of Dagbon descended directly from those early rulers.

In the typical accounts of invasion and of the usurpation of the *tindanas*, it seems that the Dagbamba are portrayed as almost two groups: a ruling elite and a larger population of indigenous people who have been brought under the influence of the elite's centralized and patrilineal political organization. The chiefs who move from town to town as they ascend the chieftaincy hierarchy are considered "strangers" to the towns, and, with a few exceptions, it is the chiefs and the princes from the chieftaincy line who are qualified to contend for chieftaincy. Perhaps the ancient *tindanas* were already evolving into a stable political system, as some historical data suggest (see Skalnik 1978, 469–93; 1979, 197–213), and the cultural transition under the conquerors was relatively seamless. The longevity of the ruling dynasty is itself a kind of evidence that the establishment of the Dagbamba state did not involve immense cultural conflict. In the simplest yet most profound terms, what holds the Dagbamba together is the understanding that they are one family. This understanding is the foundation of the social cohesion that prevented constant political contestation and even occasional civil war from destroying the unity of the state.

It need be noted that the Dagbamba are distinguished from their neighbors by their elaborate political organization, a hierarchy of patrilineal chieftaincies that exerts authority over those who live in the towns and villages of the Dagbamba state. Their paramount chief, known as the Yaa-Naa, is in Yendi, and most other chiefs move from town to town, shifting their positions upward within a complex system with twelve major divisional chieftaincies under the Yaa-Naa (see Blair and Duncan-Johnstone 1931; Ferguson and Wilks 1970; Ghana Government Reports of the Yendi Skin Affairs Committee of Inquiry 1974; Report on the Yendi Skin Enquiry 1968–69).

Chieftaincy, the Drummers, and Storytelling

While it is true that the story of such a distant time of the people is shrouded in darkness and secrecy, it is claimed that the traditional historians of Dagbon, a lineage-based guild of drummers, possess some historical facts and know the most about the first chiefs of the towns. Dagbamba drummers say that there is no Dagbana whose family cannot be traced to some point on the line of the chiefs, and that there is no one whom they cannot praise with the proverbial praise-name of a former chief.

According to the drummers, the Dagbamba came as warriors under a single leader. At that time, there were no Dagbamba. Later, a quarrel among brothers, the children of the regional cultural icon named Naa Gbewaa, caused the group to separate, with some going north to found the Mamprusi state and others south to found the Nanumba state, each brother carrying the seed of chieftaincy. All three groups trace their starting to Naa Gbewaa. The Dagbamba chief who remained, Naa Shitobu, instructed his son, Naa Nyaysi, to wage war and place Dagbamba chiefs to rule over the towns, thus to secure chieftaincy for his descendants. At the time, each town was ruled by a local priest of the land. Such a land-priest is called *tin-dana*[2] in Dagbani. At the present time there are *tindanas* throughout the region and into the Mossi area of Burkina Faso. *Tindana* comes from *tina,* meaning "town" or "land," with the suffix -*lana,* which means "holder" or "owner." In this case, the notion of stewardship of the well-being of the town predominates over the notion of actual ownership, for the notion of *tina* includes the land within and around the town that is related to the god or shrine of the place, known in Dagbani as the *bu li* (plural *bu a*), to which the *tindana* must make appropriate sacrifices. The usurpation of the *tindanas* was not complete, for the chiefs could not perform the sacrifices to local spiritual manifestations, and the surviving *tindanas* or their heirs returned to the towns for that purpose.

At towns or villages with major chieftaincies, the installation of a new chief is often accompanied by a performance of the drum history, which is normally beaten only during the two festivals noted above. This performance will typically move to conclude with the line of the new chief. The drum history tells a chief about his forefathers and lets a chief know chieftaincy. And for any Dagbana, whether man or woman, it tells that person who he is. The drum history will open his eyes to the old talks that are inside his family, and it is inside his praise that he will know his relationship to chieftaincy. During the performance, an animal is sacrificed. There are two explanations given for the sacrifice. The first reveals that the history often contains accounts of wars and bloodshed, and that the blood of the sacrifice is necessary as commemoration. Second, the spirits of the past chiefs are still around, roaming, and they are dangerous because they do not like to be talked about, but they can be placated with the blood of the sacrifice. Such ritual relations between living and dead are an important aspect of the association of history and ancestorism, in which the past chiefs are ancestors with regard to whom the living stand in ambiguous moral relation. The history itself has several examples of sitting chiefs who are reminded of the dead chiefs if they do not rise to the level of the tradition they have inherited.

The ceremonial environment of chieftaincy is extremely dense, and many customs serve to affirm the relationship between past and present chiefs. When a Yaa-Naa is installed, he wears or sits on or comes into contact with the regalia of the dead Yaa-Naas—gowns, amulets, hats, walking sticks, stools. When a chief dies, Dagbamba say, "The chief is not dead. He is roaming." Formerly when a Yaa-Naa was terminally ill, nobody even saw him die. An elder would tie a bell to his leg, with the belief that when a person dies, he shakes himself. After the ringing of the bell, the elders would wait. If the bell did not ring again, they would call a person with medicine to look into the room to see if the chief was dead or had transformed himself and gone away. Then they would announce simply, "The earth has shaken." When any major chief is buried, his body is lifted up and he is made to walk to his grave. When the new chief is installed, they say, "The chief has roamed and come back." The office of chieftaincy itself is called "the skin," after the animal skins on which the chief sits. The office, which represents the tradition of chieftaincy as well as the family of the chiefs, seems larger than the person holding it. During the time before the final funeral observances are performed and a new chief is chosen, anywhere from three months to a year, the eldest son of the dead chief sits in his father's place as the *Gbonlana*, the "holder of the skin." When a new chief is chosen, he makes sacrifices at the shrines that have precedents in custom, not only to the *bu li* of the town but also to places of significance in the history of that chieftaincy. The installation is attended by other chiefs or their representatives, with various protocols of greeting and gift giving that solidify the sense of a family among the royals as well as put to rest the contentions of the unsuccessful rival claimants.

It is the Yaa-Naa who gives major chieftaincies, and although he is supposed to respect the recommendations of other chiefs and elders as well as the traditions of the various towns and villages, these chieftaincies are acknowledged as being given to "the one the Yaa-Naa wants." The Yaa-Naa himself, however, is chosen in an ambiguous way from among several people who are qualified for the chieftaincy by virtue of their position in the hierarchy. When the Yaa-Naa is not there, it is the elders of Yendi who choose the new chief by consensus, but the selection is not represented in that way. Rather, the selection is often represented as based on the divination of soothsayers, a point reminiscent of the selection of *tindanas*. In reality, the many titled elders in Yendi include several who have relatively greater say in the choice, as well as important roles in the installation procedures, as do powerful "elder" chiefs, particularly the chief of Gushengu. A large number of elders are each responsible for discrete sections of installation, and the failure of any one of them to perform his part can throw the whole proceeding into question. Nonetheless, the soothsayers are given the credit for finding a chief who will benefit the people. The one chosen is "the one God wants," not the one elders want. If they decide to talk about the selection, most drummers will say that the soothsayers do not choose the Yaa-Naa. One learned drummer compared the involvement of soothsayers to a large mat that is hanging in front of the selection proceedings. What they are covering up is the role of the elders. Otherwise, the disappointed claimants would have cause for complaint. The mystical element of the soothsayers' vision prevents the highly politicized selection from appearing overtly political. The traditions surrounding the installation regalia lend further authority to the choice. The selection and installation of a Yaa-Naa involve many people, and their efforts are testimony to a sensitivity regarding the way in which the heritage continues to solve their problems for them.

God in Dagbamba Worldview

The idea of God as the ultimate reality behind any other agent is a familiar motif in African religions. Dagbamba say, "Nothing can be compared to God." God is therefore beyond knowledge, with a presumed will or purpose that cannot be questioned. The indigenous view fits nicely with Islamic motifs, and it is difficult to separate the fundamental inspiration of piety between Muslims and traditional religious believers, despite their many differences in practice. They both observe the limits of human power. They note the scale of the earth and the scale of human endeavor. They note the transformations of germination and growth. And most conclusively, perhaps, they note that a human being cannot prevent the death of loved ones. Their frequent references to God remind them of both their intentions and their limitations and reinforce their piety.

When drummers pick up their drums for any important event, they start to beat a number of proverbs praising God. They start the drum history and many other types of beating with a song called *Dakoli N-nye Bia* (A Bachelor is a Child), which has many variations that address the Dagbamba belief in God. The phrases are responded to with the refrain: "Truly, it is the Chief of chiefs." The phrases affirm the omnipotence, omnipresence, and omniscience of God. They tell of God's capacity and choice to make and destroy, to uplift and bring down, to provide and withdraw, to make rich and make poor, and so on.

Dagbamba who are asked about God might frame their reply with images or ideas from this well-known song in their musical heritage.

The gods of the Dagbamba land are many and diverse. Every Dagbamba town has at least one *bu li*, but there are a number of important *bu a* that attract supplicants from other towns. Most notable are the Pong Tamale *bu li* at the town of the same name, and Naawuni, at the river between Dalun and Singa: both of these *bu a* are known for acting strongly in cases of witchcraft and theft. There are also *bu a* through which one may beg for children or for health. Some of the important *bu a* are beyond the borders of Dagbon. The one the Dagbamba call *Yabyili*, "grandfather's house," is in the Talensi area on the plateau above Tongo, just south of Bolgatanga. People from all the regions of Ghana and even from other countries visit the shrine at Yabyili to cure sickness or barrenness or poverty or any pressing worry. "The *bu a*," according to an informant

> were there before the Muslim religion came, and the gods are there today and tomorrow. They have been there for a very long time, and they are not for us Dagbamba alone. Yabyili is strong for every tribe. Some of the gods we have here are in other towns. Yabyili is in the Talensi land, and the *tindana* is a

Talensi. There is a god at Yapei called Bunnyamaashe, and we Dagbamba go there, but Yapei is in the Gonja land, and the *tindana* there is a Gonna. There is a god at Chito called Lansa; Chito is on the road going to Salaga, in the Gonja land. And so, it is not "This is my tribe's god" or "This is not my tribe's god." Anybody of any tribe can go to a god. That is how it is and people go to see the gods. If it is a true god, it is there for everyone.

Buxli can refer both to the god and to the place where a sacrifice is made. The gods have various forms and are frequently associated with animals. The *buxli* at Pong Tamale is rain. Naawuni is a crocodile. As noted, these two are frequently called to act in cases of theft or witchcraft. Zeyibu, the god at Tampion, is a monitor lizard, and Tampion has another *buxli* in the form of bees. The bees at Tampion will not allow taxes to be collected at the market there. Jaagbo, the god at Tolon, is in the form of a snake. There is a god at Tamale called Kpalanga in the form of trees. Takpala, the god at Galiwe, is also a small tree: one of Yaa-Naa Zanjina's wives went to Takpala to beg for a child and gave birth to Yaa-Naa Garba. It has become a custom that new Yaa-Naas must go to make a sacrifice there as well as at many other shrines. If a woman who goes to beg for a child is successful, the child often takes the name of the god. Thus, in Dagbon, someone named Lansa was either given birth to with the help of the Lansa *buxli* or named after a grandparent who was a child of that god. Similarly, someone named Tambo is named after the Tambo *buxli* at the town of Sang. Children who are from Yabyili (Grandfather's house) are called Yapaxa (Grandfather's woman) or Yabdoo (Grandfather's man). It is also typical that a *buxli* will give a sign if the chief or the *tindana* of the town is going to die; if there is an animal associated with the *buxli*, that animal will enter the town. Also, a *buxli* must be "repaired" or "made well" annually with a sacrifice, normally at the start of the planting season. Every *buxli* is unique, but the ones that are considered strongest are the Pong Tamale *buxli* Naawuni and Yabyili, as well as those to which the Yaa-Naa must sacrifice.

At the present time, most Dagbamba towns have both a chief and a *tindana*, and the *tindana* remains in charge of annual sacrifices and other matters regarding the *buxli* and the town. The *tindanas* inherit their positions in a variety of ways, mainly from father to eldest son, but matrilineal succession is not uncommon, and some *tindanas* are women.[3] In some towns, the office can pass to the *tindana*'s sister's son, or it can alternate, passing from father to daughter to daughter's son. When a *tindana* dies, divination or signs are used to determine which one of the eligible people will be the new *tindana*. A delegation of *tindanas* and elders will find the person. They will stand in a circle around him and notify him by throwing a donkey's tail at him, symbolizing the "old thing" that the *tindana* holds. At that point, the person's life just changes at once, and he or she returns home to assume the office. It is worth noting that another group of spiritual specialists, the soothsayers, inherits their bag of paraphernalia from their mother's brother. The contrast between chiefs and *tindanas* is more than a contrast of matrilineal and patrilineal customs, of older and newer systems. The chief is considered a "stranger" who has come to sit in the town and hopes to go out from the town as he advances through the chieftaincy hierarchy. The *tindana* is "a child of the town," rooted to the town by birth and by the office he will not leave until he dies. Four of the twelve divisional chieftaincies (Gushegu, Tolon, Kumbungu, and Gukpeogu) and several less powerful chieftaincies are given to commoners, that is, those who are not children or grandchildren of a Yaa-Naa. These chiefs resemble *tindanas* in that they do not move to another chieftaincy. They are from their towns and they have a more active role to play in rituals.

Ancestors and the Family Shrine

The main moral dilemma involved in Dagbamba society continues to be ancestral belief. In asserting one's unambiguous place in relation to the heritage of chieftaincy, the inheritor places himself in an ambiguous moral relationship to the past chiefs, his ancestors. Chiefs are motivated by their knowledge of the deeds of their fathers and forefathers in whose place they stand, and they measure themselves against the standards of the office they have inherited. In a crisis, they think of the past chiefs who are now dead. Their elders will remind them of what such-and-such a chief did. The drummers beat drums and address the chiefs with the praise-names of their ancestors.

Talensi and Dagbamba societies are certainly distinct from one another, but the traditional religious foundation of the region percolates through most aspects of Dagbamba spirituality. In households that are not strongly within the fold of Islam, there are family shrines, places where the family "medicine" (*tim*) is. On the walls, or just outside the walls of such compounds is designated a point where sacrifices are offered. Some households have their shrines inside a room in the house. These shrines are called *bayuya* (singular, *bayuli*), also referring to the practice of attending to the ancestors. According to my informants, the *bayuli* is the god of the house. These housegods are not gods like the gods of the land. The gods of the land are older than the housegods and they gave birth to all the people. Furthermore, Tilo, Jebuni, Wuni, and Wumbee are claimed to be the main housegods. Wuni is the Dagbani word for "god," and Wumbee is a contraction of the words *wuni* and *bia* (child), thus "god's child." These two have their shrines outside a house, while Tilo and Jebuni are located inside. Tilo is a calabash that is with an elder woman in the family; the sacrifice to Tilo involves millet beer. Jebuni is a pot, and it is repaired with a goat when the new yams are first harvested. It need be mentioned that it is not every house that has a shrine; the *bayuli* is normally at the house of the head of the family.

> The meaning of the word *bayuli* is to stand quietly or secretly and look at something, in the sense that the dead people in the family are lurking about and looking at the family. Any of the gods in a family is looked upon as the old thing or the old talk that is in that family. The typical Dagbamba take it that when they are begging from it, they are begging from their dead people. When they are going to repair the god through a sacrifice offering, they call the names of the dead people. The leader at the offering will say, "My grandfather so-and-so, this is your water I am giving you." He will pour the water on the ground. And he will say, "May grandmother so-and-so, give me good sleep to sleep." He will call all those he knows, and those he doesn't know but had been told about. If there is any child in the family who has bad luck, he will go to consult a soothsayer. He/she may be told, "Tilo says that you got and ate, and you didn't give him. That is why you are deprived of what you want." Or he may say to another person whose children are dying, "Tilo says that you have forgotten about him." The victim will then tell the family so that they will repair it for him. He could also go to meet the woman who looks after Tilo. They may go together to repair it. Somebody could be dreaming but he/she may know neither the place nor those in his/her dreaming experience. Such a dreamer is considered to be seen by his dead people. The dead people are claimed to come and stand outside the door of his room, looking at him. There is the need to repair his house god.

This description of the ancestors and the family shrines is similar to the types of descriptions that have become part of the broader ethnographic record of the region. In Dagbon, too, the family provides the context for interpreting the vicissitudes of destiny and even Muslims who have nothing to do with sacrificing to Jebuni or Wuni would acknowledge the relevance of ancestral presence. There are even Muslims, despite their grip on their faith, who would see nothing wrong with visiting a soothsayer to find out about their problems.

Divination and Soothsaying

As noted above, the main spiritual elements of solving a crisis involve finding out the cause and then determining the appropriate sacrifice. In Dagbon, it is primarily professional soothsayers who are able to discover the fundamental situation and prescribe the sacrifice. These soothsayers, *baxsi* (singular *baxa*), work with a marvelous assortment of things—bones, cowrie shells, sticks, twigs, stones, pieces of metal—kept in a bag. These are called the *baxbihi*, "soothsayer's children." The *bax' kolgu*, "soothsayer's bag," is an "old thing" that is inherited: it passes through women, to a soothsayer's sister's son, and thus if a soothsayer dies, the bag will "catch" the new soothsayer from among the soothsayer's nephews. Soothsayers "look" to see which of the nephews will be "caught" by the "old thing," and the bag cannot be refused without risking dire consequences through bad luck (*zuxu biexu*, literally, "bad head"). The new soothsayer is taught and tested by older soothsayers before beginning to practice. In Dagbon, there are others who "see," notably a group known as *jinwarba*, whose members look into fire to see; others look into a calabash of water. It is the soothsayers who are the main group of diviners. They are professionals, and they even have their own chiefs and elders.

When visiting a soothsayer who is very adept, one needs to take one's turn after many others who wait for a consultation. The actual consultation is typically a rather matter-of-fact affair. The client does not tell the soothsayer anything, but rather states the problem "in his heart." The soothsayer calls God: "This morning, what is on the earth?" throws his *ba bihi* and studies them, and then he starts to tell his client what he has seen about the client's situation. There are some situations in which the soothsayer is asked to "look" into a particular matter. Such cases include sickness, death, or the naming of a child. There are also others in which the problem is quite vague, and the soothsayer will "see" a particular interpersonal or familial dynamic and report it to the client. In some situations, of course, there is no sacrifice needed. The soothsayer may say that a particular death was natural, that is, that there was no witchcraft or medicine involved. Or the soothsayer may identify the ancestor whom a newborn baby has "inherited," that is, who has come back and whose name the baby will take. Or the soothsayer may help in making decisions where a choice is made difficult by customary processes, for example, to identify the member who is to inherit the bag of a deceased soothsayer or to identify the suitor who can be chosen to marry a widow without incurring bad luck. When, however, there is a problem involving sickness or obstruction, after the soothsayer has identified the cause, he will recommend a sacrifice, which might involve repairing the housegod but often simply takes the form of alms such as giving beancakes (*maha*) soaked in milk to children or animals.

Most people who patronize soothsayers obviously have a degree of trust in soothsaying, but they may still consult more than one soothsayer in a crisis, and the soothsaying does not appear to involve much effort at persuasion. The soothsayer is mainly concerned to see the situation clearly, to the best of his ability. There is, however, a Dagbamba proverb that says, "someone who is not a person, when he talks, don't accept it and don't refuse it." The explanation of the proverb, according to an informant, is, "If a soothsayer tells you something, you should also soothsay in your heart." That is, one needs to make sense out of what one is told to confirm the correctness of the revelation of the soothsayer. Many who go to soothsayers have strong confidence and trust in them, having been to them several times and had their problems solved. Thus, within their own context, the soothsayers are evaluated empirically, that is, by the accuracy of their revelations. This link between pragmatism and mysticism can be observed to be common to many religious traditions, for the type of insight involved in divination is limited in its application and is not analyzed or worked into a larger epistemological or theological perspective.

Sickness, Medicine, and Healing

A similar approach characterizes the Dagbamba perspective on "medicine" (*tim*), a term that includes herbal treatments for sickness as well as magical amulets and talismans. A Dagbana might compare medicines to the *bu a* in that no one knows how they work, and no one knows whether the medicine treated a person or the person got better on his own, or by any other means. In any case, a *tindana* does not necessarily have medicine, but there are some shrines where people go for treatment of sickness. *Yabili*, as noted, is known for treating infertility. Medicines themselves are distinct, each with a different name, and the knowledge involved in their acquisition and application is also particular. Someone who has medicine (a *timlana*) may be able to treat only one sickness; in other words, he has the medicine for that sickness. Moreover, someone may have medicines for many different kinds of sickness. Therefore, any person with medicine has the extent of its knowledge. Medicines are typically passed within the family from father to son and mother to daughter. The Dagbamba talk about the medicine as being "inside" the family, an "old thing" in the family—someone's grandfather "ate it and put it down for him." Medicine is also "repaired" annually, with the same sacrifices that were made when it was acquired. Apart from those medicines used to treat sickness, there are many medicines that have magical efficacy. *Liliga* (vanishing) enables one to disappear from a place of danger. *Vua* (calling) enables hunters to call bush animals and also enables its owner to attract people to himself. *Kabre* (tying) is used to immobilize people or prevent them from taking certain actions. *Tahinga* (shouting) can make an animal or a person fall down. *Sutili* protects its owner against knife or cutlass wounds. *Muhili* protects against bad medicines given in food. There is a type of chilo, the antimony that people use to line their eyes, that is, a medicine that enables one to see bad people. *Lukuri* is used to acquire wealth. *Teeli* (remembering) is used by the drummers to help them remember the vast amount of information they need to control. *Zambana* (a cat) is used by drummers to make their wrists flexible in beating. There are countless types of these medicines. One of the things soothsayers often do is to direct people to the place where they can get the correct medicines for their problems. A person looking for medicine will not ask for it directly. He or she will greet the owner of the medicine with gifts several times, until the medicine owner asks for the specific reason of his gifts. While the owner of the medicine knows what he or she wants, he also will not speak directly to ask whether the person wants medicine. The medicine can be eaten or drunk, sewn into a talisman or waistband, bathed with, or given in the form of a powder; Dagbamba speaks of all these ways that the person has "eaten" medicine.

Islam and Traditional Culture and Practices

It was at the beginning of the eighteenth century that Islam established a significant influence in Dagbon. At that time, a great Yaa-Naa, Muhammad Zanjina, brought learned Muslims to instruct the Dagbamba in the religion of Islam. The Dagbamba say that Naa Zanjina "lit a lantern and opened the eyes of Dagbon," and they call him the "light of Dagbon." However, it should be remarked that Islam was not unknown before Naa Zanjina: in the early to mid-seventeenth century, there were Muslim scholars of both Wangara and Hausa origin who passed through the Mossi state and into Dagbon and through Larabanga in the Gonja area. Nonetheless, Dagbamba attribute the introduction of Islam to Naa Zanjina because it was during his time that the people embraced Islam. Among the titled Muslim elders in the state, most are of Hausa origin, and there are only a few important titled family lines descended from Mossi and Wangara missionaries. At this time, somewhat more than half of the Dagbamba are Muslim. Many important customs are performed according to Muslim teachings, from the naming of children to weddings to funerals. In addition, there is the full complement of religious organization and practice: Arabic schools, mosques, public prayer, clerics, Ramadan fasting, festivals, and so on. Recently, the Ahmadiyya movement has established a strong presence.

Insofar as adherents consider Islam the "final" religion, combining spiritual awareness with a guide for correct living, Dagbamba Muslims look to

Islam for ideas about every aspect of life. Their splendid piety rests on the foundation of their unfaltering belief in God and their appreciation of the practical benefits of Muslim wisdom. Many Dagbamba distinguish three types of Muslims. The first category are those who are able to read the Holy Qu'ran as well as follow its teachings. The clerics are included in this group. In Dagbani, a cleric is called *afa* (plural *afanima*), and a broader term in West African English is the Hausa word *maalam*. The second group includes those who cannot read but who pray in a Muslim way. These are numerous. Both types of Muslims are considered believers, those who have faith in the Muslim religion. The third group includes those who pray and also sacrifice to a *buxli* and to household shrines. People in towns are more likely to be Muslims. Nonetheless, Kumbungu and the villages around it are known for the number of their learned Muslims. Although the people of Tolon and the villages around it are more attached to the *buxa* than to Islam, the late chief of Tolon, Alhaji Yakubu Alaasan Tali, was a figure of great national prominence and highly learned in Islam.

It is clear that by the time the militant Islam that penetrated the Niger Basin had passed through the Mossi states to reach Dagbon, it had lost much of its puritanical edge. That is not to say that Dagbamba Muslims are not devout. Dagbon was the major channel for Islam to penetrate further south in what is now Ghana, and Dagbamba *maalams* have for years, even centuries, been in attendance at the court of the Asantehene in Kumasi. Still, the overall impression is one of a society in which the practice of Islam was tempered by a number of other cultural factors. For a rather routine example, one can observe the normal situation of married women. Women are active economically, and many run their own businesses without restrictions. There are only a few households where the wives do not go outside the house; more typically, married women in public wear their veils atop their heads like scarves, without covering their faces. Nonetheless, Muslim social codes apply to women in such matters as inheritance. In many areas of Dagbamba social life, Islamic practice is compartmentalized. The most obvious illustration is the chiefs, who are Muslims and who have Muslim elders yet who also observe a number of traditional practices such as coordinating the *tindana*'s sacrifices on behalf of the town.

Major annual community celebrations are decidedly based on traditional and Islamic religious practices. The five festivals in each year are all attributed to Islamic origin. These are fire festival (*Buxim*), the birthday of the Holy Prophet (*Damba*), the whipping of guinea-fowls (*Kpini*), the end of Ramadan (*Konyuri*), and the prayers during the pilgrimage month (*Chimsi*). One focal point of the *Buxim* (Fire) festival is the opening by *malaams* of talismans projecting the type of year in store for the town, a gathering on the morning after a torch-throwing procession. No *malaam* would go near the previous night's activities, in which young people carrying weapons dance to the ancient drumming of the *tindanas* and where, in the past, grudges were often settled. *Damba* is the biggest festival. Although *malaams* go about to tell stories of the Holy Prophet, the festival is mainly a chieftaincy festival, full of dancing and processions. According to the drummers, when Damba was introduced by Naa Zanjina, he explained how Muslims were to celebrate the festival, but because the Dagbamba were not "standing all that much in the Muslim religion," they should celebrate the festival in a Dagbamba way, with drumming and dancing. Another story affirms that Damba festival began as a Muslim festival, but the chiefs "collected it and made it theirs."

The other three festivals are less elaborate. The story behind the Guinea Fowl Festival (*Kpini Chuxu*) relates to the Holy Prophet Muhammad. The Guinea Fowl Festival is celebrated by removing all the feathers of a guinea fowl, after which it is beaten with a stick. The guinea fowl is told, "You! You refused to give water to God's child, the Holy Prophet Muhammad." The guinea fowl will be whipped and abused before it is slaughtered. However, *malaams* don't participate in the Guinea Fowl Festival. The two other festivals, *Konyuri Chuxu* (the Water Drinking Festival) and *Chimsi Chuxu*, take place at the end of Ramadan and during the month of pilgrimage. All the Muslims in a town gather at one location for prayers. Apart from a few ancillary activities, the major event in towns with important chiefs is a performance by drummers of a selection from the epic body of the Dagbamba historical tradition. The drummers' performance chronicles the lives and accomplishments of the chiefs. Thus, although the rationale for the festivals is Muslim, the actual performances are directed toward many other facets of the social spectrum. These facets reflect not only pre-Islamic religion but also more particularly the deeper spiritual aspects of Dagbamba culture itself, which in this vein may be considered a reflection of a descent group.

One other area of spiritual interaction is medicine. Muslim *malaams* also have medicines that perform similar functions to those of the traditionalists. *Malaams'* medicines are in two main forms. *Walga* is made by taking an edible ink (currently made by boiling down sugar) and writing prayers on a board. The writing is then washed off the board into a container; part of the liquid will be drunk and the other part will be used in bathing. *Sabli* is a talisman made by a *malaam* who writes the appropriate prayers on a piece of paper that is then folded and sewn into a leather amulet. Muslim Dagbamba say that *malaams'* medicines come from the Holy *Qu'ran* in the form of prayers. When going to a *malaam* for medicine, therefore, one gives the *malaam* a greeting of cola and kerosene. The kerosene is for the *malaam*'s lantern, to be used for reading and praying. *Malaams* also make medicine to treat sicknesses, generally in the form of *walga*. They also prepare talismans for protection, to be buried at the sides of houses. The effectiveness of the *malaams*' medicines is attributed to the power of God, though some *malaams* also acquire reputations for greatness based on the strength of their medicines, a reflection of both their knowledge and ability to pray. Nonetheless, Muslims accept the effectiveness or ineffectiveness of medicine as ultimately beyond human control. Both muslims and traditional religious believers hold the view that medicine works with certain conditions and principles.

If it appears that the medicines of *malaams* and those of traditional believers are variations on the same theme, the underlying factor is their belief in the Supreme Being as the creator and the all-powerful who is the source of power behind the working of all medicines.

Dagbamba society displays a mixture of religious customs, but certain basic sentiments seem present throughout the variety of religious forms one sees in Dagbon. It is not merely a matter of Muslim and non-Muslim customs existing side by side or intermingled, as has been noted with regard to the major community festivals. Nor is there reason to infer that there is an issue of comparative depth of religious inspiration. There seems rather to be a continuum along which religious sentiment changes its center of attention rather than its profundity. The ancestorism that is the foundation of spirituality in the broader cultural region remains strong in Dagbon. There are strict as well as traditional religious believers. In between are a large number of people who consult specialists from either group. Strict Muslims do not keep or repair house gods, and *tindanas* do not sit down and consult with *malaams*. But there are still occasions when some Muslims go to seek advice from a soothsayer or treatment from a shrine. And there are some traditional believers who will at least learn how to pray Muslim prayers so that they might participate in the assembled prayers during the *Chimsi* and *Konyuri* festivals. The boundaries between Islam and indigenous tradition are typically well defined. However, Islam has made great contributions to Dagbamba customs. To the Dagbamba, Islam has "opened their eyes" and helped them improve many aspects of their cultural life, yet they see Islam as an agent of "increase," as something that has "added to" their tradition. When they wish to describe their culture in fundamental terms, that is, in terms of what makes them distinct as a people, most of them tend to talk about chieftaincy and, by implication, their descent group.

In much the same way that Islam has accommodated the spiritual base of its adherents' lives, the political system has developed within the fundamental context of ancestral significance. The chieftaincy is inherited; Dagbamba say that chieftaincy is "in the bone," with the implication that there is never a break between "how a person started" and what he or she is. Turning around the obvious point that one cannot contest for most chieftaincies unless one has a claim through inheritance, one can view a claim to succession as a claim to direct descent from the original conquerors. This affiliation is posited even if the relationship is not direct. Most contestants for chieftaincy are children and grandchildren of chiefs. But if a chief dies without children, it is possible for his nephew (his sister's son) or his grandson if he receives the approval to stand as his "son" who will claim his "father's" chieftaincy. Thus a direct line is maintained. (His brother's sons are already in the direct line through his father or grandfather.) When Naa Nya si placed his followers as chiefs of the towns, some of them were his father's brothers and his own brothers, but these chiefs are called "sons" of Naa Nya si, and the drummers praise them as such. Despite what an outsider might assume, such issues of fictionalized legitimacy do not present ambiguities within the patterns of succession or within the genealogy

Conclusion

Most Dagbamba look toward deeper elements of the customs they observe with an eye that respects the spiritual weight of their forebears; they experience and accept the moral authority of the sanctions that accompany their customs. They reflect on the importance of "what we grew up and met" as a benefit they can pass on to their children. They understand that it is their continuing involvement that revitalizes the heritage, but they also rely on the mystification and ritualization of enough elements of social processes to control contestation. For Dagbamba, the ancestors represent the tradition, and Dagbamba experience their tradition as a living body of thought; moreover, they acknowledge its effects in a manner that ascribes to it an intimation of agency. Their observations indicate that those who ignore its prohibitions often suffer.

In Dagbon, people's efforts to maintain and add to their tradition display a prolific reflection of ancestorism. In their religious imagination, they nurture and dwell within a deep intuition for how they started and its meaning for them. Reviewing the example of chieftaincy, it is quite easy to comprehend how the precedence of the office of chieftaincy over the person of the chief is reinforced by the broader cultural sentiments that bind the living family and the ancestors. In Dagbon, the important transition that distinguished the Dagbamba from the other cultural groups in the region can be envisioned as much in religious motifs as in political ones. The unification of the towns and villages under the rule of a centralized state is also the unification of separate families into one larger family. The evolution of hierarchical political form is also the evolution of an elaborately segmented family. From the many complexities of customs that surround the chieftaincy system, which is their central institution, the customs that reflect the way that Islam was adopted and institutionalized, and the many aspects of their daily life in which respect for older generations, origins, and the heritage of the past guide their reasoning, one needs to appreciate that much of the deliberateness with which the Dagbamba maintain their traditions is a product of religious inspiration.

Notes

1. Much of the primary data in this essay were developed with the aid of grants from the National Endowment for the Humanities, the National Science Foundation, the Social Science Research Council, and the John Simon Guggenheim Memorial Foundation. A comprehensive ethnography on the Dagbamba is in progress: John M. Chernoff and Alhaji Ibrahim Abdulai, with the collaboration of Alhaji Mumuni Abdulai, Kissmal Ibrahim Hussein, Benjamin D. Sunkari, and Mustapha Muhammed, *A Drummer's Testament: The Culture of the Dagbamba of Northern Ghana*, 3 vols. (Chicago: University of Chicago Press, forthcoming).

2. The correct plural form of *tindana* is *tindaannima* or *tindamba*, but in the context of this essay I have anglicized the plural for simplicity.

3. A female *tindana* is called *tindaampaa*.

References

Blair, H. A., and A. C. Duncan-Johnstone, eds.
   1931   *Enquiry into the Constitution and Organization of the Dagbon Kingdom*. Accra, Ghana: Government Printing Office.
Chernoff, John M., and Alhaji M. Abdulai
   forth-   *A Drummer's Testament: The Culture of the Dagbamba of Northern*
   coming   *Ghana*. 3 vols. Chicago: University of Chicago Press.
Drucker-Brown, Susan
   1975   *Ritual Aspects of Mamprusi Kingship*. Leiden: Africa-Studie-centrum; Cambridge: African Studies Center.
Fage, J. D.
   1964   "Reflections on the Early History of the Mossi-Dagomba Group of States." In *The Historian in Tropical Africa*, ed. J. Vanisina, R. Mauny, and L. V. Thomas. London: International African Institute and Oxford University Press.
Ferguson, Phyllis, and Ivor Wilks
   1970   "Chiefs, Constitutions, and the British in Northern Ghana." In

West African Chiefs: Their Changing Status under Colonial Rule and Independence, ed. Michael Crowder and Obaro Ikime. New York: African Publishing Corp.

Fortes, Meyer
1945   *The Dynamics of Clanship among the Tallensi. Being the First part of an Analysis of the Social Structure of a Trans-Volta Tribe.* London: Oxford University Press.

1949   *The Web of Kingship among the Tallensi.* London: Oxford University Press.

1959   *Oedipus and Job in West African Religion.* Cambridge: Cambridge University Press.

1987   *Religion, Morality, and the Person: Essays on Tallensi Religion.* Cambridge: Cambridge University Press.

Ghana Government
1974   *Ghana Government, Reports of the Yendi Skin Affairs Committee of Inquiry.* Accra, Ghana: Ghana Publishing Corporation.

Levtzion, Nehemia
1968   *Muslims and Chiefs in West Africa: A Study of Islam in the Middle Volta Basin in the Pre-Colonial Period.* Oxford: Clarendon Press.

Mbiti, J. S.
1970   *African Religion and Philosophy.* Garden City, N.Y.: Doubleday, Anchor Books.

Naden, Tony
1989   "Gur." In *The Languages of Ghana,* ed. M. E. Kropp-Dakubu, 12–49. London: Kegan Paul International. Also in *The Niger-Congo Languages,* ed. John Bendor-Samuel, 141–68. Lanham, Md.: University Press of America.

Report on the Yendi Skin Enquiry, December 1968 to July 1969 (Accra, Ghana: Ghana Publishing Corporation, n.d.).

Skalnik, Peter
1978   "Early States in the Voltaic Basin." In *The Early State,* ed. Henri J. M. Claessen and Peter Skalnik, 469–93. The Hague: Mouton.

1979   "The Dynamics of Early State Development in the Voltaic Area." In *Political Anthropology: The State of the Art,* ed. S. Lee Seaton and Henri J. M. Claessen, 197–213. The Hague: Mouton.

Part Three

AFRICANS' ENCOUNTER
WITH OTHER RELIGIONS

The Task of African Traditional Religion in the Church's Dilemma in South Africa

G. C. OOSTHUIZEN

Western Theology and African Alienation

THE MEANINGFULNESS of any theology rests on its relevance to the life of the members of the communities where it is applied. Many of the theologies that spun out from and were nourished in the Western intellectualist context have no roots in the life of the communities in Africa and thus "became useless verbiage." This is because Western theology has in many respects been indifferent to the church getting rooted in Africa, to its longing for Africanization. While Western theology has been the intellectual foundation of the Western-oriented churches, these dispositions blindfolded theology to the issues at the gut level of Africa's authentic existence. It smothered what is positive in the traditional African context. This is what A. D. Galloway says about European philosophy in Africa. He emphasizes that philosophies are relevant "only in so far as they assist us to formulate our own problems more clearly" (cited in Segolo 1994). This applies even more to theology.

It thus becomes disastrous in this context to produce theology for its own sake. Its usefulness to the religious and cultural situation should be closely analyzed and evaluated. This means that the emphasis is not to be put on the church as an institution but rather on the church as an organism.

Not only is the theology of the Western-oriented churches in Africa becoming progressively more suspect but also the structures of the Western-oriented churches. The imposition of Western values and institutions on indigenous African systems is seen as a major cause of the retrogression of the so-called mainline churches. There is also the growth in suspicion that

277

the Western political systems do not have the answer for the indigenous African society and its systems. The "migrant social structures," that is, the foreign artificial structures, according to Ekeh (1974), were superimposed on the indigenous African systems without the corresponding values.

The organization of the church as institution became more important to missioners than the traditional inborn sense of fellowship and mutual caring and sharing that are basic in traditional African religion. This was, however, to be addressed with the emergence of the African Independent Churches (AICs). It should be noted that only about 5 percent of the AICs have church buildings. One begins to wonder why people feel satisfied gathering in houses, shacks, shelters made from motorcar boxes, in open spaces, and a small percentage in school classrooms. This should not be interpreted merely as a reflection of poverty but as the inner need for fellowship: the need for small-scale church communities which reflect the extended family system in the ecclesiastical context. Western secular structures as well as Western ecclesiastical structures resulted in a sense of alienation with many in Africa. The vast sums spent on these Western-oriented constructions remain an obstacle to the African concept of religion as a sharing and caring phenomenon.

There is a feeling in African communities especially of being disjointed, of being out of gear, of not being able to progress. Instability prevails. The Western type of church institution is not seen as the ideal from a functional point of view. The six thousand AIC denominations in South Africa, about 90 percent of which act like the extended family system, tell a story. Africa wants face-to-face fellowship to advance the support rendered by the extended family system. This is the challenge that faces the so-called mainline churches. This is the problem that the AICs address. Political instability is due to systems that do not work. The coexistence of ruling and opposition parties is foreign to Africa. Large indigenous churches often break up because of leadership tussles. The new South Africa has perhaps found a solution whereby all the parties of any consequence can take part in the government. The greatest problem is the undervaluation of the African cultural heritage by a Western ideological system and tradition of scholarship.

Everything African was seen as hardly of any significance; thinking was here seen as based on "pre-logical mentality," that is, not really evolutionized; their achievements were treated as if next to nothing, their social systems not worth maintaining. African life was described as irrational; the Western culture as based on the so-called superiority of the science-oriented Western world; the one "primitive" and "traditional," the other so-called civilized or modern. This is the unfortunate attitude of the Western-oriented churches whose sympathy lies with so-called Western modern thought, but many Africans in these churches do not wish to lose contact with traditional approaches because of their meaningful Christian appeal.

Modern Africa is in search of viable political institutions, as Christianity in Africa is in search of relevant ecclesiastical institutions in keeping with their religious yearnings and challenges. The two worlds, the world of the modern industrial center and the known world of the traditional disposition and orientation, are responsible for the intensification of "the new dualism," which "causes a kind of mental and ethical schizophrenia in some spheres of conduct" (Wiredu 1980, 23).

The rising consciousness of the "new dualism" in Africa will become more and more an issue with which the so-called mainline churches will be confronted by their African constituencies. Furthermore, if they do not seriously tap the resources of African thinking in general and African spirituality in particular, the future of these churches will become bleak. The various mainline churches in South Africa have lost from 5 percent up to over 28 percent of their membership from 1980 to 1991. There has been a tremendous shift from these churches to the AICs, who increased by at least 20 percent during the same period. In 1950 the so-called mainline churches in South Africa had under their wings about 75 to 80 percent of all African Christians and the AICs 12 to 14 percent; in 1980 the respective percentages were 52 percent and 27 percent; in 1991 the respective percentages were 41 percent and 34–35 percent. During the first few years of the twenty-first century the AICs will be in the majority, and the so-called mainline churches will house the minority of South Africa's Christianity, making their buildings almost empty.

Mission Christianity and Identity Crisis

The major area that has been distorted by the missionary-oriented evaluation of African thinking is the area of religion. The missionary and anthropological literature has presented African religion in a most negative manner, as if it is overruled by or infested with beliefs in magic, fetishes, spirits, ancestors, and so on. Such beliefs are not the totality of African traditional religion. It is not necessary to emphasize the fact that the concept of God was always vivid in African traditional religion, although God was not directly approachable. He was always behind everything. Taking on Christianity has often led to a crisis of identity—in fact, many in the so-called mainline churches are not absolved from this crisis.

In the mainline churches the crisis of identity lies in the fact that many of their members wish to receive the benefits of traditional religion, such as their spontaneity in liturgy and their healing procedures. In this the AICs have became a significant factor, as many of their members are the children of the identity crisis; in and through them the crisis has been ameliorated and even solved. They have become masters in solving the dualism between empirical Christianity and African traditional religion. AICs are managing this dualism on their own in a masterly manner without being schizophrenic. Those in the mainline churches have much to do with the schizophrenic syndrome because they have been mentally colonized, and what they need is a mental and spiritual decolonization process in the new South Africa and Africa.

African Challenge and Indigenous Christianity

African resources and approaches should be subjected to rigorous scrutiny in order to assess how they could be utilized meaningfully in contemporary society. Folklores are still alive in the African culture and day-to-day life. They were never out of fashion but only went "underground" as a result of the misinterpretation of African culture and thought in secular-oriented society. How traditional Africans view the world, the metaphysical world with its spirit beings and forces, how they view causes of things, what is truth to them, what is quality of life—all these and more predominate in contemporary African life even in the most secularized situations. Members of the AICs utilize this aspect of African culture in their congregations to create an atmosphere and a place to feel really at home. It is important to face all these issues squarely in the religious context of philosophy of religion and theology. Traditional African spirituality and healing should be seen in the correct perspective—not as merely associated with suppression—without overvaluing it. The contemporary task of African philosophy and Africa theology should be to reconstruct African value systems (Sogolo 1994, 7). However, this should be done contextually, because secular dispositions cannot merely be ignored. Africa is in search not only of viable political institutions but also of indigenous-oriented church institutions. Africa, in the postcolonial era made strong advances in the direction of socialism, which was seen as an offshoot of traditional African communalism (Wiredu 1980, 3). The failure of its development was due to the misunderstanding of the African concept of humanity, which was based on a deep sense of interhuman relationships. Africa is in need of organizing its social and political institutions, including the church, on the basis of genuine human fellowship. South Africa is involved in the process of this social and political adjustment. The AIC phenomenon is the result of a process of ecclesiastical experimentation that started in the face of much opposition—they are changing the theological and institutional stance of the church in Africa. Here critical thinking has already taken place on the ecclesiastical level, and the AICs had the courage to go their own way after the deep self-analysis of those who left the mission churches and who have through the years left the so-called mainline churches.

In constructing a sound basis for the church in Africa, one should take cognizance of the historical churches, the traditional African religions, and the AICs. In the traditional African context, political legitimacy was derived primarily from religious assumptions. The role of traditional African religion thus will not be wiped out as the colonial christianizing efforts tried to do. It is necessary to investigate which cultural positions of the Western-oriented churches were embedded in the colonial culture, so that secular culture will survive. The Westminster and other Western political and ecclesiastical structures have not taken deep root in Africa; the ecclesiastical structures have been more successful, but the reaction from the renaissance of traditional African religious approaches should not be underestimated. Indigenous values and socio-moral injunctions based on the African cultural and religious inheritance have been underestimated and misrepresented by those who concentrate on monologue instead of dialogue when it comes to these issues.

The destruction of the traditional system of collective values by the westernization process and its extreme individualism had a negative influence on traditional African values (such as fellowship and mutual concern and respect), which are highlighted in the AICs. The collapse of values in the urban areas cannot be restored merely by economic means and methods. It is here that the church has a task, but the mainline churches especially have lost contact with the grass-roots situation. It is here that Africa's traditional moral system needs to be revived, which is in fact being done by the AICs. Traditional African moral systems had human interests at heart. As Sogolo rightly states: "an action was judged right or wrong depending on the extent to which it promoted well-being, mutual understanding and social harmony" (Sogolo 1994, 11). The emphasis on the dictum that a human being is only a human being through other human beings (which is the basis of a humanitarian morality) needs to be strengthened in modern African society. This is basic to the AICs, which accounts for their growth. African moral thinking needs to be elucidated and clearly contrasted with the misconceptions that exist in modern westernized society concerning the inherent value of morality for a healthy African society.

The AICs have been able to resolve the crisis of identity engendered by the Western missionary theological position through bringing the African value system of traditional religion into their interpretation of Christianity. Through this combination of two forces—as in traditional medicine, two medicines are more effective than one—a dynamic religious stance has been established that is evident in the impact of the AICs. The dualism that Western-oriented Christianity introduced into South Africa and elsewhere has been effectively handled in the AICs. Here the reconstructive mission of the church at the grass-roots level has begun; the fundamental principles of traditional African religion have been analyzed and integrated into the Christian context.

African religion has existentially never been "inferior" to the Christian religion—they both uphold the humanity of the human being, worship their Creator, have moral concepts, and give direction in life situations. In the human social context, however, in spite of its schools and other activities in society, human needs at the very grass-roots level have been neglected by the mainline churches. Those to whom the churches gave attention have often been alienated from the rank and file, while the AICs, with their upholding of traditional human values, have reacted with caring and sharing fellowship. This role in the rapidly changing social situation in South Africa has attracted literally millions to the AICs who have accepted the reconstructive mission. Many in the mainline churches envy them for what they do. The African theologian should examine the fundamental principles that stimulate traditional religion; look at the foreign influences and the conflicts to which these give rise; examine issues such as inter-human relationships, fellowship, healing in its holistic context, church liturgy, and spontaneous religious expression such as composition of hymns and so on. The AICs are involved in the realities of South Africa—even the political realities, but in their own way. There should thus be what Sogolo calls "a reconstructive mission" aimed at resolving major issues of intellectual conflict, as is found and expressed in the realities of contemporary life in Africa (Sogolo 1994, 12).

African cultural life has also changed and can never be the same again, although certain aspects show only minimal changes. Certain demands of modern society cannot be met in the traditional context, especially on the scientific and industrial level. The efficiency and imagination of modern civilization should, up to a certain level, be accepted, but Africa should not be overpowered by them. African approaches to its indigenous culture are, as is the case in any culture, protective of the basic aspects of various traditions. The challenges of the modern world do affect the indigenous culture to such an extent that even the balanced wisdom of centuries is negatively influenced. It is here that the AICs assist society to retain a balanced outlook within the context of the vicissitudes of urban social problems. New realities have to be faced but in a balanced manner.

Africa has been seen as a continent lacking in awareness of alternatives (see Horton 1967, 50–71, 155–87; Sogolo 1994). This misconception is challenged with the AICs as an example. Many hail from the mainline churches; others from the indigenous traditional religions. This is obvious, even among the most illiterate, and in contrast to this some scientists have a closed dogmatic approach, which is reluctant to accept alternatives (see Gellner 1974, 157). The static nature of the so-called mainline churches toward change contrasts badly over against the dynamic adaptability of the AICs. This adaptability is seen in their liturgy, choruses, and ritual innovations; their emphasis on special methods of sharing and caring in situations of rapid social change; and their methods of healing, money saving, and money lending in situations of deprivation.

References

Ekeh, Peter
   1974   *Social Exchange Theory: The Two Traditions.* London: Heinemann Educational.
Gellner, Ernest
   1974   *Legitimation of Belief.* London/New York: Cambridge University Press.
Horton, R.
   1967   "African Traditional Religion and Western Science." *Africa* 37, no. 1:50–71; no. 2:155–87.
   1994   *Patterns of Thought in Africa and the West: Essays on Magic, Religion and Science.* Cambridge: Cambridge University Press.
Sogolo, G. S.
   1994   *Foundations of African Philosophy: A Definitive Analysis of Conceptual Issues in African Thought.* Ibadan, Nigeria: Ibadan University Press.
Wiredu, Kwasi
   1980   *Philosophy and African Culture.* New York: Cambridge University Press.

13

African Muslim Spirituality: The Symbiotic Tradition in West Africa

PATRICK J. RYAN, S.J.

Spirituality on Religious Frontiers

THE DEVELOPMENT OF ISLAM in sub-Saharan Africa has followed a gradualist pattern, with Islamic practices replacing those of traditional provenance only in stages or phases. Humphrey J. Fisher has characterized the progress of Islam in this area as a threefold development; first, as represented by foreign Muslim residents; second, commanding some local support but forced to compromise with local custom; and third, able to impose reform at will. The pattern did not begin in all the areas at the same time, nor advance at the same rate, so differing stages may exist side by side (Fisher 1970, 2:345–56).

In a study of African Muslim spirituality, the first stage is of interest in so far as foreign Muslim residents have exercised a formative influence on indigenous African Muslims in the sub-Saharan zone. In the third phase, African Muslim spirituality has much in common with Muslim spirituality in other parts of the world. Such reform-minded Muslims often deny that there is anything uniquely African in their Islam, urging the thesis that Islam is one and supra-cultural.

This essay will dwell on the spirituality of a much-maligned population among Muslims in Africa, those in the second phase, the people called "mixers" (Arabic *mukhallitun*) by such reformers as ʿUthman dan Fodio (d. 1817) in what is now northern Nigeria.[1] The spirituality of these people—their inwardness as individuals or groups, their openness to Ultimate Reality—differs from individual to individual and from group to group in the way it combines aspects of traditional African approaches to the Transcendent with those of Islamic inspiration. But the common factor in the various expressions of inwardness open to the Transcendent in all of these "mixing" Muslims, from the most Africanized to the most Islamized, is the fact that they have lived their spiritual lives on the frontiers where Islam and the multiple varieties of traditional faith in Africa have met.

Although many reform-minded Muslims in Africa today would like to think that the "mixing" variety of Islam is dying out on the continent, it is sometimes surprising to discover that even some reform-minded Muslims participate in religious traditions of African traditional inspiration from time to time, and especially in moments of personal and communal crisis. Folk versions of Sufism bridge the gap between African traditional forms of faith and the piety of African Muslims. Without entering into judgment on the orthopraxy or heteropraxy of the practices described, this essay will attempt to describe how these practices reveal a spirituality of people who live on religious frontiers.

First Apprehensions of Islam in the Savanna: The Faith of Useful Strangers

It was apparently Ibadis, adherents of a moderate branch of the puritanical Kharijite movement in early Islam that had established itself by the late eighth century among the Berbers of what is now Algeria, who made the first commercial and missionary contacts for Islam among sub-Saharan West Africans. As Ibadis these Berbers acknowledged the de facto governance of the Muslim world by non-Ibadi Muslims, the purity of whose Islamic faith they questioned.

Although there were instances when Ibadis repudiated their usual policy of religious and political quietism (qu'ud), they generally managed to live under the rule of Sunni Muslim rulers, whom they considered to be virtual infidels (kuffar), even if not actually those who ascribe partners to God (mushrikun) (Lewicki 1960, 3:648–60). Perhaps it was this Ibadi tolerance of Muslim "infidels" that made it easier for them to live peaceably as well with populations that made no claim to Islam, the Traditionalist peoples who lived in "the land of the blacks" (bilad al-sudan).

Evidence of North African Ibadi commercial contact in the ninth century with Gao in what is now Mali comes from a later Ibadi source narrating how an Ibadi named Aflah ibn ʿAbd al-Wahhab, later to become the imam of the Ibadi town of Tahart, had wanted to travel for trade to Mali, but his father, the reigning imam, forbade his journey (al-Wisyani in Corpus, 90).[2] When he succeeded his father as ruler in Tahart, Aflah sent a delegation with gifts to an unnamed "king of the blacks," very likely the ruler in Gao. The leader of that delegation, Muhammad ibn ʿArafah, fascinated the African ruler. A tenth-century source narrates that the ruler "admired

[Ibn 'Arafah's] dignity, handsomeness and chivalry as he rode a horse" (Ibn al-Saghr in *Corpus,* 25). This sub-Saharan admiration for North African style, simple as it may seem, recurs as a theme over and over again in the stories of how West Africans first felt the attraction of Islam. From such peaceful encounters between Berbers and West Africans, rather than from military raids, arose the beginnings of Islam in West Africa and the beginnings as well of a type of spirituality that eventually evolved into the cultus of the Muslim holy man, or marabout, the paragon of a new style of personal interaction with the Transcendent.

Not every Ibadi who crossed the desert from North Africa did so for purely commercial reasons. An anonymous twelfth-century Ibadi source mentions a certain shaykh of a century or so earlier named Abu Musa Harun ibn Abi Imran, who called for the formation of a religious school in Ouargla, an Algerian oasis. After the Fatimid shi'i conquest of Tahart in 909, Ouargla had become the last bastion of Ibadi power in North Africa. But the Ibadi ruler in Ouargla only offered the shaykh a paltry sum for this pious cause, prompting the indignant shaykh to announce that he would travel southward to Ghanah[3] (on the borders of present-day Mali and Mauritania), the source of gold that had played an important economic role in Tahart's former prosperity. Evidently the Ibadis established in Ghanah might still be expected to fund such an expensive project. In choosing to remove to Ghanah, Abu Musa Harun was following the example of another North African Ibadi scholar named Falhun ibn Ishaq, who had died in Ghanah. Eventually, the source narrates, Abu Musa Harun went even further south than ancient Ghanah, dying at last in the gold-mining center of Ghiyara, "whose people he found to be naked."[4] Ghiyara, evidently still predominantly non-Muslim at this time, must have had enough Ibadi traders living there on whose generous benefactions the pious scholar could hope to survive.

Support for such pious exiles as Falhun ibn Ishaq and Abu Musa Harun may have been forthcoming not only from North African Ibadis living on the southern fringes of the Sahara as traders but also from their West African trading partners. Traditionalist rulers found these pious scholars useful for their literacy and knowledge of numbers and also for their religious techniques, their new methods of dealing with the Transcendent and with the unruly mysteries of this world as well. The Andalusian geographer Abu 'Ubayd Allah al-Bakri, writing in the eleventh century, gave several examples (based on the testimony of Andalusian merchants) of West African kingdoms where Muslim strangers, including professional holy men, lived and prospered among Traditionalist populations whose leadership, at least, valued their religious services, even before these rulers or their people eventually converted to Islam.

The Muslim community in ancient Ghanah lived for the most part in virtual quarantine (see Fisher 1973, 31) from the Traditionalist population of the royal capital. The Muslim residential area lay six miles away from the royal precincts to which the ruler's Muslim ministers traveled daily to fulfill their functions. For their convenience during the working hours a single small mosque adjoined the king's court of justice, whereas their own residential area boasted of twelve mosques, one of them used for the Friday congregational worship (al-Bakri in *Corpus,* 70). At the time when al-Bakri was writing (before 1068), these Muslim ministers served the ruler of Ghanah faithfully, even though they did not share his faith. Their Muslim identity accorded them privileges not available to non-Muslims in Ghanah.

When the people who profess the same religion as the king approach him, they fall on their knees and sprinkle dust on their heads, for this is their way of greeting him. As for the Muslims, they greet him only by clapping their hands (al-Bakri in *Corpus,* 80). An indication of the Africanization of Islam after quarantine broke down can be found in the fact that subsequent "mixing" Muslim rulers in West Africa demanded prostration and "dusting" from their Muslim subjects as well, a practice that modern reformers have vehemently excoriated.[5]

Even if the ruler in Ghanah remained completely Traditionalist himself, others of his West African contemporaries were beginning to take on some of the external trappings of Islam, as al-Bakri's description of eleventh-century Gao in Mali suggests. Exposed to Ibadi influence from at least the ninth century, Gao's Muslim community still lived separately from the court of Qanda, the ruler at al-Bakri's time. Only Qanda himself bridged the ritual gap between these two communities, at least to some degree. Although he presided over what seems to have been a ritual meal accompanied by dancing connected with the tutelary spirit of the Niger River, nevertheless, at his enthronement, Qanda received "a signet ring, a sword and a copy of the *Qur'an,* which, as they assert, were sent to them by the Commander of the Faithful (the Caliph)" (al-Bakri in *Corpus,* 87).

Sunni Muslims from North Africa felt some scruples about trading with "the land of the blacks," to judge from the disapproval expressed in the famous legal treatise of Ibn Abi Zayd al-Qayrawani (d. 996) (Ibn Abi Zayd al-Qayrawani in *Corpus,* 55), but Ibadis, habituated to a world of infidels, even among Muslims, looked with a more benign eye on their West African trading partners, even accepting their political dominance when this served the Ibadis' commercial purposes. The Almoravid reformers, militant Sunnis from the western Sahara in the eleventh century, reacted against this Ibadi tradition of tolerance and sowed the seeds of later forms of Islamic militancy in West Africa (see Levtzion 1973, 29–42).

Ibadi tolerance of religious diversity seems to have affected the first expressions of the Islamic tradition among indigenous West Africans themselves. Fewer more vivid examples of a certain symbiosis (or "mixing," to use the reformers' terminology) of Islamic and Traditionalist faith can be found than in the medieval empire of Mali. Our historical knowledge of medieval Mali is very partial, but the sources we do have give us glimpses of several stages in the development of a West African Muslim community that was, in its later Diaspora, to spread a symbiotic, nonmilitant form of Islam that survives in many parts of West Africa to the present day.

Symbiotic Muslim Spirituality in Medieval Mali

One of the areas of sub-Saharan West Africa visited by al-Bakri's informants was Malal, a chieftaincy generally thought to have been a constituent part of the empire later called Mali. Al-Bakri narrates how a ruler of Malal at some earlier period, perhaps the tenth century, came to be called al-Musulmani. This originally Traditionalist ruler kept as a guest in his court "a Muslim who used to read the *Qurʾan* and was acquainted with the sunnah" (al-Bakri in *Corpus*, 82). Some sources have suggested that this anonymous guest of the ruler in Malal may have been an Ibadi (al-Shammakhi in *Corpus*, 368–69), but the evidence is not conclusive (see Levtzion and Hopkins in *Corpus*, 432). It seems likely, however, that the guest was a North African. Al-Bakri never asserts that the guest had come to Malal on secular business, and the very opposite may be implied. The narrative suggests that he may well have been an early example of a widespread phenomenon in later times, the Muslim chaplain in a Traditionalist court. As such he proved his worth when drought ravaged the territory of Malal:

> The inhabitants prayed for rain, sacrificing cattle till they had exterminated almost all of them, but the drought and the misery only increased. . . . To the Muslim guest the ruler complained of the calamities that assailed him and his people. The man said: "O King, if you believed in God (who is exalted) and testified that He is One and testified as to the prophetic mission of Muhammad (God bless him and give him peace) and if you accepted all the religious laws of Islam, I would pray for your deliverance from your plight and that God's mercy would envelop all the people of your country and that your enemies and adversaries might envy you on that account." Thus he continued to press the king until the latter accepted Islam and became a sincere Muslim. The man made him recite from the *Qurʾan* some easy passages and taught him religious obligations and practices which no one may be excused from knowing. Thus the Muslim made him wait till the eve of the following Friday, when he ordered him to purify himself by a complete ablution, and

clothed him in a cotton garment which he had. The two of them came out towards a mound of earth, and there the Muslim stood praying while the king, standing at his right side, imitated him Thus they prayed for a part of the night, the Muslim reciting invocations and the king saying "Amen." The dawn had just started to break when God caused abundant rain to descend upon them, so the king ordered the idols to be broken and expelled the sorcerers from his country. He and his descendants after him as well as his nobles were sincerely attached to Islam, while the common people of his kingdom remained polytheists. Since then all their rulers have been given the title of al-Musulmani. (al-Bakri in *Corpus*, 82–83)

In this eleventh-century narrative of events in Malal, several typical elements in the earliest expression of symbiotic African Muslim spirituality manifest themselves. First and foremost, it should be noted that the ruler's Muslim guest, possibly a North African Ibadi, seems to have lived among Traditionalist West Africans without proselytizing them for some time before the events narrated by al-Bakri. It is possible that the Muslim guest, whose piety is remarked upon by al-Bakri, had come to Malal as Abu Musa Harun and Falhun ibn Ishaq came to Ghiyara and Ghana, a mendicant scholar in search of patronage. Such patronage, he may soon have discovered, was forthcoming not only from the North African merchants to whom he came but also from their non-Muslim trading partner, the local ruler. Even today Traditionalist and Christian rulers in West Africa, to say nothing of ordinary people, have selectively patronized the religious services offered by Muslim holy men. Soldiers plotting a coup, football players preparing for a crucial match and students worrying over examinations—no matter what their religious background—have sought out such Muslim specialists for appropriate amulets and powerful prayer.

In Malal the quarantine of the Muslim community had already broken down by the eleventh century, and it broke down not because of military aggression or mercantile influence but because a Traditionalist West African ruler reached out to a Muslim stranger in the ruler's time of need. The ruler in Malal who first called for Muslim religious aid was a king in terrible trouble, and herein lies a second major theme in the history of symbiotic Muslim spirituality in West Africa. The ruler in Malal faced a crisis that could have led to his deposition. When the chieftaincy in West Africa grows out of or competes with the custodianship of the earth as a numinous force, as it does in some parts of the savanna zone, the king must produce rain for his people (see Fortes 1945, 95). The Muslim guest in Malal was probably known to be a devotee of the One who causes rainfall and of him alone. To this stranger and his intercession with the heavens the beleaguered king betook himself. Over and over again the history of West

African Islam has proven its utility to kings, especially those in need of such heavenly blessings as rain.[6]

The prayer a Muslim makes in supplication for the gift of rain, *salat al istisqa*, differs from other forms of ritual worship in the Islamic tradition in that it retains, in some localities, traces of homeopathic magic in its actual performance. In Morocco, for instance, the imam who leads it reverses his outer garment and the congregation follows him, apparently acting out their desire for a change in the weather (Westermarck 1926, 2:254–55). In modern Senegal some Muslims go even further, engaging in a somewhat boisterous transvestism (Gueye 1977, 53). No specific mention of such practices is made in the text of al-Bakri, but the ruler and his Muslim guest may well have prayed for rain at an earth shrine (a mound of earth) (Ryan 1981, 384), a traditional site sought out in time of drought (ibid., 382). Such a detail may suggest that, at least at first, West Africans looked to the Islamic tradition for a supplement to or replacement for problematic techniques in their indigenous armory of magical practice. Only very gradually, over a process of centuries, did the deeper import of Islam open up before them.

The ruler in Malal and his courtiers came to a deeper understanding of Islam than did their subjects. Indeed, al-Bakri notes that the commoners of Malal remained religiously unchanged by the conversion of their king. Although the nameless Muslim guest is said to have instructed his royal proselyte "in all the religious laws of Islam" before they prayed together for rain, it may not be insignificant that the king only ordered the destruction of his idols and the expulsion of his sorcerers after the *salat al-istisqa* had produced concrete results. Al-Musulmani's faith depended on the tangible benefits to be derived from it. The spirituality of symbiotic West African Islam takes an instrumental attitude to prayer.

The conversion of al-Musulmani in Malal may well mark the beginning of Islam in the area later called Mali. The Keita clan that came to power in Mali in the early thirteenth century eventually traced their origin to Bilal, the African freedman who called the Prophet Muhammad and his companions to worship in the seventh century. Little historical credence can be given to this genealogy. Even the present-day oral epic Sundiata portrays the earliest Keita descendants of Bilal as hunter-kings who communicated more with spirits of the bush (assimilated to jinn) than with God (Niane 1965, 2–3).

Sundiata's eighth successor on the throne of Mali, Mansa Musa, left a lasting impression on the North African Muslim world during his pilgrimage to Mecca in 1324–1325. Musa struck contemporary Egyptian observers as a very devout Muslim who was, however, unaware of central precepts of

Islamic law. When Mansa Musa visited Cairo on the way to Mecca, the governor of Old Cairo befriended him. Later he passed on to the Egyptian chronicler Ibn Fadl Allah al-ʿUmari some account of the Mali sovereign's understanding of Islam.

It is a custom of his people that if one of them should have reared a beautiful daughter he offers her to the king as a concubine and he possesses her without a marriage ceremony, as slaves are possessed, and this in spite of the fact that Islam has "triumphed among them and that they follow the Malikite school (of Islamic law) and that this sultan Musa was pious and assiduous in prayer, *Qurʾan* reading and the practice of recollection (*dhikr*)" (al-ʿUmari in *Corpus*, 268).

The Egyptian governor drew this anomaly to Mansa Musa's attention and the amazed ruler declared that he would renounce such concubinage with free women forthwith. The Sufi tendencies alluded to in this passage are further expanded in the governor's account of the effect the completed pilgrimage had on Mansa Musa:

> He accomplished the obligations of the pilgrimage, visited (the tomb of) the prophet (at Medina) . . . and returned to his country with the intention of handing over his sovereignty to his son and abandoning it entirely to him and returning to Mecca the Venerated to remain there as a dweller near the sanctuary; but death overtook him. (al-ʿUmari in *Corpus*, 268)

There may be more (or less) than Sufi piety involved in Mansa Musa's desire to hand over the sovereignty to his son, whom he had earlier appointed his deputy during his absence on the pilgrimage. Such filial succession, far from established in Mali at that time, deprived Mansa Musa's brother of the throne (Levtzion 1973, 66). Whatever may have been his motivation, and despite the desire he expressed to shake off worldly concerns and dedicate himself to the things of God, Mansa Musa continued to rule for another twelve years after his return from the pilgrimage. Even if his pious aspirations proved only temporary, his friend in Cairo remembered him as one who "maintained a uniform attitude of worship and turning towards God" while in Egypt before and after the pilgrimage. "It was as though he were standing before Him because of His continual presence in his mind" (al-ʿUmari in *Corpus*, 269). Prayerfulness without much concern for other legal observances typifies symbiotic African Muslim spirituality.

Mansa Musa's son and successor, Mansa Muhammad, was probably deposed by his uncle, Mansa Sulayman, in 1341 (Ibn Khaldun in *Corpus*, 335). The indefatigable Moroccan tourist Ibn Battutah visited Mali in the reign of Mansa Sulayman between 28 June 1352 and 28 February 1353. He stayed with the expatriate North African community in the Mali capital and may have exaggerated the importance in the royal court of these foreigners and local Muslim scholars who were allied with them. One anecdote narrated by Ibn Battutah does seem to indicate that expatriate Muslim scholars wielded great power in Mali. Ibn Battutah tells how a Berber scholar, Abu Hafs, felt able to stand up in the congregational mosque of the capital one Friday and publicly call on Mansa Sulayman to rectify an economic injustice Abu Hafs had suffered at the hands of a commercial agent of the Mansa (Ibn Battutah in *Corpus,* 294). Events like this—of great interest to the Berber trading community in Mali—prompted Ibn Battutah to praise Mansa Sulayman's government for its freedom from oppression, its provision of internal security, and its respect for the rights of expatriate businessmen (Ibn Battutah in *Corpus,* 296). It may also be interpreted as indicating Mansa Sulayman's economic dependence on this resident alien mercantile community. The North African point of view enshrined in Ibn Battutah's judgments must be complemented by the evidence he also offers that certain of Mansa Sulayman's indigenous subjects—including his principal wife and a cousin—were plotting against him. Further evidence of the power of Muslim holy men in royal Mali can be gathered from the fact that the conspirator queen, when confronted with her crime, took refuge from her husband's wrath in the house of the Muslim scholar who ordinarily preached the sermon at the congregational worship on Fridays (Ibn Battutah in *Corpus,* 294–95). This unnamed preacher (*khatib*), who may also have been a Berber or at least a close associate of the expatriate community, evidently exercised considerable influence at court.

Summing up the virtues and vices of the people whom he met in Mansa Sulayman's Mali, Ibn Battutah dwells at some length on their devotion to the ritual worship and the memorization of the *Qurʾan,* a practice they enforced on children by shackling delinquents (Ibn Battutah in *Corpus,* 296). Various forms of nudity in Mali rank first among the failures he singles out. All female servants pursued their duties in complete undress, and women entered the royal presence only after removing their clothing (Ibn Battutah in *Corpus,* 296–97). Ibn Battutah seems also to have been scandalized by the way his Berber hosts in Walata, for all their devout profession of Islam, continued to practice matrilineal succession and inheritance. Worse than this, they even allowed their wives the greatest freedom in their mode of dress and association with male friends other than their husbands (Ibn Battutah in *Corpus,* 285–86). If the alien Berber Muslim community tolerated such infractions of the usual Sunni marital code, the indigenous Muslim community of royal Mali could hardly be expected to know any better.

It may not be insignificant, in this context, that Ibn Battutah met at

Zaghari, on the road to the Mali capital, a community of Malian Wangara traders living side by side with Ibadis of North African origin, the Saghanaghu (Ibn Battutah in *Corpus,* 287). In later times the Saghanaghu had intermarried with their erstwhile neighbors (Wilks in Goody 1967, 181). From the Wangara they also seem to have adopted Sunni Islam, but probably not without the Wangara taking from the Ibadis some of their quietism (*qu'ud*), their ability to live at peace with infidels. The notable lack of militance among most Wangara (Dyula) Muslims of the Mali Diaspora in later times (Willis 1979, 19–20) seems to have taken its origin from Mali, where devout Muslim men, who crowded the central mosque on Fridays, thought nothing of celebrating the Night of Power (toward the end of Ramadan) at a feast served by naked slave girls (Ibn Battutah in *Corpus,* 297). Ibn Battutah's notice of the coexistence of North African Ibadis and Wangara in fourteenth-century Mali suggests that the quietist traditions of ninth-century Tahart survived south of the Sahara long after that Ibadi community had been overrun by Muslim forces less tolerant of deviation along the Mediterranean littoral.

The Missionary Spirituality of the Muslim Diaspora from Mali

The Mali empire began to fall apart toward the end of the fourteenth century after a series of coups and counter-coups in the capital. The fifteenth century witnessed its inclusion in the rising Songhay empire. During the fourteenth and fifteenth centuries traders (variously called Dyula or Wangara) and holy men (*karamokho*) from the Mali empire had penetrated other areas of West Africa south and east of their homeland. These Malian strangers seem to have been the first Muslims to live in Burkina Faso and the northern parts of Sierra Leone, Liberia, Ivory Coast, Ghana, Togo, Benin, and Nigeria (Levtzion 1968, 3–14). Throughout this zone they created small settlements where they traded with local populations without necessarily trying to convert them. The frequency with which a Malian word for land or village, *dougou,* occurs as a suffix on the names of towns in this area testifies to the widespread influence of the Malian Diaspora.[7]

Not unlike Mansa Musa, who refrained from exacting the *jizyah* (tribute to be paid by non-Muslims in a Muslim realm) from Traditionalist goldmining populations under his sway (al-ʿUmari in *Corpus,* 272), these Wangara or Dyula found it expedient to tolerate the faith of their trading partners. In theory Muslims only interact with fellow Muslims or with "People of the Book" (Jews, Christians, and Sabʾians [*Qurʾan* 5:70]). With the conquest of Persia, however, this *Qurʾanic* category was enlarged to

include adherents of the Zoroastrian tradition of faith (Magians). The tolerated status of al-Majusiyyah was later extended to include such diverse populations as the Berbers of North Africa and the Horsemen (Buchner 1953,
300). The Arab and Berber informants of al-Bakri in the eleventh century
also described the faith of certain Sahelian populations with whom they
had extensive commercial dealings, most notably the peoples of pre-Islamic
Takrur and Ghanah, as al-Majusiyyah. Their objects of cults the Muslims
politely called *dakakir* (al-Bakri in *Corpus,* 77, 80),[8] a West African term of
uncertain provenance, rather than *asnam* or *awthan,* plain Arabic for idols.
This tradition of tolerance, evading the *Qur'anic* command to fight infidels
until they pay the *jizyah* and have been humbled (*Qur'an* 9:29), may
explain why the Traditionalist Hausa to the present day are called
Maguzawa (Greenberg 1946, 13). It may also explain the genesis of the
Dyula notion of *tabakoroni,* a purgatorial vestibule between this life and
the next, where good Traditionalists may yet have the opportunity to
embrace Islam, which J. R. Willis calls "person" (1979, 261).

Wangara holy men coming from Mali probably reached Hausaland in
present-day northern Nigeria as early as the fourteenth century. The Kano
Chronicle, an anonymous Arabic account of the rulers in that city, ascribes
their advent to the reign of the Sarkin Kano Yaji (1349–1385; Palmer 1928,
3:104). A seventeenth-century source dates their arrival to the reign of
Muhammad Rumfa (1483–1499; al-Hajj 1968, 12). No indication is given in
either version that the Wangara migrants came as traders, and both accounts
make much of their identity as holy men. The name of their leader, 'Abd al-
Rahman Zaghitay (Diakhite), suggests that he may have been a Jakhanke
tracing his ancestry to Diakha-Bambukhu in Mali. Holy men of Soninke
descent spreading out from this center have developed over many centuries
into a distinctive caste of Muslim scholars, the Jakhanke (Diakhanke).
Known not only for their scholarship but also for their pacifism, even to the
point of renouncing militant struggle in the cause of Islam (*jihad*), the
Jakhanke have contributed a great deal to the peaceful growth of Islam in
many parts of West Africa (Sanneh 1989, 33).

Even before the coming of the Wangara, the Kano Chronicle portrays
the somewhat shadowy predecessors of Yaji as chiefs in political tension
with the spirit resident in a tree and a snake venerated in what may have
been an earth shrine (Palmer 1928, 3:103–4). The Kano rulership traced its
origins to immigrants coming from the northeast, the sons of Bagauds.
Bagauds's tenth successor, Yaji, found in Islam a sacral power that could
overcome the resistance of Traditionalist religious symbols. Not only did
the Wangara initiate the practice of *salat,* but they surrounded the chief
with a retinue of new sacral functionaries: imam, muezzin, qadi, butcher

(Palmer 1928, 3:105). The last-named, by no means an unimportant figure, has introduced Islam into many communities in the history of West Africa. Even where Muslims make up only a tiny minority, they tend to monopolize the provision of butchery services for their non-Muslim neighbors. Just as butchers have made Islamic ways relevant to the lives of non-Muslims, the Wangara holy men who came to Kano gradually inserted themselves into the Sarkin Kano's struggle with the sacred tree.

The sarki gave orders that every town in Kano country should observe ritual prayer and they did so. He built a rectangular mosque under the previously mentioned (sacred) tree and the five prayers were recited there. But the Sarkin Garazawa was opposed to the practice of *salat,* and after they had prayed and returned to their homes he came with his followers and they excreted in the mosque, covering it with filth. In consequence Dan Buji was appointed to patrol around the mosque with armed men from the evening until daybreak, keeping up a constant halloo during the patrol, whereupon the pagans sought to deflect his company and succeeded in detaching some of them, but he and the rest refused. But the defilement of the mosque continued until Sheshe and Fa-Mori announced, "There is no remedy against the pagans except prayer," and the people agreed. So they gathered on Tuesday night in the mosque and prayed from sunset until sunrise against the heathens, not returning to their homes until the forenoon. God answered their prayer. The leader of the pagans was struck blind that very day, and subsequently all who had taken part in the defilement together with their women. After that all the pagans were afraid. Yaji (the Sarkin Kano) dispossessed the chief of the pagans from his office, saying to him, "Be thou chief of the blind."[9]

The Sarkin Garazawa, priest-ruler in one of the areas near Kano that had formerly acknowledged the religious centrality of the shrine of the sacred tree, rejected its Islamization by Yaji and the Wangara. The Kano Chronicle deftly contrasts how a Hausa military patrol, of wavering loyalty to Yaji's cause, and the Wangara holy men, faithful courtiers, undertook to defeat the Sarkin Garazawa and his company of vandals. The superiority of prayer to military action comes in for further emphasis in the account of how the Wangara came to Yaji's aid in the conquest of Santolo, another religious center to the southeast of Kano. Entering into the fray as chaplains to the Hausa army, the Wangara marched around Santolo and prayed for its downfall, not unlike Joshua and the priests at the battle of Jericho. Their prayers eventually achieved their military aim, when the names of the eight principal men of Santolo were revealed to the Wangara, a detail which suggests that these Mali-descended holy men were not averse to directing their prayers against specifically named enemies (Palmer 1928, 3:105–6).

Holy men from the Mali Diaspora seem to have played a role as well in the military foundation in the sixteenth century of the Gonja suzerainty in what is now northern Ghana. The migrants who founded the royal traditions of the Gonja were not Muslims themselves, but probably came from the Mali Diaspora to their present homeland (Tamakloe 1931, 257). These migrants are summed up in the oral tradition in the figure of Ndewura Jakpa, a title indicating that its bearer became the master of many towns through his use of the spear (Goody 1967, 187). Jakpa called into his service a Muslim chaplain remembered as Fati-Morukpe (or Fatigi-Morukpe), a title denoting that its bearer was a Muslim scholar (*fotigi*) and a white man (*moro-kpe*) (Levtzion 1968, 52 n. 3). Very likely this figure also represents a type rather than an individual. Several sources affirm that white Muslims, probably of North African background, lived in the Mali Diaspora of the southern savanna and the forest zone. One of these Muslims, Muhammad al-Abyad (Muhammad the white man), is said in an eighteenth-century Arabic source to have come north from a Malian trading post in the Akan forest, Begho, to act as chaplain for a Gonja ruler whom he eventually converted to Islam (Levtzion 1968, 51–52; Wilks, Levtzion, and Haight 1986, 92).

Were these white Muslims in the Mali Diaspora descended from the Ibadis Ibn Battutah met at Zaghari in the company of Wangara? Possibly, but no positive evidence for their identity as Ibadis can be offered, although their quietistic complacency with their Traditionalist environment might suggest this hypothesis. Pere Labat, an early-eighteenth-century chronicler of the travels of the Chevalier des Marchais in West Africa, describes two "Malais" slave traders, one black and the other white, whom the Chevalier met at the port of Ouidah (in present-day Benin) on the Atlantic coast. Labat could not be absolutely sure whether these "Malais" were Jews or Muslims for reasons he details:

> That which might make one think they are Jews is that they do not eat all kinds of meat. They choose the land animals they want to eat, kill and prepare them for themselves. But this choosing of meats and their solicitude not to be served with meat other than what they have prepared for themselves is (also) a practice among Mohammedans. However, they both drink alcohol and even liqueurs and wine, which does not fit in with (their being) strict Mohammedans. They speak pure Arabic, pray to God several times a day. They have neither fetishes nor amulets (gris gris) and they do not wash themselves at all before making their prayers. They read and write their language very well. (Labat as quoted in Marty 1926, 9)

The intriguing combination of observance and laxity in the Muslim practice of these "Malais" slave traders had its parallel in the Christian practice of the European traders who planted the cross on the West African coast in the late fifteenth century. And yet, by a peculiar irony, it was from the exemplarity of such fallible men of faith that a new stage in the history of religion in West Africa began. Their spirituality was somewhat rough and ready, pragmatic in its almost magical reliance on prayer, but far from consistent in its attitude toward the Islamic moral code (*shari'ah*). Prayerful but not legalistic, they lived out their spiritual lives on the frontiers between Islam and Traditionalist faith. Like all people who live on frontiers, they sometimes crossed and recrossed the borders between these forms of faith.

First Apprehensions of Islam in the Forest: The Faith of Those Who Pray and Write

How were these holy men from North Africa and the Malian cultural area received by the Traditionalist populations of the forest zone, among whom some of them eventually settled?

The sources available for such information are scanty, to say the least, but oral tradition preserves piquant hints of how the earliest Muslims and their new religious practices were understood. Although very little concretely can be said about Malian influence in Yoruba land (in present-day Nigeria), Islam as a religious tradition and Muslims themselves are referred to in Yoruba as Imale or Onimale. Archaeological research at the site of Old Oyo, the ancient Yoruba capital, may someday reveal whether this city had experienced the presence of Malian traders as early as Kano and the Brong area of the Akan forests (fourteenth to fifteenth centuries).

Whether the first Muslims to live among the Yoruba came from Mali or not, some of the references to Muslim beginnings in Yoruba oral tradition may well illustrate early Yoruba reactions to Islam (Abimbola in Biobaku 1973, 57). Verse compositions from the *Ifa* divination corpus, especially those connected with the figure (*odu*) called *otua-meji*, reflect a certain competitive hostility between the custodians of Ifa divination (*babalawo*) and Muslims, especially those Muslim holy men who may have proffered their own techniques of geomantic divination (*khatt al-rami*, "sand-cutting") as a substitute for the indigenous Yoruba system. The Ifa estimate of the Islamic religious tradition presents an outsider viewpoint, generally unsympathetic. Nevertheless it may serve as an indication of what the Traditionalist Yoruba first noticed about the spirituality of the stranger populations who had settled among them. External acts of piety are often oddly interpreted.

The fast of Ramadan did not appeal to the Traditionalist Yoruba diviner. In much of West Africa, fasting implies mourning. One Ifa verse composition playfully interprets the fast of Ramadan as punishment inflicted on a Muslim who had so neglected his mother as to cause her death by starvation. Another verse composition interprets the practice of the five daily times of worship (*salat*) as punishment inflicted on Muslim yam-thieves caught in the act by a farmer named Sala (Ryan 1978, 88–89).

These brief satirical interpretations of the Ramadan fast and the practice of *salat* must be complemented, however, with a longer verse composition associated with *otua-meji* that suggests—not without some satire as well—that Islam in Yoruba land derives from Ifa, begotten by the *orisha* Orunmila, who presides over this elaborate divinatory process. Some scholars have tried to suggest the very opposite, that the Levantine geomancy called *khatt al-rami* in Arabic and popularized in Africa by Muslims has begotten the externals of the Yoruba system (Hebert 1961), if not its essential core, the verse compositions. The witty ethnocentrism of the suggestion that Orunmila fathered Yoruba Muslims need not be taken seriously as history, but it does capture an early Yoruba perception of Islam as another version, possibly counterfeit, of something the indigenous Yoruba tradition already offered. Orunmila's three Muslim sons go beyond what their father taught them (both Ifa and *khatt al-rami*), but he tolerantly allows them to take the religious path they have chosen:

> They took their father's agbada garments
> And their mother's gele head-dress.
> They put on the agbada garments,
> And curled the gele head-dress massively on their heads.
> They stretched out on the floor four pieces of wood side by side,
> And stood inside the enclosure so formed.
> They started to utter some words silently,
> They were placing their heads against the floor,
> And standing up again.
> They were kneeling down,
> And getting up again.
> Their father was just looking at them in amazement.
> They were doing that five times a day.
> He then remembered the warning,
> Which his diviners had given him,
> And he did not quarrel with them.
> (Ryan 1978, 86–87; see Abimbola 1969, 2:97)

Orunmila's tolerance of his Muslim sons, albeit tinged with a certain irony, has corresponded to the general Yoruba Traditionalist attitude toward Muslims down to the present day. Half or more of the Yoruba today would describe themselves as Muslim in one sense or another.

Although very few Yoruba today would openly profess their commitment to the Traditionalist religious system of their ancestors, Ifa and the other salient features of the Yoruba religious tradition play a large role in the spiritual lives of Muslim and Christian Yoruba alike. If Orunmila has tolerated the religious deviations of his sons, his sons have not wandered very far away from their father's household.

The symbiosis between Islam and the Traditionalist faith of the Yoruba finds little parallel in the Akan cultural area (in modern Ghana) despite many centuries of Muslim presence there. The matrilineality of the Akan and their traditional dislike of circumcision, very different from Yoruba cultural norms, may be cited among the reasons for the general reluctance of the Akan to adopt a religious tradition that could cut them off from inherited wealth or succession to rulership. Those Akan who are Muslims today are called *kramo*, a word derived from the Malian term for holy man, *karamokho*. It is not at all unlikely that many of the Muslims in the Akan areas are descendants of Muslim holy men and traders who settled and married in urban centers like Bondoukou and Kumasi. Virtually no Akan in the chieftaincy estate has become a Muslim; the Asantehene Osei Kwame, enstooled at the age of twelve in 1777, was deposed twenty-two years later precisely because it was thought by the king makers that he had become too close to the alien Muslim community (Wilks 1975, 253–54).

Nevertheless, for all the tension between Islam and Akan culture, Muslim symbols have sometimes entered into certain aspects of royal Akan regalia and even the printed designs of adinkra cloth (Rattray 1927, 20–21). Muslims may possibly have influenced the development of the seven-day week in the Akan division of time. Muslim holy men are still revered in the Akan areas for the varieties of Levantine magical practice they make available to their non-Muslim neighbors. Oral tradition in Asante recalls the services of Muslim amulet makers as a vital supplement to the magical and protective means offered by the Asantehene's chief officer in charge of such services, the Nsumankwahene (Garrard 1980, 27).

The ability to read and write, interpreted by literate populations in purely pragmatic terms, strikes the illiterate as somehow uncanny. In many parts of West Africa, including both Yoruba land and the Akan areas today, Arabic script is valued as a device redolent with mysterious power. In an earlier period amulets containing verses from the *Qurʾan* and even whole volumes of the Muslim scriptures were revered for their numinous potency (Biobaku 1957, 25). In more than one part of West Africa unread copies of the *Qurʾan*, wrapped in hides and buried, have been transformed into shrines thought deserving of sacrificial offerings (Johnson 1921, 4; Levtzion 1968, 65–66, 73, 144). All such practices would seem to derive their origins from the earliest perceptions of the alien religious tradition by peoples who were as yet incapable of comprehending the revealed word contained in these scriptures. Thus has the faith of peaceful strangers been misunderstood, or only partly understood, transformed by the religious imaginations of those among whom they settled.

Those who have been willing to travel over long distances have often been the agents of religious change in West Africa. Hunters in ancient times brought down from the zone that is now the Sahara and the Sahel the mysteries they had learned while tracking their prey. To the hunter is often ascribed the beginning of chieftaincy in various parts of West Africa or the introduction of cultic innovation. More mobile than the herdsmen whose cattle move more gradually and survive only with difficulty the disease characteristic of the forest zone, the hunter can live by his trade while traveling farther away from his homeland.

Muslim traders and holy men in West Africa have likewise traveled, sometimes over long distances, introducing dramatic changes in spirituality as they went. Sometimes the former were less interested in such religious change than the latter. As in the nineteenth-century Christian experience in West Africa, the trader and the missionary have sometimes found themselves at odds, despite their common provenance. But the coming of any long-distance traveler, no matter how insouciant his faith, has often sparked a religious revolution in West Africa. The advent of those who came as strangers willing to live in peaceful symbiosis with Traditionalists far from their native territories has opened up vistas larger than those who have never traveled had previously imagined. Both the Muslim strangers and their Traditionalist hosts were changed by this experience of symbiosis.

North Africans other than the Ibadis, Sahelian kingdoms other than Mali, and Muslim migrants other than the Wangara have made their presence felt in more southerly areas of West Africa over the last millennium. The Mali and the Wangara have been singled out in the preceding pages as examples of the peaceful penetration of Islam into West Africa. The forces of Islamic militancy, often associated with reform movements, have also promoted the growth of Islam among Traditionalist populations in West Africa. But quietistic tolerance and pacific penetration, less well documented in the Arabic sources of West African history, have come in for less scholarly examination than they deserve. The priority given to economic explanations in much of modern historiography has also tended to exaggerate the influence of traders (Dyula or Wangara) rather than holy men (*karamokho*) in the Mali Diaspora. Without denying economic aspects of the diffusion of Islam in much of the West African savanna and forest areas, the preceding pages have been intended to suggest that religious functionaries have played important roles as well, and in particular those Muslim holy men who were able to live among Traditionalist populations in a pacifistic spirit and offer new religious solutions to old problems (drought, warfare) when and if opportunity arose. They stimulated a transformation in West African spirituality, creating a new amalgam of Traditionalist and Islamic forms of faith. Subsequent Muslim reform movements have condemned this amalgam as tantamount to infidelity (*kufr*), but for those who lived on these religious frontiers, it signified a revolutionary new perspective on the Transcendent, one that needs more sympathetic understanding than it often receives in Africa today.

Notes

1. ʿUthman dan Fodio 1897–98, 58–59 (Arabic)/300–301 (French). See also al-Maghili 1985, 22–25 (Arabic)/76–79 (English).

2. *Corpus* = N. Levtzion and J. F. P. Hopkins, eds., *Corpus of Early Arabic Sources for West African History,* trans. J. F. P. Hopkins, Fontes Historiae Africanae IV (Cambridge: Cambridge University Press, 1981). This invaluable sourcebook does not include the actual Arabic texts of the works excerpted. In some instances I have made slight changes in the translations to conform with the style of this essay (e.g., *Qurʾan* for Koran) or because my own reading of the Arabic text differs from that of *Corpus.* The editions of the Arabic texts used are cited in full in *Corpus.*

3. This transcription of Arabic is used to distinguish ancient Ghanah from the modern nation of Ghana, so named in 1957.

4. From the anonymous Siyar al-mashayikh in *Corpus,* 91.

5. ʿUthman dan Fodio 1960, 563 (Arabic)/569 (English). For a more recent expression of this condemnation, see Mohammed and Gumi 1987, 37.

6. Rain making has also played a significant role in the coming of Christianity to some savanna populations, most notably the Dagaba of northwestern Ghana (see McCoy 1988, 112–24).

7. Examples include Ferkessedougou and Bondoukou in Ivory Coast and Ouagadougou, Knodougou, and Dedougou in Burkina Faso.

8. This is where the translator renders al-majusiyyah as "paganism."

9. Translated in Trimingham 1962, 131. See also Palmer 1928, 3:105.

References

Abimbola, W.
    1969   *Ijinle Ohun Enu Ifa,* vol. 2. Glasgow: Collins.
    1973   "The Literature of the Ifa Cult." In *Sources of Yoruba History,* ed. S. O. Biobaku, 41–62. Oxford: Clarendon.

Biobaku, S. O.
   1957   *The Egba and their Neighbors, 1842–1872.* Oxford: Clarendon.
Biobaku, S. O., ed.
   1973   *Sources of Yoruba History.* Oxford: Clarendon.
Buchner, V. F.
   1953   "Madjus." In *SEI = Shorter Encyclopedia of Islam,* ed. H. A. R.
                 Gibb and J. H. Kramers. Leiden: Brill.
Fisher, H. J.
   1970   "The Western and Central Sudan and East Africa." In *The Cam-
                 bridge History of Islam,* ed. P. M. Holt, A. K. S. Lambton and B.
                 Lewis, 2:345–405. Cambridge: Cambridge University Press.
   1973   "Conversion Reconsidered," *Africa* 43:27–40.
Fortes, M.
   1945   *The Dynamics of Clanship among the Tallensi.* London: Oxford
                 University Press.
Garrard, T.
   1980   *Akan Weights and the Gold Trade.* London: Longman.
Goody, J.
   1967   "The Over-Kingdom of Gonja." In *West African Kingdoms in the
                 Nineteenth Century,* ed. D. Forde and P. M. Kaberry, 179–205.
                 London: Oxford University Press.
Greenberg, J.
   1946   *The Influence of Islam on a Sudanese Religion.* Reprint. Seattle:
                 University of Washington Press, 1966.
Gueye, M.
   1977   *Le Droit Chemin dans la Pratique Islamique Parfaite.* Dakar: Les
                 Nouvelles Editiones Africaines.
al-Hajj, M.
   1968   "A Seventeenth Century Chronicle on the Origins and Mission-
                 ary activities of the Wangarawa." *Kano Studies* 1, no. 4:7–48.
Hebert, J.
   1961   "Analyse Structurale des Geomancies Comoriennes, Malgaches
                 et Africaines." *Journal de la Société des Africanistes* 31:115–208.
Johnson, S.
   1921   *The History of the Yorubas from the Earliest Times to the Beginning
                 of the British Protectorate.* Reprint. London: Routledge & Kegan
                 Paul, 1966.
Levtzion, N.
   1968   *Muslims and Chiefs in West Africa: A Study of Islam in the Middle
                 Volta Basin in the Pre-Colonial Period.* Oxford: Clarendon.
   1973   *Ancient Ghana and Mali.* London: Methuen.
Lewicki, T.
   1960   "al-Ibadiyya." In *NEI = The Encyclopedia of Islam.* New ed., ed.
                 H. A. R. Gibb et al., 3:648–60. Leiden: Brill.

al-Maghili, M.
1985   *Shari'a in Songhay: The Replies of al-Maghili to the Questions of Askia al-Hajj Muhammad*, ed. and trans. J. O. Hunwick. Fontes Historiae Africanae V. Oxford: Oxford University Press for the British Academy.

Marty, P.
1926   *Etudes sur l'Islam au Dahomey*. Paris: Lerous.

McCoy, R.
1988   *Great Things Happen: A Personal Memoir*. Montreal: Society of Missionaries of Africa.

Mohammed, Y., and A. B. M. Gumi
1987   "Interview with Sheikh Abubakar Mahmoud Gumi." *Quality* 1, no. 2:34–39.

Niane, D. T.
1965   *Sundiata: An Epic of Old Mali*. Trans. G. D. Pickett. London: Longman.

Palmer, H. R.
1928   *Sudanese Memoirs*, vol. 3. Lagos: Government Printer.

Person, Y.
1979   "Samori and Islam." In *Studies in West African Islamic History*, vol.1, *The Cultivators of Islam*, ed. J. R. Willis, 259–77. London: Frank Cass.

Rattray, R. S.
1927   *Religion and Art in Ashanti*. London: Oxford University Press.

Ryan, P. J.
1978   *Imale: Yoruba Participation in the Muslim Tradition*. Missoula, Mont.: Scholars Press for the Harvard Theological Review.

1981   "Drought and Faith: (1) Prelude to Dialogue in West Africa." *The Month* 242, no. 11 (November):380–86.

Sanneh, L.
1989   *The Jakhanke Muslim Clerics: A Religious and Historical Study of Islam in Senegambia*. Lanham, Md.: University Press of America.

Tamakloe, E. F.
1931   "History of Dagomba." In A. W. Cardinall, *Tales Told in Togoland*, 237–79. Reprint, Westport: Negro Universities Press, 1970.

Trimingham, J. S.
1962   *A History of Islam in West Africa*. London: Oxford University Press.

ᶜUthman dan Fodio
1897–98   *Nur al-Albab*, in L. Hamet, "Nour-El-Eulbabe (Lumiere des Coeurs) de Cheikh Otmane ben Mohammed ben Otmane dit Ibn-Foudiou," *Revue Africaine: Bulletin des Travaux de la Société Historique Algerienne*, 41:297–320; 42:58–81.

1960   *Kitab al-farq.* In M. Hiskett, *Kitab al-farq: A Work on the Habe Kingdoms Attributed to 'Uthman dan Fodio, Bulletin of the School of Oriental and African Studies* 23:558–79.

Westermarck, E. A.
1926   *Ritual and Belief in Morocco,* vol. 2. Reprint. New Hyde Park: University Books, 1968.

Wilks, I.
1968   "The Transmission of Islamic Literacy in the Western Sudan." In *Literacy in Traditional Societies,* ed. J. R. Goody, 161–97. Cambridge. Cambridge University Press

1975   *Asante in the Nineteenth Century.* Cambridge: Cambridge University Press.

Wilks, I., N. Levtzion, and B. Haight
1986   *Chronicles from Gonja: A Tradition of West African Muslim Historiography.* Cambridge: Cambridge University Press.

Willis, J. R.
1979   "Introduction: Reflections on the Diffusion of Islam in West Africa." In *Studies in West African Islamic History,* ed. J. R. Willis, 1:1–39. The Cultivators of Islam. London: Frank Cass.

14

Patterns of Islam among Youth in South Africa

ABDULKADER I. TAYOB

R ELIGIOUS PRACTICES are interwoven with cultural, social, and political values from which they cannot be easily extracted. Even if such an extraction were possible, the religious values or practices so found would be transformed beyond recognition. Recognizing the difficulty of identifying such values, this paper will be focusing on the activities and ethos of a number of Muslim youth organizations that have emerged during the second half of the twentieth century. The organizations provided a home for the religious values and practices of most Muslim youth in South Africa. To be sure, these organizations did not exhaust the experience of the youth. Nevertheless, they provide a useful starting point for discussing such values and practices. Several of these organizations have had fleeting life spans. Others have matured as the key members have aged. But they all expressed, at one time or another, some of the religious values and sentiments of Muslim youth in the second half of the twentieth century.

Muslims in South Africa

Muslims in South Africa constitute one percent of the total population of forty-three million. The first group of Muslims came to the Cape in successive waves from 1658 to the end of the eighteenth century. According to Frank Barrow, the origins of the slave population, and thus the Muslims, during the seventeenth century were divided between Madagascar, Ceylon, India, Indonesia, Malaya, Indo-China, and Japan. The majority of Muslims

305

appear to have come from islands in the Malay archipelago and locations around the Bay of Bengal. They came as servants, political exiles, convicts, and slaves (Da Costa 1990; Bradlow and Cairns 1978). The prominent figures were religious leaders like Shaykh Yusuf (d. 1699), Tuan Said Aloewie, and Tuan Guru (d. 1807), who were instrumental in founding the first Islamic institutions in South Africa.

It is this general Malay origin for which Cape Muslims are identified as Malays, and not for any historical or ethnic reason.[1] The Muslim community in the Cape today also consists of a large number of converts. During the nineteenth century, Islam became a cultural and religious home for the under classes. The leadership of the imams and the rites of passage that they administered to the people of Cape Town attracted many converts to Islam (Shell 1984, 7–8).

The second wave of Muslims to arrive in South Africa were entirely from India. Most Indians came to work on the sugar plantations of Natal, and there was a small group of Muslims among them (7 to 10 percent). Another group of Indians, in which the Muslims were a majority, came as "passenger" Indians, so called because they paid their own fares to South Africa. The Indians, numbering fewer than one million, were classified as a separate group under apartheid, and Muslims constituted 16.8 percent of the total.

These two groups and their descendants constitute the dominant groups among the Muslims in South Africa. They have been in South Africa for a long time and enjoy a history unique to it. Their social and religious institutions of mosques, schools (*madrasah*), *ʿulamaʾ*, and service organizations cannot be extricated from the history of South Africa as a whole.

The youth organizations of the second half of the twentieth century form an important part of this history. They emerged after the Second World War and responded to the institutionalized racism of the ideology of apartheid. In addition to the political context of apartheid, the youth organizations were also Islamic responses to general social changes in the country. These include modernization and bureaucratization of schools in particular and society in general. The patterns of religiosity among youth bear the mark of both the particular experience of apartheid and the general modernization of South Africa.

Islamic Youth Organizations in South Africa

It is possible to distinguish two general phases of post–World War II Islamic youth organizations in South Africa. This first phase ended with the death in state detention of Imam Abdullah Haron in 1969. The youth organizations until then were mainly concentrated in the provinces. Nevertheless, they laid the basis for the national organizations that followed.

Youth Organizations up to 1969

Islamic youth organizations in the Cape were closely associated with modern schooling. From 1913, a total of fourteen Muslim mission schools were established by the Muslim community in order to provide Muslim children with modern schooling. The main initiator of the Muslim mission schools was a medical doctor and political person, Dr. Abdullah Abdurahman, who felt that Muslims should not reject modern schooling because of its domination by Christian missionaries (Ajam 1989). The Muslim mission schools made modern education for Muslim children accessible. Within the schools, traditional Islamic education was provided by local 'ulama' during special periods. The Muslim mission schools were the first institutional base where Muslim youth were exposed to some form of integration between the Islamic world and the modern world.

Not surprisingly, the first organization to articulate the aspirations of the youth in Cape Town was the *Muslim Teachers' Association*. It was established in 1951 by the teachers of the various Muslim mission schools in Cape Town. The Muslim Teachers' Association was a variation of the Teachers' League of South Africa, a nonracial teachers' body in South Africa, formed in 1943. The latter took an active role in resisting the plans of the Afrikaners to subject the Cape coloreds to the comprehensive design of apartheid. This meant, in particular, the erosion of the limited rights enjoyed by coloreds in the Cape province.[2] The Muslim Teachers' Association was part of a growing group of intellectuals and educated individuals in the Cape who resisted the emerging apartheid ideology.

The Muslim Teachers' Association rejected the attempts by apartheid ideologue I. D. du Plessis to delineate a neat cultural and racial entity for Cape Muslims. They rejected Du Plessis's *The Malay Quarter and Its People,* which attempted to create divisions among Muslims. A statement issued by the teachers declared that "the book propagates Islam as a Malay religion whereas Islam is a universal religion and has only one law for all Muslims throughout the world" (Jeppie 1987, 80).

As an organization, the Muslim Teachers' Association was successful in dissuading the Moslem Judicial Council (est. 1945), the 'ulama' body of Cape Town, to participate in the Van Riebeek festival of 1952 (Jeppie 1987, 78). Jan Van Riebeek was the first Dutch colonial governor who occupied the Cape in 1652.

The Muslim Teachers' Association was followed by the *Muslim Youth*

Movement of District Six in 1957. Consisting entirely of youth, this organization held meetings and discussion groups on various religious and political topics at the Zinat al-Islam Mosque, popularly know as the Muir Street Mosque in District Six. A wide variety of speakers were invited to address Muslim youth on, *inter alia*, the Muslim world at large and the nature of apartheid ideology being implemented step by step in South Africa (Larney 1989, 12–13, 24).

With the removal of black people from District Six under the Group Areas Act, the Muslim Youth Movement was involved in frequent clashes with the police. As a result of the overt political nature of their meetings and the subsequent police attention this entailed, the organization was asked by the Muir St. Mosque trust to find another venue (Larney 1989, 27). Nevertheless, the Muslim Youth Movement inspired other youth in towns around Cape Town to establish similar organizations in Paarl, Worcester, Strand, Athlone, and Claremont (Larney 1989, 30). A contemporary of the Cape Muslim Youth Movement, and apparently more successful was the *Claremont Muslim Youth Association*, established by Imam Haron at the Stegman Road Mosque in the Claremont suburb of Cape Town. Imam Haron managed to work closely with both the teachers and students around Claremont. He recognized and responded to their alienation and marginalization from the religious centers in the community. He taught and encouraged them to prepare the Friday talks and preside over the religious ceremonies in the community. He also provided a venue for the discussion and dissemination of social and political issues facing the community under the threat of apartheid. In this way, the youth of the new association became directly involved in the affairs of the mosque, and Imam Haron was himself exposed to the currents of political discourse at the time (Haron 1986, 69; Omar 1987, 17).

The Claremont Muslim Youth Association expressed their ideas in a newsletter called *Islamic Mirror*. It relied on the writings of contemporary Islamic resurgent thinkers like Sayyid Qutb (d. 1964) and Abul A'la Mawdoodi (d. 1979). The youth of Claremont found the political and social focus of their writings a refreshing alternative to the traditional discourse of the ʿulamaʾ (Haron 1986, 69).

Both the Cape Muslim Youth Movement and the Claremont Muslim Youth Association were instrumental in putting apartheid on the Islamic agenda of Cape Town. The high point of their success in the city was the convening of the Cape Town Drill Hall meeting of ten thousand Muslims representing a wide range of mosque, welfare, and social organizations. In spite of the repressive climate of apartheid, the mass meeting of Muslims issued a declaration, called the Call of Islam, which unequivocally condemned the system of apartheid:

For too long now have we been together with our fellow sufferers, subjugated, suffered humiliation of being regarded as inferior beings, deprived of our basic rights to earn, to learn and to worship freely to the Divine Rule of Allah. . . . By proclamations under the Group Areas Act we are deprived of our homes and places of worship. Even if our sacred mosques are not removed, the fact that we will be driven out of our settled homes is an act of tyranny, a transgression on our fundamental rights which no true Muslim should allow to pass. (Haron 1986, 300)

The meeting and resolutions were so enthusiastically received that a committee was established to look into the formation of a Cape Islamic Federation to campaign against apartheid. The state, however, began to exert pressure on the anti-state activities of Imam Haron and the Claremont Muslim Youth Association (Omar 1987, 35; Haron 1986, 88).

Imam Haron extended his political activities by providing assistance to state detainees' families. In this way, he became a safe channel for information between activists, particularly within the Pan Africanist Congress. The security apparatus of the state finally closed in on him and detained him in 1969. After five months in prison, he was found dead in his cell on 27 September 1969, like many a previous political detainee. The state attributed his death to natural causes (Haron 1986).

The anti-apartheid campaign of the Muslim youth organizations did not enjoy unconditional support in the community. The Moslem Judicial Council, of which Imam Haron was a member, and the *Muslim News*, of which he was the editor, distanced themselves from his political activities during his detention. Imam Haron was thought to be involved in the political struggle purely in his personal capacity, and not on any religious grounds. Some *'ulama'* in the Cape defended their complacency by stating that Imam Haron was used by the political parties (Omar 1987, 47, 73). In spite of the anti-apartheid focus of the Call of Islam many in the Muslim community believed, as they put it, that one could not "treat the community's political ailments if you still have to establish Islamic values among yourselves" (Omar 1987, 31).

Imam Haron's involvement in the political struggle was accompanied by parallel missionary efforts in the black townships. He was among the first prominent Muslim leaders to support small groups of Africans who had converted to Islam. His work led to the formation of the *Nyanga Muslim Association* in 1960. This was the first organized body working among African Muslims in Cape Town (Abrahams 1981).

The *Muslim Assembly*, established in 1967, was very different from the organizations mentioned so far. It was founded by a medical doctor, Dr. Kotwal, to "cater to the spiritual, moral, educational and economic upliftment of the Muslims" (Omar 1987, 33–38 passim). The political concerns in general, and apartheid in particular, were conspicuously absent from their primary considerations. The Muslim Assembly represented a non-clerical group of professionals, led by a medical doctor. Their Islamic ideas were also drawn from the Islamic resurgent literature of Mawdoodi and Qutb. However, unlike the Cape Muslim Youth Movement and Clare-mont Muslim Youth Association, the Muslim Assembly maintained a more moderate approach to the state in South Africa. For example, it proudly announced its successful visit to the South African military cadet camp at Faure, set up exclusively for "Cape Colored." This visit to an apartheid state facility took place in November 1969, not very long after Imam Haron's death in detention. The Muslim Assembly was not totally oblivious to apartheid, however. At a 1970 Muslim Assembly conference, the sociologist and anti-apartheid activist Fatima Meer focused on the nega-tive effects of removals and resettlement under the Group Areas Act (Omar 1987, 63, 70).

Another organization representing youth in the Cape was the *Muslim Students' Association*, formed in 1968. It was founded at the University of Cape Town, mainly by medical students. The students' major activity was the organization of prayer facilities for students on campus. In general, they tried to create an Islamic space for Muslims coming to the new and strange environment of university. In 1974, the Muslim Students' Associa-tion became a national student body with representative structures on the English-speaking campuses of South Africa (Bradlow 1983).

The youth organizations in Natal also originated within the context of modern schooling and education. A group of young businessmen and some professionals in Natal advocated the integration of Islamic and Western education in the province. The key organization within which this aspira-tion was articulated was the *Natal Muslim Council*, a federal organization of mosque, welfare, and educational bodies in the province. Founded in Dur-ban in 1943 with twenty-two affiliated bodies, it promoted modern profes-sional education for men and women and insisted on Arabic as the religious medium for Muslims in Natal. It called for a more rational approach to organization of welfare and charity in Muslim society.[3] Two conferences, one held in 1944 and another in 1952, were convened to promote modern Islamic education in Natal. The first was designed "to awaken the con-sciousness of the Muslim public to their general backwardness and inspire them to undertake measures leading to their regeneration and progress." At the second of these conferences, Mawlana ʿAbd al-ʾAlim al-Siddiqi was invited from Pakistan to support the integration of Islamic and secular edu-cation in South Africa (Moolla, 2). At the second conference, a resolution was passed that the community should put together its resources for an institute of higher Islamic studies, a Dar al-ʾulum whose graduates would be able to "lecture on Islamic subjects" and would be "qualified in religion, modern technique and modern education." Moreover, the conference also resolved that the ʿulamaʾ had to be "trained in the peculiar conditions which prevailed in (the) country, aware of our great problems and trained to confront them while being free of any trammels binding them to outside sources of instructions" (Moolla, 7–8).

These goals notwithstanding, the most significant achievement of the Natal Muslim Council was its success in promoting integrated education in state-aided schools, very similar to the Muslim mission schools in the Cape. They were instrumental in providing support and community acceptance of five such schools in Durban (Yacoob Abdul Kader 1981, 40–42).

There was one further resolution of the Natal Muslim Council conference that became a significant symbol of youth groups in Natal. This was the belief that Arabic, and not Urdu, ought to be the lingua franca of Muslim religious life in Natal and the Transvaal (Moolla, 5–7). Urdu was the exclusive language of the sermons and religious instruction in the *madrasahs*. The Natal Muslim Council members wanted to replace Urdu with Arabic as the primary language of religious instruction.

The question of language became the distinctive feature of an organization that succeeded the Natal Muslim Council as the voice of Islamic resurgence in Natal. The *Arabic Study Circle* was founded in 1950 by a group of professionals and young businessmen headed by a medical doctor, Dr. Dawood Mall, which committed itself to the promotion of Arabic, through which the meaning of the *Qurʾan* could be directly accessed. The ultimate goal of learning Arabic was to understand the *Qurʾan* without having to rely on teachers.[4]

Following the Natal Muslim Council's search for "modern technique and modern methods," the Arabic Study Circle briefly published a newsletter entitled *Al Muʾminun*. A description of one issue in 1955 (vol. 1, no. 2 [August 1955]) will indicate the direction of the Arabic Study Circle's Islamic resurgence. On the title page, the newsletter committed itself to propagating the teachings of Islam in the light of the *Qurʾan* and the *ahadith*. With one exception, all the articles were written by women. This was a significant achievement, as men continued to dominate Islamic activity in Natal. An article by Bilqis Jhavery entitled "Divine Revelation" dealt with the nature of revelation during the time of the Prophet and accepted the gradual historical unfolding of the monotheistic idea in the *Qurʾan*, matching revelation with history. Zuleikha Mayet in "Women in Islam" crafted a careful role for women in society by focusing on the public role of the Prophet's wives. Another modern tendency was clear in Rokaya Mall's

"Muhammad as a Social Worker." Jeffreys in "The Home of Man," proposed that evolutionary theory was compatible with Islam because the "Qur'an does not say where man started." Clearly, judging from this issue of *Al-Mu'minun*, the Arabic Study Circle was trying to match ideal Islam with modern models of social thought and action. This was a distinctive pattern of Islamic reformist thought at the end of the nineteenth century which tried to argue that Islam was compatible with progressive scientific and social developments.

The Arabic Study Circle invited individuals who could articulate a modern approach in Islam to South Africa. The Arabic Study Circle's guest and mentor, Joseph Perdue, an English convert to Islam, was a perfect example of a modern and articulate spokesperson for Islam.[5] In a lecture tour of the country, Perdue argued that Islam had gone through three distinct phases since its inception in the seventh century. The first apostolic age lasted two hundred years after the *hijrah*,[6] followed by a caliphate of superior material and physical power. But the latest phase was a spiritual age with its own peculiarities and demands. Reminiscent of the caliphate debates in the early part of the century, Perdue came to the Egyptian ʿAli ʿAbd al-Raziq's rejection of the caliphate as an essential aspect of Islamic belief (Binder 1988, 131). Like ʿAbd al-Raziq, Perdue angered the community when he suggested that the spiritual and material dimensions of Islamic civilization ought to be separated in the spirit of evolution and progress. The ʿulama' in Natal, organized in the Jamʿiyyat al-ʿulama' Natal, devoted a number of pamphlets and lectures to criticizing Perdue and the Arabic Study Circle.[7]

In 1964, the Arabic Study Circle organized scholarships for two students, Ebrahim Mahida and Farouk Vanker, to pursue the study of Islam in Pakistan. Unlike the ʿulama' trainees, these students were sent to the University of Pakistan. In addition to these long-term sojourns, the Arabic Study Circle members also attended Islamic conferences.[8]

The third organization that may be said to represent trends among youth in Natal was the *Islamic Propagation Centre*. Established by Ahmad Deedat in 1957, it has since become internationally famous for its crude criticism of Christianity and Hinduism. The organization projected the idea that Islam was rational and modern and that Christianity and the Bible were irrational and inconsistent. Deedat's selective use of biblical criticism provided ready material for the second image to attract some Christians to Islam, or at least to prevent Muslims from abandoning their religion (Jamal 1991).

The Natal Muslim Council, the Arabic Study Circle, and the Islamic Propagation Centre were the major organizations representing the Islamic youth in Natal before 1969. Unlike the anti-apartheid focus of some of the Cape organizations, these were considerably more conservative toward the state. Nevertheless, they too provided a home for educated youth searching for Islamic roots.

The case of the Transvaal is unique in terms of Muslim youth organizations. The widely dispersed Muslim population in the region and the strength of the ʿulamaʾ and the mosque committees precluded the emergence of significant support for youth organizations.[9] There were, however, three organizations—one in Pretoria and two in Johannesburg—that indicate the place of Muslim youth in the Transvaal before 1969.

The first, the *Universal Truth Movement*, was launched in 1958 in Pretoria by two young ʿulamaʾ, Ismail Abdul Razack and Cassim Sema. It enjoyed the support of ʿulamaʾ in both the Cape and the Transvaal, but most of its members were youth from Pretoria. Like other youth Islamic organizations in the country, the Universal Truth Movement made contact with international Islamic groups like the Muslim Brothers and the Jamate Islami.[10] Its major activity was propagation of Islam through the translation of the *Qurʾan* and other Islamic writings. On a smaller scale, it made an attempt to lodge objections against distorted images of Islam in society.[11] The organization also organized very popular Mawlood[12] celebrations in Pretoria where academics from the University of Pretoria were invited. The latter were not converts but Islamicists like J. Knappert, an authority on Islam in Africa, and A. van Selms, who was the first person to publicize the Arabic-Afrikaans writings of the Cape Muslims. Even in the presence of ʿulamaʾ, these guests were key speakers on the Prophet Muhammad. Clearly, the Universal Truth Movement echoed the Arabic Study Circle's own search for a modern articulated Islam.[13]

The second youth organization in the Transvaal was the *Young Men's Muslim Association*, formed by a group of youth in Johannesburg in 1955. Mawlana Abdul Razack of the Universal Truth Movement was regularly consulted for its newsletter, *Awake*. Like the Islamic Propagation Centre in Durban, the Young Men's Muslim Association's early activity seems to be concerned with pointing out inconsistencies in the Bible. With the Group Areas Act, the Young Men's Muslim Association split into Benoni and Lenasia branches, on the east and west of Johannesburg respectively.

The Lenasia branch disappeared, but the Benoni branch has become a champion of traditional Islamic values in the South Africa.[14] The third organization in the Transvaal, the *Islamic Missionary Society*, was founded in 1958 by M. S. Laher. It operates closely with the Islamic Missionary Society in Durban, on whom it relies for pamphlets and material for Islamic mission in the black township of the Transvaal.[15]

The period leading up to the death in detention of Imam Abdullah Haron in 1969 was characterized by a wide array of youth religious responses in South Africa. The organizations representing the youth were concerned with Christianity as the major religion in South Africa. Second, they were interested in a modernized expression of Islam. Third, some groups in the Cape had a clearly anti-apartheid focus.

Youth Organizations after 1969

The youth organizations after 1969 projected national goals and aspirations as opposed to the more regional characteristics of the pre-1969 organizations. The first truly national organization of Muslim youth was the *Muslim Youth Movement*.

Founded in Durban in December 1970, it spread rapidly to the Transvaal and then to the Cape.[16] The Muslim Youth Movement went through a series of changes. Initially it took the Islamic resurgence ideas of its predecessors in Natal and launched them on a national scale. Conferences, international guests, missionary activity, women's participation, a newspaper (*al-Qalam*), and the use of English (and not Urdu) were some of the early issues taken up by the organization.

The Muslim Youth Movement flourished on the university campuses, where Muslims had increased considerably. During this period, the *Muslim Students' Association*, which was launched in 1969 as a Cape body, became a national student body in 1974. The student body was closely aligned with the Muslim Youth Movement and organized annual national conventions where Muslim students gathered to share their views and ideas.

After the Soweto riots of 1976, deliberations within the Muslim Youth Movement and Muslim Students' Association increasingly included apartheid and the state. After an absence of some years since the death of Imam Haron, the apartheid focus was returned to the agenda of the youth.

From the Islamic side, the *ʿulamaʾ*, particularly trained in India and Pakistan in Deobandi institutions, began to question the modern features of the youth organizations. They demanded a more literal following of the teachings of Islam from the students. At the same time, the 1979 success of the Iranian revolution also presented an alternative Islamic outlook to society and politics.

In response to the *ʿulamaʾ* and the Iranian revolution, the Muslim Youth Movement adopted an ideological approach to Islamic education and mobilization. It derived its inspiration from the Muslim brothers and the Jamate Islam, two key proponents of Islamist ideology in the twentieth century. In South Africa, this meant that the Muslim Youth Movement rejected racism and called for equity and justice. But more significantly, it posited individual training in the Islamic tradition and organizational cohesion as prerequisites for an Islamic solution to South Africa. In a statement issued against the apartheid regime, it reaffirmed its particular notion of struggle:

> To attain this vision we have to struggle. Our first priority is an improvement of the self. The struggle to total change begins with change in the individual. The struggle for real freedom begins with freedom of the individual.[17]

The Muslim Youth Movement later changed its approach to the political and social issues facing Muslims in the country. While earlier it had pinned its hopes on individual development and ideological clarity, it now argued for a contextual reading of the Qur'an in South Africa with regard to women's rights, Africanization, and workers' rights.

In contrast, Qiblah was launched by a veteran anti-apartheid activist, Achmat Cassiem, who had been imprisoned on Robben Island and banned several times.[18] Qiblah believed that the Islamic revolution of Iran was a model for an Islamic solution to South Africa. He thus called for a revolution that would, as in Iran, bring about the alleviation of oppression for the masses of South Africa. Qiblah tried to convene rallies and mass meetings to register Muslim opposition to the state. Later, some of its activists also left the country for military training.

Yet a third alternative was that of Fareed Esack, who broke away from the Muslim Youth Movement to found an organization that was not committed to what he called "outside models of Islam" or tied to "international developments in the Muslim world" (Esack 1988, 491, 492). Taking the anti-apartheid 1961 manifesto as the name of the new organization, the Call of Islam was specifically interested in generating Muslim support against apartheid, nothing more nor less. The Call of Islam joined the United Democratic Front established in 1983 to oppose the white minority regime's attempt to include coloreds and Indians as junior partners of apartheid. While Qiblah and the Muslim Youth Movement refused to join the United Democratic Front because it was not based on any ideological principles, the Call of Islam championed it for that very reason (Tayob 1990).

As the numbers of Muslims on campuses increased, trends of retraditionalization also began to make their appearance in the early 1980s. Blessed by the Deobandi 'ulama', the Tablighi Jamat began activity on university campuses, especially in Natal and the Transvaal. Unlike the other youth groups, the Tablighi Jamat did not articulate a modern expression of Islam. It too, however, was selective about aspects of Islam: the declaration of faith (shahadah); worship (salah); respect toward a Muslim (ikram Muslim); the acquiring of religious knowledge ('ilm); going out in the path of Islam (fisabil Allah); and spreading the message of Islam (tabligh). These six points became the principal elements of the outlook of the *Tablighi Jamat* in South Africa.

By limiting itself to these key points as interpreted by the 'ulama', moreover, the Tablighi members became a major force for retraditionalism on campuses. In their view, for example, women had no role on campuses, their place being at home. At the campus of the University of the Witwatersrand in Johannesburg, in particular, they have prevented women from joining Friday worship.

The Tablighi Jamat youth recruitment and activities were not confined to university campuses. Especially in Natal and the Transvaal, they also targeted adolescents, mainly male, in the communities for recruitment. These young adults were taken on trips during which they were introduced to the movement's six-point outlook of Islam. Only a fraction actually joined the organization, but a large number become potential supporters of the organization. Most of them, however, were initiated into the organization's understanding of Islam.

Yet another organization representing mainly young African Muslims has emerged in South Africa. *Da'wah* (mission) since the 1950s in South Africa resulted in a number of conversions in the African townships. However, the older Muslim communities did not accept the new converts as equals, leading to frequent accusations of racism. In 1983, a British visitor, himself a convert, 'Abd al-Qadir al-Murabit, successfully recruited a number of black African Muslims into a new group called the *Murabitun*. The Murabitun consisted of both African and non-African members, sometimes advocating parallel groups to deal with racism in the communities. They also advocated a vigorous retraditionalism under the guide of Malikism, a legal school said to be closest to Africa because of its widespread dispersion in North and West Africa. Unlike the Tablighi Jamat, the Murabitun did not shun political transformation. It insisted, however, that political activity must take the form of traditional Islam. In this regard, they have introduced the leadership roles of *amir* (commander) and *qadi* (judge) in their midst and have demanded that Muslims in South Africa pay allegiance to their decisions.

Qiblah, the Call of Islam, the Muslim Youth Movement, the Tablighi Jamat and the Murabitun compete with each other for the allegiance of the youth. On the campuses, the Muslim Students' Association is led successively by students who favor one of these groups.

Patterns of Islamic Faith and Practice among Youth

Some key patterns of youth Islamic values and practices in the second half of the twentieth century in South Africa will now be considered. As the major articulators of youth experience, the organizations are useful media from which these patterns can be extrapolated. These patterns are not to be found in each and every youth in Muslim society. They are presented here as the recognizable markets by which Muslim youth experience of religion in South Africa may be appreciated.

Islamic Mission and Apologia

Observers of Islam in the modern world have identified apologia as a major characteristic of modern Islamic thought (Smith 1959, 119–65). In South Africa, this has taken the most visible form in Islamic *daʿwah* (mission). The well-known Ahmad Deedat of the Islamic Propagation Centre has been criticized by the Muslim Youth Movement and the Call of Islam for his vicious attack on Christianity and Hinduism. Both these organizations have favored an interfaith approach to Islam's relations with other religions. However, Deedat's approach to Christian missions in particular, and Christianity in general, appealed to Muslim youth. The approach emphasized that Islam stood high above religions as ideologies in the modern world. The booklets printed by Deedat vindicated Islam in a quasi-rational, logical, and factual contest. Biblical criticism provided Deedat with regular material with which to criticize Christianity for failing to be rational, logical, and most of all, historically accurate.

This approach of Deedat was based on a kind of cognitive accent on religion where the factual, logical, and rational took precedence over the emotional and irrational. It was this accentuation that was prominent in other forms of Muslim youth activity in South Africa as well. A few exceptions aside, Muslim youth exalted the historical and rational over the mystical and spiritual. Their religiosity was based on values celebrated in the social and political sphere, the debating halls, and the print media. While this approach to religion was most visible in the missionary activity of the youth, it was also present in the political and social focus of the Muslim Youth Movement and the Call of Islam.

Islam as Identity

A key aspect of Islamic youth experience was undoubtedly linked with labeling. In a country where people have been labeled and relabeled in racial categories, it is not surprising to see how Islam became a counter-label for Muslim youth. The first visible location of this labeling was in the 1950s in Cape Town. Muslim youth there challenged the labels of "Colored" and "Malay" applied by the state, and offered "Muslim" as an alternative label for South Indians and Malays.

The second location of Islamic identity was the campuses of the black universities of apartheid, particularly the University of Durban-Westville and the University of the Western Cape, established by apartheid for Indians and colored students respectively. Like other black universities throughout the country, these campuses witnessed a rise of black consciousness movements in the 1970s, which rejected the ethnic divisions of apartheid. The Muslim Youth Movement and the Muslim Students' Association on these campuses championed Islam as an alternative to the racial identities assigned by apartheid.

Muslims on campus did not totally reject black identity. For the increasing number of Muslims at the campuses, however, the Islamic youth organizations provided a sense of belonging within a religious identity. At the same time, they provided an immediate vehicle, a symbol, by which apartheid could be rejected. As part of the colored and Indian groups in South Africa, black identity was not always the most obvious choice for many Muslim youth. "Muslim," then, was another label for nonracialism. It became the symbol by which Muslim youth could find their way to a South African identity, as black was a symbol for many African youth.

A very revealing measure of Muslim youth making the pilgrimage from local community to South African national identity was the issue of language in the youth groups. English has become the lingua franca of Muslim youth, the adoption of which has involved a departure from traditional language media.

Cape Muslim history was inextricably linked with the emergence of Afrikaans. A. van Selms was the first person to identify the unique Afrikaans religious literature of Cape Muslims written in Arabic script. Amchat Davids followed this with an extensive study of the orthography and context of what has now been called Arabic-Afrikaans. By the middle of the twentieth century the Afrikaans-Arabic literature tapered off in the community. Afrikaans continued to be used in most mosques, but the youth organizations preferred the use of English in lectures, seminars, newsletters, and discussion groups. The preference for English signified the difference between youth and adult groups in their appropriation of an Islamic identity.

The language difference was evident in Natal and the Transvaal as well. Among Indian Muslims, Urdu was the language of religious discourse. The youth groups, epitomized by the Arabic Study Circle, championed the cause of Arabic against Urdu. Indian Muslim youth who were using English felt no compulsion to learn Urdu for religious purposes. For them, Arabic was the obvious language for Muslims.

In the 1970s, the Muslim Youth Movement continued to champion the cause of Arabic against Urdu, which still dominated religious discourse. Now, however, English had become the language of Muslim youth, and the Muslim Youth Movement demanded that it ought to be used in Islamic discourse wherever possible. Even where Arabic had to be used for liturgical and ceremonial purposes, English translations were demanded. As with Muslim youth in the Cape, English came to be regarded as the acceptable language for Islamic discourse. Arabic was still important, but it was accepted as a second language for Muslims. In Natal the transition from Urdu to English was accomplished through the Arabic bridge.

The adoption of English was a significant aspect of Islamic practice among youth in South Africa. English replaced Afrikaans and Urdu, which had sustained and nurtured religious meaning. English, as the language that bridged all communities in South Africa, was the choice of Muslim youth who were part of an emerging national identity.[19]

Traditionalism versus Modernism

Among youth in South Africa, a tension existed between those who favored some form of modernism and those who insisted on the traditional practices of Islam. The Tablighi Jamat was the chief proponent of traditional values and practices. Complete female seclusion, special dress consisting of a long cotton shirt (*khurta*) and headgear, and unconditional allegiance to the ʿulamaʾ as religious leaders, were the major symbols of traditional Islam, projecting stability and assuring familiarity for most youth.

In response, the modernists, chief among them the Muslim Youth Movement and the Call of Islam, considered such traditional aspects to be at best cultural practices, and at worst, features of patriarchalism and literalism. The wearing of traditional dress, for example, was a literal interpretation of the Prophet's teachings that ignored the principles therein. On the other hand, the resistance to female participation in Islamic affairs along with men was regarded as a particular form of sexism that had to be overcome.

The attraction of familiar models and images of Islamic religiosity was difficult to resist. In the choice between traditionalism and modernism, most favored the former. Youth committed themselves to traditionalism in the private sphere of mosque and home, while reconciling themselves to modernized approaches in the workplace.

Ideology versus Contextualism

The contest between traditionalism and modernism took on a particular shape in the political map of South Africa. The youth groups were divided along three lines, the Call of Islam and the Muslim Youth Movement in the first group, Qiblah and the Murabitun in the second, and the Tablighi Jamat in the third.

On the one side, the Tablighi Jamat placed a fideistic hope in the traditional practices and beliefs of Islam. Members of the group believed that the perfection of faith (*iman*) ought to precede political action. In practice, political discussion or action had no place in the Tablighi Jamat's outlook or activities.

In contrast, the other youth groups were committed to Islam in its political and social manifestations. They believed that Islamic teachings projected values for the world in political and social contexts. There were, however, two trends: the first, represented by Qiblah and the Murabitun, insisted on a purely Islamic solution to South Africa. In this view, Islam was an ideology with a clearly defined set of beliefs and a clearly defined action plan. Even though Qiblah and the Murabitun had a different understanding of the terms of the Islamic ideology, they both emphasized the unalterable and eternal principles and terms of Islamic values.

In contrast, the Call of Islam, followed by the Muslim Youth Movement, believed in a contextual approach to Islamic values. In their approach, the teachings of Islam had to be expressed in the local context of the struggle for justice against apartheid. These values could not simply be reproduced from the experience of Muslim minority countries. They could not even be reproduced from the example of the Prophet Muhammad fourteen hundred years ago.

Conclusion

I have identified five patterns and symbols that characterized Muslim youth activity in South Africa. A great number of youth found in Islam a historical mission and a rational plan. Both political activists and missionaries were eager to define Islam as a this-worldly historical religion that could alternatively contribute or compete in the country. The youths were also involved in different levels of identifying themselves. In the context of South Africa's racial history, they used Islam as an identity to mediate a South African identity denied to them by apartheid. Some youth found their identity in traditional time-honored forms and symbols, while a small minority were prepared to experiment with new forms. The black struggle against apartheid provided the ground where such an experimentation could take place. All Muslim youth, modern and traditional, made the pilgrimage from Afrikaans and Urdu to English. The transition to English among them was a symbol of the transformative nature of Muslim youth experience in South Africa in the second half of the twentieth century.

Notes

1. The Muslims of the Cape are often misrepresented as Malays in a racial sense. The most notorious abuse of this labeling was apartheid ideology's attempt to assign a uniform racial characteristic to the Muslims of Cape Town (Jeppie 1987).

2. Until the advent of apartheid, blacks in the Cape province enjoyed the right to vote and to be represented in provincial and city councils (Thompson 1949, 32–36)

3. See my *Islamic Resurgence in South Africa: The Muslim Youth Movements* (Cape Town: University of Cape Town Press, 1995).

4. Arabic Study Circle pamphlet, undated, circa 5 December 1965.

5. Interview with Ismail Manjra, member of the Arabic Study Circle, December 1992.

6. The *hijrah* was the migration of the Prophet Muhammad from Mecca to Medina, from which date the Islamic calender is counted.

7. Interview with Ismail Manjra and Perdue's defense pamphlet "Answers to Mr. Bawa and explanation of all other Misunderstandings."

8. An Arabic Study Circle member attended one such conference on education held in Mecca in 1965 (1965 pamphlet).

9. I have discussed the absence of significant support for Islamic resurgence in the Transvaal in my *Islamic Resurgence in South Africa.*

10. In the annual brochure of 1964, the Universal Truth Movement had messages of support from Mawlana Mawdoodi and Said Ramandan from the Jamate Islamic Muslim Brothers respectively.

11. For example, it objected to the Transvaal Education Department for its negative portrayal of the Prophet Muhammad in school textbooks (Universal Truth Movement General Report and audited financial statement and balance sheet, 1964).

12. The Mawlood, also called *mawlid* and *milad,* is a gathering that celebrates the birthday of the Prophet Muhammad.

13. Universal Truth Movement General Report and audited financial statement and balance sheet, 1963.

14. "Glimpses into the Past," *Awake to the Call of Islam* 5, no.2 (Ramadan, 1413/Feb.-March, 1993): 2–19.

15. Information obtained from Omar Deedat in Cape Town, 2 May 1994.

16. I have dealt extensively with the Muslim Youth Movement and its contemporaries in my *Islamic Resurgence in South Africa.*

17. Muslim Youth Movement's *The Muslim Response: Our Vision for South Africa* (November 1983).

18. *Inquiry,* "Annals of South Africa," February 1988, pp. 55–56.

19. The history of Afrikaans in the mosque and its replacement by English has not been studied in detail. I suspect that it has everything to do with the emergent teachers and students who studied at English-speaking colleges and universities in Cape Town.

References

Abdul Kader, Yacoob
    1981   "Islamic Religious Education in the Durban and Surrounding Areas 1860–1979: A Historical-Philosophical Perspective." Diss., University of Durban-Westville.

Abrahams, Zainulghoes'n
    1981   "The Growth and Spread of Islam in Langa, Nyanga and Guguletu in Cape Town." Honors Paper, University of Cape Town.

Ajam, M. T.
    1989   "Islamic Schools of Cape Town as Agencies of Socialization." *Journal for Islamic Studies* 9:70–98.

Binder, Leonard
    1988   *Islamic Liberalism: A Critique of Development Ideologie.* Chicago: University of Chicago Press.

Bradlow, Adil
    1983/1984   "The Muslim Students Association of South Africa: Building and Islamic Future." History III Project, University of Cape Town.

Bradlow, Frank, and Margaret Cairns
    1978   *The Early Cape Muslims: A Study of Their Mosques, Genealogy and Origins.* Cape Town: A. A. Balkema.

Da Costa, Yusuf
    1990   "The Spatial Origins of the Early Muslims, and the Diffusion of Islam to the Cape Colony." *Journal for Islamic Studies* 10 (November): 45–67.

Davids, Achmat
    1991   "The Afrikaans of the Cape Muslims from 1815 to 1915: A Sociolinguistic Study." Master's thesis, University of Natal.

Esack, Fareed
    1988   "Three Islamic Strands in the South Africa Struggle for Justice." *Third World Quarterly* 10 (April): 473–98.

Haron, M.
    1986   "Imam Abdullah Haron: Life, Ideas, and Impact." Master's thesis, University of Cape Town.

Jamal, Riaz Cassiem
    1991   "The Role and Contribution of the Islamic Propagation Centre International in the Field of Da'Wah." Master's thesis, University of Durban-Westville.

Jeppie, M.
    1987   "Shamiel: Historical Process and the Constitution of Subjects: I. D. Du Plessis and the Re-invention of the 'Malay.'" Honors Paper, University of Cape Town.

Larney, Ebrahim
    1989   "The Muslim Youth Movement of District Six." Honors Paper, University of the Western-Cape.

Moolla, A. M.
n.d.   *The Problem of Muslim Education.* Durban: Natal Muslim Educational Committee.

Omar, Abdul Rashied
1987   "The Impact of the Death in Detention of Imam Abdullah Haron on Cape Muslim Political Attitudes." Bachelor's Paper, University of Cape Town.

Shell, Robert C.
1984   "Rites and Rebellion: Islamic Conversion at the Cape, 1808 to 1915." *Studies in the History of Cape Town* 5.

Smith, Wilfred Cantwell
1959   *Islam in Modern History.* New York: New American Library.

Tayob, Abdulkader I.
1990   "Muslims' Discourse on Alliance Against Apartheid." *Journal for the Study of Religion* 3 (September): 31–47.
1995   *Islamic Resurgence in South Africa: The Muslim Youth Movements.* Cape Town: University of Cape Town Press.

Thompson, L. M.
1949   *The Cape Coloured Française.* Johannesburg: South African Institute of Race Relations.

15

Sufism in Africa

LOUIS BRENNER

And when I have fashioned him and breathed into him of My Spirit, then fall down before him prostrate. (38:72)

THIS QUOTATION from the *Qur'an*, which refers to God's command to the angels to bow down before Adam, is seen by many Muslims as a reference to the spiritual aspect of Islam known as Sufism. Sufism, or *tasawwuf* in Arabic, is a spiritual discipline intended to liberate the human spirit from its corporeal shell and enable it to move closer to God. To be more precise, the human spirit, having been breathed into its recipient by God, is of divine origin. The Arabic word for spirit, *ruh*, also means breath. The human spirit, therefore, has the same source as the divine breath. It is a divine substance contained within each human being.

Freed of all encumbrances, the spirit will move of its own accord toward God. But the spirit is encased within the human being and hindered from this natural movement by the *nafs*, soul. The Muslim concept of *nafs* is different from the Christian concept of soul. The *nafs* is associated with all aspects of personality, that is, one's emotions and desires, abilities and disabilities, strengths and weaknesses, but also with the animal characteristics of humans, such as sexuality. The *nafs* is malleable and changeable, responding to all kinds of social and personal stimuli. For these reasons, the *nafs* can be referred to as the carnal soul. By contrast, the spirit is stable and unchanging, reflecting its transcendent, divine origin.

The spiritual discipline to which a Sufi acolyte submits is designed to control the carnal soul so that the spirit can move toward God. The process, in Muslim literature, is often likened to a kind of internal warfare, *jihad al-nafs*, or struggle to control the carnal soul. In its most common

324

usage, the word *jihad* refers to a holy war to defend the Muslim faith against its enemies. By analogy, one engages in the *jihad al-nafs* to defend the spirit against the spiritually debilitating characteristics of the carnal soul. The Prophet Muhammad, often quoted by Sufis in *hadith*, is said to have remarked, upon returning from a battle against those who opposed his nascent Muslim community:

> We have returned from the lesser *jihad* to the greater *jihad*.
> And they said, "What is the greater *jihad*, O Messenger of God?"
> He said, "The struggle with the carnal soul and with the passions."[1]

So difficult and elusive are the demands of the spiritual discipline of Sufism that attempts to describe it with metaphorical allusions to warfare may seem quite appropriate to those engaged in the process. By contrast, however, the transformational process in which the Sufi engages may appear relatively simple and even passive to the outside observer, since it consists primarily of devotional exercises.

This observation points up one of the major difficulties that confront those of us who study Sufism from the outside, because the understanding that can be acquired through study is of a qualitatively different nature from the understanding that Sufis seek through their devotional exercises. It is the difference between an understanding acquired through the intellect and an understanding that an individual obtains through a kind of revelation, what Ibn Khaldun referred to as "supernatural perception" (1958, 1:214). The Sufis are sensitive to these distinctions, which have been the source of mutual criticism and even conflict between themselves and some of their intellectually oriented opponents in many parts of the Muslim world. Such conflict, however, was rare in sub-Saharan Africa, where, until recently, most of the leading scholars have also been adherents of Sufi spiritual practice.

An influential Sufi of the early nineteenth century, Ahmad Ibn Idris, described these distinctions in the following manner:

> The people of (the scholastic or philosophical) persuasion believe in God according to what they understand, while the people of God are people who believe in God inasmuch as He makes Himself known to them. And what a great difference there is between the two persuasions, because he who believes inasmuch as God makes Himself known to him places his intellect behind his belief, so that he believes whether his intellect accepts it or not. And he who has this kind of belief, God informs him of what he did not know before by means of revelation, not through the intellect. He who only believes in what he understands, he goes no further than "the letters."[2]

This passage touches on an idea that has been central to Sufi thinking through the centuries, that God continues to provide glimpses of supernatural perception to a select few among his worshipers through certain kinds of revelations, or visions. These are not the revelations of prophecy, which concluded with Muhammad, but these insights are related to prophecy in that they have a divine source. Ibn Khaldun, for example, was of this view, and he expanded on the notion, employing the idea introduced above that the human soul can be transformed. He concluded that there exist at least three kinds or levels of human soul. The first perceives through the senses and the imagination, but it is limited by the capacities of the human body—this is the soul of ordinary persons and of the scholars.

The second kind of soul is capable of direct spiritual perception that is neither limited by nor requires the intermediation of bodily organs—this is the soul of the saints and mystics. The third kind of soul is that of the prophets, which is elevated above both the physical and spiritual and attains the level of the angels.[3]

If God created the prophets with the express intention that they should know him, the saints usually referred to in the African literatures as "friends of God" (*wali*) receive their spiritual knowledge and insight as "a gift from God" in response to the sincerity of their profound faith and their prayers. In theory, this elevation might be received by any person who is able to submit to the requisite spiritual discipline, expressed through their complete and utter submission to God. The word *Islam*, after all, means submission to God. But this is a two-way process; the individual must be prepared to engage in the spiritual quest, although the ultimate initiative comes from God. Ahmad Ibn Idris expressed it thus:

> May God include us and yourself among those who fear God and who have drawn near unto Him with their whole being. Thus no preoccupation has diverted them from God, outwardly as well as inwardly, and God has taken them as His friends through His solicitude. Their love for God Most High has been purified in every way. Their state has become such that when they stand, they stand because of God and for God; they do nothing, except they do so because of God and for God. Both their movement and their being at rest are because of God.
>
> And may your tongue habituate itself to the invocation (*dhikr*) of God Most High, so that it overwhelms your heart and you become one of "Those who remember God whether they stand, sit or recline, and who consider the creation of the heavens and the earth." (III:191): I pray to God the Gracious, lord of the tremendous Throne, that He may grant us and yourself the sweetness of complete faith in which the heart submits to God Most High, in every way and at all times, and that He may grant us and yourself the desire to be united with Him the Most High, at every drawing of breath. (Quoted in O'Fahey 1990, 175–76)

The reference to *dhikr* in this passage alludes to the devotional practice which is at the center of Sufi spirituality. The sustained remembrance of God by means of invocation is the ultimate aim of the Sufi and the primary focus of her or his efforts. No description of Sufism can be complete without an attempt to comprehend the implications of such devotional practice.

These brief introductory comments are based on classical references to Sufism as they have been expressed in the African context. What is attempted in this essay is an elaboration of these basic concepts, focused on two central themes: the broader epistemology in which Sufi ideas are located, and the range of practices that give effect to these ideas. A third theme is the relationship of Sufism to the social context in which it appears. The influence of Sufism has been pervasive in much of Muslim Africa, although its impact has varied considerably over time and in different places. For one thing, Sufi expression has changed and evolved over the centuries. For example, the Sufi order or brotherhood did not take hold in sub-Saharan Africa until the eighteenth century. At that time, Sufi practice was limited primarily to the scholarly classes. During the latter nineteenth and twentieth centuries, Sufism took a more populist turn, attracting active adherents from all walks of life. There is considerable variation between the perceptions of Sufism held by a well-read scholar and by a less well educated Muslim, as the following examples will illustrate.

As suggested in the passage from Ahmad Ibn Idris quoted above, scholars such as himself orient all their activities toward a search for God. This is their primary goal, alongside of which everything else is secondary. They engage in their religious devotions and spiritual exercise for the transformation of their state of being. This attitude places considerable emphasis on the passivity of humans in relation to God; even if the individual Sufi must commit him- or herself to the efforts demanded, the actual transformation comes only from God. Being transformed into *walis*, they are in effect passive agents of God; all their actions are inspired by Him. The miracles and marvels that are often attributed to such *walis*, and which are seen as the signs of their spiritual elevation, are not of their own making. These events happen around them or through them, but in the classical view are in fact sent by God as trials to divert such persons from their constant objective, which is always the search for God. No importance should be accorded to them. Al-Hajj ʿUmar referred to them as the "menstruations of men."[4]

If such is the view of the most learned of the scholarly classes, it is not shared by the majority of Muslims, who see the *walis*, or even local Muslim clerics, as powerful intercessors capable of responding to their needs. Such persons often look to holy men to resolve the problems of everyday life, to heal illnesses, to bring adequate rain for their crops, to provide effective blessings for themselves and their families, and so forth. For them, Muslim clerics have access to a supernatural power, which they are able to employ as they wish, and local Muslim lore, both oral and written, is filled with accounts of their exploits. One example, drawn from recent research in Mali, will illustrate the phenomenon.

Alfa Amadou Gidaado, who died about 1950, resided north of Mopti in the tiny Peul village of Tambieni for most of his adult life. He was reputed to be a very learned and accomplished scholar, renowned in the region as a teacher and an ascetic. At its height, his school attracted more than three hundred pupils and students, who were all fed and lodged from the income Alfa Amadou received in alms. In contrast to the practice of most Muslim clerics, he refused to allow his students to farm on his behalf, preferring to rely solely on God for his own subsistence. A profound mystique surrounded the memory of the man, nourished by the many miraculous stories about him that circulated among the people who had known and studied with him. For example, that he had performed the pilgrimage to Mecca more than forty times without ever leaving the village, and that he had protected the village from swarms of locusts and other epidemics that had ravaged the surrounding region, and so on.

The persons recounting these events, which many claimed to have seen with their own eyes, clearly considered Alfa Amadou to be the absolute master of these extraordinary powers, as the following story demonstrates. A young man residing in a distant village had been given the task of conveying a sack of grain to Alfa Amadou as an offering of alms. The sack was placed on the back of an ox (oxen were employed in the region as beasts of burden). Later, when the young man was well on his way and far from any village, the sack fell from the back of the ox, and he was unable by himself to lift and replace it. In his despair, he said, "If Alfa Amadou is truly a saint, may God send someone to help me." Some moments later, a man appeared and helped him to replace the sack of grain. When the young man reached his destination, he was amazed to discover that the person who had helped him in the bush was none other than Alfa Amadou himself, who had not left his own lodgings for days. When the young man attempted to inquire about this extraordinary and seemingly impossible event, Alfa Amadou commanded him to keep silent.

What we cannot know is how Alfa Amadou himself would have reacted to such accounts about himself, and whether he in fact encouraged or disavowed these kinds of tales. After all, his silencing of the young man might have been intended to inhibit the spread of stories about him, although the individual who recounted the story in my presence did not share this view. It would be extremely valuable to have knowledge of Alfa Amadou's own views on these matters, which would inform us about his personal interpretations of Muslim concepts and doctrines. But whatever his views and interpretations, they would not much affect the recounting of such tales, which form an integral part of the local religious culture.

Indeed, the classical claims of the most highly reputed scholars, that miracles are sent by God to test them, only reinforce the role that miraculous stories have played in society. In the past, virtually no one denied the possibility of their occurrence, even though there may have been debates about whether a particular event should be considered a miracle and who precisely was responsible for it.[5]

In spite of differences of interpretation or explanation, popular and scholarly perceptions were completely interrelated.

If the people of Tambieni thought that Alfa Amadou brought them health and prosperity through his religious powers, such eminent figures as Shaykh ʿUthman b. Fodiye and al-Hajj ʿUmar Tal justified the *jihads* which they led in order to cleanse and spread Islam by claiming that their actions had received divine authorization in visions.[6] All of these ideas were of a piece, generated by an epistemology that was common to both Muslims and non-Muslims in Africa.

The Epistemological Foundations of Sufism

Our discussion of Sufism opened with reference to the potential for human beings to attain what Ibn Khaldun called supernatural perception. This idea is based on the belief that there is a reality which, although hidden from the view of the majority of humanity, can be glimpsed by individuals who have achieved a certain degree of spiritual development. Sufis discuss this spiritual evolution from various perspectives, for example, the stages of purification through which the carnal soul must pass in order to free the spirit to move toward God, or the kinds of knowledge to which one has access through this opening of the spirit to receive it. It seems justifiable to begin the present analysis with an epistemological approach because so much of what Sufis discuss concerns the different kinds of knowledge that exist and how to achieve access to them.

An idea central to Sufi epistemology is that everything created in the universe consists of two aspects, the manifest *(zahir)* and the hidden *(batin)*. These two Arabic terms can also be translated respectively as "external" and "internal." The universe itself, as well as all created knowledge, is comprised of both manifest and hidden aspects. It is from this basic concept that Ibn Khaldun's discussion of supernatural perception emerges. Sufis have reflected on and elaborated this idea in many different ways over the centuries. The following quotation from Ibn ʿArabi provides one example:

Know that God Almighty has given to each thing an external aspect and an internal or hidden aspect. The human soul also possesses an external and an internal aspect because it is included among the things created (by God). What man comprehends by means of the external aspect of his soul is interpreted through image, imagination and the senses; these are not comprehended by his internal soul at all. That which is comprehended by means of the internal aspect of the soul is knowledge which is communicated directly to the internal soul (batin) and is characterized by sound experiences, the secret of gnosis and the secret of the unity of God. . . . The manifestations of God Almighty through His Secret Name to the internal soul are communicated by means of the eye of discernment and not by means of thoughts or theories. He who perceives through the eye of discernment knows truths and hidden meanings. . . . When these revelations enter into his internal soul, he becomes the master of the divine sciences, of the secrets and hidden meanings of all which is associated with the beyond, and of direct knowledge of the unity of existence. (Quoted in 'Ali Harazim, 1:23)

This quotation appears in the biography of Ahmad al-Tijani, eighteenth-century founder of the Tijaniyya Sufi order, which spread extensively in West Africa in the nineteenth century under the leadership of al-Hajj 'Umar Tal. Al-Tijani was a near contemporary of Ahmad Ibn Idris, and both were products of the religious culture of the Maghreb. It is therefore not surprising to find Ahmad Ibn Idris propounding very similar ideas, here about the manifest and hidden aspects of the *Qur'an*:

The Koran has an interior, an exterior, a limit, a starting point. Its interior is known to the elect; its exterior is the science of the *Sharia*. The limit means that the Koran encompasses all the Gnosis of God, whereas the starting point is known only to God Most High, and He makes it known to whomsoever He wishes. (Quoted in O'Fahey 1990, 196)

It will be useful to expand on certain aspects of this quotation. The *shari'ah* is of course the religious law of Islam, which is here described as the exterior aspect of the *Qur'an*, whereas its interior aspect is known only to a select few, presumably the *walis*. Similar language was commonly used by African scholars to describe Islam itself, which they claimed was divided into three elements: *shari'ah*, the law; *tariqa*, the way, meaning the Sufi way (a Sufi order or brotherhood is referred to in Arabic as *tariqa*); and *haqiqa*, the truth or divine reality. To attain *haqiqa* is the ultimate achievement of the religious quest according to the Sufis, the reward of the *walis*, those who have been "opened" by God to the most profound forms of supernatural perception. Such persons, it is said, have united *shari'ah* and *haqiqa* within themselves, that is, they have brought together both the manifest and the hidden (the external and internal) aspects of their religion.

Of course, this kind of religious thinking has profound social implications. Only a tiny minority of persons—the elect, as Ibn Idris referred to them—will attain these levels of spiritual achievement. Only they have penetrated the deepest secrets of God's revelations, and consequently they are best qualified to interpret God's laws. By extension, it could be argued that only they are qualified to occupy the roles of leadership in a proper Muslim society. This is precisely the kind of reasoning which was employed by such leaders as al-Hajj ʿUmar and Shaykh ʿUthman b. Fodiye to justify their own leadership of the *jihads* which they led in the nineteenth century.[7]

The concepts of *shariʿah, tariqa,* and *haqiqa,* therefore, emerge from an epistemology which presupposes a hierarchy of different kinds or qualities of knowledge that are not equally accessible to all Muslims. All Muslims, without exception, must submit to the *shariʿah,* the divine law which is based on the *Qurʾanic* revelation. According to the Sufis, the spiritual discipline of the *tariqa* enables the disciple in effect to go beyond the *shariʿah,* to penetrate its deeper and hidden significances, ultimately to attain the supernatural perception that is associated with *haqiqa.*

This hierarchical conceptualization of knowledge has characterized Muslim thought in Africa over the centuries, reflecting the deep influence of Sufi ideas on the leading theologians in the region. For example, in his *Kitab ʿulum al-muʿamala* (Book of the Sciences of Behavior), Shaykh ʿUthman b. Fodiye set out to provide a basic explanation of three theological concepts: *islam, iman,* and *ihsan* (ʿUthman b. Fodiye 1978). Islam here referred to an individual's personal submission to God's law; Shaykh ʿUthman equated this submission with the religious science of *fiqh,* which he described as the outward requirements of religion. In this section of his book he discussed the rules for ablution, prayer, and other basics or religious practice which every Muslim must know. *Iman,* which literally means faith, was equated with *tawhid,* or theology, the study of the unity of God; under this rubric Shaykh ʿUthman discussed the attributes of God and of the prophets. *Ihsan,* which means exemplary behavior, was based on the science of *tasawwuf,* which concerns the inner aspects of religion, the acquisition of praiseworthy qualities and the elimination of blameworthy ones. *Tasawwuf,* according to Shaykh ʿUthman, aided the Muslim in purifying the heart from the whisperings of *Satan* and from such moral disabilities as conceit, pride, false hope, anger, and envy.

The religious sciences of *fiqh, tawhid,* and *tasawwuf* together constituted the full range of religious studies which an accomplished scholar would pursue, complemented of course by other subjects. But these three fields of study also reflect the hierarchical structure of Islamic knowledge because of the differing demands which their study places on the student. For example, those aspects of *fiqh* to which Shaykh ʿUthman refers under the category of *islam*, primarily ablution and prayer, can be learned by mere imitation. The theological concepts of *tawhid*, however, require considerably more intellectual application, even if they are simply committed to memory without any very deep understanding, as was often the case. But *tasawwuf*, which for Shaykh ʿUthman was a science of inner transformation, requires an even more sophisticated level of personal application. Study and reading, as well as the imitation of a teacher or *shaykh*, might encourage and support one's search for the development of inner qualities, but they cannot alone produce them. The methods associated with the religious science of *tasawwuf* were developed and transmitted in the formal context of a Sufi order, under the direction of a spiritual guide who authorized one to recite certain prayers and directed one in specific exercises that were intended to aid one's inner development.

Muslim scholars consistently reflected on these three concepts of—*islam*, *iman*, and *ihsan*, which they presented to their students in various permutations. A more simple version is the following:

Islam consists of five obligatory actions:
- the articulation of the *shahadatain:* "I bear witness that there is no god but God, unique and without partner; and I bear witness that Muhammad is His servant and His messenger."
- the performance of five daily prayers
- the payment of *zakat* (the annual tithe intended for the poor)
- the fast during the month of Ramadan
- the pilgrimage to the sacred House, to Mecca (required only of those able to accomplish it)

Iman consists of belief in six principles:
- God
- the Last Judgment
- the angels
- the revealed Books (including those which preceded the *Qurʾan*)
- the prophets of God
- the decree of God (the belief that everything comes to us from God)

Ihsan commands that one must:
- adore God as if you see Him because if you do not see Him, He sees you.[8]

These principles form part of an orally transmitted Muslim catechism which had been designed to present the most fundamental tenets of Islam. But this same catechism continues to a second level of teaching in which Sufi principles are presented. Here the concepts of *islam, imam,* and *ihsan* are reformulated in terms of *taqlid*, literally imitation, here referring to imitation of one's Sufi *shaykh* or teacher; *nazar*, literally, "to see," but in

Sufi terminology referring to the profound intellectual understanding of religious principles; and *dhawq*, literally, "taste," but here referring to experiential knowledge, the direct and unmediated perception of hidden truths.

Four different triads of Islamic principles have now been introduced, which can be presented in tabular form in the following manner:

Islam (submission to God)	*Iman* (faith)	*Ihsan* (upright behavior)
Fiqh (the study of inner jurisprudence)	*Tawhid* (the study of theology)	*Tasawwuf* (the pursuit of purity)
Shariʿah (the religious law)	*Tariqa* (the Sufi way)	*Haqiqa* (the Truth)
Taqlid (imitation)	*Nazar* (understanding)	*Dhawq* (taste)

Some of the epistemological principles previously introduced can be reviewed with reference to this table. The terms in the left-hand column of the table refer to external aspects of religious practice and comprise visible and manifest elements of Islam, the *zahir*, whereas the terms in the right-hand column refer to its inner or hidden aspects, the *batin*. The religious individual is encouraged to move from the outer to the inner, to seek a deeper experience of his or her religion; the terms in the middle column mediate this movement.

This idea of mediation is perhaps most clear with reference to the concept of *tariqa*, the Sufi way that provides the spiritual discipline necessary to move from a practice of Islam based on conformity to religious law to an Islam informed by the direct experience of divine Truth. The word *tariqa* specifically connotes movement because it means "path" or "way." But all four triads are conceptually parallel to one another, and the middle term in each is perceived by African Muslims as mediating between the two adjoining religious principles. The table therefore illustrates a basic principle of Sufi thought, that knowledge acquired through the intellect, although essential for the good Muslim, is only a step on the way to another kind of knowledge which is obtained through direct experience and which does not depend on the intellect. This is the principle to which Ibn Idris was referring in the quotation cited above when he spoke about the person who "places his intellect behind his belief, so that he believes whether his intellect accepts it or not."

This table is presented as a heuristic device to illustrate the epistemological principles that are here under discussion. Sufi thinkers have reflected and expanded upon these concepts in many different ways, and a table of this sort is inadequate to capture the complexity of their thought and experience. However, the following commentary about faith (*iman*) can go some way to demonstrating the subtlety and expressive beauty with which some Sufis transmitted their teachings. These are the words of Cerno Bokar Saalif Tal, who died in French Soudan (now the Republic of Mali) in 1940. Elsewhere in his commentaries, Cerno Bokar spoke about faith as if it were a kind of material substance within the human being that could be heated up through the effects of religious devotion. For him the nature of faith varied according both to its "heat" and to the life conditions of different individuals. Here he is responding to a question about the different kinds of faith:

> For me faith is, in part, the sum total of trust that we have in God, and in part our fidelity toward our Creator. Faith experiences both moments of elevation and moments of decline. It varies according to people and their circumstances. . . .
>
> The first degree of faith, *sulb*, is solid faith. It is suitable for the common man—the masses—and for the teachers who are attached to the letter (of the law). This faith is channeled by prescriptions imposed by a law drawn from revealed texts, be they Jewish, Christian or Islamic. At this level faith has a precise form. It is subject to a rigorous determination which admits no foreign element. It is intransigent and hard like the stone from which I draw its name. . . . Faith at the degree of *sulb* is heavy and immobile like a mountain. At times it prescribes armed warfare if this is necessary to gain respect and to assure its position.
>
> *Saʾil* (liquid) faith is that of men who have worked and successfully faced up to the trials of *sulb*, of the rigid law that admits no compromise. They have triumphed over their faults and have set out on the way which leads to truth. The constituent elements of this faith derive from understanding. It values truths from wherever they come, considering neither their origin nor the date of their existence. It gathers and assembles them in order to make from them a body in perpetual movement. The parts of this body do not arrange themselves in one particular form. They effect a flow which is constantly forward, like the flow of the molecules of water which emerge from the mountain hollows and trickle across varied terrain, flowing together and increasing in size to streams which finally, as rivers, are thrown into the ocean of Divine Truth. This faith, due to its subtle, liquid nature, is strong and undermines the faults of the soul, erodes the rocks of intolerance and spreads out, taking on a shape which is not fixed as in the case of *sulb* faith but borrows the form of its recipient. This faith penetrates individuals according

to the accidents of their moral terrain, never changing its essence and never retreating whatever detour might be necessary to avoid temptation, an obstacle which Satan places on its road.

Saʾil faith manifests itself as gigantic mystical waterfalls, falling from the mountain into the ravine of active life. It contracts into a sinuous thread in order to traverse the steep pass which Satan has placed on its route. It expands into a great flood, playing across a country worn flat by the adoration of God and made favorable to its full extension. *Saʾil* faith disciplines the adept and makes of him a man of God capable of hearing, listening to and appreciating the voices of those who speak of God. This faith is vivifying. It is of the middle degree. It can solidify like hailstones when it must move to the range of souls of the degree of *sulb*. Similarly, it can become more subtle and rise as vapor toward *ghazi* faith in the heaven of absolute truth. This faith is that of men who walk in the straight way which leads to the city of peace where man and animal live in common and in mutual respect, where the elements of the three kingdoms live in brotherhood. The adepts of this faith stand against war. This faith is the ante-chamber of truth.

Ghazi (vaporous) faith is the third and final form. It is decidedly more subtle, and it is the attribute of a specially chosen elite. Its constituent elements are so pure that, void of all material weight which would hold them to the earth, they rise like smoke into the heaven of holy souls, expanding to fill them. The faith of the sphere of truth emerges entirely from this last form. Those who reach this faith adore God in truth in the light without color. On this sublime plane *sulb* faith, which has emerged from revelation and *saʾil* faith, which has emerged in turn from this uncompromising way, both disappear to make a place for one sole thing, the Divine Truth which flourishes in the fields of Love and Truth. (Quoted from Brenner 1984, 170–72)

The three kinds of faith described here form yet another triad that could be added to our table. Although the imagery that Cerno Bokar employed of solid and vaporous forms of faith differs from the concepts we have been discussing, these are clearly analogous to the manifest and hidden aspects of Islam. And "liquid" faith, the mediating state between the other two, is associated with movement; indeed, "liquid" faith works to create a "body in perpetual movement."

Spiritual movement is the essence of Sufi religious practice and will be examined in the next section of this essay. But before turning to that subject, we must explore one other significant dimension of the epistemology that is being elucidated here. The idea that the deeper, more profound, or more spiritual aspects of Islam are to be found in its hidden aspects applies to all created things. This principle has profoundly permeated Muslim thought in Africa and extends from the most abstract kinds of theological reflection to the mundane affairs of everyday life.

This observation can be demonstrated with reference to the *Qur'an*, which Muslims believe to be God's final revelation to humankind. Muslims believe that many prophets preceded Muhammad, beginning with Adam, and that God revealed to each of them a part of the divine law. Muhammad was the last of the prophets, and he was given the last of God's revelations in the form of the *Qur'an*. But many Sufis also believe that there is an unrevealed aspect of the divine law as well as a hidden aspect of the *Qur'an*, which can be explored through the religious science of *ta'wil*, the esoteric interpretation of the *Qur'anic* text. In addition, they believe that the words of the *Qur'an*, being the words of God, are possessed of particular powers in themselves, having originated in the hidden world of the *batin*.

These ideas gave rise to what might be called the applied Muslim religious sciences, those practices which were designed to tap the hidden or esoteric power of the *Qur'anic* word for the benefit of society. These sciences became highly systematized and were known generically as *tasrif* (see Sanneh 1989, 158–59).[9] *Tasrif* included such fields of knowledge as *'ilm al-huruf*, the science of letters, and *'ilm al-awfaq*, the science of magic squares, both of which involved numerological manipulations based on the idea that the hidden aspect of each letter of the alphabet (each letter in the *Qur'an*) could be expressed by a numerical equivalent. Therefore, words and letters, transformed into their numerical equivalents, could be manipulated and juxtaposed with one another to produce particular results.

These concepts and practices formed the basis of a wide range of healing and ameliorative activities for which Muslim clerics were well known, especially the production of protective and curative amulets. Such amulets were invariably based on *Qur'anic* words and phrases, often translated into their numerological equivalents and arranged according to various patterns into more or less complex versions of the magic square.

Many other practices were also based on the notion that the words of the *Qur'an* contained power. *Qur'anic* erasures, for example, involved the writing of *Qur'anic* phrases on a wooden slate, then washing off the ink and drinking the solution, thus placing the word of God within one's body. Like amulets, erasures were employed for protective and curative purposes. The emphasis placed on the efficacy of repeated recitation of various prayers is also based on the concept that *Qur'anic* words contain transformative power.

Healing in the African context is concerned not only with the treatment of physiological disorders and disease but also with addressing all kinds of social and individual misfortunes. Depending on their symptoms, illnesses and misfortunes are referred to different specialists; some complaints are seen to be susceptible to Muslim treatments and others to non-Muslim

treatments. Because of this, and because healing by its very nature is a pragmatic process, Muslim and non-Muslim religious experts have tended to
interact rather freely in their roles as healers. Over the centuries, this interaction has led to extensive mutual borrowing of ideas and procedures,
which according to some Muslim scholars allowed practices unacceptable
to Islamic precepts to contaminate the legitimate practice of *tasrif*. The first
major book written by Shaykh ʿUthman b. Fodiye (n.d.) addressed this
problem in considerable detail.

In the twentieth century, of course, many of these practices are rejected
in their totality as either superstitious (the usual secularist accusation) or as
illicit innovation contrary to Muslim religious law (*bidʿa*). But historically
the application of the Muslim religious sciences to healing has probably
been the element of Islamic religious culture which initially brought most
non-Muslims into direct contact with Islam. And *tasrif*, like *tasawwuf*,
received serious attention from the scholarly community. It was included
among the most advanced stages of the religious studies curriculum precisely because it concerned hidden and potentially powerful knowledge.
And as with Sufism, knowledge of it was not attained through the intellect,
as indicated by Ibn Khaldun (1958, 174), here quoting al-Buni: "One should
not think that one can get at the secret of the letters with the help of logical
reasoning. One gets to it with the help of vision and divine aid."[10]

These esoteric and healing sciences were based on the sacred nature of
the *Qurʾan*. According to Ahmad Ibn Idris, "in every letter [of the *Qurʾan*]
is every thing, and in its every letter are all the letters. And this is the same
for the human world, all of it from beginning to its end, all that is within it,
is in each person" (O'Fahey 1990, 196). According to this way of thinking,
all created things have been created in the image of one another: all the elements of the created universe are contained within the *Qurʾan*, indeed, are
contained within its individual letters. By analogy, all the human world is
contained within each individual. The Sufi spiritual quest has been
explained and elaborated with this manner of reflection about the role and
place of humanity in God's universe.

This kind of thinking also justifies for Muslims why their religious
search must begin and end with the study of *Qurʾan*, which is the most
complete expression God has given to humankind of his universal design.
And study of the *Qurʾan* follows precisely the pattern that has been expli-
cated above, moving from its external to its internal aspects. The child
begins to learn the *Qurʾan* with a rote memorization of the text. At this
early stage no effort is made to convey the meaning of the text; all emphasis
is placed on precise and correct recitation. Only those relatively few students who continue their studies to advanced levels will learn the Arabic
language well enough to understand the meaning of the *Qurʾanic* text,

which will be pursued in conjunction with the study of other classical religious texts, virtually all of which are themselves based on aspects of the *Qurʾanic* message. The formal study of the meaning of the *Qurʾan* is known as *tafsir*, an advanced subject in the religious studies curriculum which is mastered by those to whom Ibn Idris refers as the elect. *Taʾwil*, the interpretation of the hidden or esoteric meanings of the *Qurʾan*, is a level of understanding beyond that communicated by the intellect and is reserved for the very few who have achieved direct knowledge of the Divine through gnosis.

The epistemology that has been presented here can justifiably be described as an esoteric paradigm of knowledge because its foundations rest on the idea that a secret and powerful knowledge exists that is available to those who can gain access to it, both through their own efforts and by the grace of God. All scholarship, learning, and teaching focus on the idea that it is always possible to deepen one's understanding of one's relationship to God, although it is also accepted that not all individuals have the same capacity for either intellectual or spiritual achievement. This situation produces a social hierarchy based on the nature and depth of one's religious understanding.

The religious, social, and political reforms initiated by Shaykh ʿUthman b. Fodiye in the early nineteenth century were based on this kind of social understanding. He was quite explicit in some of his writings that the religious knowledge of most Muslims will never extend beyond the external aspects of *shariʿah* (or of *islam*, in the triad explained above). It was adequate, or rather, obligatory, that these people should imitate the outward behaviors of their religious betters, the advanced students of the religious sciences who understood the requirements of *shariʿah* in detail. Above the level of the accomplished scholars were those who had also mastered the inner spiritual disciplines of *tasawwuf*, who had brought together *shariʿah* and *haqiqa* in the manner they lived their lives. These were the *walis*, the role models and leaders for the proper Muslim society.

The Devotional Practice of Sufism

The intellectual and spiritual disciplines of study and religious devotions provide the means for an individual's personal development as a Muslim. The *Qurʾanic* school, which offers an elementary form of religious education, and the *majlis*, which is the center for the advanced study of the religious sciences, are formalized educational institutions. The Sufi order, or *tariqa*, is fundamentally a religious rule which prescribes a set of prayers or litanies to be recited, a set of spiritual exercises to be pursued, and various disciplinary injunctions which define the relationship between the acolyte or disciple (*murid*) and his or her spiritual guide (*murshid*). The *tariqa* provides a context and a method for spiritual development, which is transmitted in an initiatic fashion from guide to aspirant.

Initiation into a *tariqa* is effected by an agreement to submit to its disciplinary injunctions and by the granting of formal permission to recite its litanies. A newly initiated disciple is allowed to recite the basic litanies of the order and with time will normally be authorized to recite additional prayers. But, it is believed, none of these prayers can be efficaciously recited without formal authorization by a recognized superior.

These litanies and special prayers are often referred to as secrets *(asrar)*. They are believed to be imbued with spiritual power which is activated through their repeated recitation. This power derives from the fact that Sufi prayers have originated in the hidden domains of the *batin* and have been transmitted in dreams or visions to the founders of the various Sufi orders by the Prophet Muhammad himself or by an earlier deceased *shaykh*. In other words, they are direct evidence of the supernatural perception of notable Sufi *shaykhs* or *walis*.

The Sufi orders are therefore associated with and named after their founders, whose personal religious experience became the basis of their religious rule and spiritual discipline. Among some of the more significant orders in sub-Saharan Africa are the following.

The Qadiriyya, which derives its name from ʿAbd al-Qadir al-Jilani, a Sufi of twelfth-century Baghdad, is one of the most widespread in the Muslim world and it was present in Africa from an early period. Among its most important adherents there were Shaykh ʿUthman b. Fodiye (d. 1817) and Sidi al-Mukhtar al-Kunti (d. 1811), who was responsible for reinvigorating the order in the region. The Mourides of Senegal, founded by Amadu Bamba (d. 1927), are a branch of the Qadiriyya. The Qadiriyya also became influential in East Africa during the late nineteenth and early twentieth centuries, where it was spread by Shaykh Uways b. Muhammad al-Barawi (d. 1909).

The Tijaniyya was founded in the Maghrib by Ahmad al-Tijani (d. 1815), and was spread extensively in West Africa during the nineteenth century primarily through the influence of al-Hajj ʿUmar al-Futi (d. 1864). Of the more important sub-branches of the Tijaniyya to appear in the twentieth century have been the Hamalliyya, founded by Shaykh Ahmad Hamallah (d. 1943) and the Niassiyya or Ibrahimiyya, founded in Senegal by Shaykh Ibrahim Niass (d. 1975). The Niassiyya is based in Senegal, but has attracted large numbers of adherents in Ghana, Nigeria, and Sudan, and has recently begun to spread in the United States among African American Muslims.

Ahmad Ibn Idris (d. 1837) did not himself claim to found a *tariqa*, although several of his followers were responsible for establishing Sufi

orders which became some of the most influential in nineteenth- and twen-
tieth-century Africa. Muhammad al-Sanusi (d. 1859) was the founder of the
Sanusiyya order, which came to predominate in Libya and the central
Sudan. Muhammad ʿUthman al-Mirghani (d. 1852) was founder of the
Mirghaniyya or Khatmiyya order in the Sudan. From the teachings of
Ibrahim al-Rashid (d. 1874), another student of Ibn Idris, there emerged
three Sufi orders that would become influential in northeastern Africa and
beyond: the Rashidiyya, the Salihiyya, and the Dandarawiyya.

The Sufi orders differed from one another in various ways, for example,
in the content of their prescribed prayers and litanies, and in the way in
which their leaders conceptualized the organization of the *tariqa*. Occasionally the contrasts were extreme. For example, Ibn Idris resisted the tendency of those around him to organize his followers into a structured
organization, whereas Ahmad al-Tijani encouraged his followers to consider themselves the members of a highly exclusive religious order that was
superior to all others. Although these variations have been socially and
politically significant, we cannot trace their histories here. Our discussion
will therefore concentrate on the nature of the spiritual discipline that all
the orders pursued in common.

As suggested above, the founders of all the Sufi orders are considered
walis, having received the inspiration for their spiritual practices in dreams
and visions, often from the Prophet Muhammad. Their personal experiences then become the model for the spiritual discipline that they recommend to their followers, which is transmitted personally through an
initiatic process. An initiatic chain of transmission (*silsila*) is therefore
established that has its origins with the Prophet and links him to the
founder and in turn to his many spiritual subordinates, usually known as
the *shaykhs* or *muqaddams* of the order, whose spiritual attainments have
qualified them to initiate others into the order. Viewed from the opposite
perspective, from that of an individual adherent, we see that each member
of a Sufi order is connected, through a *silsila*, first to his or her initiator or
shaykh, then to the founder of the order, and ultimately to the Prophet.

This initiatic practice therefore conforms to the hierarchical principles
that were explored above in the epistemological section of this essay. The
silsila constitutes a tangible link between the manifest and hidden worlds of
zahir and *batin*. Through it have been transmitted the prayers and litanies
of the order, the *wird* and *dhikr*, which provide the practical means for an
individual to engage in personal spiritual development. Through the chain
of transmission, Sufi aspirants also receive the *baraka*, or spiritual grace, of
the founder to protect and sustain them in their efforts. Al-Hajj ʿUmar
described this mutual exchange via the *silsila* as follows:

Each time that a disciple recites the *dhikr,* he should hold the image of his *shaikh* in his heart and seek his aid. The heart of this *shaikh* is similarly turned toward the heart of his own *shaikh,* and so on right to the Prophet. And the heart of the Prophet Muhammad is continually turned toward the Divine Presence. In this way, when one recites the *dhikr,* one should visualize his *shaikh* and seek the aid of his sanctity. Such aid will pour forth from the Divine Presence to the Prophet, and will then flow from the heart of the Prophet to the hearts of all the *shaikhs* of all ranks, and in the same way to the heart of his own *shaikh* from where it will penetrate his own heart. (ᶜUmar b. Saᶜid al-Futi, *Rimah* 2:3).

The litanies of the Tijaniyya order can provide an example of the kinds of recitations required of a Sufi initiate. In addition to the five daily prayers that are obligatory for all Muslims, Tijanis are required to recite three sets of invocations, known respectively as the *wird,* the *wazifa,* and the *hadra.*

The *wird* includes three invocations to be recited twice daily—in the morning before the dawn prayer, and in the afternoon:

1. 100 times the formula "I beg forgiveness from God."
2. 100 times the *salat al-fatih:* "O God, bless our master Muhammad, who opened what had been closed, and who is the seal of what had gone before; he who makes the Truth victorious by the Truth, the guide to Thy straight path; and bless his household as is the due of his immense position and grandeur."
3. 100 times "There is no god but God," called the *hailala.*

The *wazifa* includes four invocations recited at least once daily—before the morning prayer—but a second time in the evening if one wishes.

1. 30 times the formula "I ask forgiveness from God, the Great, of whom there is no other god but Him, the Living and the Self-subsisting."
2. 50 times the *salat al-fatih,* as above.
3. 100 times "There is no god but God."
4. 11 or 12 times the *jawharat al-kamal:*

> O God, send benediction upon and salute the source of divine mercy, a true ruby which encompasses the center of comprehensions and meanings, the son of Adam, the possessor of divine Truth; the most luminous lightning in the profitable rain-clouds which fill all the intervening seas and receptacles; Thy bright light with which Thou has filled Thy universe and which surrounds the places of existence.
>
> O God, bless and salute the source of Truth from which are manifested the tabernacles of realities; the source of knowledge, the most upright; Thy complete and most straight path.

O God, bless and salute the advent of the Truth by the Truth; the greatest treasure, Thy mysterious Light. May God bless the Prophet and his household, a prayer which brings us to knowledge of him.

The *hadra* is a group recitation held each Friday afternoon during which the *hailala* or simply the name Allah is recited. The number of recitations is not specified. (Brenner 1984, 193–94).[11]

We must now attempt to explore how invocations of this kind can form the basis of a spiritual evolution. Of course, the act of receiving a Sufi initiation and agreeing regularly to perform even these simple prayers is a major commitment. Sufis refer to it as a conversion (*tawba*), a conscious commitment to reorient one's life to an internal spiritual quest. We can obtain some insight into the impact of such devotional exercises from the comments of Saada Oumar Toure, a Tijani Sufi from Mali, who is here talking about reciting the *wird:*

When one adopts the Tijaniyya order and begins to perform the required invocations morning and evening, the adherent simulates making a visit to God, that is, he performs a spiritual ascension. Of course, the adherent must not present himself before his Lord in a defiled state, so after performing his ablutions, he begins to say: "I beg forgiveness from God." He asks God's forgiveness because God himself promised in the *Qur'an* to purify all those who asked His forgiveness. In this way, the adherent's clothes are clean, his body is clean, and now his soul is being washed of the sins which would defile it in the presence of his Lord.

For this spiritual ascension, one needs a guide, which in this case is the Prophet Muhammad. Therefore, the adherent begins to pray for him (by reciting the *salat al-fatih*). Now, with his companion and guide, the adherent continues on his way passing through all the stages until he presents himself before his Lord. He says, I bear witness that I am far from all the attributes which one assigns to You my Lord. With this introduction, the pious visit has begun, and the adherent recites "There is no god but God" one hundred times. After this, he takes his leave, rejoins the Prophet Muhammad and returns. Each morning and evening, the adherent performs this spiritual ascension. In this way, he accustoms his soul to being near to God.

In the Tijaniyya, you are given the *wird* to use like soap and water. It is now up to you to know how to wash properly, that is to concentrate while performing the invocations. First to clean the soul by asking God's forgiveness, then to seek the company of Muhammad who will guide you on the spiritual way until you have attained your goal, when you recite "There is no god but God." The process is like a file which little by little removes the rust from an object until it is completely rust-free. That is the aim. The adherent who does not concentrate properly during his invocations will not achieve much of a result.[12]

Saada Oumar is referring here to the *jihad al-nafs*, or struggle against the carnal soul, introduced at the beginning of this essay. According to his understanding, a major weapon in this struggle is the concentration of the adherent, the intensity of which determines the efficacy of the invocations. If the *wird, dhikr,* and other devotional prayers are recited with proper concentration, an internal process is activated that will begin to cleanse the carnal soul of its impurities. Saada Oumar's comments recall those made about "liquid faith" by Cerno Bokar when he speaks about a moral terrain "worn flat by the adoration of God." Both men are describing a process in which an action is initiated (the devotional invocations), the desired effect of which (internal spiritual transformation) cannot be directly willed by the adherent. This pattern of relationship between the outer and inner aspects of the individual (the manifest and the hidden) is completely compatible with the concepts already elaborated in this essay. The language which Sufis employ to discuss this spiritual transformation, at least in its initial stages, is highly moralistic. But here we can begin to gain some insight into the distinctions they draw between *ihsan* as upright behavior and *tasawwuf* as the pursuit of inner purity. They are speaking about two aspects of morality, the manifest and the hidden; consequently the two moralities cannot be perfected in the same manner.

Later in the same interview, Saada Oumar draws attention to this distinction by comparing the effects of Sufi invocations with those of the five daily prayers (*salat*):

> [The Sufi adherent] must struggle against himself, which can be accomplished both by these invocations and by prayer, because God tells us in the *Qur'an* that "Prayer banishes shameful and evil actions." This is because if someone presents himself before his Lord in the morning and promises that he will not again succumb to the same sins, if he is conscientious, then he is obliged to fulfill his promise by setting aside all the things which might lead him again into these sins. This is repeated five times a day. If he is sincere, I believe that he is going to abandon a lot of things. . . . A true Muslim, a true believer, is ashamed to return to his Lord defiled with the same sins. All day long, he is obliged to adopt the behavior of which he has spoken to God while praying, if he has shame; if he is really a Muslim. In this way, little by little, one distances oneself from one's passions.

Here Saada Oumar is speaking about the external aspects of morality, which one must address through sincerity and conscientiousness. By contrast, the weapon one must use in the internal struggle against the carnal soul is concentration. This precept is repeated constantly in the Sufi literature.

The development of such concentration depends on the capacity of the individual to place his or her full attention on the devotional exercises. It is virtually impossible to describe how such a state of concentration is developed because it is a highly subjective experience. Furthermore, it is an experience which, as it deepens, becomes less accessible to processing by the intellect and therefore moves even further from the realm of possible discourse. Sufis refer to such experience in terms of "taste" (*dhawq*); the sensations of taste are not easily reduced to words. Nonetheless, some Sufis do attempt to talk about it, and we can do no better than explore some of what they have said about this internal transformation.

Like so much else in Islam, this process begins on a relatively simple level. New initiates into the Tijaniyya order agree to conform to twenty-one conditions or rules, among which are stipulations about the proper recitation of the *wird* and *dhikr;* these include directives about the cleanliness of one's clothing and body as well as of the place in which one recites the invocations, as well as warnings about not being distracted during the invocations. But there are two additional conditions for those who can accomplish them: first, that while reciting the invocations one should envisage Ahmad al-Tijani, or preferably the Prophet; and second, that one should call to mind the meanings of the formulations of the invocations if one is able to understand them (Brenner 1984, 195–96). These two additional demands greatly increase the level of concentration one must bring to these devotional exercises. Of course, adherents who cannot accomplish these two additional requirements will still receive spiritual benefits from the invocations, but they will be limited in their spiritual development.

Ever deeper levels of concentration are sought. According to al-Hajj 'Umar:

> You must place the meaning of the *dhikr* in your heart each time that you repeat it; and during the *dhikr,* you must pay attention to the heart while evoking this meaning, until it is the heart which is reciting it and you who are listening to it. ('Umar b. Sa'id al-Futi, *Rimah* 2:4)

This comment seems to suggest that the Sufi aspirant can achieve a state of being in which the recitation of *dhikr* is carried out by a part of the self which is other than one's conscious mind. Cerno Bokar spoke about a similar state, in which one is constantly reciting the name of God, that is, endlessly reciting *dhikr*. *Dhikr* itself has been defined as "a spiritual exercise designed to render God's presence throughout one's being" (Trimingham 1971, 302). In a similar vein, we have the injunction of the fifteenth-century North African Sufi Muhammad b. Yusuf al-Sanusi, that one should frequently recite the *shahada* ("There is no god but God, and Muhammad is the Messenger of God") "while calling to mind that which it contains from the articles of faith until it, with its meaning, mingles with his flesh and blood. Then, if God wills, he will behold some of his boundless secrets and wonders" (1986, 10 [Arabic]/17 [French]).[13]

Al-Sanusi's text reminds us that, whatever the efforts of the Sufi aspirant, actual spiritual transformation comes only from God. Sufi doctrine is very clear that spiritual evolution is a gift from God that is beyond the will and efforts of the individual. That which is within the capacity of the individual adherent to achieve, for example, the various levels of concentration, Sufis refer to as *maqam*. The spiritual transformation of one's state of being, which can only come from God, they refer to as *hal*. Al-Hajj ʿUmar pointed out the difference in the following passage:

> The intention of spiritual exercises is the cleansing and purification of the essence from any slackness, so that it will be capable of bearing the burden of the secret. This is not possible unless wrongdoing is eliminated from it, and unless vanity and falsehood are prohibited from coming into contact with this objective. When for a time these are separated from it, (the essence) exists with only the attributes of its true nature, and God Almighty might purify it without any intermediary. (ʿUmar b. Saʿid al-Futi, *Rimah* 1:132–33)

The language here is again couched in moral terminology, but by now the reader should be better able to understand the different levels of interpretation which such language is able to convey. A less moralistic and somewhat different perspective on the effects of such spiritual exercises was recorded by Shaykh ʿUthman b. Fodiye:

> When I reached thirty-six years of age, God removed the veil from my sight, and the dullness from my hearing and my smell, and the thickness from my taste, and the cramp from my two hands, and the restraint from my two feet, and the heaviness from my body. And I was able to see the near like the far, and hear the far like the near, and smell the scent of him who worshipped God, sweeter than any sweetness; and the stink of the sinner more foul than any stench. And I could recognize what was lawful to eat by the taste, before I swallowed it; and likewise what was unlawful to eat. I could pick up what was far away with my two hands while I was sitting in my place; and I could travel on my two feet (a distance) that a fleet horse could not cover in the space of years. That was a favour from God that He gives to whom He will. And I knew my body, limb by limb, bone by bone, sinew by sinew, muscle by muscle, hair by hair, each one by its rank, and what was entrusted to it. Then I found written upon my fifth rib, on the right side, by the Pen of Power, "Praise be to God, Lord of the Created Worlds" ten times; and "O God, bless our Lord Muhammad, and the Family of Muhammad, and give them peace" ten times; and "I beg forgiveness from the Glorious God" ten times; and I marveled greatly at that. (Quoted in Hiskett 1973, 64–65)

These comments are as indicative as any of what a Sufi aspirant might experience in his or her spiritual search. The closer the aspirant moves toward the ultimate goal, which is to draw near to God with their whole being, the less communicable is the experience. We must accept that there is a limit to the understanding of the Sufi experience that is accessible to us.

Conclusion

We can summarize the preceding discussion as follows. The spiritual work that is Sufism aims at the transformation of the hidden or inner aspect of the human being. The Sufi aspirant enters into this spiritual work through an initiatic relationship with a guide or a teacher who has himself engaged in similar efforts under the guidance of his own spiritual teacher. The aspirant's efforts are focused on deepening the state of concentration in which he or she recites the invocations. The ultimate aim is to reach a state in which, as Ahmad Ibn Idris said, no preoccupation can divert the aspirant from God, outwardly or inwardly. Such persons "do nothing, except they do so because of God and for God." The quest for this state, which itself comprises an internal, transformative movement, constitutes the essence of the Sufi way, a path toward God that is opened to the aspirant only as God wills regardless of the personal efforts expended. It is a spiritual path which offers no certitude about its ultimate result, and which consequently demands a profound faith from anyone engaged in it. The person of such faith, who can "place his intellect behind his belief," is informed by God directly through revelations. The nurturing of such faith is an essential part of the Sufi initiatic process. This process demands a struggle with oneself, with the carnal soul, which is so firmly attached to the external, manifest world. The great paradox of Sufism is that, while the struggle with the self is so long and demanding, the ultimate goal is always so very near, indeed, within each human being, because God has breathed into each human being a part of his Spirit.

Sufism in Africa differs little from the Sufism that has developed in other parts of the Muslim world. The basic principles and spiritual practices are very similar, although there are many variations in the specific features of the different orders. Of course, Sufism is an Islamic religious expression, and Sufism in Africa is based on universal Muslim principles. But as a spiritual discipline, Sufism shares many epistemological and practical features with non-Muslim African religious practice. One must naturally be cautious not to generalize too broadly about religion in Africa, but the following observations might encourage readers of this book to reflect further on the relationships between different religious practices on the continent.

Indigenous African religious practitioners posit the existence of a manifest world in which the living community functions, and an invisible, hidden world which is occupied by various spiritual entities and forces. In a manner similar to the Sufi epistemology explained in this essay, African religious epistemology is based on the idea that the welfare of the living community, and of the entire manifest world, is dependent on maintaining a proper relationship with the entities and forces of the invisible world. This relationship is maintained by religious experts, whose specialized knowledge is often secret, in that it is not shared with the community as a whole, and who are prepared for their religious roles through a transformative initiatic process in which the transmission of intellectual knowledge is often secondary to an experiential praxis. Equally important is the personal transformation of the individual to enable him or her, in their future religious role, to sustain the necessary relationship with the entities of the invisible world, be they the ancestors, various spirits, or deities. Religious experts must be specially prepared for their duties, because proximity to spiritual entities entails dangers which ordinary persons cannot sustain.

The initiatic process therefore transforms an individual by imbuing him or her with new powers which give direct access to the hidden world. Such persons can "see" what others cannot see. They learn how to conduct rituals that manipulate the forces of the other world and to tap the hidden powers of the world around them, particularly in plants and animals, to manufacture healing and protective medicines, much as Muslims employ the hidden powers of the *Qur'anic* word.

If a major part of Islamic doctrine is addressed to converting unbelievers to the religion of Islam, these few brief references to similarities in religious concept and practice seem to suggest that on another level Muslims and non-Muslims may have shared some similar forms of religious experience. The extent to which religious persons in Africa in the past may have sought to explore these similarities has yet to be seriously researched.

Notes

1. Quoted in ʿUmar b. Saʿid al-Futi, "Rimah hizb al-rahim ala nuhur hizb al-rajim" (published in the margins of ʿAli Harazim, *Jawahir al-maʿani* [Beirut: n.d.]).

2. The teachings of Ahmad Ibn Idris were seminal for the spread of Sufism in nineteenth-century Sudan and eastern Africa. The quotation is taken from O'Fahey 1990, 74.

3. Ibn Khaldun was particularly interested in the human capacity for supernatural perception. References cited here are from Ibn Khaldun 1958, 1:184–88, 197–99.

4. ʿUmar b. Saʿid al-Futi, *Rimah*, 1:131. This kind of remark is evidence of the extent to which Sufi ideology was male-oriented. Although some women did achieve noted status as scholars and even Sufis, Muslim literature rarely notes or places emphasis on this fact.

5. During the twentieth century this situation has been modified through two

very different but complementary influences: the secularism of much Western education, especially in French-speaking Africa, and the anti-Sufi doctrines of the Wahhabi school of Muslim thought, which began to penetrate sub-Saharan Africa in the 1940s. These two influences have combined to produce what I have called a "rationalistic paradigm of thought," which is now replacing the "esoteric paradigm," which formerly prevailed and of which Sufism is one aspect. For a discussion of the impact of this process on Muslim education, see Brenner 1993, 159–80.

6. The *jihad* led by Shaykh ʿUthman began in 1804 in what is now northern Nigeria. He was a highly prolific scholar and devout Sufi; see Last 1967. The *jihad* led by al-Hajj ʿUmar lasted from 1852 until his death in 1864 and focused primarily on regions that are located in the present Republic of Mali. ʿUmar was also an accomplished scholar and a Sufi; see Robinson 1985.

7. A detailed discussion of the political applications of Sufi thought is beyond the scope of the present essay, but see Brenner 1988.

8. Taken from a Muslim catechism developed by Cerno Bokar Saalif Tal in Mali during the first half of the twentieth century. See Amadou Hampate Ba 1980, 210–12; Brenner 1984, 188.

9. References to *tasrif* occur among other clerical groups in West Africa in addition to the Jakhanke, who were the focus of Sanneh's study.

10. Ahmad b. ʿAli al-Buni (d. 1225), a North African scholar, was one of the leading experts in the esoteric sciences of letters and numbers. Ibn Khaldun is here quoting his *Shams al-maʿarif*, which was widely used in Africa.

11. Based on information in ʿUmar b. Saʿid al-Futi, *Rimah*, 1:229–30.

12. Interview with Saada Oumar Toure, Segu, Mali, 5 February 1978.

13. For a discussion of the significance of al-Sanusi's thought for African Sufism, see Brenner 1984, 79ff.

References

ʿAli Harazim
    n.d.   *Jawahir al-maʿani*. Beirut.
Ba, Amadou Hampate
    1980   *Vie et enseignement de Tierno Bokar: Le sage de Bandiagara*. Paris: Editions du Seuil.
Brenner, L.
    1984   *West African Sufi: The Religious Heritage and Spiritual Search of Cerno Bokar Saalif Taal*. London: C. Hurst & Co.; Berkeley: University of California Press.
    1988   "Concepts of Tariqa in West Africa: The Case of the Qadiriyya." In *Charisma and Brotherhood in African Islam*, ed. D. Cruise O'Brien and C. Coulon. Oxford: Clarendon Press.
    1993   "Two Paradigms of Islamic Schooling in West Africa." In *Modes de transmission de la culture religieuse en Islam*, ed. H. Elboudrari, 159–80. Cairo: Institut Français d'Archéologie Orientale.

Hiskett, M.
1973 *The Sword of Truth: The Life and Times of the Shehu Usuman dan Fodio.* New York: Oxford University Press.
Ibn Khaldun
1958 *The Muqaddimah.* Translated from Arabic by Franz Rosenthal. London: Routledge & Kegan Paul.
Last, Murray
1967 *The Sokoto Caliphate.* London: Longman.
Muhammad b. Yusuf al-Sanusi
1986 *Al-ᶜaqida al-sughra.* Algiers.
O'Fahey, R. S.
1990 *The Enigmatic Saint: Ahmad Ibn Idris and the Idrisi Tradition.* London: Hurst & Co.
Robinson, David
1985 *The Holy War of Umar Tal: The Western Sudan in the Mid-Nineteenth Century.* Oxford: Clarendon Press.
Sanneh, Lamin
1989 *The Jakhanke Muslim Clerics: A Religious and Historical Study of Islam in Senegambia.* London: University Press of America.
Trimingham, J. S.
1971 *The Sufi Orders in Islam.* London: Oxford University Press.
ᶜUmar b. Saᶜid al-Futi
n.d. "Rimah hizb al-rahim ᶜala nuhur hizb al-rajim" (published in the margins of ᶜAli Harazim).
ᶜUthman b. Fodiye
n.d. *Kitab Ihyaʾ al-sunna wa ikhmad al-bidᶜa* (The Revival of the Sunna and the Suppression of Illicit Innovation).
1978 *Kitab ᶜulum al-muᶜamala.* Translated from Arabic by ᶜAisha ᶜAbd ar-Rahman al-Tarijumana. In *Handbook of Islam.* Norwich: Diwan Press

16

Roman North African Christian Spiritualities

Margaret R. Miles

IN THE THREE-HUNDRED-year period of Christianity's greatest strength in North Africa, between the late second century C.E. and the mid-fifth century, distinctive forms of Christian spirituality emerged. The geographical context was a relatively small area of Roman North Africa, including the provinces of Numidia, Mauretania, and Proconsular Africa. In Roman North Africa, Christianity showed both continuities of characteristic problems, attitudes, ideas, and practices, and changes as the social and political position of North African Christians changed.

Attention to this small geographical area over a limited time period exemplifies the inadequacy of generalizations about "the early church." In a time before public communication media, local configurations must be respected as carefully as temporal distances. Moreover, the particularities of Christian spiritualities on Roman North African soil come clearly into focus only when Christian ideas and practices are approached from a comparative perspective, that is, one in which the primary native religions of North Africa are understood both as informing and as competing with Christianity. An ecumenical perspective is also essential to recognizing the distinctiveness of North African Christianity.

Traditional histories of Christianity usually begin from the hindsight of a late-fourth-century triumphant church and proceed to reach behind that *fait accompli* to identify its development or emergence. This, however, puts the cart before the horse. Not only does it mask the continuous conflict in which dominant interpretations of Christian belief and practice emerged, but it also—and more seriously—ignores the committed intellectual and ethical commitments of the full spectrum of North African Christians. Interpretations of Christian belief and practice that later came to be understood as heretical or schismatic from an orthodox perspective, flourished in

Roman North Africa as attractive explanations of Christian beliefs and values. I will, then, adopt both comparative and ecumenical perspectives in the following discussion. I will regard Christian groups that identified *themselves* as Christian as alternative interpretations of Christian belief and practice rather than as heretics, especially in the time periods before the ecclesiastical decisions that branded them as such were made.

Roman North Africa

Three racial strains converged to produce "native" North Africans: semi-nomadic Libyans or Berbers, an indigenous race with roots going back to the ninth millennium B.C.E.; Phoenicians, a seafaring people from the eastern Mediterranean who gradually established themselves in North Africa, founding the city of Carthage (now Tunis), according to tradition, in 1186 B.C.E.; and the Italians who recolonized North Africa after the Punic Wars. By the Christian era, it was language, not race, that distinguished Berbers, Phoenicians, and Latin-speaking Romans in contemporary literature.

Carthage, the "New City," was, by the Roman period, a great Mediterranean power based largely on its agriculture and shipping. Carthage was the breadbasket of the Mediterranean, a practical hegemony that was maintained until the fifth century C.E. Its ship-building industry created and maintained the Roman navy. Explorers from ancient Carthage may have sailed as far as England and Ireland. Moreover, it was an international center of education and artistic activity; for example, mosiacs were invented in Carthage. Its power rivaled and threatened Rome, leading to three Punic Wars between 246 and 146 B.C.E., in which ancient Carthage was destroyed and subsequently recolonized. By the mid-third century C.E., Carthage was again equal in wealth and productivity to Alexandria, and second only to Rome in power. Carthage was also an important center of Christianity.

Christianity in Roman North Africa

The origins of North African Christianity are lost in obscurity. The two most plausible theories are that Christianity emerged from the large Jewish community in Carthage in the second century, or that traders and immigrants from the eastern Mediterranean carried Christianity to North Africa. Even the African Christian author Tertullian, writing at the end of the second century, did not know the origins of North African Christianity; he reports legends concerning its origins in his *Prescription against the Heretics*. All Christian liturgies and literature in North Africa—as elsewhere in the empire—were in Greek until the beginning of the third century, when Tertullian wrote several of his treatises in Latin. The first Latin versions of the New Testament came from North Africa, and the Latin liturgy also originated there (Saxer 1969, 11–12).

Christianity was a popular movement in Roman North Africa. About 150 names of bishops in Mauretania, Numidia, and Proconsular Africa are known from the period up to the mid-third century. Only one of these had a Punic name, while about a dozen more were non-Latin. By the beginning of the fifth century, about seven hundred bishops were listed, though it is important to note that bishops often existed in towns less than ten miles apart. Christianity flourished in North Africa until the seventh century, when it was replaced by Islam.

The first extant reference to North African Christianity is in the mid-second-century C.E. African secular author Apuleius, who remarks scornfully on Christians in his *Metamorphoses*. The first extant document of African Christianity is the *Acts of the Scillitan Martyrs*, which describes the trial, on 17 July 180, of seven men and five women who were accused of being Christians and were sentenced to death on the arrival in Carthage of a new governor, Vigillius Saturninus. One of the governor's first official acts was to condemn to death these twelve African Christians with native names from a small town near Carthage. As they were led to execution, it is recorded that they cried, *"Deo gratias!"* "Thanks be to God!"—a phrase which was to become a rallying cry of African Christianity for several centuries (Musurillo 1972, 86–89).

Three powerful and influential authors are primarily responsible for forming the Roman North African Christianity that, by the beginning of the fifth century, was synonymous with Catholic Christianity. In different social and political circumstances, Tertullian (d. 220 C.E.), Cyprian (d. 258 C.E.), and Augustine (d. 430 C.E.), shaped the religious life of Christians in relation to secular society, to dissident Christians, and to the church. Each author dealt, on location and under pressure, with issues of church discipline, the establishment of an authoritative church hierarchy as the basis for a heavily advocated but slenderly achieved Christian unity, and the crafting of a stable relationship between church, society, and Roman government. These three authors' interpretations of Christian values, lifestyle, and institutions came to be normative in North Africa, as well as influencing the development of the Catholic Church across the Roman empire. Although later authors revered the earlier—Cyprian called Tertullian "the Master," and Augustine acknowledged the great respect North African Christians felt for Cyprian, the martyr-bishop of a century and a half before—each rejected particular decisions made by their antecedents in their different social and institutional circumstances. What these North

African Christian authors shared, then, was not unanimity in belief and practice but commitment and creativity in interpreting Christianity in relation to the needs and opportunities of their own time.

Two characteristic preoccupations of North African Christianity make it distinctive: preoccupation with martyrdom and interest in the activity of the Spirit in Christian communities. One might without exaggeration characterize North African Christian spirituality as passionate, often to the point of fanaticism, and uncompromising, sometimes to the point of violence. Frequently unhappy with a geographically distant and, by the fourth century, wealthy imperial church, many North Africans chose Christian groups in which they could pursue extra-scriptural knowledge (the Manichaeans), or worship in locally governed Christian groups (the Donatists) or in groups in which the Spirit was still believed to speak immediately and directly through prophets who were not necessarily ordained to professional Christian leadership (Montanists). These groups dissented from Catholic belief, organization, and/or practice, but this essay will endeavor to demonstrate that they insistently preserved characteristically North African religious interests and values.

Roman Religion in North Africa

Archaeological and literary evidence for the practice of the cult of Saturn in North Africa is fragmentary but fascinating. The Saturn cult was a Punic religion, adopted by the African Berbers and popular primarily among the lower classes in Roman North Africa. It is striking that the only two Christian authors to report accusations of child sacrifice against Christians were Africans—Tertullian and Minucius Felix (Rousselle 1988, 109). Did Africans find such accusations plausible because the practice of infant sacrifice continued in indigenous religions in remote regions in secret, as Tertullian claimed (*Apology* 9.3), even in his own day?

Archaeological discoveries in Carthage have revealed numerous trophets, or urns for human sacrifice. More than four hundred urns have been excavated, containing human and animal bones buried between 700 and 146 B.C.E. (Charles-Picard 1954). Lawrence Stager estimates that between 400 and 200 B.C.E. alone, about twenty thousand urns were buried, each containing at least one human baby, an average of one hundred sacrifices a year (Stager 1980). Thirty percent of the bones analyzed from the early period were those of infants under four. Of urns containing a single child, 68 percent contained a child of one to three years; the rest were young infants. Thirty-two percent of the urns contained two or more children. The ancient writer Diodorus Siculus described these public sacrifices:

The people were filled with dread because they believed that they had neglected the honor of the gods that had been established by their fathers. In their zeal to make amends for their omission they selected 200 of the noblest children and sacrificed them publicly; others who were under suspicion sacrificed themselves voluntarily, in number not less than 300. There was in their city a bronze image of Cronus, extending his hands, palms up and sloping toward the ground, so that each of the children when placed thereon rolled down and fell into a sort of gaping pit filled with fire. (Quoted in Stager 1980, 11)

Child sacrifice seems to have functioned either as expiation for guilt, as described above, or as a bid for success. A third-century B.C.E. document, reports that "the Carthaginians, whenever they seek to obtain some great favor, vow one of their children, burning it as a sacrifice to the deity, especially if they are eager to gain success" (quoted in Stager 1980, 6).

As archaeological evidence demonstrates, the substitution of animal for human sacrifice began in the second century when the cult of Saturn was romanized. Depictions of Saturn from this period represent the god as a bearded Roman in a toga. Rather than understanding the cruelty and violence of the Saturn cult as discontinuous with Roman culture, however, it needs to be placed in the context of a violent society. One form of violence was the brutal wars by which a fifth to a sixth of the then world's population was brought under Roman jurisdiction in the last two centuries B.C.E. Another was violent public entertainment in the cities of the Roman empire. An "atmosphere of violence, even in peace" was maintained by public execution of prisoners, fights to the death between hundreds of gladiators, and the "indiscriminate slaughter of domestic and wild animals" (Hopkins 1983, 2). The popularity of these bloodbaths is attested by the huge colosseums in cities of the empire. Public killings were a common spectacle of Roman life.

Were there continuities between human sacrifice and Christian martyrdom in North Africa? It is not a stretch of the imagination to interpret gladiatorial fights to the death, public punishment and execution of criminals, and martyrdom of Christians as replacements for the human sacrifice abolished by Tiberius. Spectacles of the colosseum incorporated symbolic reference to North African religions. The Carthaginian martyrs Perpetua and Felicity were ordered, when they entered the arena, to put on the robes of a priestess of Ceres, while their male companions were to don the robes of priests of Saturn. Moreover, like the victims of infant sacrifice, Christians condemned to death were given a feast the day before their execution. When Saturus was attacked by a leopard, the crowd's exclamation on seeing Saturus's blood was *"Saluum lotum! Saluum lotum!"* "Well washed; well washed!" which may have been a ritual exclamation during a sacrifice to Saturn.

A final parallel between human sacrifice and Christian martyrdom in North Africa is even more illuminating. Sacrificial ritual required that the victim die happily—or "appear" to die happily. In the case of infants, "the parents played with them so that they would die laughing for the salvation of themselves, the city, and their family" (Rousselle 1988, 119; see also Reinach 1911). In *Apology* 8.7, Tertullian describes the "ritual laughter or at least gaiety which was supposed to accompany human sacrifices to Saturn: 'You need a baby which is still tender and which does not know of death and laughs as you raise your knife.'" Like sacrificial victims in the Saturn cult, African Christian martyrs are consistently reported to have met their deaths joyfully, embracing martyrdom as the "baptism by blood" that was believed to anticipate the general eschaton and guarantee them instant reception into heaven. The association of joyful death with individual and communal salvation was an ancient one in North Africa.

Martyrdom and North African *Acta*

In *Confessions* 6.11, Augustine, bishop of Hippo, near Carthage, describes the immense interest the spectacles of the colosseum held for fourth-century Romans. He narrates the addiction of his friend and fellow African Alypius to gladiatorial fights and other entertainments. A century before, Christians had themselves been part of the spectacle as they were thrown to wild beasts, burned, and stabbed. Christian martyrdom made a lasting impression on North African liturgy and spirituality. *Acta*, accounts of the trials, tortures, and death of the martyrs were read on the anniversary of the martyr's death in North African liturgies (Saxer 1980, 157). Moreover, martyrdom as a fact of church life through the second and third centuries set an intransigent and lasting standard for radical commitment to Christianity.

Martyrdom was not, of course, uniquely the experience of North African Christians, but by the third century a "developed cult of martyrdom" can be identified in North Africa (Saxer 1980, 154). The leaders of African Christianity wrote treatises encouraging Christians to aspire to martyrdom. Tertullian and Cyprian—himself a martyr and the first African bishop to be martyred—urged steadfastness in the face of imprisonment, torture, and execution. Confessors—those who awaited death after condemnation for their Christian witness—were so revered in North Africa that their perceived power to forgive sin and to adjudicate differences among Christians was sometimes feared and resisted by church leaders.

North African Christian *acta* consistently emphasize the happiness of martyrdom. Clearly, the laughing infants sacrificed to Saturn hover in the common cultural background of North Africans. One of the most poignant documents of Roman North African Christianity, the *Passio Sanctarum Perpetuae et Felicitatis* (Musurillo 1972), describes the trial, imprisonment, and martyrdom of Perpetua, an educated member of an upper-middle-class family, and her slavewoman, Felicity. Perpetua and Felicity were arrested early in 203 C.E. for confessing adherence to Christianity. The central sections of the *acta* are widely accepted as the prison journals of the twenty-three-year-old Perpetua. The *acta* narrates the events just before their martyrdom. On the occasion of the confessors' last meal, Perpetua and her companions spoke to the crowd of curious voyeurs, "stressing the joy (*felicitatem*) they would have in their suffering." On the day of their martyrdom—the "day of their victory"—the editor of the *acta* writes:

> They marched from the prison to the amphitheatre joyfully ("hilares") . . . trembling, if at all, with joy ("gaudio") rather than fear. . . . Perpetua went along with shining countenance and calm steps, as the beloved of God, as a wife of Christ . . . they rejoiced at this that they had obtained a share in the Lord's sufferings. (18)

The Holy Spirit in North African Christianity

The second emphasis of North African Christianity—interest in the continuing activity of the Holy Spirit—is also associated with martyrdom. By Tertullian's time it was commonly believed that the Holy Spirit accompanied persecuted Christians from the time of their arrest, through their time in prison, and to the moment of their translation into heaven. The expected spiritual privilege of the confessor is evident as Perpetua relates that she received visions, prayed for—and was assured of—the healing of her long-dead brother, and experienced the immediate cessation of physical and mental distress when her nursing infant son was taken from her. The prologue of the *acta* describes North Africa's interest in the *present* activity of the Spirit:

> Let those then who would restrict the power of the one Spirit to times and seasons look to this: the more recent events should be considered the greater. . . . We hold in honor and acknowledge not only new prophecies but new visions as well. . . . Thus no one of weak or despairing faith may think that supernatural grace was present only among those of ancient times, either in the grace of martyrdom or in visions, for God is always working as he promised.

North African Montanists

Perpetua and Felicity's *acta* seem to have emerged from a group of Montanist Christians, judging from their lively interest in the present activity of the Holy Spirit. Montanism originated in Phrygia in Asia Minor, but its importance within the history of Christianity lies in its development in North Africa. In a treatise from his Montanist period, *De pudicitia*, Tertullian acknowledges Montanism as threatening ecclesiastical hierarchical authority: "The church is not a conclave of bishops but the spirit manifested through a spiritual person" (21.17). Despite this, Montanism almost gained ecclesiastical recognition, as Tertullian testifies. The evident attraction for North African Christians of a Spirit-directed church is apparent in the fact that Montanism was still acceptable in North Africa as late as 203 C.E., a decade after its rejection in Rome. If we place Montanist dissent in the context of pervasive North African Christian interest in the guidance of the Spirit, Montanists appear less as dissidents in relation to Catholic Christianity than as faithful to one of African Christianity's strongest values.

Frequently, dissenting Christian interpretations—and groups of earnest and committed people—can be reconstructed only from the writings of their victorious opponents. However, Tertullian himself became an adherent of the "New Prophecy," and it is primarily from the writings of his Montanist period that one can reconstruct the interests, values, and practices of Montanists. An ecumenical perspective reveals the North African Montanists as a group committed to maintaining what they legitimately considered the core of African Christianity (Ash 1976).

Was Montanism in North Africa a separate church? Was it a "holy club" within North African congregations? It was apparently neither a heresy nor a schism, but it does appear to have been an enthusiastic and intransigent group characterized by adherence to a stricter discipline as well as to ongoing revelation as part of the Spirit's present activity. According to his own testimony, Tertullian was attracted both by the discipline and by Montanists' attention to the present prophetic activity of the Holy Spirit. Women prophets were associated with Montanus; before she died in 179 C.E., the prophet Maximilla, speaking as the voice of the Spirit, said: "I am driven as a wolf from the sheep. I am not a wolf; I am word, spirit, and power." Montanism continued to be referred to in writings until the eighth century, but no development can be discerned past the third century C.E.

In discipline, Montanists insisted on stricter and more frequent fasts than were customary for Catholic Christians. In addition to more demanding fasts, Montanists were expected to practice the xerophagy, or dry fast, two weeks (five days each) a year. There may be a connection between Montanist food practices and their interest in ecstatic prophecy and visions, both of which can be stimulated by fasting. Moreover, Montanists protested an increasing institutionalization of prescribed fasts, insisting on the time-honored practice of tailoring ascetic practices both to individual abil ity and to the goal for which the fast was undertaken. Montanists preferred self-discipline to external discipline, or legislation of common—and therefore necessarily nondemanding—fasts for the whole church. Tertullian notes that Catholics compared Montanists' fasting practices to those of pagans in that they lacked the element of communal, externally imposed discipline.

Montanists also proscribed second marriages, even when one of the partners had died. Tertullian's treatise *De monogamia*, connects insistence on one marriage to belief in one God, claiming that, although not to be found in scripture, "the Paraclete has taught" the restriction of marriage to one partner. Finally, Montanists rejected the prerogative of flight in times of persecution, a much-debated issue in North Africa. Claiming that because persecution represents "the just judgment of the Lord," Tertullian said that Christians must not endeavor to escape it. He especially deplored "persons in authority" taking to flight. However, the widespread rejection of his interpretation of Christians' duties is suggested by the fact that, as far as we know, no African bishop was martyred before Cyprian suffered martyrdom in the Decian persecution of the 250s C.E. Cyprian himself fled in the first wave of persecution, understanding this action as nothing more or less than judicious and in the best interests of the church for which he was responsible. Yet the intransigent and heroic Christianity represented by Montanist belief and practice needs to be understood in the context of an indigenous church whose origins come to light in the account of the uncompromising and joyful Scillitan martyrs, who departed to their death saying, "Thanks be to God! Today we are martyrs in heaven!"

Donatists

Like Montanists, Donatists differed from North African Catholics not in theological doctrine but in values and ecclesiastical loyalties. Originating in the persecution of Diocletian at the beginning of the fourth century, the Donatist church was, by Augustine's time, the majority Christian church in North Africa. By the end of the fourth century, a long history of dispute, debate, and violence separated Catholics and Donatists.

Donatists alleged that a Catholic bishop, Caecilian, was ordained in 311 C.E. by Felix of Aptunga, who had become a *traditore* by surrendering the holy scriptures to authorities of the Roman state during the persecution. His ordination was condemned by eighty Numidian bishops, but recognized by a greater majority of North African bishops. Throughout the fourth century the schism widened as intermittent persecution by imperial forces polarized the division between a "persecuted church" and a "persecuting church." At the beginning of the fifth century when public debates by Catholics and Donatists conducted under imperial sponsorship failed to bring the desired "unity," imperial laws were enacted against Donatists. Donatist clergy and lay people were required to become Catholic; Catholics were given Donatist property; Catholic bishops were charged with identifying Donatists who declined to transfer their allegiance to the Catholic Church, and Donatist clergy and lay people of all classes were fined for refusing to join Catholics. Formally, this was the end of the Donatist church, but underground Donatism persisted in North Africa until the Christian church in Africa was destroyed in the seventh and eighth centuries.

Did Donatists, like Montanists, perpetuate some ancient and thoroughly African religious values and attitudes? Donatism was the majority interpretation of Christianity on North African soil. And Donatists apparently held to ideas of ritual purity and the danger of contamination that can be related directly to the constant threat, and frequent reality, of martyrdom in the time before Constantine extended legitimacy and support to Christianity in 312 C.E. As confessors had rejected the assimilation of Christianity to the Roman state, so Donatists refused to participate in a Catholic church they believed to be tainted by apostasy and actively engaged in spreading contamination through its sacraments.

Donatists also valued a self-governing North African church, autonomous in relation to the Roman empire. They seem to have supported the campaigns of two Moorish counts—Firmus in 372–375 C.E., and Gildo in the 390s—to rule Africa. Augustine mocked the Donatists on grounds that reveal his awareness of their nationalism. He ridiculed their view that they alone—a tiny branch of Christianity in relation to a world church—could claim to be a "pure" church. Their appeal to a time before the empire and the church were partners in governing society exposes their unwillingness to reconcile the contradiction between a Catholic Church in partnership with the formerly persecuting Roman state and their self-identification with the local martyrs of the earlier North African church. The radical fringe of Donatism, the Circumcellians, who were especially active in the province of Numidia, dramatized this identification with African martyrs by their use of the Scillitan martyrs' cry, "Deo gratias." They sacked and whitewashed Catholic churches, captured, tortured, and murdered

Catholics, and even, in states of ecstatic frenzy, flung themselves to death over cliffs—martyrs, in their view, for Donatist Christianity.

Donatist spirituality and ritual practice were partly a protest against a Catholic Church that had become a venue for social upward mobility and privilege. Donatists criticized Augustine's acceptance of the church as a *corpus permixtus*, in which blatant sinners and "convalescent" Christians rubbed elbows. Augustine acknowledged, in *De cat. rud.* 25.48:

> One who enters [the church] is bound to see drunkards, misers, tricksters, gamblers, adulterers, fornicators, people wearing amulets, clients of sorcerers, astrologers . . . the same crowds who press into the churches on Christian festivals also fill the theatres on pagan holidays.

Augustine's favorite metaphor for the Christian church was the parable of the wheat and the tares lying together on the threshing-room floor until authoritatively separated on the day of judgment. By contrast, Donatists invoked scriptural metaphors that refer to the church as bride of Christ "without spot or wrinkle." Tyconius, a Donatist theologian, was the first to use a metaphor of the church in the world later made famous by Augustine: the two cities, radically separated by their loyalty either to this world or to God.

Donatists were well aware that their debates with Catholics did not occur in a situation in which political power was evenly distributed. Identifying the "true church" as the persecuted church, Donatists cited scripture to argue that Christ did not use force. Augustine reports the Donatist Petilian as saying: "'Blessed are they which are persecuted for righteousness' sake, for theirs is the kingdom of heaven.' You are not blessed, but you make us martyrs to be blessed" (*Ad Petilianus* 72).

Repetitiously citing "unity" as a greater and more essential value than purity of sacraments, Augustine gave an elaborate rationale for coercion of Donatists. His *Epistle* 185 (417 C.E.) to Boniface, tribune and count in Africa, enumerates a sad list of rationales for coercion. Initially opposed to coercion, Augustine writes, he became convinced of its usefulness when Christians who had been forced to join the Catholics testified that they are grateful to have been shown the error of Donatism. Citing the forcible conversion of the apostle Paul, Augustine outlined a method for coercion: "As in the case of the Apostle Paul . . . let them acknowledge in him Christ first compelling and afterward teaching, first striking and afterward consoling" (22). In the face of the established Roman virtue of tolerance, Augustine argued that there are situations in which tolerance is nothing more than laziness and negligence. In fact, Augustine concluded,

If you were to see the effects of the peace of Christ: the joyful throngs, their eagerness to hear and sing hymns and to receive the word of God, the well-attended, happy meetings; the sentiments of many among them, their great grief in recalling past error, their joy in contemplating the known truth . . . you would say that it would have been excessively cruel for all these to be abandoned to eternal loss and to the torments of everlasting fire. . . . (32)

Some of Augustine's rationalizations for coercion have had a very long history of use in situations far removed from that of the minority North African Catholic Church.

The theological consanguinity of Donatism and Catholic Christianity is evident in the fact that Donatist laypeople were admitted to the Catholic Church without rebaptism, and Donatist clergy retained their former ranks and offices within the Catholic Church after a brief period of repentance. Although theological differences between Donatists and Catholics were insignificant, the *religious* values and therefore the spirituality of Donatists and Catholics differed. A full picture of Donatist spirituality cannot be reconstructed from the "fragments that remain" of this vigorous movement. However, if one respects Donatists' intense attention to ritual purity, more can be detected in Donatism than the belligerent and obstinate self-isolation described by Augustine.

Moreover, the Donatists' fierce protection of Christian sacraments was directly in line with the martyr-bishop Cyprian's insistence that those who had been baptized in dissident Christian groups must be rebaptized upon joining the Catholic Church. Donatists rightfully claimed to be the faithful successors of Cyprian's views. Augustine was very aware that his claim that the sacraments belong to Christ and are not tainted by the imperfection of the minister was in conflict not only with Cyprian's insistence on rebaptism but also with Tertullian, who had been the first to declare non-Catholic baptism invalid. Tertullian had argued, in De baptismo, that because the Holy Spirit was not present in "heretical" baptism, it could not be effective.

Augustine's treatise De baptismo against the Donatists begins by acknowledging that Donatists are citing Cyprian's authority for their belief that the sacraments must be maintained in purity, but he argues: "The authority of Cyprian does not alarm me, because I am reassured by his humility." Cyprian, who died before there was a final resolution of issues surrounding rebaptism, was more concerned, Augustine insisted, about the *unity* of the church than about his own views on rebaptism. His final appeal, in De baptismo, dismissed a view of Christianity he had come to see as provincial, for that of a Catholic Church:

how much more readily and constantly should we prefer, either to the authority of a single bishop, or to the council of a single province, the rule that has been established by the statutes of the universal church.

Manichaeans in North Africa

Mani, a Persian who called himself the "apostle of Jesus Christ," claimed to offer a revelation that superseded that of Christ's earthly teachings. He taught that the Holy Spirit, promised three centuries before, had finally descended in him. Mani was martyred by crucifixion in 276 C.E. at the instigation of Zoroastrian priests. Manichaeism was a missionary religion with claims to universality. Within Mani's lifetime it had spread beyond Mesopotamia to Iran and adjoining parts of the Roman empire. Advancing along commercial routes, Manichaean groups were also in Arabia, Armenia, Syria, Asia Minor, including Palestine, the Balkans, Italy, Spain, and Gaul. Manichaeism spread from Egypt to North Africa at an early date, nearly twenty years earlier than the first reference to Manichaeism in Rome.

Manichaeism was syncretistic, incorporating features of Buddhism, Zoroastrianism, Taoism, Confucianism, and Christianity. It was suspect in the Roman empire, however, not only for its ideas but even for its place of origin—Persia, the third-century "California" of new religious movements. And this most persecuted of heresies was not accepted by the religions with which it sought to affiliate, perhaps largely because Mani claimed to have the only true interpretation of each. Despite its claims to possess Truth, the virtual absence of polemical literature in Manichaeism is striking in comparison with the volume of anti-Manichaean literature.

Latin translations of Manichaean texts appeared at the end of the third century, less than a century after the first North African Christian writings in Latin. The aesthetic qualities of the great tomes which contained Mani's teachings were not the least of Manichaeism's attractions; they were inscribed with graceful calligraphy and lavishly illustrated. According to tradition, Mani himself was a skillful painter.

Only twenty years or so after Mani's death, sometime between 31 March 297 and the same date in 302, the emperor Diocletian dispatched the first prohibition of Manichaeism to Julianus, the proconsul of Africa. The rescript demanded that "Manichees and magicians and their sacred books" be burned. Yet, in the West, the fourth century was the time of the greatest numerical and geographical development—and the greatest persecution—of Manichaeism. Following Diocletian's edict of 297 outlawing Manichaeism, emperors throughout the fourth century reiterated and attempted to enforce the edict—Constantine in 326, Valentinian in 372, and Theodosius in 381. Yet Manichaeism survived both the Arian Vandal rulers of fifth-century North Africa, and Justinian's (sixth century) reconquest of North Africa, which brought renewed Catholic persecutions of Manichaeans. As late as 724, Pope Gregory II cautioned against the ordination of Africans who had fled to Italy from Islamic invaders because many of them had strong connections with Manichaeism. In North Africa, traces of Manichaeism can be identified until Christianity itself was extinguished by Islamic invasions.

At the time of Augustine's encounter with the Manichaeans, Manichaeism had been established in North Africa for almost a century. It flourished within Catholic congregations, claiming to be an intellectually sophisticated and rigorously ascetic version of Catholic Christianity, a Christianity of the inquiring mind. In his *Letter* 236, Augustine acknowledged that one of his subdeacons had been a Manichaean Hearer for years without being detected by the Catholic congregation to which he ministered. Differences between Catholics and Manichaeans seem to have been less evident on location than in retrospect. Both the popularity of Manichaeism and its compatibility with Catholic Christianity made it especially difficult to extirpate from North Africa.

Ironically, Augustine himself was repeatedly and throughout his life accused of Manichaeism. In his youth, he had been a Manichaean Hearer for nine years; his *Confessions* describe both his attraction to Manichaeism and his subsequent disenchantment. His ordination to Catholic priesthood was delayed while suspicions that he had not decisively broken with Manichaeism were investigated. Moreover, as a Catholic priest and bishop, his commitment to ascetic monasticism, and his teaching that marriage and sex are inevitably implicated in the transmission of original sin repeatedly sparked accusations that he had never completely departed from the religion of his youth. Perhaps his personal vendetta against Manichaeism was motivated at least in part by his eagerness to demonstrate his orthodoxy. His harshness toward the priest who simultaneously discharged his duties as a Catholic priest and participated in a Manichaean cell also witnesses to Augustine's need to demonstrate his lack of sympathy for the Manichaeans.

Manichaeans were dualists, positing a kingdom of light and a kingdom of darkness eternally at war with each other. Their primary appeal to the young Augustine lay in their clear and satisfying answer to the problem of the origin of evil. The kingdom of darkness, eternally at odds with the kingdom of light, was the cause of pain and evil; it was also the home of bodies and the natural world. However, Manichaeans' metaphysical dualism was tempered by their recognition that "in experience," the kingdom of darkness and the kingdom of light—the material and the spiritual worlds—were intertwined. This meant that all material things contain particles of spiritual light and thus are sacred. Manichaeans believed that these particles of light are sentient, suffering in their entrapment in the material world of bodies and objects, yearning to breathe free of their prisons and reunite with their spiritual homeland.

The suffering of all things did not, for the Manichaeans, remain an abstract notion; rather it was vivid and concrete. For example, the *Cologne Codex* relates that before Mani organized his own religion, while he was still a member of the Elchasaios sect, he was forced to do agricultural work. As he worked he found that "blood oozed from the places where the plants had been hurt by the blows of the sickle. They also cried out with a human voice because of the blows they received" (Lieu 1985, 34).

Manichaean literature resounds with the poignant longing of the light particles to return to the Kingdom of Light, a longing believed to be at its most acute in human beings. "The drama . . . centers on the redemption of the Light Elements which have been swallowed by the archons of Darkness and have thus become mixed and sullied" (Lieu 1985, 14). One Manichaean understanding of Jesus—an understanding documented only in North Africa—was that of *"Jesus patibilis,"* Jesus as the prototypical and quintessential living soul (*viva anima*), perennially trapped and suffering in the world of the senses. Augustine quotes the Manichaean Faustus's description of the suffering Jesus: "The Holy Spirit, by his influence and spiritual infusion, makes the earth conceive and bring forth the mortal Jesus, who, as hanging from every tree, is the life and salvation of humanity" (20.11).

From Augustine's perspective, North African Manichees displayed a virtually neurasthenic sensitivity to all kinds of sufferings—human, animal, plant, and mineral.

Manichaeism was also a highly disciplined way of life. Augustine is the source of a rich store of information about Manichaean practices in North Africa. These must be described under two categories: those required of Hearers, and those expected only of the "Perfect" or Elect. Regulations for both were designed to avoid actions that might harm the light particles or further entrench them in matter. For Manichaeans, nothing short of the redemption of God was at stake: God is Light, trapped in the material world. The release of the light will actively serve to speed the "Future Moment" in which, the liberation of the Light nearly completed, the material world will be abandoned to its native evil and warfare. The faithful will be translated to the kingdom of light, there to participate in and enjoy this blissful reward—Hearers at the right hand of the triumphant Jesus, while the Elect are transformed into angels.

Hearers lived as fully functioning members of secular society. They were permitted to marry, but encouraged not to bear children. Their duties to the sect consisted primarily of a "soul service" in which they cared for the elect, providing and preparing their daily ritual meal. The *Kephalaia of the Teacher*, a fourth-century Egyptian document, describes the connection of food practices to the release of the light particles: "The alms which pass over to the Elect are made like many Icons, and they are purified, and they depart to the Country of the Living" (Wimbush 1990, 205). At their death, Hearers could expect to be reincarnated, and the body to which they were reassigned was contingent on the quality and faithfulness of their service to the elect.

The practices of the Elect were considerably more strenuous. They were contained in the "Three Seals" that Augustine described in *De moribus manichaeorum*: the Seal of the Mouth, the Seal of the Hands, and the Seal of the Breast. What leaves the mouth as well as what enters is governed by the Seal of the Mouth: blasphemous speech was prohibited, as was the eating of meat and drinking of wine. Vegetarianism was prescribed because the bodies of animals contain fewer light particles than the plants. Animals ingest light by feeding on plants, but a portion of this light was believed to be obliterated in the transfer. Wine was forbidden because it induces intoxication and the forgetfulness of one's real self and home in the kingdom of light, a forgetfulness that Manichaean teachings, doctrines, hymns, and prayers resisted.

The Seal of the Hands stipulates that the faithful must not perform any task that might harm the particles of light. By this Seal, they were "forbidden to till the soil, or to pluck fruit, or to harvest any plant or to kill any animal, no matter how small" (Lieu 1985, 20). Bathing was also forbidden: Manichees emphasized the pollution of the water by dirt from the body rather than the cleansing of the body. The Seal of the Breast forbids sexual intercourse in that its result is the propagation of more flesh in which light particles are painfully enslaved.

In the West, the ritual practices of Manichaeans were conducted in private homes. Once a day Hearers and Elect gathered, the Hearers to prepare and witness the meal—in North Africa it was called "eucharist"—consumed by the Elect. At this solemn ritual, the beautiful and haunting Manichaean hymn cycles and psalms were also sung. A weekly confession of sins—Hearers to Elect, and Elect to Elect—completed Manichaeans' ritual practice. Different religious sensibilities underlie Augustine's theology and that of the Manichaeans. In contrast to the Manichaeans' "emotional" view of the suffering universe, Augustine argued in his *Epistle of Manichaeus Called Fundamental* that the only "just judgment" results from a mind "composed," rational, and free of emotion. Augustine's idea of God's participation in the universe is interdependent with his view of suffering. Augustine's God is "present by the power of divinity, for administering and ruling all things, undefilably, inviolably, incorruptibly, 'without any connection with them.'" According to Augustine, the Manichaeans' God, by contrast, was "everywhere mixed up in heaven, in earth, in all bodies, dry and moist, in all sorts of flesh, in all seeds of trees, herbs, humans and animals . . . fettered, oppressed, polluted (*Nature of the Good* 46.44). The Manichaeans' God was intimately and integrally engaged in the world and its processes, deeply interior to the universe.

The continuity of Manichaeism with North African Christianity, and therefore the attractiveness of Manichaeism in North Africa, can be seen in its strict discipline and in its clear distinction of spiritual from physical. Manichaeism's claim to a revelation beyond scripture is also reminiscent of the Montanists' interest in the present prophetic activity of the Holy Spirit. Moreover, Manichaeism was a martyr church, the most persecuted of any Christian sect. Clearly, these strong connections with the earliest African Christianity contributed to its popularity in North Africa.

North African Catholics in the Roman Period

North Africa was the volatile location for the emergence of a constantly contested consensus on issues of ecclesiastical organization and order. Although the subject of this essay is not the practical matters of church authority and discipline that North African Christians struggled over, the spiritualities of these Christians cannot be treated in separation from these struggles. I have endeavored to demonstrate the continuity of these controversies with both the earliest Christianity and with indigenous religion in North Africa.

One group of Christians remains to be discussed—North African Catholics, especially as represented by their most prolific and influential bishop, Augustine of Hippo, pervasively affected the subsequent development of Christianity in the West to our own day. Augustine inherited North African Christian emphases and interests, but his sense of a broader world and a Catholic Church that could claim universality was the result of his sojourn as a successful young teacher of rhetoric in the imperial capital of Milan. Augustine revised characteristic North African Christian emphases and interests in the direction of bringing them into accord with a world Christianity and thus transmitted North African Christianity to the medieval West. Augustine was also the influential articulator of a model of Christian spirituality that has become the dominant model of Western Christianity.

Among Christian authors of the first centuries of the Christian era, Augustine is unique in his presentation of theological ideas in the context of his own life and experience. He was the first Christian author to demonstrate how his religious sensibilities were formed by people and events. His *Confessions* details the long and circuitous path by which his intellectual quest and his experience in relation to family, friends, and lovers brought him to understand God's activity in his life. Pursuing sex, professional success, and social position with all his energy, he came at the end of this exhausting agenda to understand his complete dependence on God's grace for salvation and nourishment. He named this agenda *concupiscentia*, a compulsive grasping at every object that crossed his path in the fear that something would be missed. Intellectual questions such as the origin of evil intermingled with personal unhappiness to lead him, at the age of thirty-two, to a more cosmopolitan version of the Catholic Church of his North African childhood.

The central moment in Augustine's autobiography, the moment for which the book is justly famous, is that of his conversion. Curiously, it was not a moment of intellectual insight; intellectual insight preceded and informed the moment of his conversion of the will, but it was not sufficient for this. Nor was it a moment of belief or religious ecstasy. Augustine narrates this experience quite explicitly as a conversion from compulsive sexual activity to continence.

Throughout the *Confessions*, prefiguring and mirroring his conversion account, Augustine described himself as alternatively distracted and dispersed among temporary pleasures or gathered and collected in a disciplined "return" to himself and to God. His model of the spiritual life as recollection has become the dominant model of Western Christian subjectivity and spirituality and has, in the twentieth century passed into secular culture in the form of numerous varieties of psychotherapy and secular spirituality. The model is one of centering, of arresting the hemorrhage of energy and attention that flows out of the self onto other human beings and objects of all sorts, and pulling that energy within—collecting, focusing, centering. Augustine's clearest definition of the model occurs in the *Confessions* 11.29:

> I have been spilled and scattered among times whose order I do not know; my thoughts, the innermost bowels of my soul, are torn apart with the crowding tumults of variety, and so it will be until all together I can flow into you [God], purified and molten by the fire of your love.

Continence was the key to changing not only the course of Augustine's life but also the direction of his longing and passion. But continence was more than a resolution of his compulsive sexuality. It was also symbolic of a unified and unifying affection and attention. Thus, continence defined the form and dynamic of the spiritual life for Augustine and, as a result of the strength and beauty of his description, for Western Christianity.

Augustine was ordained priest by congregational acclamation, and subsequently bishop, in the town of Hippo Regius as he and several companions were passing through the town on their return to North Africa. From this institutional base, he became a major figure in the translation of Christianity from a persecuted sect to the official religion of the Roman empire. Augustine's mature theology was formed in the heat of polemical struggle against the alternative interpretations of Christian faith that flourished in North Africa, especially Donatism, Manichaeism, and, later in his career, Pelagianism. Each of these controversies centered on conflicting interpretations of the human being and thus had, as we have seen in discussing Donatism and Manichaeism, implications for spirituality.

In Augustine's conflict with Pelagius, and later with Pelagius's younger advocate, Julian of Eclanum, Augustine articulated his sense of human beings as helpless infants, utterly dependent on God's grace for the accomplishment of every good act. Pelagius taught that the grace bestowed on each human being in her/his creation was a sufficient basis for accomplishing good. He advocated Christian adulthood, urging that people take responsibility for their actions and actively endeavor to perform the good. "Since righteousness is possible," he wrote to Demetrias, a prospective nun, "righteousness is obligatory."

Augustine saw in Pelagius's teaching a fatal temptation to Christians to depend on their own efforts rather than on God's grace. Augustine's development of the doctrine of original sin responded to Pelagius's optimistic view of the inherent goodness of human nature. Moreover, Augustine understood the inevitable undermining of human goodness and happiness not simply as a flaw, wound, or weakness as Tertullian had named it—vitium—but as peccatum, sin, a strand of sinfulness intimately woven into the character of each human being. In the last decade of his life, in his encounter with Julian of Eclanum, he identified the transmission of original sin as occurring at the moment of conception, an analysis that subsequently contributed to an institutionalized lack of esteem for human sexuality as a gift of God.

Augustine's own experience of sexuality as a "tyrant," in Plato's expression, and his much later identification of original sin as transmitted by sexual activity is strangely dissonant with his lifelong committed effort to understand human bodies as integral and permanent to human persons. As he studied the scriptures and considered the doctrines of creation, incarnation, and resurrection of the body. He recognized that the classical philosophical description of human beings as hierarchically layered parts—that is, rational soul on top, then irrational soul, and body at the bottom—could not be integrated with those Christian doctrines that insisted on human bodies (both of male and female) as the good gift of a generous God.

Augustine's integration of body as essential to human beings and the condition of human salvation incorporated Tertullian's strong sense of the Christian sacraments as conjunctions of material and spiritual. In the context of conflict with Marcion, who believed that the body was accidental and incidental to human being and could not participate in the salvation of the soul, Tertullian had written:

> To such a degree is the flesh the pivot of salvation, that since by it the soul becomes linked with God, it is the flesh which makes possible the soul's election by God. For example, the flesh is washed that the soul may be made spotless; the flesh is anointed that the soul may be consecrated; the flesh is signed that the soul too may be protected; the flesh is overshadowed by the imposition of the hand that the soul may be illuminated by the Spirit; the flesh feeds on the body and blood of Christ so that the soul may become fat with God. (*De carne christi* 4)

Incorporating this strong view of the role of the body into the Christian faith, Augustine contributed the philosophical rationale for the body being an integral and permanent feature of the human being. This contribution further supported an enriched—and now institutionalized in the universal church—view of the Christian sacraments as a material vehicle of efficacious grace. Augustine described a complex theological system in which the union of body and soul in a single human being became the model and exemplar of the union of Christ and the Church as made present—localized—in the union of spiritual and material in the sacraments. He thus articulated—and his institutional authority stabilized—a strongly corporate spirituality practiced within the liturgy of the Catholic Church.

Augustine pictured all human beings as engaged in a long struggle toward the differing objects of each person's longing, desire, and delight. He distinguished the human race into two groups according to the objects of their desire. Those who belong to the "earthly City" pursue the powerfully attractive objects of sex, power, and possessions; and those of the "City of God" journey on pilgrimage toward the ultimate completion and fulfillment of human perfection in the resurrection of the body. Yearning for the moment beyond time and space when the resurrected body will be reunited with the redeemed soul, Christian pilgrims struggle across time toward a happiness and pleasure never fully present in the transitory world of present human existence. Briefly rewarded and nourished by glimpses of that future satisfaction, Christians journey in faith toward a moment when, Augustine wrote, the "eyes of the body" will somehow gaze on the incorporeal God.

Conclusion

This survey of Roman North African Christianity has endeavored to demonstrate the convergence of alternative interpretations of Christian belief and practice in the theology of Augustine of Hippo. Modified and philosophically examined in Augustine's writings, Augustine's interest in human bodies, in the activity of the Spirit symbolized in the sacraments, and in his acknowledged fanciful picture of the completion and fulfillment of the work of human salvation in the resurrection of the body form the characteristic interests of North African Christianity. It was Augustine who inherited, interpreted in the context of his own time, and transmitted these interests to Western Christianity. Both his model of individual spirituality as centering—returning to God through returning to self—and his construction of corporate spirituality as focused by the sacraments have become characteristic of Catholic Christianity. This mainstreaming of African spirituality was, however, not without loss, as lively dissident Christian groups were increasingly marginalized and gradually faded from the historical record. Ironically, it is because of this incorporation in "universal" Catholic belief and practice that the roots of Western spirituality in the characteristic interests and concerns of ancient North Africa have been forgotten. Western Christianity in all its modern branches owes a tremendous debt to the passionate spirituality of a Christianity defined by martyrdom and the ongoing activity of the Holy Spirit. North African Christian spirituality was redefined when martyrdom was no longer a threat. It was redefined to meet the demand of the corporate spiritual nourishment through the practice of sacraments and individual spirituality. It aimed at centering of attention and affection in longing and a delight that, as Augustine said, can be trusted to "order the soul" (*De musica* 6.11.29), for "my weight is my love; by it I am carried wherever I am carried" (*Confessions* 11.13).

References

Ash, James L., Jr.
    1976   "The Decline of Prophecy in the Early Church." *Theological Studies* 37, no. 2 (June).

Bergman, Martin S.
1992   *In the Shadow of Moloch*. New York: Columbia University Press.
Charles-Picard, G.
1954   *Les religions de l'Afrique antique*. Paris.
Frend, W. H. C.
1988   "The End of Byzantine North Africa: Some Evidence of Transi-
            tions." In *Archeology and History in the Study of Early Christian-
            ity*. London: Variorum Reprints.
Hopkins, Keith
1983   "Murderous Games." In *Death and Renewal*. Sociological Studies
            in Roman History 2. Cambridge: Cambridge University Press.
Kader, Aicha Ben Abed, and David Soren
1987   *Carthage: A Mosaic of Ancient Tunesia*. New York: American
            Museum of Natural History.
Lieu, Samuel N. C.
1985   *Manichaeism in the Later Roman Empire and Medieval China: A
            Historical Survey*. Manchester: Manchester University Press.
Miles, Margaret R.
1979   *Augustine on the Body*. Missoula, Mont.: Scholars Press.
1992   *Desire and Delight, A New Reading of Augustine's "Confessions."*
            New York: Crossroad.
Musurillo, Herbert, ed.
1972   *Acts of the Christian Martyrs*. Oxford: Clarendon Press.
Pedley, John Griffiths
1980   *New Light on Ancient Carthage*. Ann Arbor: University of Michi-
            gan.
Reinach, S.
1911   "Le rire rituel." *Revue de l'Université de Bruxelles*.
Rousselle, Aline
1988   *Porneia, Desire and the Body in Antiquity*. Oxford: Basil Black-
            well.
Saxer, Victor
1969   *Vie liturgique et quotidienne à Carthage vers milieu du IIIe siècle*.
            Vatican City: Pontificio Istituto di Archeologia Cristiana.
1980   *Morts, martyrs, reliques en Afrique chrétienne aux premiers siècles*.
            Paris: Beauchesne.
Stager, Lawrence W.
1980   "The Rite of Child Sacrifice at Carthage." In *New Light on
            Ancient Carthage*, ed. John Griffiths Pedley. Ann Arbor: Univer-
            sity of Michigan.
Wimbush, Vincent L., ed.
1990   *Ascetic Behavior in Greco-Roman Antiquity: A Sourcebook*. Min-
            neapolis: Fortress Press.

17

Asante Catholicism: An African Appropriation of the Roman Catholic Religion

PASHINGTON OBENG

THE FOLLOWING DISCUSSION, while addressing the Asante integration of Roman Catholicism into the lives of Christians in Ghana, also highlights how they as actors employ both Asante topography, gestural idioms, and Christianity for self-definition and community building. In the process of living out their faith, these Christians become social critics and religio-cultural architects as they redraw the contours of both the Roman Catholic and Asante cultures.

With its large membership of over seventy million, a highly trained local and foreign clergy and lay apostolate, and rapidly expanding ministries, African Roman Catholicism has become a powerful religious and social reality in Africa (Hastings 1989, xi). It has a commanding lead in professionalism, financial support (Hastings 1979, 261), and a strong hierarchically structured institution. In its postconciliar movement, the church has aggressively embarked on vernacular liturgy, healing services, publications in local languages and in English, scripture translation, retreat centers, social concerns, and intense training of local clergy and other church personnel. The church is also making serious efforts to combine indigenous African religio-political elements with Christianity. The church has come to see itself as "one in diversity" whereby "Catholicity," or "universality," does not mean uniformity (Abega 1978, 597–605). Christ's incarnation becomes concrete through every people's God-given ways within which all humanity can have access to him.

The joyous and solemn celebrations of Christian festivals, liturgical renewals such as that of Ndzon-Melen in Cameroon, Benedictine and Cistercian monasteries in Dzogbegan in Togo, Bouake in the Ivory Coast, Koubri in Burkina Faso, and Lumbwa in Kenya have become the focus of scholarly inquiry (Becken 1976; DeCraemer 1977; Abega 1978; Shorter

1973; Hastings 1979, 1989). The African church has developed charismatic renewal groups and pilgrimage and healing centers by tapping indigenous religious experience and Christianity, especially Catholic mysticism, to help mold the identity of the African Christian. Factors that have given birth to such developments in African Christianity are vast and varied. Under both external and internal stimuli, Africans draw on their world-views and values to respond to the new cultural and religious circumstances. Asante Catholicism is therefore a specific African response to world Christianity by which the Asante of Ghana define themselves and make meaning of life as well as contribute to religious transformation.

The sheer numbers of Catholics in Ghana and the apparent deterioration of appearances of indigenous shrines and temples have led casual observers to conclude that Christianity has dominated the indigenous religions, customs, and attitudes of the Asante of Ghana. The following essay seeks to shed light on how Catholicism has come into continuity with Asante religious and cultural history. Thus, we will briefly touch on the significance of healing in the Akan understanding of health and wholeness and the importance of Asante dance within Catholicism.

In order to understand some basic features about Roman Catholicism as a faith that was brought by missionaries to Ghana, it is important to touch on some principles that have governed its spread. In responding to a plural landscape of religions, cultures, languages, and peoples with their communicative imperative, Catholicism has developed an institution and polity for controlling ethics, knowledge, and identity of all who convert to that faith (Hefner 1993, 25–35). The management and standardization of belief and practice are accomplished through the following: the church defines the boundaries and membership of its religious community, establishes the relationship between religion and political power, and promotes over-arching ethos among its pan-ethnic community.

Roman Catholicism in Ghana was a latecomer on the missionary scene after many false starts between the fifteenth and nineteenth centuries. However, it restarted after the 1880s under the S.A.M. (Society of African Missions) and later local agents and has now become the largest denomination in Ghana with about three million members.

The Asante Diocese, which is the focus of this paper, is one of nine dioceses in the country and has a membership of over four hundred thousand, with Bishop Peter Sarpong, a social anthropologist and an Asante, as its diocesan pastor. The Asante are an Akan-speaking people of Ghana, West Africa. They occupy mainly the Asante region, but some of them are found in other parts of the country such as the eastern, western, central, and Brong Ahafo regions. The Kumasi Diocese covers an area of 9,700 square miles and has hospitals and clinics, agricultural projects, literacy programs, a press, seminaries, schools, clergy, sisters and brothers, nuns, and a strong lay apostolate.

Postconciliar Asante Catholicism has become vibrant because the leadership is seeking to fuse Asante ways of life with Christian ritual practice. In spite of Vatican II's encouragement for local churches to incorporate their indigenous values into Christianity to enrich the latter, such "culture building" or reforging of values has become a delicate dance. It is a delicate dance because the Asante Diocese, like others in Africa, tries to appropriate and articulate a Roman Catholic religion by retaining its canonical links with the Vatican, thus having communion with the universal church, while at the same time remaining authentically African. In that sense Roman Catholicism becomes an Asante religion since it is integrated into Asante religious history and practice. It is worth noting that as the two religious traditions encounter each other there arise areas of conflict, innovation, and accommodation. Such innovations, conflicts, and accommodations result from the fact that Catholicism enters a well-structured religious and cultural system and both traditions seem to have some correspondences and divergences between their form and structure.

Apparent Convergence

Indigenous religious life and practice involve ritual and sacrifice, protective amulets, herbs, incantations, the use of sacred space and time, color, and bodily gestures to convey religious meaning. The Catholic Church with its "liturgical color of vestments . . . , holy water, medals, guardian angels, prayers for the dead" provided some "symbolic and structural continuity" (Hastings 1979, 71) with Asante indigenous religious experience. The Hebrew scriptures contain examples of sacred space, place, and time. Mountains, desert spots, and Jerusalem were sacralized as places where God and humans encountered each other. Such pilgrimage centers resonate with African notions of sacred groves, sacred mountains, rocks, towns, and shrines. Thus, when the worshipers select a hilly and rocky place to consecrate it for healing, worship services, and pilgrimage (such as Buoho near Kumasi), they are extrapolating from both the Bible and their indigenous religious experience, using their imagination to create a new phenomenon to meet their psychological, social, and spiritual needs. Despite the apparent congruence between the externals of Asante indigenous ways and Christian values and ritual practice, the following discussion will touch on how there are divergences in content and referents within the congruencies.

For our purposes, we will examine an Asante Catholic healing center and their celebration of Corpus Christi.

Postconciliar Liturgical Renewal

Prior to Vatican II, traditional Catholic mass was said in Latin, starting with prayers, praise in the *Gloria,* and repentance for sin in *Confiteor, miseratur* (Abega 1978). In the area of religious singing, the canticles and songs written in Latin with European melodies were hopelessly meaningless to the local people. Moreover, the priest stood apart from the worshipers in location, language, and the meaning of what he did. The congregation appeared passive as mere spectators. The liturgical style was alien to the worshipers. But in this postconciliar period, under the Asante Diocesan Liturgical Committee, the church has translated songs into Asante Twi, composed new songs with Christian images and personalities and Asante rhythmic melodies and idioms (Obeng 1996). By so doing, religious singing has been brought within the reach of the African Christian. Asante mass is now celebrated differently.

In response to the spirit of Vatican II's *Sacrosanctum concilium,* the Ghana Bishops Conference, including Bishop Peter Sarpong of Kumasi, have put forward the following:

> The mystery of the incarnation demands that Christianity be inculturated. . . . The Christian faith should be implanted in all cultures. In view of this, African thought patterns, life-style, dress, ways of celebrating, art, music, preferences for colour and materials, etc., must be reflected in our being church and incorporated in our Christian liturgy, catechesis and theologies.

The bishops further assert that the African for many years is "still not at home with Christianity," since in its "theologies, spirituality, style of worship, prayers, rites, structures, and even architecture" it is European.

The Asante Diocese under Bishop Sarpong has translated liturgical rites and the Bible into Asante Twi; uses Asante symbols in liturgical celebrations; has composed and employs liturgical songs based on local tunes and idioms; and makes use of local musical instruments such as drums, flutes, shakers, and xylophones. In addition, the diocese has decorated some walls of their congregations with Asante religious art forms, as well as employing locally woven cloths and vestments for their priests.

Bishop Sarpong, for example, enters St. Peter's Cathedral and other churches to the sound of *kete* (the Asante king's drums) accompanied by songs and the sound of castanets. As he approaches the altar, he removes his sandals and miter before he genuflects. He then sits on an *asipim* (an Asante king's ceremonial chair) under a special large umbrella. Sarpong's crozier, which is held to accompany him like a linguist staff (held by the king's spokesperson), bears Asante proverbial emblems. One of such is the two-headed crocodile with one stomach, which is an Asante symbol of unity in diversity. This Asante symbol, called *nkabom,* is the heart of their concept of *abusua,* or clan system, purporting that they all descended from a common ancestress.

Anointing of the Sick/Healing: Health and Wholeness

Asante indigenous medicine and techniques were in use before the arrival of Western medicine and Christian healing practices. At the moment many healing rituals coexist in the Asanteland. For the Asante, a breach in their interpersonal and human–spirit relationships not only threatens the well-being of the community but also affects the individuals who constitute the social unit. According to the Asante, *yadee* (illness) is expressive of disturbed relationships affecting others and the spirit world and may be attributed to punishment from the *nananom nsamanfo,* bad magic from someone, or an enemy who uses sorcery.

Given the above cognitive map, even if an indigenous Asante cannot give reasons for some misfortune in her/his life, the individual believes that nothing happens by chance. The Asante may consult an oracle to divine the cause. Consequently, healing involves the righting of relationships with humans and the spiritual beings (Twumasi 1975, 4f.). Indigenous healing mobilizes the Asante worldview to frame and reframe illness and therapy. The acknowledgment that illness is not simply caused by physical and biological dysfunction and thus has to be cured with spiritual assistance provides a basis for the Catholic sacrament of the anointing of the sick. The Asante Catholic Church draws on a fusion of worldviews (Asante, Christian, and Western biomedical) to reformulate concepts of illness and therapy.

After Vatican II, the church emphasized the anointing of the sick, which is conferred on sick members who are not necessarily at the point of death. The church's shift of emphasis from "extreme unction" (meant for assisting a person's soul as it enters eternity) to ensuring that a person receives both physical and spiritual wholeness, was greatly accepted because it meets critical needs in the lives of the worshipers. The rite is given to a person before surgery, at home, or during mass, as will be discussed here later.

In its Five Year Development Plan of Health Services (1987–1992), the Kumasi Diocese states in its preamble:

> The Church is committed to the total development of Man and is involved in promoting health as a continuation of Christ's healing works. The plight of the poor, deprived and neglected is of great concern to the church. . . .

Not only does the church affirm its commitment here to holistic healing for the human being; it also reiterates the same commitment elsewhere. For instance:

> The sick have a privileged place within the Body of Christ, and ought to receive special care and love from the community. Sick persons who accept their sickness in surrender to the will of God and in union with the suffering Christ, "make up all that has still to be undergone by Christ for the sake of His Body, the Church (Col. 1:24–25) and become the source of saving grace, not only for themselves but for the whole Body of Christ and society as a whole. (Catholic Diocese of Kumasi, 1984, sections 5, 16)

> The diocese expresses a commitment to healing ministry which is exercised through the sacrament of anointing to provide "inner healing, inner peace, and consolation, through repentance, forgiveness and reconciliation" for the sick person. "Bodily healing," it states, "is a sign of faith for the person and for the whole Body of Christ." Thus the diocesan health policy embraces the provision of bodily and spiritual health care through its hospitals and clinics, primary health care and healing ministry. Healing ministries have been developed at all parish levels at which prayer for healing is "part of Catholic life" in the Diocese of Kumasi. (1984, 17)

Prayers for healing that I gathered in 1988 underscored how and why selected aspects of God, the Holy Spirit, and Jesus Christ were mobilized during the anointing of the sick. For instance, although the Asante priests and their parishioners did not dismiss the fact that some people still believe in witches and other malevolent spirit beings, they emphasized the sovereign power of God above all powers. Their prayers and songs referred to the God who is always able to heal, and Jesus who raised the dead. Christ is king because he has power above all powers on earth and sickness. The acceptance of some elements of Asante belief system and their teaching that Christ's authority is able to effect some transformation in the people's life enhances confidence in some of the Catholics to seek healing in the church and not elsewhere. The church's teaching and practice, including healing, help make Jesus relevant to their present needs. For those who appropriate the healing powers of Jesus Christ, he is real, here and now, and he works for them. It is no accident that a rocky hill outside of Kumasi has become a Roman Catholic shrine where people go for healing and other miracles.

Buoho Catholic Shrine

The shrine was built on the idea of Lourdes, where people go to meditate and say prayers and receive healing. According to the Catholic priest who was the founder of the shrine and was then head at the center, the shrine was built to help people appreciate the gospel and Christ's life "visually and pictorially." Through that experience he noted that people can deepen their faith. The shrine was constructed on a rocky landscape on a hill at Buoho, outside of Kumasi. The various stations of the cross and scenes from Christ's last days are strategically constructed to reenact Christ's passion during his final hours on earth. According to the priest, as visitors and clients climb the hill and feel physical exhaustion they are better able to seek spiritual renewal.

For almost sixty years the center has attracted people from all parts of Ghana and other West African countries such as the Ivory Coast, Togo, and Nigeria. On Fridays people spend the night there praying for various needs. It has a small community of about twenty people who have farms around the shrine. They help the sick and their families when they visit to seek healing. The community also has people who help in the upkeep of the shrine by clearing bushes and running errands for the director and others.

Like healing centers in independent African churches and indigenous religions, the shrine has facilities for families that need to stay with relatives who visit to receive healing. On my visit I met a seventy-year-old man and his family and a fifteen-year-old girl whose mother and some of her siblings were also there. The seventy-year-old was said to have suffered a stroke and was paralyzed on one side. According to the director, he prayed for the man, anointed him with oil, and made the client walk up the hill of the "Stations of the Cross," and "he was able to regain the use of his arm and walk properly," according to the priest. The fifteen-year-old suffered from what the priest called "madness" inflicted on her by evil spirits. When the girl was brought to the shrine, her hands were tied because "the spirit in her was potentially dangerous to others and herself," said Father Tawia. Like the other case, the priest was able to heal the girl after praying over her and anointing her with oil to cast out the spirit that brought the madness on her. These two success stories, according to him, were only two of many such miracle stories at the Buoho shrine.

Indigenous religious life and practice of sacred groves, mountains, and spots have found literal and symbolic correspondence with the Bible at Buoho. The people also draw upon such sacred places for worship, healing, and fasting. A sacralized Asante mountain spot has become a place for spiritual renewal. Here again we observe how pilgrims to the shrine and relatives who take their sick people there seem to articulate a belief that illness can be cured by spiritual means and that miracles do still occur. Besides the practical purposes such as cooking for the sick and taking care of them, families do provide group solidarity for the sick.

A site that was the worship place of local divinities still has social and religious significance. The sacred aspect of Buoho has been reinterpreted to provide continuity as well as discontinuity. It is the same site, but at present it is the Catholic Church that administers healing there. Since Buoho is visited by both Christians and non-Christians, Ghanaians and other nationals, the church is continuing to translocalize an Asante sacred spot. This spot, according to the caretaker, was frequented by people from all over West Africa before the church came to build a shrine there. The diocese has not limited its medical care to healing rituals. It also has hospitals and clinics, as discussed elsewhere (Obeng 1996, 161–64).

Finally, the timing, process, and content of Asante Corpus Christi will reveal ways in which this Roman Catholic feast has been incorporated into the rhythmic cycle of Asante *adae* (fortieth day and annual festivals).

Corpus Christi

All religious activity is designed to achieve some kind of union between the divine and the human. Whatever means (symbols, gestures, rites) are employed for this purpose have a "sacramental" character. They are external signs by which God encounters man, and man encounters God. . . . The transcendental has intervened decisively in . . . history in the person and ministry of Jesus Christ. The sacramental, and, therefore, liturgical life of the church exists to dramatize publicly and symbolically what has taken place, is about to occur in the future and is actually happening here and now. (Sarpong 1979, 3)

The feast of Corpus Christi is one more concrete situation in which the Kumasi Diocese under Bishop Sarpong applies "true evangelization" (Pope Paul VI, encyclical *Evangelii Nuntiandi*, "Evangelization in the Modern World") to the life situations, sensibilities, aspirations, hopes, anxieties, and paradigms of the Asante people.

From 1246 to 1264 Corpus Christi was first celebrated only in the diocese of Liège when Pope Urban (1261–1264) decreed its observance throughout the Catholic world. The Council of Trent (1545–1563) described the feast as a "triumph over heresy and condemned those who protested against the procession of the Sacrament" (Cowie and Gummer 1974, 106).

The feast of Corpus Christi (Body of Christ) is celebrated after Pentecost, whereas Christ the King feast occurs on the last Sunday of the Catholic Church's ecclesiastical calendar. Asante Catholicism has combined the two feasts into one, and it is celebrated on the last Sunday of the church calendar. As a result of this combination, the external celebration and the solemnity of the feast of the Body of Christ have been reworked into the feast of Christ the *ohene*, held annually in Kumasi.

The striking novelty about the festival lies in its timing and the process, form, and content of the celebration. The "coincidence of timing and congruence of functions" (Brooks 1984) of Asante Corpus Christi will reveal how the apparent unchanging Catholic feast with its symbolic structure intersects with Asante festivals, royal titles, colors, and ritual practice.

Asante Corpus Christi is aimed at portraying Jesus Christ as the *ohempon* (ultimate king) to the Asante nation. As *ohene* he greets and blesses the people as he is carried in an *apakan* (palanquin) processing through the major streets of Kumasi. He is enthroned at one stage for people to pay homage to him. At different phases, the feast is marked by ritual and recreational acts of singing and dancing, performed by a variety of actors.

African dance as an important marker of inculturation when Christianity interacts with indigenous religions has received much attention (Bame 1991; Kane 1991; Isichei 1995). T. A. Kane's discussion in particular stresses the liturgical importance of African dance by stating that "the experience and history of a particular tribe or community is the starting place to express the deepest Christian mysteries" (1991, 1). This focus seeks to tell us about the cultural relevance of African dance for translating the mysteries of the church. It does not, however, address the psychosocial dimensions of those who dance. Ranger's analysis of the *beni ngoma* of East Africa, rather raises some more interesting points for our present discussion. T. O. Ranger asserts that the *beni ngoma* dance was part of how the East African dancers were writing themselves into modernity, resisting colonialism, structuring their independence, entertaining themselves, and so on in the urban areas (1975). Dance can thus be utilized to accomplish a variety of goals. Besides its polyvalent nature, dance is at times gendered in Africa.

With the exception of men's secret society dances, women tend to be involved in all dances in Africa. Women play both key and minor roles in performances that range from recreational to possession dances. Dance is an integral part of African life. The African dances when a child is born, during puberty rites, marriage, funerals, religious ceremonies, festivals, and for recreation (Opoku 1968; Nketia 1973; Chernoff 1979). Africans also use dance idioms to express hostility, cooperation, friendship, and expectation (Agordoh 1994, 3). Africans therefore through this meta-language live, reflect on life, and communicate with one another and with the spirit world. In addition, the Blakelys point out that a combination of "verbal art" and "artful gesture" such as dance provides interactional resources during which profound statements are made by individuals and groups. "Dialogue" and decision making occur instead of "straight-line logic, plain talk" (1994, 438). Dance is not an avoidance strategy. It can be a meaningful avenue to address issues in the open.

In light of the above, we will look at specific Akan dance forms, examining women's roles in them to understand how the indigenous contexts for dance may have changed but women are able to recall indigenous dance narratives to address new social and religious circumstances.

Dance in the Indigenous Settings

Adakam is an Akan recreational dance found among the Brong Ahafo region of Ghana (Bame 1991, 10). It derives its name from its main musical instrument, which is a wooden box (*adaka,* an Akan Twi word). During the dance women form a chorus, clapping their hands, singing, and dancing. The women dancers also embark on congratulatory dances by going around the other dancers and waving handkerchiefs over their heads. Dancers may dance solo or with the opposite sex. The body language in this dance involves dancers keeping their upper torso slightly tilted forward as they move "forward in measured steps with a handkerchief in the right hand and waving the two hands in criss-cross pattern" (ibid., 11). Although women engage in the dance, they tend to be those who acknowledge the skilled dancers when they circle the dancers while waving their handkerchiefs.

Another Ghanaian dance is the *Akom,* or possession dance. It involves varying dance gestures which an indigenous priest/ess employs to enter a trance or get out of it. During the trance, such religious specialists are able to communicate with spirit beings. They may receive messages about how to cure diseases, who are sorcerers in the community, who commits antisocial acts, and so on.

Before the priest/ess does the possession dance, women and drummers gather to perform singing, drumming, and dancing to prepare the devotees and spectators. The tempo of the drumming and singing increases when the priest (*okomfo*) or priestess (*okomfobaa*) wearing raffia skirt, besmeared with white powdered clay emerges. The *okomfo* or *okomfobaa* wears talismans and may hold a cow tail (*bodua*) or a ritual stick (*kotokoro*). The ritual stick or cow tail is used by the religious specialist to acknowledge the Supreme Being and at times point out antisocial people in the crowd. The *okomfo,* according to Opoku,

> walks around greeting people and dispensing powdered clay .... He acknowledges God who is the spirit of the earth, the source of physical strength and material well-being. He also acknowledges the four winds which

carry to him the words of God. He then begins the *ntwaaho* circling in a series of pivot turns, to illustrate the perfection, wholeness and oneness of God. Then follows the *adaban*, a retreating and advancing movement of great power and fascination combined with spins and turns in the air. (1968, 10)

By their dance, the priests/esses utter their religious beliefs. Aspects of their faith embedded in dance movement are annunciated: human inescapable dependence on the Supreme Being for sustenance and revelation, as well as the Supreme Being's wholeness and perfection. Since both men and women do the *akom*, it follows that they both receive revelations from spirit beings, communicate with such entities, and also engage in social critique.

At the Buronyaa shrine in Juaso in the Asante region of Ghana, the *okomfobaa's* husband is her attendant and he interprets her messages to her devotees when she is in a trance. Here, it is a woman at center stage. Her role is not to simply acknowledge skilled dancers.

There are other dance forms in which both men and women wield equal communicative power to address the community. Among such dances are the *fontomfrom*, *adowa* suite, and the *nwonkoro* (exclusively performed by women in the indigenous communities). Since all three dances are discussed below, we will only highlight some aspects at this stage.

Fontomfrom dance consists of a series of gestures some of which are mimes of combat, showing valor, and others are the queen mother's dance of peace, stability, and motherliness (Opoku 1968, 38). When a chief or king dancing to the *fontomfrom* music points his forefinger to the sky, the ground and to his chest, he asserts: "Except God and Mother earth, there is none besides him in authority" (Bame 1991, 25). When any other dancer uses similar gestures but at the end points to the chief or king, it implies that the dancer acknowledges the authority of that chief or king. When queens or chiefs dancing the *fontomfrom* point their right hand to the north, south, east, and west, and then cross their arms over their chest and stamp on the ground, they mean they own all they survey; also, they will trample on their enemies (Bame 1991, 26).

A queen mother or any woman who has lost a dear one, can use the *fontomfrom* suite to express her loss and pain as well as her hope. For instance, she may point her right finger at her eyelid, thereby implying, "look what has happened to me." Sometimes she may put both palms against her lower abdomen with her upper torso tilted forward a little, or use the palms to support her tilted head or put the palms over her head during the dance all to embody and convey pain and dejection (Bame 1991, 26). The woman dancer may throw herself into the hands of a chief, family elder, or a person she regards as the source of her support. The one into whose hands she throws herself is expected to catch her. This gesture reminds the source of support of his responsibility toward her, and at the same time assures the bereaved person that she has someone on whom she can depend. But women dancers do more than simply remind others of their responsibility.

Adowa dance consists of graceful and elegant gestures accompanied by drumming and singing. Men and women dancers hold the left hand forward as they make a series of motions over the left with their right hand. The dancer may turn, spin, and bow depending on the drum beat and the messages being communicated. Bame states:

> two women rivals may employ symbolic gestures to vent the feelings they harbor against each other. One rival may stretch a right thumb overclenched fingers pointed towards the other thus telling the other that "she is a beast." The other also may briefly stop dancing, focus on her rival and then give a right-hand brush of her whole foot to signify that she regards her rival as a chicken or she has no regard for her; she brushes her aside. (1991, 27)

Consequently, *adowa* can be deployed to generate and express resentment and animosity between people in the open. There are times when men and women dance to articulate conflicts in their social relationships. Dance in such contexts is disruptive because it can widen the rift between people. Like the *adowa*, *nwonkoro* suite is used for praise and critique. This orchestra has traditionally been composed only of women. As mentioned above, some of the open criticism and countercriticism does not always lead to peaceful resolution, since animosities may deepen between some individuals in society.

Although nonverbal, nondiscursive, and non–straight-talk, Akan dances provide social avenues for people to make open issues that matter to them by criticizing others or praising them, for entertainment and for religious purposes. Skilled dancers, in addition to helping others to focus on specific messages, also gain the admiration of members of their community. As in every endeavor, dancers who do very well are applauded by their people and that enhances their self-esteem. For instance, the woman whose dance is at the heart of this discussion was applauded by people in the crowd including her bishop. Sometimes spectators acknowledge a dancer's skills by posting money on the dancer's foreheads, which is ego boosting.

The above discussion has touched on the multiple uses to which Akan dances are put. Such disciplined use of the body to convey a wide range of emotions, beliefs, and expectations, occurs within some culturally appropriate and meaningful modes. Let us now turn to how the Asante woman dancer has not forgotten dance in the face of social and religious changes. How relevant is the Akan dance narrative during this period of postmodern communication technology? The Akan have always used dance to order their lives, relate to one another and outsiders, and for promoting peace and tranquillity as well as channeling frustrations.

Since its inception in the Asante region in the early 1900s, the Roman Catholic Church has provided health centers, schools, agricultural projects, and so on (Obeng 1996). The church has also become a crucial mediating institution for the rearticulation of Asante dance narratives and the narratives of the dancers, with their attendant religious and social implications.

Within the celebration of Corpus Christi among the Asante, Asante Catholics create their own world for religious and cultural renewal. It is in this new cosmos that women dancers recreate and redeploy culturally meaningful and transforming gestural idioms that extend beyond Asante sociopolitical systems. The women utilize their dance lexicon to reevaluate and challenge aspects of the Catholic Church and, by so doing, ratify and reinvigorate Asante women dancers' role as social critics and cultural innovators.

Kinship and royal descent among the Asante are understood and interpreted in structures of matriliny, and festivals such as *adae* (nine cycles of forty days during which royal ancestors are communed with) and *odwira* (celebration in which the nation and community are sanctified or blessed) processions "might freely and openly acknowledge the generic and social significance of . . . matriliny" (McCaskie 1995, 166). T. McCaskie points out that despite the importance of matriliny, such celebrations articulate male-dominated power. Thus, when the Asante Catholic Diocese incorporates aspects of such male-dominated tradition into its liturgy, the obvious conclusion one may hastily make is that women's role in the feast of Corpus Christi is either negligible or nonexistent. However, Asante Corpus Christi opens and holds up intriguing possibilities for women dancers to take center stage to foster the restructuring of power relations within the church and outside of it.

Before 1970, Corpus Christi was celebrated with pomp and pageantry, accompanied by the playing of a brass band. According to Bishop Sarpong during an interview in November of 1979, "when we were using a brass band to accompany Christ, many people did not know what we were doing. Now that we use Asante instruments such as regalia borrowed from the *Asantehene*, even non-Christians know at least that we are presenting Christ as the ultimate *ohene*."

The incorporation of Corpus Christi into the Asante calendrical rhythmic cycle of *adae* (clarified below) creates new avenues for a new cast of actors and ritual performances with their attendant power relations. For example, the indigenous Akan *nwonkoro* or *adowa* woman singer's and dancer's roles are recast in a Roman Catholic context. When women dancers and singers perform their function in their new context as Christians, they affirm the existence and importance of their indigenous roles as those who perform and sing songs about social conditions and power relations. Their new function therefore points to the cultural implications of their indigenous role by way of symbol synonymy, since the meanings of their visual action and symbols tend to be influenced by the emotions and concepts their society utilizes in defining and experiencing analogous roles.

Asante Corpus Christi therefore presents, *inter alia*, two distinct spheres of influence for the worshipers. The first arena is the spatio-temporally formed sanctuary experience where male priests are the chief officiants. The second is the *Asantehene Manhyia* (place of gathering, the Asante King's palace grounds). It is here that the body of Christ in a monstrance (silver or gold vessel for carrying the consecrated Host) is enthroned for worshipers to renew their allegiance to Christ by singing and dancing. Women dancers in the latter sphere are able to mobilize Asante indigenous songs and bodily gestural idioms to reevaluate and restructure their status and make social comment. Further, the setting becomes a sacred space for worship, during which dancers provide leadership in orienting the gathered community toward Jesus Christ.

During my stay in Kumasi in 1979, I observed a woman dancer whose encoded message mentioned at the beginning of the paper needs explaining here. While she was dancing at the king's palace grounds, she employed dance gestures to ask permission from Jesus Christ, who was enthroned by bowing before him and then repeating the bow before the singers, drummers, and the hierarchy of the church. After that she pointed both hands skyward, thus indicating that she looked to God for guidance, protection, and courage. Having taken permission and alluded to the fact that she "looked up to God," she followed that gesture with the kinesthetic statement that implicated a particular priest, as mentioned above. My interview with her later revealed that she was unimpressed by the behavior of a particular priest and so she was expressing the fact that in the presence of Christ, both priest and parishioner need to be humble.

Thus, during dance a laywoman parishioner has evoked conceptions of appropriate power relations between priests and parishioners and reconstructed the setting by drawing on her indigenous metaphors that submit priest and parishioner to the authority of Christ.

Hence, within the intended purpose of Asante Corpus Christi, with its prefabricated cast of characters, there emerges a range of possibilities for women dancers to articulate and redefine power relations and their identi-ties. The above example shows that within each seemingly unchanging celebration of Corpus Christi lies the critical variable of the current psy-chosocial concerns of the participants. Further, the discussion will shed light on how dance idioms are marshaled to blur the lines between priest and parishioner at the king's palace grounds (*manhyia*). Such blurring of boundaries rearticulates legitimate spheres of power relations, pregnant with symbolic ambiguities, enabling the dancer to transmit visually per-formed messages to Jesus Christ (the host of the feast), the priestly authori-ties (who are male), and to the gathered community (male and female, both the living and the dead who come to witness and participate). Finally, the dancer redefines her role as a social critic and thereby puts on public record the relevance of that function for self-critique as well as reviewing power relations within the church and the larger community.

I draw attention to the above example because neither the indigenous Asante society nor the Roman Catholic Church has satisfactorily dealt with why women are sometimes treated as second-class people. Much scholarly literature has been devoted to the larger issues of gender relations, but my concern here is a limited one. I focus on the flexibility within Asante Corpus Christi for real people engaged in ritual action to negotiate and transform "shifting configurations of power" (Gilbert 1994, 118).

Attention has also been given to the significant roles of Asante queen mothers, and to the fact that women in matrilineal societies prolong the longevity of their lineage because of their *mogya* (blood), which reproduces society. Further, a queen mother, for instance, in her own right as a woman possesses "moral quality of wisdom, knowledge, emotion, compas-sion . . . symbolically, not granted by man, but as a person with the innate quality of a woman who moves in a man's sphere of action; a person with-out formal political authority in a court of male power" (Gilbert 1993, 9f.).

In spite of the above attributes and the importance the Akan descent sys-tem attaches to women, only postmenopausal women are able to perform religious ritual acts in their own right in the indigenous society. The Catholic Church, on the other hand, disqualifies all women from exercis-ing priestly and thus sacramental duties. It is within the context of such "matriphobic practice" (Taylor 1990, 244) and the liturgical regimen of Corpus Christi that this discussion presents the Asante Catholic woman dancer as an interpreter and architect of power relations. One context in which women dancers have always pledged their loyalty and honor to their political leaders is during festivals such as the *adae*.

A brief description of an Akan *adae* here will help contextualize the symbolic continuity that arises between Corpus Christi and Asante calen-drical rhythm and illuminate the latitude that exists for participants.

A Brief Outline of Adae

The Akan calendar year has nine cycles of forty days that are called *adae*. An *adae* may fall on a Wednesday (*Wukudae*) or on a Sunday (*Akwasidae*). Each *adae* is a day of celebration and worship. *Adae Kese* (Big *Adae*) marks the end of the year. During an *adae*, the chief or king and his elders go to the stools-room (*nkonguafieso*) to feed the stools in which reside the royal ancestors. The day before an *adae* is called *dapaa*, which is a day of preparation. Townspeople clear bushes from their surroundings and clean their houses. They also re-clear paths to farms, rivers, and wells (Opoku 1970, 7f.). As the other citizens tidy up their surroundings, stool carriers and court officers also clean court paraphernalia such as white stools, cooking and drinking utensils, and drummers and horn blowers tune up their instruments for the next day. The preparation is of both hygienic and cosmological significance. They clear their surroundings and clean the instruments and utensils, to welcome the ancestors who will be participating in the next day's festivities.

On the day of *adae*, the king's chief drummer, rising early in the morning, recounts the history of the people and praises the royal ancestors as well as the ruling leader. Some of the phrases he uses in his drum language are:

> Mighty and valiant king
> I salute you sir . . .
> I bid you *adae dawn*
> King that captures kings

After that the drummer continues to use praise poems for the king:

> Great and valiant . . .
> King of hosts
> Who is ever sought for an ally in battle
> Benevolent one
> Unconquerable one . . .
> He that balances the keg of gunpowder upon his head
> And somersaults over the flames
> Out, and come with me!
> Out, and come with me!

The chief or king and his elders then come out to go to the stool house. They all remove their sandals and tuck their clothes around their waists as a sign of reverence before their elders the ancestors. As the king puts mashed yam and egg on the stools, he invites the spirits to come using words such as the following:

> Spirits of my grandsires,
> Today is *adae*

Come and receive this food
And visit us with prosperity;
Permit the bearers of children
To bear children [etc.]

The *apae* (prayer and praise) is marked by ceremonial horn blowing, recounting the great feats of the ancestors, and praising them, at the same time exhorting the ruling king to emulate the greatness of his ancestors.

When the spirits of the ancestors arrive to eat, an attendant rings a bell and everyone is silent. After the ritual the chief changes his dark cloth (which marks mourning) into brightly colored cloth and goes to meet his townspeople. The climax of the public ceremony is when the chief holds a durbar in his courtyard and his subchiefs and citizens pay homage to him as they also hear him promise to use his office to protect their well-being.

The king's procession in his palanquin, with his subchiefs under their large umbrellas, through the major streets of town is marked by pageantry during which power, gold, and wealth are displayed. Ritual objects captured in war, royal artifacts, and other regalia are expressive of the king's political and military powers (Gilbert 1994). Other visual objects symbolic of the king's power are skulls of enemy kings who were killed during Asante wars. These skulls are hung on the *fontomfrom* (king's drums). Such intentional show of the king's possessions and power enhances the dignity and importance of the ruler as well as helping people appreciate their rich heritage.

Although the king's roles as judge and military leader and notions of his personal sanctity have changed, the deployment of his symbolic status serves to unite the community. His ritual role (ideally) fosters the political unity of his people. As the king accompanied by the *nsumankwahene* (chief priest) and other religious specialists perform their rites during *adae*, the community is believed to be cleansed from all the pollution that results from various human infractions of community laws and taboos during the year. The festival reconstructs by reenacting and expressing the "transformational movement from defilement toward purification; from disintegration toward integration" (McCaskie 1995, 212).The Asante festival stresses the renewal of the community's well-being at the end of a cycle or a year as it is ushered into a new year and the significant role ancestors play in renewing the community and fertility of the land and humans. Also, the symbolic and literal power of the king as made manifest in royal artifacts, the retinue accompanying him, the size of his umbrella, and the gold and colors with which he adorns himself are highlighted. Of interest to us is how the form and content of an Asante *adae* have been reconfigured to articulate a pan-ethnic religious festival such as the Roman Catholic Corpus Christi.

At Manhyia (the King's Palace Grounds)

Groups and individuals went to pay homage to Christ and to be blessed by him. As Christ arrived, the bishop, *Asantehene*'s spokesperson, and all genuflected.

They then sang:

Ote ho daa	He lives forever
Yesu ote ho daa	Jesus lives forever
Oye nyanka Yesu	He is the Jesus of orphans

The monstrance made of gold was placed on the *asipim* (the *Asantehene*'s ceremonial chair). It bears a combination of geometrical figures such as squares and circles called *Nyame Ntaakyire* (God's spiritual support and protection) (Sarpong 1974a, 101). When the king sits in state on the chair, he symbolically seeks God's help in the exercise of his royal authority. The figures convey feelings of warmth, welcome, and security (ibid.). Jesus Christ had then been enthroned. Mary's statue was raised beside the Host with large fans lying beside her. This was after she had accompanied Christ during the procession through the town. The *menson* (seven horns) were sounded at that stage because Christ had sat in state.

All the priests bowed and knelt before the king Jesus. At that stage the bishop invited all to come and bow before the Blessed Sacrament in a certain order—priests, the Apostolic Pro-Nuncio, then sisters, followed by the *Asantehene*'s representative, the seven horn blowers, then two police officers, and so on. After those acts of paying homage, some traditional dance ensembles played and danced in honor of Jesus. The first of the groups to dance was the *Adowa*, followed by the Fante Catholic Union. Other groups that followed suit were the Frafra, *Nwonkoro* performers, and Eve group, which sang and danced *agbadza*, and the *Kasena Nankani*.

Following the singing and dancing, the bishop carried the monstrance to bless the people, escorted by two Knights of Marshal and the six sword bearers. After the blessing he put the monstrance back on the throne. When the grand durbar in honor of Christ was over, the people went back to the cathedral to end the feast.

The pomp and pageantry that greet the *Asantehene* when he emerges from the stools room are similar to what happened when the Host (Jesus Christ), borne in an *apakan*, came out of St. Peter's Cathedral. In the procession were many choirs and church organizations in addition to people of varying ecclesiastical ranks. Behind Christ were the *mpintin, kete,* and *fontomfrom* drums playing. Right in front of Christ's *apakan* were two mass servers, one carrying the *asipim* chair followed by another who carried a pillow that is often placed on the chair. This assignment of positions in the procession replicates that which occurs when the *Asantehene* is carried in procession during a festival.

Like the *Asantehene,* when Christ sat on the *asipim* on a podium at Manhyia, the faithful came and bowed before him. So did musical groups play in his honor. In addition, beside Christ's throne was Mary, mother of Christ, just like the Asante queen mother. If Corpus Christi were simply a matter of replacing Christian elements with Asante ones, the discussion would end here. In order not to gloss over the problems that emerge as the Asante Catholic Church applies Asante sociopolitical structures and values to Christian ritual communication, it is important for us to examine some aspects of divergences.

In addition to festivals being occasions for leaders of the Asante and their people to affirm their values and reinforce their relations, they also help people to celebrate life as a whole. *Adae,* for instance, is when the ancestors are fed. Corpus Christi as an annual feast provides opportunity for the faithful to renew their faith in Christ by affirming their togetherness as a people of God, and to publicize Christ as the *ohene* whom they worship. The *Asantehene*'s authority is exercised in Asante. On the other hand, Christ's sphere of influence as declared during the feast extends beyond Asante to other parts of the world. In that sense the *Asantehene* becomes a subject of Christ, according to the bishop. This assertion is borne out by the *Asantehene*'s offering some of his regalia to be used by the Catholic Church on the occasion of the feast. When Asante "object language" such as designs, regalia, clothing, and all kinds of adornment are used (Morain 1987, 119), it is supposed to enhance the power of the Asante king and nation. During Corpus Christi, however, the redeployment of the same object language presents an aspect of Christianity that ideally replicates a universal culture.

Corpus Christi drew from Kumasi ethnic groups in the church who brought their music and dancing. The *nwonkoro* group performed when Christ was enthroned at Manhyia. *Nwonkoro* songs are sung among the Akan of Brong Ahafo like Wenchi, Abetifi, Kwahu, and Oda of the Eastern region and can be heard in Mampong and Kumasi in the Asante region. According to Nketia, the themes of the songs relate to "loved ones, relations and prominent men of a locality" (1973, 17). They also contain ideas of praise, hope, satire, disappointment, and death. These songs are often sung by adult women.

On the day of Corpus Christi the Asante Catholic *Nwonkoro* group sang, amidst clapping and dancing, *Nana eba o, nana eba. Awurade Yesu ba o, Nana eba!* (Jesus Christ as *ohene* or *nana* is arriving!) The women were using the same traditional melody, rhythm clapping, and cantor-chorus style of singing to praise Jesus. The difference, however, was that *Nana eba* was not alluding to an earthly king. It was Christ whose arrival was being heralded. As the singing, clapping, and dancing continued, the women one after the other stepped out of the semicircle they formed before Christ and danced. They all completed their turn by bowing before the enthroned Christ.

The *Adowa* band, whose melodic characteristics resemble those of *Nwonkoro*, also played and danced. The *Adowa* band had three cantors singing the lead one after the other as the chorus joined in. During the singing, the gongs and drums such as the hourglass drums and *atumpan* (talking drums) were being beaten. As Bishop Sarpong points out, "Dancing depends very much on bodily movements. Foot-work, manipulation of the neck, manual gestures, gesticulations with the arms . . . pliability of the torso, shaking of the lower part of the trunk" (1974b, 123).

The gestural language conveyed as the female dancer stepped forward made the bishop stretch his right hand, parting his index finger from the middle finger to acknowledge the dancer's skill and elegance. Mobilizing Asante gestural idiom, the woman dancer pointed to her left and right using both hands and then pointed both hands toward Christ.

Dance among the Asante of Ghana is used for other purposes as well. A chief may dance and mime his own political power, which would appear to threaten that of the king, but through body language, the chief enhances his own reputation (Gilbert 1994, 118). Thus, dance is a way of knowing, reflection, expression of the self, and relating to self and others. Asante dance is utilized for ordering experience and articulating the nature of relationships, be they positive or negative. Blacking (1973, 28–30) points out that music and dance that express and comment on relationships between individuals and community tend to have political ramifications. He asserts also that the effectiveness of nonverbal symbols articulated in dance enables people to appropriate personal power as they participate in culturally constructed actions. Thus, people's personal and social identities become intertwined in real ways, since the self develops through its interaction with others in varying social contexts. Consequently, the dancer is able to restructure relations of power and identity.

The Asante also through dance articulate and create conceptions of social relations, stabilize society, validate one's own authority over others, and pay homage to a deity or a person in authority. According to J. L.

Hanna (1979, 136–46), dance may be used by people to cope with subordination, to constrain political power, and for redress and transformation of individual and society.

Of interest in this paper is the function of dance for symbolic self-assertion to redefine one's identity in the face of perceived or real domineering authority. This is when dancers seek to publicly restructure and establish their worth in relation to "the powerful" without any apologies. The Christian women dancers recontextualize themselves in their indigenous cultural values to assert their identity and simultaneously claim membership in the Roman Catholic culture. Such a double heritage enables them to utilize Asante singing and dance to instruct and impose restraint on any abuse of power within the church. Thus, through "cybernetic . . . psychobiological patterns, and persuasion dynamics," the dancers create an interrogative dance (Hanna 1979, 128).

Such condensed symbolic action recasts the cultural history of gender relations in which women rework names, events, and personal experiences into their songs either to praise or castigate people of the community, particularly men. As the women utilize their bodies in motion marked by delicately executed steps, disciplined in action and purpose, their dance opens up a range of possibilities for restoring order and equity. The public gains access to aspects of certain behavior patterns as they are dramatized through the sensory-motor images and idioms by the dancers. Dance therefore becomes a medium for people to "transact relationships more favorably, affect the dynamics of a corporate group, and sanction correct relations" (Hanna 1979, 118). The dance and song evoke the power of women as well as the cultural foundations of such intentional nonverbal kerygmatic idiom to restructure and transform male–female relations. The female dancers may be titleless and ordinary parishioners, but their message is aimed at priests, lay people of the church, and non-Catholics because their "congregation" is larger than that of the faithful who only gather in the sanctuary and therefore come under the direct sway of male priests.

The women dancers do not structure their notions of themselves as social and religious critics along the priestly line of power. In fact that avenue is not available to them. They reassert themselves along those indigenous routes of body language and the music of their culture. By their critique, they step outside "the cone of authority" (Matory 1993, 68) and create their own legitimate authority to proclaim a message that both enhances the purpose of the feast and helps restructure the identity of women.

Christ's royal power is properly placed above the ecclesiastical authority of priest and parishioner and thereby relativizes whatever perceived or real control there may be of priest over parishioner. On that field of priest and parishioner occupying the same position before Christ, the dancer maximizes the dance space and time to give meaning, express freedom for reflection and meditation, tell her story, transform the limits of priest and parishioner relations, and, ultimately, publicly give a new understanding of self and the other. By use of a delicate and successful execution of body language drawing on drama and pantomime, private and collective experience is both articulated and used to redress the wrong.

In that ritual context, gender history and ecclesiastical structure dominated by men are recalled and reviewed, and a new vision breaks loose. The new vision provides possibilities in which women can make personal and collective assertion to transform power relations within ecclesiastical structure. If before the feast of Corpus Christi, some parishioners had felt intimidated to speak to the priest in question, women have succeeded in utilizing symbolic gestures to bring into the open what bothers them.

Alternative Sacred Space

The dancers employing a set of complex gestural idioms reinforce and enrich the worship and honor of Christ. For instance, as they dance, pointing both hands or the right hand skyward, they affirm that they look to God for guidance and protection. When they roll both arms inward and the right arm stretches simultaneously with end beats of the music, they express the point that even if someone bound them with cords, they would break them into pieces with the power of God. The central role the dancer plays in this alternate arena is evidenced by the following:

> In subtle flexions of hands and fingers—our prayers; in thrusting of the arms —our thanksgiving; in leaps and turns—mockery at our foolishness; stamping and pauses—our indignation at the precariousness of the human condition; tensed frame—our defiance at that which threatens human well-being; halting steps and a bow—reverence and allegiance. (Opoku 1968, 21)

The mood and temperament created by music and dance foster an experience in which the dancers and the gathered community participate in the drama of worship.

It is worth observing that the specific Asante drum languages such as those of the *kete*, *fontomfrom*, and *mpintin*, which are reserved for the *Asantehene*, enhance the honor the faithful give to Jesus Christ. The *kete* drumming, according to Nketia, has an *akatape* piece that says *sre sre bi di nye akronobo* (to beg here and there for something to eat is not stealing). The piece does not encourage laziness and begging. Rather it stresses the interdependence in society and, subsequently, the mutual dependence between humans and spirit beings. Another piece of the *kete* is *adinkra*. That piece says *Yede brebre bekum adinkra* (Steadily, we shall kill Adinkra). Adinkra was an *ohene* of the state of Gyaman, who fought the Asante on several occasions until he and his people were defeated. It was thus played by the Asante to celebrate that defeat and to honor the Asante king and his soldiers for their persistence and courage. A spokesperson of the *Asante-hene* who also is a Catholic informed me that since the Asante wars ended between 1896 and 1900, the piece is now used to publicize Christ's power, achievement, and victory over all his enemies, death, and evil. The *mpintin* drumming also has a piece which, Nketia says (1963, 132f.), is used to close the dance at *Adae* ceremony. It is called *Akwadaa mo* (well done or bravo, young one). The words are as follows:

Akwadaa mo	Well done, young one
Yaa nua mo	Thank you, brother or sister, well done.

The *mpintin* provides processional music to which the *Asantehene* marches or when he is carried aloft in an *apakan*. The *fontomfrom* also has variant pieces. Among them is the *nnawea*, which Nketia points out is the music for a dance of joy, a "triumphant music" played behind the *ohene* when he is returning from a celebration to his palace or sits in state. The rhythms, he continues, mean:

Efiri tete	It is an ancient truth
Banin ko, banin dwane	A man fights, a man flees
Okofo dammirifua.	Condolences, warrior
Banin ko, banin dwane.	A man fights, a man flees. (1963, 138)

The war imagery in the above pieces cannot be overemphasized. As powerful Asante kings sought to add to the power and wealth of the nation, drummers and various dance ensembles composed pieces to honor the achievements of those kings.

Clearly, the Catholic Church uses Asante regalia, songs (with their form, mclody, rhythm, and messages), musical instruments, and dances prominent in the worship of local deities and heroes, to praise and honor Jesus Christ and to reorder the lives of the worshipers. For example, *fontomfrom* dance, which is a series of victory dances, recounts the achievements of a warlord, during which the dancer asserts the warrior's supremacy. Such dances publicly portray the prowess of the valiant fighter by using symbolic gestures to mime combat motifs. Such motifs are also manifested in the dancer's slow procession and trekking, marked by occasional halts, during which brief episodes are expressed. The episodes may articulate relaxation movements when warriors rested. Sometimes the episodes allude to Asante warrior retreats and sudden attacks that they launched on their enemies. The heroic deeds of their past are recalled, embodied, and renarrated by the dancers during a Christian worship.

When the dances are performed during harvest festivals, they also express thankfulness for the fruits of the earth, which are symbolic of new life. Other songs previously used only in the context of puberty rituals, funerals, recreation, durbars, and festivals were decontextualized and incorporated into the feast of Corpus Christi. In the recontextualized situation, praise chants used at *ahemfie*, love songs, and others were all reutilized in the service of Jesus Christ.

As the dancers take hold of a Catholic feast such as Corpus Christi, they incorporate it into their dance, their own history, as well as celebrate the kingship of Jesus Christ. The successful execution of the dancers' delicate steps, and other body language, become a dramatic and ritually expressive way in which Jesus Christ is reconfigured and honored. Through what Brooks calls "social and cultural exchanges" (1984, 28) between Asante cultural history and Roman Catholicism, Asante Catholics make Corpus Christi their own and thereby allow for "mutual accommodation" (ibid.) and purging between Christianity and Asante indigenous religion.

It should also be said that the Asante Catholic Church's multiethnic character was expressed, affirmed, and drawn upon by the church to declare *Yesu Kristo* (Jesus Christ) a pan-ethnic spirit being who cares for both Asante and non-Asante peoples. The presence of the Dagaba, Kasena, Nankani, and Frafra dance ensembles, originally from Northern Ghana, the Kpalogo group from the Ga Adangbe in and around Greater Accra, and the Eve singers and dancers of Volta region was a testimony to the above assertion. The Fante union also added great ethnic diversity to the celebration. They each brought a specific variant of their culture to honor Christ as *ohene*. All those people participated because of their common faith and allegiance to Christ. Asante *adae*, during which the chief or king processes through the streets amidst community singing and dancing and later holds a durbar, has found apparent congruence with Corpus Christi.

Most of the songs used during the whole ceremony could be sung by both literate and illiterate people. The fact that such songs were easily accessible to Catholics and non-Catholics made it easy for the spectators to join with the Catholics in singing and dancing throughout the celebration in town.

In one of my interviews with him in November of 1979, Bishop Sarpong argued that the active participation of the worshipers was "both Roman Catholic and Asante." He continued, "Stereotyped, read-to-use prayers, which give no room to free reverent expression of one's innermost cravings and experience would be contrary to the Ghanaians' religious sensibility and traditions." The feast of Corpus Christi, he contended, must speak to the "different existential situations of the faithful. Christ must mean something to them in the diversity of situations."

Asante Corpus Christi is much more than "culture building," and a reworking of the worshipers' histories and identities. It also provides the worshipers with the fabric to weave Christian theology that bears affinity with the Judeo-Christian titles of Christ as king and priest. Yet beyond such affinity, the Judeo-Christian titles and their significance transform Asante kingly titles. For example, Christ or Messiah was an important title, since it was for the one in whom God's hope for Israel was to be fulfilled. The title Messiah, which means "anointed one," was conferred on the king of Israel (Judges 8:22f.; 1 Samuel 8:7). Saul and David were invested with that title in 1 Samuel 12:3 and 16:6 respectively. S. G. Hendry points out that the title is also given to the high priest in Leviticus 4:3f. (1969, 54). In Jesus Christ the expectations of Israel are reconfigured. The roles of priest, king, and prophet came to fruition in him as the one who by his life renews the covenant between God and God's people. In Christ the people know and experience the will and purpose of God for their lives. He is thus a prophet par excellence. By his life, death, and resurrection, Jesus Christ as priest offers himself in order to cleanse God's people of all sin and further to reunite them with God. The eschatological dimension of Jesus is also manifest in his role as the Christ (anointed) to be king whose reign transcends death and decay because he rose from death. In that role Jesus Christ's reign is eternal and he is able to raise his people "to new life in obedience to God" (Hendry 1969, 55) to participate in his royal realm (1 Peter 2:9; Revelation 5:10) until he comes again (Matthew 25:34, 40; Acts 10:42, 17:31). As Asante Catholics celebrate Corpus Christi in time, space, and in their own cultural history, they are also proclaiming and ushering in Jesus Christ, who is the ultimate king, priest, and prophet. There is thus symbolic, structural, and institutional continuity and mutual transformation between Roman Catholicism and Asante lifeways.

As Christians seek meaning and redefine their personal and social identities, they create and recreate, interpret and reinterpret new ideals for themselves. They do not simply internalize and reproduce their past but reforge that experience in new situations, thereby lending a startlingly new slant to Catholicism in Asante. Corpus Christi, like an Akan *adae*, provides worshipers with an occasion to renew their loyalty and faith in Jesus Christ the *ohempon*. Further, as their religiopolitical institutions resonate with Judeo-Christian traditions, the Bible comes alive, the worshipers are helped to renew themselves, and their indigenous traditions are reinvigorated.

The feast of Corpus Christi in Kumasi has become spiritually elevating and emotionally scintillating. To those people Christ's kingdom comes in continuity with Asante *ahenie*. Moreover, people who thought that the Catholic Church's worship style was stale and dry are pleasantly surprised to observe the spontaneity with which the faithful are singing, dancing, and clapping like members of the indigenous churches.

Finally, within the latitude and confines of Vatican II, Asante Catholics are using Asante topography such as indigenous sacred places and Corpus Christi to rearticulate and reorder their personal and collective religious and cultural histories. Thus, as pilgrims visit sacred spaces for health and wholeness, they reclaim the religious sites to address their needs. In the context of male-formulated and male-dominated church doctrine, which excludes women from holding priestly office, women dancers reassert their didactic and social critic's role by appealing to their pre-Christian dance idioms. Their dance gestures of submission to Jesus Christ are symbolic acts of freedom from the pyramid of authority with male priests at the top and a refocusing of attention on the cosmic power of Jesus Christ. In appealing to Asante sacred mountain and in dance to a cosmic Christ, Asante Christians deepen and extend Asante Catholic ritual, restructure their role, win the admiration of others by their skillful performance, and open up new visions to renew the lives of women and men.

References

Abega, P.
 1978   "Liturgical Adaptation." *Christianity in Independent Africa*, ed. E. Fasholé-Luke et al. Bloomington, Ind., and London: Indiana University Press.

Agordoh, A. A.
 1994   *Studies in African Music.* Accra, Ghana: Printhony Press.

Appiah-Kubi, K.
 1981   *Man Cures, God Heals: Religion and Medical Practice Among the Akans of Ghana.* New York: Friendship Press.

Bame, N. K.
 1991   *Profiles in African Traditional Popular Culture: Consensus and Conflict: Dance, Drama, Festival and Funerals.* New York: Clear Type Press.

Becken, H.-J.
 1976   "On the Holy Mountain: A Visit to the New Year's Festival of Nazaretha Church on Mount Nhlangkazi, Jan. 1976." *Journal of Religion in Africa* 1, no. 2:138–49.

Blacking, J.
 1973   *How Musical Is Man?* Seattle: University of Washington Press.

Blakely, T. D., et al., eds.
1994   *Religion in Africa: Experience and Expression.* Portsmouth, N.H.: Heinemann.

Brooks, G. E.
1984   "The Observance of All Souls' Day in Guinea-Bissau Region: A Christian Holy Day, an African Harvest Festival, an African New Year's Celebration, or All of the Above (?)." *History in Africa* 11:1-34.

Catholic Diocese of Kumasi
1984   *Acts and Declarations of the First Synod of the Catholic Diocese of Kumasi.* Kumasi, Ghana: University of Science and Technology Press.

Chernoff, J. M.
1979   *African Rhythm and African Sensibility: Aesthetics and Social Action in African Musical Idioms.* Chicago: University of Chicago Press.

Cowie, L. W., and J. S. Gummer, eds.
1974   *The Christian Calendar.* Springfield, Mass.: G. & C. Merriam.

DeCraemer, W.
1977   *The Jamaa and the Church: A Bantu Catholic Movement in Zaire.* Oxford Studies in African Affairs. Oxford: Clarendon.

Fasholé-Luke, E., R. Gray, A. Hastings, et al., eds.
1978   *Christianity in Independent Africa.* Bloomington, Ind., and London: Indiana University Press.

Firth, R.
1970   *Rank and Religion in Tikopia: A Study in Polynesian Paganism and Conversion to Christianity.* London: Allen & Unwin.

Gilbert, M.
1993   "The Cimmerian Darkness of Intrigue: Queen Mothers, Christianity and Truth in Akwapern History." *Journal of Religion in Africa* 23, no. 1.
1994   "Aesthetic Strategies: The Politics of a Royal Ritual." *Africa* 64, no. 1.

Hanna, J. L.
1979   *To Dance Is Human: A Theory of Nonverbal Communication.* Chicago: University of Chicago Press.

Hastings, A.
1967   *Church and Mission in Modern Africa.* London: Burns & Oates.
1976   *African Christianity.* New York: Seabury Press.
1979   *A History of African Christianity 1950–75.* Cambridge: Cambridge University Press.
1989   *African Catholicism: Essays in Discovery.* Philadelphia: Trinity Press International.

Hefner, R. W.
1993   "World Building and the Rationality of Conversion." In *Conversion to Christianity: Historical and Anthropological Perspectives on a Great Transformation*, ed. R. W. Hefner. Berkeley: University of California Press.

Hendry, S. G.
1969   "Christology." In *A Dictionary of Christian Theology*, ed. A. Richardson. London: S.C.M. Press.

Hillman, E.
1993   *Toward an African Christianity: Inculturation Applied*. New York: Paulist Press.

Isichei, E.
1995   *A History of Christainity in Africa: From Antiquity to the Present*. Grand Rapids: Eerdmans.

Kane, T. A.
1991   *The Dancing Church: Video Impressions of the Church in Africa*. Mahwah, N.J.: Paulist Press.

Matory, J. L.
1993   "Government by Seduction." In *Modernity and Its Malcontents: Ritual and Power in Postcolonial Africa*. ed. Comaroff and Comaroff. Chicago: University of Chicago Press.

McCaskie, T.
1995   *State and Society in Pre-Colonial Asante*. Cambridge: Cambridge University Press.

Morain, G. G.
1987   "Kinesics and Cross-cultural Understanding." In *Toward Internationalism: Readings in Cross-cultural Communication*, ed. J. Luce et al. New York: Newbury House.

Nketia, J. H.
1963   *Drumming in Akan Communities of Ghana*. London.
1973   *Folk Songs of Ghana*. Accra: Ghana University Press.

Obeng, P.
1996   *Asante Catholicism: Religious and Cultural Reproduction among the Akan of Ghana*. Leiden: E. J. Brill.

Oduyoye, A. M.
1983   "Wholeness of Life in Africa." In *An African Call for Life*, ed. M. Ma Mpolo. Geneva: WCC.

Opoku, A. A.
1970   *Festivals of Ghana*. Accra: Ghana Publishing Corp.

Opoku, A. M., ed.
1969   *The Ghana Dance Ensemble*. Accra: Pierian Press.

Peel, J. D.
1968   "The Christianization of African Society: Some Possible Mod-

els." In *Christianity in Independent Africa*, ed. E. Fasholé-Luke et al. Bloomington, Ind., and London: Indiana University Press.

Ranger, T. O.
1975   *Dance and Society in Eastern Africa, 1890–1970, the Beni Ngoma.* London: Heinemann.

Ray, B.
1993   "Aladura Christianity: A Yoruba Religion." *Journal of Religion in Africa* 23, no. 3.

Sarpong, P.
1974a   "African Theology and Worship." *Ghana Bulletin of Theology* 4, no. 7. Accra: Presbyterian Press.

1974b   *Ghana in Retrospect.* Tema, Ghana: Ghana Publishing Company.

Shorter, A.
1973   *African Culture and the Christian Church: An Introduction to Social and Pastoral Anthropology.* London: Geoffrey Chapman.

1985   *Jesus and the Witchdoctor: An Approach to Healing and Wholeness.* Maryknoll, N.Y.: Orbis Books.

Taylor, M. K.
1993   *Re-membering Esperanza.* Maryknoll, N.Y.: Orbis Books.

Thomas, J. C.
1974   "Society and Liturgical Reform." *The Ghana Bulletin of Theology* 4, no. 6.. Accra: Presbyterian Press.

Twumasi, P.
1975   *Medical Systems in Ghana: A Study in Medical Sociology.* Teama, Ghana: Ghana Publishing Corporation.

Part Four

AFRICAN SPIRITUALITY
IN THE AMERICAS

Forms of African Spirituality in Trinidad and Tobago

RUDOLPH EASTMAN AND MAUREEN WARNER-LEWIS

ETWEEN THE SEVENTEENTH and nineteenth centuries Africans were brought by Europeans to the southerly and neighboring Caribbean islands of Trinidad and Tobago, which in the 1890s became a unitary administrative colony within the British empire. The controlling force exercised by the European operators of sugar, tobacco, and cocoa plantation economies, and the superiority of master over slave and indentured laborer meant that African mind-sets and forms of cultural behavior were disparaged and outlawed, while European religions and worldview were promoted. For this reason, positive recognition of African-based forms of spirituality is of recent date, beginning toward the close of the colonial period after the Second World War and increasing tentatively as national self-confidence has grown following political independence in 1962. This means that despite ethnic links, Caribbean societies have been historically colored by hostility toward and ignorance of Africa and its cultures. All the same, some African cultural traits have continued a vibrant existence. But their expression has assumed a correlation with class and educational status. Thus, African cultural manifestations have traditionally been strongest among the peasantry, the working class, and the lumpen. However, black power militancy during the 1970s has led to a resurgence of interest among the educated in traditional ethnic cultural forms, and African-based religions have attracted intellectual interest, religious membership, and cultural status because of the changed ideological climate. There is thus less tendency for upper- and middle-class persons to be embarrassed about their association with such religions—an association that has historically existed but at a clandestine level (see Henry 1983, 63–69; 1991, 53–62).

Individual Acts of Spirituality

Obeah is a pan-Caribbean term expressive of a belief in the power of a spiritually endowed individual, on behalf of the self or another, to manipulate spiritual forces to procure good or to activate evil or to counter evil. Rituals involved in *obeah* practice require herbal, magical, and spiritual knowledge. Services dispensed by *obeah* practitioners include "spiritual" or "bush" baths, the manufacture or empowering of charms or "guards" to be worn, the placing of charms or drawing of "seals" over entrances, and the "mounting" of cultivation plots against predial larceny and "evil eye" or *maljo* by the suspension from trees of blue bottles containing antidotes. Over the period of the islands' histories several *obeah* specialists have been brought before the law courts for these legally offensive acts. According to Ordinance 6 for the Suppression of Obeah passed in 1868, a person so convicted faced up to six months imprisonment and the possibility of corporal punishment (see Trotman 1986).[1]

Masquerade occasions have also involved the practice of African spirituality. This is because masquerade groups have grown out of secret societies on the West African model. These societies, once known as *convois,* or regiments, served under slavery to coordinate rebellious action as well as to bind their members in mutual welfare associations. They also had a religious focus. But after emancipation in 1838, the *convois* and African ethnic associations, whether Rada or Congo or Yoruba, converted themselves on occasion into costumed groups and processionals. One such occasion was participation in the carnival season of masked revelry enjoyed by the French and Spanish landed gentry. Some masquerades represent spirits: the *jab molasi* or *jabjab,* based on the Efik *ekpo* ancestor masquerades; *juju warriors,* recalling the scouts of the southern Igbo oracular deity; *moko jumbi,* an ethnically composite ancestral figure on stilts; "Black Indian" or "wild Indian," a reinterpretation of the Onitsha Igbo *igele* representation of a deceased potentate; and "midnight Robber," who, wearing a Niger Delta chieftancy hat, boasted of conquests over humans and spirits with supernatural strength (see Warner-Lewis 1991b, 180–86). Undertaking such masquerades was, however, perceived as a spiritual challenge: the would-be masquerader faced illness, even death, in assuming this daring encounter with the spirit world. Masks were reported to have moved as if propelled by nonhuman force, and therefore had to be destroyed rather than be worn (Eastman 1980).

Oracular blessing of a marital union occurs through the medium of an ancestral possessed person at Tobago's Wedding Reel. This premarital ceremony involves dancing to the music of fiddles, tambourines, and drums; it also involves libation and ancestor veneration. The possessed individual advises on the desirability of the proposed union and warns of future problems. In Tobago as well, fishing boats and seines (fishing nets) are christened by a Christian churchman. Thereafter the owner sacrifices a hen and a cock and spills their blood on the seine along with raw rice, corn, and bread, symbols of prosperity. Libations of sugared water or rum and water are poured to invoke the ancestors, and offerings of saltless rice and boiled eggs are placed near the seine for them.

African-based Religious Congregations

Orisha Religion

The focus of worship in this religion is Orisha (deities). In Trinidad and Tobago, the Orisha are also called "powers," "the old people," and "saints." The Orisha represent natural forces and historical persons given superintendence by the Supreme Deity, Olorun, over certain aspects of the natural order (see Idowu 1962; Simpson 1970; Bascom 1972; Warner-Lewis 1991c). The Orisha pantheon comprises Esu, the link between the human and the spirit world and inspector of sacrificial offerings; Orunmila, the divination principle, patron of lawyers and other intellectuals, whose complex system is not practiced in Trinidad and Tobago but who is identified with St. Anthony; Obatala, ruler of the head, the residence of fate and the seat of mental clarity and maturity; Ogun, natural energy that keeps matter in motion, and patron of hunters, warriors, farmers, and those who work in metal; Oshosi the hunter whose speed and accuracy of arrow link with telepathy and logic; Shopona or Babaluaye, representing disease, suffering, and death; Mama La Te, the Yoruba Onile, earth or fertility principle; Osanyin, expert in herbal medicine; Ibeji-Olokun, identified with Sts. Peter and Paul and associated with Olokun, the sea; Erinle, associated with the ocean; Shango, divine retribution as manifest in thunder and lightning, whose fertility is the rain; Yemoja, symbol of motherhood and the fullness of the sea; Oya, the hurricane, air, the lungs; and Oshun, symbol of female beauty and ruler of the veins of the body. Because of the prominence of West African Yoruba among slaves and immigrants brought to Trinidad, the name of Shango, a king of Oyo state, became generic to Orisha worship, the state religion of Oyo and its politically affiliate city-states. However, adherents of this religion in Trinidad and Tobago describe the worship as *ebo*, "Yaraba/Yoruba work," "African work," "Orisha work."

Although Orisha affiliation is not accounted for in Trinidad and Tobago censuses, there are about six dozen compounds with thousands of adherents and marginal supporters. Membership in the Orisha faith is attained not through proselytization but through possession by an Orisha, or mediated through dreams, visions, and divination. The initiation process covers nine to fourteen days and involves a symbolic death and rebirth, expressing the neophyte's break with the past. Initiation marks the surrender of one's "head" and formally continues with seclusion within an inner sanctum. The ritual activities performed here are secret and sacred. Conventions to be observed after this induction set parameters for ritual defilement, behavioral attitudes to elders and strangers, marital behavior, and social interaction among adherents. The spiritual family becomes an important nexus, forming a surrogate extended family. Emphasis is placed on discipline, respect, and purity of thought as indicators of good character. There is no clear line of demarcation between good and evil, but it is recognized that magic, medicine, and other mystical powers should not be used maliciously. That is, they should not be applied against someone without his/her knowledge; however, the use of these powers to neutralize the efforts of an individual's or community's enemies is acceptable.

In its original setting, separate festivals and rituals were held for individual Orisha. However, subethnic clustering and conditions of exile have caused the clustering of ceremonies for the Orisha into a single ceremony called *ebo* (sacrifice), or feast. Such ceremonies take place at various times of the year, normally between June and November. A feast lasts from a Sunday night to Saturday morning or from a Tuesday night to Saturday morning. This is followed by an interval of one week after which another feast called "the return" is held. Birthdays of the Orisha are marked by feasts. However, a "one-day feast" can be held at any time as requested by the Orisha or for the purpose of initiation or to deal with a particular problem.

There is no order of priests and priestesses associated with a specific Orisha, as in Nigeria, another aspect of the amalgamation of worship in the Western Diaspora. However, as in Yorubaland, succession to leadership is achieved through kinship inheritance or by spiritual calling. Both instances are likely to be preceded by a learning process that takes a semi-apprentice form involving observation and practice. The calling comes through fasting and divination and often results in the adherent establishing his/her own compound, sometimes with the concurrence of his/her leader, who assists in the laying of the stools or earthen altars, and in conducting various rituals. Leaders provide spiritual, medical, and psychological services to clients who visit on days set aside for this purpose. Such clients come not only from the Orisha membership but from persons of other religious affiliation and from all strata of society.

Most Orisha ceremonies take place in the compound of the head of the shrine or sometimes at the compound of the sponsor. In the compound are the residential area; an area set aside for cooking ritual food; the *palais*, or public covered area for ceremonies; the *chapelle*, or secluded room for storing ritual implements; and ground shrines called "stools" (*perogun*). Most *palais* are not very large (twenty by twenty feet), are partially enclosed, with an earthen floor, seating along the sides and covered either with palm leaves or with corrugated iron sheets. The *chapelle* is a small shrine located very near the *palais*. Inside the *chapelle* is an altar with vases of flowers and ritual paraphernalia, ground shrines of some Orisha, and chromolithographs of Christian saints. The ground shrines start from the entrance of the compound and go along the side of the premises. A stool is a mound of earth about eight inches high; buried within it are ritual substances which localize the power or *ashe* of the Orisha to whom that altar is dedicated. Around each stool are placed the ritual paraphernalia of the particular Orisha, such as a sword or cutlass for Ogun or a broom (*sheshere*) for Babaluaye, along with goblets of water, and bottles of olive oil and honey. Bamboo poles flying rectangular flags to the deity are also planted next to the "stool."

Each shrine has a male or female head (*amongba*), who is fully in charge of all members and activities. The head is assisted by relatives or adherents who are delegated during ceremonies to perform various functions such as cleaning and preparation of the *chapelle*, and ritual food offerings and meals for participants. The drummers who play for the ceremonies as well as the individual delegated to kill the sacrificial animals receive special attention during the preparations. Three drummers play the kongo-mother drum, the *bembe*, and the *umele* (*omele*) with curved sticks similar to those used to play the Yoruba *dundun* drum. Other instrumentation is provided by shak-shaks and the clapping of participants who dance counterclockwise and clockwise in a circle within the *palais*.

A typical ceremony begins around 9:00 P.M. and goes until dawn. After Christian prayers are said, the officiant proceeds to sing chants to placate Eshu. These chants are followed by the ones chanted for Ogun, the clearer of the path, and those to other Orisha follow according to the particular deities being invoked. The chants contain invocation and praise, as they highlight aspects of the Orisha's life, personality, and prowess. They also include pleas for their assistance and protection. The chanting, dancing, and drumming precipitate the possession of adherents by the Orisha. The possessed adherent is termed a "horse" (*hunsi*). The *hunsi* becomes a conduit between the human world and the spirit world, identified with the Orisha, and is referred to and treated as such since the qualities peculiar to the Orisha are exhibited in the dance of the *hunsi*. Under possession, the Orisha's benevolence may take the form of distribution of olive oil for other adherents to drink or to have rubbed on their bodies, or the sick may be healed, blessings and admonishment dispensed, and the future foretold.

Possession is the ultimate experience of an Orisha adherent, and during the period of a feast an adherent may be possessed several times by his/her patron Orisha(s) or even by other Orisha. Sometimes too a noninitiate or a newly initiated person may "fall to the drums" and become inducted into Orisha worship by rolling on the ground upon becoming possessed. This experience may happen several times before the "horse" begins to stand up and dance in the appropriate manner.

When the Orisha "mounts" a seasoned "horse," the latter goes to salute the corners and entrances of the *palais,* the stools, the drums, the officiate, and sometimes all present. It is very important that the possession is a strong one, that is, one in which the subject loses consciousness of self and of actions. Strong possessions command the respect and admiration of participants and are assessed according to the dancing and healing performed, the accuracy of predictions, and the quality of advice given. On the other hand, false possessions invite disdain from the membership. In earlier times an individual so suspected was invited to walk or dance in front or wash hands and face in hot olive oil brought in a large calabash, much to the chagrin of the faker. A possession may also be suspected of being anti-Orisha or evil, in which case the officiate proceeds to dismiss it from the ceremony and then ritually purify the *palais* and surroundings.

The Orisha normally indicates readiness to leave the head of the *hunsi* when the latter spins rapidly and falls to the ground or onto the spectators or drummers. The *hunsi* may go into the *chapelle* and lie down. The recovered adherent appears to awaken from a deep sleep; water is poured on the ground; and the adherent is given some to drink. Sometimes a transition stage in exiting from possession is possession by a *were* or *rere.* This messenger of the Orisha induces the horse to act in a childlike manner and to play pranks on participants. Despite this childishness, however, the *were* is acknowledged as a disciplinarian, and therefore to be disobedient or disrespectful toward it is to cause trouble or disaster.

Blood sacrifice is offered at dawn to a designated Orisha and is seen as a means of protection against evil involving the substitution of animal lives for human life. The animals and birds are ritually washed by persons designated to assist in the slaying, and then ritually fed. Before the sacrificial offering, the officiate divines with *obi* seeds (kolanut) to inquire if the Orisha will accept the sacrifice. This divination is accompanied by the prayers of the congregation. The blood of the sacrificial animal or bird is spilled on the shrine and symbols of the Orisha.

At that moment a lot of energy is released, and it is not unusual at that time for the Orisha to mount their *hunsi.* After this some participants leave to attend to their daily affairs while others begin preparation of the sacrificial food. The latter is cooked without salt (Warner-Lewis 1993, 108–23) and is served to the Orisha on leaves placed in front of the appropriate "stool." Some of this food is shared with the drummers, then with adherents of the particular Orisha, and then with other devotees

Divination and sacrifice constitute the main pillars on which Orisha worship is grounded. Divination helps the adherent interpret and understand his/her choice of destiny made by the individual at the moment of one's creation. There are several types of divination practiced by the Yoruba: Ifa (performed by a priest of Orunmila called a *babalawo*) (see Bascom 1969; 1980), *Owo Merindinlogun,* or sixteen cowries; *Obi* (kolanut) divination; water gazing; trance; and utterance. In Trinidad and Tobago, Obi divination is the most widespread form and is sometimes combined with water gazing. In addition to divination, the adherent must align himself with an Orisha, who will guide him throughout a pre-allotted life span.

The idea that one is punished after death is foreign to Orisha belief. In keeping with African systems of thought, judgment proceeds during physical life in the form of retributive justice. However, death is not an end but a physical separation from family and community, and life as an ancestor extends to the spiritual realm. The ancestor acts as guardian of family affairs and can be contacted through dreams, trances, and divination. In addition, the ancestor waits for his turn to be reincarnated into the world of human beings. Although there are no *eegun* (ancestor) festivals within Orisha worship in Trinidad and Tobago,[2] acts of veneration and commemoration take the form of wakes, nine nights, and annual ceremonies for the dead at the New Year and at the commencement of the annual *ebo.* At such times a series of chants for the dead is sung and saltless food is offered together with libation of alcohol and water.

Vodunu

In Trinidad the religion dedicated to the vodun from Dahomey is known by the names *vodunu* and Rada (see Carr 1953), the latter being the name by which the Trinidad-based Fon-speaking people from Dahomey are called. *Vodun* are deities. Among those worshiped in Trinidad are Ogu, patron of iron and war; Hebioso or Sobo, associated with thunder; Dangbwe, the rainbow or sacred serpent; Age, patron of the hunt; Sakpata, representing the earth and smallpox; and Legba, the divine messenger between the vodun and humankind. As with Orisha, sacrifice, divination, ritual song and dance, possession by the vodun, and the use of magic and medicinal herbs are characteristics of this religion.

Its main center of worship is located on Belmont Valley Road on the outskirts of the capital city of Port of Spain. It was established in the late nineteenth century by an African immigrant, Robert Antoine (known as Papa Nanee). His compound was dedicated to Dangbwe or Da Ayido Hwedo, and was called Dangbwe Comme (House). The faith still survives but is practiced mainly by the Antoine family descendants, some of whom return to Trinidad annually from North America to perform rituals at the family shrine. As there had traditionally been cooperation between Orisha and Rada adherents in the mounting of ceremonies, it would appear that the more widespread Orisha has absorbed would-be members of the Rada religion.

The Spiritual Baptist Faith

The origins of the present-day Spiritual Baptist religion in Trinidad and Tobago lie in the ecstatic revivalist forms of Protestant religion practiced by European and African descendants in the United States (see Brewer 1988; Herskovits and Herskovits 1947; Stewart 1976, 17–25; Simpson 1978; Glazier 1983; Thomas 1987). This type of religion was introduced into the Caribbean by way of the settlement during the nineteenth century of various waves of African Americans. For instance, between May 1815 and August 1816, 781 African-American ex-soldiers and their families were evacuated to Trinidad from Nova Scotia; they had belonged to the defeated British army in the American war of independence and were settled in five villages in Trinidad. Other groups came from Baltimore and Pennsylvania in 1841 and 1851. In the 1840s the Baptist Missionary Society of England attempted to bring the "Merikins" into line with their more restrained approach to religious expression, but the Merikin preachers were unwilling to do away with shouting or "catching power" during acts of worship. Such groups became known as the "Disobedients." The Independent Baptist Church was another split-off. By 1900, Shouters, Shakers, Wayside Baptists, and the Converted were various names for Baptist sects, with the terms Shouter Baptist and Spiritual Baptist emerging by the mid-twentieth centiury. These forms of Christian worship cross-fertilized with cognate practices among immigrants from other West Indian islands, notably St. Vincent and Grenada. But in the view of official and established Christianity the Baptists' ringing of bells and blowing of horns constituted "disgraceful and riotous meetings," so that the Shouters Prohibition Ordinance was proclaimed in 1917. This ordinance gave the police authority to search without warrant any house or place where they had reason to suspect that Shouters' meetings were held. The building of churches was prohibited. Adnerents were beaten, arrested, and fined or imprisoned.

Baptists believe in the efficacy not of infant baptism but of immersion of the reasoning adult in water, in a pond, a river, or at the seashore. A later water ritual sometimes performed is called "emerging," in which the already baptized member is reconsecrated by immersion. Total immersion symbolizes death of the old life and rebirth into a new spiritual life. After baptism the adherent is sworn in as a member of the faith by being given the "hands of fellowship." In addition, s/he is given a new spiritual name and a password, the first of many to be received during a lifetime of spiritual elevation in the faith. Adherents also receive "spiritual clothes" at the end of their fast. These clothes represent spiritual rank as well as the power and burdens associated with the office to which they are designated. Among the offices are Leader, Mother, Pointer, Teacher, Prover, Driver, Captain, Matron, Stargazer, Watchman, Shepherd, Bell-ringer, Zion Waker, and Nurse. Sometimes these offices are combined, for example, Teacher Pointer.

Another central ritual is fasting, which is also known as Mourning, Building, Throne of Grace, or Taking a Light. Fasting involves seclusion and secrecy, and only those adherents who are spiritually knowledgeable are allowed to participate in some parts of the ritual. Fasting is the main vehicle by which an adherent can realize his spiritual destiny. It also involves additional vows and responsibility and can be undergone several times during a lifetime. Fasting may involve drinking water exclusively or a sparse diet of biscuits and herb tea; such abstinence together with constant prayer and meditation may last from three to twenty-one days, during which the adherent is known as the pilgrim or candidate, and the officiant or instructor as the Pointer. During the fast, the pilgrim calls up "tracks" (tracts), which are told to the Pointer, who interprets them to the pilgrim, especially if the latter is a neophyte. As in baptism, the pilgrim's eyes are covered by eye-bands, on which the Pointer draws iconographic forms in chalk. These forms are then traced and sealed with the wax of a lighted candle; hence they are called "seals." The use of chalk signs compares with its use in various indigenous African traditions, such as the mystic drawings of the Kongo/Angola, the *nsibidi* of the Ekpe/Ngbe lodges among the Efik and Ejagham from west Cameroon and southeast Nigeria, the *Orhue* of the Edo of Benin, and the sacred drawings of the Fon of Dahomey. These practices are repeated in the *veve* of Haitian vodun, the *pontos riscados* of the *Candomble* and *Macumba* of Brazil, the *anaforuana* of Cuban Abakua, and the *afaka* of the Juka people of Surinam.

Thanksgiving offering is held annually or at regular intervals by the adherent or by a sponsor who may be a client of a center's head. Thanksgiving takes the form of feeding the poor, feeding children, or shrine-sponsored pilgrimages. Thanksgivings are accompanied by some type of feasting and express gratitude for blessings from the Almighty received for the period past. Failure to hold thanksgivings is believed to result in loss of the benefits already received and those to come. An individual may also give a thanksgiving in response to spiritual instruction, or to ward off some misfortune. When the poor are fed, the food is taken to the destitute and shared together with money. Sometimes the sponsor goes to a home for the aged or to an orphanage to perform this service. On the other hand, children are fed either at the shrine or at the individual's home. Shrine members, friends, and nearby children are invited to partake. A table covered with a white tablecloth is adorned with flowers, candles, and sometimes a bell. Sweet and salted bread, soda pop, sweet biscuits, seasonal fruits, milk, wine, honey, olive oil, sweets, and other delicacies are displayed here. The sponsor states the reason for the thanksgiving, after which hymns are sung, prayers said, and the table blessed. Food items are then put into bags and distributed to the children present.

Pilgrimages take place at various times of the year when members and supporters travel to another shrine. Members travel by chartered buses singing hymns and songs from Sankeys' sacred hymnbook. Upon arrival, they are greeted by the head of the host shrine in a very elaborate ceremony designed to test the spiritual knowledge of the elevated ones. This ceremony is followed by a service where gifts are exchanged and various aspects of the scriptures are expounded upon by individuals. Another type of pilgrimage terminates at sacred places in forested areas, at waterfalls, rivers, or the seashore. Services are conducted there and offerings made of pigeons or chickens or ducks, together with cakes, fruits, sweets, milk, sweet wine, candles, flowers, and perfume. Wayside preaching, also called "Mission" is an important aspect of Spiritual Baptist activity and was one of the reasons for the enactment of the Shouters Prohibition Ordinance. Adherents receive instructions through dreams and visions to keep a wayside service at a specific location and to read particular scriptural passages and the requisite message to be delivered. Sometimes the adherent is instructed to deliver the message along the way before keeping the service at a specified venue. Messages range from warnings of impending disaster to extolling a clean and holy life, and the need to repent and be baptized.

Spirit possession, called "shouting," "bringing 'doption," or "catching power" is central to the Spiritual, London, and Independent Baptist faiths and is encouraged by highly rhythmic singing as well as dancing, though controlled trances also occur. Glossalalia (speaking in tongues or unknown languages in spirit) may take place during possession.

Conclusion

The religious beliefs and observances presented above coexist symbiotically even as they may be differentiated one from the other. As indicated, *obeah* is an informal, wide-spectrum belief system whose adherents and officiants fall both within and outside the three formal congregational groups described here. Indeed, there is considerable overlap between the membership of the three religious bodies and the membership of Euro-American Christian denominations. This is so not only because an individual may, during a lifetime, change religious allegiance but also because some people simultaneously hold plural affiliations. Lay members of both Orisha and Spiritual Baptist faiths may be categorized as those with and those without connection in the other. It is also obvious that this intense interfaith contact involves Hinduism in a donor relationship with African-based religions, both in respect of iconography and followership: Hindu symbols and converts from Hinduism are to be found in some Orisha and Spiritual Baptist congregations.

It is therefore natural that the religions in question face dilemmas as to their identity and the extent of the African rituals in their acts of worship. The three formal religions share elements of African ritual: trance-possession, initiation ceremonies, visionary-*cum*-apprenticeship priesthood processes, noncentralized shrine and priesthood structures. Not surprisingly, however, the Spiritual Baptist community, as the group most strongly syncretized with Christianity, has tended since its "unbanning" in to approximate to practices observed by its Christian counterparts. This is evident in the adoption of a centralized hierarchy headed by an archbishop; the replacement of titles Mother and Leader with Pastor, Reverend, Mother or Father, and Bishop; increasing male-gender monopoly of the priesthood; the establishment of dioceses; the use of Catholic and dog-collar vestments by priests; Christian church layout and architecture; and the administration of holy communion. There are, however, several competing branches of Spiritual Baptists, so that the movement toward the Christian model is not uniform. Instead, some Spiritual Baptists include in their rituals libation and animal sacrifice, some employ the drum for musical accompaniment, and some shrines recognize the "spiritually called custodian," an adherent who can become possessed by an Orisha and who receives dream instructions to hold Orisha ceremonies for a particular purpose.

Meanwhile both the Orisha and Spiritual Baptist faiths have won recognition from a number of ecumenically minded Christian churches and from government officials regarding participation in interdenominational services. Considerable television exposure came by way of a 1983 series called "The African Presence in Trinidad and Tobago." Internally, the Orisha religion has already begun the process of centralization, with two organizations now officially registered. These organizations provide occasional media coverage concerning the religion and agitate for the parliament to legalize marriages performed by the faith's officiants. Participation by educated devotees also exerts pressure in the direction of leadership training and formal instruction in the philosophy and liturgy of the religion. These westernizing tendencies are countered by a greater interest in acquiring the Yoruba language, moves to excise Christian elements from the liturgy, and the forging of international ties with practitioners of other Orisha-based religions in Brazil, the United States, and Nigeria.

While there are levels of stability in the occurrence of African-derived religions on the two islands, it is clear that they are in a state of dynamic interrelation with other religions in their vicinity, even as they seek both pragmatism and idealism in their response to the human need for spiritual, emotional, and material support.

Notes

1. Between 1868 and 1871 and 1875 and 1899, some fifty-three persons were imprisoned for practicing *obeah* (Trotman 1986, 224).

2. In Trinidad and Tobago ancestor veneration is performed in ceremonies such as *saraka* and *nation dance,* outside of ceremonies for the Orisha. However, ancestor veneration is incorporated into some Yoruba-derived religions in the West Atlantic. See Warner-Lewis 1991a, 63–80.

References

Bascom, William
    1969   *Ifa Divination: Communication between Gods and Men in West Africa.* Bloomington: Indiana University Press.
    1972   *Shango in the New World.* Austin: University of Texas Press.
    1980   *Sixteen Cowries: Yoruba Divination from Africa to the New World.* Bloomington: Indiana University Press.
Brewer, Peter David
    1988   "The Baptist Churches of South Trinidad and Their Missionaries, 1815–1892." M.Div. dissertation, University of Glasgow.
Carr, Andrew
    1953   "A Rada Community in Trinidad." *Caribbean Quarterly* 3, no. 2: 36–54. Republished, Port of Spain: Paria Publishing, 1989.
Eastman, Rudolph
    1980   "Africa and Carnival: Myth or Reality." Typescript, West India Reference Library, Central Library Services, Port of Spain.

Glazier, Stephen
1983   *Marchin' the Pilgrims Home: Leadership and Decision-Making in Afro-Caribbean Faith.* Westport: Greenwood Press.

Henry, Frances
1983   "Religion and Ideology in Trinidad: The Resurgence of the Shango Religion." *Caribbean Quarterly* 29, nos. 3–4:63–69.
1991   "The Changing Functions of the Shango Religion in Trinidad." In *African Creative Expressions of the Divine,* ed. Kortright Davis and Elias Farajaje-Jones, 53–62. Washington, D.C.: Howard University School of Divinity.

Herskovits, Melville, and Frances Herskovits
1947   *Trinidad Village.* New York: Alfred A. Knopf.

Idowu, Bolaji
1962   *Olodumare: God in Yoruba Belief.* London: Longman.

Simpson, George Eaton
1970   "The Shango Cult in Trinidad." In *Religious Cults of the Caribbean: Trinidad, Jamaica and Haiti.* San Juan: Institute of Caribbean Studies.
1978   *Black Religions in the New World.* New York: Columbia University Press.

Stewart, John O.
1976   "Mission and Leadership Among the 'Merikin' Baptists of Trinidad." In *Contributions to the Latin American Anthropology Group,* ed. N. Whitten, 17–25. Washington, D.C.: Latin American Anthropology Group.

Thomas, Eudora
1987   *A History of the Shouter Baptists in Trinidad and Tobago.* Ithaca, N.Y.: Calaloux Publications.

Trotman, David
1986   *Crime in Trinidad: Conflict and Control in a Plantation Society, 1838–1900.* Knoxville: University of Tennessee Press.

Warner-Lewis, Maureen
1991a   "The Ancestral Factor in Jamaica's African Religions." In *African Creative Expressions of the Divine,* ed. Kortright Davis and Elias Farajaje-Jones, 63–80. Washington, D.C.: Howard University School of Divinity.
1991b   "Mind-Set, Myth and Masquerade." In *Guinea's Other Suns: The African Dynamic in Trinidad Culture,* 175–86. Dover, Mass.: Majority Press.
1991c   "Yoruba Religion in Trinidad: Transfer and Reinterpretation." In *Guinea's Other Suns: The African Dynamic in Trinidad Culture,* 125–40. Dover, Mass.: Majority Press.
1993   "African Elements in Rastafari Belief." *Caribbean Quarterly* 39, nos. 3–4:108–23.

19

The Music of Haitian Vodun

GERDÈS FLEURANT

T HE PEOPLE OF HAITI, the second independent republic in the
Americas, evolved from three cultural sources: African, Amer-
indian, and European. The most prominent and, indeed, dominant of the three is the African. Central to the African heritage of
the Haitians is Vodun, the religion of the majority of the people. But
Vodun is more than simply a religion, for to a greater or lesser extent, the
totality of the Haitian population is influenced by some of the beliefs
springing from Vodun, understood here as a comprehensive system of universal knowledge that includes an economic, political, social, and techno-
logical component, but in which the cultural and most important spiritual
dimensions are pronounced. Yet, in the popular mind, Vodun is associated
with witchcraft and magic, a label that was attached to it by the early writers and propagandists of the nineteenth century who could not make their
peace with an independent Haiti. This is why in this article, I use the more
appropriate orthography *Vodun* instead of the popular spelling *Voodoo*,
often found in journalistic writings.

In this article I will refer to many African and Creole terms. The African
words are retained from the Fon, Kongo, Yoruba, and other African languages spoken by the ancestors of the Haitians brought to the Americas
from the sixteenth to the eighteenth century. Creole (whose lexicon consists largely of seventeenth-century French words superimposed on an
African syntax) is the language of the Haitian people, most of whom are
illiterate, because the Haitian establishment does not deem it crucial to
make all Haitians literate. Vodun's wisdom and music are thus preserved
through the oral tradition, and many of the African and Creole words cannot be readily translated into English. For these words I have attempted to
give an approximate explanation or translation. For example, the Kongo
word *lwa* is translated in the literature as "god," but this does not render

the true meaning of the Vodun conception of that term. For Vodun practitioners, the term refers to spiritual entities.

A Conceptual Framework

It is encouraging that academia has recognized the value of the "reflexive approach" (Turner 1969), which consists of an attempt to study a culture from an insider's view and on its own terms. Consequently, researchers now through initiation into Vodun (moving from the *bosal* to *Kanzo* or *pridezye*) have access to more accurate data and are beginning to report more sensibly on the subject. This new development makes it possible to arrive at an enhanced appreciation of the Vodun belief structure and its concomitant artistic dimension, particularly in the music.

Vodun and its music, the subject of this article, hail from Africa, the cradle of human race. The oldest of the world's great religions (in 1983 the World Council of Churches recognized Vodun officially), Vodun is the least understood of all the non-Western forms of worship. In the United States, politicians have made it a practice to equate Vodun with any schemes they deem to have little chance to work. "Voodoo economics" is one of the favorite terms commonly used in this regard (George Bush, 1980 presidential campaign), and now some scholars have joined the dance with "Voodoo academics." Vodun, however, is much scrutinized. Since the publication of Moreau de Saint-Mery's *Description Topographique de L'Isle de Saint-Dominique* in 1797, this faith of the Haitian people has been the object of numerous studies, ranging from the journalistic and popular to the scientific. The frenzied proliferation of such publications prompted VèVè A. Clark (1982) and this author (Fleurant 1987) to devise the model "*bosal, Kanzo, pridezye,*" which emerges from the nomenclature of Vodun (initiates move progressively through those three levels while acquiring knowledge about the religion) to help evaluate the voluminous literature in terms of its importance for an understanding of the subject. They found that the majority of works on Vodun fall into the *bosal* category, which corresponds to the least informed level of understanding about Vodun.

The more informative categories of *Kanzo* and *pridezye* are few. Among the authors who have studied Vodun in some depth are Maya Deren, Alfred and Rhoda Metraux, Melville and Frances Herskovits, James G. Leyburn, Harold Courlander, Zora Neale Hurston, Suzanne Comhaire-Sylvain, Katherine Dunham, Milo and Odette Rigaud, Leslie Desmangles, Laennec Hurbon, VèVè A. Clark, Michel Laguerre, Michel Leiris, Guerin Montilus, George E. Simpson, Remy Bastien, Emmanuel C. Paul, Max Benoit, and Karen McCarthy Brown. There is an interlocking relationship between Vodun as a belief system and its music. Any discussion of the music of Vodun must be preceded by a review of Haiti's ethnographic history, since the two derive from the historical context of the Haitian community and they further constitute the live current of the people.

The Ethnographic History

Haiti, which shares the western third of the island of the same name with the Dominican Republic and with a land surface of 10,714 square miles, is one of the Greater Antilles of the Caribbean sea. Before Christopher Columbus's encounter with the area in 1492, its first inhabitants were the Arawak, the Ciboney, and the Carib, who came from the southern mainland and gave their name to the region. The Africans were brought into the area in 1502 by the Spaniards to replace the first occupants, whom they had enslaved and called Indians, because Columbus assumed that he had reached India. Those were not the first Africans to arrive in the region, for some had accompanied Columbus during his voyage, and, according to Ivan Sertima, Africans lived in the area long before Columbus arrived.

The island of Hispaniola, its name given by the Conquistadores, the site of many wars of influence between the European powers over the control and exploitation of its resources, goods, and spices, gradually became divided between the French in the west and the Spaniards in the east. The French section, with the Treaty of Ryswick in 1697 became known as St. Domingue and emerged as France's richest colony, whose motor was African slavery. The black population by 1789, the date of the French Revolution (an event that changed the political map of the world) outnumbered the white by fifteen to one. St. Domingue's population at that time counted some forty thousand French people (differentiated in three status groups), who formed the upper class; forty thousand colored/freed people (from the union of the white men and black women), who constituted the middle class; and seven hundred thousand African captive workers, who occupied the lower rungs of the social ladder and were the people who produced the wealth that made the colony the richest land of the Americas for most of the eighteenth century. The laboring class, made of captive workers who, coming in majority from the west coast of Africa, were the Fon, Ewe, and Yoruba of Dahomey, the Bambara, Wolof, and Mandingo of Senegambia, Hausa, Fulani, and Ibo of present-day Nigeria, Akan of Ghana, Kongo, Luongo, and Wangol of the Angola-Congo axis, to mention but the most important ethnic groups.

According to C. L. R. James, Africans came from all over the continent, with captives taken as far away as Mozambique on the eastern side of

Africa. The fusion of these people's religious practices gave Haiti its Vodun, a Fon term that means "spirit" or "power," which Haitians called *lwa*, a Kongo word. Vodun was the cement that bound together all of these people and allowed them, after the religious and political congress of Bwa Kayiman, held near Cap Français, on August 14, 1971, to earn their independence in 1804. In effect, on the appointed night, the leaders of all the major plantations in the northern plain of Haiti gathered at Bwa Kayiman to hold a ritual and confer about the plans for a general revolt of the slaves or captive workers. To hold a religious ceremony before any major actions are undertaken is a gesture grounded in the African conceptions of the order and forces of the universe. Many Haitians believe the war of liberation (1791–1803), inspired by the African belief system of Vodun, which preceded the birth of the nation, accounts largely for most of the hostility (whose effects are felt even today) that the European colonial powers have shown Haiti and Vodun in particular.

Vodun Belief and Structure

Vodun, which shares the African belief system with religions such as the Candomble of Brazil, the Santeria of Cuba, the Kumina of Jamaica, Shango of Trinidad and Tobago, in Haiti comprises many rites such as the Rada, Ibo, Kongo-Petro, Makanda, and Nago. In practice, Haitian Vodun is divided into two major rites (or styles of worship): the Rada, whose music and structure are retained quite faithfully from the Fon/Ewe and Yoruba of Dahomey, and the Kongo-Petro, which emerged from the crucible of the plantation system. Contrary to what many authors seem to think, the division between the Rada and Kongo-Petro rites is not rigid, for Vodun results from the fusion of what the Haitians call the 21 nations of lwa— some others even talk about 101 nations. Many lwa, known as *an de zo*, or in two rites, are worshiped on both the Rada and Kongo-Petro sides.

Vodun is primarily a family religion in the sense that many ceremonies are held within the family circle. The ritual has a sacerdotal hierarchy made up of the *oungan*, or priest, and the *manbo*, or priestess, and their assistants, the *laplas*, or swordbearer, *ounsi*, or spouses of the spirits, *oungenikon*, and *ounto*, who are respectively the chorus leader and drummers whose functions are crucial for the success of a ceremony. In the absence of priests, the head of the family, indeed a traditional paterfamilias, conducts the service. The Haitian family in this context is first and foremost an extended socioeconomic unit living in the *lakou*, or compound, whose center is the *ounfo* (temple), to which is attached the peristyle, the public dancing space, for Vodun is primarily a danced religion. The center post, or *potomitan*, which literally occupies the center of the peristyle incarnates all the ancestral and spiritual forces of the community. The people dance around the *potomitan*, for it is the point of departure of essential segments of the ritual process.

The fundamental beliefs of Vodun can be summarized as follows: God, or *Bondye*, the Supreme Being called Mawu-Lisa among the Fon and known as *Olorun* among the Yoruba, created the universe, and thus the lwa, human beings, animals, vegetables, and minerals. After creating the world, God retired far into the sky and left the management of all earthly matters to the lwa with dominion over specific areas such as fire, water, wind, trees, and plants, including the secrets of their medicinal properties, illnesses, and their cures; in sum, all actions, sentiments, and virtues. In Vodun beliefs, one finds a series of spiritual entities, often syncretized with the Catholic saints, with specialty in certain tasks that maintain human existence.[1] For example, Legba, the opener of the cosmic gate, must be invoked at the beginning of all undertakings; Azaka presides over agriculture; Ezuli's domain is love; and Ogoun, the entity of defense, stands on guard. The knowledge and teaching of Vodun are preserved in the songs and dances which also contain the attributes of the lwa, or spiritual entities. The following songs to Legba, Kouzen Zaka, Erzuli, and Ogoun present some of the characteristics of the lwa just mentioned:

Kreyòl	English
Legba lan barye a	Legba at the cosmic gate
Se ou ki pote drapo	You are the flag bearer
Se ou ka pare soley	You will prepare the way
Pou lwa yo	For the lwa
Bonjou Kouzen(Zaka)	Good morning Cousin
Bonjou Kouzin-o	Hello my (female) Cousin
O kou yo wem' nan	I may be humble and poor
Konsa mwen danjere	But I am still a proud man
Ala yon bel fanm	What a beautiful woman
Se Erzuli	That Erzuli is
Erzuli map' fe w oun kado	I will give you a present
Avan ou ale, Abobo	Before you leave, Abobo
Ogoun-o, nèg gè	Ogoun-o, man of war
Kanno tire	They fired the cannon at us
Nou pa pran yo	We didn't get hurt

In this sense, Vodun is also a practical religion, where relations between humans and spirits are maintained through exchanges and mutual reinforcement of energies, and the solutions to concrete problems are designed according to a system established through ancestral tradition passed down orally from generation to generation. The vodunist serves the lwa, who come to his/her aid in difficult moments, and the lwa rely on the "servitcur," or those who serve the lwa for their needs to partake in human actions, such as dancing and feasting. This is why music and dance are central elements of Vodun, because it is through them that the community calls the lwa, who must come to participate in the feast offered in their intention, for the religious service consists also in the preparation of favorite ritual food of the lwa whose guidance one is seeking. In this regard, the *oungenikon* (chorus leader) and the *ounto* (drummers) are important people, chosen for their knowledge of ritual matters as well as their artistry.

The Music of Vodun

Dancing, drumming, and singing are the main components of the music of Vodun. Studies on the music or the dance of Vodun are few, but growing steadily since the 1990s. The pioneer in this area is Harold Courlander, who contributed two books and several professional articles on the music of Vodun. His best-known works are *Haiti Singing* (1939) and *The Drum and the Hoe: The Life and Lore of Haiti* (1960). Courlander's musical analyses are provided by ethnomusicologist M. Kolinski, who contributed the article on the music of Haiti for the *Grove Dictionary of Music* (1980). Haitian scholars Lamartiniere Honorat and Jean Fouchard contributed works on the ritual dance and méringue, the national music. Katherine Dunham (1969) and Lavinia Yarborough-Williams (1964) have also published excellent works on the dances of Vodun. But the works of Claude Dauphin (1986) and this author (Fleurant 1987; 1996) are the first in-depth continuation of the research undertaken by the pioneers of a generation earlier. Now a growing crop of young ethnomusicologists are making some interesting contributions to the music of Haiti with some reference to Vodun.

Ignorance of the organizing principles of African music prevented serious and more accurate study of the music of Haitian Vodun until the 1960s. The turning point occurred with the shift within the discipline of ethnomusicology from armchair to fieldwork and the rise of the concept of bi-musicality (Hood 1960.) Ethnomusicologists became convinced of the need for fluency in two musical cultures and for performing the new music one is studying. The leaders in this respect were A. M. Jones (1959), J. H. Kwabena Niketia (1959; 1963; 1974), Hewitt Pantaleoni (1972), David

Locke (1979), and John Miller Chernoff (1979). Their work allowed us to decode the principles of African music, thus opening the way for understanding the logic of Haitian Vodun music. The principles of African music can be summarized as follows:

1. The predominance of complex rhythms with a 3-against-2-beats pattern; the presence of multiple meter/polymeter and polyrhythms.
2. Off-beat phrasing as one encounters in a series of breaks in the flow of the music, known in Haiti as *kase*.
3. Antiphonal form, call and response, polyphony and the A/B binary form of the songs.
4. The use of a time line realized by the bell pattern as the guiding principle on which the ensemble is built.
5. Collective participation, improvisation, and a metronome sense or learned sense of rhythm.
6. The discovery of the three-drum chorus, from Senegal to Angola and beyond.
7. The use of the press/bounce technique of sound reproduction, tonal language and the use of talking instruments to communicate messages of both practical and aesthetic values.

Vodun Music in Context: Music to Call the Lwa

The music, which follows the logic of African music, not only accompanies the ritual but is essential to most phases of the ceremony. There are songs and special rhythms for each group of lwa, songs for the human participants in the service such as *oungan/manbo, oungenikon, lapla, ounsi, ounto,* and songs for sacred objects such as *drapo* (flag), *govi* (earthen jar), *zen* (fire pot), *dife* (fire), *kolye* (necklace), *tanbou* (drum), *vèvè* (ritual drawing). Here is an example of a song for *oungan, ounsi,* and *vèvè,* and another one for the necklace:

Kreyòl	English
Ounsi la yo	My dear Ounsi
Kouman nou ye	How are we doing
Kote oungan nou	Here is your oungan
Kap' simen farin ate	Drawing the veve
Ounsi layo	My dear ounsi
Kouman nou ye	How are we doing
Aleksina, wa rantre	Aleksina, go inside
Lan ounfo a	The ounfo

| Wa pran potel ban mwen | You'll see the veve necklace |
| Wa pran potel' ban mwen | Take it and bring it to me |

I have already mentioned that the Rada and Kongo/Petro have emerged as the principal rites (styles of worship) of Haitian Vodun. Milo Rigaud reports the existence of some three hundred lwa from both rites (1953). But in Bopo, Arcahaie, and Mirebalais, where I did my fieldwork (and for that matter in most of Haiti), some fifteen to twenty major Rada lwa and five to ten major Kongo/Petro entities are usually saluted at services in the following order:

The Rada Lwa

Legba Atibon
Loko Atisou
Ayizan A-Velekete
Marasa Dosou Dosa
Danbala & Ayida Wèdo
Sobo & Badè
Agasou Jèmen
Agwe Taroyo
Bosou Kanblanmen
Agarou Tonè
Azaka Mede
Belekou Yenou
Metrès Erzuli Freda
Sen Jak Majè
Ogoun Feray
Osanyen Megi Melo
Ogoun Badagri
Ibo Lele
Gede/Bawon Samdi

The Kongo-Petwo Lwa

Kalfou
Simbi Andezo
Gwan Bwa Ile
BawonLakwa
Marinet Bwa Sech
Ti Jan Danto
Limba Za w
Zando

Kongo Savann
Bawon Samdi

Although the music for the Rada and Kongo-Petro spirits will be discussed later in greater detail I will summarize them now.

The musics played for the Rada are the *yanvalou*, *mayi*, and *zepol* or *yanvalou debout*. Among the Rada, the Marasa are saluted with the beat *twa rigol* and not the *pas rigole*, as it has been referred to in the literature. Kouzen Zaka takes the *dyouba/matinik* and Ogoun takes the *nago grankou*, *nago cho*, or *yanvalou debout* and *mazoun*. The lwa of the Guede family, entity of life and death, found in both rites (this is true for several other lwa), dance to the music of *banda* or *mazoun*.

In Bopo, a suburb located some ten miles north of Port-au-Prince, which could be considered a prototype for most of Haiti, five major Kongo/Petro lwa are worshiped. They dance to the rhythms of *boumba*, *kita sech*, and *kita mouye*. However, the late Philocle Rosenbère a.k.a. Coyote, one of the last authentic *ounto*, or master drummer, Maya Deren's teacher and my principal consultant/teacher, contends that there are no such things as *kita sech* or *kita mouye*. There is only one *kita* rhythm, he insists, which is played to salute all the lwa in the Kongo-Petro category. For him the music of Kongo-Petro consists of *boumba* and *kita*. In the Artibonite Valley, in the *lakou*, or compound, of Soucrie, near the city of Gonaives, the site of the Haitian Proclamation of Independence in 1804, where the Vodun tradition has been maintained faithfully, only the Kongo rite is observed. Its music is identical, in many respects, to that of Petro, a fact that led me, after a conversation with Abudja, a Vodun leader and promoter of the "root music" movement, to conclude that the Petro should be called Kongo-Petro (August 1991).

Before discussing the songs and drum rhythms of Vodun, it is important to introduce the reader to some of the structural terms and symbolic concepts used in the music, such as the *kase*, or break, some issues pertaining to the songs' interpretation, and the symbolism of the rhythms and their healing values.

The *Kase*, or Break

In both Rada and Kongo-Petro drumming ensembles, a special off-beat phrasing occurs at certain moments during the performance. This is the *kase*, or break, whose main function is not only to add elegance to the music but to facilitate possession, the coming of the lwa. Possession is considered the climax of the ceremony, for immanence (God in us and with us) is central to Vodun. The *kase* thus enhances the structure of the musical performance by breaking the fluidity of the cyclical development characteristic of a Vodun piece, a fact that is aesthetically generated as well as spiritually grounded.

The Meaning of the Songs

Vodun songs are interpreted at two levels, the manifest and latent, or the surface and deep levels (Laguerre). Songs of the lwa, or songs uttered by a person in trance, and songs which reveal the attributes of the lwa, can be interpreted at even deeper levels depending on the interpreter's degree of *konesans*, or knowledge about ritual matters. Some songs are in ancient Dahomean languages, like Fon, Mahi, or Yoruba, generically called *langaj*, for they may contain words from other African tongues as well. Others are part in *langaj* and part in Creole. Songs entirely in Creole may be obscured by a hidden meaning, known as *pwen*, or the "point" (Brown 1976), where the reference may be either to sacred/ritual matters, sociohistorical issues, community sanction, or plain gossip. For example:

Kreyòl	English
Oungan pa manke	Oungan are numerous
An efe, se bon ki ra-e	The good ones are few
O Legwa-e	O Legwa-e

This song refers to a *oungan*'s ability and willingness to serve the community and to maintain the dignity of the faith. This song also signals that the presence of a particular *oungan*, who may have violated the code of ethics, may be unwelcome at a ceremony.

Songs of Action/Direction

Songs about *drapo* (flag), *vèvè* (ritual symbols drawn on the ground with flour, corn powder, ground coffee, or cinder ash), *govi* (earthen jar containing ritual ingredients), *kolye* (necklace), *zen* (pots made in either ceramic or iron used for boiling herbs and other ritual objects), and *bwapen* (pine wicker) are usually straightforward and mean just what is being sung. I call them songs of action/direction, for they indicate an impending action or an action in progress. For example:

Kreyòl	English
Aleksina wa antre la ounfor-a	Aleksina go in the ounfo
Ou a we yon kolye vèvè	You'll see a ritual necklace

| Ou a pran potel, ban mwen | Take it, bring it to me |
| Aleksina anko mwen malere | Aleksina, is it because I'm poor? |

This song refers to both the action indicated and the *pwen* (point) about the status of the person making the request. The emphasis here is on communication, learning by doing, the power of observation and the ability to grasp figurative language and maximize the use of one's sense. The scientific apprehension of the person's total environment, material and spiritual, seems to be the aim expressed in this song.

Symbolic Rhythms and the Healing Drums

Some rhythms and dances are symbolic of the action, either impending or in progress. The *yanvalou* is a prayer, an invitation, a dance of body purification in keeping with the African holistic principle of body and soul as one. The African conception of time (past, present, and future) as one is symbolized in the music/dance *twa rigol* (danced for the lwa Marasa or the Twins entity), whose pulses appear in groups of three. The reference here is to the three healing leaves, three healing roots, three lines of descent, three moments of time/existence and the enduring nature of the family (mother, father, child) as the guarantor of the human race. The music reflects and symbolizes the drama of human existence as it unfolds on the African continent and in its Diaspora.

In spite of the great depth reflected in the symbolic meaning of the music and dance, care is taken to keep the ritual songs and dances simple in order to facilitate collective participation, for an overriding principle in African life, as in Haitian life, is inclusion. The restoring function of participation has long been recognized in Haitian traditional circles. A patient brought to the peristyle, or Vodun temple, for treatment is invited to participate in his/her own cure by learning the songs and the dances of Vodun when the person is well enough to do so. Traditional African society, the Vodun community or the Lakou, is democratic. Simplicity of action and word is highly prized in an effort to be nonexclusive. Everyone participates, everyone is healed. In this sense, the conception of the universe in Vodun circles is communalistic and what I call humanocentric (the person as the essence of the discourse), for the person regardless of ethnicity or gender is welcome to participate fully in the spiritual and community's encounter with the lwa.

Finally, the songs and dances contain the wisdom of a community facing severe stress both internally and externally. A Haitian saying goes as follows, "*fo w konn viv, pou viv lan lakou malviv,*" meaning that one has to be diplomatic to get along in a community under stress. This is particularly true of the Haitian situation today. The lwa taught the people how to navigate their way through the turbulent waters of national and international politics from the revolutionary war (1791–1803) to the new world order; people who don't hesitate to take literally to the high seas in search of a new day away from oppression. Part of this wisdom and determination to survive is summarized in the following song:

Kreyòl	English
Si se pate bon Ginen sa-a	If it weren't for the lwa
Nou tout ta peri deja-e	We would have all perished
M'di Gras papa Ginen	Have mercy, papa Ginen
M'di Gras manman Ginen	Have mercy, manman Ginen
Si se pate bon Ginen sa-a	If it weren't for the lwa
Nou tout ta peri deja-e	We would have all perished.

The Vodun Orchestra

The Vodun orchestra, as in most of West Africa, consists of a battery of three conic drums, bells, and rattles that accompany a chorus of singers and dancers. The instruments used in the Rada and Petro rites vary slightly because of the material employed in their construction and the manner in which they are played.

In the Rada rite, the three conic drums are named in relation to their size and function. The smallest, which measures about twenty-four inches in height with a head surface diameter of eight inches and foot opening exterior diameter of four and one-half inches, is called *boula*. Played with two sticks in a continuous and regular pattern, it produces a high pitch. The middle-sized drum, *segon*, measures twenty-four and one-half inches high, with a drumhead diameter of eight and one-half inches and a base or foot opening exterior diameter of seven inches. It too is played with two sticks, one straight and the other, called *ajida*, curved like a half moon. The drum provides the cyclical patterns to which the participants in a ceremony dance. The largest drum, the *manman*, is thirty-eight inches high, with a drumhead diameter of eleven inches and a foot exterior diameter of seven and three-fourths inches. It is played with one bare hand and a hammer-shaped stick, also known as *baget ginen*. The *manman* punctuates and choreographs the dance movements.

The Rada drums are made with hard wood such as mahogany or oak and are covered with cowhide attached to the drumhead by means of pegs inserted on the side of the instrument. The use of cowhide is explained by the fact that it is a material strong enough to withstand the heavy blow of the stick players.

In the Kongo-Petro rite, three conic drums are used equally. They measure roughly the same size as those of the Rada rite, but are made of softer wood such as pine. Goatskin is used to cover them, and they are attached to the drumhead by means of laces. The use of a softer wood and skin to cover the head accounts for the fact that these instruments are played with bare hands and are often used in procession-like rituals, such as Mardi Gras and its concomitant rural festivity held in the spring, the Rara, which involves carrying them around. Technically, two drums form the core of the Kongo-Petro chorus, but a third, the smallest, is often added to lend color to the ensemble. The small drum, called *kata* or *katabou*, an onomatopoeia that refers to the sound that it produces, plays a regular and continuous patter and as such sounds in the high register. The middle-sized drum, the *ti baka* or *gwonde*, a name that also refers to the low roaring sound and pattern it produces, sounds in the middle register. The largest drum, called the *gwo baka* or *manman*, plays the variations that punctuate the general choreography.

In both the Rada and the Kongo-Petro rites, bells and rattles are used. They will be discussed later in our consideration of the ritual functions of the music of Vodun.

The Songs and Drum Rhythms of Vodun

In this section, I will discuss the ritual functions of the music played for fifteen of the major Rada lwa (spirits of Vodun) worshiped in most of Haiti. The music of the Rada rite consists of the following rhythms: *yanvalou, twarigo, mayi, zepòl, kongo, dyouba/matinik, nago grankou, nago cho, mazoun,* and *Ibo.*[2] Although they are not linked here with any particular ceremonies, these Rada rhythms are presented in the order in which they would appear if they were performed at a ritual. For each rhythm I will focus on three aspects: the origin of the term, its meaning, and its function in the ritual process. Then, I will turn to what I call the "*yanvalou* trilogy" (which consists of *yanvalou, mayi,* and *zepòl*), and the "*nago/mazoun* sequence." The "*yanvalou* trilogy" will be discussed after the presentation of the first four Rada dances/musics; the "*nago/mazoun* sequence" will follow the discussion of *nago* and *mazoun*. A table summarizing the respective music performed for the fifteen major Rada lwa considered here should help to further clarify the discussion. A musical transcription of the *ogan, houla,* and *segon* patterns in *yanvalou, mayi,* and *zepol* will appear at the end of this chapter. Before discussing what music is played for which lwa, it may be good to recall the role and function of the Rada instruments.

There are six instruments in the Haitian Rada orchestra: the bell, the rattles, the *bas*, or small tambourine, the middle, and low drums.[3] Of these six instruments, the drums are the most prominent. We should recall that the small drum is called *boula*, the middle-sized drum *segon*, and the lead drum *manman*. The bell and the rattles are idiophones (self-sounding) and play a vital role in the ensemble. The bell in particular is the pace-setting instrument of the Rada battery. As in Africa, among the Adja-speaking people (Fon, Eve, Mahi), the bell seems to be the instrument on which the whole ensemble rests. The rattles in the Rada ensemble are both a musical and ritual instrument. Handled by the *oungan*, or priest, *manbo*, or priestess, who uses them to punctuate the ritual process, the rattles, which are called *ason*, play in counterrhythms with the bell and other instruments. As a ritual instrument, the *ason* is used to call the lwa (spirits of Vodun), and as such constitute the very heart of priestly practice. The *boula*, or small drum, plays a high tone and maintains a regular pattern; the *segon*, or second, sounds in the middle tone and plays in dialogue with the *manman*, or lead drum, which speaks in the low register.

Yanvalou

The origin of *yanvalou* can be traced to the Fon people of Dahomey, present-day Benin in West Africa (Herskovits 1967; Dunham). Literally, the term means "come to me." It is both an invocation and a supplication dance/music, which must be played first at all ceremonies for the Rada rite. It is known also under the name *yanvalou doba* (lowered-back *yanvalou*) because it is danced on bent knees, a stance that symbolizes supplication (Paul).

Yanvalou is the dance that begins the Vodun or Rada worship. (The terms Vodun and Rada are used interchangeably in the ritual process, although in the general context Vodun refers to the totality of the practice including all the other rites, such as Ibo, Kongo, Petro, and Makanda.) It is through the singing, playing, and dancing of the *yanvalou* that vodunists establish contact with the ancestors in Lafrik Ginen or Guinea Africa. *Possessions*, which are a means of communication between lwa and vodunists, are expected to occur during the performance of *yanvalou*. The lwa must respond to the insistent appeals of the drums, the dancing, and the singing of worshipers. Therefore, the ritual function of *yanvalou* is to call the lwa, whose manifest presence is considered a "good sign," for people who serve the lwa believe that a successful Vodun ceremony is one in which many possessions occur. This is why *yanvalou* is the ubiquitous music of the Rada rite played and danced for all the Rada spiritual entities.[4]

Twarigol

Twarigol replaces *yanvalou* when the Marasa, or the entity of the Twins, is invoked. The origin of the term is traceable to the northern region of Haiti, particularly Cap Haitian, where it is known under the name of *dereal* (Coyote, personal communication, 1982). The term *dereal* means "of the king" and refers to Haiti's only kingdom, under Henri Christophe, from 1807 to 1820. In the literature, *twarigol* has been referred to as *pas rigole,* or steps of the stream (Honorat; and Yarborough-Williams). However, Coyote, as well as most people in Bòpo, insist that the correct term is *twarigol.* Let us look further into the matter.

The number three is important in Vodun. The Marasa, although they are twins, do come in sets of two and three. In the latter case, they are referred to as "Marasa Twa" or twins of three. The term *Marasa Dosou Dosa* is also used. Dosou is the name of the male child born before or after the Marasa, and Dosa, the female child of the same order. Such a child, Dosou Dosa is considered spiritually powerful, even more so than the Marasa themselves.

Therefore, the number three seems a logical characteristic of the Marasa. Three streams or the music that is played for them may connote the idea of three lines of descent. *Twa fey, twa rasin,* or three leaves, three roots, is a recurring idea in many Vodun songs.

Kreyòl	English
Twa fey, twa rasin-o	Three leaves, three roots
Jete bliye,	Cast away and forget
ranmase sonje	He who picks up remembers

It is important to mention that this song, which expresses the importance of the number three in the Vodun worldview is at the same time a *pwen* (point) about the fact that he who dishes out forgets, but the person who is the butt of a raw deal always remembers. Vodun songs are laconic and axiomatic. In a few words they can express some rather deep ideas or verities about Haitian culture.

The music also reflects a threefold character. The *segon,* or second drum, plays a pattern of three strokes, which is the basic feature of the *twarigol,* or three streams. The musical structure is complex. To most *segon* players, the *twarigol* constitutes a challenge, and in a sense may be a real test of their ability, for *twarigol* allows for only two sets of dialogues between the *segon* and *manman*. Therefore its interest resides in the accuracy and the particular timbre of the *segon* player, who sets the pattern of three strokes answered in dialogue by the lead drum.

The performance of a *twarigol* may last as long as any *yanvalou,* from ten to fifteen minutes depending on the ritual action in process.

Mayi

The *mayi,* the dance/music named after the Mahis people, a neighboring ethnic group of the Fon of Dahomey, West Africa, follows the performance of *yanvalou* at the Rada ritual. It functions as transitional music between *yanvalou,* because Rada lwa are welcomed to the sound of several *yanvalou. Mayi* is played after an lwa has already arrived. Thus, in order to move on to the next lwa, a *mayi* is played. Then a *yanvalou* is intoned to welcome the next spiritual entity. *Mayi* is played for five of the Rada lwa. Executed faster than *yanvalou, mayi* can be of short duration. Its performance seldom lasts more than three minutes (unless a person possessed by the lwa requests that it be played, so the lwa may dance), for its ritual function consists in sending away a lwa that has been saluted. In this regard, along with *zepol, mayi* is a part of the *yanvalou* trilogy.

Zepòl

Zepòl, the dance of the shoulders, is so named because dancers move their shoulders back and forth while they perform it. The word *zepòl* means "shoulders" in Creole. Like *yanvalou,* the origin of *zepòl* can be traced to West Africa, particularly to the Adja-speaking people of Benin, Ghana, and Togo. In Haiti, this dance/music is known as *yanvalou debout/*standing *yanvalou,* a reference to the erect position assumed by the dancers (Honorat). *Zepòl* is sometimes referred to simply as vodun and is considered one of the most beautiful dances of the Haitian traditional repertoire. This is expressed in the following song:

Medam katye Morin	Katye Morin women
Medam ki gen talan	Are women with talent
Pou yo danse vodun	To dance vodun

Katye Morin, situated in the northern part of the country, is a village near Cap-Haitien, the historic capital of Haiti, a town that in the 1700s was considered the "Paris of the Antilles." The elegance of northern women is proverbial, particularly in their ability to dance vodun. (For a visual reference to *zepòl,* see Deren 1953.) Like *mayi, zepòl* is also a transitional music played between *yanvalou.* It is performed in honor of all the Rada lwa with the exception of Marasa and Azaka Mede. *Zepòl,* the fastest dance/music of the "*yanvalou* trilogy," can be of short duration because its main function, in the absence of possession, is to placate an entity.

The Yanvalou Trilogy

The *yanvalou, mayi,* and *zepol* form a musical unit that is the most important one and the basis of the Rada rite. I call this unit the "*yanvalou* trilogy" because these three dances/rhythms function as an obligatory ritual sequence. The Rada invocation cycle consists of several *yanvalou* followed by a *mayi* or a *zepol.* Most lwa require either the *mayi* or the *zepòl,* while others—Agasou, for example—demand both the *mayi* and the *zepòl.* The chart below illustrates the "*yanvalou* trilogy" within the Rada cycle.

Rada Invocation Cycle

1. Two or more *yanvalou* _____ one *mayi*
2. _____ *yanvalou* _____ one *zepol*
3. _____ *yanvalou* _____ one *zepol* _____ one *mayi*

Mayi and *zepòl* are the ritual complements of *yanvalou,* for they are performed for the same lwa, a fact that distinguishes them from the other dances/musics that are played for specific entities at specific times during the ritual process. Both *mayi* and *zepòl,* which are danced standing up (as opposed to *yanvalou,* which is danced on bent knees and with the back lowered, a movement that can be tiring indeed), function as relievers of tension. They are rhythms of transition in the invocation cycle of the Rada rite. Their main function is to send away a lwa on a positive and happy note. A more practical function of *mayi* and *zepòl* is to give a well-deserved rest to the dancers, since a *yanvalou* may last as long as twenty to thirty minutes depending on the ritual action. In such a case, the *yanvalou* is often interrupted by a series of *kase*/breaks, during which time the dancers assume a standing position before resuming the traditional lowered-back posture of *yanvalou.*

Kongo Rada

The origin of the kongo dance/music has been traced to the Congo people in central Africa (Moreau de Saint-Mery 1796, in Fouchard). Their territory covers present-day Zaire and part of Angola (Thompson; Fleurant). There are six varieties of kongo dances/musics in Haiti: *kongo fran, kongo siye, kongo laroz, kongo payet, kongo sosyete,* and *kongo rada.* Of interest here is *kongo rada,* which is played for La Sirèn, a water entity and one of Agwe's wives, or spiritual complements. Besides its association with the female water entity, *kongo rada* is played as intermission music at Vodun ceremonies conducted for the Rada rite. In this context, it is usually of very short duration and rarely exceeds two to three minutes. Its function is that of a tension releaser, for after several rounds of the demanding *yanvalou, mayi,* and *zepol,* the *kongo rada* is introduced, because drummers, dancers, and singers are in need of a music of *rejouissance.* The *kongo rada* is often played by the drums alone with no song melody or lyrics. The singers in such a case simply take a well-deserved rest. At other times, if the situation warrants, one may hear this popular lyrics:

Kreyòl	English
Yo vini gade	They come to look
Yo vini gade	They come to look
Pou yale pale	In order to gossip
Kongo men yo	Kongo, here they are
Pinga dyòl yo	Keep your mouth shut
Eyap eyap	Eyap, eyap
Pinga dyòl yo	Keep your mouth shut

This is a *chante pwen* (see Brown 1976), whose message is directed at all those who may be gossiping about the unfolding of the ceremony or other matters of the Vodun temple. Again, only two or three strophes are sung. The point is made briefly, and one hears soon after the drumbeats of the next *yanvalou* round that will welcome and salute another lwa.

The Yanvalou-Kongo Rada *Sequence*

When *kongo* is played and danced for the lwa La Sirèn, one of the spiritual complements of the salt-water entity Agwe, it becomes part of an obligatory sequence, the *yanvalou-kongo rada* sequence. La Sirèn's song cycle requires the performance of several *yanvalou,* the *zepòl,* and the *kongo-rada* to complete the round. La Sirèn along with its female companion La Balèn form an important part of Agwe's escort or squad, which is a group of lwa who walk and work together, as the Haitians put it. Songs intoned in honor of La Sirèn forcibly include La Balèn as a member of this indissoluble unit. A most commonly heard chant, in this regard, to conclude the Agwe-La Sirèn-La Balèn cycle is this one:

Kreyòl	English
La Sirèn La Balèn	La Siren La Balen
Chapom' tonbe lan lanmè	My hat fell into the sea
M'ap fe bcbcl ak La Sirèn	I was flirting with La Siren
Chapom' tonbe lan lanme	My hat fell into the sea

Dyouba/Matinik

The origin of this dance/music has been said to be traceable to some European dances, the minuet for example, that the slaves learned during the colonial period. Emmanuel C. Paul (1962, 64) refutes the idea and asserts that *dyouba matinik* came from Dahomey, West Africa. To him, it is none other than the *calinda* dance which Moreau de Saint-Mery (1796) described in his essay on dance (Fouchard). In Haiti, the *dyouba matinik* is danced in honor of the lwa Azaka Mede, who appears dressed as a peasant. Azaka Mede is also known in Africa (Herskovits). Azaka or Papa Zaka is the entity which protects agriculture, and when he enters someone's head, the person dances *dyouba matinik*. The term *matinik* or Martinique means that the dance came to Haiti via the neighboring island of the same name (Honorat). One of the characteristics of this music is that the *manman*/lead drum part is played with both hands, instead of the customary stick used to beat the lead drum of the Rada orchestra. The *manman* in this case plays some of the most intricate patterns in cross rhythm with the *segon*/second drum, which dialogues or answers the patterns of the *ogan*/bell, when one is used. If no *ogan* is used, the *boula*/small drum plays the *ogan* part. Another way of playing the *dyouba matinik* is for the player on *boula* to play its regular pattern with two sticks on the side of the *manman* drum, put lying down, while the lead drummer sits horse-riding style on the lead drum and hits the drum head with his hands and heels as well.

Nago

Two *nago* dances/rhythms are known in Haiti: *nago gran kou*/big neck and *nago cho*/hot *nago*. *Nago cho* is faster than *nago gran kou*. This dance/music can be traced back to the Anago of Yorubaland, in present-day Nigeria, West Africa. At Rada ceremonies, nago is the music played for the Ogoun family member, which in Haiti are numerous. They include, among others, Sen Jak Maje, Ogoun Feray, Ogoun Balindjo, Ogoun Badagri, Ogoun Panama, and Osanj Megi Malo (Paul 1962). The close relationship of the Yoruba and the Adja-speaking peoples (Bertho 1949) accounts for the syncretism of their music and rituals which occurred in Haiti. The drum rhythms *nago cho, yanvalou debout,* and *zepol,* which share a similar musical structure, are considered equivalent also in the ritual context. The ritual function of *nago gran kou,* like *yanvalou,* is to welcome the lwa and the *nago cho,* like *zepol* or *yanvalou debout,* to send him off on a positive note.

Mazoun

The *mazoun,* in the Rada ritual process, is associated with the Ogoun family. It is performed after the *nago gran kou* and the *nago cho.* The term *mazoun* is a contraction of the word Amazon, the legendary female warriors of Dahomey. In the Rada ritual context, *mazoun* functions in a transitional way between *nago,* because Ogoun Feray and Ogoun Badagri are saluted one after the other with a sequence of *nago gran kou, nago cho,* and *mazoun.* It serves also as a tension releaser after the *nago gran kou* and *nago cho,* which are austere in character. In this regard, its performance is always of short duration, lasting no more than two to three minutes. It is a part of what I call the "*nago/mazoun* sequence."

The Nago/Mazoun Sequence

The *nago gran kou, nago cho,* and *mazoun* are played one after the other for the Ogoun family. The order in which they are played is an obligatory sequence to salute, receive, and send away an Ogoun entity. Why the *mazoun* came to conclude the *nago* sequence is not known, but I suspect that it may be because of the origins of the dance's name. According to Henock Trouillot, *mazoun,* known as the dance/music of the Amazon, was introduced into the Rada rite in 1816. It seems clear that the *mazoun* came from the Amazon dance which evokes a defense and war dance since the latter took its name from the Dahomean female warriors. Therefore, it may have become natural to associate the Amazon with the *nago* dance, which is played in honor of the entities of war and defense, the Ogoun, for military and political leadership are characteristics associated with these lwa.

Ibo

The *Ibo* dance/music is discussed last in this presentation of the music of the Rada rite, because it is seldom played at a Rada service. It is the only rhythm linked with a particular ceremony, while the other dances/musics of the Rada rite are associated with a specific lwa. The *ibo,* the music of the

Ibo people, from Africa, is performed at a special service known as *kase kanari ibo,* or breaking the *ibo* jar, a rarely observed family ritual. Musically, however, the *ibo* is close to the *kongo* and is sometimes referred to as *ibo-kongo.* In fact, at a special session taped at Coyote's home (my main informant/consultant) on the afternoon of January 15, 1983, where I asked Coyote, TiBe, and Edner (two of Coyote's assistants) to play all the Rada and Petro drum rhythms, the *ibo* was presented as the "same thing" as *kongo.* The *ibo* rhythm, however, may be played at the Vodun/Rada service on the special demand of a person in trance if an *ibo* lwa were to mount a *chwal* or horse.[5]

The Rada Lwa and Their Respective Dances/Musics

The table on the following page summarizes the dances/musics of the Rada rite. It shows the rhythms played for each of the fifteen Rada lwa worshiped in most of Haiti. It further demonstrates that *yanvalou* is played for all the Rada entities with the exception of Ogoun. *Twarigol* is performed to invoke the Marasa. *Mayi* is played for five lwa, and *zepòl* played in honor of thirteen entities including Ogoun. When played for Ogoun, the *zepòl* is known as *Nago Cho. Kongo rada* is the dance/music played for La Sirèn and in conjunction with *yanvalou* forms the "*yanvalou-kongo rada* sequence," and *dyouba/matinik* is performed in honor of the peasant lwa, minister of agriculture, Azaka. *Nago* is the music of the Ogoun family, whose cycle requires also the performance of the *mazoun,* which gives rise to the "*nago/mazoun* sequence." *Ibo* is played only if an *ibo* lwa is present and may be heard during the ritual *kase kanari ibo.*

The music of Vodun is manifest in the rituals of its major rites and can best be understood when considered in its natural sequence, which is usually the Rada followed by the Kongo-Petro. While ceremonies held on the Rada rite are most elaborate, those conducted on the Kongo-Petro rite, its counterpart, are no less sophisticated.

The Kongo-Petro Rite

The Kongo-Petro rite, whose origin is to be found in Africa, evolved from the crucible of the plantation slavery system in St. Dominique. In the literature on Vodun, the Kongo-Petro rite, referred to simply as Petro, is presented as the negative or even the "evil" side of Rada. To many, Petro is considered an aggressive practice, a set of powerful recipes that the Haitians use against their enemies. Others confess that if such practices exist, they are a result of the brutality of Haitian history. From the colonial times to

The Rada Lwa and Their Respective Music and Dance

LWA	Yanvalou	Twarigol	Kongo Mayi	Dyouba/ Zepol	Rada	Matinik	Nago	Mazoun	Ibo
Legba/Gran chimen	x	x	x						
Loko Atisou	x		x						
Ayizan Velekete	x		x						
Marasa Dosou Dosa	x	x	x						
Danbala and Ayida Wèdo	x		x						
Sobo and Badè	x		x						
Agasou Jemen	x	x	x						
Agwe Taroyo and La Sirèn	x	x	x	x (La Sirèn)					
Bosou Kanblanmen	x		x						
Agarou Tonè	x		x						
Azaka Mede	x	x		x					
Belekou Yenou	x		x	x					
Metrès Ezili Freda	x	x	x						
Sen Jak Majè	x		x		x	x			
Ogoun Badagri	x		x		x	x			

the recent military dictatorships, Haitians had to devise ways, they contend, to deal with the horrible conditions that the people have endured in the past two centuries. This is why, both sides concede, the music of Petro reflects the rage of the oppressed. While there is an element of truth in such an assertion, the record should be set straight.

First, the rite should be called Kongo-Petro, as I have called it here, for it evolved through the years, like its counterparts, the Nago, Ibo, or the Rada, for example, and absorbed a variety of minor rites from the passage from Africa to the Americas. As mentioned earlier, Vodun, the generic term used for all the traditional religious practices retained from Africa, encompasses the rituals of "101 *nanchon*" or ethnic groups. Thus, none of the rites alone could be a typical product of the new milieux. They are grounded in African traditional practices reconstituted, and indeed seasoned with the means of the new environment, to meet the people's needs to survive. The division of Vodun rituals into categories such as Rada, Nago, Kongo, Ibo, and Petro is more a matter of conceptual convenience, an attribute of all intelligent people (and the Haitian practitioners of Vodun are no exceptions) rather than one of rigid distinction. Milo Rigaud, one of the most perceptive practitioners and analysts of Haitian Vodun, put it this way: "It is useless to try to separate the Kongo rite from the Anmine, the Anmine rite from the Petro, the Petro rite from the Rada or the Nago. Between these 'rites' or 'nations of lwa', there is rather some practical difference in the manner in which the magical science is applied, for nothing scientific could be substracted from those great fundamental lwa" (1953, 159). And finally, the Petro rite was reconstituted from the major elements of a variety of Kongo practices, a fact well documented (see Thompson 1984) which warrants joining the two terms to express the ritual and musical realities of this aspect of Haitian Vodun.

The Music of the Kongo-Petro Rite

The music of Kongo-Petro consists of dancing, drumming, and singing, which as in most African traditional music, forms the core of the ritual process. As mentioned earlier, only drumming and singing will be discussed in this chapter on the music of Vodun. Let us discuss now in greater detail the instruments of the Kongo-Petro rite.

The drumming here, one of the most electrifying styles in Haitian Vodun, includes three instruments of varying size. The biggest one, known as *gwo baka* (or *manman*), produces the grave tone called *rale;* the sound of the second, called *ti baka,* is referred to as *taye* or *gwonde;* and the third and smallest drum is the *kata* or *katabou,* an onomatopoetic name from the sound it produces. It should be said that the *kata* is often omitted in Kongo-Petro music. This chorus of drums also includes an "iron" or bell, known as *ogan,* as in Rada music, whose pattern serves as the guiding principle of the instrumental battery. Finally, one or several rattles called *cha cha* are used to provide the underlying beat in counterrhythm to the other instruments. Thus, the instruments of the Kongo-Petro style consist of three drums, a bell, and rattles made of a dry and emptied gourd calabash filled with pebbles through which a stick has been attached. The rattle can also be made of used tin cans in place of calabash. But the metallic instruments are found primarily in the Mardi Gras and Rara, which will be discussed later in this paper.

An offshoot of the Kongo-Petro rite is the *Makanda,* or rite of the secret societies. The music of Makanda is called *chica* or *kongo-sosyete,* and the drumming consists of two portable instruments because these societies often move about town during their night rounds. The main drum in this case is the *timbal,* a double-headed instrument played with two sticks with a small board fixed to its casing to serve as a percussion devise. According to Metraux (and I have had the opportunity to confirm this during my work with a secret society in Arcahaie, a town located some fifty miles north of Port-au-Prince), the *timbal* gives the *kongo-sosyete* its true character, while the other drum(s) are merely there to back it up with *siye* and *rale.*

A public version of the music of the secret societies can be found in the Mardi Gras and Rara, bands which operate under the principles of Kongo-Petro. Mardi Gras, the well-known pre-lenten festival which takes place from January to Ash Wednesday, primarily in the urban areas, is also referred to as carnival. Although rooted in the Vodun, it has incorporated elements of Christian festivities and cosmopolitan values, as well as European-made instruments. Rara follows in the wake of carnival and lasts from Ash Wednesday to Easter Sunday. Rara, found primarily in the countryside, managed to remain as close as possible to the African model of African spring/harvest festivals. However, closer to the capital city of Port-au-Prince, European instruments such as trumpets and saxophones can be found in some Rara bands. The bands are attached to a Vodun temple, and the music they perform is a variety of Kongo-Petro derivatives.

The Rhythms of Kongo-Petro

The rhythms of Kongo-Petro are the following: the *kita sech, kita mouye,* and the *boumba.* To this we have to add the variety of *kongo* and *kongo* derivatives such as *chica, kongo-savann,* and the much-prized *piyinp,* which has all but disappeared. From a musical point of view, these rhythms are in 4/4 time and based on the principle of 2 against 3, or that of cross-rhythms and syncopation. The difference between *kita* and *boumba,* for example, is only one of degree, nuance, and emphasis on where the accents are placed in the articulation of the various parts. The *kita* and *boumba* form a sequence which is played to salute, welcome, and placate the Kongo-Petro lwa. Without getting into the structural detail of the musical ensemble, on the next page is a possible notation of the bell pattern for the *kita* and *boumba.*

As mentioned before, the bell pattern is the guiding principle of the ensemble, and a modification or change of emphasis in the *ogan*/bell also accounts for a difference here warranting a different terminology. Thus, to

Bell Pattern for the *Kita* and *Boumba*

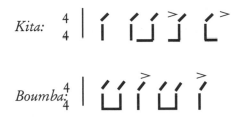

the unaccustomed ear, the distance between the *kita* and *boumba* seems slight. Yet to the practitioners of Vodun such as dancers, musicians, and priests/priestesses, those differences entail not only aesthetic values but also liturgical significance, for they will tell you that the lwa themselves require a different beat in order to manifest themselves according to the traditional sequence, procedure, or protocol. A consideration of the Kongo-Petro songs should help to further our understanding of the music of Vodun.

The Songs of the Kongo-Petro Rite

The songs of the Kongo-Petro rite are among the most assertive of the Vodun repertoire. Some writers (Courlander, Deren, Dunham, and Metraux) used terms such as "aggressive" and "evil magic" to characterize the tenor of this rite, an accepted fact in the literature of Haitian Vodun. We should offer an alternative explanation, which emerged from my research and practice of Vodun. The songs of Kongo-Petro refer to the many trials and tribulations of the African in exile. They speak of the mistrust that existed among the captive workers on the plantations of St. Domingue, the former name of Haiti. They also mention the need for secrecy and swift action as the fundamental dimension of the liberation process. We must recall the socioeconomic structure of the plantation as a productive unit, based on the exploitation of the captive workers for the benefit of the owners. The divide-and-rule tactic, which consisted in driving a wedge between the different ethnic/language groups by favoring certain elements to the detriment of others, was a major determining factor in the behavior of the Africans in captivity in colonial Haiti. Yet the people forged bonds of solidarity in establishing an underground trail leading to the mountains, the land of the maroons, where they reproduced their social organization, the center of which was their cultural and religious practice of Vodun. The plantation workers realized early that their salvation resided in their strategic unity, a feat they achieved in the face of the most brutal repression. Thus, the songs of the Kongo-Petro rite have their roots in the social organization of the maroon societies, the precursors of the Bizango, or secret societies of present-day Haiti. They have their roots also in the Bwa Kayiman ceremony of August 14, 1791, a turning point in the struggle, which led to the independence of Haiti on January 1, 1804. But, while independence brought relief from slavery, it did not translate ipso facto into complete liberation from class oppression, for the favored literate minority composed of both blacks and mulattos arrogated to themselves the spoils of the independence war. The songs of Kongo-Petro in this sense, reflect also the class and status differentiation of post-independence Haiti. To describe the tone of this rite only in terms of its aggressiveness or its propensity toward evil (something that is being done to this day in most writings on Vodun) is to miss the mark entirely as far as the sociohistorical context of Vodun in Haitian life is concerned. Let us consider some songs of Kongo-Petro taken from my fieldwork in Bòpo and Arcahaie:

Kreyòl	English
Legwa o, Legwa e	Legwa o, Legwa e
Legwa lan barye e	Legwa at the gate
Papa Legwa Papa	Papa Legwa Papa
Na veye zo nou	You watch out for us
Legwa Kalfou Legwa	Legwa of the Crossroads
Lan Barye e	You stand at the gate

Legwa of the Crossroads not only opens the cosmic gate but also stands guard at the gate to protect the servants of the lwa. The crucial point here is *"na veye zo nou,"* a Creole idiom which means that a person should look after his/her welfare, physical and spiritual, for a more literal translation of this expression reads "we will watch over our body." The "we" refers here to the dialectical conception of the body and soul (the person and the lwa) as one. The next two songs refer to the socioeconomic context of Haiti and show the little guy, the poor, the peasant in his every day struggle with an oppressive structure:

Kreyòl	English
Mwen di de o	I say two
Mwen di de o jiska twa e	I say two, even three
Yo fe conplo pou yo touye m'	They are plotting to kill me
Le yo rive	When they arrived at
Gangan yo mande non m'	Gangan's who asked my name
Yodi yo pa konnen m'	They could not remember it

Se we yo we mwen	For they only see me, and
Yo pa konnen mwen	Have no idea how strong I am

This song clearly uses the structure of Vodun (the possibility that one can be hurt through magic) to express one of the concerns of the community. The point here is that they are plotting to kill the poor, but with the help of the "guard" of the Kongo-Petro spirits, the oppressed will survive. The oppressors could not even remember the victim's name, for they know little of the strength and ability of the poor to overcome Haitian history and its legacy of misery. Vodun songs, grounded in the African circumlocutions, are often ambiguous. Only a deep level interpretation (Laguerre) may begin to unravel the extent of the coded message lodged into them. The next song seems even opaque in its use of Vodun beliefs to express a collective claim:

Kreyòl	English
Legwa fem' sa anye	It is Legwa that did it to me
Legwa fem' sa anye	It is Legwa that did it to me
Legwa Petro a	It is Legwa Petro
Kap fem'mande charite	That caused me to beg

It is easier, indeed safer, to put the blame on Legwa Petro than to confront the sociopolitical system, known historically for brutally repressing the masses' attempts to vindicate their rights. It is clear that Legwa Petro whose function is to protect the worshipper, could not cause the serviteur to go out and beg, in other words, to be reduced to an abject state of poverty. Thus, the songs of the Kongo-Petro rite, using a figurative language, contain the essence of a whole new side of Haitian life that many researchers seldom associate with Vodun consciousness. The democratic aspirations of Vodun communities as expressed in the song lyrics are a subject worthy of scholarly attention. In the last ten years, the quasi totality of the Vodun *lakou* responded enthusiastically to the dialectic of the theology of liberation preached by Aristide, who confessed that before he was a Roman Catholic priest, he was Haitian, and therefore he must be connected with Vodun. He was referring of course to the revolutionary dimension of the Kongo-Petro rite. Ayibobo!

Conclusion

In this chapter, I have attempted to present the music of Haitian Vodun in a new light. This analysis could not have been possible without the work of pioneers like Courlander, Comhaire-Sylvain, Dunham, and Kolinski, on the one hand, and the contributions of informants/consultants/teachers such as Coyote and TiBe, on the other. The concept of "bi-musicality," which favors apprenticeship, and the reflexive approach, which suggests initiation as a means to acquire much richer data, made it possible for me to study the music of Vodun from an insider's perspective. It has been possible to establish that the music of Vodun, grounded in the functional and structural principles of African art and life, is the foundation of the ritual process. The music is the central element of the Vodun ceremony, and as such, drummers and song leaders are indispensable individuals chosen as much for their artistic talents as for their liturgical knowledge. Furthermore, Vodun as a comprehensive system of universal knowledge requires a high moral conduct from its priests, priestesses, participants, and practitioners, precisely because information is power. But that power must be used for the benefit of the community. It is through the songs and dances that much of this information is passed down to the generations. Thus, the music of Vodun has not only great aesthetic value, but it is also a means of teaching the moral values of the community. The songs are an instrument of socialization. In the *lakou*, the extended-family compound, people sing all day long, even outside of the ritual context, for music forms the matrix of community living, where the lwa, the spiritual entities of Vodun, are always present, whether they are manifest or not. Thus, it is no exaggeration to say that the music of Vodun constitutes the foundation of Haiti's musical life. The major contributions of the music of Vodun should be summarized as follows: The folk music and popular music of the past two centuries have emerged from the beat of Kongo-Petro rhythms. In the past fifty years, the Jazz des Jeunes, one of the major dance bands, founded in 1943, has used extensively and successfully both Rada and Kongo-Petro beats in their compositions. Artists and singers such as the late Lumane Casimir, Haiti's Billy Holiday, who performed to great acclaim in the 1950s, Martha Jean-Claude, the grand dame of committed music who has resided in Cuba since the 1950s, and Emerante de Pradines, one of the first elite members to promote Vodun music, used Rada and Kongo-Petro rhythms as the basis of their much-prized recordings. Vodun music was the constitutive element of the "Freedom Culture" movement of the 1970s, an affirmation movement that preceded the popular "Rasin" or "Roots" music of today, of which the best known bands are Boukman Eksperyans, Boukan Ginen, Foulah, RAM, Racine Mapou, and Azor. Finally, the music of Vodun influenced the music of other Latin American countries, and the much vaunted Afro-Cuban style, so popular in the United States since the 1940s, has been influenced by the Haitian *calinda*, a dance/music grounded in the Kongo-Petro style. But, most important is the spiritual dimension of the music, the centerpiece of Vodun which is itself the "center post" of Haitian society. The music of Vodun has indeed been the common denominator of Haitian musical life. It only took us some time to recognize it. Ayibobo!

The *Boula,* or Small Drum

Boula Patterns in Yanvalou

1.

Boula Patterns in Mayi

1.   2.

Boula Patterns in Zepol

1.

The *Segon,* or Middle-sized Drum

Segon Patterns in Yanvalou

1.   2.

Segon Patterns in Mayi

1.

Segon Patterns in Zepol

1.

The *Ogan,* or Bell

Ogan Patterns in Yanvalou

1. 𝅘𝅥 𝅘𝅥 𝅘𝅥· 𝅘𝅥·   2. 𝅘𝅥· 𝅘𝅥· 𝅘𝅥 𝅘𝅥 𝅘𝅥

3. 𝅘𝅥 𝅘𝅥 𝅘𝅥 𝅘𝅥𝅮 𝅘𝅥 𝅘𝅥𝅮 𝅘𝅥   4. 𝅘𝅥 𝅘𝅥 𝅘𝅥𝅮 𝅘𝅥 𝅘𝅥 𝅘𝅥𝅮 𝅘𝅥

Ogan Patterns in Mayi

1. 𝅘𝅥 𝅘𝅥 𝅘𝅥 𝅘𝅥· 𝅘𝅥·   2. 𝅘𝅥· 𝅘𝅥· 𝅘𝅥 𝅘𝅥 𝅘𝅥

3. 𝅘𝅥 𝅘𝅥 𝅘𝅥𝅮 𝅘𝅥 𝅘𝅥 𝅘𝅥𝅮 𝅘𝅥

Ogan Patterns in Zepòl

1. 𝅘𝅥 𝅘𝅥 𝅘𝅥 𝅘𝅥· 𝅘𝅥·   2. 𝅘𝅥 𝅘𝅥 𝅘𝅥 𝅘𝅥𝅮 𝅘𝅥 𝅘𝅥𝅮 𝅘𝅥

3. 𝅘𝅥 𝅘𝅥 𝅘𝅥𝅮 𝅘𝅥 𝅘𝅥 𝅘𝅥𝅮 𝅘𝅥

Notes

1. The term "syncretism," the meeting of two cultures whose fusion gives birth to a new form is being challenged in these days. Leslie Desmangles (1992) substitutes instead the concept of symbiosis, which he sees as a cohabitation of cultural elements living side by side.

2. Singing, drumming, and dancing are the three main structural components of Rada music. Only singing and drumming patterns will be considered.

3. Several authors mentioned the use of a seventh instrument: the triangle (Rigaud 1953; Herskovits), but it is no longer in use.

4. The only exception is Ogoun, from the Nago family, who is usually considered part of the Rada rite.

5. When a person is possessed by a spiritual entity, it is said that such a person is being ridden by the lwa. Therefore, the person becomes the *chwal,* or horse, of the lwa.

References

Bertho, Jacques
  1949   "La Parenté des Yoruba aux Peuplades de Dahomey et Tog."
              Africa 19, no. 2:121–32.
Brown, Karen
  1976   "The Vèvè of Haitian Vodou: A Structural Analysis of Visual
              Imagery." Ph.D. Dissertation, Temple University.

Chernoff, John M.
1979   *African Rhythm and Africa Sensibility.* Chicago: University of Chicago Press.
Clark, VèVè A.
1978   *Kaiso! Katherine Dunham: An Anthology of Writings.* Berkeley: University of California Press.
1982   Lecture at the *Arts Connection,* New York, April.
1983   "Fieldhands to Stagehands in Haiti: The Measure of Tradition in Haitian Popular Theatre." Ph.D. dissertation, University of California, Berkeley.
Courlander, Harold
1939   *Haiti Singing.* Chapel Hill: University of North Carolina Press.
1960   *The Drum and the Hoe: The Life and Lore of Haiti.* Berkeley: University of California Press.
Dauphin, Claude
1986   *La Musique du Vaudou: Fonctions, Structures et Styles.* Naaman, Canada.
Deren, Maya
1953   *Divine Horsemen: The Living Gods of Haiti.* London: Thames & Hudson.
Desmangles, Leslie
1975   "God in Haitian Vodun." Ph.D. dissertation, Temple University.
1992   *Faces of the Gods: Vodou and the Catholic Church in Haiti.* Chapel Hill: University of North Carolina Press.
Dunham, Katherine
1969   *Island Possessed.* New York: Doubleday.
1983   *Dances of Haiti.* Los Angeles: CAAS. Copyright 1947.
Fleurant, Gerdès
1973   "Caste, Class Conflict, and Status Quo in Haiti." In *Ethnic Conflict and Power,* ed. D. Gellfand and R. Lee, 178–93. New York: John Wiley.
1987   "The Ethnomusicology of Yanvalou: A Study of the Rada Rite of Haiti." Ph.D. dissertation, Tufts University.
1996   *Dancing Spirits: Rhythms & Rituals of Haitian Vodun, The Rada Rite.* Westport, Conn.: Greenwood Press.
Fouchard, Jean
1967   *La Meringue: Danse Nationale d'Haiti.* Lemeac, Quebec, Canada.
Herskovits, Melville
1973   *Dahomey: An Ancient West African Kingdom.* Evanston, Ill.: Northwestern University Press.
1971   *Life in a Haitian Valley.* New York: Doubleday. Copyright 1937.
Honorat, Lamartiniere
1972   *Les Danses Folkloriques Haitiennes.* Port-au-Prince: Imprimerie de L'Etat.

Hood, Mantle
1960 "The Challenge of 'Bi-Musicality.'" *Ethnomusicology* 4:55–59.

Hurbon, Laennec
1972 *Dieu dans le vaudou haitien.* Paris: Editions Payot.
1987 *Le barbare imaginaire.* Port-au-Prince: Editions Henri Deschamps.

Jones, A. M.
1959 *Studies in African Music.* 2 vols. London: Oxford University Press.

Kolinski, Mieczyslaw
1980 "Haiti." In *The New Grove Dictionary of Music and Musicians,* ed. Stanley Sadie, 33–37. New York: Macmillan.

Laguerre, Michel
1980 *Voodoo Heritage.* Los Angeles: Sage Publications.

Locke, David
1979 "The Music of Atsiagbeko." Ph.D. dissertation, Wesleyan University.
1981 "Drum Language in Agzogbo." *African Music* 6, no. 1:32–51.
1982 "Principles of Offbeat Timing and Cross-Rhythm in Southern Eve Dance Drumming." *Ethnomusicology* 26, no. 2:217–46.

Lomax, Alan
1969 "Africanism in New World Music." In *Research & Resources of Haiti,* ed. Richard P. Schaidel, 118–54. New York.

Maximilien, Louis
1945 *Vodou: Rite Rada-Kanzo.* Port-au-Prince: Imp. de l'Etat.

Mbiti, John S.
1969 *African Religions and Philosophy.* Garden City, N.Y.: Doubleday.

Metraux, Alfred
1959 *Voodoo in Haiti.* New York: Oxford University Press.

Montilus, Guerin C.
1981 "African in Diaspora: The Myth of Spring Dahomey in Haiti." *Journal of Caribbean Studies* 2:73–84.
1986 *Dieux en Diaspora: Les Loa Haitiens et Les Vaudou du Royaume d'Allada (Benin).* Niamey: CELHTO.

Nketia, J. H. Kwanbena
1959 *African Music in Ghana.* Evanston, Ill.: Northwestern University Press.
1963 *Drumming in Akan Communities of Ghana.* London: Thomas Nelson & Sons.
1974 *The Music of Africa.* New York: W.W. Norton.

Pantaleoni, Hewitt
1972 "The Rhythm of Atsia Dance Drumming Among the Anlo (Eve) of Anyako." Ph.D. dissertation, Wesleyan University.

Paul, Emmanuel C.
    1962   *Panorama du Folklore Haitien.* Port-au-Prince: Imprimerie de l'Etat.
Price-Mars, Jean
    1973   *Ainsi Parla 'Oncle.* Paris: Lemeac. Copyright 1928.
Rigaud, Milo
    1953   *La Tradition Voudoo et le Voudoo Haitien.* Paris: Editions Niclaus.
Roumain, Jacques
    1943   *Le Sacrifice du Tambour-Assoto(r).* Port-au-Prince: Imprimerie de L'Etat.
    1944   *Masters of the Dew.* London: Heinemann.
Simpson, G. E.
    1970   *Religious Cult of the Caribbean: Trinidad, Jamaica and Haiti.* University of Puerto Rico.
Thompson, Robert Farris
    1968   "An Aesthetic of the Cool: West African Dance." *African Forum.*
    1984   *Flash of the Spirit: African and Afro-American Art and Philosophy.* New York: Vintage Books.
Turner, Victor
    1969   *The Ritual Process: Structure and Anti-Structure.* Ithaca, N.Y.: Cornell University Press.
Wilcken, Lois
    1962   *The Drums of Vodou.* White Cliffs, Ariz.: Augustin.
Yarborough-Williams, L.
    1964   *Haiti-Dance.* Frankfurt am Main: Bronners Druckerei.

Selected Discography

Ritual & Folk Music of Haiti

Auguste, Annette (Sō Ann). *Haiti Folk Voodoo Songs.* J. D. Productions, 1839-3.
Beauvoir, Mathilda. *Le Vaudou: Chants & Dancses d'Haiti: Ceremonie Vaudou.* CBS Inc., 1973. Pressed in France.
Boukan Ginen. *Jou a Rive.* Cine DISC, Haiti, 1993.
Boukman Eksperyans. *Vodou Adjae.* Mango Records, TM 1990.
———. *Nou La.* TCD Productions, 1991.
Courlander Harold. *Calypso and Meringues.* Folkways Records.
———. *Folk Music of Haiti.* Folkways Records, FE 4407, 1952.
———. *Songs and Dances of Haiti,* Folkways Records, FE 4432, 1952.
Deren, Maya, (Ito). *Divine Horsemen: The Living Gods of Haiti.* Lyrichord, LLST 7341, 1978. Music recorded 1947–1953.
Gillis, Verna, and Roman Martinez. *Rara in Haiti, Gaga in the Dominican Republic* FE 4531-1978.

Hill, Richard, and Morton Marks. *Voodoo Tance Music: Ritual Drums of Haiti.* Lyrichord LLST 7279, 1974.

Jean Claude, Martha. *Songs of Haiti.* Rumba Records 55503.

La Troupe Makandal. *A Trip to Voodoo.* LP 1374, Stero Saryleen Records, Brooklyn, N.Y., 1983.

RAM. *Aibobo.* Cine DISC, Haiti, 1993.

Roots of Haiti. *Voodoo.* Mini Records, No>y. 1978. Vols. 1–3.

——. *TiRoro.* Mini Records, 1978. Vol. 4.

——. *Rara Grap Plezi.* Mini Records, 1979. Vol 5.

Sharing Heritage. Savary & Son Records, New York, 1980. Center for African Studies, Haiti.

Solèy Leve. *Chansons & Poesies Patriotiques.* Haiti, Soley SOS 001, 1973. Vol. 1.

——. *Peyi an Mouin.* SL-1974A. Vol. 2.

——. *Ayiti Demain* Peze Kafe. 1976. Vol. 3.

TiRoro and His Voodoo Drums. Request Records, Elmhurst, N.Y.

Wawa and His Group. *Le Vaudou Haitien.* Michga Records, Vols. 1–6.

——. *Le Vaudou Haitien.* "Baron," Michga Records.

Wawa. *Et Les Camisoles Bleus.* Vaudou, Coumbite, March Record, 1240. Copyright 1970.

——. *Et Les Camisoles Bleus.* Vodou March Record 276. Copyright 1979.

zobop. [Haitian Vodun]. Haiti Editions R-10008. Copyright 1979.

Films

There are many films on Haiti with both Creole/French and English dialogues. The titles listed below focus primarily on Vodun and use English as the feature language.

Black Dawn. Green Valley Media, Burlington, Vermont, 1985.

Divine Horsemen: The Living Gods of Haiti. Deren/Ito, New York, 1978.

Haitian Pilgrimage. Green Valley, Burlington, Vermont, 1991.

Haitian Song. Karen Kramer, New York, 1984.

Legacy of the Spirit, Karen Kramer, New York, 1986.

Mete Pye w Lan Dlo (Put Your Feet in Water). Haitians, Health Care and AIDS, Boston City Hospital, 1991.

Voodoo and the Church. Nine Morning Productions, Inc. Chicago, 1989.

Voyage of Dreams. Ray Cajuste, Peter Davis et al., New York, 1984.

20

African-derived Religion in the African-American Community in the United States

MARY CUTHRELL-CURRY

FRICAN-DERIVED RELIGION is defined here as a religion in the United States that had its origin in Africa and is now practiced by native-born African Americans. This does not include religions totally restricted to immigrant communities, nor does it include religions developed in the United States with an African inspiration. Consequently, in this article, African religions practiced by immigrant Africans or Haitian Vodun as well as religions that are "reconstructed" Africanism are not considered. While the latter have no connections to continuing traditions, the former are largely restricted to their own communities and have not had a large impact on native-born African Americans. Hence, my discussion is confined to Yoruba-derived religions in the United States.

Since the 1960s, as one walks through New York City and other major urban centers, one occasionally sees a man, woman, or child dressed all in white with numerous beaded necklaces in different patterns and a beaded bracelet worn on the left wrist. This is an initiate in the Santeria or the Yoruba Religion. Also commonly found around Latin or more rarely African-American neighborhoods are stores called botanicas. These stores have a bewildering selection of merchandise in their windows: statues of saints, American Indians, or perhaps even Hindu deities; candles, covered bowls, clothing made of gingham and burlap; books in Spanish and English; beads; and so on. These stores sell the materials used in the Santeria and in the Latin version of spiritualism, Espiritismo.

The dress of initiates and botanicas are the only two visible manifestations of the Yoruba Religion that a casual observer sees. The Religion (in most instances) does not have churches or buildings devoted to its practice. Rituals take place in the homes of its practitioners or occasionally in halls rented especially for the occasion. But beneath the visible surface of major urban centers, behind the facades of brownstones and hidden by apartment walls, one notices a quietly thriving religion growing in its influence over the cultural life of major urban centers—finding expression in music and dance, and in painting and sculpture.

Historical Background

The Yoruba Religion (also called Santeria and Ocha but most commonly the Religion) is an African-derived religion that has survived despite the enslavement and persecution of its adherents. It originated in West Africa, where it was the society-wide religion of Yoruba kingdoms. During the slave trade, it was introduced into the Caribbean and Latin America, especially Haiti, Cuba, Trinidad, and Brazil.

When slavery ended, the followers of the religion were persecuted as criminals in Catholic countries. Indeed, the very first studies of the religion were written by a physician of forensic medicine (the work of Nina Rodrigues—*L'Animisme Fetichiste des Negres de Bahia* [1900]) and as criminology by Fernando Ortiz (*La Hampa Afro-Cubana—Los Negros Brujos* [1906]). Police raided houses of worship and confiscated religious objects. In Brazil, this continued until the 1950s. In her book *The Divine Horsemen,* Maya Deren (1953, 174) describes the sounds of a vodun ceremony masked by the music of a popular band in order to evade the police. In Protestant countries, with the exception of Trinidad,[1] the religion ceased to exist during slavery or had never existed at all.

Yoruba-derived traditional religion quietly entered the United States in the 1960s (during a period of political, social, and religious ferment—the time of the civil rights and black power movements). Despite the existence of the Yoruba Temple in Harlem, the Religion was overshadowed by other religious groups such as the Nation of Islam and the followers of Malcolm X and the major political events of the decade. For many Afro-Americans conversion to the Yoruba Religion meant a rejection of Christianity and a searching for a religious perspective that would foster African-American identity.

Continuously since the 1960s, concurrent with large-scale Cuban immigration (as a result of the Cuban revolution), the Yoruba Religion has been steadily growing in African-American and Latin communities in the United States in addition to attracting a smaller number of white adherents

(Marks 1974). In the United States, outside of the Cuban community, the Yoruba Religion is spreading by conversion, yet it does not actively seek converts. Still, it has become an important cultural element in the life of major urban centers, especially New York City, finding expression in painting, sculpture, and the performing arts (Brandon 1983; Friedman 1982; Hunt 1979; and Murphy 1981; 1988).

Cuba and the Development of Yoruba Religion

One significant factor that contributed to the popularity and development of this religion was the immigrating to the United States of the Cubans since about 1840 (Office of Pastoral Research 1982). My informants, however, date the beginning of the influence of Cubans on the African-American community from the 1940s. That influence was initially felt in the performing arts, that is, Afro-Cuban jazz and the dance. It was noted, however, that major ceremonies in the Religion were not practiced in the United States until the 1960s (Weaver 1986; Brandon 1983).

The Cuban revolution made initiations in this country necessary, and the arrival of Cuban ritual specialists in the United States made them possible. My informants mention two particular Cubans, one *babalawo*,[2] Pancho Mora (Gonzalez-Whippler 1983) and one Oriate.[3]

The first Afro-American priest was Nana Oseijeman Adefunmi (born Walter Eugene King), who went in search of an African religious expression for African Americans. This search made him leave Detroit (where he was born in 1928) and go to Cuba's Matanzas Province, where he was initiated as a priest of Obatala[4] on August 28, 1959. Accompanying him and initiated as a priest of Aganju[5] on the same day was the late Christopher Oliana, a black American of half-Cuban ancestry. During his youth, Adefunmi had performed with the Katherine Dunham dance troop and had founded a study group on Afro-American religions which was called Damballah Wedo.[6] In 1970 Adefunmi left Harlem and established the village of Oyotunji (Oyo rises again)[7] in Sheldon, South Carolina.

Adefunmi's story is important because he was the first African-American priest initiated into Yoruba Religion and the founder of the Yoruba Temple, which was a well-known part of the Harlem scene from 1960 to 1970 (Clapp 1966). Many members of the African-American community first became aware of the Yoruba Religion through the Yoruba Temple and participated in its activities. A number of African Americans received their African names from Adefunmi, and some of these began to wear African dress, whether converted to the Yoruba Religion or not.

When Adefunmi left New York City in 1970, he took only a small number of his followers with him. Some joined him after the founding of Oyotunji Village. Many of Adefunmi's former followers and casual visitors to the Temple became members of Cuban or multiethnic Houses.[8] Many of them were referred to these Houses by Adefunmi himself because at that time he was prohibited from initiating people into the Religion. Out of these Houses, African-American Houses developed. (Clapp 1966; Brandon 1983).

Up until 1960, the date of the Cuban revolution, initiations into the priesthood were conducted in Cuba. After that date they were conducted in Puerto Rico. By 1962 the Cubans in New York City had begun to do initiations, and ultimately the late Marjorie Baynes Quiñones, a young African-American woman was made a priest of Shango—thus becoming the first African American to receive a full Yoruba initiation in the United States. She went on to initiate twenty-one priests.

The late Asunta Seranno, a Puerto Rican priest of Obatala who founded a large multiethnic House, initiated a number of African-American priests. Adefunmi also referred a number of African Americans to Seranno (Brandon 1983, 98). Since the closing of the Yoruba Temple, the Religion in the African-American community has grown. It is a small but distinct presence in the African-American community in the United States.

The Scope of Yoruba Religion in the United States

The two largest concentrations of practitioners of the Yoruba Religion in the United States are in Miami and New York City.

> While Cuban immigrants have tended to concentrate in a few major settlements, the 1970 census found Cubans living in every state except Wyoming and Vermont. More than 40 percent of all Cubans in the United States resided in Metropolitan Miami in 1970. Most of the rest lived in New York City, Northern New Jersey, Los Angeles or Chicago. (Office of Pastoral Research 1982, 2:104)

There are smaller concentrations of worshipers in Philadelphia, Gary, Indiana (Bascom 1972), Boston, Cleveland, Chicago, San Francisco, and Los Angeles (Brandon 1983). It is probable that there are practitioners of the Religion in all major cities of the country. However, there is no adequate count or estimate of the total number of practitioners for the entire country. Adequate answers to the questions of precise size and scope are issues of further investigation. However, it is reasonable to assume that although reliable figures are unavailable, both the literature and reports from practitioners indicate that Yoruba Religion is widespread in the United States and that its two primary areas of concentration are Dade County, Florida, and the greater New York metropolitan area. It is also clear that the number of African-American adherents is much smaller than the number of Latin ones.

Beliefs and Practices

Yoruba Religion consists of (1) ideas of destiny and reincarnation, (2) a cosmology that places human beings at the center of a nexus of forces, (3) a complex ritual system that consists of divination and sacrifice, and (4) a rich system of ceremonies.

The Concept of Destiny

The ideas of destiny and reincarnation are the basic components of Yoruba Religion. The Orisha[9] serve as organizing principles for understanding the world. The Yoruba use their characteristics as premises in a system of analogies. Ori, the Yoruba word for destiny, is a complex multivalent term. It means simultaneously the physical head, destiny, potentiality, the quality of a person's character, the ancestral guardian spirit, and the individual's personal deity or Orisha. It is connected to ideas of predestination, reincarnation, and struggle in the world, and it is the focal concept of Yoruba religious life.

Ori is the Yoruba word for head, or the top of anything. To the Yoruba, the physical head is sacred because it is the seat of divinity. It is the symbol of the link between the divine and human and between the ancestors and the living. The outer physical head is the manifestation of the inner person. The Yoruba believe the person to be made of several spiritual and physical elements. The spiritual elements are the heart, *Okan*, which in some circumstances can leave the body and act on its own, and *emi*, or breath, the essence of a person or the seat of living. The physical elements are the body *(ara)*, shadow *(ojiji)*, which the Yoruba think of as an embodiment of a person's inner self, and *iye*, part of the mind resident in the brain. The head coordinates these different elements into a composite being.

Yoruba religious life is centered on the concept of destiny—the self-chosen pattern of a person's life. The Yoruba concept of "predestination" contains a preponderant element of choice. According to the oral tradition, a person kneels in heaven before Olodumare to choose his or her lot in life. The Yoruba believe that the person is allowed to make any choice, and that, within reason, Olodumare grants that choice. Destiny involves the individual's personality, his or her occupation, his or her luck, and the date of his or her death. Yet even this choice is not determinate, for the Yoruba conceive of destiny only as potentiality. The person, through his or her own efforts, must bring it into manifestation. Human beings or opposing spiritual forces may seek to work against a person achieving all that is destined for him or her.

The Ifa and Merindinlogun oral literatures contain countless stories to explain and illustrate the ramifications and permutations of destiny. The stories show that choices may be wise or unwise. At birth, the person forgets the choice. Priests and *babalawos* perform divination for the person to ascertain that pattern which the person chose in heaven, in order to remedy it through sacrifice or to ensure that those who work against it will not succeed.

The person can achieve his or her potential destiny only with struggle, the aid of supernatural forces, and the failure of those, human or other, who would work to oppose its actualization. There are active negative forces, supernatural and human, that actively work against the achievement of one's destiny. These negative forces are called *ajogun,* or enemies against man. *Ori* is a choice-potentiality-to-be-realized-through-struggle. This conception of predestination emphasizes the person's own self-creation.

Although a person's destiny may contain honor, wealth, and long life, it does not automatically come to him or her. The good things in life will happen only through unceasing effort. The person has divination performed to ascertain what his or her destiny is and makes sacrifices to repair an unfortunate destiny, to ensure the maintenance of a fortunate destiny or to placate or oppose those who would obstruct its manifestation. Nevertheless, the person has to pay attention to other areas of life. S/he has to carry out purely secular[10] activities. Food must be cooked, houses built, crafts and professions practiced—the "logical" activities to achieve one's goals. If the person has chosen a good destiny, has struggled and has overcome opposition, then s/he will have a good life in this world.

The Yoruba Religion is a life-affirming religion. There is no dichotomy between an "evil world" and a "good heaven." Heaven is a holy place, but so is the earth. It is also a religion that models itself on the family as a corporate group. The living, the dead, and the unborn are all part of the family group. They interchange states but stay in the same group. Life and death, then, are cycles within the family group.

A person kneels in heaven before Olodumare and chooses his or her destiny. That person is born as the youngest and least senior of the group. As s/he grows, others are born or married into the family and s/he gains a measure of seniority. As the person grows older, s/he gains in seniority so that by the time s/he is old, s/he will be the most senior person and therefore the person closest to the ancestors in the family group or lineage. The person dies and becomes an ancestor. In some way the spirit of that ancestor can be reborn in a number of descendants. A family then can be conceived of as a set of constantly circulating spirits.

The Yoruba see the world as a good place. Only those who have lived their lives in such a way that they are sent to the heaven of potsherds[11] will not be reincarnated again in their families. The Yoruba do not seek release from the chain of rebirth; indeed the ultimate tragedy is to be barred from it. Life on earth is good, and life in heaven is good. The person experiences and reexperiences both. There is no eternal salvation or eternal damnation. A person who is unworthy is not dammed. S/he is discarded from the cycle of life.

Ori is also the word for ancestral guardian spirit. The Yoruba believe that one component of that composite which a person is considered to be is the soul of one of his or her ancestors. This ancestral guardian spirit has chosen to come back to earth and guard the person. Ori is also the name given to a person's personal Orisha. Worshipers believe that of all the gods, only a person's Ori will go with him or her throughout all his or her difficulties. What a person's Ori ordains, no one can prevent, and what his or her Ori denies, no other Orisha can cause to happen. Thus, for any person, the most powerful of the gods is that person's own personal Orisha.

Destiny is also connected to the idea of character. A person's individual traits or proclivities will affect/determine what happens to him or her. It is in the meaning of character that Yoruba morality and ethics are found. Robert Farris Thompson discusses what he considers to be the three cardinal values of the Yoruba Religion: *ashe*, the power-to-make-things-happen; *iwa*, character; and *itutu*, coolness or grace under pressure (1983).

In the Western Hemisphere, the idea of respect is that aspect of good character that is most emphasized: respect for authority, respect for oneself, and indeed respect for everything and everybody. An important consideration in this regard is context. The situations of life require flexibility. Different emphases on particular values may be more appropriate in one situation than another.

Steven Gregory describes another prime Yoruba component of character.

> Each encounter with nature and society is thought to be meaningful, revealing both the interrelations among phenomena and the potential with which these relations are impregnated. The ability to realize, in the double sense of this word, the meanings immanent within these relations constitutes spiritual power, or *Ashe*. Comprehending these inter-relations is dialectically linked to the act of making them real. In the realm of human social relations, this realization entails the maintenance of a multi-dimensional reciprocity. (1986, 99)

Ori is consequently a densely packed concept with implications for many areas of Yoruba belief and practice. Almost any major practice can be traced to it. Divination and sacrifice are centered on the concept of destiny. The belief in destiny gives worshipers their reason for being.

Divination

The Yoruba believe that, although a person chooses his or her destiny in heaven, this choice is forgotten when the person is born into this world. However, there are means of communication between the human and divine. Those means are the various forms of divination. Orunmila, the deity of divination was present at each person's choice and therefore knows what is allotted to him or her. Consequently, if a person needs such information, s/he goes to a priest to obtain it through divination.

The priest divines to determine the pattern of life the person chose in heaven so that the person can remedy his or her life pattern through sacrifice or s/he can placate or successfully oppose those who work against the desired flowering of his or her destiny. Divination is usually an individual affair. A person seeks divination because s/he has an individual difficulty, and it is the duty of the diviner to help solve that person's problems when s/he is consulted. There are times, however, when divination is communal, that is, when it is performed for a group.

Three major forms of divination are common among the Yoruba: Ifa, Merindinlogun, and Obi. Of these three, Ifa is the most prestigious. Priests of Ifa (the *babalawom*, Father-of Secrets or Father-Knows-the-Secret) specialize in divination. They are philosophers, experts on religious life, and custodians of Yoruba oral culture.

Ifa is much more culturally prominent in Nigeria than it is in the Western Hemisphere. Slavery did not allow the leisure to memorize and reflect on the tremendous amount of materials in the Ifa corpus. Nor did slavery encourage traveling from expert to expert to learn, which is a pronounced feature of the training of a *babalawo* in Nigerian culture. It was especially impossible for *babalawos* to congregate and chant the verses of Ifa (Weaver 1986; Gleason 1973). A *babalawo* can really have no other occupation. Additionally, Ifa is considered to be a man's cult, although such a rule is not absolute in Nigeria. There are women *babalawo*, according to E. McClelland (1982, 88):

> Great surprise was caused by the appearance of a woman babalawo in this seeming inviolate men's preserve but inquiry yielded the information that s/he had only reached the first stage and would not go further. However, s/he was competent, set out his or her little statue of Eshu, laid down his or her equipment on a mat and proceeded to divine with his or her chain.

In the Western Hemisphere, the rule is followed absolutely—no woman may be a *babalawo*. This difference may be a result of change. The older (pre–slave-trade rule) may be that no woman is permitted to be a *babalawo* and in this the practitioners in the West may be more traditional.

Ifa is a kind of geomancy[12] that depends on the generation of certain signs (called Odu in Nigeria and/or letters in Cuba) and the interpretation of their meaning. There are two methods of generating *odu*, or letters. The *babalawo* shifts them rapidly from hand to hand. If one is left in one hand, he makes two marks in a tray that contains a powder. If two are left in one hand, he makes one mark on the tray. If more are left, the procedure is repeated until one or two are left. This entire process is repeated four times until an *odu* is generated. The second, a faster method, is by the use of an *opele*, a chain that has eight seeds, which when spread open have naturally concave and convex surfaces. One toss of the *opele* will produce a sign. Both maneuvers have the potential of producing 256 different signs. Each sign, called an odu, has verses[13] (Nigeria) and stories (the Western Hemisphere) attached to it. These stories sketch a predicament faced by its protagonists, and the stories are assumed to contain the answer to the questioner's difficulties. The solution almost always takes the form of a sacrifice. Ifa, then, is a repository of human problems and their solutions. Although Ifa exists in the United States (the *babalawo* are consulted every day in New York, for example), Merindinlogun, a system closely related to Ifa but which can be used by the priest of any Orisha, is much more culturally prominent in the Western Hemisphere.

In Merindinlogun, the second form of divination, the diviner uses sixteen cowries to generate the signs. Priests file the backs of the cowries off to reveal the inside. The cowries are thrown on a basket tray or a mat and the number face up are counted. An *odu* is attached to each number. According to William Bascom, the *odu* of Ifa and Merindinlogun are similar. To each *odu*, a story is attached, as in Ifa. Also, solutions to problems are deemed to be sacrifices.

Any priest or priestess may use the Merindinlogun. Merindinlogun is much more culturally prominent in the Western Hemisphere than is Ifa, where there are many more women diviners than there are men. Moreover, Merindinlogun is much easier to learn than is Ifa. A more important factor in its prominence may be that in the Western Hemisphere—perhaps because of literacy—a priest is not expected to memorize all the stories of the corpus. Instead, priests have notebooks in which they record the teachings of their elders—a change from a preliterate to a literate tradition.

The third type of divination that is available to both priests of Ocha and the *babalawo* is *obi*. In Nigeria, the kind of *obi*, kola nut, that is used for divination is the one that breaks into four lobes. Since kola nuts do not grow in the United States and Cuba, the coconut is substituted for them. In the Western Hemisphere, the coconut is called Obi. The diviner breaks a coconut and divides the meat into four pieces. The inside of the coconut is white and its outside is brown; this allows five patterns to be perceived when four pieces of coconut are thrown simultaneously and allowed to fall.

Obi has no stories attached to it. It is used to obtain answers to yes/no questions. The various combinations of *obi* give n + 1, that is, five combinations. There seemingly are various nuances of yes and no.

If manifestation of a favorable destiny is the main concern of the practitioners in the Yoruba Religion, then divination is its principal means of diagnosis and sacrifice is the paramount means of setting things right. If Ori is the predominant belief in the Yoruba religion, then sacrifice is the foremost practice. The oral tradition constantly emphasizes the theme of sacrifice. The basic pattern is: So-and-so had such-and-such a problem. S/he was told to perform such-and-such a sacrifice. At this point, the person performed the sacrifice and his or her problem was solved, or the person did not perform the sacrifice and the problem remained unsolved; or the person performed part of the sacrifice and the problem was partially solved.

Oral traditions give all kinds of reasons that a person might not comply with the directive to sacrifice: "He took Ifa for a liar and Eshu for a thief"; "She sacrificed for children but did not sacrifice so that his or her children should not be enemies"; and so on. Wande Abimbola (1973, 11) emphasizes the importance of sacrifice in the Yoruba Religion and finds it to be central to the Religion. The purpose of sacrifice is to achieve or restore a state of balance between the individual and supernatural forces (Zuesse 1979, 218).

The Yoruba pantheon consists of God, the earth, the ancestors, and the Orisha. The Orisha operate as a framework for understanding humanity and nature. Above all other deities, on another plane altogether, is Olodumare, also called Olorun (the Owner of Heaven), or, in the United States and Cuba, Olofin. He is supreme. Yet there is no cult attached to him; he receives no direct organized worship; and he has no shrines. The Yoruba say: "Who would dare offer sacrifice to Olodumare." Olodumare is considered to be the creator of heaven and earth. He is the source of all destinies and the ultimate source of good and evil, yet he is above the human distinctions of good and evil. He is a combination of opposite polarities, the ultimate balance of all contradictory powers. Robert Farris Thompson (1983) conceives of him as the totality of all the forces of the universe. According to Ulli Beier (1975, 34):

... the Orisha are part representations of Olodumare. Each Orisha is the universe looked at from another angle. Olodumare is the sum total of all the complexities, he is the universe concentrated into one intelligence ... one could conceive of God as the one force from which everything emerges—or else one could see him as the coexistence of all the complexities.

God, then, is a perfect dynamic balance of forces of the totality, which makes him ultimately neutral. He is the ultimate balance and the ultimate coolness. "Coolness" is an extremely important concept. It includes notions of balance, proper behavior, respect for the authority of the elders, and grace under pressure. The universe is the dance of interacting forces. The totality is beyond comprehension, but individual parts can be grasped. God, then, is the creator, the source of destiny, greater than the heavens. He is omnipresent, omnipotent, and omniscient. God is not remote, but the Orisha are more approachable, both in requests for help and in the grappling of understanding.

In Nigeria, Onile (the-Owner-of-the-Earth) has his or her own particular cult, the Ogboni, or Society of Elders. Onile sanctions covenant breaking and the shedding of blood. In Yoruba society, the Ogboni served as a counterbalance to the power of the king and conducted a court in which to try offenses against the earth. They had the power to ask the king to go to sleep (commit suicide) if they felt he was in some way unsuitable. Since the period of colonization, the Ogboni have lost considerable political power, but remain a powerful moral force.

The cult of the earth, as such, did not translate to Cuban and American cultures (although it did to the Brazilian culture) but the religious valuation of the earth did. Sacrifices are made to the earth, and s/he is held in reverence.

For the Yoruba, life does not really end; the person changes from one state of existence to another. Their belief in reincarnation and life continuing in heaven much as it does on earth means that for them there is a cycle of existence in which the living become the ancestors and the unborn are born again in their descendants. Death does not break relationships. It changes their character.

Orisha are difficult to define. They are complex, multivalent beings (Beier 1975, 34). Each Orisha is considered to have a particular domain, physical manifestations, and psychological correlatives in the human mind and other symbolic extensions (Gregory 1986, 90). Orisha are considered to be aspects of God, forces of nature, or the universe viewed from different angles. According to John Mason, the Orisha are specialized forms of the Supreme God. They are analogous to the saints of the Catholic Church—hence the Spanish term "Santo"—in that they are conceived to be intermediaries between human beings and God. Yet the parallel ends there. The saint is separate from God, not a part of him. Moreover, the Yoruba insist that the Orisha be responsible to humanity in a way that no European would (Soyinka 1976, 14–15).

Orisha are also thought of as psychological forces in the human mind. It is also believed that each person has an Orisha assigned to him or her at birth and that this Orisha and the person (called his or her child) share the same character. There is a proverb which says: "The character of the person is the character of the Orisha," or in Haitian, "*Temperament mun, ce temperament loa-li*" (Deren, 1970). Shango,[14] for example, is described as the wrath of God, or Yemonja[15] as his mercy. A person described as a child of Shango could very well be characterized as one with an explosive temper, whereas a child of Yemonja as unusually tolerant. None of these portrayals of Orisha is inaccurate or exhaustive. Rather, they are all simultaneously accurate and incomplete. On a moral plane, no Orisha is totally good or totally evil. Each force has positive and negative manifestations. Some show more of their positive face, some more of the negative.

The Religion is organized into structures of ritual kinship called Houses of Ocha.[16] The word House describes a group of people, the relationship between them, and lines of descent of Orisha. A House of Ocha is called by the name of the priest who is its head, for example, Peter's House. Members of the house are the godchildren of the priest who heads it. Godchildren are godbrothers and godsisters to each other. Other terms modeled on kin relationships are also employed. There are grandparents-in-*ocha;* aunts- and uncles-in-*ocha;* and nieces- and nephews-in-*ocha,* and so on.

Of these relationships, the most important is that between godparent and godchild. It is the key relationship in the House of Ocha. Godparents and godchildren have complementary responsibilities. The godparent is responsible for the godchild's growth in the Religion. S/he oversees all necessary divinations, sacrifices, and initiations for the godchild. S/he has the duty to instruct the godchild in religious knowledge, ritual, and duties. S/he must give the godchild aid up to and including taking him or her home and providing a funeral and burial if the blood family is not capable of doing so. Reciprocally, the godchild is expected to assist the godparent in rituals or to do work in the godparent's home that is connected with religious activities. This would include cooking and cleaning in preparation for a religious ceremony. Moreover, if the godparent is performing an important ritual, the godchild is expected to attend. Twice a year, on the Orisha day of the godparent and on the anniversary of the godparent's initiation into the Religion, the godchild is expected to bring a ritual gift called an *ashe-di.* This consists of two candles, a coconut,[17] and $1.05.[18]

It must be emphasized that the term House refers to a group of people, and not a physical location. A House of Ocha does not have physical space separate from the homes of the priests. Each home of a priest is a shrine, but there may be many priests in a House. The houses or apartments of priests contain shrines of the Orisha but, on casual observation, do not appear to be religious centers. The home of a priest is also a ceremonial center in which religious rituals and/or ceremonies are held. Although a House may have many possible places of worship, the main one will be the home of the head of the House.

Life Cycle Ceremonies

Yoruba Religion is rich in ceremonies and ritual. When a child is born, its father announces its name on the seventh day after its birth at its naming ceremony. The ceremony occurs as early in the morning as possible. Before the ceremony, the child's parents choose a godfather and godmother.

The ceremony begins with a sacrifice to the ancestors. The sacrifice announces the birth to the ancestors and is in thanksgiving for the child and the safe delivery by the mother. Then the child is taken outside; its head is uncovered, and it is lifted up toward the sky—showing the child to Olodumare. Then the officiating priest divines for the child using Merindinlogun. After the priest asks the father what name has been chosen for the child. The father announces the child's name to the community for the first time.

Next comes the food-tasting ceremony. The food consists of nine items: (1) a jikora[19] of water, (2) a bottle of gin, (3) a saucer of honey, (4) a saucer of guinea pepper, (5) a saucer of grated coconut, (6) a saucer of salt, (7) a saucer of sugar, (8) a saucer of cayenne pepper, and (9) a saucer of palm oil. The godfather chooses each of the saucers in random order and puts a small amount in the child's mouth and then passes the saucer around so that everyone present tastes a small amount. Priests present explain the symbolism of each food. Next each person present dances with the baby beginning with the godfather and ending with the mother. While dancing, everyone whispers a blessing in the baby's ear. After the dancing, guests give money and gifts to the baby.

When two people decide to marry, their respective parents and they themselves, along with the priest who will officiate, conduct a negotiating session in order to develop a marriage contract. Each person present airs his or her concerns about the proposed marriage.

The wedding itself consists of a sacrifice before the shrine of the ancestors to announce the marriage and pray for happiness. Before the wedding, the women of the house come together to prepare the bride for marriage. This consists of giving her a perfumed bath, dressing her, and giving her any advice they may deem necessary. They and the bride then go to the place where the marriage is to be held. They leave their cars a short distance away and in a procession they dance and sing. The groom and his party meet them at the building where the ceremony is performed. After that, the new spouses and their guests dance and feast.

When a person dies, prefuneral ceremonies are performed. Before the funeral of an *Alejo,* the godparent will go to the funeral home and break the *Alejo's ilekis.*[20] The funeral would proceed according to the wishes of the family. If the deceased was a priest, there would be an additional ceremony called an *itutu* before the funeral.

Other ceremonies are performed that can but do not necessarily have to result in initiation into the priesthood. *Ilekis* are bead necklaces made in color schemes appropriate to the various Orishas. The color scheme and numerical pattern vary from house to house. For example, Shango's *ileki* is red and white, one red bead alternating with one white bead. Yemonja's colors are blue and crystal. In one house her *ileki* would be one blue bead alternating with one crystal bead or seven crystal beads alternating with seven crystal beads. Many people undergo an additional initiation called receiving warriors, in which they acquire the implements of certain Orisha.

Initiation into the priesthood is the final ceremony in the series of initiations. An initiation ceremony is a seven-day event. The initiate remains secluded for seven days and returns home on the seventh day. Thereafter s/he must dress in white for a year and follow certain other restrictions. After the year is over, the initiate is a full-fledged priest. Annually on the anniversary of his or her date of initiation, a priest celebrates his or her Ocha birthday.

The Yoruba Religion is steadily growing in the United States. Its growth is most noticeable in the non-Cuban Latin and African-American communities.

Notes

1. Trinidad was originally colonized by Spain. After the Haitian revolution, it gained a large number of French immigrants. Consequently, it had a large number of Catholics in its population. Only after the British takeover was there a significant Protestant presence.

2. Priest of Orunmila, the Orisha of divination. A *babalawo* is considered a high priest and specializes in divination.

3. An especially knowledgeable elder priest whose function is to ensure the correctness of rituals.

4. The most senior deity in the Yoruba pantheon.

5. The deity of volcanoes. The Cubans adapt him as St. Christopher.

6. Damballa Wedo is the Haitian Loa (deity) that is most closely associated with the ancestors. He represents all the unknown ancestors (Herskovits 1967; Deren).

7. Oyo was a Yoruba empire that held political sway over much of Yorubaland and Dahomey—now the Republic of Benin.

8. House is the name given to a group of worshipers.

9. Deities of the Yoruba religion.

10. If there is such a thing in this context.

11. The heavenly rubbish heap.

12. Divination by figures or lines, usually drawn on the earth's surface or a substitute therefor.

13. Poetry facilitates memory. The character of Yoruba as a tone language allows the verses to be chanted. Spanish does not permit patterns of Yoruba versification based on tones (which Spanish lacks). Consequently, in the move from Yoruba to Spanish, stories in verse became stories in prose.

14. The Orisha of Truth, Justice, Thunder and Lightning, to be discussed below.

15. The Orisha of Motherhood, Mercy, and Continuity, to be discussed below.

16. Shortened form of Orisha. Name given to the physical symbols of the Orisha, that is, the covered dishes in which they are kept. Also a synonym for the Religion.

17. Two coconuts if the godchild has been initiated into the priesthood.

18. An amount equal to the number associated with one's Orisha multiplied by $1.05 (for example, a priest of Obatala would bring $8.40).

19. A small gourd used on ceremonial occasions.

20. Beaded necklaces, the symbol of one's connection to the Orisha.

References

Abimbola, Wande
    1973   *Ifa Divination Poetry.* Bloomington: Indiana University Press.
Awolalu, J. Omosade
    1979   *Yoruba Beliefs and Sacrificial Rites.* London: Longman.
Barnes, Sandra T.
    1980   *Ogun: An Old God for a New Age.* Occasional Paper, No. 3.
                Philadelphia: Institute for the Study of Human Issues.
    1989, ed.   *Africa's Ogun: Old World and New.* Bloomington and Indianapolis: Indiana University Press.
Bascom, William
    1972   *Shango in the New World.* Austin: University of Texas Press.

Bastide, Roger
  1971   *The African Religions of Brazil: Toward a Sociology of the Interpen-
              etration of Civilizations,* Trans. Helen Sebba. Baltimore: Johns
              Hopkins University Press.
Beier, Ulli
  1975   *The Return of the Gods: The Sacred Art of Suzanne Wenger.* Cam-
              bridge: Cambridge University Press.
Brandon, George Edward
  1983   "The Dead Sell Memories: An Anthropological Study of Santeria
              in New York City." Ph.D. dissertation, Rutgers University.
Caribbean Cultural Center
  n.d.   *African Religion in the Caribbean: Santeria and Voudon.* New
              York: The Caribbean Cultural Center, An Affiliate of the Phelps
              Stokes Fund.
Clapp, Steven
  1966   "A Reporter At Large: African Theological Archministry."
              Unpublished. Ms. Schomburg Collection, New York.
Deren, Maya
  1953   *Divine Horsemen: The Living Gods of Haiti.* London and New
              York: Thames & Hudson.
  1970   *Divine Horsemen: The Voodoo Gods of Haiti.* New York: Dell.
Friedman, Robert A.
  1982   "Making an Abstract World Concrete: Knowledge, Competence
              and Structural Dimensions of Performance Among Bata Drum-
              mers in Santeria." Ph.D. dissertation, Indiana University.
Gleason, Judith A.
  1973   *Recitation of Ifa, Oracle of the Yoruba.* New York: Grossman.
  1975   *Santeria.* New York: Atheneum.
  1987   *Oya: In Praise of the Goddess.* Boston: Shambala.
Gonzalez-Whippler, Migene
  1983   "Pancho Mora: Babalawo Supreme and Oracle Orunla." *Latin
              New York* 6, no. 9 (September): 27–28.
Gregory, Stephen
  1986   "Santeria in New York City: A Study in Cultural Resistance."
              Ph.D. dissertation, The New School for Social Research.
Herskovits, Melville J.
  1967   *Dahomey: An Ancient West African Kingdom.* 2 vols. Evanston,
              Ill.: Northwestern University Press.
  1971   *Life in a Haitian Valley.* Garden City, N.Y.: Doubleday, Anchor.
Hunt, Carl M.
  1979   *Oyotunji Village: The Yoruba Movement in America.* Washington,
              D.C.: University Press of America.
Idowu, E.
  1962   *Bolaji Olodumare: God in Yoruba Belief.* London: Longmans.

Laitin, David
    1986   *Hegemony and Culture: Politics and Religious Change Among the Yoruba.* Chicago: University of Chicago Press.

Marks, Morton
    1974   "Uncovering Ritual Structures in Afro-American Music." In *Religious Movements in Contemporary America,* ed. Irving I. Zaretsky and Mark P. Leone. Princeton: Princeton University Press.

Mason, John
    1985   *Black Gods—Orisha Studies in the New World.* Brooklyn, N.Y.: Yoruba Theological Archministry.

Mbiti, John
    1975   *Introduction to African Religion:* New York: Praeger.

McClelland, Elizabeth
    1982   *The Cult of Ifa Among The Yoruba.* Vol. 1, *Folk Practice and the Art.* London: Ethnographica.

Murphy, Joseph M.
    1981   "Ritual Systems in Cuban Santeria." Ph.D. dissertation, Temple University.
    1988   *Santeria: An African Religion in America.* Boston: Beacon Press.

Ortiz, Fernando
    1973   *La Hampa Afro-Cubana—Los Negroes Brujos.* Miami: Ediciones Universal, P.O. Box 450353 (Shenandoah Station), Miami, Florida

Office of Pastoral Research of the Archdiocese of New York
    1982   *Hispanics in New York: Religious, Cultural and Social Experiences.* 2 vols. New York: Office of Pastoral Research.

Soyinka, Wole
    1976   *Myth, Literature and the African World.* Cambridge: Cambridge University Press.

Thompson, Robert Farris
    1983   *Flash of the Spirit: African and Afro-American Art and Philosophy.* New York: Random House.

Weaver, Lloyd
    1986   "Notes on Orisha Worship in an Urban Setting: The New York Example." Paper read at The 3rd International Conference on Orisha Tradition(A) July 1–6, 1986, University of Ife Ile Ife, Nigeria.

Zaretsky, Irving I., and Mark P. Leone, eds.
    1974   *Religious Movements in Contemporary America.* Princeton: Princeton University Press.

Zuesse, Evan M.
    1979   *Ritual Cosmos: The Sanctification of Life in African Religions.* Athens, Oh.: Ohio University Press.

Contributors

JACOB KEHINDE OLUPONA, editor of this volume, is Professor and Director of African American and African Studies and Director of the Religious Studies Program at the University of California, Davis. He has recently been named the E. Desmond Lee Professor of African and African American Studies at the University of Missouri, St. Louis. He is the author and editor of several works in Religion and Africana studies, including *Kingship: Religion and Ritual in a Nigerian Community,* and *African Religions in Contemporary Society and Religious Plurality in Africa: Essays in Honor of John S. Mbiti* (co-edited with Sulayman Nyang).

M. F. C. BOURDILLON is Professor of Sociology at the University of Zimbabwe, Harare, Zimbabwe.

LOUIS BRENNER is Professor of the History of Religion in Africa at the School of Oriental and African Studies, University of London, U.K.

JOHN M. CHERNOFF is resident in Pittsburgh, Pennsylvania, and is a research affiliate of Trinity College, Legon, Ghana.

MARY CUTHRELL-CURRY is Associate Professor in the Department of Sociology at the University of Houston, Texas.

UMAR HABILA DADEM DANFULANI is a lecturer in the Department of Religious Studies, University of Jos, Jos, Nigeria.

RUDOLPH EASTMAN is a babalorisha of the Orisha religion, diviner in the Merindilogun system, and Chairman of the Central Committee of the Orisha Movement of Trinidad and Tobago (Egbe Orisha Ile Wa) Inc. 1981. He is also an independent cultural researcher and publicist for the Orisha tradition.

GERDÈS FLEURANT is Professor of Music at Wellesley College, Wellesley, Massachusetts.

SABINE JELL-BAHLSEN holds a Ph.D. in Anthropology from the New School for Social Research. She has taught at The Rhode Island School of Design in Providence, Rhode Island. She is also a research affiliate of the Architectural Heritage Center of the University of Technology in Lae, Paua, New Guinea.

OGBU U. KALU is Professor of Church History in the Department of Religion at the University of Nigeria, Nsukka, Nigeria.

FLORA *EDOUWAYE* S. KAPLAN is Professor of Anthropology and Museum Studies, New York University, New York.

CHARLES LONG was until recently Professor of the History of Religions and Director of the Black Studies Center, University of California, Santa Barbara.

WYATT MACGAFFEY was until recently Professor of Anthropology at Haverford College, Pennsylvania.

MARGARET R. MILES is Professor and Dean, Graduate Theological Union, Berkeley, California.

KATHLEEN O'BRIEN WICKER is Professor of Religion at Scripps College, California.

PASHINGTON OBENG is Assistant Professor, Wellesley College, and Lecturer, Harvard University, Cambridge, Massachusetts.

G. C. OOSTHUIZEN was until recently Professor in the Department of Religious Studies at the University of Durban, Durban Westville, South Africa.

BENJAMIN RAY is Professor of the History of Religions, University of Virginia, Charlottesville.

PATRICK J. RYAN, S.J., is an Islamicist and was Professor of Religion at the University of Cape Coast, Cape Coast, Ghana.

ABDULKADER I. TAYOB is Professor of Islamic Studies, University of Cape Town, Cape Town, South Africa.

MAUREEN WARNER-LEWIS is Professor of African-Caribbean Language and Orature in the Department of Literatures in English at the Mona, Jamaica campus of the University of the West Indies.

DAVID WESTERLUND is Associate Professor of Religion in the Department of Theology, University of Uppsala, Sweden.

DOMINIQUE ZAHAN was a professor of African religions in France.

Photo Credits

THE EDITOR AND PUBLISHER wish to thank the varied museums, institutions, and individuals for providing photographs and granting permission to reproduce the illustrations in this volume.

Chapter 5
1, 2, 3, 4. Umar Habila Dadem Danfulani.

Chapter 6
1, 4, 6. Collection of Flora E. S. Kaplan. Photographs by S. O. Alonge.
2. Manchester Museum, The University of Manchester.
5. The Brooklyn Museum.
7. The Glasgow Museum.
8, 9, 10, 11, 13, 15. Collection of Flora E. S. Kaplan. Photographs by Flora E. S. Kaplan.
12. Courtesy of Priest O. Ebohon.
14. Courtesy of the Enogie of Obazuwa-Iko.
16, 17, 18. Collection of Morton Lipkin. Photographs by Morton Lipkin.
19. The Liverpool Museum.

Chapter 9
1. Patricia Ranieri.
2, 3. Allan W. Wicker.
4, 5, 6, 7, 8. Kathleen O'Brien Wicker.

Index

Abdulai, Alhaji M., 273
Abdul Kader, Yacoob, 311, 322
Abdurahman, Abdullah, 307
Abega, P., 372, 375, 397
Abimbola, Wande, 110, 298,
    301, 459, 464
Abrahams, R. G., 164, 172
Abrahams, Zainulghoes'n, 309,
    322
Achebe, Chinua, 44, 45, 49n. 8;
    50n. 11; 51, 223, 252
Achebe, Chinwe (Ms), 50n. 12;
    51
Admas, M., 237, 252
affliction: as punishment, 159,
    162–63; symbolic meaning
    of, 89
Afigbo, A. E., 72, 81
African-derived religion,
    450–66
African Independent Churches
    (AICs), xxi, xxviii–xxix,
    278–83
Agordoh, A. A., 380, 397
air: shrines and, 17–18
Ahrauran (prince), 127
Ajam, M. T., 307, 322
Akan adae, 387–89
Akenzua II (Oba), 124, 136
Akyeampong, Emmanuel, 199,
    205, 213, 214n. 4
Aladura (Independent
    churches), 73, 74
'Ali Harazim, 330, 347n. 1; 348
altars, ancestral, 13
ancestors, 41; as agents of ill-
    ness, 164–68, 172n. 18; and
    art, 238–41; beliefs concern-
    ing, xx; cult of, 10–14; and
    Dagbamba pepole, 264–65;
    meaning of, 11; newborn
    children and, 12, 93, 119;
    Obas and, 121–24; Odo cult

of, 61–70; rituals concerning,
    12; as source of affliction, 94;
    as spiritual entities, 164–65;
    spirituality and, 54–84; ven-
    eration of, 167–68; and
    Yoruba Religion, 462–63
Ani/Ala (Igbo mother earth
    goddess), 44, 50n. 12
Aniakor, C., 51, 242, 253
Anyimadu, Amos, 209, 215
Arabic Study Circle, 311, 313,
    318, 321nn. 4, 5, 8
Arhem, Kaj, 159, 161, 163, 172
art, African: characterizations
    of, 224; cosmology and,
    233–35; and masks, 226–33;
    and spirituality, xxvi–xxvii,
    223–256
artists: attitudes toward, 250;
    status of, 250
Asante Catholicism,
    xxxiii–xxxiv, 372–400;
    anointing of the sick in,
    376–77; Buoho Catholic
    Shrine, 377–79; celebration
    of Corpus Christi in, 374,
    379–81, 384–86, 393–97;
    dance in, 381–86; postconcil-
    iar liturgical renewal in,
    375–76
Asanti (Ashanti) people: altars
    of, 13; shrines of, 31–32;
    stool ceremonies of, 31–32
Ash, James L., Jr., 357, 370
Augé, Marc, 206, 215
Augustine, 352, 355, 360–62,
    363–70
Awolalu, J. Omosade, 36, 464
Awoonor, Kofi, 207

Ba, Amadou Hampate, 348n. 8;
    348

al-Bakri, Abu ʿUbayd Allah,
    286–87, 288, 289, 294
balance: in Igbo cosmology,
    41–42
Bamba, Amadu, 339
Bambara, 5, 7, 8, 18, 21
Bame, N. K., 380, 381, 382–83,
    397
al-Barawi, Uways b. Muham-
    mad, 339
Barnard, Alan, 170n. 2; 173
Barnes, Sandra T., 36, 464
Barrow, Frank, 305
Bascom, William R., 110, 409,
    414, 453, 464
Bassing, A., 241, 252
Bastien, Remy, 417
Bastin, M.-L., 239, 252
Baxter, P. T. W., 182, 195
Becken, H.-J., 372, 397
Beier, Ulli, 459–60, 465
Ben-Amos, P., 234, 243, 252
Benedict, Ruth, 60–61
Benin, 138n. 4; ancestor wor-
    ship in, 122; sacred kingship
    in, 114–39
"Benin Massacre," 115
Benwell, Gwen, 200, 201, 215
Berg-Schlosser, Dirk, 168–69,
    173
Bertho, Jacques, 434, 445
Biebuyck, D., 246, 252
Binder, Leonard, 312, 322
Biney, C. L., 206, 215
Biobaku, S. O., 297, 299, 302
Blacking, J., 391, 397
Blair, H. A., 259, 273
Blier, Suzanne Preston, 199,
    202, 210, 215
Boddy, J., 252n. 6; 252
Bourdillon, M. F. C., 187, 195
Bradbury, Robert, 115, 121,
    126–27, 137n. 3; 139

Bradlow, Adil, 306, 322
Brain, R., 250, 252
Brandon, George Edward, 452, 453, 465
Brandstrom, Per, 164, 171n. 3; 173
Bravmann, R. A., 226, 252
Breidenbach, P. S., 251, 253
Brenner, L., 335, 342, 344, 348nn. 5, 7, 8, 13; 348
Brewer, Peter David, 410, 414
Brooks, G. E., 380, 395, 398
Brown, Karen McCarthy, 417, 425, 433, 445
Buchner, V. F., 294, 302
al-Buni, Ahmad b. ʿAli, 337, 348n. 10
Burton, J. W., 249, 253
Buxton, J., 249, 253
Bwa people, 5, 7
Bwiti cult: shrines of, 33–34

calendar, xxiii; agriculture and, 50n. 19; ritual and, 50n. 19
Call of Islam, 315, 316, 317, 319
Cape Muslim Youth Movement, 310
Carr, Andrew, 409, 414
Cassiem, Achmat, 315
Chavunduka, G. L., 194n. 2; 195n. 6
Chernoff, John M., 273, 380, 398, 422, 446
chi (life force/soul), xxii, 41–44, 50n. 17
Christianity: indigenous, 280–83
Clapp, Steven, 453, 465
Claremont Muslim Youth Association, 308–10
Clark, VèVè A., 417, 446
clothing, ritual: for Pa diviner, 101–2
Cole, Herbert M., 36, 51, 242, 253
colonialism: and African religious traditions, xv
colors: significance of, 43, 61, 117–18, 169, 171n. 12; 233
Comhaire-Sylvain, Suzanne, 417, 442
Connah, Graham, 121, 139
Cornet, J., 234, 256

Corpus Christi, celebration of, 374
Courlander, Harold, 417, 421, 440, 442, 446
Crawford, J. R., 193, 195
creation, 4–6, 8–10
Cuba: and Yoruba Religion, 452–53
custom (omenala), 38, 39, 50nn. 12, 16
Cyprian, 352, 355, 358

Da Costa, Yusuf, 306, 322
Dagbamba people: religion and culture of, xxvii–xxviii, 257–74
"dance of power" (n/um tchai), 27–28
Dandarawiyya order, 340
Danfulani, Umar H. D., 110
Danquah, J. B., 55
Danto, Arthur, 225, 253
Dapper, Olfert, 116, 139, 224, 253
Dauphin, Claude, 421, 446
D'Azevedo, W. L., 250, 253
death, 54; Igbo belief about, xxii; and witchcraft, 181
DeCraemer, W., 372, 398
Deedat, Ahmad, 312, 317
De la Burge, R., 239, 253
Deren, Maya, 417, 424, 432, 440, 446, 451, 461, 465
Derrick, J., 251, 253
Desmangles, Leslie, 417, 445n. 1; 446
dhikr (invocation), 326–27
Dieterlen, G., 236, 247, 253, 254
Diodorus Siculus, 353–54
Diop, Birago, xxii, 54
divination: and Dagbamba people, 265–67; Ifa, xvi; and Igbo people, 45; Pa, xxii–xxiv, 87–113; and Yoruba Religion, 457–62
diviner: in Pa divination, 100–109
divinities: of Dagbamba people, 262–63; female, 38–50; as intermediaries, 6–8; water, 198, 200
Dogon people, 5, 7, 8, 13, 14, 19, 21; art of, 246–48; cos-

mology of, 247; masks of, 247–48
Donatists, 353, 358–62
Drewal, Henry John, xxvi, xxvii, 200, 201, 202, 205, 215–16, 227–28, 253
Drewal, M. T., 228, 253
drought: causes of, 91–92
Drucker-Brown, Susan, 258, 273
drummers: of Dagbamba people, 259–61
Duncan-Johnstone, A. C., 259, 273
Dunham, Katherine, 417, 421, 429, 440, 442, 446
du Plessis, I. D., 307

earth: shrines and, 16–17
Eastman, Rudolph, 404, 414
Edo people, xxiv, 138n. 4; sacred kingship and, 114–40
Efe/Gelede masquerades, 227–29
Egharevba, Jacob U. (chief), 114, 120, 133, 137n. 2; 139
Ehengbuda (Oba), 126–28
Eisenhofer, Stefan, 114, 139
Ekeh, Peter, 278, 283
Eneasato, M. O., 72, 81
Eni, Emmanuel, 208, 216
Erediauwa (Oba), 120, 127, 128, 136, 137n. 1; 138n. 5
Esack, Fareed, 315, 322
Esigie (Oba), 127, 133
Eto, Victoria, 207, 216
Evans-Pritchard, E. E., 37, 152, 173, 177, 180, 181, 195
Ewedo (Oba), 120
Eweka I (Oba), 119
Eweka II (Oba), 116, 119, 123, 124
Ewe people, 4, 5, 6; altars of, 13
Ewuare (Oba), 120–21, 127
Eyo, E., 244, 253
Ezra, K., 248, 253

Falhun Ibn Ishaq, 286, 289
Falola, Toyin, 114, 140
Favret-Saada, J., 194, 195
Feierman, Steven, 152, 173
Fernandez, James W., 37, 236, 253

Ferguson, Phyllis, 259, 273
festivals: *Agugu*, 50n. 19; among
  Dagbamba people, 269–70;
  Pa divination and, 90
Field, M. J., 192, 195
fire: shrines and, 17–19
Fisher, Humphrey J., 284, 287,
  302
Fleurant, Gerdès, 417, 421, 432,
  446
Fon people, 4, 6, 7, 18
Fortes, Meyer, 186, 195, 274,
  289, 302
Foss, P., 244, 254
Fouchard, Jean, 421, 432, 434,
  446
Fraser, Douglas, 200, 216
Fratkin, Elliott, 169, 173
Freedberg, D., 251, 254
Friedman, Robert A., 452, 465
Fry, P., 252n. 6; 254

Galaty, J. G., 160, 172n. 28; 173
Gallois-Duquette, D., 24, 25
Galloway, A. D., 277
Ganda people: royal shrines of,
  26–27
Garrard, T., 299, 302
Gauguin: and African art, 224
Gidaado, Alfa Amadou, 328, 329
Gilbert, M., 229, 254, 386, 388,
  391, 398
Gilroy, Paul, 199, 216
Glaze, A., 237–38, 254
Glazier, Stephen, 410, 415
Gleason, Judith A., 457, 465
Gluckman, M., 181, 195
Goldblatt, John, 207, 216
Gonzalez-Whippler, M., 452,
  465
Goody, J., 296, 302
Grau, Ingeborg Maria, 49n. 3;
  51
Greenberg, J. H., 227, 252n. 5;
  254, 294, 302
Gregory, Steven, 456, 460, 465
Greschat, Hans-Jürgen, 214n. 5;
  216
Griaule, M., 236, 247–48, 254
Griffith, Lee Ellen, 201, 216
Group Areas Act, 313
Guenther, Mathias G., 154,
  172n. 26; 173

Gueye, M., 290, 302
Gumi, A. B. M., 301n. 5; 303
Gusinde, Martin, 159, 170n. 2;
  173

Hackett, Rosalind I. J., 214n. 1;
  216
Haight, B., 296, 304
Haiti: ethnographic history of,
  418–19; music of, 416–49
al-Hajj, M., 294, 302
al-Hajj ʿUmar Tal, 327, 329–
  331, 348n. 6
Hamallah, Ahmad, 339
Hamalliyya order, 339
Hammond-Tooke, D., 183, 195
hand: as central symbol in
  Benin art, 118–19
Hanna, J. L., 391–92, 398
haqiqa (truth or divine reality),
  330, 331, 333, 338
Haron, Imam Abdullah, 306–7,
  308, 309, 310, 313–14, 322
Harris, M. D., 223, 254
Hartwig, G. W., 249, 254
Harwood, A., 180, 196
Hastings, A., 372, 373, 374, 398
Hatfield, C. R., Jr., 164, 173
Hauge, Hans-Egil, 171n. 11;
  172n. 27; 173
Heald, Suzette, 178, 186
healing: among Dagbamba,
  267–68; cults of, 29–30; *Pa*
  divination and, 88; and
  trance dance, 156–57; Uham-
  miri priests and, 39
health, 88–89, 376–77
Hebert, J., 298, 302
Hefner, R. W., 373, 399
Hendry, S. G., 396, 399
Henry, Frances, 403, 415
Hersak, D., 237, 254
Herskovits, Frances, 410, 415,
  417
Herskovits, Melville, 410, 415,
  417, 429, 434, 445n. 3; 446,
  465
Hiskett, M., 345, 349
Hocart, A. M., 120, 139
Home, Robert, 115, 139
Honko, Lauri, 98, 110

Honorat, Lamartiniere, 421,
  430, 434, 446
Hood, Mantle, 421, 447
Hopkins, J. F. P., 301n. 2
Hopkins, Keith, 354, 371
Horton, Robin, 50n. 13, 51, 55,
  82, 180, 196, 198, 216, 283
Hunt, Carl M., 452, 465
Hurbon, Laennec, 417, 447
Hurskainen, Arvi, 171n. 18; 173

ibn Abi Imran, Abu Musa
  Harun, 286, 289
Ibn Abi Zayd al-Qayrawani,
  287–88
Ibn ʿArabi, 329–30
Ibn Battutah, 291–93, 296
Ibn Idris, Ahmad, 325–27,
  330–31, 337, 339–40, 346,
  347n. 2
Ibn Khaldun, 291, 325–26, 329,
  337, 347n. 3; 348n. 10; 349
Ibrahimiyya order, 339
Idike, Emmanuel, 74, 81n. 3; 83
Idowu, E. Bolaji, 214, 216, 415,
  465
Igbo people, xxi; arts and, xxii;
  belief about death, xxii;
  christianization of, 71–75;
  cosmology of, 38–50; deities
  of, 58–59, 61–64; *mbari*
  shrines of, 30–31; pantheon
  of deities of, 39–41; women's
  war, 48n. 1
ihsan (upright behavior), 333;
  command of, 332
ikegobo (altars-of-the-hand), 118
illness, xxiv; among Dagbamba
  people, 267–68; anointing of
  the sick, 376–77; human
  agents of, 152; natural causes
  of, 168; social causes of,
  168–69; spiritual agents of,
  152–75; *see also* health
iman (faith), 333, 334; six principles of, 332
immortality of the soul, xxii
Imperato, P. J., 247, 254
incest: witchcraft and, 181
initiation: allotactic, 22–25;
  epispanic, 22; rites of, 21–25
Inneh, Daniel E., 124, 138n. 3;
  140

Isichei, E., 380, 399
Islam: meaning of the word, 326; modern characteristics of, 317–20; obligatory actions of, 332; among Dagbamba people, 257, 268–72; Diaspora from Mali, 293–97; in medieval Mali, 288–93; Mami Water in, 208–9; submission to God, 333, 338; in West Africa, xxix–xxx, 284–304; among youth in South Africa, xxx–xxxi, 305–23; see also Sufism
Islamic Missionary Society, 313
Islamic Propagation Centre, 312, 317
Iyoba (queen mother), 116, 118

Jahn, J., 54, 82
Jamal, Riaz Cassiem, 312, 322
James, C. L. R., 418–19
Jege, Emmanuel, 251
Jell, George, 49n. 6; 50n. 20; 53
Jell-Bahlsen, Sabine, 38, 48nn. 1, 2; 49nn. 6, 9, 10; 50nn. 18, 19, 20, 21, 22, 23; 51–52, 53, 203–4, 216–17
Jenkins, Della, 204, 205, 217
Jeppie, M., 307, 321n. 1;, 322
jihad (holy war), 329, 331; spiritual, 324–25
Johnson, S., 299, 302
Jones, A. M., 421, 447
judgment, final: absence of, in African religions, 3
Jules-Rosette, Bennetta W., 214n. 1; 217

Kalu, O. U., 61, 71, 74, 82
Kane, T. A., 380, 399
Kaplan, Flora Edouwaye S., 52, 116, 120, 123, 124, 127, 129, 133, 136, 140
Kasfir, Sidney, 52, 205, 217, 244, 254
Katz, Richard, 155–57, 168, 170n. 2; 174
Kavuna, S., 240, 254
Keim, C. A., 249, 251, 256
Khatmiyya order, 340
King, Noel Q., 214n. 1; 217

kingship, sacred: among Edo (Benin) people, xxiv, 114–40; colonialism and, 115–16; as unifying element of religion, xviii
Knappert, J., 313
knowledge: as a spiritual force, 226
Kolinski, M., 421, 442, 447
Komo people: art of, 248–49; masks of, 248–49
Kramer, F., 233, 250, 254
Krieger, K., 249, 255
Kung San people, 27–28, 152–59; see also San people

Lagerwerf, L., 182, 196
Laguerre, Michel, 417, 425, 447
Lamp, F., 234–35, 255
Larney, Ebrahim, 308, 322
Lawal, Babatunde, 37, 229, 239, 240, 255
Lawrence, Bruce, 213, 217
Lawson, E. Thomas, 214n. 1; 217
Leach, Edmund, 98, 110, 223
Lee, Richard B., 155, 159, 170n. 2; 174
Leiris, Michel, 417
Levtzion, Nehemia, 274, 288, 291, 293, 296, 299, 301n. 2; 302, 304
Lewicki, T., 285, 302
Lewis-Williams, J. David, 155, 174
Leyburn, James G., 417
libations: ancestors and; see also sacrifices
Lieu, Samuel N., 364, 371
Lifschitz, E., 246, 255
Lionnet, Françoise, 199, 217
lithomancy. See Pa divination
Locke, David, 421–22, 447
Luba people: art of, 230–31

Maasai people, 152–53; God as agent of illness among, 159–63
MacGaffey, Wyatt, 231, 255
Mall, Dawood, 311
Mami Water, xxv–xxvi, 198–222; cultural strands in,

199–203; functions of, 203–9; name, 199
Mamiwater, Togbe Abidjan (Adawuso Dorfe), 209–13; shrine of, 211–13; rituals of, 213
Manichaeans, 353, 362–66
Mansa Muhammad, 291–92
Mansa Musa, 290–91, 293
Mansa Sulayman, 291–92
Manu, Igse O. C., III, 81n. 7; 83
Maquet, J., 224–25, 252n. 2; 255
market days: in Igbo land, 46
Marks, Morton, 452, 466
marriage: Pa divination and, 93; in Yoruba Religion, 462–63
Marshall, Lorna, 37, 155, 159, 168, 170n. 2; 171n. 8; 174
Marty, P., 296, 303
Marwick, M. G., 183, 185, 187, 189, 190, 196
masamva (spiritual entities, among Sukuma), 164–68, 172n. 20
masks, xxvii, 35; African art and, 226–33; idea of, 229; of kings, 229–30; and social hierarchies, 241–43; Yoruba ancestor mask (egungun), 35
Mason, John, 460, 466
masquerades, xxvii; Odo, 66–68; in Trinidad and Tobago, 404–5
Matory, J. L., 392, 399
Maximilien, Louis, 447
Maurer, E. M., 234, 255
Mawdoodi, Abul A'la, 308, 310
Mawdoodi, Mawlana, 321n. 10
Mbiti, John S., 214n. 1; 217, 274, 447, 466
Mbuti people: molimo ceremonies of, 28–29
McCaskie, T., 384, 399
McClelland, Elizabeth, 457, 466
McCoy, R., 301n. 6; 303
McLeod, M. D., 229, 255
McNaughton, P. R., 248–49, 255
medicine: and religion, xxiv
Mendonsa, Eugene, 110
Merker, M., 161, 168, 174
mermaids (and mermen), 214n. 3; in African art, 200, 202;

mermaids (*cont.*)
  and African water divinities,
  200–201
Metraux, Alfred, 417, 447
Meyer, Birgit, 207, 208, 217
Middleton, J., 178, 196
Miles, Margaret R., 371
al-Mirghani, Muhammad ʿUth-
  man, 340
Mirghaniyya order, 340
mission Christianity, 279–80
Mitchell, R. C., 73, 82
"mixers" (*mukhallitun*), 284–85
Mohammed, Y., 301n. 5; 303
Mol, Frans, 171n. 14; 172n. 28;
  174
monotheism: of Maasai, 171n.
  18
Montanists, 353, 357–58
Montilus, Guerin, 417, 447
Moolla, A. M., 310, 311, 323
Morain, G. G., 390, 399
Moslem Judicial Council, 307
Mossi people, 5; ancestors and,
  11
Mourides of Senegal, 339
moyo (soul, in Sukuma), 164
Muhammad b. Yusuf al-Sanusi,
  340, 344–45, 348n. 13; 349
al-Mukhtar al-Kunti, Sidi, 339
Mupun people: *Pa* divination
  and, 90, 92
al-Murabit, ʿAbd al-Qadir, 316
Murabitun, 316, 320
Murphy, Joseph M., 452, 466
music: of Haitian Vodun,
  xxxiv–xxxv, 416–49
Muslim Assembly, 309
Muslim Brothers, 313
Muslim Students' Association,
  310, 314, 316
Muslim Teachers' Association,
  307
Muslim Youth Movement,
  314–16, 317, 318, 320,
  321nn. 16, 17
Muslim Youth Movement of
  District Six, 307–8
Muslim youth organizations,
  305–23
al-Musulmani, 290
Musurillo, Herbert, 352, 356,
  371

Mwaghavul people: *Pa* divination and, 90, 92
mysticism, 20–21

Nadel, S. F., 184, 186, 196
nafs (soul): meaning of, in
  Sufism, 324–25
Natal Muslim Council, 310–11
Nevadomaky, Joseph, 124,
  138n. 3; 140
Ngas people: *Pa* divination and,
  90
Ngubane, H., 252n. 6; 255
Niass, Ibrahim, 339
Niassiyya, 339
Nketia, J. H., 380, 390, 393,
  394, 399, 421, 447
nkisi (power object), 213–32,
  240
Nnadozie, J. A. W. E., 75–78,
  81n. 9; 83
Nne Mmiri/Uhammiri (Igbo
  supreme water goddess), 44
North Africa, Roman,
  xxxii–xxxiii; Catholics in,
  366–70; Christianity in,
  350–71; martyrdom in,
  352–53, 354, 355–56; Roman
  religion in, 353–55
Nooter, M. H., 230, 233, 242,
  252n. 3; 255
Nuer people, 29; religion of,
  152
num (spiritual energy), 155–56,
  171n. 6
n/um tchai ("dance of power"),
  27–28
Nwanunobi, Cyril, 55, 82
Nwapa, Flora, 50nn. 14, 15, 23;
  52
Nyanga Muslim Association,
  309
Nzomiwu, J. P. C., 80–81, 82

Oakes, C., 194n. 1; 197
Oba (sacred king), xxiv, 115–40;
  ancestors and, 121–24; court
  of, 124–28; funeral ceremonies for. 123–24; as mediator, 117; pre-destiny and,
  119–20; regalia of, 117–18;
  secrecy and, 129–32; wives
  of, 128–29

Obeng, Pashington, 199, 215,
  375, 379, 384, 399
Obetta, Akubui S., 81n. 10; 84
Obiora, Leslye A., 38, 50n. 16;
  52
Ochiam, Patrick, 81n. 6; 84
Odo ancestral cult, xxii, 61–70;
  female roles in, 70
Oelman, A. B., 241, 255
O'Fahey, R. S., 330, 337, 347n.
  2; 349
Offiong, D. A., 189, 194, 196
Ogbonnaya, A. Okechukwu,
  213, 217
Ogbuide. *See* Uhammiri/
  Ogbuide
Ogun (Yoruba god of iron,
  war, and hunting), 33, 117,
  234
Oguola (Oba), 120
Oha, Obodimma, 48n. 2; 53
Ohen (Oba), 133
Ojo, J. R. O., 246, 255
Okechukwu, C. U., 81n. 5; 84
Olivier de Sardan, J.-P., 226,
  255
Olokun (Lord of the Dry
  Land), 116–17, 138n. 6; 234
Olsson, Tord, 161–62, 168, 174
Omar, Abdul Rashied, 308,
  309, 310, 323
omenala (custom). *See* custom
Onyeama, D., 71–72, 83
Opoku, Kofi Asare, 55, 83, 198,
  213, 215n. 6; 217, 380,
  381–82, 393, 399
Orhogbua (Oba), 127
Orisha religion, 404–9
Orishas (divinities), 6, 227; in
  Trinidad and Tobago, 404–9;
  in Yoruba Religion, 454–63
Oru Igbo people, 49n. 4; cos-
  mology of, 38–50; *see also*
  Igbo people
Ottenberg, S., 238, 255
Ovonramwen (Oba), 116
Ozolua (Oba), 128, 133

Pa: divination, xxiii—xxiv,
  87–113; etymology of the
  term, 88; process of, 98–109
Palmer, H. R., 294–95, 301n. 9;
  303

Pantaleoni, Hewitt, 421, 447
Parrinder, G., 6, 25, 49nn. 8, 9, 10; 53, 214n. 1; 218
Paul, Emmanuel C., 417, 429, 434, 448
Paxson, Barbara K., 200, 201, 202, 214n. 2; 218
pebbles: *Pa* divination and, 99–109, 112, 113
Peek, Philip M., 87, 111
Peel, John D. Y., 73, 83, 399
Pemberton, J., 229, 234, 240, 253, 256
Perdue, Joseph, 312, 321n. 7
Phillips, James R., 115
Phillpotts, Beatrice, 201, 218
Platvoet, Jan, 214n. 1; 218
Pollock, A., 250, 252
prayer, 19–20; disease and, 163
pre-destiny: in Benin, 119
priesthood, 19–20
puberty rites, 93; *Pa* divination and, 93
"Punitive Expedition," 116

al-Qadir al-Jilani, ʿAbd, 339
Qadiriyya order, 339
Qiblah, 315–16, 320
Qutb, 310

Ranger, T. O., 380, 400
al-Rashid, Ibrahim, 340
Rashidiyya order, 340
Rattray, R. S., 37, 299, 303
Ray, Benjamin C., 37, 400
redemption: absence of, in African religions, 3
reincarnation, 44, 55; in Benin, 119; in Yoruba Religion, 454–57
religions, revealed, 3
religions, traditional: concept of God in, 4–6
Richards, A. I., 189, 196
Rigaud, Milo, 417, 423, 438, 445n. 3; 448
rituals, xvi; agriculture and, 117–18; of ancestor propitiation, 165
ritual symbolism: *Pa* divination and, 98–103
Roberts, Allen F., 214, 218, 226, 234, 255, 256

Robinson, David, 348n. 6; 349
Rogers, Susan, 48n. 1; 53
Ross, D. H., 251, 253
Rousselle, Aline, 353, 355, 371
Ruel, M., 192, 193, 196
Ryan, P. J., 290, 298, 303
Ryder, A. F. C., 115, 137n. 3; 140

sacred space, 393–97
sacrifices, 117; among Dagbamba, 260; ancestors and, 12; animal, 354; child, 353–54; and disease, 163, reconciliation and, 97
Salihiyya order, 340
Samba, Cheri, 207
Sanneh, L., 60, 83, 294, 303, 336, 348n. 9; 349
San people, 152–53; illness causation among, 153–59
Santeria, 450–51
Sanusiyya order, 340
Sarpong, Peter (bishop), 373, 375, 379, 384, 389, 391, 395, 400
Sawyerr, Harry, 55, 83
Saxer, Lawrence W., 352, 355, 371
Sayyid Qutb, 308
Schapera, Isaac, 155, 174
Schildkrout, E., 249, 251, 256
Schmidt, Wilhelm, 159
shariʿah (religious law of Islam), 330, 331, 333, 338
Shelton, A. J., 66, 83
Shorter, A., 372, 400
Shostak, Marjorie, 159, 174
shrines, xx–xxi, 14–19; air and, 17–18; Benin, 122–23; as channels of communication, 26–36; earth and, 16–17; fire and, 17–19; water and, 15–16
al-Siddiqi, Mawlana ʿAbd al-ʾAlim, 310
silsila (transmission), 340–41
Simpson, George Eaton, 410, 415, 417, 448
sin: concept of, among Maasai, 162–63; illness and, 163; *see also* affliction, as punishment
Siroto, L., 238, 256
Skalnik, Peter, 258, 274

slave trade: and African religious traditions, xv
smallpox, 6–7
Smith, Wilfred Cantwell, 317, 323
snake: *Ashe* manifested in, 49n. 10; meaning of, 40; python, 49nn. 8, 10
Søderberg, B., 240, 256
Sogolo, G. S., 280, 281, 282, 283
sorcerers: as one who harms people, 172n. 28; as agents of disease, 152, 166
sorcery, 169
Sörensen, J. P., 99, 111
soul: in Sufism, 324
Soyinka, Wole, 461, 466
Spencer, Paul, 160, 162, 163, 171nn. 13, 14; 172n. 27; 174
Sperber, D., 179, 196
spirit: in Sufism, 324–26
spirits, xx; of nature, 153–54
Spiritual Baptist Faith, 410–12
spirituality: ancestors and, 10–14; and economic and social life, 154
Stager, Lawrence, 353–54, 371
Steves, Guy W., 172n. 29; 175
Stewart, John O., 410, 415
Stoller, Paul, 194n. 1; 197
stool ceremonies, 31–32
Sufism (*tasawwuf*), xxxi–xxxii, 324–49; devotional practice of, 338–46; epistemological foundations of, 329–38; orders of, 339–42
Sukuma people, 152–53; ancestors as agents of illness among, 164–68
Supreme Being, xxix–xx; Chi-Ukwu, 39–50; as Creator, 4–6, 7, 8–10, 154; Dagbamba idea of, 262–64; *enkAi* as, 160, 171n. 11

Tablighi Jamat, 315–16, 319
Tal, Cerno Bokar Saalif, 334, 335, 344, 348n. 8
Talbot, P. Amaury, 140
Tamakloe, E. F., 296, 303
Tanner, Ralph E. S., 164, 166, 171n. 3; 172n. 23; 172n. 29; 175

taqlid (imitation), 332–33
tariqa (Sufi way), 330, 331, 333, 338–39, 340
tasawwuf. See Sufism
Taylor, M. K., 386, 400
Tayob, Abdulkader I., 323
Tcherkezoff, S., 171n. 3; 175
Teachers' League of South Africa, 307
Tertullian, 351–52, 353, 355, 357–58
theology, Western, 277–79
Thomas, Eudora, 410, 415
Thomas, Linda E., 214, 218
Thompson, Robert Farris, 49n. 10; 52, 211, 218, 234, 256, 432, 448, 456, 459, 466
Thompson, L. M., 321n. 2; 323
Thurner, Ingrid, 154, 175
al-Tijani, Ahmad, 330, 339, 340, 344
Tijaniyya order, 330, 339–40, 341–42, 344
time, xvii–xix; cyclical, 3, 41–42, 55–56; linear, 3; ritual; *Pa* divination and, 89–90
Tobago. *See* Trinidad and Tobago
tok kum (communication with deities), 88; in calendrical rituals of passages, 90–91; for individual afflictions caused by human agents, 94–95; for individual afflictions caused by spiritual agents, 94; in life crisis rituals, 92–93; for national calamities, 91–92
Toure, Saada Oumar, 342–44, 348n. 12
trance dance: of San people, 155–59
tree: prayer and, 171n. 17; significance of, 18
Trimingham, J. Spencer, 208, 218, 303, 344, 349
Trinidad and Tobago: African spirituality in, xxxiv, 403–15
Trotman, David, 404, 414n. 1; 415
Tuan Guru, 306
Tuan Said Aloewie, 306
Turner, Harold W., 214, 218

Turner, Victor, 37, 98, 111, 417, 448
Twumasi, P., 376, 400

Uchendu, V., 41, 44, 53
Udeaguala, J. C., 81n. 8; 84
Ugwuta/Oguta: lake, 38–50; town, 49n. 5
Uhammiri/Ogbuide (lake goddess), xxi, xxii, 38–50, 204
Ukpong, J., 60, 83
ʿUmar b. Saʿid al-Futi, 339, 340–41, 344, 347nn. 1, 4; 348n. 11; 349, 345
al-ʿUmari, Ibn Fadl Allah, 291, 293
Umeh, Marie (ed.), 53
United Democratic Front, 315
Universal Exposition of 1889, 224
Universal Truth Movement, 313, 321n. 10
Unrug, K., 240, 256
Urashi (river god, husband of Uhammiri), 38, 47
Usuanlele, U., 114, 140
ʿUthman b. Fodiye, 329, 331–32, 337, 338, 339, 345, 348n. 6; 349
ʿUthman dan Fodio, 284, 301nn. 1, 5; 303–4

VanAllen, Judith, 48n. 1; 53
Van Riebeek, Jan, 307
Van Riebeek festival, 307
van Selms, A., 313
Vodun, 6; belief and structure of, 419–21; Mami Water and, 210; music of Haitian, 416–49; in Trinidad and Tobago, 409–10
Vogel, Susan, 207, 218, 252n. 3; 256
Voshaar, Jan, 162, 171nn. 14, 16; 172n. 27; 175

Wahhabi school, 348n. 5
wali (friend of God), 326, 327, 330, 340
Walker, Sheila S., 206, 218
Warner Lewis, Maureen, 404, 409, 414n. 2; 415

water: divinities, 198; goddess, 38–50; shrines and, 15–16
Waugh, Arthur, 200, 201, 215
Weaver, Lloyd, 452, 457, 466
Wendl, Tobias, 205, 206, 218
Westerlund, David, 171n. 3; 172n. 19; 175
Westermarck, E. A., 290, 304
Wicker, Kathleen O'Brien, 213, 215n. 6; 217
Wilks, Ivor, 259, 273, 293, 296, 299, 304
Williamson, Kay, 49n. 8; 53
Willis, J. R., 293, 294, 304
Willis, R. G., 189, 190, 197
Wilson, M., 184, 197
Wimbush, Vincent L., 365, 371
Wiredu, Kwasi, 223, 225–26, 256, 279, 280, 283
witchcraft, xxiv–xxv, 91–92, 94–95, 169, 172n. 29; and society, 176–97; eradication of, 188–91
witches: as agents of disease, 152, 166, 172n. 28
women: and African spirituality, xviii, xxii; and Efe/Gelede masquerades, 227–29; roles of, in African religions, 19–20; roles of, in Asante dance, 380–86; roles of, in Odo ancestral cult, 70
Wyllie, Robert W., 170n. 1; 175, 192, 197

Yarborough-Williams, Lavinia, 421, 430, 448
Yoruba-derived religion, xxxv–xxxvi, 450–66; Cuba and, 452–53
Yoruba people, xvi, 7, 34–35; cosmology of, 234; Islam among, 297–301; masks and, 227–29, 239–40; shrines of, 33
Young, Robert, J. C., 198, 199, 218
Young Men's Muslim Association, 313–14
Yusuf, Shaykh, 306

Zahan, Dominique, 5, 25
Zuesse, Evan M., 98, 459, 466